Astrology

FOR

DUMMIES®

2ND EDITION

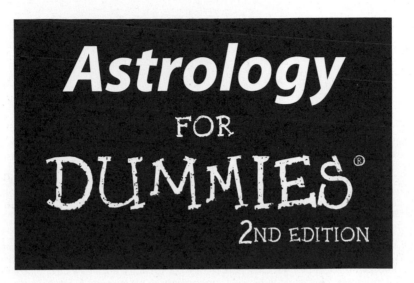

Astrology
FOR
DUMMIES®
2ND EDITION

by Rae Orion

BICENTENNIAL
1807
WILEY
2007
BICENTENNIAL

Wiley Publishing, Inc.

Astrology For Dummies®, 2nd Edition

Published by
Wiley Publishing, Inc.
111 River St.
Hoboken, NJ 07030-5774
www.wiley.com

WILEY

About the Author

Rae Orion has been casting horoscopes since the Ford Administration, when she became the court astrologer for a metaphysical bookstore on the West Coast and began to prognosticate for strangers. She has taught astrology to high school students, social service professionals, friends, and relatives, and has written monthly horoscope columns and articles about astrology (among other topics) for *New Woman* and other magazines. She lives in New York City.

Dedication

For George, always

Author's Acknowledgments

Two Capricorns deserve extravagant praise: my husband, George, and my editor, Chrissy Guthrie. Both are thoughtful, serious, organized, kind, and a lot more fun than is generally advertised for that sign. I also want to thank Tracy Boggier, who reintroduced me to the *For Dummies* way of life; Ethel Winslow, who is a fine astrologer as well as an editor; and others at Wiley, including Jessica Smith, David Lutton, the people in Composition Services, and Christy Beck, whose behind-the-scenes presence was always a comfort. Without Reid Boates, this book would not exist.

Publisher's Acknowledgments

We're proud of this book; please send us your comments through our Dummies online registration form located at www.dummies.com/register/.

Some of the people who helped bring this book to market include the following:

Acquisitions, Editorial, and Media Development

Senior Project Editor: Christina Guthrie

(Previous Edition: Christine Meloy Beck)

Acquisitions Editor: Tracy Boggier

Copy Editor: Jessica Smith

Technical Editor: Ethel Winslow

Editorial Manager: Christine Meloy Beck

Editorial Assistants: Erin Calligan Mooney, Joe Niesen, David Lutton

Cover Photo: © Mary Evans Picture Library / Alamy

Cartoons: Rich Tennant (www.the5thwave.com)

Composition Services

Project Coordinator: Heather Kolter

Layout and Graphics: Carl Byers, Brooke Graczyk, Joyce Haughey, Stephanie D. Jumper

Anniversary Logo Design: Richard Pacifico

Proofreaders: Aptara, David Faust

Indexer: Aptara

Special Help

David Lutton

Publishing and Editorial for Consumer Dummies

> **Diane Graves Steele,** Vice President and Publisher, Consumer Dummies

> **Joyce Pepple,** Acquisitions Director, Consumer Dummies

> **Kristin A. Cocks,** Product Development Director, Consumer Dummies

> **Michael Spring,** Vice President and Publisher, Travel

> **Kelly Regan,** Editorial Director, Travel

Publishing for Technology Dummies

> **Andy Cummings,** Vice President and Publisher, Dummies Technology/General User

Composition Services

> **Gerry Fahey,** Vice President of Production Services

> **Debbie Stailey,** Director of Composition Services

Contents at a Glance

Table of Contents

Introduction

Astrology can change your life. It did mine. Astrology illuminates the secret corners of the self, provides a key to understanding others, contributes a useful method for scrutinizing relationships, and even offers a glimpse into the future. Beyond that, as with all great areas of knowledge, astrology has the power to alter perception. Once you know something about it, you never see the world in the same way again.

Using a vocabulary that's both objective and poetic, astrology enlarges your curiosity (because after you absorb its principles, everyone you meet, no matter how dull the person or how fleeting the encounter, becomes a mystery waiting to be solved); it expands your insight into behavior and motivation; and most of all, it increases your compassion. Some people think that astrology divides all human beings into 12 groups. How wrong they are! Astrology teaches that all human beings are subject to universal needs and desires — and that every individual is entirely and splendidly unique.

About This Book

Astrology has many forms. In this book, I focus on *natal astrology,* the interpretation of a birth chart to gain insight into yourself and others. Using real life examples, I show you how to construct your birth chart (or how to get it on the Internet), how to interpret its component parts, and how to use that information to gain insight into yourself and others.

I consider astrology a tool — an objective tool — for understanding self, assessing relationships, examining your potential, and even making some basic decisions. In this book, I show you how to use that tool.

Conventions Used in This Book

One of the most charming aspects of astrology, in my opinion, is that virtually all birth charts, calendars, and books on the subject are strewn with tiny, mysterious-looking symbols. Until you know those symbols by heart, their presence can be distracting and confusing. That's why I usually spell out the names of the signs, planets, and aspects. With actual birth charts, however, words are insufficient. I present those horoscopes just the way a professional astrologer would — covered with symbols.

Memorizing those symbols is incredibly useful. But you don't have to do it. Instead, you can turn to the Cheat Sheet at the beginning of this book, where you can find a neat list of every symbol you need to know. The Cheat Sheet enables you to translate the symbols back into English. That way, when you're looking at a birth chart and you see something like this:

☽26♊23

you'll know that it means that the Moon (☽) is in Gemini (♊) at 26 degrees 23 minutes.

In this book, whenever I refer to a planetary position such as the one in the preceding example, I describe it as 26°23' Gemini. I usually don't spell out the words *degree* (°) and *minute* ('). I assume that you know them. On birth charts, I go further and omit those two tiny symbols. Instead, the charts in this book announce planetary positions by using boldface type for the degrees and regular type for the minutes, as follows: **26** 23.

What You're Not to Read

I'd like you to read every word in this book, but you don't have to. You can safely ignore the paragraphs marked with the Technical Stuff icon, and you can even skip the sidebars (the gray-shaded boxes that are scattered throughout the book). Although reading these sections will enhance your understanding, you'll get along fine without them.

Foolish Assumptions

Despite the title of this book, I assume that you're no fool. I assume that you're intrigued by the art of astrology because you're seeking fresh ways of understanding. I also assume that, whether you're a newcomer or a longtime follower, you're primarily interested in your own horoscope.

I assume that you have access to a computer and can get on the Web, where you can easily obtain your birth chart. (You can also cobble one together yourself, using only the material in this book.) That horoscope combined with this book enables you to explore astrology in a multitude of ways.

My final assumption about you is simply that you have some sense; that you expect insight from astrology, not winning lottery numbers; that you understand that astrology isn't about fate or even about luck. It's about possibility, propensity, and potential. An old maxim, taught to every generation of astrologers, says it all: The stars impel, they do not compel.

How This Book Is Organized

Astrology For Dummies, 2nd Edition, follows a logical sequence. It starts with an overview, offers various methods for getting your chart, and then explores the Sun signs and the other components of the chart in detail. After that, it expands into relationships, leaps into ways of using astrology on a daily basis, and concludes with a section on talents and timing.

Part I: Mapping Your Place in the Cosmos

These three chapters cover the basics. Chapter 1 briefly discusses the Sun, the Moon, the planets, the rising sign, and the 12 houses. Chapter 2 tells you how to get your chart via the Internet or computer software. And Chapter 3 tells you how to construct a rough copy of your chart using the tables in this book. After that, you're ready to dive into the rest of the book.

Part II: Here Comes the Sun

Astrology is an interpretative art that can lead in many directions. It starts here with four chapters about the Sun signs organized according to element. Chapter 4 surveys the fire signs (Aries, Leo, and Sagittarius); Chapter 5 explores the earth signs (Taurus, Virgo, and Capricorn); Chapter 6 talks about the air signs (Gemini, Libra, and Aquarius); and Chapter 7 considers the water signs (Cancer, Scorpio, and Pisces).

Part III: Everything Else in the Cosmic Cookbook

Sun Sign astrology, albeit fascinating, leaves many questions unanswered. The chapters in this part help fill in those blanks. Chapter 8 illuminates the Moon and the Nodes of the Moon in all 12 signs. Chapters 9 and 10 discuss Mercury, Venus, Mars, Jupiter, Saturn, Uranus, Neptune, and Pluto — plus the asteroid Chiron, which was discovered in 1977 and is now routinely included in horoscopes by many astrologers. Chapter 11 talks about the Ascendant, and Chapter 12 describes the influence of the planets in each of the houses. Finally, Chapter 13 looks at the way the planets interact by analyzing the *aspects,* or geometrical relationships, that link them together.

After you've looked up your planetary placements, you may find yourself suffering from information overload. Never fear — Chapter 14 shows you how to winnow that data down to its most essential components by looking for patterns that characterize your chart as a whole.

Part IV: Using Astrology Right Now

Gaining insight into your psyche is a worthy enterprise, but most people interested in astrology have other topics on their minds: like relationships, which I discuss in Chapter 15. Included in that chapter is an assessment of all 78 Sun sign combinations — plus tips on how to capture the heart of each sign of the zodiac.

In Chapters 16, 17, and 18, I tell you how to squeeze the maximum benefit out of astrology. Chapter 16 explains how the current positions of Mars, Jupiter, Saturn, Uranus, Neptune, and Pluto affect you — and what you can look forward to in the future.

Chapter 17, the most hands-on chapter in the book, focuses on only one planet (and I'm using that word loosely): the Moon. Its monthly swing through all of its phases and all 12 signs brings days when the cosmos is with you — and days when it's decidedly not. In this chapter, I tell you how the position of the Moon can help you decide when to take the initiative, when to hang back, when to start projects, when to wait, and more.

Chapter 18 addresses a phenomenon that never fails to annoy people: retrograde Mercury, which is famous for generating bouts of delay and aggravation. I'm generally quite sanguine about this passing influence. After all, it happens three times a year. What's the big deal? Or so I used to think. Recently, though, retrograde Mercury put me on the wrong train twice in a week, swallowed up a crucial e-mail, and lobotomized my iPod. In this chapter, I tell you how to cope better than I did.

Part V: The Part of Tens

After you understand the Sun, the Moon, and the planets, you have the basics down. In this part, I apply that information in two ways. In Chapter 19, I reveal the planetary components of ten different talents. And in Chapter 20, which addresses the fine art of astrological timing, I tell you when to throw a party, when to launch a business, when to buy a computer, even when to get married — by the stars.

You'll also find the Appendix, which lists the positions of the Sun, the Moon, and the planets, including Chiron. This is the section of the book to turn to when doing a birth chart. It tells you where the planets were (and will be) between 1930 and 2012.

Icons Used in This Book

Four icons sprinkled throughout this book serve as road signs. Here's what the icons mean:

In an ideal world, every planetary placement, aspect, and transit discussed in this book would be accompanied by an example from the life of a flesh-and-blood human being. In the real world, book space is limited, so I'm able to use only a few such examples. This icon highlights those examples. In many cases, real-life examples feature movie stars, politicians, and other public figures. Occasionally, I focus on people I know personally. In those instances, the names are changed. The astrology remains the same.

Certain facts and principles are essential. I discuss most of them in the early chapters. But when you need to recall a fact in order to understand another aspect of a birth chart, I try to remind you, gently, using this icon.

It's impossible to talk about astrology without coming smack up against astronomy and mathematics. Whenever I give a nuts-and-bolts scientific explanation of an astrological phenomenon, I warn you upfront with this icon. Want to skip the explanation? Go ahead. Most of the time, you can ignore it and still be on track.

A paragraph marked with this icon may suggest an easier way of doing something. It may point you to a book or a Web site that covers material similar to that being discussed in the text, it may suggest a way to offset a problem that arises with a particular configuration in a chart, or it may tell you how to, say, seduce a Capricorn. Never let it be said that astrology isn't useful.

Where to Go from Here

If you're a novice, you may as well know the truth: Astrology is a complicated system. The only way to describe it is to begin at the beginning, which is what I do. But I've seen the way people leaf through astrology books, and I have written it with the understanding that you may open it anywhere.

So consider this book a reference. You don't need to read the chapters in any particular order. You don't even have to remember much from one chapter to the next because this book is filled with cross-references and reminders. If you know a little bit about the subject, you can jump in anywhere.

Nonetheless, you may want to start at the beginning and read a chapter or two before you plunge into the rest of book. If you know your sign but nothing else, turn to Chapter 2, which tells you how to get an accurate horoscope. If you already have a copy of that essential document, you're ready to begin. I invite you to take a random walk through the book.

I find the knowledge I've gained from astrology to be consistently fascinating and helpful. It's my hope that you, too, will rejoice in — and benefit from — the wisdom of the stars.

Part I
Mapping Your Place in the Cosmos

The 5th Wave · By Rich Tennant

"I was born under the 'Parking' sign. My mother never made it from the car to the hospital."

In this part . . .

"**K**now thyself," the Delphic Oracle said. It's still good advice. But suggestions like that are never easy to implement . . . unless you know astrology. An ancient and evolving system, astrology illuminates the secret corners of the psyche and points the way to self-knowledge. Astrology enables you to recognize your strengths, to acknowledge your weaknesses, to accept your needs, and to understand the otherwise incomprehensible behavior of the people you know. But first, you need a copy of your chart. This part tells you how to get one.

Chapter 1

An Astrological Overview: The Horoscope in Brief

*L*egend has it that Sir Isaac Newton, widely considered the greatest genius of all time, may have explored astrology. Newton had a complex, curious mind. In addition to inventing calculus and discovering the universal law of gravity, he was interested in alchemy (the quest to turn ordinary metals into gold), the Bible, and astrology. When his friend Edmund Halley (after whom the comet is named) made a disparaging remark about it, Newton, a conservative Capricorn, shot right back, "Sir, I have studied the subject. You have not." Or so the story goes.

Like every other astrologer, I like to think that story might be true. After all, astrology has faded in and out of fashion, but it has never lacked followers. Catherine de Medici had Nostradamus as her astrologer, Queen Elizabeth I consulted John Dee, and other astrologers advised Napoleon, George Washington, J. P. Morgan, and Ronald Reagan. Yet in all that time, no one has provided a satisfying explanation as to why astrology works. Over the centuries, proponents of the ancient art have suggested that gravity must be the motor of astrology . . . or electromagnetism . . . or the metaphysical "law of correspondences." Carl G. Jung summarized that view when he wrote, "We are born at a given moment, in a given place, and like vintage years of wine, we have the qualities of the year and of the season in which we are born."

I don't know why astrology works, any more than Sir Isaac did. But I can assure you that it does work. The pattern that the planets made at the moment of your birth — that is, your birth chart or horoscope — describes your tendencies, abilities, challenges, and potential. It doesn't predict your fate, though it does make some fates more easily achievable than others. The exact shape of your destiny, I believe, is up to you.

In this chapter, I delve into the astronomy behind astrology, the signs of the zodiac, and the components of the birth chart.

Looking at the Starry Sky

Picture, if you will, our solar system. In the middle is the Sun. Spinning around it are the planets and asteroids, whose orbits surround the Sun roughly the way the grooves on a record album encircle the label in the center.

That idea, drilled into us in childhood, would have astonished ancient stargazers. They never doubted that the Sun, Moon, and planets revolved around the Earth. And although we know better, thinking so didn't make them stupid. The Sun really does look as if it revolves around the Earth. It seems to rise in the east and set in the west. And it always stays within the confines of a ribbon of space that encircles the Earth like a giant hoop. That strip of sky is called the *ecliptic*.

Following are the three most important facts about the ecliptic:

- The ecliptic represents the apparent path of the Sun around the Earth — apparent because, in fact, the Sun doesn't spin around the Earth at all. It just looks that way.

- Like a circle, the ecliptic is divided into 360 degrees — and each degree is, in turn, divided into 60 minutes. The first 30 degrees of the ecliptic are Aries, the next 30 degrees are Taurus, and so on.

- The stars that are scattered like dust along the entire length of the ecliptic form the constellations of the zodiac.

Here comes the confusing part: The signs of the zodiac and the constellations that share their names aren't the same. The signs are divisions of the ecliptic, each exactly one-twelfth of the total length — 30 degrees. The constellations have nothing to do with the signs. I explain this sorry state of affairs in the sidebar "The signs, the constellations, and the precession of the equinoxes."

The signs, the constellations, and the precession of the equinoxes

Thousands of years ago, when the Babylonians were establishing the principles of astrology, the constellations and the signs of the zodiac were in alignment. On the *vernal equinox* (the first day of spring), the Sun was "in" the constellation Aries: That is, if you could see the Sun and the stars simultaneously, you'd see the Sun surrounded by the stars of the Ram. In those happy days, the signs and the constellations coincided.

Alas, this is no longer the case. On the vernal equinox today, the Sun shows up amidst the (dim) stars of Pisces the Fish — a very different kettle indeed.

The reason for this shift is that the Earth wobbles on its axis, which traces a circle in space like the spindle of a spinning top. As the axis shifts, the constellations seem to slip backwards. The amount of slippage over a human lifetime is minuscule, but over generations it adds up. As a result, every equinox takes place a little earlier in the zodiac than the one before. This process is called the *precession of the equinoxes*. It explains why the vernal equinox, which used to occur in the constellation Aries, now takes place in Pisces.

When the equinox moves back even further, to the constellation of the Water Bearer, the Age of Aquarius will officially begin. Astrologers differ about when that will be. Some are convinced that it's happening now. Others believe that it's decades — or centuries — away. Eventually, the cycle will begin again. Around the year 23800, the vernal equinox will return to Aries, and astrologers will be able to skip this entire explanation. Meanwhile, constellations of the zodiac and the signs of the zodiac aren't the same.

Skeptics who attack astrology — and for some reason, these wary souls can be amazingly hostile — often point to the changing position of the constellations and the precession of the equinoxes as proof that astrology is bogus. The truth is that astrologers are well aware of this phenomenon. They consider the constellations as signposts and little more. What matters is the division of the ecliptic. The stars, glorious though they are, have nothing to do with your sign.

Identifying the Signs of the Zodiac

The sign that the Sun occupied at the moment of your birth is the most basic astrological fact about you. It defines your ego, motivations, needs, and approach to life. But the Sun isn't the only planet that affects you. (For astrological purposes, both luminaries — the Sun and the Moon — are called planets. Do yourself a favor and don't use this terminology when talking to astronomers.) Mercury, Venus, Mars, Jupiter, Saturn, Chiron, Uranus, Neptune, and Pluto, not to mention the Moon, represent distinct types of energy that express themselves in the style of the sign they're in.

Nevertheless, astrologically speaking, your Sun sign is the most essential fact about you. To determine your sign, use Table 1-1. Keep in mind that the dates vary from year to year. After all, although a circle has 360 degrees, and each sign has precisely 30 degrees, it's an inconvenient fact that a year has 365 days — not counting leap years. As a result, the signs don't divide into the days as neatly as you would want. If you were born on the first or final day of a sign, you may want to check your birth sign by using the tables in the Appendix, venturing onto the Internet, or consulting an astrologer.

Table 1-1	The Sun Signs	
Sign	*Dates*	*Symbol*
Aries the Ram	March 20–April 18	♈
Taurus the Bull	April 19–May 20	♉
Gemini the Twins	May 21–June 20	♊
Cancer the Crab	June 21–July 22	♋
Leo the Lion	July 23–August 22	♌
Virgo the Virgin	August 23–September 22	♍
Libra the Scales	September 23–October 22	♎
Scorpio the Scorpion	October 23–November 21	♏
Sagittarius the Archer	November 22–December 21	♐
Capricorn the Goat	December 22–January 19	♑
Aquarius the Water Bearer	January 20–February 18	♒
Pisces the Fish	February 19–March 19	♓

Understanding the Signs

Like any truly satisfying system, astrology classifies and interprets its basic building blocks in a number of ways. Just for starters, each sign is defined by a *polarity* (positive or negative reaction pattern), a *quality* or *modality* (form of expression), and an *element* (describing basic temperament).

Polarity: Dividing the zodiac by two

You can figure out the polarity of each sign by dividing the zodiac in half. Beginning with Aries, six *positive* or *masculine* signs alternate with six *negative* or *feminine* signs. The sexist language, I regret to say, is traditional. Many astrologers use the terms yin and yang instead. Call them what you will, the meanings are as follows:

✔ **Positive** (yang) signs are more extroverted, objective, and assertive.

✔ **Negative** (yin) signs are more introverted, subjective, and receptive.

The zodiac can also be divided into pairs of opposing signs. The opposite signs are: Aries and Libra; Taurus and Scorpio; Gemini and Sagittarius; Cancer and Capricorn; Leo and Aquarius; and Virgo and Pisces.

Modality: Dividing the zodiac by three

The three modalities describe different forms of expression, as follows:

✔ **Cardinal signs** are enterprising. They initiate change and make things happen. The cardinal signs are Aries, Cancer, Libra, and Capricorn.

✔ **Fixed signs** consolidate and preserve change. They're focused and determined. The fixed signs are Taurus, Leo, Scorpio, and Aquarius.

✔ **Mutable signs** are flexible and versatile. They adapt and adjust. The mutable signs are Gemini, Virgo, Sagittarius, and Pisces.

Within the cycle of the zodiac, the three modalities occur in sequence. Cardinal energy initiates change, fixed energy digs its heels in and maintains the status quo, and mutable energy adapts to shifting circumstances.

Elements: Dividing the zodiac by four

Describing the temperament of each sign of the zodiac by assigning it to one of the four ancient elements is probably the most famous method of classification. The four elements are fire, earth, air, and water:

✔ **Fire** brings vitality, excitement, and intensity. The fire signs are Aries, Leo, and Sagittarius.

✔ **Earth** gives stability, common sense, and the ability to get things done. The earth signs are Taurus, Virgo, and Capricorn.

✔ **Air** enlivens the intellect and enhances sociability. The air signs are Gemini, Libra, and Aquarius.

✔ **Water** strengthens the emotions and the intuition. The water signs are Cancer, Scorpio, and Pisces.

Putting the zodiac back together

Once you know the order of the signs, it's easy to assign them to their correct polarity, modality, and element because those classifications always occur in sequence. (You can clearly see that sequence in Table 1-2.) Those classifications convey a great deal of information. If all you know is the polarity, modality, and element of each sign, you know a lot.

Table 1-2	The Qualities of the Signs		
Sign	*Polarity*	*Modality*	*Element*
Aries	Positive	Cardinal	Fire
Taurus	Negative	Fixed	Earth
Gemini	Positive	Mutable	Air
Cancer	Negative	Cardinal	Water
Leo	Positive	Fixed	Fire
Virgo	Negative	Mutable	Earth
Libra	Positive	Cardinal	Air
Scorpio	Negative	Fixed	Water
Sagittarius	Positive	Mutable	Fire
Capricorn	Negative	Cardinal	Earth
Aquarius	Positive	Fixed	Air
Pisces	Negative	Mutable	Water

For example, take Cancer the Crab. It's the sign of negative cardinal water. This tells you that Crabs tend to be internal and receptive (negative), with a heavy dose of initiative (cardinal), and strong emotional awareness (water).

The Zodiac Man

The zodiac arcs across the cosmos, huge and impossibly remote. Its symbolic equivalent, small and incredibly close, is the human body. Two thousand years ago, a Roman astrologer named Manilius correlated each sign of the zodiac to a part of the body in a sequence that starts at the head with Aries and runs down to the feet, which belong to Pisces. Medieval art, both European and Islamic, includes many fine renderings of the so-called Zodiac Man, which also appears in ancient medical texts. Indeed, medicine as it was once practiced relied on astrology not only for its understanding of disease but also for its cure.

I have my doubts about medical astrology (though I have to say, I have seen cases in which it's weirdly, even disturbingly, accurate). However, I love this diagram because it reminds me that the spectrum of experience represented by the signs of the zodiac is universal and lives in everyone.

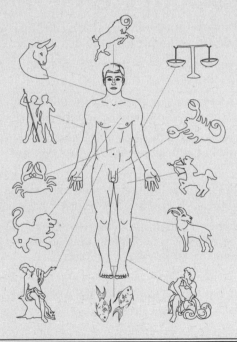

Or consider Leo, which lives next door to Cancer but boasts a very different personality (as is always the case with adjacent signs). Leo is the sign of positive fixed fire. This means that its natives tend to be outgoing (positive), determined (fixed), and full of flash (fire).

...y, modality, and element provide a rudimentary sense of what ...s about. For a detailed description of the signs, turn to Part II.

...g the Sun, the Moon, and the Planets

The Sun, the Moon, and the planets play individual parts in your horoscope. Their meanings are as follows:

- ✔ **The Sun** represents your essential self, will, individuality, vitality, and desire for power. More than any other planet, it represents who you are. It also symbolizes men in general.

- ✔ **The Moon** represents your emotions, subconscious, instincts, habits, and memory. It also represents women in general.

- ✔ **Mercury** symbolizes your style of communication, your reasoning ability, and the way you think.

- ✔ **Venus** represents those parts of your life that are concerned with love, attraction, beauty, possessions, and the arts.

- ✔ **Mars** is the planet of desire and aggression. It represents your physical energy, combativeness, enterprise, and courage.

- ✔ **Jupiter** is the planet of expansion and good fortune. It represents growth, prosperity, abundance, wisdom, generosity, and the higher mind. Jupiter's position in a horoscope tells you where you're lucky.

- ✔ **Saturn** represents limitation, restriction, caution, organization, endurance, and discipline. It tells you where you have to face your fears — and also where you're ambitious.

- ✔ **Chiron,** a dwarf planet discovered in 1977, represents past hurt and future healing. Astrologers, not all of whom use Chiron, often associate it with holistic medicine.

- ✔ **Uranus** represents originality, independence, rebelliousness, inventiveness, insight, and everything unexpected.

- ✔ **Neptune** represents spirituality, dreams, psychic ability, intuition, disintegration, compassion, self-sacrifice, deception, and illusion.

- ✔ **Pluto** represents elimination, destruction, regeneration, renewal, and transformation.

One way to simplify all this is to assign a single word — or, as astrologers prefer to say, keyword — to each planet. These keywords, which summarize each planet's meaning, appear in Table 1-3.

Table 1-3	Keywords for the Planets	
Planet	*Keyword*	*Symbol*
Sun	Self	☉
Moon	Emotion	☽
Mercury	Communication	☿
Venus	Love	♀
Mars	Action	♂
Jupiter	Expansion	♃
Saturn	Restriction	♄
Chiron	Healing	⚷
Uranus	Revolution	♅
Neptune	Imagination	♆
Pluto	Transformation	♇

Who Rules? Discovering the Rulers of the Signs

In an ideal world, each planet would work well in each sign. But in fact, some placements are better than others. The sign in which a planet seems to function most effectively is the sign that it is said to rule. Two thousand years ago, when astrologers only had to worry about the Sun, the Moon, and five planets, they assigned the rulerships this way:

✔ The Sun ruled Leo.

✔ The Moon ruled Cancer.

- ✔ Mercury ruled Gemini and Virgo.

- ✔ Venus ruled Taurus and Libra.

- ✔ Mars ruled Aries and Scorpio.

- ✔ Jupiter ruled Pisces and Sagittarius.

- ✔ Saturn ruled Aquarius and Capricorn.

After Uranus was discovered in 1781, followed by Neptune in 1846 and Pluto in 1930, astrologers modified the system. Today, the most commonly accepted planetary rulers are as follows:

- ✔ The Sun rules Leo.

- ✔ The Moon rules Cancer.

- ✔ Mercury rules Gemini and Virgo.

- ✔ Venus rules Taurus and Libra.

- ✔ Mars rules Aries.

- ✔ Jupiter rules Sagittarius.

- ✔ Saturn rules Capricorn.

- ✔ Uranus rules Aquarius.

- ✔ Neptune rules Pisces.

- ✔ Pluto rules Scorpio.

In recent years, astronomers have discovered legions of asteroids, moons, and other celestial bodies in our solar system. One of them is *Chiron,* which was discovered in 1977. Some astrologers believe that Chiron is the ruler of Virgo. Others associate it with Sagittarius. Many don't bother with it at all, and it has yet to be assigned the rulership of a sign.

Assessing the Ascendant and the Houses

The planets aren't the only essential components of your chart. The *Ascendant* or *rising sign* — the sign that was climbing over the eastern horizon at the moment of your birth — is equally important. It refers to your mask or persona — the face that you show the world. It also marks the start of the 12 houses.

The Ascendant

Have you ever had a friend who was Miss Congeniality — until you got to know her? Did you ever encounter anyone who seemed standoffish and cold at first but warmed up later on? Do you know anyone whose devil-may-care, lighthearted attitude masks a calculating, manipulative mind? And have you ever wondered how you strike other people, especially when they don't know you well? Your horoscope provides the answer. While your Sun sign may not be apparent to people, they definitely notice your Ascendant. It's your image, your facade, your surface personality. Whether it clashes or harmonizes with your Sun sign, it describes the way people see you and the impression that you make. Indeed, some astrologers consider the ruler of the Ascendant — that is, the planet that rules the rising sign — to be the overall ruler of your chart.

No matter what your Sun sign might be, any one of the 12 signs might have been on the eastern horizon when you were born. If you were born around dawn, when the Sun was peeking over the horizon, you already know your rising sign: It's the same as your Sun sign. If you were born at any other time of day, your rising sign and Sun sign differ.

For those people whose Sun signs and rising signs are identical, the surface and the substance are the same. For everyone else, what you see isn't necessarily what you get.

Consider Whoopi Goldberg: She has Aquarius rising, so she appears progressive, sociable, and eccentric — a personality with a lively mind and a detached, observant approach to life. In fact, her Sun is in Scorpio, so beneath her brilliant Aquarian surface, she's intensely emotional, passionate, and secretive — not detached at all.

To determine your rising sign, you need to know the time of your birth. When you have that, turn to Chapter 3, which gives you a rough estimate of your rising sign. Then go to Chapter 11 for an interpretation.

Besides shaping your personality, the Ascendant serves another function: It opens the door to the houses. For more about that subject, read on.

Taking the house tour

It makes no difference whether you're a fun-loving Leo or a workaholic Capricorn, you still have to deal with relationships, money, health, career, and so on. Those areas come under the authority of the *houses*, which divide the sky into 12 parts, beginning with the Ascendant, which marks the start of the first house. The meanings of the houses are summarized in Table 1-4.

Table 1-4	Houses and Their Significance
House	*Areas of Concern*
First house	Your appearance and surface personality
Second house	Money, possessions, values
Third house	Communication, short journeys, brothers and sisters
Fourth house	Home, roots, one parent, circumstances at the end of life
Fifth house	Romance, children, creativity
Sixth house	Work and health
Seventh house	Marriage and other partnerships
Eighth house	Sex, death, regeneration, other people's money
Ninth house	Higher education, long journeys, religion, philosophy
Tenth house	Career, status, reputation, the other parent
Eleventh house	Friends and aspirations
Twelfth house	Enemies, seclusion, secrets

Just as every birth chart includes all the planets, every horoscope has all 12 houses. The sign on the *cusp*, or beginning of the house, describes your approach to it. For instance, if the sign of the bull is on the cusp of your house of work, your attitude toward your job is Taurean, making you dependable, productive, and a bit of a plodder, regardless of whether that house is crammed full of planets or empty.

The word *cusp* is used in two ways in astrology. When people say they were born "on the cusp," they mean that their birthday falls at the end of one sign and the beginning of another. They usually think that they have qualities belonging to both signs. (I discuss this issue in Chapter 3.) When astrologers refer to the cusp of a house, they mean the house's starting point.

Chapter 2

Getting Your Precise Horoscope: The Old Way versus the Easy Way

*W*hat could be more fabulously arcane than an astrological chart? Well, lots of things: Alchemical sigils, kabalistic diagrams, magic spells — you name it. But this book isn't about them. It's about astrology, which only seems strange. That's because an astrological chart, with all its mysterious-looking symbols, has nothing mystical about it. It's a representation of the real world, and it isn't peculiar at all. An astrological chart is a picture, in streamlined form, of the solar system at the time of your birth. It's that simple.

To visualize the cosmos as it was then, imagine standing on the Earth at the precise moment of your birth. Imagine, too, that you're facing south and look-ing at a gigantic clock face that has been superimposed on the sky. To your left, in the nine o'clock position, is the eastern horizon. That's your Ascendant. If you were born around dawn, that's also where your Sun is. The twelve o'clock position is high in the sky in front of you. That's where your Sun is if you were a lunchtime delivery. To your right, in the three o'clock position, is the western horizon. If you were born around dusk, your Sun is there. And if you snuck into this world around midnight, when the Sun was illuminating the other side of the planet, your Sun is in the six o'clock spot.

If you know the phase of the Moon at your birth, you can locate it in a similar way. Were you born under a new moon? Then your Moon and Sun are in roughly the same place. Born under a full moon? Then the Sun and Moon are opposite each other — 180° apart. If one is rising, the other is setting.

The point is this: The horoscope is neither a metaphysical construct nor a mystical symbol nor a psychological portrait. It's a map. Your horoscope shows the position of the Sun, Moon, and planets at the moment of your birth. The astrologer's task is to look at that map and figure out its meaning. But first you have to get your hands on the map. In this chapter, I tell you how to do just that.

Gathering the Information You Need

If you're like most people, you won't have any trouble finding your birth information. Here's what you need:

- ✔ Your month, day, and year of birth
- ✔ The place of your birth
- ✔ Your exact birth time — or as close to it as you can get

Without an accurate birth time, you can never know what your Ascendant is (see Chapter 11 for more about Ascendants). You won't have trustworthy house placements for your planets. You may not even know your Moon sign because it changes signs every two or three days. Without an accurate birth time, interpreting your chart correctly will be challenging. And predicting the future will be close to impossible.

Fortunately, finding the exact time is usually easy. But don't be surprised if your mother's memory of what must surely have been the highlight of her entire life turns out to be spotty. Since I haven't done a survey, I have no statistics to bandy about, but I will say this: It's shocking how many parents can't remember when their children were born. They don't know if it was 2:05 or 5:02. One mother even confessed to me that she wasn't sure who was born at 10:06 a.m.: her daughter or herself. That's why I recommend that you corroborate your birth time through the official record — your birth certificate.

To get your birth certificate online, check out the National Center for Health Statistics at www.cdc.gov/nchs and click on the link that says "Help obtaining birth, death, marriage, or divorce certificates."

Dealing with approximate birth times

What if no one thought to look at a clock when you were born? First, keep in mind that an approximate time is better than nothing — much better. If all you know is that you came into this world before breakfast or during the *Late Show with David Letterman,* that's useful information, even if it's not exact.

If you aren't sure of your birth time, you might consider asking a professional astrologer to *rectify* your chart. Rectification is a complex process. It involves working backwards from major events in your life (such as marriage, divorce, or the death of a parent) to make an educated guess about your probable birth time. Some astrology software includes rectification modules. Even so, it's wise to proceed with caution: Unless the astrologer has considerable experience, rectification isn't a sure bet.

Coping with an absence of information

A more significant problem arises when you have no idea what time you were born. I have a beloved friend, one of many children, who never knew her birth time. And then one day, things got rapidly worse. During an astonishing conversation with an older sister, she discovered that no one in her family could vouch with 100 percent certainty for the day of her birth — or even the month. Suddenly she wasn't sure whether she was a Libra (no way) or a Scorpio (yes). This rare situation is an astrologer's worst-case scenario.

More typically, people know the day, month, and year of their birth — but not the time. That's not a tragedy. Even without the time, you can uncover a wealth of information about yourself. However, when you go online to get your horoscope — or even when you do it yourself — you have to adjust for the missing information.

In the absence of anything resembling an accurate birth time, I recommend that you do what professional astrologers do: Pretend that you were born either at noon or at dawn (my preference) and proceed accordingly. (In Chapter 3, I tell you more about what to do if your birth time is lost in space.)

What It Takes to Cast Your Chart the Old-Fashioned Way

In the past, before the computer infiltrated every corner of human existence, figuring out the positions of the planets was a challenge. It required patience, hours of free time, a fearless approach to mathematics, and an eagerness to grapple with the kinds of boring details that drive most people nuts.

For instance, you had to look up the longitude and latitude of your birth place, and you had to correct for its distance from the standard time meridian for that location. You had to distinguish between local time and Greenwich mean time, not to mention standard time, daylight saving time, and war time. Then you had to calculate the movement of the planets using, among other tools, a table of proportional logarithms. Most people didn't want to bother.

I always felt differently. I liked staying up late surrounded by numerical tables, volumes of astrological data, pads of yellow paper, and the special horoscope blanks I bought at a metaphysical bookstore. As I calculated each planetary position and house cusp, drew the symbols of the signs and planets onto the chart, and counted up how many planets were in fire signs, in earth signs, and so on, the chart — and the person —slowly grew clear in my mind.

That process takes time, and I don't do it anymore. Instead, I use a computer, like every other astrologer I know. With a computer, you can get an accurate chart without even thinking about math. Later in this chapter, I tell you how.

Still, the best way to understand astrology is to cast a chart the old-fashioned way. Here's what you would need to calculate it yourself:

- **The precise longitude and latitude of your birthplace.** You can figure it out from a map or look it up in a book like *The American Atlas: U.S. Longitudes and Latitudes, Time Changes and Time Zones,* by Thomas G. Shanks (ACS Publications), which includes an international atlas.

- **The details about your time of birth.** Just because you know the exact moment of your birth doesn't mean that your problems with time are over. You also have to know what time zone you were born in — and this is an area riddled with quicksand.

  For instance, Tennessee is divided down the middle, half in one time zone and half in another. Most places in Texas observe central standard time — but El Paso doesn't. And if you were born in Indiana between 1955 and 1965, you're in deep trouble. During those years, the powers-that-be, unable to choose between central and eastern time, decided to carve up the state and assign different regions to each time zone. Each year, they did it in a different way. If you were caught in this civic calamity, you have no choice: Go to a professional astrologer. Or log on to one of the Web sites listed later in this chapter.

  Then there's daylight saving time. Until 2007, it ran from late April to late October, but the exact days differ from year to year and from state to state. For example, if you were born in California on October 27, 1963, you were born under daylight saving time. But if your birthday is a year later, on October 27, 1964, you were born under standard time.

  And did you know that during World War II, the entire U.S. operated under war time? It began on February 9, 1942, about two months after Pearl Harbor, and ended on September 30, 1945. (It was also in operation in some places during World War I.)

  To account for these variations in time, you need a trustworthy source. Again, I recommend *The American Atlas: U.S. Longitudes and Latitudes, Time Changes and Time Zones,* compiled by Thomas G. Shanks.

- **A table of houses.** This book-size table tells you what degree of the zodiac is rising at any given moment according to the time and latitude of your birth. It also tells the degrees that appear on the other house

cusps. One resource for this information is the *Michelsen Book of Tables* by Neil F. Michelsen (ACS Publications), which includes two popular types of house division as well as a worksheet for casting a horoscope the old-fashioned way.

✔ **An ephemeris for the year you were born.** The Rosetta Stone of astrology, an *ephemeris* is an almanac that lists the positions of the Sun, Moon, and planets for every day of the year, either for midnight or noon in Greenwich, England (the basis for Greenwich mean time, from which all time zones are determined). So if you were born on the stroke of midnight in Greenwich, you don't have to do a thing to determine the position of your planets. You can read them right out of the book.

If you were born at any other time or place, you have to make adjustments. Using an ephemeris, a table of houses, and the principles of high school algebra, you can come up with a close approximation of your chart. Should you insist on precision (perhaps because you have a dose of Virgo in your birth chart), you need one more item, which I explain in the following bullet.

✔ **A table of proportional logarithms.** Using this numerical chart makes your calculations precise. But if going to the mat with a table of logarithms sounds like a fight you won't win, do yourself a favor: Skip the calculations and go directly to the Internet.

To get your hands on any of these books, go to a well-stocked astrological or New Age bookstore — if you can find one. Or check out The Astrology Center of America at www.astroamerica.com. The folks who run this place have virtually everything (including software), and they comment on much of it, so you can do a little comparison shopping right there. Plus, if you're intrigued by Tarot cards, you'll enjoy this site, which lets you peek into about a hundred different decks. Contact The Astrology Center of America via the Web, by phone at (410) 638-7761, or at 207 Victory Lane, Bel Air, MD 21014.

Getting Your Horoscope in a Nanosecond

The easiest way to get an accurate copy of your horoscope is to log on to the Internet, go to one of the sites in the following list, and type in the date, year, time, and place of your birth. Here are three of the best sites to visit:

✔ **Astrolabe** (www.alabe.com): Astrolabe offers an excellent, free birth chart along with about three pages of interpretation. Feed your birth date into their form, send it off, and seconds later, it comes back to you, complete — and I mean complete. In contrast to other Web sites with seemingly similar offers, Astrolabe supplies not only some basic interpretation but also an image of the actual chart, with the Sun, Moon, and planets placed clearly within the zodiac wheel. Astrolabe also offers other services, for which you have to pay.

✔ **Astrodienst** (www.astro.com): You can get a free birth chart (or "portrait") at this absorbing Web site — and lots more, including lengthy daily horoscopes, a report on "love, flirtation, and sex," a relationship chart and analysis, and a six-month forecast based on the changing position — or transits (see Chapter 16) — of the planets. All these freebies are abbreviated versions of longer reports you can buy. I don't have a problem with that. The only missing ingredient here is that your actual chart — the round emblem that suggests a personal mandala — is not shown. You have to construct it yourself. (I show you how in Chapter 3.)

✔ **Chaos Astrology** (www.chaosastrology.com): The free birth chart offered at this Web site is longer than most — plus, it includes the actual chart, if you know where to look. The trick is simple: After you feed in your birth information and your astrological profile appears on the screen, click on the sun/moon icon at the top of the page. Lo and behold: Your actual birth chart appears.

Investing in DIY Software

Nothing in the astrological world is more fun than being able to cast accurate charts for anyone at a moment's notice. Astrological do-it-yourself software is endlessly diverting. It enables you to calculate natal charts, compare charts, determine how the planets may affect you in the future, and, in short, entertain yourself for hours. Software isn't cheap, but if you decide it's worth the expense, the following sections give you a few recommendations.

Maximizing the Mac

If you use a Macintosh (as I do, and I'm not backing down), you have only two choices:

✔ **Io Programs:** Time Cycles Research Programs offers a wide selection of software which includes the following:

- Io Edition, their core program, which does all manner of calculations but offers no analysis.

- Io Interpreter, which provides interpretations and creates written reports. It's available with a choice of modules, including Io Horoscope, the basic interpretation program; Io Child, which analyzes children; Io Relationship, which compares horoscopes; Io Forecast, which tells you what the future may hold; and Io Body and Soul, which suggests, among other things, what vitamins you ought to take.

- Io Detective, which allows you to research all kinds of cosmic phenomenon in the charts of thousands of famous people.

- Io Midnight Ephemeris, which provides a full ephemeris page for every month between January 1850 and December 2049.

Io programs cater to professionals. I've been using them for years, but they're expensive (about $200 each) and complicated. Reach the people at Time Cycles by phone at (800) 827-2240 or (860) 444-6641, by e-mail at astrology@timecycles.com, or on the Web at www.timecycles.com.

✔ **TimePassages:** Astrograph Software designed this software as a universal starting point, appropriate for both beginners and professionals, and Mac advocates and PC fanatics. The top-of-the-line program, with a myriad of astrological functions you can play with, costs about the same as a single Io program, while the basic edition, which provides natal charts, compatibility charts, and two ways of forecasting the future, runs about $50. The savings are considerable.

This program is a lot of fun as well as an effective way to master the topic. Click on any element of a chart — a planet, a house cusp, an asteroid — and an explanation pops up. If you're a newcomer to astrology, this product could be just what you're looking for. Call (866) 77-ASTRO or go to www.astrograph.com, where you can download a free demo with over 200 celebrity charts, including Angelina Jolie, Brad Pitt, and J. K. Rowling. (To get the demo, click on any one of the software choices and then go to "Downloads.") Even if you don't spring for the software, you can get a free copy of your chart along with a mini-interpretation of the Sun and Moon placements. (Just click on Horoscopes and go to the bottom of the page, where you can create an account for free.)

Playing with the PC

I love the Mac. I think Steve Jobs is a genius. But I've started to wonder why there's so much great astrological software for the PC and hardly any for the Mac. I also wonder what it would be like if I, you know, fooled around on a PC. Would it be wrong?

The software options for PC are beyond tempting and too numerous to do justice to here. I asked astrologer Hank Friedman, a software guru and frequent software reviewer for *The Mountain Astrologer* magazine, to make a few suggestions. His recommendations include — but were not limited to — the following:

✔ The Electronic Astrologer Series by ACS (www.astrocom.com). ACS produces three basic programs that can be purchased separately or bundled together at a savings: "The Electronic Astrologer Reveals Your Horoscope," "The Electronic Astrologer Reveals Your Future," and "The Electronic Astrologer Reveals Your Romance."

These programs include plenty of helpful information, but primarily they simply generate reports. To get an idea of what they're like, go to the Web site, click on the "Electronic Astrologer Series," and then click on the program that interests you. Free sample printouts appear at the bottom of the page. The free natal and future reports are written for Willie Nelson. The romance report is written for an imaginary couple: Drew Barrymore and the debonair Cary Grant, 71 years her senior. Except for the fact that he died in 1986, she could do worse (and has).

✔ Kepler 7.0. This amazingly comprehensive, exciting program includes 47 lessons in astrology, an astrological encyclopedia, over 19,000 charts, and a mind-boggling collection of functions. Want information on Vedic astrology, fixed stars, or the dark moon Lilith? It's all here, along with the basics: natal charts, transits and progressions, and comparisons, for about $300. Go to www.patterns.com for more information.

✔ AstrolDeluxe ReportWriter by Halloran Software; Win*Star Express; Janus; and the list goes on and on. Which is why you might want to get some additional help before making a purchase.

Seeking out advice

If you've decided to invest in astrological software, it's smart to talk to someone who's knowledgeable about both the software you want and the hardware you have. Here are two ways to get trustworthy information:

✔ Visit the Astrology Software Shop (www.astrologysoftwareshop.com) or e-mail the shop at info@astrologysoftwareshop.com.

✔ Contact Hank Friedman for assistance in choosing software that's right for you. The consultation is free, and he sells all the software at a real discount. You can e-mail him at stars@soulhealing.com or give him a call at (888) 777-7366.

Above all, visit his Web site at www.soulhealing.com. There you can find detailed discussions of astrological software, fascinating articles on many other aspects of astrology, and a stunning collection of recipes involving chocolate — because man cannot live by stars alone.

Chapter 3

Estimating Your Horoscope Using the Tables in This Book

Doing your chart the old-fashioned way provides the best possible introduction to the science behind the art of astrology. But it's a time-consuming process. Plus, if you make a mistake — and believe me, it's easy to make a mistake — your efforts will be wasted. I know. When I first cast my own chart, I looked the results up in a book and was astonished to learn that I was the kind of extroverted person who rises to prominence in every group. Since, in reality, I was so shy that I sat in the back of every classroom and dreaded going to parties, I decided to try another book. This one opined that I was thin and bony, with a firm sense of self-discipline. If only.

Either I was living someone else's life or astrology was wrong. I decided to recalculate. That's when I discovered that I had subtracted when I should have added. It was a small error on the page, but it made a substantial difference in the interpretation.

You don't have to make a mistake like mine. By getting your chart on the Internet or by using astrological software — two options I discuss in Chapter 2 — you can be confident that the computations are accurate. And it only takes a moment.

But what if you're outside the reach of a computer? What if you're all alone on that mythical desert island, leaning against that palm tree, reading this book? Using only the information contained here, you can construct a rough version of your horoscope (or anyone else's) — and for most purposes, that approximation will do just fine. First, copy the blank chart form on the Cheat Sheet, either by machine or — if that desert island doesn't happen to have a Kinko's — by hand. Next, follow the instructions in this chapter.

Using the Tables in This Book to Identify Your Planets

To figure out your planets, turn to the tables in the Appendix. For each planet, flip to the year of your birth and jot down its position, beginning with the luminaries:

✔ **The Sun:** Its position is your Sun sign — your sign of the zodiac.

If you were born on a day when the Sun moved from one sign to the next (that is, if you were born "on the cusp"), you need to take an extra step to identify your Sun sign, but you can only do it if you know the time of your birth. What you want to figure out is this: Which came first, your birth or the passage of the Sun into the next sign?

For instance, consider the horoscope of rocker Bruce Springsteen, born September 23, 1949. On that day, the Sun moved from analytical Virgo to Libra, the sign of relationships. Which one is he? According to the table at the back of this book, the Sun made its move that day at 4:06 a.m. eastern standard time (EST). (All the tables in this book are EST.) Bruce was born well after that, at 10:50 p.m. So he's a Libra.

Making this calculation is more difficult if you were born in another time zone — but only slightly. The introductory material to the Appendix tells you how to account for time differences.

✔ **The Moon:** Figuring out the placement of the Moon, which represents your emotions, can be challenging because the Moon swings into a new sign of the zodiac every two or three days. Here too, the exact time of your birth can make a difference.

For instance, director Oliver Stone was born on September 15, 1946. Turn to the Moon Table in the Appendix. Since his birthday isn't listed, check out the closest preceding day. You can see that on September 14 the Moon entered Taurus. It didn't change signs until the 16th, when it entered Gemini. On the 15th, the Moon was still in the sign of the Bull. (And does Oliver Stone seem like a willful, emotional person who doesn't let go easily and cares about money more than you might think? Makes sense to me.)

Identifying the Moon sign is more difficult in a case like that of actress Kate Hudson. She was born in Los Angeles on April 19, 1979, at 10:51 a.m. Pacific standard time (PST). On that day, according to the Moon Table in the Appendix, the Moon entered Aquarius at 15:02 (that is, 3:02 p.m.) eastern standard time. So is her Moon in Aquarius or is it in Capricorn?

To answer that, you need to figure out what time it was in California when the Moon changed sign. Since it's three hours earlier on the West Coast, figuring out California time means subtracting three hours from EST. When it's 3:02 p.m. in the East (or 15:02, as the table says), it's 12:02 in L.A. That's when the Moon slipped into Aquarius. Since Kate was born prior to that, at 10:51 a.m., her Moon is in Capricorn.

Of course, the Sun and the Moon aren't the only celestial bodies that may have changed signs on the day you were born. On December 10, 1982, for example, Mercury, Mars, and the Moon all changed signs. If you were born on that eventful day, you would have to calculate the positions of all three. Or — as I suggest in Chapter 2 — you could skip the hard work and go directly to the Internet. But you should know: Those of us who learned how to cast horoscopes back when "Apple" was nothing more than a snack and a record label consider that a cheat.

What if you were born on a day when the Moon (or any other planet) changed sign but you don't know the time of your birth? You have to guess. Read the descriptions of both signs to see whether one of them rings true. You may know immediately: One placement sounds just like you and the other sounds like no one you've ever even met. But don't be surprised if it's difficult to decide. First, every sign in the zodiac appears in your chart somewhere, so some part of you identifies with every sign. Beyond that, other planets may blur the picture. For instance, the Moon may have moved from Taurus to Gemini on the day you were born. But if you also have Jupiter in Taurus and Venus in Gemini, you already have qualities associated with both signs, and it may be hard to isolate the effect of the Moon based solely on intuition. You need mathematics.

In most cases you can identify the signs occupied by the planets in your chart simply by looking them up in the Appendix, no calculation required. Just jot 'em down, using the following list:

- **Mercury:** The planet of communication has to be in one of three signs: Your Sun sign, the sign that precedes your Sun sign, or the sign that follows it. If Mercury is anywhere else, you're reading the tables wrong.

- **Venus:** The planet of love and beauty is always within 48° of your Sun. So if your Sun is at 15° Gemini, your Venus could be as far away as 3° Leo or 12° Aries. Venus can never be farther than two signs away.

- **The rest of the planets:** They can be in any sign of the zodiac, regardless of your Sun sign.

Figuring Out Your Ascendant or Rising Sign

Figuring out the sign that was rising over the eastern horizon at the moment of your birth is the hardest part of casting a chart, but it's essential because the Ascendant or rising sign represents the part of you that other people see (and sense) first.

Although figuring out the Ascendant isn't for the faint-hearted, there's a logic to it. At any given moment, one sign of the zodiac is rising in the east and its opposite sign is setting in the west. If you were born at dawn, when the Sun was on the horizon, your rising sign is the same as your Sun sign. If you have the Sun in Aries, you're Aries rising — a double Aries, as they say, and a formidable example of fire signs in action. If you were born at sunset, your rising sign would be the opposite of your Sun sign: That is, if you're an Aries born at dusk, you have Libra rising — and Aries setting.

The *ecliptic* — the path followed by the Sun as it moves across the sky (see Chapter 1) — surrounds the Earth like a gigantic ring. That ring is divided into 12 equal segments, one for each sign. As the Earth rotates on its axis, it spins past each segment — all 12 signs in 24 hours, or approximately one sign every two hours (although latitude makes a difference and some signs hang around longer than others). The segment of the zodiac that happens to be coming up over the horizon at the moment of your birth is your rising sign.

Finding your rising sign in three easy steps

Here's how to figure out your rising sign the easy way:

1. **Turn to Figure 3-1.**

2. **Locate your birth time in the boldface horizontal row at the top of the table or in the boldface horizontal row in the middle of the table.**

3. **Find your Sun sign in the column on the left side of the table.**

   The point where the horizontal row and the vertical column intersect shows your probable rising sign.

Don't forget daylight saving time, which has usually been in operation in the United States from the last Sunday in April to the last Sunday in October. You can account for it by subtracting one hour from your birth time.

As an example of how this table works, consider the actress Nicole Kidman, a Gemini born June 20, 1967, at 3:15 p.m. in Honolulu, Hawaii (although, yes, she grew up in Australia). Find her Sun sign (Gemini) in the column on the left. Now run your finger across the Gemini row until you reach the column labeled "2 p.m. – 4 p.m." The sign that appears there — Scorpio — is her rising sign or Ascendant. Precise calculations bear that out. (Note that although Nicole was born between April and October, it isn't necessary to make an adjustment for daylight saving time because it isn't observed in Hawaii.)

Sun Sign	4 a.m. - 6 a.m.	6 a.m. - 8 a.m.	8 a.m. - 10 a.m.	10 a.m. - 12 p.m.	12 p.m. - 2 p.m.	2 p.m. - 4 p.m.
Aries	Aries	Taurus	Gemini	Cancer	Leo	Virgo
Taurus	Taurus	Gemini	Cancer	Leo	Virgo	Libra
Gemini	Gemini	Cancer	Leo	Virgo	Libra	Scorpio
Cancer	Cancer	Leo	Virgo	Libra	Scorpio	Sagittarius
Leo	Leo	Virgo	Libra	Scorpio	Sagittarius	Capricorn
Virgo	Virgo	Libra	Scorpio	Sagittarius	Capricorn	Aquarius
Libra	Libra	Scorpio	Sagittarius	Capricorn	Aquarius	Pisces
Scorpio	Scorpio	Sagittarius	Capricorn	Aquarius	Pisces	Aries
Sagittarius	Sagittarius	Capricorn	Aquarius	Pisces	Aries	Taurus
Capricorn	Capricorn	Aquarius	Pisces	Aries	Taurus	Gemini
Aquarius	Aquarius	Pisces	Aries	Taurus	Gemini	Cancer
Pisces	Pisces	Aries	Taurus	Gemini	Cancer	Leo

Sun Sign	4 p.m. - 6 p.m.	6 p.m. - 8 p.m.	8 p.m. - 10 p.m.	10 p.m. - 12 a.m.	12 a.m. - 2 a.m.	2 a.m. - 4 a.m.
Aries	Libra	Scorpio	Sagittarius	Capricorn	Aquarius	Pisces
Taurus	Scorpio	Sagittarius	Capricorn	Aquarius	Pisces	Aries
Gemini	Sagittarius	Capricorn	Aquarius	Pisces	Aries	Taurus
Cancer	Capricorn	Aquarius	Pisces	Aries	Taurus	Gemini
Leo	Aquarius	Pisces	Aries	Taurus	Gemini	Cancer
Virgo	Pisces	Aries	Taurus	Gemini	Cancer	Leo
Libra	Aries	Taurus	Gemini	Cancer	Leo	Virgo
Scorpio	Taurus	Gemini	Cancer	Leo	Virgo	Libra
Sagittarius	Gemini	Cancer	Leo	Virgo	Libra	Scorpio
Capricorn	Cancer	Leo	Virgo	Libra	Scorpio	Sagittarius
Aquarius	Leo	Virgo	Libra	Scorpio	Sagittarius	Capricorn
Pisces	Virgo	Libra	Scorpio	Sagittarius	Capricorn	Aquarius

Figure 3-1:
Identifying
your
Ascendant.

Does that Scorpio Ascendant make sense? To my mind, it describes perfectly her intense, mysterious appeal. Think of *To Die For,* her break-out movie, in which she plays an upbeat Gemini-like weather girl with a dark, seductive, manipulative — dare I say Scorpionic? — bent. Despite her sunny beauty and high-profile status as a fashion icon, there's something enigmatic and opaque about Nicole. Who is she, really? I mean, has anyone out there seen *Dogville?*

Beware of the limitations

Although this method for estimating the rising sign works for Nicole Kidman, it's by no means a perfect technique. Often, precise calculations don't square with the results of the table. One reason is that the Earth revolves around the Sun at a tilt. As a result, some signs (like Gemini) take longer to rise over the horizon than others (like Pisces). So the two-hour blocks I divided the day into are artificially equal.

Geography also matters. Imagine two babies born in New England on January 1, 2001, at 11 a.m. The one born in Portland, Maine, has Aries rising, as predicted by the table. But the Earth is curved, and a few hundred miles away, in Hartford, Connecticut, Aries has yet to climb over the horizon. The child born there has Pisces rising. I hate to admit it, but the table will not reflect that difference.

So when you use this table, know that it can't be fully trusted. More than half the time, it's right on the money. The rest of the time, it's wrong, generally by one sign. If the sign given as your Ascendant doesn't sound right to you, contemplate the signs on either side (with particular attention to the sign that comes first). For example, if the table says you're Gemini rising, but in real life you're the strong, silent type, consider the possibility that Gemini may not be your Ascendant, and read Taurus instead.

Determining Your Houses

Once you have identified your rising sign, your troubles are over. If you haven't already done so, go to the Cheat Sheet and make a copy of the blank chart. (Or draw a circle and divide it into 12 pie-shaped pieces, representing the houses.) Now all you have to do is label the houses with the appropriate signs.

Begin by labeling the first house with the name (or better yet, the symbol) of your rising sign. Then move counterclockwise around the circle, labeling the second house with the sign that follows your rising sign, the third house with the sign that follows that, and so on. No matter what your rising sign is, the signs always follow in their usual order: That is, they begin with Aries and proceed to Pisces, going counterclockwise. (See the Cheat Sheet.) Thus, if you have Aries rising, then Taurus is on the cusp of the second house, Gemini on the cusp of the third, and so on to the twelfth house, where Pisces presides. And if you're Scorpio rising, you have Sagittarius on the cusp of the second house, Capricorn on the cusp of the third, and so on, right up to Libra, which is the sign on the cusp of the twelfth house. In that case, the wheel of your chart should look something like Figure 3-2.

Dividing the houses

Astrologers have long debated the best way of slicing up a chart. The most common approaches are the Koch system, a time-based method introduced in 1962, and the Placidus system, an equally complex technique named after Placidus de Tito, a 17th-century astrologer who got it from an Arabian astrologer of the 8th century. Placidus is difficult to calculate and grossly inaccurate in northern latitudes. Nonetheless, because it's widespread, it's the system I use for the charts in this book.

The simplest system — well, actually the second simplest — was invented by Ptolemy almost 2,000 years ago. It's called the equal house system because it assumes that all the houses are the same size. In this system, if your Ascendant is 12°26' Leo (like Johnny Depp's), you have 12°26' Virgo on the cusp of the second

house, 12°26' Libra on the cusp of the third, and so on around the chart.

The most straightforward system of house division comes from Hindu astrology. It aligns the houses with the signs and puts 0 degrees on the cusp of every house. (The Ascendant is, therefore, not the cusp of the first house but simply a point within it.) So if you have Sagittarius rising, all of Sagittarius is in your first house, all of Capricorn in your second house, and so on. In this chapter, I recommend this method. Although this system isn't used extensively in Western astrology, the astrologer Robert Hand recommends its revival — and there's much to be said for it, especially when you suspect that the birth time is incorrect. If that's your situation, I recommend this system. Put your Sun sign on the cusp of the first house (at nine o'clock) and continue from there.

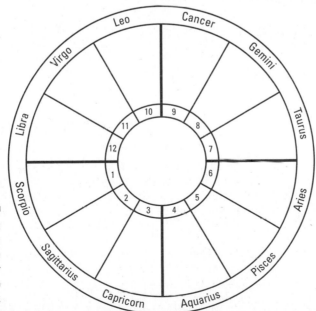

Figure 3-2:
A basic horoscope wheel for Scorpio rising.

The first house begins at nine o'clock and extends counterclockwise to eight o'clock, the second house begins at eight o'clock and goes to seven o'clock, and so on.

Creating a Horoscope

Putting together a basic birth chart involves these steps: Looking up the planets, figuring out your Ascendant, making the wheel of the horoscope, and placing the planets on the wheel. After that, you're ready for the true art of astrology: interpretation.

To illustrate the process, let's go back to Nicole Kidman, who was born on June 20, 1967, at 3:15 p.m. in Honolulu. To make her birth chart, begin by looking up her planets in the Appendix. Here's what we find for that day:

Her Sun is in Gemini.

Her Moon is in Sagittarius.

The North Node of the Moon is in Taurus (which means that the South Node is in Scorpio).

Mercury is in Cancer.

Venus is in Leo.

Mars is in Libra.

Jupiter is in Leo.

Saturn is in Aries.

Uranus is in Virgo.

Neptune is in Scorpio.

Pluto is in Virgo.

The next step is to figure out her rising sign, which we did earlier in the chapter. It's Scorpio.

Now take a blank horoscope wheel like the one on the Cheat Sheet and assign Scorpio to the first house, Sagittarius to the second, and so on, as shown in Figure 3-2. Write the symbols for the planets (or their names) in the correct houses. If you're a beginner, you may want to do this in plain English, a process that yields a chart that looks something like Figure 3-3.

Better yet, memorize the beautiful and mysterious astrological symbols. (The Cheat Sheet at the beginning of the book can help.) That way, you end up with a chart that looks like Figure 3-4.

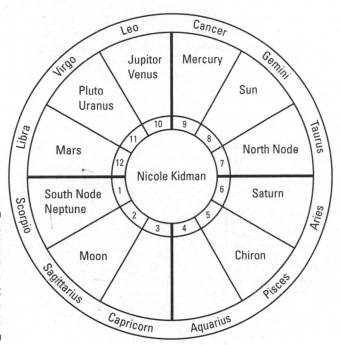

Figure 3-3:
Nicole Kidman's approximate birth chart in plain English.

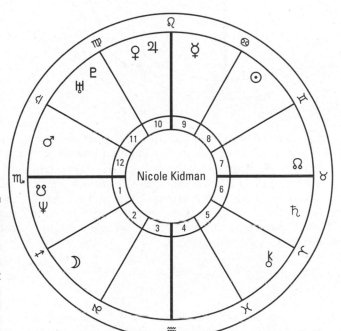

Figure 3-4:
Nicole Kidman's approximate birth chart using astrological symbols.

Of course, the best possible chart is more specific. If you get your chart from the Internet or generate it yourself using astrological software, you'll get something like Figure 3-5. This figure shows Nicole's horoscope, adjusted for place (Honolulu) and calculated to the minute via computer, using the Placidus system of house division (see the sidebar "Dividing the houses" for more on this system).

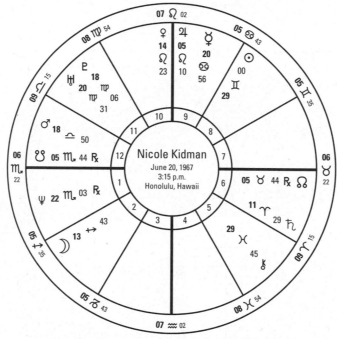

Figure 3-5: Nicole Kidman's precise, computer-generated birth chart.

Are there differences between these methods? There are, though in Nicole's case, the differences aren't dramatic. The main difference is that an exact chart provides specific degrees for the planets, the Ascendant, and the house cusps. That information is crucial, especially for timing predictions. Nonetheless, an estimated chart is still stuffed with information about your personality, your talents, your weaknesses, your desires, your love life, your career, and even your future. It's not perfect. But it's thought-provoking and absorbing, and a good place to start.

Part II

Here Comes the Sun

The 5th Wave   By Rich Tennant

...and in the corner to my right, weighing 217 pounds, fighting as a Capricorn with Capricorn rising and Mars conjunct Uranus in the fifth, out of Beaufort, South Carolinaaaa...

In this part . . .

When I was in college, I picked up my first astrology book virtually by accident, and my understanding of life was transformed. The book — it was one of many by Zolar, a name used by a succession of astrological writers — described the people I knew with uncanny accuracy based solely on their sign, which is determined by the position of the Sun. My parents, my roommate, my so-called boyfriend — all were there, in stunning detail. During those first few hours, I discovered that, all by itself, the Sun sign is amazingly revealing.

Later, I realized that an astrological chart is as complicated as a long-running soap opera (and in the hands of a skilled astrologer, almost as predictable). A chart includes the Sun, the Moon, eight planets, twelve houses, and more. But the core of almost every horoscope is the Sun.

In this part, you can check out of the implications of your Sun sign. Whether it's a fire sign, an earth sign, an air sign, or a water sign, your Sun sign reveals your intrinsic self and illuminates your chart, just as the blazing Sun dominates the sky.

Chapter 4

Fire Signs: Aries, Leo, and Sagittarius

*T*he first of the four traditional elements is fire, and you don't need to be an astrologer to guess what it means. Ancient astrologers linked fire with the vital force of creation. (Think of the original fireball: the Big Bang.) This association stands. Fire generates heat in the form of excitement, activity, and desire. People born under these dynamic, extroverted signs are vigorous and volatile, enterprising and courageous. They're also restless and impatient, with a ready supply of creativity and vision. But they have trouble accepting limits — which may be why they're prone to burn out.

In the cycle of the zodiac, every element has its function. Earth offers stability. Air communicates. Water imparts emotion. But only Fire can provide the initial burst of energy — the creative spark that sets the world in motion.

Figure 4-1, which combines the circle of potential with the dot of individuality, represents the Sun. The Sun's placement in the sky at the moment of your birth determines your sign. If you have any doubt about your Sun sign or were born at the beginning or end of a sign, check out Chapter 1.

Figure 4-1:
The symbol
of the Sun.

Astrologers allot three signs of the zodiac to each of the four elements. The fire signs, which are known for their energy and drive, include the following:

✔ Aries the Ram (March 20 to April 18), the sign of cardinal fire. It's impulsive, daring, and gifted at setting things into motion.

✔ Leo the Lion (July 23 to August 22), the sign of fixed fire. It's vibrant, confident, and brimming with determination.

✔ Sagittarius the Archer (November 22 to December 21), the sign of mutable fire. It's independent, adventurous, and spontaneous.

Even though these signs differ in many ways, they share the life-affirming vitality that fire brings. In this chapter, I discuss the fire signs. If you were born under one of them, you're in the right place. Here I present your good traits and your not-so-good traits, as well as information about work and relationships.

Each sign has an element (fire, earth, air, or water), a polarity (positive or negative), and a quality or modality (cardinal, fixed, or mutable). For more on those terms, turn to Chapter 1.

Aries the Ram: March 20–April 18

The astrological year starts on the spring equinox, which is the first day of Aries, the sign of the Ram. Because you're ruled by Mars, the planet named after the Roman god of war, you're spirited, straightforward, courageous, and enterprising. Yours is the sign of new beginnings.

The *glyph* (written symbol) of Aries appears in Figure 4-2. It signifies the head of the ram, a gushing fountain of energy, or the eyebrows and nose of a human being — a part of the face that's well-defined and graceful on a typical Aries.

Figure 4-2:
The symbol
of Aries
the Ram.

The sunny side

Enthusiastic, inspiring, and exhilarating, Aries is a force of nature like no other. Blessed with boundless energy and a bold, appealing personality, you have a zest for life that other signs can only envy. You're intrepid, passionate, and courageous — a firebrand, glowing and full of flash. Unconventional and joyously individualistic, you display a robust sense of who you are and an

eagerness to follow your own intuition. You have a sense of purpose and a distinct personal style, and you refuse to let others define you. Often a creature of extremes, you react quickly and make instantaneous decisions. You believe in action and proudly stand up for what you know is right, even if it conflicts with commonly held notions. Neither a joiner nor a follower, you're a natural-born leader because you have a clear, decisive mind combined with total faith in your own reactions and plans.

At your audacious best, you're untiring, ardent, and thoroughly original. You're an activist on your own behalf, and you have initiative. A risk-taker with a pioneering spirit, you have a deep need to prove yourself. So when a fresh idea or a groundbreaking mission captures your imagination, you rush in. Later on, if your interest falters or your hopes don't pan out, you move on, undaunted. Life is too short to waste on anything that fails to please you.

The sorry side

Like a child, you can be self-centered, inconsiderate, and intent on doing things your way. Your determination is often unbreakable. When you really want something, you can be combative, brash, and even ruthless in your efforts to get it. You're willing to take risks and you do a lot of rule breaking, a trait that doesn't always work to your benefit. Rather than bending to someone else's requirements, you prefer to simply obey your instincts. At times you exhibit a woeful lack of foresight, and you often lack diligence. Although your enthusiasms are many, you easily become restless and your initial interest soon fizzles. Your impatience is legendary. For that reason, you find greater satisfaction with short-term ventures than with lengthy ones.

Emotionally, you find it difficult to imagine how other people feel. You can strike people as insensitive, egocentric, and self-absorbed. And there's no avoiding the fact that you have a white-hot temper: It comes and goes in a flash, but when it appears, you're terrifying. You hold strong opinions, and you're not afraid to express them, no matter how impolitic (or impolite) they may be. You figure it this way: If expressing your views causes others discomfort, let them nurse their fragile sensibilities on their own. You have too much to do to sit around obsessing over hurt feelings, criticism, or the sorrows and injustices of the past.

Relationships

Anyone who knows you — from friends and family to the most casual of acquaintances — knows where you stand. Outspoken and direct, you don't hesitate to express yourself, and you have little patience for those who can't take the heat. Besides, you enjoy your own company entirely too much to tolerate anyone who requires coddling. Self-sufficient and independent, you

prefer your friends to be as on-the-move as you are, and you can't bear whining. As for love, you're an exciting person to be around, overflowing with enthusiasm and joie de vivre. Although you suffer from jealousy and can be competitive, you enjoy the chase — not that you let it drag on for too long. You're not a game player. You know what you like, and when you find it, you go for it. And did I mention that you're sexually ravenous?

At the same time, you're an idealist who's fully prepared to hold out for the real thing. You demand equality, and if you don't get it, you make your displeasure clear. With Mars, the warrior planet, as your ruler, you seldom shy away from confrontation. And even though you don't mean to be contentious, at times you can't help yourself. You're not one to suppress your feelings or to spend endless hours delving into the intricacies of your own — or anyone else's — psyche. You'd rather face the issues head-on. Your combustible, intimidating exterior may mask feelings of inferiority, but most people won't realize that. All they know is that you're a force to be reckoned with.

For information on your relationships with other signs, flip to Chapter 15.

Work

With your executive decision-making ability and general verve, you're a self-starter and an effective leader who likes to initiate change. Ambitious and competitive, you rise to a challenge. But you're a sprinter, not a long-distance runner. You love the unmistakable thrill that comes at the beginning of an undertaking, when creative momentum is high and the possibilities are wide open. You're delighted to experiment and innovate. But once things have settled into a routine and the endeavor becomes weighted down with procedures, precedents, and supervisors, your excitement wanes. You find it irritating and dispiriting to spend time focusing on details and loose ends or doing standard maintenance tasks. Not surprisingly, quitting too soon is one of your worst — and most frequent — mistakes.

You're happiest working on your own or being the boss, preferably in an enterprise that allows you to be in charge of your own schedule. Physical activity is a definite plus, as is the opportunity to participate in a variety of tasks. You're easily bored, and your need to express yourself is stronger than your need for security. Pie-in-the-sky careers for Aries include being a film director like Francis Ford Coppola, an action star (or motorcyclist) like Steve McQueen, a military leader like General Colin Powell, or a talk show host like David Letterman. Surgery is said to be an Aries profession, as is anything that involves fire (including cooking) and anything with a high risk quotient. Whatever your true vocation, it's not something you choose for money or prestige. Instead, you're drawn to it because it offers you a way to make an impact on the world — and at the same time to express your incomparable, amazing self.

Classic Arians

- ✔ Marlon Brando, Booker T. Washington (Moon in Aries)

- ✔ Norah Jones, Quentin Tarantino, Robert Downey, Jr. (Moon in Taurus)

- ✔ Reba McIntyre, Leonard Nimoy, Harry Houdini (Moon in Gemini)

- ✔ Charles Baudelaire, Aretha Franklin, Robert Frost (Moon in Cancer)

- ✔ Joseph Campbell, Gloria Steinem (Moon in Leo)

- ✔ Emmylou Harris, William Wordsworth (Moon in Virgo)

- ✔ Rosie O'Donnell, Maya Angelou (Moon in Libra)

- ✔ Mariah Carey, Eric Clapton, Francis Ford Coppola (Moon in Scorpio)

- ✔ Thomas Jefferson, Vincent Van Gogh (Moon in Sagittarius)

- ✔ Al Gore, Kate Hudson, David Letterman (Moon in Capricorn)

- ✔ Johann Sebastian Bach, Steve McQueen, Conan O'Brien (Moon in Aquarius)

- ✔ Kareem Abdul-Jabbar, Sarah Michelle Gellar (Moon in Pisces)

If you work for an Aries, your boss will most likely be assertive, enterprising, and impatient with anyone who can't keep up or who requires a lot of supervision. Your best move is to work independently — and don't take those angry outbursts personally.

Aries: The Basic Facts

Polarity: Positive	Favorable Colors: Red and white
Quality: Cardinal	Lucky Gem: Diamond
Element: Fire	Part of the Body: The head
Symbol: The Ram	Metal: Iron
Ruling Planet: Mars	Key Phrase: I am
Opposite Sign: Libra	Major Traits: Energetic, impetuous

Leo the Lion: July 23–August 22

I used to imagine that I was somehow unique in having so many Leo friends. I have come to understand that Leos are so outgoing and warm that they accumulate friends the way other people collect shoes. Fact is, I've met very few people who don't have a Lion or two among their closest companions.

The swirling glyph of Leo (see Figure 4-3) represents the lion's tail, the lion's mane, or the creative force of the Sun.

Figure 4-3:
The glyph of
Leo.

The sunny side

You've got flair. If you're a typical Leo, you're outgoing, loyal, determined, cheerful, and likable. You're active, with an astoundingly busy social calendar and a pile of responsibilities. Whatever you may do for a living, your schedule is crammed full. You aim to live life to the fullest — and have a good time while you're at it. Even in ordinary conversations, you fall into the role of entertaining other people because you love to be the center of attention — and with the Sun as your ruling planet, you really do light up the room. Equipped with a lively sense of humor, vividly rendered opinions, and the ability to have fun even under adverse conditions, you present yourself with confidence and pizzazz. Radiant and proud, you have charisma to burn.

You also have a king-of-the-jungle sense of dignity — and an equally regal sense of entitlement to go with it. You appreciate luxury and glamour in all their forms. (Your color is gold, your metal is gold, and your aura is gold.) Yet despite your aristocratic ways and your need to be pampered, you respect hard work and are willing to shoulder more than your share of the responsibility. Although you can be demanding, you value loyalty and return it in kind. You're helpful and generous, a staunch supporter of an underdog or a friend in distress. And you bring the party with you. Naturally, you want to be acknowledged. What's wrong with that?

The sorry side

Beneath your flamboyant exterior, you would be humiliated if anyone ever knew how hard you try or how vulnerable you feel. In your desperate efforts to get people to like you, you hog center stage, sometimes reducing everyone around you to audience members. (You should know that most people don't enjoy that role.) You're inclined to tell people what you think they want to hear, even if it means weaseling out later when the truth is revealed. You tend to exaggerate, partially because you want to tell a riveting story and partially because you want to cast yourself in a flattering light. It's a matter of strategy: You figure that if you play your cards right, you'll triumph.

You can also be arrogant, overbearing, vain, self-aggrandizing, and histrionic — a real drama queen. You can be dogmatic about the tiniest things — shampoo, say. Or barbecue sauce. Or what other people ought to do with their lives. I don't mean to be harsh, but your urge to give unsolicited advice gets old, even though your motivation is noble. An idealist of the first order, you know what life ought to be. If only you could figure out how to make it happen — and how to convince other people to play their parts. You're more demanding than you realize — and more controlling. And you find it difficult to admit mistakes. When you calm down and stop manipulating, your warmth and generosity come through, and you command the adoration that you crave.

Relationships

Your self-assurance and easy-going humor draw a crowd. The center of any social scene, you're an accomplished party-thrower and a sought-after dinner guest. Although you like to maintain the upper hand in a relationship, and you rely on the attentions of others to keep your ego in shape, you also know how to bestow affection and admiration. People feel privileged to be your friend.

As for romance, Leo loves to be in love and believes in everything symbolic of that state — from Saturday night (which is sacred) to flowers, phone calls, breakfast in bed, loads of sex, and plenty of bling. (I've known Leos to leave dog-eared copies of the Tiffany catalogue on the breakfast table, just to make sure the message comes across.) You're definitely high maintenance, though you undoubtedly think otherwise. When times are good, you're passionate, accommodating, supportive, and adoring. When things are falling apart, you do too, becoming domineering, arrogant, and jealous. Should a hot affair cool into dull predictability, you may even stir things up, just to keep life interesting. And when your beloved disappoints you, you're devastated, even if you don't let it show. For all your bluster, you have a tender heart.

Finally, I want to add a note about animals. In traditional astrological lore, pets aren't associated with Leo. But I have noticed that the people I know who treat their pets like family, cart them around in Louis Vuitton cases, purchase wardrobes for them, publish books about them, or appear on television with their squirming bulldogs on their laps to protest against puppy mills, are overwhelmingly Leos. Not every Leo has a pet, and some wouldn't dream of it. (They don't want to be upstaged.) But those who do value their four-legged friends invest themselves fully in the relationship.

For information on Leo's relationships with other signs, take a look at Chapter 15.

Classic Leos

- Jacqueline Kennedy Onassis, Andy Warhol, Jennifer Lopez (Moon in Aries)

- Bill Clinton, Mick Jagger, Kyra Sedgwick (Moon in Taurus)

- Amelia Earhart, Tony Bennett (Moon in Gemini)

- Emily Brontë, Annie Oakley, Sean Penn (Moon in Cancer)

- Charlize Theron, Halle Berry (Moon in Leo)

- Madonna, Dustin Hoffman, J. K. Rowling (Moon in Virgo)

- Fidel Castro, Belinda Carlisle, Julia Child (Moon in Libra)

- Alfred Hitchcock, Ben Affleck, Steve Martin (Moon in Scorpio)

- Herman Melville, Magic Johnson, Martha Stewart (Moon in Sagittarius)

- Napoleon Bonaparte, Arnold Schwarzenegger (Moon in Capricorn)

- Sandra Bullock, Beatrix Potter (Moon in Aquarius)

- Coco Chanel, Robert De Niro (Moon in Pisces)

Work

Because Leos enjoy basking in the limelight, people occasionally assume that you aren't hard-working. This judgment couldn't be further from the truth. Leos are hugely ambitious and somewhat opportunistic. You're resourceful and productive, a skilled organizer with a sharp business sense. Many Leos speculate with abandon. You seek recognition more than most, fantasize about fame, and are willing to work at maximum intensity. If you're at the top of the heap, even in a tiny, home-based business, you feel powerful and magnanimous. You happily make room for others, both as partners and as employees, and you're not afraid to get your hands dirty or to share a pizza with the part-time staff.

But no matter how gratifying your job may be in other respects, you can't exist without a little razzle-dazzle. Ideal careers are musician (Madonna), actor (Halle Berry), clothing designer (Coco Chanel), politician (Bill Clinton, Barack Obama), and anything that's likely to put you in front of a group of people. Fifth-grade teacher? Fine. Lawyer? Sure, especially if you can strut your stuff in court. President of anything? Absolutely. Star of screen and stage? Now you're talking.

If you work for a Leo, be prepared to work intensely (except when your boss is in the mood to talk), to shower him or her with respect and compliments, and to step politely aside whenever the spotlight is turned on. Your allegiance and your skill will be privately recognized — and rewarded. Leo is warm and generous. But remember, Leo rules. The term of art here is "benevolent despot."

Leo: The Basic Facts

Polarity: Positive

Quality: Fixed

Element: Fire

Symbol: The Lion

Ruling Planet: The Sun

Opposite Sign: Aquarius

Favorable Colors: Gold and orange

Lucky Gem: Ruby

Parts of the Body: Heart and spine

Metal: Gold

Key Phrase: I will

Major Traits: Extroverted, demanding

Sagittarius the Archer: November 22–December 21

Independent, lively, and brimming with an irrepressible sense of possibility, you feel most vibrantly alive when you're having an adventure in the world. For that you can thank Jupiter, your ruler, the planet of expansion and good fortune.

The glyph of Sagittarius (see Figure 4-4) represents the centaur's arrow and your high aspirations.

Figure 4-4: The symbol of Sagittarius.

The sunny side

At your happiest and best, you're a free spirit, a cheerful wanderer, an honest and intelligent companion, and a philosopher who likes to ponder the big questions — preferably with a few pals and a plentiful supply of snacks. You see life as an ongoing quest for experience and wisdom, not as a search for security. Restless and excitable, with a rapid-fire wit, you chafe under restriction and demand autonomy, which you happily extend to others.

In your eternal quest for experience and knowledge, you pursue a multitude of interests and you set ambitious, wide-ranging goals for yourself. You want to see the world and understand it, which is why your sign rules travel, philosophy, religion, law, and abstractions of all kinds. Sagittarius is free-thinking, casual, open-minded, and optimistic (though a couple of planets in

Scorpio can dampen your spirits and add a touch of melancholy). You connect easily with all kinds of people and are said to be lucky. The truth is that your spontaneous decisions and out-there gambles occasionally pay off, but what benefits you the most is your fearless attitude. Sure, troubles may come. No one is immune to that. But ultimately, buoyed by your curiosity and belief in the future, you bounce back. You look at it this way: What other choice is there?

The sorry side

Like the centaur, your half-human, half-horse symbol, you're divided. Part of you aspires to party into the night (that's the quadruped half). The other part of you aims high, longing to expand your mind and explore the infinite reaches of the spirit. Sounds good, but you can be a blowhard — and without a target, you flounder. Impractical and disorganized, you're easily sidetracked and must battle a tendency to procrastinate. You fritter away endless amounts of time and energy (and money). Moreover, you can be unreliable, with an unfortunate tendency to promise more than you can actually deliver. You don't mean to misrepresent yourself; it's just that your innate optimism causes you to overestimate your ability.

A peculiar fact about Sagittarius is that although you supposedly love the outdoors, you may not spend much time there. (As Sagittarian Woody Allen said, "I'm at two with nature.") And though you thrive on exercise, you can be physically clumsy. More significantly, you can be dogmatic and fanatical, with an exasperating propensity to preach. Finally, there's your legendary tactlessness. You haven't learned to lie, even when it's a kindness to do so. A friend shows up with badly cropped hair or a hideous new outfit? You blurt out the unflattering truth. It's the flip side of your honesty — and it's nothing to be proud of.

Relationships

Funny, generous, enthusiastic, and direct, the Archer loves to talk and makes friends easily. Stimulating conversation and a clever sense of humor carry a lot of weight with you. You also prize personal freedom, making romance much trickier than friendship. Despite a tendency to take risks in other areas, you tend to hold back romantically and are famous for being resistant to commitment. Whether you come across as a Don Juan, an inconstant lover, or a monk-in-training, you usually manage to maintain your independence, even at the cost of occasional loneliness. Besides, you're an optimist (though you may think otherwise). So why settle for someone who's less than perfect when Match.com alone offers thousands of eligible soul mates at the click of

a mouse? No wonder it's hard to choose. Denizens of other signs may rush to the altar, anxious to pair up and settle down. You have fantasies aplenty — but they're not about weddings, gift registries, mortgages, or twins. You'd just as soon see the world and develop some of your own talents.

When you do ultimately connect (and fear not, it happens all the time), you sincerely hope that the relationship will lead to a larger, more fulfilling life — not a more constrained one. You have nothing against domesticity, but it is not your dream, and stability is not your guiding principle. Instead, you seek a life of adventure, be it literal, intellectual, or spiritual, with plenty of laughs along the way — and an active, accomplished companion who doesn't mind being with someone as independent as you. Even in a fully committed, deeply passionate relationship, Sagittarius always needs some space.

For information on the Archer's relationships with other signs, turn to Chapter 15.

Work

Sagittarius is the sign of higher education, and the professions associated with the sign reflect that. Blessed with a love of learning and a yearning to do something that matters, you're well suited for teaching, publishing, journalism, law, religion, communications, and anything involving international relations or travel. You dislike bureaucracy and grow restless in a rigidly structured organization. Whatever you do, your intellect needs to be engaged. Versatile and quick, you're easily distracted and may accept a hodgepodge of assignments just to keep things interesting. Big projects and high ideals excite you. Bookkeeping doesn't. Financial management doesn't. Indeed, it's the small stuff that trips you up — and yet your professional success depends upon your ability to handle the details.

Learning to delegate is another one of your challenges. A natural egalitarian, you hate to request assistance and are uncomfortable asking others to perform the dull tasks you'd just as soon dodge yourself. Finally, you may face issues of time management. In a world full of fascinating distractions, it's essential to use your time to advantage. But you already know that.

If you work for a Sagittarian, your essential task is to keep the big picture in mind and make sure things are moving forward. If your work is generally on target, the Archer won't nitpick you to death. Sagittarius isn't a micromanager. On the other hand, if you need help with something specific, you may not get it. After all, you already received a rundown of the situation — right? And be prepared: Detail-averse Sagittarians don't object to working overtime. If you're a strict 9-to-5er, the Archer may question your commitment.

Classic Sagittarians

- Mark Twain, Tyra Banks (Moon in Aries)

- Christina Aguilera, Lucy Liu, Jim Morrison, Diego Rivera (Moon in Taurus)

- Jeff Bridges, Edith Piaf, Tina Turner (Moon in Gemini)

- William Blake, Jimi Hendrix (Moon in Cancer)

- Winston Churchill, Katie Holmes (Moon in Leo)

- Frank Zappa, Samuel L. Jackson (Moon in Virgo)

- Jane Austen, Emily Dickinson, Jay Z (Moon in Libra)

- Scarlett Johansson, Bruce Lee, Steven Spielberg (Moon in Scorpio)

- Ludwig von Beethoven, Joan Didion, Jon Stewart (Moon in Sagittarius)

- Brad Pitt, T. C. Boyle (Moon in Capricorn)

- Woody Allen, Britney Spears, Caroline Kennedy (Moon in Aquarius)

- Joe DiMaggio, Frank Sinatra (Moon in Pisces)

Sagittarius: The Basic Facts

Polarity: Positive	Favorable Colors: Purple and blue
Quality: Mutable	Lucky Gem: Turquoise
Element: Fire	Parts of the Body: Hips and thighs
Symbol: The Centaur	Metal: Tin
Ruling Planet: Jupiter	Key Phrase: I see
Opposite Sign: Gemini	Major Traits: Adventurous, independent

Chapter 5

Earth Signs: Taurus, Virgo, and Capricorn

*J*ust as the universe burst into existence with the fireball of the Big Bang, the cycle of the zodiac lifts off with a blast of fire, the most energetic of the four traditional elements. Fire creates heat, light, and movement. But what's the point of all that combustion if it leads to nothing? Without earth, fire would burn itself out like a spray of fireworks against the night sky. Earth signs ground the energy of fire by turning the sizzle into something tangible. Cautious where fire is bold, earth signs are stable, sensible, productive, persistent, and materialistic — and I don't mean that in a bad way. Unlike less realistic signs, earth signs understand and respect material things, including money. They're also sensuous, responsive human beings who glory in the physical world in all its splendor.

Fire sends off sparks, no question. Air talks up a storm. And no one understands the impact of emotion like Water. But if you want to actually get something done, look to Earth.

Astrological tradition allots three signs to each of the four elements. The earth signs, recognized for their productivity and pragmatic approach to life, include the following:

- ✔ Taurus the Bull (April 19 to May 20), the sign of fixed earth. Taurus is known for its persistence, its longing for security, and — in case you thought that earth signs are only about practicality — its love of pleasure.

- ✔ Virgo the Virgin (August 23 to September 22), the sign of mutable earth. Virgo is famed for its analytical mind, its attention to detail, and its tendency to be a perfectionist.

✓ Capricorn the Goat (December 22 to January 19), the sign of cardinal fire. The Goat is resourceful, conscientious, and ambitious.

These signs share a desire to make a tangible contribution. If earth is your element, read on. In this chapter, I present your great traits and your grating traits, along with information about relationships and work.

The sun's position in the heavens at the time of your birth determines your sign. If you were born at the beginning or end of a sign or you're unsure about your sign, turn to Chapter 1 and read the section entitled "Born on the Cusp." Also, in addition to its element, each sign has a polarity (positive or negative) and a quality or modality (cardinal, fixed, or mutable). For more on these terms, refer to Chapter 1.

Taurus the Bull: April 19–May 20

When Harry Truman was president, a sign in the oval office read "The buck stops here." That's just what you might expect from a Taurus. In good times and in bad, you're steadfast, dependable, and willing to accept responsibility. But Taurus also has a pleasure-loving side, for it is ruled by Venus, the guardian of love and art. Truman knew something about that part of life too. A devoted husband and fiercely protective father, he was a gifted piano player who thought about becoming a professional musician. He decided that he didn't have what it takes. "A good music-hall piano player is about the best I'd have ever been," he said. "So I went into politics and became President of the United States." Taurus has the stamina and the persistence to make something like that possible.

The symbol (or glyph) of Taurus, shown in Figure 5-1, represents the head and horns of the Bull — or the circle of potential topped by the crescent of receptivity.

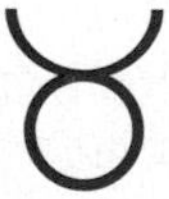

Figure 5-1:
The symbol of Taurus.

The sunny side

In the cycle of the zodiac, Aries, the pioneer, arrives first, spewing energy in every direction. Taurus, the second sign, brings that energy down to earth and uses it to build something solid. As a fixed earth sign, you're cautious,

grounded in reality, steady on your feet, and utterly reliable. Because you have an intense need for security, both emotional and financial, you make conservative choices and try to avoid change. You hold on tightly, only giving up when there's no other option. But once you've made a decision, nothing can convince you to change your mind. Concrete goals make the most sense to you. You pursue them quietly and with single-minded determination. It's true that you may not reach your destination quickly — but like the legendary tortoise to whom you're often compared, you do get there.

As an earth sign, you're at home in your body and attuned to your environment. Romantic and sensuous, kind and gentle, you're responsive to comforts of every kind, and your senses are wide open. You love slow, languid sex; the textures of silk and velvet (and corduroy); freshly baked bread; full-bodied red wine; nature in all its seasons; and handcrafted objects, which you acquire with ease and never cease to enjoy. Taurus is also creatively gifted. Chances are you have talent in at least one of the arts, including music, dance, sculpture, painting, design, architecture, cooking, gardening, and the fine art of relaxing.

The sorry side

Although your dedication is impressive, your leisurely pace can drive other people to distraction. You start slowly, tend to plod, and refuse to be rushed. You can be stodgy at an early age, and you can easily fall into a rut. Plus, you're incredibly stubborn. Your well-known tenacity is a positive trait when it means sticking up for moral principles (think of Coretta Scott King or Bono, the Taurus rock singer who was nominated for a Nobel Peace Prize). Too often, though, it means refusing to change, no matter what the circumstances. I've seen Taureans cling to outmoded, self-destructive patterns for years just because they didn't want to risk trying a new approach or making amends. That's what being bull-headed can mean.

As long as we're discussing your negative traits, let me add that you can be greedy, status conscious, acquisitive, gluttonous, self-indulgent, and self-pitying. Normally, you're hard-working and persevering, but when you're down, you become apathetic. You can also be possessive, dependent, jealous, insensitive and, at your worst, a user. You don't intend to exploit other people. But — you know — things happen.

One more thing: Taurus, unlike Aries, doesn't get angry easily, for which the rest of the world is grateful. But when you do blow up . . . let's just say that some of the worst mass murderers and dictators in history — men like Hitler, Lenin, and Saddam Hussein — were born under the sign of the Bull.

Relationships

With Venus as your ruling planet, you're appealing and affectionate, and you effortlessly attract friends, lovers, and sidekicks. Romance is hugely important to you but (with rare exceptions) you won't go after it aggressively. Quietly seductive, you give subtle signals, and if the object of your desire turns out to be immune, you look elsewhere.

Your feelings run deep, but it's not excitement you seek; it's sanctuary. In your heart, familiarity breeds contentment. You relish the daily, domestic rituals along with the security of a long-running relationship. When you're in a secure partnership, you hold on tightly. You're loving, protective, and supportive, even if you're also dependent and possessive.

Although you dislike conflict and try to avoid it, you don't back down either. If a relationship is on shaky ground, you can hardly bear the tension. Some people (Leo and Scorpio, for example) get all caught up in those romantic ups and downs. They throw themselves into the drama and even find it titillating. Not Taurus. Sincere and intense, you play for keeps because you're not playing. For you, love isn't a game.

For the lowdown on your relationships with other signs, turn to Chapter 15.

Work

Because you adore the creature comforts and lack that manic hit that often characterizes high achievers, people may assume that you're lazy. They couldn't be more wrong. Though your ability to lounge around on weekends is without equal, you're diligent, productive, and organized when you want to be, with an inborn need to do something constructive. Security is essential to you, whether that means money in the bank, real estate, a first-rate pension plan, or all of the above. And yet, that's not where you live. At bottom, it's more important for you to believe in what you're doing and to find a modicum of creative expression. When you identify an area that satisfies those needs, you're willing to make financial sacrifices.

Whatever you choose, you work at a steady pace. And unlike other signs, you aren't constantly trying to elbow your way into the spotlight. Naturally, people come to rely on you. And yes, it sometimes feels as though you're doing more than your share of the work for less than your share of the recognition. That's one of the drawbacks of being an earth sign.

Working with the Bull is easier if you accept the fact that he knows what he wants and he's unlikely to change. He values productivity, follow-through, loyalty, and the ability to stay cool. As for those brilliant ideas you have about how to shake things up, keep them to yourself. They will only make him distrust your judgment.

Classic Taureans

- Stevie Wonder, Cate Blanchett (Moon in Aries)

- Katharine Hepburn, Kelly Clarkson (Moon in Taurus)

- Sigmund Freud, Fred Astaire (Moon in Gemini)

- Benjamin Spock, Ulysses S. Grant (Moon in Cancer)

- Barbra Streisand, Renee Zellweger, James Brown (Moon in Leo)

- Michelle Pfeiffer, Jay Leno, Jack Nicholson, Shirley MacLaine (Moon in Virgo)

- Billy Joel, Rosario Dawson (Moon in Libra)

- Bono, Harry S. Truman (Moon in Scorpio)

- Frank Capra, Al Pacino, Sue Grafton (Moon in Sagittarius)

- Cher, George Clooney (Moon in Capricorn)

- Charlotte Brontë, Uma Thurman, David Beckham, George Lucas (Moon in Aquarius)

- Audrey Hepburn, Jerry Seinfeld, Leonardo da Vinci (Moon in Pisces)

Taurus: The Basic Facts

Polarity: Negative	Favorable Colors: Greens and browns
Quality: Fixed	Lucky Gem: Emerald
Element: Earth	Parts of the Body: Neck and throat
Symbol: The Bull	Metal: Copper
Ruling Planet: Venus	Key Phrase: I build
Opposing Sign: Scorpio	Major Traits: Productive, obstinate

Virgo the Virgin: August 23– September 22

The mind of a Virgo is a wondrous thing. Thanks to Mercury, the planet named after the quick-witted god of communication, you're observant, insightful, capable, and articulate. You're also discriminating and critical, especially of yourself. Constantly in search of self-improvement, you consider yourself a work in progress.

The symbol of Virgo the Virgin (see Figure 5-2) resembles an M with a closed-in loop. It signifies the female genitals, in contrast to Scorpio, which represents the male.

Figure 5-2:
The symbol
of Virgo.

Ⅶ

The sunny side

Nothing sneaks past you. You have an eye for detail, an inborn sense of efficiency, and a supreme sensitivity to the implications of language. Smart, funny, and engaging, you can claim extraordinary analytical abilities, a rare clarity of mind, an enviable capacity for concentration, and a love of learning that isn't just for show. On top of that, you're considerate and appealingly modest. You know you're not perfect — but you're doing just about everything you can to get there. Like the other earth signs, you're conscientious, industrious, and efficient. Unlike them, you're also an idealist. You know how things ought to be, and you're certain that you can make them that way, one detail at a time. Armed with your lengthy to-do list, you're organized and disciplined, ready to push yourself to the limit. You're equally willing to assist other people, an offer that extends way beyond your immediate circle. You have a strong moral core and can be helpful to the point of selflessness. People often forget that Virgo is the sign of service. (Think of Mother Teresa.) Acting on behalf of others makes you feel good about yourself.

The sorry side

You're too hard on everyone, yourself included. You nag. You criticize. You can't distinguish between that which is acceptable (your spouse) and that which is ideal (your spouse, if only he would shape up). You can be incredibly demanding — and incredibly disappointed when your demands aren't met. At times you act the part of the martyr who's compelled to put up with the inadequacies of others, but you also suffer from waves of guilt, inferiority, shyness, and anxiety. You worry about the air, the water, global warming, war, calories, the homeless person you passed on the street, the insensitive remark you're afraid you may have made, your investments, and your body. In the life of a typical Virgo, hypochondria is a dragon you have to slay (which is one reason Virgos often immerse themselves in the Merck Manual or become fascinated by alternative healing techniques). A healthful diet, sufficient exercise, and a reliable method for reducing stress are essential.

A note on neatness: No matter what you may have heard, not all Virgos are neatness fiends. Not that it doesn't happen: I've known Virgos who can't rest unless everything in the refrigerator is arranged parallel to the door. I've known Virgos who have genuine opinions about tile cleansers. I've also

known Virgos who are incapable of throwing things out. Their intention is to do something with all that stuff. Meanwhile, they don't look compulsive in the least; they look like world-class slobs.

Relationships

You'd think that a sign supposedly as critical as Virgo would have trouble making friends. But this isn't the case. Virgos love to converse, excel at analyzing other people, dote on exploring new ideas, and maintain a multitude of interests. Conversation with a Virgo is never dull. Virgos also remember birthdays, bring chicken soup and DVDs to ailing friends, and generally extend themselves. So you don't lack for a busy social life — even if you are a little heavy-handed with the advice from time to time.

In a committed relationship, you're most comfortable when your role and responsibilities are clearly defined. When you don't know what to expect or those roles are shifting under the pressure of circumstances, you become jittery, insomniac, withholding, and — your worst mistake — controlling. You don't mean to be — you just want to make sure that everything is on course. You have a powerful sense of the way things should be, and when reality conflicts with your impossibly high standards, you slip into a state of denial and see what you want to see. When breakups occur, you're stunned. For all your good sense, a Virgo with a broken heart is a pathetic creature indeed. Fortunately, you aren't one to spend your life sobbing into your limited-edition designer brew. Inevitably, you find a way to turn things around. You have no trouble attracting admirers, for Virgo can be incredibly seductive, despite its virginal image. (Iconic Virgo sex symbols include Sean Connery, Richard Gere, Sophia Loren, and Greta Garbo.) But that's not what helps you get through tough times. It's your mental ability to reframe a situation. Sure, things may look bad from one angle. But from another . . .

For the scoop on Virgo's relationships with other signs, check out Chapter 15.

Work

It's difficult to imagine an organization that wouldn't benefit from having a Virgo or two around. The master of multi-tasking, you easily juggle hundreds of details and dozens of conflicting demands. Organized and meticulous, you're skilled at teaching, writing (and other forms of communication), and anything that requires an analytical mind and attention to detail. But no matter what direction you go in, more work ends up on your desk than on anyone else's because, guess what? You're more efficient than anyone else. That's why the powers-that-be keep calling on you. No one else is up to the job — and you may not want to do it either. Even so, you produce accurate,

Classic Virgos

- Ingrid Bergman, Lily Tomlin, Roald Dahl, Pink (Moon in Aries)

- Oliver Stone, Cameron Diaz, Hugh Grant (Moon in Taurus)

- Claudia Schiffer, Cathy Guisewite, John Cage (Moon in Gemini)

- Julio Iglesias, Elvis Costello, Dave Chapelle (Moon in Cancer)

- Garrison Keillor, William *"Lord of the Flies"* Golding, Ludacris (Moon in Leo)

- Sean Connery, Lance Armstrong, Rachael Ray, Leo Tolstoy (Moon in Virgo)

- D. H. Lawrence, Agatha Christie (Moon in Libra)

- Beyoncé Knowles, Bruno Bettleheim (Moon in Scorpio)

- Mary *"Frankenstein"* Shelley, Stephen King (Moon in Sagittarius)

- Dorothy Parker, Brian de Palma, John McCain (Moon in Capricorn)

- Sophia Loren, Samuel Goldwyn, Bill Murray (Moon in Aquarius)

- Michael Jackson, MacCauley Culkin (Moon in Pisces)

timely results because you can't resist rising to a challenge. Might as well admit the truth: You can't resist the compliment, and you take secret pleasure in tucking in every last detail. You're the ideal employee, like it or not — which may be why Virgos often fantasize about owning their own businesses. The degree of control you gain as an entrepreneur is tonic for your soul.

If you work for a Virgo, follow instructions to the letter and obey the unstated rules of the workplace. On the surface, the environment may be casual and egalitarian. Nonetheless, the standards are strict. So go ahead and request instruction and clarification when you need it. Virgo will respect you for asking. Similarly, feel free to ask for feedback. But understand that after you receive advice, you must make a sincere effort at following it. Otherwise, Virgo may perceive your request as a waste of time. And take my word for it: You don't want to waste a Virgo's time.

Virgo: The Basic Facts

Polarity: Negative

Quality: Mutable

Element: Earth

Symbol: The Virgin

Ruling Planet: Mercury

Opposite Sign: Pisces

Favorable Colors: Navy and neutrals

Lucky Gem: Peridot

Part of the Body: The nervous system

Metal: Mercury

Key Phrase: I analyze

Major Traits: Analytical, fault-finding

Capricorn the Goat: December 22– January 19

Somebody has to uphold tradition. Somebody has to follow the rules. For that matter, somebody has to write them. With somber Saturn, the planet of structure, as your ruler, it may as well be you.

The glyph of Capricorn (see Figure 5-3) represents either the mountain goat with its curling horns or the mythical creature who is a goat above and a fish below.

Figure 5-3:
The symbol of Capricorn.

The sunny side

You're productive, responsible, competitive, and mature. You're an adult — even as a child. Indeed, Capricorn often has a tough time as a youngster because you're more serious than most people. You come into your own in adulthood, and you age beautifully. Although there may be occasional dips along the way, it's a well-recognized phenomenon that the older you get, the happier you become. It's the miracle of Capricorn.

You're ambitious. Like the mountain goat that clambers over rocky terrain to reach the summit, you have your eye on a distant peak — and you've figured out a strategy for getting there. Patient, industrious, and thrifty, you bravely weather any difficulties you encounter along the way. Society depends on Capricorn because you have the ability to step outside of yourself, to consider the needs of others, and to develop realistic strategies for fulfilling those needs. You're a natural leader.

Though you may panic internally during times of stress, externally you stay calm. Unlike other signs I can name (Sagittarius, say, or Pisces), you know how to apply self-discipline — and, unlike Virgo, you can do so without making a fetish of it. Your control is obvious in every cell of your body. You're cool, reserved, dignified, and authoritative. As an earth sign, you see what needs to be done and you act expeditiously. And though you often have trouble loosening up, you have that earth-sign sensuality to indulge in. You respond to timeless art, true love, and the pleasures of the kitchen, the bedroom, and the boardroom — up to and including a nice fat investment portfolio. Say what you will, money does provide security.

The sorry side

A natural-born conservative, no matter what your politics may be, you have a plan (and a budget) for everything. Status-conscious and money-minded, you can be fearful, repressed, and pessimistic. You have such a deep sense of purpose that you find it difficult to relax: Taking time off feels like breaking stride to you, and you don't want to do it. After all, there's more to be done . . . much more. You're frustrated by your slow progress. The truth is that if it weren't for other people, you'd live on the treadmill. You're the least spontaneous sign of the zodiac. A little resiliency would lighten your considerable load but it isn't easy for you to bend. I hesitate to say "You work too hard" only because I know that you will agree — and secretly take it as a compliment.

Here's another problem: Emotional issues can be threatening to a Capricorn. Even with friends, you'd rather not discuss feelings at all, thank you. No one likes to reveal weakness, but for you it's especially painful. So you suffer in silence and are prone to denial. Why see what you don't want to see? What's the point of gazing into the heart of darkness — or the void at the center of a bad relationship — if you aren't prepared to do anything about it? It may be better not to know. Right?

Right. Except that sometimes facing the truth is the only way to make things better.

Relationships

Begin by acknowledging that Capricorn has a strong sense of privacy, propriety, and emotional reserve. Even your oldest friends don't get too close. You admire them for their accomplishments and sympathize with them for their troubles. You're not unkind. But you're uncomfortable with emotional displays and would just as soon not have to be there during times of major crisis. (You would rather help by doing something practical.) In love, too, you go out of your way to avoid pyrotechnics. You just can't stand it.

On the other hand, you're a traditionalist with a strong sex drive and a deep need to be comforted, admired, and connected. Your ideal partner is accomplished, well put-together, and worthy in the eyes of the world. You can't help responding to the confidence that success brings. What's so terrible about that?

When you find the right person — and it can take awhile — you're faithful and devoted. Playing around isn't your style. Playing traditional gender roles is. Although you believe in gender equality, you still feel comfortable with a standard male/female role division. If there is a problem, it may be simply that you take everything very seriously. A pillow fight on a weeknight? No way! You

need 7.5 hours of sleep, and not a nanosecond less. An afternoon tryst with your beloved? Are you joking? You have a job! In Capricorn relationships, it's generally the other person who tries to provide the laughs (and the spontaneity). Someone's gotta lighten things up — and it probably won't be you.

For specifics on the Goat's interactions with other signs, flip to Chapter 15.

Work

Can you say workaholic? Capricorn is the most ambitious, industrious sign of the zodiac. You accept responsibility without complaint. You know how to operate within an organization, large or small, and when a structure is lacking, you know how to create one. You may not like bureaucracy, but you understand it, and you're at home in a corporation. Naturally you crave recognition. And let's face it: Although recognition comes in many guises, its primary form is money. You understand the stuff. Occasionally, you even become obsessed with it because money is a sign of accomplishment. Consider, for example, this remark from the eccentric, obsessive-compulsive tycoon Howard Hughes. "I'm not a paranoid deranged millionaire," he said. "Goddamit, I'm a billionaire."

So, yes, some Capricorns are covetous and materialistic. Most are not. And many of you have a little-recognized ability to put the good of others ahead of your selfish desires. Not for nothing was Martin Luther King, Jr., a Capricorn. Those born under the sign of the Goat, despite a reputation for capitalist venality, often have a social conscience. They just don't think they should have to suffer for it.

 If you work for a Capricorn, everything you ever learned about how to behave at work applies: Be on time, dress for the next level up, anticipate your boss's needs, be organized, and so forth. Avoid office pranks: Naked pictures on the copier won't amuse your straight-arrow boss. And make sure that nothing suspect appears on your computer screen — and that includes solitaire. Remember: Capricorns wrote the rules. You'd be a fool to break them.

Capricorn: The Basic Facts

Polarity: Negative	Favorable Colors: Dark green and brown
Quality: Cardinal	Lucky Gem: Onyx
Element: Earth	Parts of the Body: Bones and teeth
Symbol: The Goat	Metal: Silver
Ruling Planet: Saturn	Key Phrase: I use
Opposite Sign: Cancer	Major Traits: Goal-oriented, rigid

Classic Capricorns

- Albert Schweitzer, Diane von Furstenberg, Elizabeth Arden (Moon in Aries)

- Carlos Casteneda, Naomi Judd (Moon in Taurus)

- Joan Baez, Jim Carrey (Moon in Gemini)

- Robert F. Kennedy, Jr., Mary Tyler Moore, Janis Joplin (Moon in Cancer)

- David Bowie, Mao Tze Tung, Marilyn Manson (Moon in Leo)

- Stephen Hawking (Moon in Virgo)

- Nicholas Cage, Jude Law (Moon in Libra)

- Henry Miller, Orlando Bloom, Kate Moss (Moon in Scorpio)

- Henri Matisse, Tiger Woods (Moon in Sagittarius)

- Clara Barton, A. A. Milne (Moon in Capricorn)

- Cary Grant, Richard M. Nixon, Denzel Washington, Muhammad Ali (Moon in Aquarius)

- Edgar Allen Poe, Elvis Presley, J. R. R. Tolkien (Moon in Pisces)

Chapter 6

Air Signs: Gemini, Libra, and Aquarius

A ir represents intelligence and reason. It's the element of the intellect, and those born under its influence are known for their ability to connect the dots. Air signs are bright, curious, versatile, and intellectually restless. Their minds are always active, always searching for understanding. Crazy as it may sound, natives of those signs actually think about things, and they try to do it objectively and in depth. They value ideas and revel in conversation.

Despite their reputation for sometimes being a little too objective and detached — let's just say that Mr. Spock was definitely an air sign — they're also supremely social, linking friends, relatives, and random strangers into networks of relationships.

By long astrological tradition, each of the four elements has been assigned to three signs of the zodiac. The air signs, which are legendary for their mental acuteness, include the following:

✔ Gemini the Twins (May 21 to June 20), the sign of mutable air. Gemini is known for its curious, lively mind, sparkling personality, and capricious ways.

✔ Libra the Scales (September 23 to October 22), the sign of cardinal air. Libra is recognized for its balanced intellect, sense of fairness, and aesthetic sensitivity, as well as for the importance it places on partnership.

✔ Aquarius the Water Bearer (January 20 to February 18), the sign of fixed air. Aquarius is celebrated for its forward-looking ideas, unique and often eccentric interests, and free-spirited personality.

If your birthday falls at the beginning or end of a sign, double-check your Sun sign by turning to Chapter 1 and reading the section entitled "Born on the Cusp."

Air signs share a desire to make connections and to communicate. If air is your element, your essential qualities are discussed here. In this chapter, I present your most appealing traits and your most irritating ones, along with information about relationships and work.

Besides its element, each sign has a polarity (positive or negative) and a quality or modality (cardinal, fixed, or mutable). For more on those terms, see Chapter 1.

Gemini the Twins: May 21–June 20

Agile and articulate, Gemini is lively, bright, thoroughly engaged, and incredibly persuasive. That's because you're ruled by quick-witted Mercury, the trickster god who could wiggle his way out of anything.

The two pillars of Gemini (see the glyph in Figure 6-1) represent the mythological twins: Castor, the human son of a man, and Pollux, the immortal son of Zeus, king of the gods. They also symbolize the two sides of your double-sided nature.

Figure 6-1:
The symbol
of Gemini.

♊

The sunny side

Forever young, they say. You're clever, inquisitive, gregarious, and cheerful — and it shows in your face. In your never-ending quest for stimulation, you habitually veer off in unexpected directions. Effervescent and up-to-date, you're invigorated by the latest toy, the hottest band, the most shocking news story, and the juiciest gossip (because really, isn't that how you learn the ways of the world?). You're clever and quick, excited by everything life has to offer. You pursue a multitude of interests and love to immerse yourself in new endeavors. When you enter a new world, you feel as if doors are swinging open and the possibilities before you are infinite.

But you're also impatient and easily bored. To fend off the threat of ennui, it reassures you to have two (or more) novels on your bedside table, two jobs (preferably part-time), two love affairs (or a main one and a backup), and at least two phones. You also maintain an ever-expanding legion of friends. Your enthusiasm is infectious, and nothing delights you more than discovering — or forging — connections between unexpected people or unrelated ideas. You're in constant motion, and you make a point of cultivating spontaneity, at least in theory. In reality, you sometimes load yourself down with so many activities that spontaneity becomes essentially impossible. You're forever squeezing in another meeting, another project, another errand, another friend. Inevitably, you end up doing a lot of juggling. Yet the truth is this: When you're overcommitted and ever-so-slightly frazzled, much as you might complain, you feel content and at home in the world.

The sorry side

A hostage to hyperactivity, you squander your resources because you can't resist the immediate gratification of conversing, cavorting with the cat, going online, or simply doing something else. If you could, you'd rather be in two places at once. Impatient and inconstant, you chatter too much, have a short span of attention, and too often, drop the ball simply through inattention. You're easily distracted and often find it difficult to concentrate — or even to sit still. In many ways, you're like a child. When you find something that excites you, you accelerate into overdrive. But you can exhaust your own enthusiasm by talking it into the ground. You don't hesitate to sing your own praises. And although you may not notice, your intense, narcissistic focus sometimes drains other people. Take my word for it: They aren't as fascinated as you think.

At your worst, you can be deceptive, superficial, and fickle — the living, breathing incarnation of hot air. Astrologers (and jilted lovers) often accuse you of being emotionally shallow. Actually, you experience real emotions — just not for long. When troubles come, you see no point in dwelling on them. Instead, you push your feelings aside and adapt to the changed circumstances — and you do it with stunning ease. A lover breaks up with you? Your supervisor locks your computer and escorts you to the Exit sign? No problem. You rewrite history, and pretty soon you're the one who walked. You'll deal with the repercussions down the road (if at all). Meanwhile, you may be a bundle of nerves, but you're busy writing a new chapter. Like Gemini Bob Dylan, you don't look back.

Relationships

Those who have been burnt in a relationship with a Gemini often accuse members of your sign of being unfeeling and fickle. This is unfair. I know Geminis who have enjoyed monogamous relationships for decades. There are many factors in a horoscope, and the Sun is only one of them.

But I've also known Geminis who fit the stereotype perfectly. Playful and engaging, you love the excitement of making conquests. The banter of courtship amuses you. As much as you may long to be in a committed relationship, you're easily bored and essentially restless, and you soon grow disenchanted. The ideal partner for you is multifaceted enough to provide the stimulation you seek, confident enough to let you have the freedom you enjoy, and witty enough to make you laugh. You can't help responding to someone who presents a challenge. An on-again, off-again relationship, I'm sorry to say, piques your curiosity. Ultimately, you don't need a profound emotional connection. You also don't need off-the-charts sex (which is not to say that you don't appreciate it). What you need is a lively connection that generates sparks and engages your mind.

For details about your relationships with other signs, turn to Chapter 15.

Work

Versatile and cerebral, you have fine motor skills and are a wizard with words. Whether you're writing a roman à clef or building a Victorian birdhouse, ideas readily come to you because you're stimulated by everything. Smart and buoyant, you pick things up so fast that you practically don't *have* a learning curve. But in work (as in love), you grow quickly bored. Jobs that require a lot of repetition, no matter how outwardly rewarding, are always a mistake for you. You require mental stimulation, plenty of opportunity to socialize, and a mixture of responsibilities. The best professions for you offer variety and take advantage of your ability to communicate. Classic Gemini careers include education, travel, writing, and anything connected with newspapers, magazines, radio, or TV. Blogging was made for you. Inventive and entrepreneurial, you're skilled at creating original business ventures. Even though the freelancer's life isn't for everyone, you bask in its variety and manage the challenges (no security, no predictability, and no schedule) with confidence. Just make sure you hire a sensible Taurus or a Capricorn to look after your finances. Handling money is *not* your strength.

Working with the Twins is a challenge because they're always prepared to change directions on a whim — and they expect everyone else to follow suit. If you're working with a Gemini, your only move at these times is to shift gears and pretend you aren't rattled. "But you told us last week . . ." carries no weight with a Gemini. Geminis value new ideas, flexibility, and rapid response. They don't care about consistency.

Gemini: The Basic Facts

Polarity: Positive	Favorable Color: Yellow
Quality: Mutable	Lucky Gem: Agate
Element: Air	Parts of the Body: Arms, shoulders, lungs
Symbol: The Twins	Metal: Mercury
Ruling Planet: Mercury	Key Phrase: I think
Opposite Sign: Sagittarius	Major Traits: Clever, superficial

Libra the Scales: September 23– October 22

I grew up surrounded by Librans, and I can tell you this: Libra is the sign of civilization. Ruled by Venus, the planet of love and beauty, you act rationally, believe in fairness, and are usually easy to be around.

The glyph of Libra (see Figure 6-2) represents a simple balance or the scales of justice. It also suggests the setting Sun, which reflects the fact that the first day of Libra is the fall equinox, when day and night reach a point of perfect equilibrium.

Figure 6-2:
Libra's
glyph.

The sunny side

Where elegance meets cool, and sense meets sensibility: That's Libra. Refined and even-tempered, amiable and observant, you're the ultimate diplomat (when you want to be). You seek serenity, respond strongly to art and music, and thrive in aesthetically agreeable surroundings (though ordinary nuisances like noise make you tense and tired). Your artistic sensibility is highly developed, your social sense even more so. Easy-going, graceful, smart, and charming, you're a sought-after dinner party guest who very much wants to be liked. And although you can't stop being flirtatious, you're also a committed partner for whom relationships are indispensable.

At the same time, as an air sign, you have a sophisticated intellect and you pride yourself on your sensible approach to life. You're conscious of the implications of any and all decisions. You seek out information and opposing points of view, and you do your best not to jump to conclusions, often arguing a point just to work your way around all sides of an issue. (Plus, let it be said that you enjoy a good debate.) Because reason is a high value for you, you naturally try to be objective. That's the meaning of the scales, your symbol, which represents your ability to weigh both sides of an issue as well as your need to achieve emotional balance. (Libra is the only sign symbolized by a physical object rather than a living creature.) Most of the time, your thoughtful, objective approach works. The harmony and balance that you seek are achievable.

The sorry side

As Eleanor Roosevelt, a classic Libran, once said, "Nobody can make you feel inferior without your consent." Well, no problem: You consent. Your amiable personality may conceal a festering dissatisfaction and a terrible struggle with emotional complexities. You have a deeply ingrained predisposition to worry, combined with — at your sorriest — a woeful lack of confidence. (If you have planets in Virgo, as many Librans do, you're undoubtedly your own harshest critic.) Anxious for the good opinion of others, you may try too hard to satisfy. And yet in other ways, you don't try hard enough. When you're down, you can be vague, dependent, self-indulgent, and withdrawn, and your refined sensibilities are so easily injured that it's sometimes laughable.

You can't bear squabbles — and yet you're more than capable of generating them. Like Librans Mahatma Gandhi, the prophet of nonviolence, and John Lennon, the antiwar rock star, you're more contentious than your reputation suggests.

And as much as you need balance, you have trouble maintaining it. Because you're a serious thinker, you can be indecisive to the point of paralysis, especially when you need to make a serious choice. Uncertainty undoes you. You wobble back and forth, balancing pros and cons. You compare and contrast. You work yourself up into a tizzy, becoming distant, argumentative, or obsessed. Making up your mind so that you can move forward can be your greatest challenge. In your search for peace, beauty, and equilibrium, you can wear yourself out. Your best approach is the Roman one: Moderation in all things.

Relationships

What a bundle of contradictions Libra can be. On the one hand, you're ruled by seductive Venus, and relationships are essential to you. Longing for love, you instinctively look to romantic partners to balance your inadequacies and stabilize you. On the other hand, you're an air sign, ruled by your head — not your heart. Thanks to your refined sensibilities and visceral distaste for tear-soaked melodramas, you unconsciously preserve a distance meant to protect you from conflict and emotional chaos. In relationships, as in other areas of life, you often end up in an internal tug-of-war, first drawing close to the object of your affection, and then pulling away. Not surprisingly, your ambivalence may strike the other person as manipulative.

And what is it that you seek? The right partner has to come equipped with the whole package: looks, brains, energy, style, manners, and a dash — or more than a dash — of status. When you find that person, as most Librans do, you're loyal, loving, generous, and proud. Meanwhile, thanks to your ineffable charm and your ability to keep the conversation interesting, you need never dine alone.

For insight into your relationships with other signs, go to Chapter 15.

Work

For Libra, life would be much more pleasant without the irksome necessity of work. Because your aesthetic sense is directly related to your mood, it's imperative that your workspace be clean and airy with plenty of opportunities for face-to-face socializing. Finding an environment that supports you both intellectually and socially is equally important. You aren't enormously ambitious, perhaps because you underrate yourself. Money is seldom your chief motivation, but you know what you're worth, and you're confident enough to ask for the recognition you deserve. Still, the day-to-day quality of your work is what matters most.

Ideal fields include all aspects of the arts, including the visual arts, theater, and music. Cultural organizations are natural spots for you. You can also express your artistic talents in fashion, graphic design, interior decoration, architecture, photography, cinema, and related fields. Other areas for which you are equally well suited include diplomacy, mediation and negotiation, the law (Libra makes a fine judge), and anything that requires making contact with the public.

REAL LIFE EXAMPLE

Classic Librans

- E. E. Cummings, Anne Rice (Moon in Aries)

- Sigourney Weaver, Carrie Fisher (Moon in Taurus)

- Gwyneth Paltrow, T. S. Eliot (Moon in Gemini)

- Paul Simon, Gwen Stefani (Moon in Cancer)

- Mahatma Gandhi, Oscar Wilde (Moon in Leo)

- Serena Williams, Pancho Villa (Moon in Virgo)

- Bruce Springsteen, Joan Jett, Kate Winslet (Moon in Libra)

- Will Smith, William Rehnquist (Moon in Scorpio)

- Friedrich Nietzsche, Christopher Reeve (Moon in Sagittarius)

- Susan Sarandon, Matt Damon, Jesse Jackson (Moon in Capricorn)

- John Lennon, Annie Leibovitz, Eminem (Moon in Aquarius)

- Eugene O'Neill, Chuck Berry, Catherine Zeta-Jones (Moon in Pisces)

TIP

If you work with or for a Libra, you have the opportunity to observe the power of reason close up. Libra respects rational decision-making and analysis. Gifted with poise and intelligence, Libra tries to be fair and expects you to share in the spirit of compromise. It's true that Libran decision-making can be a lengthy process. Libra values your input. But after a decision has been reached, Libra moves with dispatch. Two pieces of advice: Present your ideas calmly and logically. And look your best. Libra may pretend that appearance doesn't matter. But others know better than to believe it.

Libra: The Basic Facts

Polarity: Positive	Favorable Colors: Blues and pastels
Quality: Cardinal	Lucky Gems: Sapphire, jade, and opal
Element: Air	Parts of the Body: Kidneys and skin
Symbol: The Scales	Metal: Copper
Ruling Planet: Venus	Key Phrase: I balance
Opposite Sign: Aries	Major Traits: Cosmopolitan, indecisive

Aquarius the Water Bearer: January 20–February 18

You're an original. With unpredictable Uranus as your ruler, you're progressive, future-oriented, and prone to dazzling flashes of insight. You're also more idiosyncratic than you may realize.

The glyph of Aquarius the Water Bearer (see Figure 6-3) represents the waves of water or, better yet, waves of sound, electricity, and light.

Figure 6-3:
The symbol
of Aquarius.

The sunny side

Very much a member of your own generation, you're a natural visionary and a humanitarian of the first order — at least in theory. You have high-minded principles, and you try to live by them. Altruistic and issue-oriented, you believe in the equality of all human beings, and you're interested in everyone, regardless of class, race, age, sexual orientation, or any of the other concerns that shape life today. Exquisitely aware of the impact that those factors can have, you possess the ability (when you so choose) to set them aside and connect with the real human being. The terrible things that happen in the world appall you, the issues of the day animate you, and you aren't one to follow a party line just because that's what your friends believe. You have a capacious brain, and you think for yourself.

A maverick with a lively, inventive mind, you have an off-beat set of interests and habits. Science fiction and technology are Aquarian; so is video art and everything indie. But whether you resonate to those particular areas isn't the point. (After all, not all Sagittarians go horseback riding, and — surprise! — not every Cancer loves to cook.) The point is that you lean into the future, not away from it. Intrigued and unafraid, you're utterly contemporary, a composition in avant-garde. You're also congenial and charismatic. You accumulate a variety of friends (and to your perverse joy, they often disapprove of each other.) Your likeable personality and open-minded intelligence are the draw.

The sorry side

Your unconventional, independent outlook can morph into eccentricity, thoughtlessness, pointless rebellion, and strange hair. You can be contrary and childish, a foot-stomping rebel who's never willing to go along. As a fixed sign, you tend to be stubborn, and it's rare for you to give up a cherished idea, no matter how outmoded it may become. And your famous humanity, perhaps your finest trait, can seem false. You may strike people as distant and aloof because you recoil from intimacy and even go out of your way to erect barriers against it. For you, detachment is a natural state. More comfortable with ideas than with emotions, you can be warm on the surface but chilly underneath. You're a visitor to spaceship Earth — alert but uninvolved. Although your idealism runs deep, and you truly want the best for yourself and others, you don't necessarily express these thoughts in a positive way. Emotionally, you may strike people as peculiarly insensitive, even as they strike you as bizarrely thin-skinned. The truth is that you just don't get it. At your worst, I'm sorry to say, you're an android.

And there's another element to you that's easily overlooked. Beneath the dazzling surface of your personality and your remarkable, inventive mind, you can be stunningly insecure. Other people may not notice this (they may think, instead, that you have an overinflated ego). In fact, your self-doubt hampers you and is something to fight.

Relationships

Given that Aquarius is the sign of humanity, you might imagine that your relationships would be role models for the rest of the world. And in some ways, they are. Fair and friendly, you're interested in people from every corner of society. You extend your friendship to oddballs, geniuses, extremists, and the kid across the street. So what if you eventually drop most of these relationships? You also maintain a few friendships for life.

Romance is more complicated. Although you pride yourself on your tolerance, certain established customs — getting engaged, for instance, or reserving Saturday night for your beloved —seem phony or old-fashioned to you. You're often astonished by the conventional expectations that people hold dear, and you resent having to go along with those antiquated notions. Trouble is, people misinterpret your independent ways as rejection — and, yes, they take it personally. Those needy folks probably strike you as unreasonable and demanding. See it that way if you wish. But remember: Intimate relationships have their own rhythm, which sometimes requires you to offer reassurance and to behave according to — please excuse the expression — the rules. In maintaining a relationship, make sure that your assumptions are shared.

Classic Aquarians

- Virginia Woolf, Chris Rock, Ellen DeGeneres (Moon in Aries)

- Bill Maher, Sheryl Crow, Jackson Pollock, Ronald Reagan (Moon in Taurus)

- Gene Hackman, Jack Benny, James Spader (Moon in Gemini)

- Lord Byron, Mischa Barton, Franklin D. Roosevelt (Moon in Cancer)

- James Joyce, Judy Blume, Paris Hilton (Moon in Leo)

- John Travolta, Vanessa Redgrave (Moon in Virgo)

- Natalie Cole, Stonewall Jackson, Edouard Manet (Moon in Libra)

- James Dean, Bob Marley, Molly Ringwald (Moon in Scorpio)

- Wolfgang Amadeus Mozart, Oprah Winfrey, Justin Timberlake (Moon in Sagittarius)

- Charles Darwin, Thomas Alva Edison, Abraham Lincoln, Betty Friedan (Moon in Capricorn)

- Joan of Arc, Jackie Robinson, Angela Davis (Moon in Aquarius)

- Susan B. Anthony, Toni Morrison, Paul Newman, Lisa Marie Presley (Moon in Pisces)

For the lowdown on your relationships with other signs, flip to Chapter 15.

Work

Why would anyone want to follow the beaten path? Striking out for terra incognita is much more entertaining. If you can create your own schedule, you're even better off. Late-night hours don't scare you; mind-numbing tasks and banal co-workers (a curse of your life) do. What matters most is that your job is future-oriented and focused on change. That's where you find the most personal satisfaction. Fields that are a fit for Aquarius include social work, politics, technology, science (and medicine in particular), academia, environmentalism, civil rights, and anything that pushes the boundaries in a progressive direction. Politicians like Abraham Lincoln, thinkers like Charles Darwin, inventors like Thomas Edison, and TV personalities like Oprah Winfrey demonstrate the impact that your sign can make. Innovative Aquarius sees the future before anyone else and knows how to react to it. Technology, by the way, is oxygen to your soul. Even if you think you don't like modern technology — maybe you're an aficionado of vinyl or a collector of portable typewriters — you still benefit from it.

If you work with or for an Aquarian, be prepared to argue your viewpoint effectively and to do your job without prodding. Aquarius wants independence and is glad to grant the same privilege to you — assuming you don't take advantage. Don't force a showdown.

Aquarius: The Basic Facts

Polarity: Positive

Quality: Fixed

Element: Air

Symbol: The Water Bearer

Ruling Planet: Uranus

Opposite Sign: Leo

Favorable Colors: Electric blue and glow-in-the-dark shades

Lucky Gem: Amethyst

Parts of the Body: Ankles, circulatory system

Metal: Aluminum

Key Phrase: I know

Major Traits: Progressive, rebellious

Chapter 7

Water Signs: Cancer, Scorpio, and Pisces

I have often wondered: If it were possible to choose my sign, what would I want to be? Rams have tons of energy, but they can be clueless. Geminis sparkle, but they try so hard, it's exhausting to contemplate. Capricorns have traits I wish I possessed, but they have a rough time loosening up. And so it goes around the zodiac, each sign in turn presenting its attractions and its liabilities. I don't know what I'd pick.

I do know this: I wouldn't choose to be a water sign. Don't get me wrong: I adore people who were born under water signs, and I treasure the (abundant) water in my own chart. I also know that water represents emotion, and those born under its influence tend to be swamped by their sentiments. Profoundly sensitive, they're vulnerable and reactive, first responders on the most human front of all. They're also hugely intuitive and occasionally psychic with what some commentators have suggested is a deep spiritual bent.

But is it easy to be a water sign? All things being equal, I'd rather be a Leo.

The water signs, which are known for their emotional responsiveness, include the following:

✔ Cancer the Crab (June 21 to July 22), the sign of cardinal water. Cancer is famed for its emotional acuity, sympathetic nature, and love of home.

✔ Scorpio the Scorpion (October 23 to November 21), the sign of fixed water. Scorpio is recognized for its intensity, magnetism, and ability to burrow deep, both psychologically and intellectually.

✔ Pisces the Fish (February 19 to March 19), the sign of mutable water. Ruled by elusive Neptune, Pisces is compassionate, impressionable, gentle, and imaginative.

The water signs share an emotional sensitivity and a well-developed sense of intuition. If water is your element, this chapter describes you. In these pages, I present your most commendable traits and your most pitiful ones, along with information about relationships and work.

In addition to its element, each sign is assigned a polarity (positive or negative) and a quality (cardinal, fixed, or mutable). For more about these terms, flip to Chapter 1. Also, don't forget to check out Chapter 1 if you were born on the cusp of any of these signs — meaning the first or last day.

Cancer the Crab: June 21–July 22

Ruled by the ever-changing Moon, you're introspective, intuitive, security-conscious, and exceedingly aware of your emotional environment. You're also determined to conquer your vulnerabilities and achieve your goals.

The glyph of Cancer (see Figure 7-1) represents the breasts (and hence the mother), the claws of the crab, and the fluid nature of emotion.

Figure 7-1:
The symbol of Cancer the Crab.

The sunny side

You embody an intriguing paradox. Because you're a water sign, you're emotionally wide open with an intense inner focus. Because you're also a cardinal sign, you're enterprising and ambitious, with a strong outer focus. No wonder you're known for your fluctuating moods. Your emotional sensitivity is one of your greatest assets. It serves as a barometer to the atmosphere around you, and the more tuned into it you are, the better. You're shrewd and insightful. When you trust your intuition enough to act in accordance with it, you can steer in any direction and navigate through the roughest storm.

You also maintain a strong tie to the past, both personal and historical, and you have a powerful longing for home, family, domestic tranquility, and emotional security. Loyal, affectionate, kind, and supportive, you never give up on someone you love — and if that means clinging or being overprotective, so be it. Your ability to nurture others parallels your need to care for and comfort yourself.

At the same time, you're intent on initiating activity. Whatever your emotions may be, you don't let them stop you from setting far-reaching goals and resolutely going after them. Your determination is extraordinary. Despite your doubts and insecurities, you forge ahead valiantly, though not without some tears along the way. At your best, your internal awareness supports your outer ambition, just as your knowledge of the past forms a sturdy foundation for your forays into the future. The fact that you have the best memory on the planet is yet another strength.

The sorry side

Picture the crab. Vulnerable and soft within its protective armor, it approaches its target sideways and, when frightened, scuttles back into its shell. You do the same. Fretful and high-strung, afraid of addressing a problem directly, you defend yourself well — sometimes to your own detriment. At times you're so defensive, so imprisoned by your anxieties, that movement becomes impossible. You withdraw or enter a state of total denial, where you become unreachable. At your worst, your need for security paralyzes you.

Yet there's no avoiding your powerful emotions, which can wash over you as suddenly as a tidal wave. Those moments of sheer emotion are an indelible part of who you are, and you don't always deal with them well. With other people, you can be stunningly possessive and demanding. Spurred by your fear of being abandoned, you cling ferociously, holding on to relationships — and jobs — way past their expiration dates.

Avoiding the quicksand of insecurity and the snake pit of depression are challenges you must confront; getting to the bottom of your deepest fears and complicated psyche is another.

Relationships

As the most maternal sign in the zodiac, Cancer has an instinct for closeness that few signs can equal. The family you were born into never ceases to play a central role in your consciousness, whether positive or negative (or, more likely, a confusing amalgamation of both). You lavish attention on friends and lovers alike, and in the absence of a committed romantic partner, you turn friends into family. Children claim a special place in your heart.

Love affairs absorb you, but you're most comfortable in a committed, traditional relationship. Shyer than you appear to be, you long for someone with whom you share a soul connection. When you feel cherished and recognized, you're utterly devoted and supportive. When you feel insecure, it's another matter. Fearful of being alone and yet unwilling to engage in conflict, you hold on too tightly for too long. When a relationship falls apart, you're devastated,

even if you're the one who made the decision. You withdraw into the safety of your shell. Many tears are shed. And then — it's amazing — you're fine. Although astrologers always say that the Crab moves sideways (and I've said it myself), it's not always true. Sometimes you move forward with giant strides. I have seen Cancer soar from abject misery to honeymoon cruise within a matter of months. In romance, as in other areas, your ability to take action and to recognize opportunities pays off.

For more on your relationships with other signs, turn to Chapter 15.

Work

It's true that yours is the sign of domesticity. That doesn't mean you want to stay home all the time making tea and crumpets. As a cardinal sign, you're happiest when you're actively involved in the world. You shine in fields that rely on your emotional sensitivity. You excel in medicine, teaching, social work, child psychology, marriage counseling, and any other form of therapy. Because you have a deep love of home (and house), you can also succeed at real estate, architecture, cooking, restaurant management, and so on. Finally, thanks to your interest in the past, you're drawn to history, antiques, and museum work. You're great with children. You're also supremely responsive to the elderly and would do well in geriatrics. Whatever you do, it must offer fulfillment as well as material security. Your occupation needs to captivate you, and there's no reason to settle for anything less.

Despite your doubts and hesitations, taking the initiative is your best move. Within an organization, you quickly form alliances and generally rise to a position of leadership. You're well-organized and energetic, but you also become emotionally involved in your work, and you tend to take it home with you. It helps to find a mentor. Establishing a personal tie with someone who has the authority and expertise you lack can fortify and reassure you. Similarly, after you have accumulated some experience, you find it gratifying to become a mentor.

If you work with or for a Cancerian, be prepared to give your all. Crabs try to create family, even at the office. They want to forge strong connections and therefore try to create a positive atmosphere. At least in theory, the office door will be open, and criticism will be constructive. If you need help, say so. (They tend to slip into a parental role.) If you have a legitimate complaint, address it in a private meeting. But don't sneak around complaining to one and all behind your boss's back. Cancerians may hide their emotions, but they're astute enough to sense betrayal.

REAL LIFE EXAMPLE

Classic Crabs

- Kevin Bacon, Pamela Lee Anderson (Moon in Aries)
- Meryl Streep, Frida Kahlo, Lindsay Lohan (Moon in Taurus)
- Henry David Thoreau (Moon in Gemini)
- Tom Cruise, Harrison Ford, Courtney Love (Moon in Cancer)
- Tom Hanks (Moon in Leo)
- The Dalai Lama (Moon in Virgo)
- Twyla Tharp (Moon in Libra)
- Rembrandt van Rijn, Gisele Bundchen (Moon in Scorpio)
- Rubén Blades (Moon in Sagittarius)
- John Glenn, Ernest Hemingway (Moon in Capricorn)
- Princess Diana (Moon in Aquarius)
- Robin Williams (Moon in Pisces)

Cancer: The Basic Facts

Polarity: Negative	Favorable Colors: White and silver
Quality: Cardinal	Lucky Gems: Pearls and moonstones
Element: Water	Parts of the Body: Stomach and breasts
Symbol: The Crab	Metal: Silver
Ruling Planet: The Moon	Key Phrase: I feel
Opposite Sign: Capricorn	Major Traits: Intuitive, moody

Scorpio the Scorpion: October 23– November 21

Intensity is the key to Scorpio. Ruled by Pluto, the (dwarf) planet of transformation, you're a compelling personality — and a creature of extremes. Emotionally or otherwise, in fact or in fancy, you live on the edge.

The glyph of Scorpio (see Figure 7-2) represents the male genitals or the piercing barb of the Scorpion's tail.

Figure 7-2:
The symbol
of the
Scorpion.

The sunny side

Vibrant, magnetic, and passionate, you're a person of depth and complexity who participates in life fully. You're perceptive and sensual, and your senses are alert. So are your powers of observation. As a Scorpio, you're aware of the spoken message as well as the subtext and the body language, and you can't help relishing the melodrama of it all. Your insights into human psychology are discerning, in part because you have such a wide range of experience. Your mood seesaws between ecstatic heights and nightmarish depths, and there's hardly an emotion that you haven't felt right down to your soul. You're also curious about other people. Although you value your privacy and are often quite reticent, you're skilled at ferreting out the secrets of others. Mysteries fascinate you, which is why astrology books inevitably recommend that Scorpios become detectives or spies.

Here's another positive trait: You're determined. When you apply yourself, your willpower is astonishing (although you can also take it too far: Eating disorders are a blight on your sign). You're resourceful, too. You make careful plans, and if the time's not right, you wait. You don't ever give up. You aim for the highest — or the lowest. That's why, unlike any other sign, Scorpio has three symbols: the scorpion, which crawls through the dust; the eagle, which soars through the air; and the phoenix, which burns itself up in the heat of its passion and is reborn. Like that mythical bird, you have the ability to rejuvenate yourself.

The sorry side

Let me be honest: Scorpio has some deeply nasty traits. You can be obsessive, jealous, secretive, manipulative, and arrogant. You have an exceedingly wicked tongue. You know how to wound, and if you're backed into a corner, you don't hesitate to do so. Once you decide that you've been crossed, you're unforgiving. You can be vengeful, spiteful, and disturbingly cold-hearted — or so it appears. When Scorpio (sign of Charles Manson) is bad, it's downright scary.

But in my experience, most Scorpions keep that side of their personalities under wraps. Instead, you struggle with depression. When times are tough, you plummet to the bottom of the sea. Other signs don't begin to comprehend the bleak despair that pulls you down. Yet this is an essential component of

being a Scorpio. It works like this: You sink into darkness, claw your way through the underworld of the psyche, and wrestle with your own worst qualities and darkest fears. And then you emerge. Before Pluto was discovered in 1930, astrologers regarded Mars, the planet of war (and desire), as the ruler of Scorpio. And indeed, you pursue your demons like a warrior, fighting relentlessly, even against addiction and other tribulations. In your quest for renewal and transformation, you're unflinching.

Relationships

No one said relationships were easy. That's because casual liaisons don't satisfy you. Even your friendships are serious. Growing up, you understood the concept of blood brothers or sisters (even if you never found a friend who qualified), and you longed for that kind of connection. As an adult, you still want to bond on the deepest of levels. That's especially true in your romantic life. Ardent, mysterious, and magnetic, you long for blazing sex, conversation that breaks all barriers, and total immersion. When you fall in love, it's theatrical and impassioned — a drama for the ages.

At its finest, that intensity helps you create the kind of fully intertwined partnership you crave. At its worst, it causes you to become suspicious, possessive, and resentful. Issues of power and control arise, and you can become painfully obsessive. When you feel injured or when a relationship is disintegrating, you unleash the deadly sting for which the scorpion is famous. If you cut someone off, it's forever. No one feels ecstasy the way you do; and no one suffers more.

Finally, I want to point out that, despite your desire to mind-meld with another human being, Scorpio also requires privacy. Without it, your peace of mind unravels, and anyone involved with you must understand that. Solitude, like sex, is a necessity.

Wondering how you get along with other signs? Turn to Chapter 15.

Work

Scorpio brings energy and ambition to the workplace, and your goals are generally of the highest order (though, for the record, I must acknowledge that Scorpios can also be adept as scam artists, drug dealers, and low-level thugs). Astute and insightful, you make a fantastic advocate for anyone in need. Plus, you're a fighter. You're also fascinated by power and money, which gives you the motivation to excel at business (think of Bill Gates) or politics (consider Hillary Clinton). Whatever field you find yourself in, trivialities don't interest you. Nor do you have to be center stage (unless, of course, you have a lot of Leo in your chart). But you do need to be involved in an

enterprise that matters. Scientific research, surgery, various kinds of counseling, community organizing, investigative reporting, investment banking, politics, and various aspects of psychology all come to mind. As I noted earlier, detective and spy are two positions traditionally considered Scorpionic. But did I mention mortician? Magician? Obituary writer? Mystery writer? Guru? Poet? Greatest artist of the 20th century (Picasso)? The list goes on and on.

If you work with or for a Scorpio, you'll see what it means to be committed. Industrious, disciplined, and demanding, Scorpios know how to concentrate (unless, of course, they can't, in which case, you get to see the miserable, sulky Scorpio). Because they know how to keep a secret, you can trust Scorpios with yours. But they're also inscrutable. They nurture their accomplices — and demolish their enemies. If you have a Scorpio boss, do your best — and don't try any fancy stuff. She'll see it coming, and you'll pay for your presumption. No one, and I mean no one, wants to have a Scorpio for an enemy.

Scorpio: The Basic Facts

Polarity: Negative

Quality: Fixed

Element: Water

Symbol: The Scorpion

Ruling Planet: Pluto

Opposite Sign: Taurus

Favorable Colors: Dark reds and black

Lucky Gem: Opal

Part of the Body: Reproductive organs

Metal: Steel or iron

Key Phrase: I desire

Major Traits: Passionate, obsessive

Classic Scorpions

✔ Bill Gates, Jamie Lee Curtis, Sally Field (Moon in Aries)

✔ Demi Moore, Prince Charles (Moon in Taurus)

✔ Bonnie Raitt, Goldie Hawn (Moon in Gemini)

✔ Condoleezza Rice, Keith Urban (Moon in Cancer)

✔ Julia Roberts, Kurt Vonnegut (Moon in Leo)

✔ Jodie Foster, Sean Combs, Matthew McConaughey (Moon in Virgo)

✔ Leonardo DiCaprio, Billie Jean King, Sylvia Plath (Moon in Libra)

✔ k.d. lang, Björk, Whoopi Goldberg (Moon in Scorpio)

✔ Pablo Picasso, Larry King, Kelly Osbourne (Moon in Sagittarius)

✔ George Eliot, Anne Tyler, Bernard-Henri Lévy (Moon in Capricorn)

✔ Calista Flockhart, Neil Young (Moon in Aquarius)

✔ Hillary Rodham Clinton, Joni Mitchell (Moon in Pisces)

Pisces the Fish: February 19–March 19

Yours is the sign of dreams, imagination, poetry, and matters of the spirit. Ruled by mysterious Neptune, the planet of glamour and illusion, your challenge is to find a way to live in a workaday world when you have an out-of-this-world sensibility.

The glyph of Pisces (see Figure 7-3) connotes two forms of experience, internal and external. Alternatively, it represents two fish tied together. When they cooperate, they navigate their watery domain with ease. When they pull in opposite directions, neither gets anywhere.

Figure 7-3: The symbol of Pisces the Fish.

The sunny side

You want sensitive? Pisces is sensitive. Every tiny bounce in the emotional weather sends your internal compass into a spin. Sympathetic and receptive, you receive a constant barrage of impressions and information, and you can be weirdly psychic. But protecting yourself is difficult because you lack boundaries. All your membranes are permeable. When the people upstairs have a fight, you feel battered. When bad things happen to good people, you're horrified. And when good things happen to people you love, you rejoice. (It's one of your most magnificent traits.) You're generous, bighearted, insightful, and truly compassionate. You're also innately spiritual.

Another strength is your powerful imagination. Your dreams (and daydreams) can be a vivid source of inspiration and even problem-solving. Your intuition is equally powerful. You sense what's going on way before it registers on the seismograph. But you can also become trapped in a web of illusion (see the upcoming section, "The sorry side"). At your intuitive best, your refusal to get hung up on the limitations of reality enables you to leap over obstacles and to make surprising breakthroughs and turnarounds. Unlike more "realistic" signs, you embrace change and are willing to take enormous risks. Often your gambles succeed. When they don't, you're philosophical about it. As Albert Einstein, a prototypical Pisces, said, "A person who never made a mistake never tried anything new."

The sorry side

At your out-to-lunch worst, you're gullible in the extreme, irrational, and so easily hurt that you're practically an open wound. Because the requirements of ordinary life can overwhelm you, you're prone to wishful thinking and out-right fantasy, often combined with a sense of entitlement that boggles the mind. Indecisive and weak, you're readily deceived.

But that's not the most serious problem. More often, you delude yourself by simply refusing to accept reality. Your grasp of reality is tenuous at best, and you often refuse to accept even a little responsibility for your situation. Even when you're miserable, your passivity can bypass all reason. Instead of taking action when you're feeling trapped, you wait to be rescued, often sinking into a melancholy pattern of brooding and procrastination. (I've seen men do this as well as women, by the way.) Moreover, when your efforts come to nothing or your dreams are thwarted, you tend to be overcome by lethargy, self-pity, depression, guilt, or resentment. Sleep — too little or, more commonly, too much — can defeat your most heartfelt resolutions. And did I mention sub-stance abuse? Let's just say that you're susceptible. More than most, you're your own worst enemy. And, more than most, you have the capacity to turn your circumstances (and your attitude) around.

Relationships

A faithful, generous friend, a whimsical, starry-eyed lover, and a tender spouse, you have a certain sweetness that can't be denied, and your ability to love is without equal. You see the best in those you care for, even when they don't see it themselves, and you delight in cheering them on, in part because you crave that kind of encouragement yourself.

A genuine romantic, you yearn to be swept away — and supported — in true Hollywood style. You're also capable of falling for a homeless bum just because you sense the potential beneath the plastic poncho. Friends may object. But once your feelings are engaged, your ability to make rational judgments evaporates like mist. As you wander around in the fog of infatuation, totally lost, you spin a fantasy that enables you to ignore unmistakable flaws (alcoholism and infidelity, say). It's a strange phenomenon: You're supremely responsive to other people. In many situations, your intuition is flawless. Yet at other times, you suffer from a dangerous Piscean malady: a deep-seated, willful refusal to face reality. For Pisces, seeing clearly is always a worthy goal.

For a glance at your relationships with other signs, turn to Chapter 15.

Work

In Utopia, these are a few of the jobs that Pisces would happily hold: poet, artist, musician, clairvoyant, palm reader, sailor, filmmaker, actor, wine taster, spiritual healer, hypnotist, yoga teacher — and anything concerning tropical fish, the ocean, or ballet.

Given those career choices, you may expect Pisces to be a failure in the real world. But you'd be wrong. It turns out that Pisces is strangely adept at handling enormous sums of money. According to a 1995 study done by *Forbes Magazine,* more of the 400 richest Americans are Pisceans than any other sign. Why would that be? Well, you really do have a creative mind. It's not just a matter of coloring outside the lines; you have the ability to toss the book aside and design something completely original. Plus, unlike more realistic signs (Capricorn, for example), you dream big. If you can harness that vision to an old-fashioned work ethic, you can accomplish anything. If your job also benefits humanity, you'll be even happier. Pisces aspires to be of service, and you'll feel better about yourself if you are. That's why, besides the utopian trades in the previous paragraph, you may want to consider medicine, social work, philanthropy, education, environmentalism, cuisine, oceanography, and — yes — finance.

If you work with or for a Pisces, stay tuned — and I mean every minute. Any bad vibes you detect, Pisces notices too. Sympathetic and broad-minded, Pisceans support their staff and don't get stuck on minor points. But they're strivers, both more opportunistic and less secure than they may appear. If a Piscean senses dissension in the ranks or anything less than total loyalty, you'll be fish food.

Pisces: The Basic Facts

Polarity: Negative	Favorable Colors: Sea green and lavender
Quality: Mutable	Lucky Gem: Aquamarine
Element: Water	Parts of the Body: Feet and immune system
Symbol: The Fish	Metal: Platinum
Ruling Planet: Neptune	Key Phrase: I believe
Opposite Sign: Virgo	Major Traits: Sensitive, escapist

Classic Pisceans

- Eva Longoria, Galileo Galilei (Moon in Aries)

- Edgar Casey, Bobby Fischer (Moon in Taurus)

- Lee Radziwill, Benicio del Toro, W. H. Auden (Moon in Gemini)

- Kurt Cobain, Drew Barrymore (Moon in Cancer)

- Paula Zahn, Ralph Nader, Queen Latifah (Moon in Leo)

- Gabriel Garcia Marquez, Jack Kerouac (Moon in Virgo)

- Nat King Cole, Patty Hearst (Moon in Libra)

- Elizabeth Taylor, Johnny Cash (Moon in Scorpio)

- Albert Einstein, Sharon Stone (Moon in Sagittarius)

- Anais Nin, Philip Roth (Moon in Capricorn)

- Glenn Close, Carson McCullers (Moon in Aquarius)

- Michelangelo, Steve Jobs (Moon in Pisces)

Part III
Everything Else in the Cosmic Cookbook

The 5th Wave   By Rich Tennant

VENUS ASCENDING IN THE HOUSE OF GUCCI

In this part . . .

Your horoscope with its mysterious symbols, concentric circles, and tiny numbers may look like a magician's amulet. In fact, it's simply a map of the heavens at the moment of your birth. That celestial pattern, formed by the planets and not to be repeated for roughly 26,000 years, encapsulates the cosmic forces operating at the time of your birth. Every object in your horoscope reflects or symbolizes an aspect of who you are.

In this part, you discover the meaning of the Moon, the Ascendant, and the planets in your chart, both by sign and by house. You can also read about the ways that the planets interact. And finally, in Chapter 14, you put those cosmic ingredients together into an interpretation. Once you do that, you're cooking.

Chapter 8

Moon Signs: The Lunacy Factor

Strange but true: To an Earthling gazing at the sky, the Sun and Moon appear to be the same size. The irrefutable evidence of science states otherwise. But visually, the two are equal. Ancient mythologies shared that perception, associating the Sun and Moon with quarreling lovers, siblings, or deities.

Astrologers picture the Sun and the Moon as partners. The unvarying Sun represents your basic essence, vitality, and conscious self, while the inconstant Moon with its many phases (and occasional disappearances) signifies your emotional reactions, instincts, habits, and unconscious.

If the Sun and Moon occupied compatible signs at your birth, you're in luck. Your (solar) will and (lunar) emotions, your conscious awareness and unconscious, moony self, are in sync. That must be nice — I wouldn't know. If your luminaries inhabit clashing signs, you'll experience a storm of conflicting needs and desires. Well, that's life. Astrology just reflects it.

To discover the Moon's position in your chart, turn to the Appendix. But remember: The Moon swings into a new sign every two or three days. If it moved from one sign to the next on your birthday, you may have to do a bit of calculation to find out exactly where it was at the crucial moment.

The Moon, which shines by the light of the Sun, is symbolized by the crescent of receptivity (see Figure 8-1). To determine its placement in your horoscope, you need an accurate chart. To get one, I recommend going to the Internet (see Chapter 2 for specific advice). You could also do precise mathematical calculations, call an astrologer, or invest in astrological software. For a description of the Moon in the houses, go to Chapter 12.

Figure 8-1:
The symbol
of the Moon.

The Moon in the Signs

The sign that the Moon occupied at your birth describes your emotional reactions. It defines an area of fluctuation and instability in your chart, and it also represents women in general and your mother in particular. In this list, I describe the effect of the Moon in the signs:

- **Moon in Aries:** Instinctive and spontaneous, you form judgments instantly. Your enthusiasm is easily aroused, as is your anger. You may come across as self-absorbed because you're more insecure than you let on, and you're often remarkably competitive. You're feisty and decisive (sometimes foolishly so). You can also be selfish, irritable, impatient, and blunt. Quick-tempered and impetuous, you make sure your needs are acknowledged at the earliest possible moment. The chances are that, when you were a child, your mother reacted promptly to your insistent, fiery demands. She had no choice. As a result, you got what you wanted — and you learned to be independent, direct, and courageous.

- **Moon in Taurus:** You yearn for security, emotional and material, and you do everything you can to achieve it. Stable and stubborn, you approach change cautiously because nothing makes you more uncomfortable. But once you understand that change is inevitable, you do what you have to do. Trustworthy and congenial, you're charming, attractive, warm, faithful, and possessive. As a child, you desperately needed the security that comes from having loving, reliable parents. You still crave the pleasures of predictability and security.

- **Moon in Gemini:** You're flighty, friendly, dashing, and articulate. You express yourself with wit and intelligence, even if you strike people as glib or superficial. Nervous and high-strung, you take an essentially mental approach to matters of the heart. Although you may panic in the heat of a crisis, that reaction is a fleeting one. After the feathers settle, you look around objectively and analyze your own reactions, a process that brings you a measure of calm. As a child, you were restless, curious, and easily distracted. During stressful moments, your mother found it easy to divert you. Diversion still strikes you as a reasonable — or at least an understandable — strategy during hard times. A first-rate rationalizer, you don't hesitate to move on when the time is right.

REAL LIFE EXAMPLE

Mary Beth Whitehead

Mary Beth Whitehead, one of the first surrogate mothers, was born April 7, 1957, with all the pioneering spirit you might expect of an Aries. Thanks to her bold Aries Sun and the detached, unconventional attitudes of her Aquarian Ascendant, she agreed to become the surrogate mother for William and Elizabeth Stern, a couple who were unable to have a child. Mary Beth, who has the Moon in Cancer in the fifth house of children, was glad to help. But after she had the baby, her maternal, Cancerian Moon kicked in — and suddenly the plan didn't seem like such a smart idea. Sensing a deep connection to the child she had agreed to give up, she stubbornly refused to relinquish her. Only when a judge ordered her to do so did she finally give the baby girl (also an Aries) to the Sterns. Had she spoken to an astrologer first, she might never have agreed to the deal in the first place.

✔ **Moon in Cancer:** The Moon rules the sign of the Crab, so no matter what else is happening in your chart, you're a lunar person: moody, receptive, sentimental, vulnerable, and supremely aware of the continual flux of emotions. Tears spring from your eyes with little provocation, and you occasionally need to withdraw to soothe your surging feelings. Caring and protective, you're a truly kind person but, like people born with the Moon in Taurus, you have a rough time letting go. As a child, you were extraordinarily responsive to your mother. Her impact on you surpasses the norm, which is why, when you have children, you're likely to be an exceptionally loving, occasionally overinvolved parent.

✔ **Moon in Leo:** A Leo moon adds warmth, dazzle, and exuberance to any Sun sign. Generous, devoted, and lively, you love to laugh and are gifted with presence and joie de vivre. Although your considerable pride is easily injured (especially if you think you've been ignored), you're usually confident and upbeat. One way or another, you love to perform, and the world loves to respond. But when things are going badly or when you feel downhearted or insecure, you cover up your doubts and ambivalence with emotional fireworks. You picked up this dramatic pattern from your mother, who was somewhat of a drama queen herself. She taught you to seek recognition, and she gave you the confidence to set ambitious goals.

✔ **Moon in Virgo:** Emotionally timid and unobtrusive, you'd rather repress your emotions than articulate them. You find it difficult to confront serious issues. Instead, you distract yourself with minutiae or by working so hard you barely have a chance to breathe. You're industrious and practical. You're also fussy and hard to please. Without a doubt, you're your

own harshest critic. Where does this reprehensible quality come from? You guessed it — your mother (or whoever played that role in your life). Although her criticism, implicit or explicit, made an impact on you, she also deserves credit for several of your virtues, including the willingness to shoulder responsibility, the values you place on efficiency and organization, and your altruistic desire to relieve the suffering of others. You may be inhibited, but that doesn't mean you're blind.

✔ **Moon in Libra:** You're gracious, romantic, and artistic. You shun vulgarity, value courtesy and elegance, and try to convey your feelings in a calm, diplomatic manner. Peace is essential to you, and you will do anything to maintain balance. As a child, you learned to maintain appearances, even if you were abused. Your even temper drew praise, and people came to expect it of you. Now, as an adult, you seem unflappable. Love and relationships are fundamental to your well-being. If you're single, you feel bereft without a partner; if you're mated, you can scarcely imagine any other scenario and may be fearful of being alone. Either way, you detest confrontation and therefore may gloss over problems. Not surprisingly, distressing issues may remain unresolved for years on end; your desire for peace and harmony trumps everything.

✔ **Moon in Scorpio:** Passionate and easily injured, you're one complicated puppy. Willful, intense, and occasionally self-destructive, your emotions — to quote Herman Melville — rush like "herds of walruses and whales" beneath the surface of your personality. Hesitant to reveal the depth of your emotions, you try to keep them hidden, a task that may require a certain degree of dissembling and manipulation. Not that you mean to be controlling — you just can't help it. Covering up your feelings is something you learned in childhood. Even if your childhood looked enviable from afar, you were afraid of abandonment or rejection and were well aware of the suppressed needs and subterranean conflicts within your family. You learned to keep quiet about your own concerns. Your silence is a form of protection — and hiding. Although some people with this placement nurse fantasies of retaliation for long-ago wrongs, most simply continue to hide their feelings. Those walruses and whales may still be down there, but the surface looks smooth.

✔ **Moon in Sagittarius:** You're philosophical, outspoken, cheerful, uninhibited, well-intentioned, unrealistic on occasion, and idealistic — sometimes pathetically so. Your optimism runs deep, and as a result, you're a risk-taker, always prepared to gallop off on an adventure or to commit yourself to causes other people deem hopeless. Intellectually and emotionally, you cherish your independence above all else. Lengthy relationship discussions make you squirm. More comfortable with action than with analysis, you can be self-righteous and inadvertently hurtful, and you tend to justify your own misdeeds without blinking. Yet you mean well. And people sense that about you. Even as a child, whenever you radiated good cheer, your mother responded positively. To encourage that sort of reaction, you convey your enthusiasm more readily than your pain and, like her, you shrink from emotional displays.

✔ **Moon in Capricorn:** You're steady, reserved, self-reliant, ambitious, and well-disciplined. Even when you were small, you were serious, and the playfulness of childhood may have eluded you. Now, ever the realist, you recognize both your strengths and your limitations. Among your limitations, you suspect, is the inability to have fun. You have a tendency to descend into depression and pessimism from time to time, perhaps because your mother suffered from a case of postpartum blues. Sensing her gloom, you pulled back. You're emotionally reserved and self-conscious, especially in the face of other people's melodramatic outbursts. You can't bear those scenes. Success steadies you. You're willing to shoulder broad responsibilities because you feel more grounded, as well as more powerful and peaceful, when you have authority. Somebody's got to take control. It may as well be you.

✔ **Moon in Aquarius:** In your mind's eye, you're out to improve the world. With your progressive instincts and sympathy for others, you have the ability to alter lives for the better. You also have a gift for friendship. But at a certain point, you disappear behind the curtains because deep in your heart, you have an antipathy for intimacy. You shy away from closeness and are drawn instead to offbeat people, unconventional activities, and the world of the intellect. Thank your mom. Even if your early years were marked by turmoil, she encouraged you to express your individuality and to use your intelligence. She was less comfortable with your emotional needs. You're the same way. You find it taxing to delve into your emotions — or even to recognize them. So you pretend they aren't there — and this technique works . . . at least for a while.

✔ **Moon in Pisces:** You're gentle, sentimental, sympathetic, and ultrasensitive. Easily wounded and often shy, you feel like a hostage to your own emotions, which are difficult to control or conceal. Other people suppress their vulnerabilities — you're all too conscious of yours. You're equally sensitive to your instincts, hunches, and fantasies. At your impressionable best, you're virtually psychic. You're also artistically (or musically) talented. But you can be gullible, hopelessly unrealistic, and self-indulgent. And you have trouble standing up for yourself. Being kind to others is often easier than helping yourself. This goes back to childhood. Ever alert to your mother's shifting moods, you learned to do what you could to improve the emotional atmosphere — even if that meant disregarding your own needs. Your continuing challenge is to be as compassionate to yourself as you are to others.

The Nodes of the Moon

Among astrologers in India, the Nodes of the Moon are considered a vital part of every horoscope, as necessary as the Sun and just as influential. But when I began to study astrology, my teachers barely mentioned the Nodes of the Moon. Even now, introductory astrology books often omit them. One reason

is that even though the Nodes of the Moon occupy two sensitive degrees in your birth chart, there's no celestial body at either spot. In a strictly physical sense, the Nodes of the Moon don't exist. As Gertrude Stein said in a different context, "There's no there there." Nevertheless, the Nodes of the Moon have a long and splendid astrological history.

The Nodes of the Moon are the points where the Moon, in its orbit around the Earth, crosses the *ecliptic,* which is the apparent path of the Sun across the sky. The spot where the Moon climbs over the ecliptic is the *North Node;* the point where it sinks below the ecliptic is the *South Node.* The Nodes, which are exactly 180° apart, gradually shift backwards, spending about a year and a half in each sign and progressing through the zodiac in about 19 years.

To ancient astrologers, the North Node (or Dragon's Head) was beneficial, allied with prosperity and luck, while the South Node (or Dragon's Tail) was Saturnian in flavor, a point of loss or adversity. Well into the 20th century, astrologers still occasionally described the South Node as evil — a distressing comment to anyone with the South Node in a prominent position.

Practitioners of Western astrology generally agree that the North Node illuminates your spiritual path and the constructive yet demanding choices that promote growth. For those who believe in reincarnation, the North Node signifies your path in this life — an evolutionary journey for which you may feel unprepared because it's a trip into the unknown. In contrast, the South Node supports habit over effort, stagnation over growth, and experience over exploration. It's your default method. It feels right because you've traveled that road before, perhaps in earlier lives.

I admit that the South Node's reputation isn't good. Neither is it completely negative. It represents a set of talents and skills you've already mastered. The danger lies not in using those qualities but in placing undue emphasis on them and thus distorting them. The South Node is your launching pad; the North Node is your destination.

The North Node (see the left-hand image in Figure 8-2) is a point of expansion, potential, and growth. Among Vedic astrologers, it is called *Rahu.* The South Node (see the right-hand image in Figure 8-2), known to Vedic astrologers as *Ketu,* symbolizes deeply entrenched patterns and habits that no longer profit you.

To figure out the position of the Lunar Nodes, turn to the Appendix and look up the year of your birth. The essential fact to remember about this table is that it tells you only the position of the North Node. You have to figure out the position of the South Node, which should take about one second.

As an example, say you were born in 1978. That year, according to the table, the North Node, spinning in a retrograde direction (that's what the R means) slipped into Virgo on July 5 at 5:41 a.m., eastern standard time. If you were born after that, your North Node is in Virgo. To figure out what sign the North Node was in prior to that, you need to check out the previous entry. In this case, it was January 7, 1977, when the North Node entered Libra. It remained there until July 5, 1978. So if you were born in 1977 between January 1 and July 5 (at 5:41 a.m.), your North Node is in Libra.

Notice, too, that the North Node is usually retrograde. As a result, it travels through the signs in the reverse direction, going from Libra in 1977 to Virgo in 1978, and eventually to Aries in 1986.

Once you know where your North Node is, you can quickly locate your South Node because it's always in the opposite sign, exactly 180° away. To wit:

If Your North Node Is In . . .	*Your South Node Is In . . .*
Aries	Libra
Taurus	Scorpio
Gemini	Sagittarius
Cancer	Capricorn
Leo	Aquarius
Virgo	Pisces

The Nodes in the Signs

The Sun, the Moon, and the planets are substantial, massive objects. Whether they're solid and rocky like the Moon and Mars, or gas giants like Jupiter and Neptune, they're distinct, visible worlds with their own geography and

their own chemistry. This isn't so of the Nodes. The Nodes are mathematical points — not places. They lack features of any kind. Nonetheless, they carry meaning.

The North Node and the South Node are a matched pair, equal but opposite. They inhabit opposite signs and opposite houses. (For information on the Nodes in the houses, turn to Chapter 12.)

The following list identifies the areas of growth and stagnation marked by the North and South Nodes of the Moon:

- ✓ **North Node in Aries/South Node in Libra:** You yearn to move in the Aries direction, toward assertiveness, self-sufficiency, and bold action. When you obey your impulses and act independently, you flourish. But all too often, instead of mustering up the courage you need, you give your power away to others. You may fear that if you assert yourself fully, you'll never find the relationship you want (or you'll destroy the relationship you have). On the contrary: Submerging your identity in another person is a mistake. Ultimately, the more independent you are, the more contented you will be, whether you're in a relationship or not.

- ✓ **North Node in Taurus/South Node in Scorpio:** Sex, lies, manipulation, and other people's money fascinate you, as do the churning melodramas and intense relationships you often attract. Trouble is, after a while, those soap operas start to go stale. Rather than continuing to immerse yourself in the *sturm und drang* of your obsessions, you gain from building a secure base for yourself. Your best moves are to gather the material resources you need (however slowly), to cultivate patience, and to let your most cherished values be your guide. What you need above all is self-worth. And it wouldn't hurt you to learn to manage money.

- ✓ **North Node in Gemini/South Node in Sagittarius:** How delightful to sit around theorizing about life, death, and the meaning of existence. How nice to know it all. And what a pleasure to convey your brilliant thoughts to your grateful audience (or, in any case, to your beleaguered friends and family). Sadly, it's also a waste of energy. With your unstoppable curiosity and ability to communicate, you benefit from accumulating information and employing it for useful purposes. You're a journalist, an artist, a teacher — a clear thinker, yes, but get the facts. Leave those philosophical musings on the conundrums of life to others. You have too much to do in the here and now.

- ✓ **North Node in Cancer/South Node in Capricorn:** Ambitious and controlling, you readily accept responsibility because you're intent on achieving respect and gaining a position in society. Yet that's not where your greatest joy lies. Despite your thirst for authority and status, you have a more compelling need for home, family, and emotional security. Although revealing your hopes and fears may cause you to feel distressingly weak, the key to your evolution rests in your ability to trust and to act in a caring fashion.

✔ **North Node in Leo/South Node in Aquarius:** Many problems need to be addressed these days, and you'd like to do your part. You'd be delighted to devote yourself to an organization with a noble purpose — at least you think you would be. In fact, though, your fulfillment lies elsewhere. To be the person you were meant to be, you must risk expressing your desires, no matter how selfish that may seem. As admirable as it seems, quietly striving for peace on Earth won't bring you happiness. The issue is simple: You don't want to be an anonymous part of a crowd. You need an outlet for self-expression and you need to be acclaimed for what you are, quirks and all.

✔ **North Node in Virgo/South Node in Pisces:** The realm of the spirit has an irresistible pull for you. But immersing yourself in that world can feed your escapist tendencies. You're better off putting away your Ouija board and attending to the routine details that vex us all, as boring as they may seem. Your need to be a victim or a martyr (the two can be indistinguishable) is chilling, and your sense of inferiority limits your possibilities. Your path to fulfillment runs straight through the workaday world of getting organized, returning phone calls, taking care of business, and being conscious of the needs of others. You don't need to sacrifice yourself. You just need to focus. Pay attention to the small stuff, and you'll be amazed at how contented you will feel.

✔ **North Node in Libra/South Node in Aries:** You're courageous, daring, and self-reliant. You're comfortable asserting yourself (even if you do have a temper), and you're an effective leader and decision-maker. But you're also self-centered, and the advantages of a loving partnership may elude you. Your challenge is to cooperate, be supportive, and mind the needs of others (listening is key). By balancing their needs with your own, you move in the direction of inner peace and contentment.

✔ **North Node in Scorpio/South Node in Taurus:** You think of yourself as a practical person who allocates your resources, financial and otherwise, with care. You believe that material security provides the foundation for psychological strength. You can keep that fantasy if you wish, but you should know that your deepest fulfillment has little to do with material possessions or sensual pleasures, much as you appreciate them. Instead, you benefit from digging into your psyche, sharing your secrets, and dredging up the courage to overcome your resistance to change. In truth, you crave nothing short of total metamorphosis. By getting involved with others and learning to accept their input, you can, at minimum, begin that process.

✔ **North Node in Sagittarius/South Node in Gemini:** It's easy for you to stumble into a life of trivial pursuits or to get lost in a labyrinth of personal gossip, rumor-mongering Web sites, and a never-ending supply of celebrity scandals. But just as Brad Pitt is not *your* boyfriend (e-mail me if I'm wrong), the path of supermarket tabloids (and other time wasters) is not right for you. With your North Node in the sign of religion, law,

travel, and education, you need to get your mind around the big picture. Seek knowledge. Learn a language. Look for a philosophy that aids your understanding. On antique maps, areas of unexplored territory were decorated with images of dragons, which were meant to warn travelers away. You need to sail into those unknown waters, dragons and all. Exercise helps. Spending time in nature is also valuable. Above all, you need to trust your intuition and step into the world. That's where you can find the balm you need the most: adventure.

✔ **North Node in Capricorn/South Node in Cancer:** You have a streak of domesticity, an interest in the past, and a lively appreciation for the simple pleasures of home and family. Alas, as lovely as that sounds, it's not your path. Instead, you require real-world achievements, the kind that are born in ambition, shaped through self-discipline, and rewarded with money and prestige. Much as you adore your home and family, you won't gain much satisfaction sitting in the parlor. And although your shifting moods may distract and disturb you, you still need to exercise your talents — despite your fears and insecurities. You have the ability to achieve your goals and to influence the wider community. Knowing that the fates are with you may boost your confidence and help you recognize opportunities.

✔ **North Node in Aquarius/South Node in Leo:** Creative self-expression comes easily to you, and you attract the kind of notice that most people never get. You know what you want and you have the drive to get it. But you're inclined to take over, and you overwhelm people with the force of your personality. For true growth, you need to team up with others and broaden your vision. Getting involved in a societal cause is a wonderful step for you. By attaching your urge for self-expression to a cause that's larger than yourself, you transcend your ego and move in the direction of fulfillment.

✔ **North Node in Pisces/South Node in Virgo:** Work we must: That's your motto. You have a legion of responsibilities, and you get so caught up in those dreary tasks that there's room for nothing else. To combat anxiety, you do your best to maintain order and to repel the encroaching forces of chaos. But there's only so much you can do. You certainly can't allow yourself to drift. And yet, drift you must. By letting your mind wander, by putting aside your dreaded to-do list, and by being alert to your dreams and fantasies, you allow yourself to glimpse another aspect of experience and to explore the province of the spirit. Yoga, meditation, and anything that can help you relax are indispensable tools. Your ultimate goal is enlightenment.

Chapter 9

The Personal Planets

In This Chapter

▶ Contemplating the personal planets in astronomy, mythology, and astrology

▶ Understanding the planets in the signs

▶ Interpreting Mercury, Venus, Mars, Jupiter, and Saturn in your chart

*T*he Sun and the Moon carry masses of information. All by themselves, they provide a skeleton key to your psyche. But to fully grasp the complexity of your own horoscope, you need to include the planets.

To ancient astrologers, that meant noting the positions of Mercury, Venus, Mars, Jupiter, and Saturn — the only planets visible from Earth. For thousands of years, stargazers assumed that there were no other planets. Then, in 1781, an amateur astronomer in England discovered another planet, and the race was on. Today, astronomers argue over how many planets there are in the solar system. Some claim there are only eight. Others insist there are 23 — and counting. The answer depends entirely on whom you ask.

Astrologers regard those five planets, the ones you can see for yourself in the night sky (and sometimes during the day), as the ones with the most immediate impact on the individual. That's why Mercury, Venus, Mars, Jupiter, and Saturn are known as the *personal planets.* The *outer planets,* which aren't visible without a telescope, are less personality-driven and more generational in their effects (with exceptions that I note in Chapter 10).

Locating Your Planets

If you've slogged your way through Chapters 2 and 3, you probably have a copy of your chart in hand, in which case you already know your planetary placements. If you don't have a copy of your chart, return to those chapters —

Chapter 2 if you want to get your chart from the Internet or Chapter 3 and the Appendix if you plan to cobble it together yourself using the tables in this book.

To figure out what those placements mean, list your planets by sign and by house and then look them up in this chapter (for the personal planets), Chapter 10 (for the outer planets), and Chapter 12 (for the house placements).

Each planet performs a different function in your horoscope. To clarify the distinctions between them, bear in mind that each planet has at least one *keyword* that summarizes its meaning. Table 9-1 lists the keywords, along with the mysterious little symbols that represent the planets.

At first, the information you find may seem random. After a while, certain ideas will repeat themselves, and a coherent picture of your own possibilities will start to emerge.

Table 9-1	Planetary Keywords and Symbols	
Planet	*Keyword*	*Symbol*
Mercury	Communication	☿
Venus	Love	♀
Mars	Activity	♂
Jupiter	Expansion	♃
Saturn	Restriction	♄
Chiron	Healing	⚷
Uranus	Revolution	♅
Neptune	Imagination	♆
Pluto	Transformation	♇
North Node	Potential	☊
South Node	The past	☋

Don't worry if you notice occasional contradictions as you look up your planetary placements: They're inevitable. As Walt Whitman said, "Do I contradict myself? Very well then I contradict myself, (I am large, I contain multitudes.)" Concentrate instead on the ideas that pop up again and again. Once you identify those themes, you're on your way to being an astrologer.

Mercury: Communicating with Style

Astrologers get their understanding of the planets from many sources, including science, mythology, and the astrological tradition.

In astronomy, the little planet Mercury is distinguished by its rapid pace — it whirls around the Sun in a mere 88 days — and its proximity to the Sun.

In mythology, the Roman god Mercury, known to the Greeks as Hermes, is also recognized for his speed. In his winged sandals and cap, he was the messenger of the gods as well as a thief, musician, trickster, and accomplished liar who could talk his way out of anything. A master of spin, Hermes escorted dead souls into the underworld. The ancients worshipped him as the god of travel, speech, roads, boundaries, sleep, dream, and the nameless places that fall between here and there. Two of those in-between spots deserve special recognition: the shadowy realm between wakefulness and sleep, and the transition between life and death.

Astrologers see Mercury as the symbol of communication, speech, writing, knowledge, the intellect, reason, wit, and learning. Its position in your birth chart determines the way you think, the speed with which you gather facts and process information, the style with which you express yourself, and your ability to tell a story (truthful or otherwise), give a speech, and use language.

Because it orbits the Sun so closely, Mercury is always either in the same sign as the Sun or in an adjacent sign — and in no case is it ever more than 28° away from the Sun. To discover its position in your chart, turn to the Appendix.

Mercury's symbol has three metaphysical components: the cross of earth or matter, the circle of spirit, and, perched on top, the crescent of personality looking like a tiny satellite dish, ready to receive information.

For a description of the way your mind operates, look up Mercury in the Appendix and read the appropriate paragraph in this list:

- **Mercury in Aries:** Never slow to jump to conclusions, you have a lightning-fast mind and a direct, forceful way of expressing yourself. Though you can be impatient, competitive, and irritable (and often find it difficult to concentrate), you're never boring or wishy-washy. You're willing to lay down the law if you must. You express yourself assertively, and people generally know what you think. (However, if Mercury is in your twelfth house, you may try to conceal your opinions, usually without success.)

- **Mercury in Taurus:** You're thoughtful, conservative, and remarkably sensible. You gather your facts, construct a careful argument, and present it diplomatically. After that, you only appear to consider other

points of view. In fact, having reached a reasoned decision with all deliberate speed, you see no reason to alter your opinion. You tend to be inflexible, and it's difficult to argue with you, in part because you have the facts, and in part because opening up to fresh ideas is not easy for you. You already know what you think.

✔ **Mercury in Gemini:** You're smart, inquisitive, perceptive, persuasive, humorous, slapdash, and clever. Your intellectual agility is extraordinary. Your curious mind engages easily, you juggle a multitude of interests, and you talk like the wind. You also bend with the wind. All too adaptable, you can rationalize anything. Still, this is an enviable placement. Mercury rules Gemini (and Virgo), so it works very effectively here.

✔ **Mercury in Cancer:** Sensitive and empathetic, you're insightful, reflective, and exceedingly well tuned-in. You can communicate with verve and compassion, and you absorb information readily. You have an amazing memory and a remarkably intuitive mind. But your moods may swamp your better judgment, and you're prone to wishful thinking.

✔ **Mercury in Leo:** Dramatic, dignified, and ambitious, you think creatively, express yourself vividly, and are confident in your opinions (though less so if your Sun is in Cancer). An opinion leader, you usually see the big picture and are persuasive, eloquent, and organized in your thinking. You can also be dogmatic, boastful, and unreserved in your enthusiasms. Okay, sometimes you go overboard. As often happens with Leo placements, your warmth overcomes your tendency to show off and carries the day.

✔ **Mercury in Virgo:** You're smart, subtle, persistent, knowledgeable, analytical, and sharp. Nothing escapes your notice, including logical inconsistencies. A secret idealist who bemoans the distance between how things are and how they ought to be, you can be a nitpicker, a critic, or a prosecuting attorney. You're also a brilliant thinker and a first-rate conversationalist. Mercury rules Virgo, so this planet-sign combination works exceptionally well. Feel confident: You have a fine mind.

✔ **Mercury in Libra:** Rational in thought and elegant in expression, you seek a balanced viewpoint and intuitively understand that the best solution is generally the simplest. Prudent, discreet, and possessed of a strong aesthetic sense, you manage to be objective in a charming, diplomatic way. You love to debate and are interested in the opinions of those you respect. In the privacy of your own mind, you bounce up and down on the seesaw of uncertainty, and because you try to consider all sides of a question, it takes you awhile to reach a decision.

✔ **Mercury in Scorpio:** You have a penetrating, resourceful mind that continually probes beneath the surface. At your best, you're an eagle-eyed observer and a profound thinker. You take nothing at face value, and often suffer from suspicion and even paranoia. You're also analytical, shrewd, incisive, and capable of digging out all sorts of information. This is a great position for a detective, a researcher, or a therapist. It can be dangerous too, because it also confers a biting wit and a persistent tendency to use words as a weapon.

✔ **Mercury in Sagittarius:** You have a searching intellect and a wide-ranging mind. When mulling over the big questions, as you love to do, you can be inspired in your insights and grand in your philosophizing. As a conversationalist, you're entertaining and wise. You can also be dogmatic, hypocritical, and weak when it comes to details, and direct to the point of tactlessness. Evangeline Adams, a great astrologer of the early 20th century, complained in *Astrology for Everyone* that people with this placement fail to keep their promises due to the "discontinuous and flitterbat quality" of their minds. Your sense of humor is your salvation. (Think of Woody Allen.)

✔ **Mercury in Capricorn:** Methodical, realistic, and organized, you're a systematic thinker. You know how to focus, and you act like an adult. Though you can be conventional, rigid, and pessimistic, you try to be even-handed in reaching conclusions, even if that means overcoming your own biases. A serious thinker who values practical information, you're responsible enough to collect the facts, and you communicate clearly and responsibly.

✔ **Mercury in Aquarius:** Fueled by ideas, you have an inventive, often brilliant mind (think of Thomas Edison). Progressive, humane, and happiest when committed to a cause, you express yourself in unique ways and often gain your greatest insight in momentary flashes of inspiration. Your perceptions are distinctly your own. You can become totally excited about a social problem or an abstract theory. Nothing wrong with that — as long as you don't become so attached to an idea that you become inflexible, refusing to let facts — or people — stand in your way.

✔ **Mercury in Pisces:** Any planet in Pisces leads to the triumph of feeling over fact. You respond to people and situations instinctively, often making the right decision without knowing why. You understand how people operate. And you find it easy to adapt to changing circumstances. Your mind is receptive, subtle, empathetic, and imaginative, but logic is not your strong suit. On the other hand, you have ready access to your intuition, which runs like a river of impressions a fraction of an inch beneath your conscious thoughts.

Venus: Love Conquers All

Whether it appears as the Morning Star or the Evening Star, Venus, the second planet from the Sun, outshines almost every object in the sky.

Astronomers say that Venus is a hothouse hell, its fractured plains and ancient volcanoes smothered beneath thick blankets of poisonous clouds. With a surface temperature of 900° Fahrenheit, a totally toxic atmosphere, and a surface pressure 100 times higher than that on Earth, it's uninhabitable, as unlovely a place as you can imagine.

The Greeks and the Romans saw it differently. In classical mythology, Venus (Aphrodite to the Greeks) was the goddess of love and beauty. She was the lover of Adonis (and others), the constant companion of the winged god Eros, and the unfaithful wife of the god Vulcan, who caught her in bed with her favorite paramour, Mars, the god of war.

Astrologers associate Venus with love, flirtation, seduction, beauty, art, luxury, harmony, and pleasure. Venus rules the force of attraction, sexual and otherwise. It describes the quality of your interactions with others, the way you express your affections, your artistic impulses, and, strangely enough, the way you deal with money.

Viewed from Earth, Venus can never be more than 48° from the Sun. That translates to a maximum distance of two signs between Venus and the Sun. To discover the position of Venus in your chart, turn to the Appendix.

The symbol for Venus includes two components from the Metaphysical tradition: the cross of earth and the circle of spirit. Most people today associate it with the biological symbol for woman.

Venus represents your romantic tendencies, values, and response to beauty, art, money, and possessions. To discover the way you express that side of your personality, look up the location of Venus in the Appendix, and then read the appropriate paragraph from the following list:

- **Venus in Aries:** Excitable, enthusiastic, and impulsive, you like to think of yourself as a romantic adventurer. You fall in love impetuously and at first sight — and fall out equally fast. More demanding than you realize (and more self-centered), you're affectionate, ardent, and easily aroused. Even though you ultimately require mental compatibility, what gets you going in the first place is physical appearance.

- **Venus in Taurus:** As the ruler of Taurus, Venus is completely at home here, making you affectionate, charming, artistic, and sensual in the extreme. All the comforts of life appeal to you, starting with rich food and ending with long, luscious sexual encounters, preferably with the same person every time. You value consistency, and though you're capable of fooling around, it's not your natural mode. You require security, comfort, cuddling, beautiful objects, an occasional push to get you moving, a committed partner, and a healthy bank account. Not to mention roses, pastry, and sheets with as high a thread count as you can possibly afford.

- **Venus in Gemini:** The planet of love in the sign of the inconstant mind produces witty banter, many happy hours of conversation and bookstore browsing, lots of light-hearted flirtation, and an irresistible attraction to people who are smart and quick. Your affections are easily swayed, and you're more than capable of carrying on a love affair entirely on the Internet. The challenge is to distinguish between what ought to be a fine romance (it sounds like a fabulous idea) and actual love.

✔ **Venus in Cancer:** A natural nester, you find your deepest pleasures in home and family. You're kind, sympathetic, sentimental, loyal, devoted, popular, and a terrific cook (or you'd like to be anyway). You may appear to be the epitome of self-confidence. Yet you require more than a little psychological support. Your fear of rejection, however you try to disguise it, may cause you to hold on too long to both lovers and friends. You don't mean to cling. It's just that when you love someone, you want it to last forever.

✔ **Venus in Leo:** Warm, outgoing, loyal, and luxury-loving, you're creative, self-dramatizing, and in love with love. You feel passionately and express yourself flamboyantly. Love is an essential part of your nature, and you tend to define yourself through it. You also love the arts. That doesn't mean you're about to run away with an unpublished poet — not unless said artiste has a trust fund. You're happiest when the cash flows freely.

✔ **Venus in Virgo:** When you're in love, you pay full attention, analyzing every interaction, rereading every e-mail, and listening to your voice mail repeatedly to make sure you've gotten every nuance. You'll do anything for your lover . . . including pointing out his flaws. You can be critical and controlling and full of opinions about how other people ought to behave. Some people with this placement have flashy personalities (those with the Sun in Leo, for instance). Most people with Venus in Virgo are modest, inhibited, and a little shy between the sheets.

✔ **Venus in Libra:** You're affectionate, gentle, warm, and willing to please. A true romantic, you idealize love and often have trouble adapting to the rough spots of a real relationship. When disappointment sets in, you take it hard for a while, and then you get moving. You're highly attractive to other people, and there's usually someone who's circling around you. This position also brings a strong aesthetic sensibility.

✔ **Venus in Scorpio:** Thanks to Scorpio's infamous sexiness, this placement sounds like a ticket to ecstasy. And sometimes it is. You get aroused in the presence of mystery, intensity, and even a subtle hint of darkness. Proud, passionate, and seductive, you're prone to deep longing, both sexual and emotional, and your love life tends to be stormy. At your best, you're deeply devoted and profoundly intimate. At your worst, you can be jealous and vengeful. You're also capable of pulling back from social interaction and isolating yourself behind an invisible shield.

✔ **Venus in Sagittarius:** Demonstrative, ardent, direct, and excitable, you see love as an adventure — not as a way to nail down a secure future. You value your freedom, and your ideal lover is someone who helps you see more of the world and experience more of life — not someone who constricts your activities. You have noble ideals and are drawn to people who are highly committed. You're also intrigued by people who come from backgrounds entirely different from your own. You don't mind shocking the folks.

✔ **Venus in Capricorn:** You're sensual in your sexual liaisons, constant in your affections, and cautious about revealing your emotions. You value stability, propriety, and rectitude. The messiness of emotional free-for-alls terrifies you, so you keep your feelings under wraps. Serious and sophisticated, you admire anything classic. In art, as in love, you understand the need for control. Sometimes you're accused of privileging status over more exalted ideals. And what's wrong with that? You're a realist, and you know that in the real world, status matters.

✔ **Venus in Aquarius:** Open-minded, friendly, and idealistic, you're drawn to mavericks and rebels, and you have a multitude of friends — which is exactly how you like it. You aren't the most passionate person on the planet, and you tend to enjoy a stimulating intellectual companionship more than a romantic one. You also need a certain amount of solitude. Ideas and causes appeal to you. Passionate displays do not. Ultimately, you're an independent sort, and your heart is difficult to capture.

✔ **Venus in Pisces:** You're sentimental, artistic, devoted, and willing to do anything for your beloved. You idealize your lovers and truly seek union with them, but you have no idea what's reasonable and what's not. Other people find it easy to abuse you, in part because you shrug your shoulders helplessly and gratefully accept crumbs. Eventually, that makes you angry, which is why you may become emotionally abusive, often in a passive-aggressive way. You truly know how to love. That's not the problem. The problem is that you're sometimes too willing to sacrifice your own needs to those of others.

Mars: Road Warrior

What a terrible reputation Mars has. Because it glows red in the sky (a result of the iron oxide in its rocky soil), the Babylonians associated it with death and destruction, Pacific Islanders thought of it as the home of a giant red pig, and New Jerseyites, listening to Orson Welles on the radio in 1938, ran screaming from their homes in fear of invading Martians. Yet people have always fantasized about living on the red planet.

To the ancient Romans, Mars was the god of war, and many festivals were held in his honor. Ares, the Greek equivalent, was not admired. Throughout Greek mythology, Ares is constantly put down by the other gods — except for Aphrodite (Venus), the goddess of love, who adores him.

Early astrologers saw Mars as the planet of violence and bad temper. As late as the 15th century, astrologers associated it with theft, murder, battle, lechery, dishonesty, and seething malice of all sorts. Astrologers continue to associate Mars with anger, accidents, and injury. They also see Mars as the planet of action and desire. It brings will, stamina, drive, strength, energy, and the courage to go after what you want. Mars makes things happen.

The fourth planet from the Sun, Mars takes almost two years — 687 days, to be exact — to spin through the zodiac. It spends about two months in a sign. (Once every year and a half, its pattern changes, and it lingers in one section of the sky, giving that particular sign an extra jolt of Martian energy). No matter what your Sun sign is, Mars can be in any of the 12 signs of the zodiac. To discover its position in your chart, turn to the Appendix.

The position of Mars in your chart indicates an area where you're energetic and forceful. In biology, this figure represents the male, just as the symbol of Venus corresponds to the female.

The position of Mars by sign describes the way in which you take the initiative, assert yourself, and dive into a new endeavor or involvement. It represents your drive and your desires. After you have located your Mars in the Appendix, you can look it up in the list that follows:

- **Mars in Aries:** As the ruler of Aries, Mars endows its natives with energy, sexual charisma to burn, and an occasionally explosive temper that you must learn to control. Fortunately, you don't hold on to your anger. After you explode, it evaporates. Enthusiastic, assertive, and daring, you're a natural leader who commands attention even without seeking it.

- **Mars in Taurus:** You're a hard-working, down-to-earth person with plenty of stamina. Determined and sensible, you can be distracted by the desires of the flesh. When you finally do commit yourself to something, whether it's a relationship or a job, you're in it for the long haul — and for the money. Born with a serious practical streak, you care about material possessions and status, often more than you're willing to admit.

- **Mars in Gemini:** With the planet of aggression in the sign of the twins, you're high-spirited, argumentative, nervous, and irritable. Your energy waxes and wanes, sometimes with startling speed. And although you love to debate, you aren't always able to distinguish between major principles and minor points. Still, you enjoy the back-and-forth. You have a lively, ingenious mind, and you're loads of fun.

- **Mars in Cancer:** You're an inherently emotional person who needs to get a handle on your moods before you can successfully accomplish your goals. Without realizing it, you tend to sulk. You're highly sensitive, but you may project signals so subtle that many people miss them. In a relationship, you can be possessive and tenacious when you ought to be angry and out the door. You stew. You bury your emotions and need to learn to be direct. You're also responsive, protective, devoted, and imaginative, in bed and elsewhere.

- **Mars in Leo:** Confident, impassioned, and tireless, you have presence and real follow-through. When committed to a cause or an activity, you're virtually unstoppable. True, you can be egotistical and arrogant, and your need for an audience can be wearing. Nevertheless, your warmth, high spirits, and willingness to take the first step bring you many admirers. You create excitement.

✔ **Mars in Virgo:** Control is an issue for you. You're hardworking, calculating, and willing to look reality dead in the eye. Sensible and methodical, you can detach yourself emotionally when your success depends on it. That quality is advantageous in your career. In your personal life, it gives you the ability to turn your sex drive on and off, seemingly at will. (Several famous military men share this placement, including Alexander the Great, Napoleon Bonaparte, and General George Patton.)

✔ **Mars in Libra:** At your best, you're friendly, flirtatious, charming, and stylish. But you're at a loss without a partner. In your love life, and even at work, you're happier when you have a partner. Also, although you pride yourself on your logical mind, you tend to cover up your uncertainties and insecurities by defending your ill-considered statements with more passion than logic. At times people are forced to agree with you, just to end the discussion.

✔ **Mars in Scorpio:** You're courageous and cunning, determined and self-sufficient. Blessed with fierce willpower and unwavering desires, you're highly sexed and intensely emotional. You may struggle with jealousy and the desire to seek revenge. Although adapting to changing circumstances isn't easy, you have a reliable source of internal energy and a great deal of personal power, making this a beneficial placement overall.

✔ **Mars in Sagittarius:** Independent and enthusiastic, you have strong convictions, a love of the outdoors, and a deep desire for adventure. But you can be slapdash and defiant, and your crusades, so eagerly launched, don't always reach completion. Early 20th century astrologer Evangeline Adams, never one to pull her punches, claims that this placement makes people "scintillating rather than solid, dashing rather than enduring." Be that as it may, you're also fair, direct, and idealistic, and you can gather your energy quickly — especially when you're off on an adventure.

✔ **Mars in Capricorn:** Your desires, sexual and otherwise, are strong, your ambitions focused. When you feel recognized, your energy is reliable and steady. When you feel thwarted, your vitality fades. Efficient and systematic, you respect tradition and authority and often rise to the top. You understand hierarchies, and in many ways you're a natural leader. But when you don't get the obedience you demand or when things simply don't go your way, you can be surprisingly cool. You usually hide your anger. On the rare occasions when it slips out, however, it's nasty.

✔ **Mars in Aquarius:** Whenever possible, you prefer the road less traveled. You're enterprising and impatient, and you don't mind taking a risk. Convention bores you, and you value the idea of progress. You're independent, idealistic, and friendly. But emotionally, you can be on the chilly side, and you occasionally rebel just for the pleasure of making a statement.

> ✔ **Mars in Pisces:** You fall deeply in love. You're generous, moody, restless, and highly intuitive. But when the emotional din becomes more than you can tolerate, you shut down. When that happens, your willpower evaporates, you have trouble getting motivated, you drive friends insane with your passivity, and your physical energy disappears. One of the central challenges of your life is regulating your energy. It's not easy to do when you're a slave to your feelings.

Jupiter: More Is Better

Looking for luck? Your search is over. Auspicious Jupiter is the lord of luck, the guardian of good fortune, and the champion of getting an even break.

Jupiter is the largest planet in the solar system by far. More massive than all the other planets combined, it could devour 1,330 Earths and still have room to burp. Its most famous feature, known as the Great Red Spot, is a 300-year-old cyclone that's double the size of the Earth.

Not surprisingly, Jupiter was named for the king of the gods, who was known in Greece as Zeus and in Rome as Jove or Jupiter Optimus Maximus — the biggest and the best, even if he was also punitive and promiscuous. The Greeks depicted him as bearded, dignified, and powerful — Zeus the father figure, surveying the universe from his home on snowy Mount Olympus.

Astrologers associate Jupiter with opportunity, expansion, growth, abundance, learning, success, optimism, and good cheer. Whatever Jupiter touches, it expands. Of course, like every planet, it can express itself positively or negatively. At its best, it brings good luck, generosity, and the ability to seize an opportunity. When it's tied to other planets through tension-producing aspects, such as squares and oppositions (discussed in Chapter 13), it expresses its shadow side by indulging in gluttony, laziness, and excess of all kinds.

Jupiter takes about 12 years to spin through the zodiac, spending about a year in each sign. To discover its position in your chart, turn to the Appendix.

Rejoice when you see this symbol in your chart, for it marks an area of opportunity. According to metaphysical tradition, the symbol is made up of two parts: the cross of matter and, rising above it, the curve of personality, indicating the expansive unfurling of the self. That's one way to remember it. Or you can think of it as looking like a highly stylized number four.

Galileo and the moons of Jupiter

About one hundred years after the birth of Christ, the astronomer Ptolemy wrote a book confidently asserting what everyone already knew: That the Earth was the center of the universe, and that everything else — the Moon, the Sun, the stars, and the planets — revolved around it.

Over a millennium later, in 1453, Copernicus showed that the Earth orbited the Sun, not the other way around. His observations were not widely accepted. Martin Luther referred to him as an "upstart astrologer" (and in fact he was an astrologer, as were most astronomers). For the most part, people continued to put their faith in Ptolemy. Few doubted that the Earth was the center of the universe.

A century and a half later, Galileo trained his telescope upon distant Jupiter and saw that it was orbited by a population of moons. (He saw four; scientists have now identified 16.) His announcement was greeted with distress, particularly by the church, because if those four moons were orbiting around Jupiter, then by definition, not everything revolved around the Earth and the Ptolemaic system had to be wrong. Galileo ended up spending the rest of his life under house arrest for his role in promoting this new view of the heavens. His ideas triumphed. Thus Jupiter and its many moons opened up a new way to see the cosmos. In an astrological chart, Jupiter has a similar function. It opens things up; it expands the possibilities.

Jupiter's position by sign describes the way you try to broaden your horizons and experience more of the world. It also indicates areas where you're likely to be lucky.

✔ **Jupiter in Aries:** You have confidence, energy, and enthusiasm. You easily get fired up, even to the point of becoming manic, and you have many interests, although you don't sustain them over the long run. It's easy for you to get wound up in your own concerns, and you must guard against the tendency to be egocentric and to lose control of the details.

✔ **Jupiter in Taurus:** You're devoted and kind; a lover of nature, material objects, and sensuous pleasures. You can easily tumble into self-indulgence. So you're great in bed — but you may also be plagued by excess weight. Fortunately, you balance your pleasure-seeking with practicality. When it comes to the bottom line, your judgment is sound.

✔ **Jupiter in Gemini:** Nothing fires you up more than a curious idea — or a game show. You're clever, multitalented, inquisitive, and easily engrossed, although you run the risk of losing your interest in a topic by talking it to death. You benefit from anything that involves writing — from keeping a journal to working in a bookstore to being a journalist.

✔ **Jupiter in Cancer:** You're openhearted, benevolent, intuitive, protective, and sympathetic — the ultimate Earth mother, even if you're a man. Understanding and forgiving (sometimes pathetically so), you love the pleasures of home, property, and parenthood. Traditional astrology holds that Jupiter is exalted in this position, and experience shows that it tends to bring luck in real estate. One downside: You may struggle with your love of good food.

✔ **Jupiter in Leo:** You're magnanimous, compassionate, exuberant, and dramatic, with enormous vitality and a deep need for recognition, respect, and power. Though you can be overbearing, you're openhearted and well liked. This position, considered a fortunate one, often brings success.

✔ **Jupiter in Virgo:** You're organized, practical, and happiest when your efforts produce concrete results. You have a fine intellect, a strong work ethic, and a tendency to put in too many hours in pursuit of perfection. Jupiter is expansive while Virgo is restrictive, so this placement gives rise to internal tension.

✔ **Jupiter in Libra:** You're likable, sympathetic, fair, and popular. Gifted with natural charm, you benefit from working with other people and have an innate attraction to the arts. You may wrestle with the classic Libran difficulty in making important decisions. Seeking balance is probably a wise idea for everyone, but it's especially rewarding for you.

✔ **Jupiter in Scorpio:** You have huge passions, a magnetic intensity that other people can sense, and a strongly sexual nature. Though you may be reserved, you're also observant, and you have a sincere interest in investigating whatever's under that rock. You're ambitious and sometimes aggressive, with a great personal pride and a ferocious willpower that can help you achieve your dreams.

✔ **Jupiter in Sagittarius:** Because Jupiter rules Sagittarius, this is considered an auspicious placement. Sagittarius brings out the best in Jupiter, making you genial, optimistic, generous, tolerant, and philosophical (so you don't obsess over the small stuff). A skilled teacher, you're drawn to foreign travel, higher education, and large, all-encompassing philosophies, religions, and belief systems. But be aware that this position also inflates your faith (or fanaticism), along with your tendency to lecture.

✔ **Jupiter in Capricorn:** With the planet of expansion in cautious, constricting Capricorn, you're ambitious, dutiful, honest, serious-minded, realistic, disciplined, and industrious, but you have a tough time relaxing. When you set a goal, your chances of achieving it are excellent. Along the way, you may have to combat pessimism, but you also find joy in accomplishment.

✔ **Jupiter in Aquarius:** Open-minded, altruistic, and innovative, you have great originality and take an interest in everything that's cutting edge. You're naturally tolerant of people, even if you're sometimes scornful of their ideas. But despite your humanitarian ideals, you don't deal with disappointment well, and you can become egotistical and overbearing.

✔ **Jupiter in Pisces:** Blessed with powerful intuitive and imaginative abilities, you absorb everything going on around you. A forgiving and empathetic person, you cherish the notion that you can make things better, even to the point of self-sacrifice. But when you feel overwhelmed, which happens more than you may want, you can turn into a hermit. Spiritual pursuits intrigue and sustain you.

Saturn: Lord of the Rings

Before the invention of the telescope, Saturn was the most distant planet that anyone could see. It marked the end of the solar system. Naturally, it came to represent limits. Today, it remains the most distant planet that's easily visible with the naked eye, so that meaning still applies. But its image has improved. Thanks to the telescope and the Voyager space missions, everyone knows what Saturn looks like. Even people who have never looked through a telescope have seen pictures of its dazzling ring structure. And they know that it's the most beautiful planet in the solar system.

The second largest planet (after Jupiter), Saturn is a gas giant surrounded by a broad collar of icy rings and at least 18 named moons (and counting). It's so large that 95 Earths could fit inside it. But its density is so low that, if there were an ocean large enough to hold the entire planet, Saturn would float.

In mythology, Saturn was originally an Italian corn god. The Romans identified him with the Greek god Kronos, who swallowed his own children and was in turn conquered by them. He's known as Father Time, the symbol of the past and the old order.

In astrology, Saturn represents the system. Its influence is serious and somber. It brings structure, discipline, limitations, boundaries, responsibility, duty, perseverance, and fear. It tests people and forces them to confront reality. As a result, Saturn has a terrible reputation, one that has been nurtured by generations of astrologers, including the great Evangeline Adams. In *Astrology for Everyone,* she explains that Saturn "blights all that he gazes on. He is the curse of disappointment, not of anger. He freezes the water-springs; he is the dry-rot and the death of the ungodly. He looks upon the Sun, despairs; in cynic bitterness his draught is brewed, and he drinks it, wishing it were poison. His breath withers up love; his word is malediction . . . But in each one of us this principle exists; it is the most inescapable of all our fates."

With publicity like that, it's no wonder that followers of astrology came to fear Saturn. Yet its reputation isn't entirely deserved because, although Saturn does bring difficulties, it also helps create order. Saturn's influence enables you to conquer your fears and to combat your inertia. If it forces you to struggle with depression, disappointment, poverty, and other obstacles, it also compels you to seek solutions, to set goals, to establish schedules, to work harder than you ever thought you could, and to get organized. Saturn is, in short, the planet of accomplishment.

Saturn takes 29½ years to travel through the zodiac. It spends about 2½ years in each sign. To discover its position in your chart, turn to the Appendix.

The symbol of Saturn, wherever it may be in your chart, marks the spot of your greatest challenges. Metaphysical astrologers describe it as the cross of matter and circumstances rising out of the crescent of personality, suggesting that humans create their own limitations and must find ways to confront them. An easier way to remember the symbol is that it resembles a curvy lowercase "h" (for "hard" or perhaps "hellish") with a slash mark across it like a French "7."

Saturn's placement by sign determines your sense of inadequacy, your fears and hesitations, the obstacles and liabilities that block your path, and the ways in which you try to overcome them.

- **Saturn in Aries:** You're an independent thinker: You can't stand to follow the leader, but you don't like directing other people either. Though you're entrepreneurial, determined, and disciplined, you can also be inconsiderate and domineering. Given a goal and a game plan, you do fabulously well. Without direction, you flounder. Nor can the goal be imposed on you by someone else. It must come from within.

- **Saturn in Taurus:** Images of the poorhouse dance in your head. You have an intense need for stability, and the thought of being without money terrifies you. So you learn to manage your resources effectively and may even become quite well-heeled. You're industrious, prudent, and methodical. The downside? You're stubborn, you lack spontaneity, and you run the risk of becoming a plodder. And although some people with this placement become obsessed with sex or other pleasures, you're secretly ambivalent about such things, and you're equally likely to deny yourself such material comforts.

- **Saturn in Gemini:** You're smart, serious, and articulate despite your fear of being considered intellectually inferior or at a loss for words. You're an excellent problem-solver, with an active mind and dozens of interests. Like any placement in the sign of the Twins, Saturn in Gemini can reveal itself in a number ways. When you're hot, your ability to concentrate is inspiring — and intimidating. At other times, you run the risk of frittering away your energy and diluting your intentions with meaningless activity and chatter. You have a clear and lucid mind, but beware: You can convince yourself of anything.

✔ **Saturn in Cancer:** Not an easy placement, Saturn in Cancer generally brings a difficult childhood with at least one parent who's cold or withholding. As a result, you may be insecure and inhibited, with a yearning for emotional control and understanding. Your attempt to win the love you lacked as a child can become the quest of a lifetime. Some people with this placement become clingy or cover up their fear of vulnerability by acting overly confident or indifferent. (The disguise, by the way, fools no one.) Most attempt to create in adulthood what they lacked in childhood by becoming tolerant, protective, loving parents.

✔ **Saturn in Leo:** Determined and dignified, you long to be creative but are afraid of expressing yourself. You want to be recognized — yet you're terrified of being mediocre. That's the Catch-22 you must overcome. Self-doubt wears you down and gets you nowhere. The challenge of this position is to acknowledge, not bury, your need for recognition and to find a way to achieve it. Similarly, your creative urges need dramatic expression and positive acceptance. Overcome a tendency to arrogance, the scourge of Leo. Dare to be dramatic. You'll be much happier.

✔ **Saturn in Virgo:** You're analytical, worried, industrious, and drawn to solitude. (In a previous life, according to one of my first astrology teachers, you may have been a medieval monk.) Because you fear losing control, you do your best to nail down every detail. Ritual relaxes you, and you rely on a string of routines you have established in your everyday life. Though you prefer things to be orderly and predictable, those routines can also limit, confine, and ultimately overwhelm you. Take as your motto this quotation from Henry David Thoreau (from *Where I lived, and What I Lived For*): "Our life is frittered away by detail . . . Simplify, simplify."

✔ **Saturn in Libra:** This favorable position makes you rational, reliable, discreet, and serious. You fear being alone, which makes you all the more anxious when you try to connect with other people. Your relationships thoroughly reflect you — yet you may not like what you see. You may feel that they somehow fail to measure up. Fortunately, you're always willing to negotiate. Although you may think you desire a passionate entanglement, you're ultimately far happier when you make the sensible choice. You tend to marry someone older, and you may marry late.

✔ **Saturn in Scorpio:** You're resourceful and powerful, with strong convictions and a great sense of purpose. Dependency issues can be tough for you, and you may struggle to define yourself as an individual while maintaining a relationship. You have compelling sexual needs, yet sex is also complicated for you. Although you're prone to jealousy and resentment, you find the courage to deal with your problems and conquer your fears, including fear of death. Mysteries fascinate you, and none more than the mystery of your own psyche.

↙ **Saturn in Sagittarius:** "Don't fence me in" is your refrain. You seek adventure, travel, and broad horizons. But unless you find a structured way to achieve your goals, circumstances may conspire to keep you from achieving them. Education is important for you, and the philosophical or moral precepts that you live by shape your life. Even though you may fantasize about being independent and footloose, what you actually need is to find meaning in your daily activities, to expand your philosophical viewpoint, and to travel widely — literally or figuratively — with purpose.

↙ **Saturn in Capricorn:** You're capable, ambitious, and pragmatic, with natural authority and obvious competence. Because you crave recognition and are secretly afraid that you won't get it, you doggedly pursue your goals and you make sure to follow the rules — even if you have to give up your more original ideas along the way. You don't like restrictions, but you know how to deal with them and can work within a structure. You can even overcome your tendency to depression. Saturn rules Capricorn, so this is considered an excellent placement.

↙ **Saturn in Aquarius:** You have a clear and original mind, an unusual sense of organization and structure, and the ability to influence others. Liberal-minded and unselfish (in part because you don't want people to think ill of you), you conceive of yourself as a member of society, a small part of a larger whole. And you're a person of principle. It's essential for your happiness and self-respect that you live in accordance with your ideals, which are generally of the noblest sort. Material success isn't a motivating force in your life — your values matter more.

↙ **Saturn in Pisces:** You're sympathetic and intuitive. Your sensitivity makes you appealing to others, and your creativity brings you satisfaction. You may also suffer from more than your share of neuroses, anxieties, and baseless apprehensions. Though you understand how other human beings operate, you may be at a loss when it comes to solving your own problems (especially if substance abuse happens to be one of them). You're afraid of chaos and isolation, and you struggle to stave off those terrors. Establishing routines is helpful. Becoming addicted is your undoing.

Chapter 10

The Outer Planets (Plus One Amazing Asteroid)

*U*ntil 1781, astrologers cast horoscopes using only the Sun, the Moon, and the five planets visible from Earth: Mercury, Venus, Mars, Jupiter, and Saturn. Then William Herschel, a professional musician and amateur telescope maker, made a momentous breakthrough. After years of staying up at night with his devoted sister and obsessively (he was a Scorpio) mapping the skies over Bath, England, he became the first human being in history to train a telescope on the night sky and discover a planet. That discovery — of the planet Uranus — rocked the astronomical world. That oddball planet, identified in the midst of the American War of Independence and only a few years before the French Revolution, transformed the commonly held view of the solar system. In astrology, it soon became associated with revolutions of all kinds, including the personal, political, and scientific.

In the next century, scientists realized that anomalies in the orbit of Uranus could be accounted for by the presence of another planet. In 1846, after a search marked by total confusion (in keeping with the nature of the planet), European astronomers identified that unknown body and named it Neptune. A third discovery further expanded the solar system in 1930, when Clyde Tombaugh, a 23-year-old amateur who was hired to examine photographic plates of the night sky, found what he was looking for: A tiny, distant body, which is now named Pluto.

Poor Pluto's demotion

When it was discovered, Pluto was hailed as the ninth planet. Since then, astronomers have discovered many small, icy, celestial objects orbiting the Sun. And so they've begun to rethink what it means to be a planet. Is it enough to simply orbit the Sun? Well, no. After all, asteroids revolve around the Sun, as do comets. Is it enough to be above a certain size? Or to orbit the Sun from within the plane of the solar system? By those standards, Pluto doesn't qualify. It's small, its orbit is tilted, and it has a peculiar gravitational relationship to its largest moon.

As a result, Pluto, the most idiosyncratic of the traditional planets, has been demoted. In 2006, astronomers dubbed it a "dwarf planet" and turned their backs on it. Astrologers are sticking with it. Okay, maybe Pluto, which is slightly smaller than our Moon, isn't as imposing as the other planets. Size isn't everything. Besides, Pluto isn't the only small object that astrologers heed. Another such body is Chiron, which wasn't discovered until 1977 and is now routinely incorporated into natal charts. (I discuss Chiron at the end of this chapter.)

All these celestial bodies — Uranus and Neptune, as well as Pluto and Chiron — differ from the visible planets of antiquity. The visible planets reflect individual disposition, and were consequently known as personal planets. Uranus, Neptune, and Pluto, which can found in the outer reaches of the solar system, don't describe personality as much as they shape generations. After all, the Sun swings through all 12 signs in a year — but Chiron takes 51 years to travel through the signs, Uranus requires 84 years to make a single orbit, Neptune needs 165 years, and tiny Pluto requires almost two and a half centuries to complete its tour of the zodiac. These celestial bodies have a minor impact on day-to-day activities. Instead, they define generations, spark momentous events, and bring hidden potentials to light.

The outer planets are also harbingers of change, both external and internal. These planets shake you up (revolutionary Uranus), inspire and confuse you (nebulous Neptune), and push you to the brink (take-no-prisoners Pluto). They represent the invincible, unstoppable, cosmic forces of change.

The generational dates given in parentheses later in this chapter for these planetary placements aren't exact. What actually happens when Neptune, Uranus, or Pluto changes signs is that for almost a year (and occasionally for longer than that), the planet appears to ricochet back and forth between the old sign and the new one. As a result, if you were born during (or even close to) the first or final year of a planet's journey through a sign, you can't rely on the ballpark dates given in this chapter. Flip to the Appendix instead. Or go to the Internet to get a copy of your chart (see Chapter 2).

Uranus: The Rebel

As the first planet discovered through the use of technology, Uranus is the planet of revolution and the modern age. It rules electricity, technology, and everything on the cutting edge. It's also said to be the planet of astrology.

Uranus is a shocker. In a birth chart, it represents the part of you that's most original and inventive, that shuns convention, craves freedom, and attracts — or creates — abrupt change. It can stir up senseless rebellion, studied eccentricity, restlessness, turmoil, and agitated states of mind. It can also herald unexpected, life-altering events, typically in areas where you haven't been paying attention. Uranus, it must be said, can shatter your world.

Uranus also generates flashes of insight, brilliant ideas, and new vistas when you need them the most. It's the iconoclastic lord of genius, inventiveness, originality, and everything that captures you by surprise. When lightning strikes, be it in the form of an unexpected pink slip or a bizarre career opportunity, love at first sight or an unforeseen divorce, a lottery win or a housing crisis, you can bet that Uranus, the emissary of disruption, is at work.

It takes 84 years — a human lifetime — for Uranus and its 15 moons to travel through the zodiac. Like Jupiter, Saturn, and Neptune, Uranus is a gas giant. But while every other planet rotates on its axis in a more-or-less upright fashion, unconventional Uranus seems to roll around on its side with its north pole pointing to the Sun. As a result, the Uranian day is 42 years long, and the night is the same length.

The symbol of Uranus (see Figure 10-1) looks like an old-fashioned TV antenna — an apt image for the planet associated with electricity, technology, and the future. The symbol also incorporates a letter H, a reminder of William Herschel, who discovered the planet in 1781.

Figure 10-1: The symbol of Uranus.

Understanding Uranus

Uranus spends about seven years in each sign. Like Neptune and Pluto, it makes its greatest impact on generations. In an individual chart, its influence is subtle — most of the time. But when it's prominent in a birth chart, Uranus is the mark of geniuses, idealists, iconoclasts, nonconformists, eccentrics, inventors, revolutionaries, and astrologers.

And when, over the course of its 84-year cycle, it stimulates the Sun, the Moon, and the other planets in a birth chart, it can beget turmoil, foolish accidents, hair-raising relationship upheaval, amazing job shifts, and — in short — whatever mayhem it takes to loosen you up and liberate you.

Uranus, like the other outer planets, primarily influences generations rather than individuals — unless it happens to occupy a strong position in your natal chart. It's prominent in your horoscope if

- ✔ It occupies an angle — that is, it's in the first, fourth, seventh, or tenth house of your chart. It's especially powerful if it's within approximately 8° of your Ascendant or Midheaven. (See Chapter 11 for more on Ascendants and Midheavens.)

- ✔ It makes a number of close aspects to other planets and, in particular, to the Sun, the Moon, or the planet that rules your Ascendant. (See Chapter 13 for a discussion of aspects.)

- ✔ You have one or more planets in Aquarius.

To check the position of Uranus in your chart, turn to the Appendix.

Uranus in the signs

The sign that Uranus occupies in your birth chart determines the way you and other members of your generation shake off the burden of expectation, rebel against the established order, liberate yourself from fear, and express your most original self.

- ✔ **Uranus in Aries (1927 to 1935):** You're feisty, indomitable, and impatient, and you value your freedom to an extraordinary degree. You're a pioneering spirit, brave at your core. When change is called for, you rush in, preferring the risks of being impulsive to the so-called safety of the slow-and-sensible approach. You're intrepid and inventive, even if your enthusiasms do flicker on and off. Change exhilarates you.

- ✔ **Uranus in Taurus (1935 to 1942):** Once you admit that you want something and begin going after it, nothing can stop you. Your willpower helps you overcome all obstacles. You also feel strongly about money and possessions and you may suffer financial ups and downs. You gravitate toward concrete, innovative methods of making money.

- ✔ **Uranus in Gemini (1942 to 1949):** You're clever, inquisitive, nervous, chatty, versatile, and mentally restless. You deal with change by reframing it — you'd rather feel like an unconscious architect of your own fate than like a victim of circumstance. You gravitate toward original ideas and new ways of communicating. You're also easily distracted with a tendency to procrastinate.

✔ **Uranus in Cancer (1949 to 1956):** You have an active imagination, a sensitive disposition, and an unusual family life. You may move frequently or experience disruptions in your home life. Much as you long for the security of a nuclear family, you also rebel against it, and when you're in a traditional family (or even a standard-issue house), you may alter its structure.

✔ **Uranus in Leo (1956 to 1962):** Assertive and freewheeling, ardent and talented, you enthusiastically throw yourself into creative endeavors. Offbeat love affairs (the more reckless the better) entice and excite you, and you approach times of change with gusto. But you can also be egotistical, imperious, and — in a word — obnoxious.

✔ **Uranus in Virgo (1962 to 1969):** Even though you have an acute and analytical mind, you rebel against routine — especially on the job, where your need for freedom takes you in surprising directions. Your approach to science, technology, and health is both original and practical. And although you rebel against routines enforced by others, you're skilled at creating your own highly individual, compulsively followed patterns.

✔ **Uranus in Libra (1969 to 1975):** You're imaginative and artistic, although members of other generations may be appalled at your taste. They may also be surprised by your relationships, romantic and otherwise, because you're attracted to unusual people and situations. In many ways your generation is forging an innovative approach to relationships — one that incorporates a high degree of personal freedom. Still, in times of stress, you're happiest with a companion by your side.

✔ **Uranus in Scorpio (1975 to 1981):** Deeply intuitive and strong-willed, you're charismatic and determined, with unusual attitudes toward sex and death, subjects of eternal fascination to you. Sudden infatuations and lengthy obsessions may plague you. Finances also absorb you, and you may experience sudden economic shifts. You're resourceful and unafraid, and when change is in the air, you choose to experience it deeply and consciously, with an eye to the future.

✔ **Uranus in Sagittarius (1981 to 1988):** You're optimistic and free-spirited, with large aspirations. You resent naysayers who denigrate your dreams, and you refuse to be constrained by practical concerns. You'd like to see the world — but not by following someone else's itinerary. You'd like to achieve spiritual enlightenment — but you rebel against standard religions. Travel and education excite you — but only when you approach them in your own unique ways. You feel liberated by the forces of change.

✔ **Uranus in Capricorn (1988 to 1996):** You're ambitious, responsible, and methodical. Yet you instinctively shun the prescribed path and the old-fashioned hierarchy. As a result, your career takes some surprising turns. If you can express your individuality within an organization or a system, fine. If not, your deep sense of discomfort forces you to bring it to its knees and create an entirely new system. You're a force for constructive change.

✔ **Uranus in Aquarius (1996 to 2003):** You're tolerant, unsentimental, humanitarian, and inventive. A nonconformist and idealist at heart, you celebrate individuality in others and number many an oddball among your friends. Amazing coincidences and strokes of luck characterize your life. Uranus works well in Aquarius, so when you embrace change, your world opens up. When you resist it, unhappiness follows. This is also a fine placement for scientific and technological explorations.

✔ **Uranus in Pisces (2003 to 2011):** Imaginative, talented, and intuitive, you're susceptible to strange dreams and psychic flashes. You have a deep sense of compassion and an attraction to unusual forms of spirituality, although you may suffer from feelings of alienation or isolation. At these times, escapism beckons and your willpower needs support. Art and spiritual pursuits provide a fulfilling path for you.

The secret of the 1960s

Why are some decades more exciting than others? The outer planets are usually to blame. They travel slowly through the zodiac. When they combine their considerable energies by moving in tandem, things start to cook.

In the 1960s, for example, freedom-loving Uranus and Pluto, the planet of transformation, were aligned in the same sign of the zodiac (Virgo) for the first time in over a century. (The previous time was around 1848, when a wave of revolutions swept across Europe.) Working together, Uranus and Pluto strengthened and stirred each other up, turning revolutionary Uranian impulses into something that made profound impressions on society and in many ways transformed it. The civil rights movement, the antiwar movement, the sexual revolution, the student movement, the Weather underground, feminism, gay rights, the Moon walk, and even the horrific assassinations that characterized the decade are all manifestations of the iconoclastic, revolutionary Uranian impulse deepened by the transformative power of Pluto.

At the time, even such cultural touchstones as Woodstock, LSD, communes, *Stranger in a Strange Land,* and vegetarian lesbian collectives (for example) seemed fraught with cosmic resonance. Not only did they symbolize the Uranian urge to rebel against the repressive adult society of the 1950s, they also took on the profundity of Pluto and the significance of philosophy — or so it appeared at the time. And if, in retrospect, a few expressions of the era look ridiculous, it's also true that many repercussions of those long-ago, tie-dyed days will simply not fade away.

If you were born between 1962 and 1969, you have both rebellious Uranus and transformative Pluto in Virgo. Although the impracticality of much of what went down in the 1960s probably irritates you, on some level you're deeply in sync with the urge to break away from old forms, alter the hidebound assumptions of mainstream society, and give peace a chance.

Neptune: The Dreamer

In 1612, Galileo gazed through his little telescope (practically a toy by today's standards) and saw what looked like a dim star — except that, unlike the other stars, it moved. He even drew a picture of it, and if he'd been thinking, he would have realized that it was a planet. Alas, he didn't put two and two together, and he missed the opportunity to identify Neptune.

Two hundred years later, Neptune continued to be elusive. By the middle of the 19th century, two scientists, one French and one English, working separately, had pinpointed the planet's location in theory but neither could gain access to a large telescope to confirm it. If they had, they would have found it in precisely the predicted spot (in Aquarius). But neither of them had the wherewithal to make it happen. Finally, in 1846, one of them asked astronomers in Germany to undertake a search for the new planet. Johann Galle, a young assistant at the Berlin Observatory, found it within an hour.

In NASA photographs, Neptune looks like a luminous turquoise marble, almost without features. Astronomers classify Neptune as a gas giant because, like Uranus, it's essentially a ball of gasses swirling around a metal core. It sports a dim halo of barely visible rings and has at least eight moons, including Triton — the coldest place in the solar system.

Neptune is named after the Roman god of the sea. Its symbol (see Figure 10-2) resembles that god's three-pronged trident.

Figure 10-2:
The symbol
of Neptune.

Assessing Neptune's influence

Impressionistic Neptune rules intuition, dreams and visions, psychic ability, imagination, glamour, and everything that flows. Neptune finds expression in dance, music, poetry, and daydreams. It stimulates compassion, dissolves boundaries, and sensitizes anything it touches. Idealistic and deeply spiritual, it also has a dark side. Neptune is the planet of illusion, confusion, deceit, vagueness, and wishful thinking. When prominent in a positive way, Neptune brings artistic talent and imagination, spiritual leanings, and psychic abilities. Under negative conditions, it accentuates the tendency to drift and increases the danger of addiction, hypochondria, and escapism.

Neptune doesn't affect everyone equally. Like the other outer planets, it tends to influence generations more strongly than individuals. But there are exceptions. How can you tell if you have a powerful Neptune? Neptune occupies a prominent position in your birth chart if

✔ It occupies an angle — that is, it's in the first, fourth, seventh, or tenth house of your chart. It's especially strong if it's near your Ascendant or Midheaven. (See Chapter 11 for more on Ascendants and Midheavens.)

✔ It makes a number of close aspects to other planets and, in particular, to the Sun, the Moon, or the planet that rules your Ascendant. (See Chapter 13 for a discussion of aspects.)

✔ You have one or more planets in Pisces.

Neptune spends an average of 14 years in each sign. To discover its position in your chart, turn to the Appendix.

Neptune in the signs

Neptune's position by sign describes the ways your generation is most idealistic — and most unrealistic. Its position in your horoscope represents an area of imagination, idealism, and spirituality (on the positive side), and aimless drifting, confusion, and deception (on the negative side).

✔ **Neptune in Aries (1861 to 1875):** Members of this generation had an intuitive sense of self and took an active approach to their spiritual life. They could be wildly inconsiderate, and they had trouble regulating their aggression, being at times far too weak (like Neville Chamberlain) and at other times far too reckless (like Winston Churchill at Gallipoli). But one member of this generation, expressing Neptune in Aries at its most rarefied, transformed the very nature of conflict: Mahatma Gandhi, the prophet of nonviolence (who was nonetheless assassinated in 1948). Neptune returns to this position in 2026.

✔ **Neptune in Taurus (1875 to 1889):** People born with this placement loved art, soft textures, rich food, real estate, the beauties of nature, and all the sensual comforts. (Casanova, born in 1725, had this placement. So did Pablo Picasso.) They were tuned into the physical world and responded intuitively to the rhythms of the body. But by and large they had difficulties in dealing with the practical stuff — finances included. Examples include Isadora Duncan, Virginia Woolf, and Albert Einstein. Neptune returns to the sign of the bull in 2039.

✔ **Neptune in Gemini (1889 to 1902):** People born during the last decade or so of the Gilded Age had subtle, clever, complicated minds along with literary talent, a tendency to be shallow, and a vast capacity for spin. (Edward Bernays, known as "the father of public relations," was born with this placement.) They idealized education and admired the intellect. But many of them struggled with the truth and may have discovered that the more you deceive others, the more you are deceived.

✔ **Neptune in Cancer (1902 to 1915):** "What a wonderful world," said the great Louis Armstrong, who was born with this placement. You agree. You're observant, receptive, and sentimental — and not just because you're old. The old-fashioned virtues of home, family, and country make you misty-eyed, and you tend to romanticize the past. (Which is not to suggest that your politics are necessarily conservative: Ronald Reagan had this placement, but so did Eugene McCarthy.) As part of the generation that experienced virtually all the great and awful events of the 20th century, you long for security and rely on family. As long as you feel protected, you're doing fine.

✔ **Neptune in Leo (1915 to 1929):** You're extravagant, artistic, and romantic — or at least you'd like to be. You idealize love, children, and the creative process. You take big risks — and you often win your outrageous bets. But you're prone to infatuation and may refuse to face reality, preferring the glitter of your fabulous ideals to the gritty imperfections of reality. And I hate to say it, but you can become so enamored of an ideal that you fail to see how moth-eaten it actually is.

✔ **Neptune in Virgo (1929 to 1942):** Neptune, the planet of murky vagueness, isn't happy in meticulous Virgo. With this placement, you can't always tell which details matter and which ones don't — so you may become anxious about all the wrong things. Hypochondria is a definite threat. But work that taps the imagination and spiritual activities that focus on service bring you joy.

✔ **Neptune in Libra (1942 to 1957):** Idealistic and compassionate, you long for tranquility, balance, and — most of all — love. You respond strongly to art and music. But romantic relationships are mystifying to you, and your high ideals about human interaction (and marriage in particular) are always bumping up against reality. If you were born with this placement, you can expect to experience great shifts in the rules of human relationships over the course of your life.

✔ **Neptune in Scorpio (1957 to 1970):** Dream interpretation, occult studies, and mystery novels pique your interest, but nothing fascinates you more than the workings of the psyche. A detective of the spirit, you project an aura of magnetic intensity and instinctively understand the concept of sexual healing. But you're also prone to sexual extremes and self-destructive behavior, and you may be unable to recognize the sources of your own pain.

✔ **Neptune in Sagittarius (1970 to 1984):** Questions of philosophy, faith, and religious values intrigue you. You find them easy to discuss but difficult to resolve. On some level, dogma makes you uncomfortable because your belief system is constantly evolving. You have a thirst for personal freedom and travel (ideally to sacred spots). But you tend to be gullible, and you're easily misled. Be cautious in dealing with anyone who wants to be considered a guru. Sooner or later, you're going to feel mighty uncomfortable about that.

✔ **Neptune in Capricorn (1984 to 1998):** You're ambitious, pragmatic, and nostalgic about the old-fashioned values of the past — or the past as you imagine it. You long for success and idealize the world of business, but you may have trouble acknowledging problems you experience there. Vagueness and uncertainty make you uneasy, and you must combat a tendency to overreact by becoming authoritarian. Your spiritual longings are best satisfied within structured organizations.

✔ **Neptune in Aquarius (1998 to 2012):** As one of the enlightenment-seeking, technologically gifted, altruistic people born since Neptune entered Aquarius in 1998, you possess an intuitive sense of the common good and a progressive approach to social reform. But you may idealize your friends, and your desire to live in a utopian community with a simpatico group of spiritually-minded, ecologically-aware individuals may be more difficult to achieve than you imagine.

✔ **Neptune in Pisces (2012 to 2026):** You have the typical traits of Pisces — squared. You're psychic, generous, creative, empathetic, mystical, gullible, possibly self-destructive, a lover of fantasy and film, an aficionado of complex (or ascetically pared-down) music, a daydream believer, and a likely candidate for all manner of addictions. Sigmund Freud, Johann Sebastian Bach, Vincent van Gogh, and Theodore Roosevelt all had this placement. The next Neptune in Pisces generation should be interesting to watch.

Pluto: The Power of Transformation

Before August 2006, Pluto was just another planet. Then the members of the International Astronomical Union pronounced it a dwarf planet. That demotion is irrelevant to astrologers. Astrologers believe that Pluto possesses the power of transformation, and nothing's going to change that.

Pluto is small, rocky, and so mysterious that astronomers aren't sure what to make of it. Its elongated orbit, which is tilted to the rest of the solar system, overlaps the orbit of Neptune. As a result, from 1979 to 1999, Pluto was closer to the Sun than Neptune. Pluto's major moon, Charon, is so relatively large

that some astronomers classified Pluto as a double planet. (That was before they decided it was a dwarf.) Other astronomers believed it to be an asteroid far away from home, a chunk of rock left over from the creation of the solar system, or a renegade moon that once belonged to Neptune. Regardless of its classification, astrologers agree that Pluto represents something profound in human nature.

In classical mythology, Pluto (Hades to the Greeks) was the god of the underworld, the king of the dead, and the god of wealth, reflecting the fact that gold, silver, and precious gems are found buried in the earth. Virtually every major character in mythology undertakes a journey to the underworld, which represents the darkest, most fear-laden part of the psyche. The return to the land of the living suggests renewal and transformation.

Thus, to astrologers, Pluto represents death, regeneration, and rebirth. It destroys, purifies, purges, and renews, bestowing consciousness on that which has been hidden and ultimately bringing transformation. The process can be tedious because Pluto moves at a glacial speed and its path is strewn with obstacles. But the rewards are life-changing.

Pluto has two symbols. One is a snazzy-looking metaphysical design: A small circle held within a crescent and balanced on a cross. I don't use this symbol because it's too easy to confuse with the glyphs of the other planets (Mercury and Neptune in particular). But many astrologers prefer it.

I'm partial to the second, more mundane symbol, which has its origins in the world of science. That symbol (see Figure 10-3) represents both the first two letters of Pluto's name and the initials of the aristocratic astronomer Percival Lowell, who was so convinced that there was life on Mars that he built an observatory in Arizona for the sole purpose of observing it. At the same time, he devoted himself to a search for the mysterious Planet X, which he believed was revolving around the sun in the outskirts of the solar system, way past Neptune. He never found it. But 14 years after Lowell's death, Clyde Tombaugh worked doggedly at the Lowell Observatory and discovered Pluto. This symbol acknowledges Lowell's contributions.

Figure 10-3:
The symbol
of Pluto.

Pinpointing Pluto's influence

Like Uranus and Neptune, Pluto primarily influences generations. Its influence in an individual's birth chart is usually subtle — unless Pluto occupies a prominent spot in your chart. Pluto is prominent if

✔ It occupies an angle — that is, it's in the first, fourth, seventh, or tenth house of your chart. It's especially strong if it's close to your Ascendant or Midheaven. (See Chapter 11 for more on Ascendants and Midheavens.)

✔ It makes a number of close aspects to other planets and, in particular, to the Sun, the Moon, or the planet that rules your Ascendant.

✔ You have one or more planets in Scorpio.

Even though Pluto spends, on average, about 20 years in each sign of the zodiac, it hurries through some signs (it's in and out of Libra in a dozen years) and plods through others (like Taurus, where it lingers for 32 long years). To discover its position at your birth, turn to the Appendix.

Pluto in the signs

Pluto's placement by sign determines the deepest obsessions of your generation as well as the style with which you approach transforming life events.

✔ **Pluto in Aries (1823 to 1852):** This generation was willful, rebellious, impulsive, and obsessed with power and independence.

✔ **Pluto in Taurus (1852 to 1884):** Security brought power for these hard-working folks, but values, particularly regarding possessions, were in flux. With Pluto in an earth sign, ownership was an issue. The American Civil War was fought during those years over that very compulsion.

✔ **Pluto in Gemini (1884 to 1914):** Wit rules. Novelty excites you. Unconsciously, you seek to transform yourself through fresh ideas. Your mind is ever young.

✔ **Pluto in Cancer (1914 to 1939):** If you were born during these years when Pluto was discovered, you belong to a generation for whom security is paramount. You were taught to hold on to what you've got, and that's what you do — even when you should know better. It's no wonder that you feel this way: The Great Depression of the 1930s was a formative event in your life or in the experiences of your parents.

✔ **Pluto in Leo (1939 to 1957):** Your desire to express yourself dramatically, creatively, and expansively can become an obsession. This placement is the trademark of the baby boomers, who look with disdain upon the

previous generation's search for security — and who are looked upon with scorn by the generations that follow because, in true Leo style, you can't help showing off.

- **Pluto in Virgo (1957 to 1972):** The excesses of the baby boomers drive you to distraction, and you react against them. You seek personal control, obsess about details, and have every intention of becoming perfect. If you were born between 1962 and 1969, you also have Uranus in Virgo, so unexpected upsets may throw you off track. But these upsets won't stop you from striving for the perfect Plutonian/Uranian transformation — the one that alters everything in a flash.

- **Pluto in Libra (1972 to 1984):** You're obsessed with balance, beauty, and social relations. You derive great power from sharing, but only if it's the real thing. You see no percentage in pretending. On the contrary, you demand a true marriage of equals. The arts have a strong impact on you.

- **Pluto in Scorpio (1984 to 1995):** You're passionate, resolute, deeply sexual, and intent on experiencing every last drop of whatever life has to offer. But controlling your desires is essential. Fortunately, you have incredible willpower. You intuitively recognize the link between money and power, and you're interested in accumulating both. This is a formidable placement.

- **Pluto in Sagittarius (1995 to 2008):** You long to find a philosophy or religion that offers intense spiritual and intellectual experiences — but you run the risk of being pompous and fanatical. Freedom is essential to you, and education and travel are transformational.

- **Pluto in Capricorn (2008 to 2024):** People born with Pluto in buttoned-down Capricorn are goal-oriented, persistent, and pragmatic, with an inborn sense of sense of how the world works. You think you've seen savvy politicians? Wait 'til these babies come along. Pluto's last sojourn in the sign of the goat was between 1762 and 1778, years that covered the American Revolution.

- **Pluto in Aquarius (2024 to 2044):** This do-your-own-thing generation is likely to have progressive ideals and to seek transformation through unconventional associations. The group will be increasingly central, but not in the limited, ethnocentric ways of the past. Remember the amazing bar scene in the original Star Wars movie? That's Pluto in Aquarius.

- **Pluto in Pisces (2044 to 2068):** This placement is bound to be intriguing. Expect to see a self-sacrificing, mystical generation that dips deep into the collective unconscious. The members of this group may face a challenge if external structures dissolve in chaos, as they did in the lifetime of Abraham Lincoln and Harriet Tubman, both of whom, like other members of their generation, had Pluto in Pisces.

Chiron: The Wounded Healer

Is it an asteroid? A burned-out comet? A planetesimal leftover from the creation of the solar system? An errant moon of Neptune, long since torn away from its original orbit? Or a particular type of asteroid called a *Centaur?* Ever since November 1, 1977, when scientist Charles Kowal discovered Chiron hurtling around the Sun between the orbits of Saturn and Uranus, scientists have been trying to make up their minds. Smaller by far than any planet (its estimated size is 200 miles across), Chiron has a peculiar orbit that causes it to spend more time in some signs (Pisces, Aries, and Taurus) than in others (Virgo, Libra, and Scorpio). A complete swing through all 12 signs of the zodiac takes 51 years.

In mythology, Chiron was a compassionate tutor whose students included three heroes: the warrior Achilles, the Argonaut Jason, and Hercules. One day, Chiron was accidentally scratched by one of Hercules's poison arrows. The pain was so intense that he wanted to die. But Chiron was immortal. Unable to die, he was forced to cope with the agony. In the process, he became expert in the arts of healing. Yet despite Chiron's knowledge, his pain never lessened. Nor did he develop a tolerance for it. He did, however, find a solution. After negotiating with Zeus, he bequeathed his immortality to Prometheus, who had given fire to mankind and was being tortured as a result. So Prometheus, having been freed from his agony, joined the society of the gods on Mount Olympus while Chiron, relieved of his agony, was allowed to travel into the underworld, release his bodily pain, and take up residence in Hades.

The symbol for Chiron looks like a letter K balanced on a circle or oval. It resembles an old-fashioned key.

Chiron's influence

In the years following its discovery, few practitioners were brave enough to insert Chiron into birth charts. It seemed too soon, and astrologers didn't know enough about it. That has changed. Today, Chiron, referred to as the Wounded Healer, is often included in interpretations. Astrologers see Chiron as both a point of pain and a source of healing — an area where you have suffered or been disappointed and where you must find resolution. Astrologers also associate Chiron with the holistic healing movement.

Note that the astrological Chiron, like the mythological figure, is more than a victim and a healer. As a tutor, Chiron was known for his wisdom and his teaching ability. Astrologer Zipporah Dobyns, PhD, links Chiron with Sagittarius and suggests that it indicates not only the quest for knowledge but also the impulse to share it with others.

Chiron is small, distant, and impossible to see without a telescope. It's prominent in your chart if

- ✔ It occupies an angle (and especially if it conjuncts or opposes your Ascendant or Midheaven).
- ✔ It closely aspects the Sun, the Moon, or the planet that rules your Ascendant.

To discover Chiron's position in your chart, turn to the Appendix, or go to the Web.

Chiron in the signs

Chiron spends, on average, a little over four years in each sign. Thus it indicates an area of concern both for you and for members of your immediate generation.

- ✔ **Chiron in Aries:** Your efforts to express your personality have been thwarted. You suffer from a bad case of fear of failure, and taking the initiative isn't easy for you. Finding the courage to do so — and you've got courage aplenty — is the only way to overcome your fears and feelings of inadequacy.

- ✔ **Chiron in Taurus:** Stability and security are key issues for you. On the one hand, you long for economic comfort. On the other hand, you struggle to manage your money. To put your desire for material goods and security into perspective, you need to pursue your deeper values.

- ✔ **Chiron in Gemini:** Communicating your ideas is a challenge, and you may not feel up to it. Seeking knowledge and acting as an educator enable you to heal this feeling of inadequacy. And here's another issue that may envelope you from time to time: gossip. It's one way people learn about each other — and yet it can be lethal.

- ✔ **Chiron in Cancer:** Your domestic life, especially as a child, may be fraught with pain. Relief comes through consciously seeking to create a supportive emotional environment. True healing comes through realizing that ultimately everyone has to nurture themselves.

- ✔ **Chiron in Leo:** In childhood, your efforts to get attention were thwarted, and you may doubt your own talents as a result. Creative expression helps heal the hurt. Acting and teaching are also beneficial because, putting aside whatever sorrows you may have suffered, everyone needs to be center stage once in a while.

- **Chiron in Virgo:** You grew up with extraordinarily rigid rules. Now you struggle with anxiety. Seek relief by focusing on wellness, by serving others without sacrificing yourself, and, above all, by refusing to be a martyr. Or try another approach entirely by taking up a craft where your perfectionism — which is so often a problem on the personal level — is actually rewarded.

- **Chiron in Libra:** Partnerships are vital to your well-being, but they're also disappointing. You're certain that a healthy relationship can heal you, and yet that doesn't seem to happen. Balancing romance with objective reality is essential. It's also important to defuse the pain of rejection. One possible way to do that is through art.

- **Chiron in Scorpio:** You long for love, passion, and phenomenal sex. But your secretive ways and deep-seated fear of revealing yourself (and hence of being rejected) make it difficult to fulfill your desires. Healing comes by plunging into your sorrows and working your way through them. Seek psychotherapy or any other form of self-knowledge.

- **Chiron in Sagittarius:** What's the purpose of life? The traditional answers leave you feeling frustrated and alone. A personal search lessens the pain. Strange as it may seem, lifelong education, designed to fit your individual requirements, can bring you healing.

- **Chiron in Capricorn:** In your heart, you long for success. You obey the rules, but they let you down. Healing comes when you turn away from society's rigid definition of status and find other ways to express your own deepest authority.

- **Chiron in Aquarius:** What's wrong with people anyway? You're sadly aware of the resoundingly negative impact of ethnic conflict, societal injustice, and isolation. Addressing those wrongs by working for the greater good can turn your life around.

- **Chiron in Pisces:** Pisces is the sign of compassion, sensitivity, and sacrifice. But you can't help noticing that many people give lip service to those qualities without actually practicing them. Your mission: To see the sorrow and react appropriately without being overwhelmed by it. Finding a spiritual base can ease your angst.

Chapter 11

What You See versus What You Get: The Rising Sign (And More)

I used to work at a bookstore with a woman who was so well-organized and in control that everyone relied on her. She knew what was on the shelves, what was on order, what was out of print, what was in the back room, and what was behind the counter. On top of that, she had read everything, including the classics that most people don't even know are classics, and she could advise the most hard-to-please customer. When she wasn't around, things fell to pieces. So I wasn't surprised when I completed her chart and discovered that she had Virgo rising. She was as intelligent, organized, and meticulous as any Virgo I knew.

But rising signs can be deceptive. Sure, on the surface she was detail-oriented and in control, just like a Virgo. But her Sun was not in Virgo. It was in sensitive, charitable Pisces, the dreamiest, most impressionable sign in the zodiac. And indeed, that sign described her more fully. She was kind, compassionate, and imaginative (that's why she was such an avid reader — she lost herself in books). She had many devoted friends, a husband she adored, a city loft filled with original artwork, and a second home — a tiny cottage — on a windswept island in a distant sea. Her life was suffused with romance, creativity, and water. But if she had experienced the poetry of Pisces, she also knew the pain of it. In one form or another, she had coped with everything from a relative in jail to alcoholism. She was a Pisces down to her toes.

Nonetheless, she looked like a Virgo. That's because Virgo was her *rising sign,* or *Ascendant.* The Ascendant describes the surface level of your personality. It is who you appear to be — the surface you present to the world. In the past,

many astrologers considered the Ascendant the most essential part of the birth chart — even more central than the Sun sign. Today, most astrologers rank the rising sign, the Sun sign, and the Moon sign as the three most important parts of a chart.

The zodiac revolves around the Earth like a gigantic ring. At any given moment, one sign of the zodiac is rising over the eastern horizon and another sign is setting in the west; one sign is riding high above you and another sign is on the opposite side of the planet. Each of these points represents one of the four main angles of your chart.

The sign on the eastern horizon is your rising sign; the exact degree of that sign is your Ascendant. The point opposite your rising sign on the western horizon is the *Descendant* or *setting sign,* which is always a full 180° away from the Ascendant. The degree at the top of your horoscope is the *Midheaven,* or M.C., and the degree at the lowest part of your chart, 180° away from the Midheaven, is the *imum coeli,* or I.C. Those four points determine the angles of your horoscope, as shown in Figure 11-1.

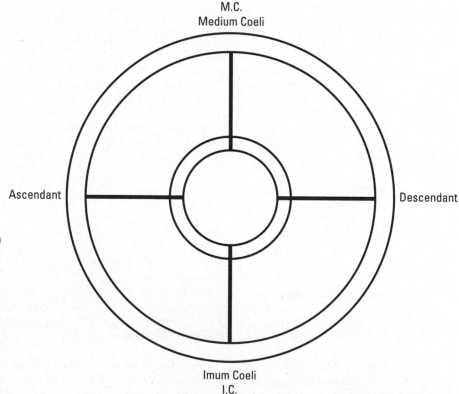

Figure 11-1:
The four angles of the chart: the Ascendant, Midheaven, Descendant, and I.C.

Identifying Your Ascendant

It's a sad fact that figuring out your Ascendant is an arduous process. To do it yourself, should you be so inclined, you have to get your hands on the full collection of astrological gear, including an atlas, a Table of Houses, and an *ephemeris* (an almanac listing the positions of the Sun, Moon, and planets for every day of the year). You also need a book to tell you what time zone you were born in (they're occasionally relocated, as in Kansas in 1967 or Nebraska in 1968) and whether you were born during standard time, war time, daylight saving time, or the unanticipated extra months of daylight saving time that marked the winter of 1974, when disco ruled and an energy crisis forced President Richard Nixon to extend the time change.

Alternatively, you could go to the Internet, as described in Chapter 2. That's the fastest, cheapest, and most reliable way to get an accurate birth chart. If going online isn't an immediate possibility, I recommend that you abandon the search for precision, at least temporarily, and make an educated guess. I tell you how to do that in Chapter 3.

After you've identified your Ascendant, either via the Internet or by following the directions in Chapter 3, I suggest that you double-check it. Begin by copying the chart on the Cheat Sheet at the front of this book. Put your rising sign at the nine o'clock spot. Then write in the other signs in a counterclockwise direction. (That is, if you're Taurus rising, put Gemini on the cusp of the second house at eight o'clock, Cancer on the cusp of the third house at seven o'clock, and so on.)

The idea is to figure out whether the Ascendant makes sense by comparing the Sun's position on your birth chart to its position in the sky at the moment of your birth. Here's how: Imagine that the Ascendant/Descendant line, which runs straight across the chart from nine o'clock to three o'clock, is the horizon of the earth. If you were born around dawn, the Sun was on or near the horizon. Its symbol in your chart should also be near the Ascendant, perhaps in the same sign. If you were born around noon, the Sun sits near the top of your chart in the ninth or tenth house. If you were born around dusk, when the Sun was setting, the Sun in your chart is once again on the horizon, this time in the sixth or seventh house, near the Descendant. And if you were a midnight delivery, the Sun lies below the horizon, in the third or fourth house.

What Your Ascendant Says about You

The Ascendant describes the surface of your personality. It's your image, your persona, your mask, your vibe. Or think of it this way: Your rising sign is

like the clothes you wear; those outfits aren't exactly *you,* but they aren't irrelevant either. They convey a powerful, unspoken message to others — and even *you* may come to associate them with your deeper self.

- ✔ **Aries rising:** You're active, assertive, adventurous, headstrong, and sometimes accident-prone. Reckless and extroverted, with an abundance of energy, you invigorate everyone around you. You take pride — for good reason — in your ability to get things moving. When you know what you want, you go after it boldly. But you can also be competitive and insensitive. You have a tendency to take over. And when obstacles block your path, your patience (which is never your high card) may evaporate. You love to be there at the start of an enterprise when the excitement is building. Later on is another story.

  Regardless of your Sun sign, your ruler is Mars, the warrior planet. Its location by sign and by house (as well as the aspects it makes to other planets) describes your energy level and the nature of your desires.

- ✔ **Taurus rising:** You're warm, generous, loyal, and a delight to be around, even if you're slow to open up and resistant to change. There's something reassuring and calming about your steady presence. You're pragmatic and patient — a reasonable person who doesn't let little things get to you. At the same time, you're affectionate and pleasure-loving, with a deep appreciation of food, drink, art, and the pleasures of the body. You care about appearances — and you aren't indifferent to money either. It brings you the security you need.

  Regardless of your Sun sign, your ruler is Venus, the planet of love and attraction. Its location by sign and by house (as well as the aspects it makes with other planets) describes the role of love, art, and beauty in your life.

The Wife of Bath

When astrologers analyze literary characters, they're usually forced to intuit what their birth dates may be. Occasionally, an author presents the essential information. Geoffrey Chaucer, for example, clearly knew his astrology. In his *Canterbury Tales,* he explained the Wife of Bath's bawdy behavior as the natural result of having a Taurus Ascendant with Mars, the planet of desire, in the same lusty sign. Don't let the 14th-century English stop you from enjoying her own explanation of her lascivious ways:

Myn ascendent was Taur and Mars therinne —
Allas, allas, the evere love was sinne!
I folwed ay my inclinacioun
By vertu of my constellacioun;
That made my I coude nought withdrawe
My chambre of Venus from a good felawe.

So who are the real-life people with Taurus rising and Mars therein? Janet Jackson is one. Barbara LaMarr is another. LaMarr, an actress from the days of silent films, married six times before her death from drug abuse at age 29.

✔ **Gemini rising:** You're talkative, excitable, funny, possibly an insomniac, and ever youthful. You pick up information in a flash and quickly adapt to changing circumstances (even if you also like to complain about them). You have a curious mind and may have writing ability. But you're restless, nervous, and easily bored, with a tendency to scatter your energy. It soothes your anxious mind to have two of everything: two best friends, two part-time jobs, two of your favorite pens, two books you're in the middle of reading.

No matter what your Sun sign is, your ruler is Mercury, the planet of communication. Its position by sign and by house, along with the aspects it makes to other planets, describes the way you speak, the way you learn, and the way your mind works.

✔ **Cancer rising:** Moody, sensitive, and imaginative, you live at a high emotional pitch. You're attuned to other people and skilled at nurturing and protecting them, yet you may feel drained by their needs and resentful of their requests. You're shrewd and ambitious, but your carefully drawn plans may crumble in the face of your emotional reactions. When you feel besieged by the needs (or criticism) of others, you withdraw into the privacy of your shell. Home, food, family, and financial well-being are essential to your peace of mind.

The ever-changing Moon is your ruling planet, no matter what your Sun sign may be. By house, by sign, and by aspect, it describes your emotions and instincts.

✔ **Leo rising:** You're flashy, fun-loving, charismatic, and friendly. The very opposite of a wallflower, you can't stand not being noticed. You have great personal pride. You do your best to appear lighthearted and confident, and you usually succeed. You're the life of the party — and more. You also have unmistakable leadership ability. You're empathetic, with a benevolent heart and a noble desire to make life better for other people. No wonder they want to bask in your glow.

The Sun is your ruling planet, regardless of the sign of the zodiac you were born under. It represents your essential self and your vitality, which is enhanced by having a Leo Ascendant.

✔ **Virgo rising:** A natural conversationalist, you have a quick, incisive mind and a thoughtful, controlled demeanor. Methodical and articulate, with an ability to juggle details that astounds the rest of the world, you communicate effectively, pick up knowledge effortlessly, and are highly observant (which is one reason you're so much fun to talk to). You make a concerted effort to engage with the world on a mental level, but emotional displays make you want to hide. Despite what you may think, your efforts to keep your feelings hidden aren't always successful. You have a tendency to worry about your health.

Regardless of your Sun sign, your ruler is Mercury, the planet of communication. Its position by sign, by house, and by aspect, describes your thinking process and the way you communicate.

Scorpio rising aliases

Some people born with Scorpio rising can't help playing around with their own identity. Examples include writer Mary Anne Evans, who published under the name George Eliot; Samuel Clemens, who wrote as Mark Twain; Washington Irving (of Rip van Winkle fame) whose aliases included Dietrich Knickerbocker and Geoffrey Crayon; Prince Rogers Nelson, who changed his name to a symbol and became The Artist Formerly Known as Prince; the spy Mata Hari; Grace Kelly, who gave up the glamorous life of a Hollywood star to become the Princess of Monaco; Jacqueline Kennedy, who left the country after the assassination of her husband and became Jackie O; David Berkowitz, the murderer who dubbed himself "Son of Sam;" and the chameleon-like comedian Tracey Ullman, whose many alter egos are of all races, genders, ages, and opinions. Why do they do it? Ask Sigmund Freud. Like other people with Scorpio rising, he too was fascinated by the mystery of identity — and the power of secrets.

✔ **Libra rising:** You're engaging, tactful, charming, refined, attractive, and easy to be around. But you have an intense need for harmony, which means you can't bear to be in a hostile environment (and you may disengage if you find yourself in one). You're also artistic and intellectually engaged, with a powerful sense of justice and a need for balance (that's what those scales are about). Partnerships, romantic and otherwise, are essential to you.

No matter what your Sun sign is, your ruler is Venus, the planet of love and attraction. Its position in your chart by house, sign, and aspect, is central to who you are.

✔ **Scorpio rising:** Traditional astrology claims that the Ascendant determines appearance. To my eye, that influence is usually a subtle one — with one exception: Scorpio rising. Dark or light, your intense eyes and personal magnetism draw people to you. You're compelling, mysterious, and sexy, with a strong sense of privacy and often a deep well of pain that can occasionally cause you to lash out. Despite whatever pain you may have experienced in the past, you're a survivor who takes control in periods of crisis. You have persuasive ability, plenty of willpower, and the ability to transform yourself, both internally and externally.

Regardless of your Sun sign, the ruler of your chart is Pluto. And don't let anyone tell you that Pluto is "just" a dwarf planet. Pluto rules destruction, transformation, and nuclear power. He doesn't have to be big. You should also know that two planets are credited with dominion over Scorpio: Pluto, the ruler of modern times, and Mars, the traditional ruler. By sign, house, and aspect, both planets play leading roles in your chart.

My friend Howard

Outgoing Leos are a dime a dozen. Hermit Leos, like my friend Howard, are a rarity. He seldom leaves the house, but when he does, he's as witty and entertaining as they get, and I don't say that just because he's my friend. So how come he shies away from relationships and prefers to stay home, nursing his modem? It's because he has Capricorn rising with stern Saturn, his ruling planet, occupying the same degree of the zodiac as his Sun. So he's a worrier, he's inflexible, and he expects the worst. No wonder he stays home.

- **Sagittarius rising:** You're outgoing, restless, and reckless. In your optimistic search for a larger, more exciting life, you cultivate people from many backgrounds, travel as widely as possible, immerse yourself in all kinds of philosophical systems (be they religious, academic, or professional), and can get all wound up over an idea. Witty and excitable, you're a lucky person with a breezy personality, many friends, and an independent attitude. When opportunities come your way, you grab them instinctively. But it's difficult for you to sacrifice your freedom for external demands, and you suffer when constrained.

  It doesn't matter what your month of birth is — Jupiter, the planet of expansion, is your ruler. Its position by house, by sign, and by aspect, indicates areas of good fortune and opportunity.

- **Capricorn rising:** Chaos makes you crazy. You're serious, reserved, reliable, and determined, with a method for everything. Ambitious and competitive, you prefer to work within an established system. You wield authority effectively and have a strong sense of ethics. You may be rigid and prone to depression, and learning to relax can be a challenge. Though your childhood may have been difficult, your outlook improves as you age (and thanks to your healthy habits, you maintain a youthful appearance).

  Saturn, the planet of discipline, is your ruler, regardless of your Sun sign. Its position by house, by sign, and by aspect, points to areas where you have to pay your dues, face down your fears, and create structures in order to achieve your potential.

- **Aquarius rising:** You have dozens of interests, legions of friends, and a cool, amiable personality. But you maintain a certain distance that can make you seem disinterested or remote, and you're unwilling to limit your options for the comfort of others. If you strike other people as willful or eccentric, well, that's their problem. Unexpected events, especially in childhood, made you wary and conscious of the need to protect yourself. More than that, you resist change and authority. Why should anyone else have power over you? You can't think of a single reason.

Rebellious Uranus, planet of the unexpected, is your ruler, regardless of your Sun sign. Before its discovery in 1781, astrologers assigned sovereignty of Aquarius to another ruler: Saturn, the planet of limitation and self-discipline. By sign, by house, and by aspect, both planets play powerful roles in your chart.

✔ **Pisces rising:** You're romantic, impressionable, sentimental, kind, and so empathetic that sometimes just being around unhappy people is more than you can tolerate. Moody and idealistic, you have powerful artistic and psychic abilities. At your most self-actualizing, you can mobilize your inner forces and turn daydreams into realities. But when wishful thinking gets out of hand, you can be gullible, passive, and too submissive for your own good. I'm sorry to say that substance abuse is a danger for you. Fortunately, you also have a yearning for creative and spiritual fulfillment that can keep you on track.

Elusive Neptune, the planet of inspiration, is your ruler, no matter what your Sun sign is. Its position in your chart by house, by sign, and by aspect, indicates an area of ideals, creativity, and spiritual fulfillment. You also have a co-ruler: Jupiter, the planet associated with Pisces prior to the discovery of Neptune in 1846.

Finding and Understanding Your Descendant

After you've identified your rising sign, you automatically know your Descendant, no calculation required. By definition, the Descendant is always exactly opposite your rising sign. For example, if you have Cancer rising, your Descendant is Capricorn.

A less powerful point than your Ascendant, the Descendant determines the approach you take toward marriage and partnerships. It describes the nature of those relationships in your life, and it indicates the kind of person you're likely to fall for. What's your type? Your Descendant provides the answer:

✔ **If you have Aries rising:** Your Descendant is in Libra. Your ideal relationship is egalitarian, and your perfect partner, unlike yourself, is poised and balanced, a force for harmony — the very quality you need the most.

✔ **If you have Taurus rising:** Your Descendant is Scorpio. Your best possible partner is sexually passionate, emotionally intense, and fully willing to engage in intimate conversation. You probably don't think you want someone who's secretive or manipulative. The evidence suggests otherwise.

✔ **If you have Gemini rising:** Your Descendant is Sagittarius, which suggests that the best partner for you is an independent person of strong beliefs who can expand your world. You romanticize relationships and may marry more than once. But since when is that a crime?

✔ **If you have Cancer rising:** Your Descendant is Capricorn, which means that you seek a solid relationship with a partner who's serious, protective, and reliable — an older or more established person who can give you the security you need.

✔ **If you have Leo rising:** Your Descendant is Aquarius, which means that although you may think that you want a dazzling, swashbuckling companion, your ideal mate is actually a unique and stimulating freethinker with whom you feel a lively mental connection.

✔ **If you have Virgo rising:** Your Descendant is Pisces, which suggests that your ideal partner is a sympathetic, adaptable person who can help you stop that crazy worrying thing you do. You may dream of someone as organized and efficient as yourself. Notice how you keep not getting it? There's a reason: It's not what you need.

✔ **If you have Libra rising:** Your Descendant is Aries, which suggests that the ideal mate for you is someone with an independent streak and a fiery personality who can stir up your enthusiasms, energize you, and help you deal with conflict.

✔ **If you have Scorpio rising:** Your Descendant is Taurus. The most natural partner for you is down-to-earth, trustworthy, and stubborn enough to resist your considerable blandishments. You may think you want someone who's spicy, complicated, and hot (like yourself). Actually, you'd be better off with someone who's as straightforward and nourishing as a fresh loaf of bread.

✔ **If you have Sagittarius rising:** Your Descendant is Gemini, suggesting that you may postpone commitment out of a fear of being tied down. When you do find the courage, the proper partner for you is an active, multifaceted person whose conversation is so stimulating that you're never bored.

✔ **If you have Capricorn rising:** Your Descendant is Cancer, which means that you need a warm, supportive mate who can soften you up by giving you the security (and the home-cooked meals) you crave. Traditional relationships are best for you.

✔ **If you have Aquarius rising:** Your Descendant is fiery Leo, suggesting that a relationship offering Leo's passion, vivacity, and personal devotion would counter your airy objectivity and bring you satisfaction. A little pizazz on your partner's side goes a long way to keeping you interested.

✔ **If you have Pisces rising:** Your Descendant is Virgo, which suggests that a mate who's practical, analytical, and meticulous with details would balance your intuitive, dreamy approach to life and help reduce the chaos that you create — or attract — without even half trying.

Looking Into Your Midheaven and I.C.

How come some people grow up in ordinary circumstances and yet end up in the strangest careers? The Midheaven, also known as the M.C. (from the Latin *medium coeli,* meaning "middle of the heavens"), frequently explains it. (Other factors in your choice of career include planets in the tenth house, the planet that rules your Midheaven, and planets in the sixth house of work.)

The Midheaven is the highest point on the ecliptic and in your chart. It doesn't determine your talents, but it affects your public persona and influences the approach you take to authority, status, and career. The M.C. also says a lot about one of your parents. Which one? Some astrologers think it refers to the mother, others to the opposite-sex parent, still others to the most influential parent. In short, it's definitely one or the other. You choose.

Directly opposite the Midheaven is the I.C., or *imum coeli* (from the Latin *imum coeli,* meaning "lowest part of the heavens"). The I.C. influences your attitude toward home and family, affects the circumstances at the end of your life, and, like the M.C., is associated with one of your parents. It's sometimes described as representing the "base of the personality," which suggests that its importance is greater than it appears.

If you have an accurate copy of your birth chart, you can find your Midheaven on or near the cusp of the tenth house at the twelve o'clock spot. If you're using the material in this book to determine your Ascendant (see Chapter 3), assume that your Midheaven is in the same sign that appears on the cusp of the tenth house. Either way, your I.C. is directly opposite the M.C., at or near the lowest point of your chart.

The easiest way to get an accurate copy of your chart is to go on the Internet. Free charts are available from www.alabe.com, www.astro.com, or www. chaosastrology.com.

The Midheaven affects your attitude toward career. The I.C. affects your attitude toward home and family.

> ✔ **Aries Midheaven:** You have a daring attitude toward your career. You respond to a challenge and are most jazzed when you're launching a new endeavor. You don't mind taking a risk. What you do mind is being powerless. Being your own boss is your best move.
>
> The planet ruling your Midheaven is Mars.
>
> Your I.C. is in Libra, indicating that while you may be willing to fight in the professional world, you need a serene and harmonious home. Take the advice of Aries artist William Morris in *The Beauty of Life:* "Have

nothing in your houses that you do not know to be useful, or believe to be beautiful." And if in doubt as to which matters more — usefulness or beauty — go for the latter.

✔ **Taurus Midheaven:** Security matters. You need to do something tangible in your career — and whatever it is, you need to receive substantial rewards. Fortunately, you have the stamina to make it happen.

The planet ruling your Midheaven is Venus, suggesting that artistic areas may appeal to you.

Your I.C. is in Scorpio, which suggests that your home is a hideaway where you can express your deepest passions and find the privacy you crave.

✔ **Gemini Midheaven:** In your career, you require diversity, intellectual stimulation, and the ability to fulfill your curiosity. Writing is favored, as is anything involving other forms of communication. You also benefit from the chance to take frequent jaunts out of the office. You don't need to go far — you just need to go *out*.

The planet ruling your Midheaven is Mercury.

Your I.C. is Sagittarius, which suggests that you move frequently (or would like to), that your domestic life is shaped by strong religious principles, or that you secretly long to be an expatriate. You agree with the Gemini writer G. K. Chesterton, who wrote in *What's Wrong with the World,* "The home is not the one tame place in a world of adventure; it is the one wild place in a world of rules and set tasks."

✔ **Cancer Midheaven:** You need a career where you can use your intuition and make emotional connections. Your stated purpose may be to provide security for your family, but you also need to be involved in the wider community and to receive recognition from authority figures there.

The planet ruling your Midheaven is the Moon.

Your I.C. is Capricorn, which suggests that you have traditional taste in interior decoration and that you take a conservative attitude toward family, an arena in which you shoulder an enormous burden of responsibility.

✔ **Leo Midheaven:** You need a career that provides room for creative expression, opportunities for leadership, and public recognition. Your pride is on the line here, so the more acknowledgment you receive for your professional efforts, the happier you will be.

The planet ruling your Midheaven is the Sun.

Your I.C. is Aquarius, which indicates that you have an idiosyncratic attitude toward home and family. As a result, there's something unusual about your domestic life — and about one of your parents as well.

Björk

Is it fair to say that the Icelandic singer/composer/performer Björk, an experimental artist who has been in the public eye since childhood, presents a supremely weird and riveting image? I think it is. What makes her unique are the two major angles of her chart: her Ascendant, which describes her persona, and the Midheaven, or M.C., which represents her career. In her case, each angle is conjunct one or more of the weighty outer planets. Her Ascendant, like her Sun and Moon, is in Scorpio, making her a triple Scorpio — an intense combination of influences. Closest to her Ascendant is Neptune, the planet of fantasy and illusion. Its prominence boosts her musical creativity. Its presence in the first house makes it easy for her to alter her image and play with her appearance in highly imaginative ways. She's no doubt a shape-shifter. What else would make her don her infamous swan dress, which looked like a cross between a dead bird and a 1980s pouf skirt? In classic Neptunian style, the meaning was indecipherable and the alluring strangeness unforgettable.

Equally important in her chart is a three-way conjunction of transformative Pluto, unpredictable Uranus, and the M.C. These heavy-duty placements suggest that she's a risk-taker with a compelling need to change the world in unconventional ways. As for her parents, they're powerful people in their own right (her father, a labor leader, was famous in Iceland before she was) and their influence on her is huge.

✔ **Virgo Midheaven:** Whatever your career (or community activities) may be, you succeed because you do your homework and pay attention to the small stuff. You work hard, and people come to rely on you. Still, you may feel that you don't receive the recognition you deserve. Keep in mind that Virgo is the sign of the martyr, and resist the temptation to torture yourself.

The planet ruling your Midheaven is Mercury.

Your I.C. is Pisces, which indicates that feelings of abandonment in childhood make you long for a serene home filled with spiritual solace. Your attitude is that of the French philosopher Gaston Bachelard, who wrote in *The Poetics of Space,* "If I were asked to name the chief benefit of the house, I should say: The house shelters day-dreaming, the house protects the dreamer, the house allows one to dream in peace."

✔ **Libra Midheaven:** You want a pleasant, rational career that enables you to balance your public and private lives. Ideally, you'd enjoy a career in the arts or one that includes plenty of socializing. You easily attract people who can help you reach your goals.

The planet ruling your Midheaven is Venus.

Your I.C. is Aries, suggesting that you can renew your energy and express your individuality most actively at home. But you can also be rebellious and short-tempered with members of your family.

✔ **Scorpio Midheaven:** You gravitate toward a career that offers you the opportunity to feel intensely and perhaps to exercise authority. Once you set your mind on a goal, you're determined to achieve it. But you can tie yourself in knots over the emotional complexity of your world, and you're always aware of the political undercurrents.

The planet ruling your Midheaven is Pluto.

Your I.C. is Taurus, suggesting that financial security and the comforts of family are extremely important to you. Owning a home and land brings you satisfaction.

✔ **Sagittarius Midheaven:** You're happiest with a career that offers independence, the opportunity to broaden your mental horizons, and plenty of frequent-flyer miles. Within your profession or community, you're known for your high ideals and powerful beliefs. You have a tendency to idealize the people you work with (or for). And although you benefit from your encounters with authority figures, they may rub you the wrong way anyway.

The planet ruling your Midheaven is Jupiter.

Your I.C. is Gemini, suggesting that your home is a busy place filled with books, magazines, and communication devices of every sort. You'd love to have two homes and you may move frequently.

✔ **Capricorn Midheaven:** Reliable and ambitious, you're willing to do whatever is necessary to achieve the success you wish for. Major responsibilities regularly end up on your salad plate. Secretly, you're complimented by the responsibility. To maintain optimism, you need clear signs of progress — things like promotions, raises, and a corner office with a ficus tree. You do well in a corporate environment.

The planet ruling your Midheaven is Saturn.

Your I.C. is Cancer, suggesting that your ties to family in general, and your mother in particular, are strong. Living near water soothes you.

✔ **Aquarius Midheaven:** Your attitude toward career and community is unconventional and unique — and so is your ideal career. Because your skills are utterly unique, your ideal job is shaped to you personally. You do well in forward-looking, progressive areas that provide benefits to the public.

The planet ruling your Midheaven is Uranus.

Your I.C. is Leo. You take pride in your home, which is a place where you can express your emotions and your creative talents. Even if you're shy elsewhere, you're the star at home.

✔ **Pisces Midheaven:** Compassion and/or imagination determine your career choices. You may be drawn to the helping professions or to an expressive field, such as music or dance. Either way, your intuition and psychic abilities guide you.

The planet ruling your Midheaven is Neptune.

Your I.C. is Virgo, suggesting that a clean, neat environment at home gives you the security and grounding that you need. You may move frequently, always in search of an ideal home.

Chapter 12

The Sun, the Moon, and the Planets in the Houses

Consider two babies born on July 6, 1935, one around 4 a.m. local time and one, in another part of the world, around 6 a.m. Their planets are in identical signs of the zodiac. But their rising signs (see Chapter 11) aren't the same, and neither are their house placements. How much difference would that make?

It would make a world of difference. One child, born with Gemini rising, Mercury on the Ascendant, and the Sun in the first house, is Candy Barr, the platinum-haired stripper who died in 2005. The other, born with Cancer rising, Pluto on the Ascendant, and the Sun in the twelfth house, is the Dalai Lama. This stark difference suggests how crucial the rising sign and house placements can be. They're as important as sign placements.

Unfortunately, it's easy to confuse the signs with the houses. One difference is that the signs, which are divisions of the ecliptic, represent various attitudes, styles, and approaches to life. The houses describe areas of interest such as money, children, health, partnership, travel, and education. In every horoscope, each planet is in a sign and a house. In this chapter, I discuss the twelve houses and offer interpretations for each planet in each house.

The planets represent types of energy, the signs represent various ways of expressing that energy, and the houses represent different areas of experience where those energies are likely to operate. House placements are based on the time of your birth, not on your sign. For instance, if you were born shortly

before dawn, your Sun is in the first house — no matter whether you were born in January or in June. To figure out your houses, get a copy of your chart online (check out Chapter 2 for details), or flip to Chapter 3 (which tells you how to set up your chart using the tables in this book). And I'm sorry to report that if you don't have a birth time that's at least fairly accurate (within an hour at the most), you may as well skip this chapter.

Taking the House Tour

Every birth chart embraces all twelve houses — no more, no less. In most charts, one or two of those houses prove to be especially important thanks to the presence of several planets. The more planets you find squeezed into a house, the more important the matters of that house are likely to be. Table 12-1 lists the twelve houses along with the areas of life that they cover.

Table 12-1	Houses and Their Significance
House	*Areas of Concern*
First house	Your appearance and apparent disposition
Second house	Income, possessions, values
Third house	Communication, writing, short journeys, brothers and sisters
Fourth house	Home, roots, one parent, circumstances at the end of life
Fifth house	Romance, children, creativity, entertainment
Sixth house	Work and health
Seventh house	Marriage and other partnerships
Eighth house	Sex, death, regeneration, other people's money
Ninth house	Higher education, long journeys, religion, philosophy, law
Tenth house	Career, status, reputation, the other parent
Eleventh house	Friends, groups, aspirations
Twelfth house	Seclusion, the unconscious, secrets, self-undoing

The following sections show how the Sun, Moon, and planets play their parts in each of the twelve houses.

The Sun in the Houses

The Sun symbolizes your will, your purpose, and your most essential self. Its house position describes the area in which you can most effectively express those aspects of your being.

- ✔ **Sun in the first house:** You're active, enterprising, and proud of your accomplishments. Your strong personality enables you to assert yourself in a natural, dignified way. This placement indicates leadership potential and success that comes about through your own efforts.

- ✔ **Sun in the second house:** You're practical, persistent, interested in money, and skilled at judging the value of things. Your possessions reflect your deeper values. Achieving financial stability gives you great satisfaction.

- ✔ **Sun in the third house:** Curious and observant, you collect information and communicate with ease, both in speech and in writing. Travel and siblings play important roles in your life.

- ✔ **Sun in the fourth house:** You're intuitive and introverted, with a strong sense of self, a close tie to your ancestors, and an interest in the past. Home and family are of primary importance. Finding your roots is essential to your sense of self.

- ✔ **Sun in the fifth house:** Pleasure-seeking and dynamic, you find happiness through romance, children, and activities that give you the opportunity to express yourself in dramatic, creative ways.

- ✔ **Sun in the sixth house:** Finding fulfilling work is essential because you devote yourself to your job and define yourself through it. Though you worry about your health, it's usually good. Regardless of your Sun sign, you tend to be a perfectionist.

- ✔ **Sun in the seventh house:** Marriage and other partnerships are essential to your identity, though you may bounce back and forth between fear of isolation and fear of commitment. Balancing power is an issue in both personal and professional relationships.

- ✔ **Sun in the eighth house:** You're a profoundly emotional person whose need to explore the mystery of your own psyche brings liberation and transformation. Sex, money, and legacies of all types play a major role in your life.

- ✔ **Sun in the ninth house:** You're a lifelong seeker who looks to find meaning and to expand your awareness through education, religion, and travel. Everyone talks about having a philosophy of life. You really mean it.

- ✔ **Sun in the tenth house:** Your determination to succeed and your desire for public recognition make you a born leader — and are excellent indicators of professional success.

✔ **Sun in the eleventh house:** You have high ideals and aspirations, many friends, a wide circle of acquaintances, and the ability to work well in a group. Indeed, becoming part of a group that expresses your most cherished values enables you to fulfill your deepest goals. Friends can be the most important people in your life.

✔ **Sun in the twelfth house:** Intuitive, reclusive, and secretive, you find nourishment in solitude and spiritual activity. You may also become involved in helping others, perhaps through large institutions, such as hospitals or prisons.

The Moon in the Houses

The house that the Moon occupies in your chart determines the area of life in which you react most instinctively. This same area is one in which you may experience all kinds of fluctuations. Yet your emotional well-being depends on the concerns of that house.

✔ **Moon in the first house:** Don't imagine that your emotions are hidden or disguised in any way. Thanks to your unconscious need to express your feelings and be accepted, they're obvious to all. Your well-being is oddly dependent on your appearance and how people perceive you.

✔ **Moon in the second house:** Although you experience financial ups and downs throughout your life, you also become increasingly persistent about holding on to the green stuff — which is fortunate, because material security is vital for your well-being. You may not think of yourself as a materialistic person; nonetheless, money matters.

✔ **Moon in the third house:** You have an adaptable, curious mind, a strong attachment to brothers and sisters, and a gift for establishing connections and linking people together. You're a skilled communicator, both in conversation and writing. In a thoroughly nonscientific survey done with a very small population base, two out of three literary agents of my acquaintance turn out to have the Moon in this position. (The other has several planets in Gemini, the sign most similar to the third house.)

✔ **Moon in the fourth house:** Your parents and family heritage are profoundly important to you, and the past has an irresistible allure. Security improves your peace of mind, and having a home that feels right is essential, although it may not be easy to find. In your search for the perfect nest, you're likely to experience many changes of residence.

✔ **Moon in the fifth house:** You're romantic, dramatic, and emotional. You're also creative and talented, perhaps in more than one field. A risk-taker, especially in the realm of love, you connect easily with children, whether they're your own or someone else's. (The most stimulating teachers I know have this position.)

REAL LIFE EXAMPLE

Walt Whitman

The poet Walt Whitman, born May 31, 1819, had the Moon in Leo in the sixth house. As a Gemini, he's known for his writing. As someone with the Moon in the house of work and health, he's also recognized for regular jobs he held during his lifetime. Among other professions, he was a journeyman printer, a journalist, a teacher, a government clerk, and a Civil War nurse, a job that was both dramatic, in keeping with the Leo placement of his moon, and service-oriented, as the sixth house demands.

✔ **Moon in the sixth house:** Until you find satisfying work, you're likely to change jobs repeatedly. Working for the money isn't enough; you need to feel productive and fulfilled. Service and health professions are satisfying. Also, you worry about your health, which can be affected by your reactions to your job.

✔ **Moon in the seventh house:** Marriage and other partnerships loom large for you, though you may feel indecisive about relationships. Once you're committed, you run the risk of becoming too dependent. In business, people seek you out.

✔ **Moon in the eighth house:** You have strongly fluctuating moods, powerful sexual urges, and the ability to heal emotional wounds for yourself and possibly for others. You're emotionally brave and willing to face reality. Financially, you may experience ups and downs, especially through a romantic relationship.

✔ **Moon in the ninth house:** The more you push beyond the boundaries of your life and seek out fresh experiences, the happier you are. You have an active imagination and a desire for knowledge. You may explore many religions and philosophies before you find one that satisfies you. Travel soothes your soul, and you take many journeys.

✔ **Moon in the tenth house:** Your peace of mind goes hand in hand with your professional accomplishments. Once you identify the right career, you pour yourself into it. Not surprisingly, your private life may suffer. The good news is that if you love what you're doing, you don't care.

✔ **Moon in the eleventh house:** Popular and easygoing, you have an instinctive understanding of other people and a remarkable capacity for friendship. Friends play a major role in your life (though you may care too much about what they think). Your goals are likely to change many times, and as they do, your circle of friends may also shift.

✔ **Moon in the twelfth house:** Digging out your secrets is no easy task. You're moody, sensitive, and intrigued by the hidden side of life. Withdrawal is your mode. You prefer to conceal your emotions (along with certain sordid episodes from the past). You may become involved with institutions such as hospitals or prisons. Clandestine relationships may offer a form of emotional sustenance that you don't find elsewhere.

The Nodes of the Moon in the Houses

Unlike the other celestial bodies I discuss in this chapter, the Nodes of the Moon don't exactly exist. They're simply the points in space where the path of the Moon crosses the ecliptic. Nonetheless, there they are in your chart: The North Node and the South Node, two sensitive spots carrying a message that some astrologers consider the most vital part of your horoscope.

Though astrologers have long debated the meaning of the Nodes, they basically agree that the North Node represents personal growth and illuminates the path to fulfillment, while the South Node symbolizes patterns established in previous lifetimes and thus represents the path of least resistance. To interpret the Nodes, consider their position by sign, by aspect, and most of all, by house.

✔ **North Node in the first house/South Node in the seventh:** You find fulfillment by expressing your personality. You stand still by surrendering your power to others and becoming too dependent (particularly on a spouse).

✔ **North Node in the second house/South Node in the eighth:** Pursuing financial security through your own efforts and in accordance with your core values brings fulfillment. Relying on others to take care of you, even through inheritance, brings disappointment, as do relationships that are entirely about sex.

✔ **North Node in the third house/South Node in the ninth:** Gathering information and using it for concrete purposes brings fulfillment; setting up a permanent residence in the airy realms of academia brings frustration. Teaching primary school, pursuing journalism, and getting involved in neighborhood activities bring benefits; philosophical and religious musings, though enjoyable, do not.

✔ **North Node in the fourth house/South Node in the tenth:** Look to family, tradition, and inner life for fulfillment. Don't expect it from the outside world. Though you may find success in a career, your greatest joy comes from getting in touch with your roots.

✔ **North Node in the fifth house/South Node in the eleventh:** Romance, children, and creative expression expand your awareness and bring fulfillment. Beware of pointless socializing — you lose your soul in the social whirl. Spiritually speaking, group activities lead nowhere.

✓ **North Node in the sixth house/South Node in the twelfth:** Satisfying work is essential to your personal development, as is a positive approach to health. Solitude and escapism limit you: Don't be a hermit.

✓ **North Node in the seventh house/South Node in the first:** Accepting the challenge of relationship and becoming an equal partner benefits you. Cooperation speeds your progress. Focusing on personal or selfish concerns slows you down.

✓ **North Node in the eighth house/South Node in the second:** You overemphasize the importance of money and material security. Instead, look for opportunities to collaborate and form intimate ties with others.

✓ **North Node in the ninth house/South Node in the third:** You tend to run around in a frenzy, gossiping and accumulating facts rather than ideas. Broaden your horizons by pursuing large ideas and philosophies. Higher education and world travel benefit you. Playing Sudoku doesn't. Don't get lost in trivial pursuits. Expand your mind.

✓ **North Node in the tenth house/South Node in the fourth:** Though it may scare you, you long for public recognition. Pursuing your career brings personal growth. Devoting yourself solely to home and family, though tempting, doesn't.

✓ **North Node in the eleventh house/South Node in the fifth:** Your tendency to focus on love affairs, personal pleasures, and children limits your development. Take a larger view. Align yourself with others in pursuit of a cause: Become political and develop a social conscience.

✓ **North Node in the twelfth house/South Node in the sixth:** Work comes your way and occasionally threatens to overwhelm you. Office politics sap your energy. Solitude, yoga, and the quest for spiritual transcendence strengthen you. Don't be a workaholic. And don't forget to meditate.

Mercury in the Houses

Mercury is the planet of communication. Its position by house suggests those areas in life that most absorb your mind and stimulate your thoughts.

✓ **Mercury in the first house:** You're a talker. You're on the ball, loquacious, and happy to share your views. You may be a gregarious storyteller, the sort of person who becomes the heart and soul of any dinner party. Even if you're not outgoing, you rise to the occasion when giving a speech. Your ability to communicate is one of your strengths, and it draws people to you.

✓ **Mercury in the second house:** You value results. By taking a systematic approach and thinking in practical terms, you can turn an idea to concrete advantage. You can also earn money by writing.

- **Mercury in the third house:** You're fortunate to possess this much-admired placement, for it gives you an alert and vibrant mind, great intellectual curiosity, and a way with words. You're an effective public speaker, a lively conversationalist, and a gifted writer.

- **Mercury in the fourth house:** Strongly influenced by your parents, you turn your home into a center of activity and intellectual stimulation. You may even work at home. Your family heritage is probably complicated in one way or another, and you must eventually deal with its repercussions head-on. At your worst, you can be narrow-minded and priggish. At your best, you're tuned in and acutely aware.

- **Mercury in the fifth house:** A fun-loving person with a variety of interests, you're a creative thinker with a weakness for speculation and a romantic history worth writing about. In love, you look for someone who gets you going mentally. As a parent, you derive enormous pleasure from your children (and you talk about them endlessly).

- **Mercury in the sixth house:** Skillful and efficient, you tend to immerse yourself in work, either handling the details with ease or becoming obsessed with them. In the absence of something important to do, you're the master of make-work — so it's essential that you find satisfying, stimulating employment. An apprehensive person, you worry needlessly and may become a hypochondriac. To ward off this possibility, take positive steps to guard your health.

- **Mercury in the seventh house:** You're a sociable person who craves lively conversation and stimulating relationships. Although you're outgoing and connect easily with others, you quickly become bored and may shy away from commitment. When you find the relationship you're seeking, the conversation never ends.

- **Mercury in the eighth house:** This placement gives you a naturally intuitive mind, the ability to ferret out secrets, amazing researching skills, and a profound mental engagement with the mysteries of life, including sex, death, money (which you resent having to worry about), and the metaphysical arts.

- **Mercury in the ninth house:** You're fortified by ideas, motivated by philosophy, stimulated by the forces of the intellect, and happy to explore the world. You enjoy grappling with ideas and meeting people, which makes education a natural field for you. (Other smart choices include law, publishing, and religion.) You find contentment in dealing with important issues but have no patience for the trivia of everyday life.

- **Mercury in the tenth house:** With this high-profile placement, you're likely to develop a stimulating career, often involving the written word. Your ideal job has great variety built into it. In the absence of that, you experience frequent job changes. You require continued mental stimulation. You prefer to be in charge and are most successful when you can pursue your own ideas.

✓ **Mercury in the eleventh house:** An active social life is essential for your well-being. You make friends easily, but if Mercury is afflicted by stressful aspects with other planets, there can be a revolving-door quality to your friendships. (See Chapter 13 for a discussion of aspects.) You find it simulating to work in a group, and you benefit from frequent contacts with people who share your ideals and aspirations.

✓ **Mercury in the twelfth house:** You're mysterious, intuitive, contemplative, and secretive. You can interpret dreams, break codes, and do all kinds of other mental tasks that require creative thinking — and a little privacy. Solitude refreshes your mind.

Venus in the Houses

The house occupied by Venus, the planet of love, indicates those areas in life that bring you pleasure and stimulate your ability to connect with others.

✓ **Venus in the first house:** Whatever appears in the first house is obvious to all. With Venus rising, you're warm, sociable, and attractive, a quality you also admire in others.

✓ **Venus in the second house:** You've heard that money can't buy you love. You just don't believe it. Money and the things it can buy matter to you, which is probably why astrologers associate this placement with shopping. Fortunately, you're adept at pulling in the green.

✓ **Venus in the third house:** You love to talk, travel, and gather information. You express yourself eloquently, and your verbal abilities attract admirers. You also interact well with your brothers and sisters. This is an excellent position for a writer or public speaker.

✓ **Venus in the fourth house:** In the absence of other factors, this fortunate placement bestows a happy childhood, a close tie to your mother, a talent for decorating, and a beautiful home.

✓ **Venus in the fifth house:** You attract love and are great with children (being somewhat of a child yourself). You respond to the arts and may be naturally talented. A delight to be around, you get along with everyone and enjoy life to the max. You'll never lack for admirers or invitations.

✓ **Venus in the sixth house:** Work is as essential to your happiness as love. When the one prospers, so does the other. You meet potential suitors through your work, and you make friends and inspire affection on the job. Fulfilling employment brings you happiness, improves your health, and makes you more attractive.

✓ **Venus in the seventh house:** Affectionate and well-liked, you're a congenial person who's happiest in a committed relationship. Thanks to your innate charm, you attract a wide selection of potential mates and have the ability to create a loving relationship, perhaps with someone in the arts. Business partnerships are also beneficial.

✓ **Venus in the eighth house:** You're seductive, manipulative, obsessive, passionate, and often under the sway of a raging storm of feelings — and that includes omnivorous sexual appetites. Your love life is probably a maze of complications. You're also shrewd with money, which often comes your way through marriage, inheritance, or savvy investments.

✓ **Venus in the ninth house:** Love comes through anything that expands your horizons, with emphasis on travel, education, law, and publishing, all fields to which you're well-suited. Philosophical and idealistic, you respond to exciting ideas and large systems of thought. You could marry a foreigner (or someone you meet while traveling), a professor, a writer, a lawyer, a member of the clergy, and anyone involved with publishing.

✓ **Venus in the tenth house:** Your career, ideally in the arts, means a lot to you. You're likable and outgoing, and people want to help you. You receive particular help from women, and your reputation is sterling — unless you make it too obvious how socially ambitious you are. You want a high-status spouse. Fortunately, people are naturally attracted to you: You don't have to push.

✓ **Venus in the eleventh house:** You're open-minded, affectionate, and cooperative, and people feel comfortable around you. You're the hub of your social circle, a natural leader within a group, and a devoted pal. You easily attract both friends and lovers.

✓ **Venus in the twelfth house:** Highly attuned to the feelings of others, you're a sensitive person with a need for privacy and a tendency to be secretive. Many people with this placement fall into clandestine love affairs, while others, suffering from shyness and vulnerability, are so easily hurt in social interactions that they pull back to lick their wounds. Solitude calms you, and art can bring you peace.

Mars in the Houses

The position of Mars by house tells you where you're most likely to act on impulse, take risks, and pursue your personal desires.

✓ **Mars in the first house:** Vigorous and passionate, you initiate activities, sometimes impulsively, and your passions (and anger) are obvious to all. This position gives you great vitality along with an assertive personality and can be a sign of the warrior.

✓ **Mars in the second house:** Competitive, acquisitive, and practical, you feel happy when you can focus on a concrete goal. You want to be rewarded for your efforts — and not only with praise. Money and material objects do the trick more effectively than mere words.

✔ **Mars in the third house:** You have a vigorous, independent, and some-times argumentative mind, and you call things as you see them — even if that means jumping to conclusions. With your razor-sharp wit, you're impatient and easily distracted, and you can be aggressive in conversation.

✔ **Mars in the fourth house:** You try to make up for a difficult childhood by focusing on your domestic life. Highly protective of home and family, you're an independent person with a sturdy constitution and an inborn vitality. Family matters consume you, but be careful not to create a home environment filled with fighting and dissension.

✔ **Mars in the fifth house:** Impulsive, excitable, and highly sexed, you're active and fun-loving, and you take pleasure in initiating creative proj-ects. You're also very involved with your offspring, whether they're lit-eral flesh-and-blood babies or children of your imagination. Although you can be impatient and competitive, you enjoy playing games, athletic or otherwise, and are energized by risk-taking.

✔ **Mars in the sixth house:** Work excites you (even if it exhausts you). You're efficient, skilled, and precise, with great physical vitality, mechan-ical skills, and a love for the tools of your trade. A dull job distresses you, and constricting organizational rules make you angry and rebel-lious. On the other hand, a challenge, even if it involves a gamble, stimu-lates you. Guard against overwork and get plenty of exercise.

✔ **Mars in the seventh house:** Partnerships energize you, but that doesn't mean you have an easy time with them. When a relationship isn't going well, you bravely confront the issues, making Mars in the seventh house the position of kiss-and-make-up. Alternatively, you may attract an aggressive partner.

✔ **Mars in the eighth house:** You have powerful desires, with determina-tion and sexual charisma to burn. A skilled researcher, you may be attracted to healing arts and occult subjects. Financial wheeling and dealing may also fascinate you, though money and inheritances can be a source of conflict. Because this position stimulates a yearning for intense experience, you fearlessly take steps that more sensible souls avoid. This placement can bring a degree of wildness, making you irre-sistible to others — and an occasional danger to yourself.

✔ **Mars in the ninth house:** You're a passionate idealist and an indepen-dent thinker with strong convictions, broad goals, and a desire to see the world. Ideas motivate you, and you're at home in the realms of law, religion, and education. But you can slip into fanaticism and must guard against becoming intolerant.

- **Mars in the tenth house:** A demanding, exciting career fills you with energy. You'd like to be famous, but more than that, you'd like to be involved in some grand effort, something that takes strategy and wits — like a war, a social protest movement, or the making of an epic film. Ambitious and aggressive, you want to make an impact on the world.

- **Mars in the eleventh house:** Your friends stimulate you and help you achieve your aspirations. In a group, you rise to a leadership position. But you can also be unreasonably demanding and may unconsciously create conflicts or be drawn to quarrelsome individuals.

- **Mars in the twelfth house:** Other people may not understand who you are because much of your energy, anger, and passion is hidden. You're hesitant to reveal these aspects of yourself, and as a result, you may feel unrecognized. Nonetheless, spending time alone revitalizes you, and you're extremely effective when you're working behind the scenes.

The Mars effect

It has long been an embarrassment to astrologers that so little research has been done in the discipline. One significant piece of astrological research was conducted in the 1950s, by Michel Gauquelin, a French statistician who explored astrology in his youth, and his wife, Françoise. They set out to prove that astrology had no basis in scientific fact. They examined the birth charts of over 20,000 people, and what they found was astrology at its finest. They didn't announce that Sagittarians were better horseback riders or that Capricorns were better CEOs — nothing that obvious. Instead, they unearthed a link between professional success and planets located near the Ascendant, Descendant, Midheaven, or I.C.

Specifically, they found that angular Jupiter appeared more often than statistically probable in the charts of successful actors; angular Moon showed up in writers' charts; angular Venus turned up in the charts of painters and musicians; angular Saturn appeared in the charts of doctors and scientists; and angular Mars showed up in the charts of champion athletes. Two positions were the most powerful:

Those close to the Midheaven (in either the ninth house or the first ten degrees of the tenth house) and those close to the Ascendant (in either the twelfth house or the first ten degrees of the first house).

Many people tried to disprove this association, and controversy raged over statistical methods. Ultimately, the phenomenon held up and became known as the *Mars effect*. Athletes who have an angular Mars include Tiger Woods, Muhammad Ali, Arnold Schwarzenegger, and Neil Armstrong, the first man to walk on the moon (and yes, in my opinion, he counts as an athlete).

Not every successful professional has one of these placements. The absence of an angular planet doesn't in any way doom you to failure. But if, perchance, Mars (or any other planet) happens to occupy the angular Gauquelin zones in your chart, that planet should be considered especially robust. In the case of Mars, it may not bestow you with the ability to outdo Shaquille O'Neal (whose Mars is in the first house). But it should at least give you a certain swagger.

Jupiter in the Houses

Jupiter's position by house determines the areas of life that are most bountiful for you — the places where benefits come most effortlessly and also the areas where you may become too complacent.

- **Jupiter in the first house:** You have an expansive, charismatic personality that naturally draws people to you. You may also have a tendency to gain weight.

- **Jupiter in the second house:** Money and prosperity come your way, often in the form of windfalls. The only downside is that your desire to spend may outweigh your ability to earn, so be prudent — if you can.

- **Jupiter in the third house:** Talkative and hungry for information, you're intelligent and well-informed, though you run the risk of filling your mind to the brim with tabloid gossip. You benefit from travel, reading, and the company of your brothers and sisters.

- **Jupiter in the fourth house:** You're a generous person who opens your home to others. Comfortable, even luxurious, housing comes your way, and you have a knack for making your home an agreeable, sustaining place to be. Life improves as you grow older, and in old age, you're surrounded by comfort.

- **Jupiter in the fifth house:** Having fun yet? If you have this placement, the answer is probably yes. This placement brings a profusion of romantic affairs, a love of entertainment, the ability to have fun even in difficult circumstances, and a joyous creativity. Although not everyone with this placement becomes a parent, those who do derive great satisfaction from it.

- **Jupiter in the sixth house:** Finding the right work is essential to your happiness, and you like to be of service. In a satisfying job, you're a devoted employee (or a happy entrepreneur) who gets along famously with colleagues. But you suffer from a tendency to overlook the details, and you may become a workaholic. In work and in health, you need to avoid excesses.

- **Jupiter in the seventh house:** You're sociable and easy to be around. Marriage and business partnerships are favored by this placement, and you have multiple opportunities to form alliances. Even in an age of divorce, people with this placement marry for life.

- **Jupiter in the eighth house:** Financially, you stand to gain from investments, insurance, inheritances, and businesses that you enter into with other people. You have a strong sex drive, a deep interest in the process of personal change, and excellent powers of recuperation.

- **Jupiter in the ninth house:** You have an expansive, optimistic attitude toward life. A natural teacher with a philosophical bent, you want to see it all and understand it all. You benefit from anything that expands your horizons, such as travel, education, religion, and publishing.

- **Jupiter in the tenth house:** With a little effort, you can fulfill your desire for recognition. You have natural leadership ability; people want to assist you, and you thrive in the public eye. This position brings success, prominence, and even fame.

- **Jupiter in the eleventh house:** You're open-minded, congenial, helpful, and fair. You work effectively with others, you know a zillion people, and your friends adore you. Large ambitions bring out the best in you. Success comes through group enterprises.

- **Jupiter in the twelfth house:** You're sympathetic, introspective, and generous. You may have psychic abilities but may suffer from a tendency to overextend yourself. Solitude and spiritual pursuits calm you down and prepare you for your forays into the world.

Saturn in the Houses

Saturn's position by house determines those areas of life in which you feel the pinch of limitation and will benefit from establishing boundaries, creating structures, and practicing self-discipline.

- **Saturn in the first house:** You're self-conscious and afraid of being hurt. You worry what people think of you, and as a result you may cloak your personality in defensive armor. Beneath your cautious exterior, you're a complicated, serious person, well worth the effort of getting to know. But you don't make it easy.

- **Saturn in the second house:** You worry about the practical side of life, and money is an issue, whether you're frugal or a spendthrift. Even when dealing with emotional concerns, you're aware of the practical implications. You'd like to win the lottery, but it's unlikely to happen (and if it did, it could bring you more trouble than it's worth). Instead, you can gain the security you seek through your own hard work.

- **Saturn in the third house:** You have a conscientious, contemplative mind and the ability to explore a subject in depth. Communication issues, whether in speech or in writing, are paramount. You have complicated relationships with your brothers and sisters, and sibling rivalry may be an issue for you.

- **Saturn in the fourth house:** Although your family is extremely important to you, you feel alienated from them (and perhaps from one parent in particular). Finding ways to interact successfully with family members (or simply to understand them) requires effort. Owning your own home is a gratifying source of identity and security.

✔ **Saturn in the fifth house:** You take a serious approach to playful things, and it's difficult for you to lighten up. You don't flirt easily and are more comfortable dating people who are older and more serious. Creativity is important to you, but because you may fear that you aren't talented, you may suppress your artistic urges. Or, you may rise to the challenge of Saturn and bring structure to your creative life. (Some people with this placement become professional artists.) As a parent, you're responsible and committed.

✔ **Saturn in the sixth house:** In your work, you're reliable, exacting, and efficient. If you have the courage to insist on doing something you love, you find fulfillment through your work. In your daily life, you pay equally close attention to your chores and responsibilities, but you're a big-time worrier, especially about your health. Reassure yourself by getting regular checkups.

✔ **Saturn in the seventh house:** You take a serious approach to marriage, but you may also shy away from it. If you overcome your fears of intimacy, you can create a long-lived, solid relationship. You'll be most comfortable with an older partner who's responsible and sober-minded.

✔ **Saturn in the eighth house:** You have great psychological insight. Your challenge is to overcome your fear of death and to face your sexual issues, which can range anywhere from total inhibition to emotionless promiscuity. Also, you're both cautious and skilled in making money — which is fortunate, because the chances are high that you'll marry someone who has financial problems.

✔ **Saturn in the ninth house:** You're a thoughtful person with wide-ranging intelligence. You're attracted to large ideas — philosophy or religion, for example — and your thorough exploration of them makes you a natural educator, writer, publisher, or lawyer.

✔ **Saturn in the tenth house:** You're responsible, ambitious, and persevering. This placement generally indicates great success, but you can also be arrogant, and you have to pay your dues before you achieve the recognition that's ultimately yours. One of your parents (most likely your father) may have been especially difficult.

✔ **Saturn in the eleventh house:** You expect great things of yourself, and you set ambitious goals, even if you fear that you aren't up to them. Fortunately, you have excellent organizational abilities and great determination, and you can mobilize the help you need. You don't make friends lightly, but the friendships you do form are long-lasting and consequential.

✔ **Saturn in the twelfth house:** Many people would be astonished to know that beneath your helpful surface, you wrestle with fear, pessimism, insecurity, loneliness, and guilt. Although you're used to working by yourself or behind the scenes, your fears become most terrifying when you're alone. You avoid solitude — and yet it's essential to your welfare. Your task is to find ways to be comfortable with it.

Uranus in the Houses

The position that Uranus occupies by house determines the area in life in which you can expect the unexpected.

- ✔ **Uranus in the first house:** You have an unusual demeanor, and you strike people as a true original. No matter how hard you try to look conventional, your attempts to pass for ordinary are doomed. From time to time, out-of-left-field events turn your world upside down.

- ✔ **Uranus in the second house:** Money and possessions come and go, arriving and departing with equal speed. You may strike oil, or you may go bankrupt. Your values can undergo a sudden turnaround.

- ✔ **Uranus in the third house:** You have an innovative mind and a clever way of expressing yourself. You could be a brilliant thinker or writer — or you could be a nut. You have unusual siblings, but your relationships with them have their ups and downs. Upsets can occur while traveling.

- ✔ **Uranus in the fourth house:** You come from or create an unconventional family. An erratic relationship with one of your parents (your mother, most likely) has a strong impact on you. You find it hard to settle down, and when you do, you set up housekeeping in a thoroughly individual way. Professional changes affect your domestic life.

- ✔ **Uranus in the fifth house:** You have a wild creative streak and an unpredictable love life. You're prone to love at first sight, preferably with rebellious types. But sudden breakups are also part of the picture. Your children may be remarkable people, though you may feel that they hamper your freedom.

- ✔ **Uranus in the sixth house:** You don't mind working, but you oppose the concept of nine-to-five. You manage to find unusual, even peculiar jobs. And even in your daily life, you do things in a unique way. Your nerves affect your health, and you benefit from unorthodox healing techniques.

- ✔ **Uranus in the seventh house:** You may marry an unconventional person, or you may create a free-wheeling relationship that acknowledges, in its radical format, your need for independence. You're liable to marry with lightning speed, but be careful — you could divorce the same way.

- ✔ **Uranus in the eighth house:** Your sex life has a remarkable, even outrageous, aspect to it, and the same is true for your finances (and those of your spouse). You benefit from unusual investment. You're also drawn to metaphysical subjects, including the idea of reincarnation. And though I hesitate to mention this, you may as well know: When it coexists with a rare pileup of especially tough aspects, this placement can indicate the possibility of sudden, accidental death — not necessarily your own. Should you worry? No. Keep in mind that literally one out of every twelve people has this placement. For further information, see the nearby "Violent death and Princess Diana" sidebar.

- ✔ **Uranus in the ninth house:** Unusual experiences come to you through travel, education, and the law. You're interested in religion but not in a conventional way, and your philosophy of life is your own invention.

- ✔ **Uranus in the tenth house:** You insist on maintaining your independence, especially regarding your career. (Fulfilling areas include — but are not limited to — social activism, computer technology, astrology, and science.) You have an original viewpoint, and professional opportunities arrive out of nowhere. Too rebellious to work in a strongly hierarchical organization, you're a natural entrepreneur or freelancer.

- ✔ **Uranus in the eleventh house:** You're a tolerant person with unusual aspirations and many highly intelligent, erratic friends who motivate you to achieve. People enter your life on a moment's notice, especially when you're involved with a cause, but you can lose contact with them just as quickly. Your many diverse friends reflect your widely scattered interests.

- ✔ **Uranus in the twelfth house:** You're a freedom-lover who requires independence and rebels against constraints. Unusual forms of spirituality attract you. You express your deepest individuality in solitude. Flashes of intuition and insight come from your core. Learn to pay attention to them.

Violent death and Princess Diana

Reading old-fashioned astrology books can be terrifying. They're filled with scary-sounding predictions of poverty, illness, and even death. These old books can be particularly nerve-wracking if you have a placement such as Uranus, the planet of the unexpected, or Mars, the planet of violence, in the eighth house of death and regeneration. It sounds bad. The truth is that many indicators are required for something as serious as violent death. Not even the presence of both Uranus and Mars in the eighth house promises such a tragedy. For that, you'd need truly horrific aspects — like those of Princess Diana, a sensitive Cancerian with the Moon in Aquarius.

Not only was Diana's eighth house home to both Uranus and Mars, it also held Pluto, the planet of transformation. In addition, Uranus formed a high-stress T-square pattern with the Moon and Venus, the planets that ruled her love life. (For a discussion of the T-square, see Chapter 14.) This is an unusually bad combination of aspects. Her chart clearly held the potential of a life-threatening accident involving a lover. In addition, at the time of her death, the position of the outer planets in the sky heightened the perils that were lying in wait in her birth chart.

But did she have to die that day, right before an eclipse? Some astrologers contend that you can't escape your fate. Others, myself among them, believe that every influence has many possible expressions. Certainly Diana's chart was under enormous stress at the time of her fatal car crash. Even in retrospect, we can't know whether Diana could have avoided this terrible accident. This much is certain, though: Taking precautions — and fastening her safety belt — couldn't have hurt.

Neptune in the Houses

The house that Neptune inhabits in your horoscope tells you where you can access the most profound level of intuition — and where you're prone to deception.

- **Neptune in the first house:** You're impressionable, dreamy, and fluid. Your intuition is acute, but you can easily become dependent. You confuse and fascinate people; they aren't sure who you are or what you're up to because your identity seems to shift. There's a good chance that you have musical or artistic ability.

- **Neptune in the second house:** You have an intuitive sense of how to make money. You can even earn money through spiritual pursuits. But you also have the ability to be defrauded because you haven't a clue about the mechanics of saving money, and as a result, your financial affairs are likely to be chaotic. Hire a responsible earth sign to help.

- **Neptune in the third house:** You're impressionable, imaginative, and highly sensitive to language. Persuasive but easily distracted, you soak up knowledge and have poetic ability. You're also gullible — and no one knows how to fool you better than your brothers and sisters.

- **Neptune in the fourth house:** The members of your family are an unusual lot. Their influence is powerful and subtle, and you find it difficult to separate from them. You may have inherited psychic ability.

- **Neptune in the fifth house:** You're artistic and sensitive, but you find it difficult to focus your creativity. Platonic relationships and secret affairs may characterize your romantic life, and you're drawn to people who mystify you. Your children (should you conquer your ambivalence about that subject and decide to become a parent) are likely to be impressionable and gentle, and you have a strong psychic tie with them.

- **Neptune in the sixth house:** You tend to get caught in the web of office politics, and the physical aspects of regular jobs — the fluorescent lights, the hideous decor — make you long for escape. Job possibilities exist in film, pharmacology, music, fashion, and anything connected to the sea. Keep in mind that your health complaints are seldom solved through Western-style medicine. Doctors have difficulty diagnosing you, and you do better with more intuitive healing styles.

- **Neptune in the seventh house:** Moody people and artistic souls attract you. You seek your spiritual soul mate, but in your confusion about relationships, you may sacrifice yourself to an image or ideal that has nothing to do with your actual partner. Idealism about relationships is wonderful, but only when it's tempered with realism.

✔ **Neptune in the eighth house:** Séances, Ouija boards, extrasensory perception, and all forms of communication with the great beyond attract you. You consider sex a spiritual exercise. But you may trust your instincts too much, especially when it comes to your money and your partner. Be careful in business partnerships.

✔ **Neptune in the ninth house:** Mystical religions and spiritual journeys are your cup of chai. You want desperately to identify a specific spiritual path, but it won't happen that way, for visionary Neptune will take you in many directions. You're also a sensitive teacher.

✔ **Neptune in the tenth house:** By choosing a profession that requires you to tap into your intuition, you find the success you covet. Following a profession just because you think it's practical (as if you would know) is a waste of time. Here are two career problems you may face: You tend to drift, and you seldom assert yourself.

✔ **Neptune in the eleventh house:** You have shifting ideals and vague aspirations, along with a large collection of inspiring, talented friends who may have drug and alcohol problems. Unfortunately, you tend to see what you want to see in your friends. Joining a spiritual organization could help you to see straight.

✔ **Neptune in the twelfth house:** You're empathetic, contemplative, reclusive, and probably psychic. You receive a continual flow of messages from your unconscious. Metaphysics, dreams, and secrets fascinate you, and you're highly responsive to those in need. Your creative efforts are best accomplished in private, and solitude is necessary for your peace of mind.

Pluto in the Houses

The house that tiny Pluto occupies in your natal chart determines the area in life where you're most likely to experience obsession and transformation.

✔ **Pluto in the first house:** You have a compulsive, controlling, and magnetic personality, along with a tendency to dominate. You make a powerful impact on people — but you may also alienate them.

✔ **Pluto in the second house:** You find concrete outlets for your abilities, but you can also become obsessed with your possessions. More importantly, money can become a battlefield, and you may struggle to control other people with it.

✔ **Pluto in the third house:** You have a profound mind, accurate perceptions, a longing to solve the mysteries of life, and an obsessive need to communicate combined with a strong sense of privacy. (Surely the inventor of the locked diary had Pluto in the third house.)

✓ **Pluto in the fourth house:** One of your parents was a force to be reckoned with; dealing with the psychological fallout is your Plutonian task. Your greatest transformations come through your family and home.

✓ **Pluto in the fifth house:** You become obsessed with romance. Yet no matter how hard you try to manipulate your lover, the person most altered by the liaison is you. Power struggles spring up around children. Creative endeavors are transformative for you. Gambling is addictive.

✓ **Pluto in the sixth house:** You have great focus and drive, and you may have healing abilities. Because your desire for power is focused on work, you may overdo it and work to the point of obsession. Your job must have meaning or your health may suffer. You need purpose.

✓ **Pluto in the seventh house:** Relationship and obsession go hand in hand with you, and marriage is a testing ground. You attract a commanding partner whose influence causes you to change in profound ways. Maintaining your sense of self in the presence of this powerful being isn't easy. Business partnerships offer similar challenges.

✓ **Pluto in the eighth house:** Life after death, extrasensory perception, and all occult subjects fascinate you, and you gain wisdom through those channels. You're intuitive, perceptive, and deeply serious. You must grapple with the truly big issues in life, including the troublesome feelings that surround sex, money, and death.

✓ **Pluto in the ninth house:** Philosophy, religion, and the law attract and strengthen you. By immersing yourself in study or becoming passionately involved with people from a culture other than your own, you deepen your understanding. Education and travel are your tickets to transformation, but you must approach them on your own terms.

✓ **Pluto in the tenth house:** You're an irresistible force in the political arena. You resent authority figures (starting with one of your parents), and yet you wish to wield authority. When you decide to seek power, you can be a real player. This position favors success.

✓ **Pluto in the eleventh house:** Friendship is a charged area for you, especially when young. But ultimately, your friends help shape your dreams and aspirations, and deeply transformative experiences come to you through those relationships.

✓ **Pluto in the twelfth house:** You're a private person with a secret life. You shy away from expressing your power, and yet you're fascinated by whatever is going on beneath the surface, especially in your own psyche. Delving into your unconscious brings transformation.

Interpreting Empty Houses

Do the math: Your chart has twelve houses, but only ten planets. This means that you're bound to have empty houses somewhere in your chart. They're unavoidable. They're also nothing to worry about.

Having an empty house of marriage, for example, doesn't mean that you'll always be single. Just ask Elizabeth Taylor, who has had eight husbands (so far), despite the fact that her seventh house is totally vacant. Similarly, an unoccupied second house of money doesn't mean you're destined for poverty. Look at Bill Gates, the youngest self-made billionaire in history. His second house is empty (as is his eighth house, which is also associated with money).

Often, an unoccupied house signifies that the usual concerns of that house are simply not a major concern. But you can't make that determination with a casual glance. Just because a house is empty doesn't mean it's unimportant. The truth is that there's so much to think about in a natal chart that even an empty house can keep you busy. To investigate an empty house, I suggest the following three-step method:

1. **Look at the sign on the cusp of the house.**

   The sign at the beginning of each house determines your approach to the concerns of that house. For example, turn to Andy Warhol's chart in Chapter 19. Notice that his second house of money is empty, with Virgo on the cusp. (The cusp of the second house is at eight o'clock, the cusp of the third house is at seven o'clock, and so on.) Thus his approach to financial matters was Virgoan: discriminating and detail-oriented. And, indeed, he made a habit of recording his daily expenses — just like a Virgo.

   Table 12-1 at the beginning of this chapter summarizes the concerns of each house. Table 12-2 suggests ways to interpret the sign on the cusp.

2. **Check out the planet that rules the sign on the cusp.**

   The position of that planet tells you a great deal. In Andy Warhol's case, Virgo, the sign on the cusp of his second house, is ruled by Mercury. It can be found in flamboyant Leo — a perfect placement for an artist who literally painted money.

3. **Look at the aspects made by the ruling planet.**

   If the ruling planet of the empty house is close to the Sun or the Moon, its importance increases. If it is conjunct Jupiter, the concerns of that house are blessed with good fortune. If it opposes Saturn, difficulties arise. And so on. For more about aspects, turn to Chapter 13.

Table 12-2	House Rulership	
If the Sign on the Cusp Is	*Your Approach to the Concerns of That House Is*	*And the House Ruler Is*
Aries	Spontaneous, energetic	Mars
Taurus	Productive, deliberate	Venus
Gemini	Flexible, communicative	Mercury
Cancer	Intuitive, defensive	Moon
Leo	Dignified, expressive	Sun
Virgo	Discriminating, detail-oriented	Mercury
Libra	Diplomatic, artistic	Venus
Scorpio	Intense, penetrating	Pluto
Sagittarius	Independent, expansive	Jupiter
Capricorn	Responsible, traditional	Saturn
Aquarius	Unconventional, detached	Uranus
Pisces	Receptive, vulnerable	Neptune

Finally, keep in mind that every year, as the Sun makes its annual pilgrimage through the zodiac, it travels through each part of your chart — every sign and every house. The Moon and the other planets visit as well, each according to its own schedule. Over time, those transiting planets activate each and every house — even if it's empty. Sooner or later, every house will have its day.

Chapter 13

Amazing Aspects: The Secrets of Cosmic Geometry

Knowing the position of the planets by sign and by house isn't enough. To comprehend the true complexity of an astrological chart, you need to know how the planets interact with each other. That information is revealed by the mathematical angles, or aspects, between the planets.

Consider the case of a woman whose Venus, the planet of love, is located within a few short degrees of Jupiter, the planet of good fortune. That combination makes expressing affection and finding love easy for her. But what if both planets are 90° from Saturn? With that harsh right angle, pessimism and disappointment enter the picture. Now you have a charming individual who easily attracts others yet is never content with them — a person who, like Groucho Marx, doesn't want to be in a club that would have her as a member.

To detect that kind of internal process in your own chart, you need to know the degree of the zodiac that each planet occupies. That information, which is beyond the scope of this book, is easy to get via the Internet. (See Chapter 2 for tips on how to do that.) Once you have a copy of your chart, you're ready to pick out the major aspects in it. Take my word for it: It's a snap.

Identifying the Major Aspects

An astrological chart, like any circle, has 360°, with each sign of the zodiac covering exactly 30°, or one-twelfth of the whole. Within that circle, each pair

of planets is separated by a specific number of degrees. Planets at certain significant distances from each other form an *aspect*. Table 13-1 lists the *major aspects,* along with their symbols.

Table 13-1		Major Aspects	
Distance	*Name of Aspect*	*Symbol*	*Effect*
0°	Conjunction	☌	Unifies or blends
60°	Sextile	✳	Supports
90°	Square	☐	Creates friction
120°	Trine	△	Assists and brings opportunities
180°	Opposition	☍	Opposes

Roughly speaking, there are three types of aspects. If two planets are within a few degrees of each other, they're *conjunct,* which means that they operate in unison. If two planets are 60° or 120° apart, they support and assist each other. These aspects — sextiles and trines — are considered *harmonious.* And if two planets are at right angles (90°) or opposite each other (180°), they're basically at war. These aspects — squares and oppositions — are considered *hard.*

Look at Oprah Winfrey's chart (Figure 13-1). She's a forward-thinking Aquarian with the Moon in optimistic, freedom-loving Sagittarius. She also has a series of aspects, both easy and challenging. They include:

- An exact conjunction between the Sun and Venus at 9° Aquarius

- A harmonious trine between Mercury, the planet of communication, at 19° Aquarius and expansive Jupiter, the planet of good fortune, at 16° Gemini

- A stressful square between aggressive Mars at 23° Scorpio and Pluto at 24° Leo

Like most people, Oprah has a mix of conjunctions, harmonious aspects, and hard aspects in her chart.

Surprisingly, an "easy" chart festooned with sextiles and trines isn't necessarily better than a "hard" chart crisscrossed with squares and opposition. Astrologers have long noted that people with harmonious charts run the risk of becoming lazy and self-satisfied, while highly accomplished achievers often have high-stress charts.

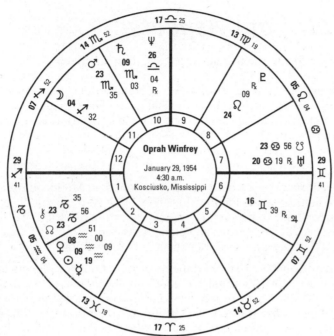

Figure 13-1:
Oprah
Winfrey's
birth chart.

The most powerful aspects occur when the distances between the planets are close to those listed in Table 13-1. A 90° square, for example, is stronger than an 82° square, regardless of the planets involved. But observation indicates that an aspect doesn't have to be precise to have an influence. So astrologers allow a little leeway on either side. This leeway is called the *orb of influence*. Astrologers differ, however, about how large that orb should be. A few generous practitioners use an orb as wide as 14°. Stricter seers permit no more than a 5° orb. Most astrologers, myself included, fall somewhere in the middle.

In general, I recommend using an 8° orb for the conjunction, square, trine, or opposition and a 6° orb for the sextile, which is a slightly weaker aspect. (Minor aspects, which I discuss later in this chapter, can handle only a 2° orb.) In each case, you can tack on an additional 2° if the Sun or Moon is involved. This means that if your Sun is at 14°, any planet between 4° and 24° of your Sun sign is considered conjunct, a planet 52° to 68° away is sextile, and so on. Remember: The tighter the orb, the more powerful the aspect.

Figuring Out Your Aspects

Here's how to locate the five major aspects in your chart:

- **Conjunctions:** You can readily detect conjunctions. If two planets are within 8° of each other (10° if the Sun or the Moon is involved), they're conjunct. For example, if you have Mars at 5° Sagittarius and Jupiter at 7° Sagittarius, they're conjunct. The same rule applies even if the two planets are in different signs. For instance, if you have Venus at 28° Capricorn and the Moon at 1° Aquarius, Venus and the Moon are conjunct.

- **Oppositions:** To pick out oppositions, look for planets on opposite sides of the chart. Planets in opposing signs often (though not always) form an opposition. To be sure, check whether they're within orb. If your Mars is at 18° Sagittarius, any planet between 10° and 26° Gemini is in opposition. A planet at 6° Gemini isn't in opposition.

- **Squares:** Squares are more difficult to spot. Look for planets in signs of the same quality (cardinal, fixed, or mutable). Then check that they're about 90° apart, plus or minus 8°. If they are, you've found the source of your deepest frustrations. In Oprah's chart, for example, Saturn, at 9° Scorpio, forms a square to Venus — which definitely puts a damper on her love life.

- **Trines:** You find trines between planets in signs of the same element — that is, both planets are in fire, earth, air, or water signs. Maybe you have Mercury in Gemini and Uranus in Libra? If they're within 8° of each other, they're trine — in which case, congratulations: You have a quick, original mind.

- **Sextiles:** The weakest of the major aspects, sextiles happen between planets that are two signs apart. In Oprah's chart, for example, Pluto at 24° Leo is sextile Neptune at 26° Libra.

Table 13-2 gives you squares and oppositions at a glance, and Table 13-3 does the same for the harmonious aspects.

Table 13-2	The Hard Aspects	
If a Planet Is In . . .	*It Squares Planets In . . .*	*And Opposes Those In . . .*
Aries	Cancer and Capricorn	Libra
Taurus	Leo and Aquarius	Scorpio
Gemini	Virgo and Pisces	Sagittarius
Cancer	Aries and Libra	Capricorn
Leo	Taurus and Scorpio	Aquarius

If a Planet Is In . . .	It Squares Planets In . . .	And Opposes Those In . . .
Virgo	Gemini and Sagittarius	Pisces
Libra	Cancer and Capricorn	Aries
Scorpio	Leo and Aquarius	Taurus
Sagittarius	Virgo and Pisces	Gemini
Capricorn	Aries and Libra	Cancer
Aquarius	Taurus and Scorpio	Leo
Pisces	Gemini and Sagittarius	Virgo

Table 13-3	The Harmonious Aspects	
If a Planet Is In . . .	It Sextiles Planets In . . .	And Trines Those In . . .
Aries	Aquarius and Gemini	Leo and Sagittarius
Taurus	Pisces and Cancer	Virgo and Capricorn
Gemini	Aries and Leo	Libra and Aquarius
Cancer	Taurus and Virgo	Scorpio and Pisces
Leo	Gemini and Libra	Sagittarius and Aries
Virgo	Cancer and Scorpio	Taurus and Capricorn
Libra	Leo and Sagittarius	Gemini and Aquarius
Scorpio	Virgo and Capricorn	Cancer and Pisces
Sagittarius	Libra and Aquarius	Aries and Leo
Capricorn	Scorpio and Pisces	Taurus and Virgo
Aquarius	Sagittarius and Aries	Gemini and Libra
Pisces	Capricorn and Taurus	Cancer and Scorpio

When planets are in the first few degrees or the last few degrees of a sign, be sure to check for out-of-sign aspects, which are notoriously difficult to detect. If you're looking at a chart with, say, the Sun at 28° Gemini and Saturn at 1° Libra, it's easy to assume that because both planets are in air signs, they must be trine. In fact, they're separated by 93° and are therefore square. This is why you should get a computer-generated chart. Even an experienced astrologer can miss an out-of-sign aspect, but you can't trick a computer.

A Note about Minor Aspects

The major aspects discussed in this chapter aren't the only geometrical relationship that astrologers consider significant. Other aspects, typically described as *minor aspects,* also connect two planets. Because minor aspects are weak, the orb allotted to them is small — only 2°.

Two minor aspects I refer to in this chapter are the *semi-sextile,* a 30° aspect that's considered mildly positive, and the *semi-square,* a 45° aspect whose influence is somewhat stressful. These minor aspects rise in importance if the chart has a scarcity of major aspects, as occasionally happens. But remember, they call them minor for a reason.

Table 13-4 lists the most important of the minor aspects.

Table 13-4	Minor Aspects	
Name	*Degrees*	*Action*
Semi-sextile	30°	Mildly supportive
Semi-square	45°	Mildly irritating
Quintile	72°	Promotes creativity
Sesquiquadrate	135°	Stressful and active
Quincunx or inconjunct	150°	Indecisive; on again/off again

Are there other minor aspects? You bet. There's the *septile,* the *novile,* and more. I've seen symbols for aspects I've never even heard of. You can reach a point when adding more aspects to a chart only obliterates the big picture. That's why I recommend sticking with the majors.

Interpreting the Aspects

In this section, I interpret the main aspects for each of the planets. I bundle sextiles and trines together as harmonious aspects. Their actions are similar, though trines are more powerful. Similarly, I tie squares and oppositions together as hard aspects, though they aren't identical either. In general, a square brings internal conflicts, while oppositions are more likely to create external obstructions.

I consider the planets in this order: first the Sun and Moon, then the planets in order of their distance from the Sun: Mercury, Venus, Mars, Jupiter, Saturn, Uranus, Neptune, and Pluto. When looking up an aspect, be sure to look for it under the planet that comes first in the list. An aspect between Mercury and Uranus, for example, appears under Mercury; an opposition between Venus and Pluto is discussed under Venus, and so on.

Aspects to the Sun

Your Sun sign represents the deepest, most essential part of your nature. The aspects it makes with other planets can help you express your potential or make it more difficult.

Sun/Moon

The Sun represents your conscious identity, while the Moon governs your innermost feelings and subconscious self. The Sun/Moon aspect shows how comfortably these two cooperate.

- **Conjunction:** If your Sun and Moon are conjunct, you were born around the time of a new moon, with all the vitality that implies. Your will and your subconscious work together, so you have strong intentions, enthusiasm, and the ability to concentrate. You may also be stubborn and closed-minded.

- **Harmonious aspects:** With your Sun sextile or trine the Moon, you're genial and energetic. Opportunities come your way. All things being equal, you're basically at peace with yourself. Consider yourself blessed.

- **Hard aspects:** If your Sun and Moon are square, your conscious self desires one thing, and your subconscious yearns for something else. So you're never truly satisfied, and you may struggle with a tendency to sabotage yourself. Interestingly, this discomfort turns out to be highly motivating. Legions of accomplished people in every field have this aspect — so many that I'm not even sure it's a disadvantage.

  If your Sun and Moon are in opposition, you were born under a full moon, a time when emotions run high. Restless and conflicted, you find it difficult to match your desires to your abilities. You attract stressful relationships and may overreact to obstacles. Although a few people with Sun/Moon oppositions screw up in astonishing ways (extreme example: Michael Jackson), the opposition also motivates them to conquer the internal divide and become hugely successful.

Sun/Mercury

The fiery Sun governs your ego while Mercury rules communication. This aspect reveals the ease with which you express your thoughts.

- **Conjunction:** These two bodies can never be more than 28° apart, so plenty of people have this aspect. It indicates a nervous, quick disposition. When the conjunction is exceptionally close, within a degree or less, it may indicate an over-the-top level of self-involvement.

- **Harmonious aspects:** Mercury and the Sun are never far enough apart to form a sextile (60°) or trine (120°). But they can occasionally be separated by 28°, making them semi-sextile, a mildly helpful aspect that strengthens your ability to communicate.

- **Hard aspects:** Mercury and the Sun are always so close together that they never form a hard aspect.

Sun/Venus

How these two planets interact influences your artistic talents, your sociability, and your ability to attract what you love — particularly with regard to relationships, money, and possessions.

- **Conjunction:** You're appealing, affectionate, and creative. You have a deep need to be in relationships, an innate capacity for intimacy, and a love of pleasure. This aspect also brings artistic talent. Because Venus can never be farther than 48° from the Sun, this is the only major aspect that these two bodies can form.

- **Harmonious aspects:** Venus and the Sun are never far enough apart to form a sextile or a trine. But if they're 30° apart, they're semi-sextile, a friendly minor aspect that supports artistic talents and the ability to express affection.

- **Hard aspects:** The Sun and Venus are never in opposition and are never square. When they're close to their maximum distance, they're semi-square, a 45° minor aspect that can stir up sexual issues and can cause you to act out. Want examples? Think of Hugh Hefner, Bill Clinton, Woody Allen, and the Marquis de Sade.

Sun/Mars

This aspect describes your ability to focus your energy and to put your intentions into action.

- **Conjunction:** You're an adventurer with energy, courage, and strong passions — sexual and otherwise. You're enterprising, competitive, and willing to take the initiative — a contender in every way.

- ✔ **Harmonious aspects:** Energy is there when you want it. You're assertive without being combative and energetic without being manic.

- ✔ **Hard aspects:** Controlling the vitality that flows through you isn't easy. You tend to overdo it, often by being a workaholic. Your temper can get out of control. You can be contentious and accident-prone, and you have a tendency to act rashly. Extreme example: Lizzie Borden.

Sun/Jupiter

Combine the Sun, which represents your potential, with Jupiter, the bringer of opportunities, and you have an enviable aspect. The challenge is to make use of the connection between the two planets — not to waste it.

- ✔ **Conjunction:** You're blessed with good fortune, a sense of humor, high intelligence, a strong spirit, and an optimistic attitude. You can also be careless and overconfident, relying on the indisputable fact that luck is with you.

- ✔ **Harmonious aspects:** This aspect brings health, success, a pleasing and positive approach to life, and a generous nature. Possible downside: You may have a tendency to kick back and be lazy.

- ✔ **Hard aspects:** You're inclined to exaggerate, to become self-important, to misjudge, and to lack a sense of moderation. Extravagance may plague you. Even so, this aspect, because it features Jupiter, can bring opportunities and is often beneficial.

Sun/Saturn

The Sun wants to dazzle. Somber Saturn advocates caution. When these two planets form a major aspect, it indicates that you feel tested in various ways. This aspect shows the way you deal with those challenges.

- ✔ **Conjunction:** Restrained but persistent, you're responsible, realistic, and introspective. You take yourself seriously. This is a taxing aspect but one that brings direction, determination, and the capacity to overcome your early sense of inadequacy through solid accomplishments.

- ✔ **Harmonious aspects:** You're industrious, goal-oriented, and willing to accept responsibility for your own situation. Purposeful and practical, you look before you leap, and your caution pays off.

- ✔ **Hard aspects:** In childhood, disappointments and frustrations may have battered your sense of self-worth. If your Sun and Saturn are square, your issues are primarily internal. If your Sun and Saturn are opposed, external obstacles or enemies may block your path. Ultimately, you have the ability to overcome everything through self-discipline, persistence, and the thing Saturn loves above all else: hard work.

Sun/Uranus

The Sun represents your core identity. Uranus represents your most eccentric side. If they form a major aspect, you can be sure of this: You aren't like anybody else.

- **Conjunction:** Independent, unpredictable, and thoroughly unique, you take an individualistic, original approach to life. You're impulsive and eccentric, a genius or a rebel, and magnetic either way. Examples: Meryl Streep and Sean Penn.

- **Harmonious aspects:** A free-spirited adventurer, you possess originality, independence, a flexible attitude, and a tendency to stumble into unexpected patches of good luck.

- **Hard aspects:** You're an unusual, dramatic person with an unfortunate tendency to act in eccentric and impractical ways and to make rash decisions. Rebellious and easily bored, you're likely to head off in unpredictable directions, especially when events take you by surprise, as they occasionally do.

Sun/Neptune

The Sun bestows vitality, while dreamy Neptune brings inspiration . . . or indolence. This combination can encourage creative potential or unrealistic schemes.

- **Conjunction:** You're a dreamer, a poet, and an inspired idealist. Intuitive, sensitive, and sometimes even psychic, you have a finely developed imagination and great creative talent for both mystical and artistic endeavors, which leaves little room for practical matters. You also have a tendency to lie to yourself (or to others) and to live in a world of fantasy, seeing only what you want to see. Drug and alcohol abuse may be a problem.

- **Harmonious aspects:** You have a strongly developed sense of intuition and the ability to use your imagination in constructive ways.

- **Hard aspects:** You have an active imagination combined with a discouraging tendency to daydream and to delude yourself. As with all Neptune aspects, deception can be a problem, either because you choose to deceive others or because you're so gullible that anyone can pull the wool over your eyes.

Sun/Pluto

If these two planets form a major aspect, control is an issue for you. This aspect reveals the way you balance your core identity with your need for power.

- **Conjunction:** A vigorous, charismatic person, you're an extremist, with strong reactions, great willpower, and the ability to transform yourself. You may struggle with a tendency to dominate or to become obsessed.

- ✔ **Harmonious aspects:** Strong-willed, persevering, and at ease with power and its uses, you have personal insight combined with the ability to adapt to circumstances and to create positive change.

- ✔ **Hard aspects:** Competition eggs you on. Acutely aware of the uses of personal power, you're manipulative, resourceful, and sometimes intimidating. The challenge, whether you're competing with others or simply trying to fulfill your own considerable ambition, is to avoid becoming overly aggressive or power-mad.

Aspects to the Moon

The Moon represents your emotions, instincts, habits, and subconscious.

Moon/Mercury

Do you have a strong need to communicate your emotions? If Mercury and the Moon form a major aspect, the answer is yes.

- ✔ **Conjunction:** You're intelligent, responsive, and in touch with your emotions. You know how to communicate confidently and with grace.

- ✔ **Harmonious aspects:** You think clearly, communicate effectively, make good use of humor, and have an excellent memory.

- ✔ **Hard aspects:** You respond quickly but often become anxious. Gifted with an unconventional mind, you often feel that people don't understand you, and you're highly sensitive to criticism.

Moon/Venus

If the Moon and Venus form a major aspect, your emotional needs and your need for love and beauty are intertwined.

- ✔ **Conjunction:** A great lover of comfort, you're responsive, appealing, kind, creative, and pleasant to be around. Your mood depends on your relationships, and you can get all wrapped up in the game of love.

- ✔ **Harmonious aspects:** You express your affections easily. You're a likable person with good taste and finely developed romantic sensibilities, even if you do occasionally stumble into the pit of self-indulgence.

- ✔ **Hard aspects:** Your love affairs travel a bumpy road of conflict and emotional frustration. Some people react by withdrawing, others by becoming demanding and possessive. Either way, you can't help feeling that you have to work harder than other people to get what you want.

Moon/Mars

If you have a major aspect between the Moon and Mars, you're assertive about the way you express your emotions.

- ✔ **Conjunction:** You're emotionally intense, impatient, and quick to anger. You let people know how you feel, and you aren't always diplomatic about it.

- ✔ **Harmonious aspects:** Courageous, energetic, helpful, and direct, you're a risk-taker who's always ready to jump into new situations.

- ✔ **Hard aspects:** Rash, defensive, and sometimes volatile, you're impulsive, competitive, and bossy. You don't hold back from expressing your emotions, and your fluctuating moods can stir up conflict. No matter what face you show the world, anger is an issue you must address.

Moon/Jupiter

The Moon wants to pour out her feelings, while extravagant Jupiter says "More is more" — which makes for a potent emotional cocktail.

- ✔ **Conjunction:** You're warm, optimistic, considerate, and empathetic, a person of huge feeling even if you do occasionally promise more than you can deliver. You have faith in your own abilities. You feel best when possibilities are multiplying and your universe is expanding.

- ✔ **Harmonious aspects:** You're highly responsive, gentle, and supportive: a genuine human being.

- ✔ **Hard aspects:** It's all or nothing with you. You're ecstatic or grief-stricken, blissed out or on the verge of collapse. In short, you have trouble controlling your feelings and you tend to go overboard.

Moon/Saturn

Saturn is the planet of restraint, and the Moon is all about unbridled emotions. This pair could be called "Sense and Sensibility."

- ✔ **Conjunction:** The past has a strong hold on you. You may suffer from self-doubt as a result of a less-than-warm relationship with your mother. Fortunately, you wield the weapon of self-control. Common sense helps you focus your feelings in a positive way.

- ✔ **Harmonious aspects:** Disciplined and sensible, you make a mighty effort to control your emotions, and you generally succeed. This explains how daredevil Evel Knievel and horror writer Stephen King can do what they do.

- ✔ **Hard aspects:** A history of emotional deprivation makes you hesitant and self-conscious. Though pessimism, repressed emotions, and difficulties with women may distress you, your understanding grows with maturity, as does your ability to find happiness and contentment.

Moon/Uranus

There's never a dull moment when the emotional Moon pairs up with the planet of unpredictability.

- **Conjunction:** Impulsive and excitable, you react in unconventional ways, attract unusual experiences, and may suffer from unpredictable mood swings. This is a volatile combination.

- **Harmonious aspects:** You rebel against restriction and convention, pride yourself on your independence, and value your autonomy, even within relationships. You're attracted to stimulating, exciting people and unusual situations.

- **Hard aspects:** Talented and easily distracted, you can't stand feeling constrained. You get worked up easily and from time to time you stir up (or attract) a crisis. To maintain your independence, you may unconsciously distance yourself from others.

Moon/Neptune

The Moon harbors the most sensitive, private side of your personality, while Neptune cloaks everything in mystery. Together this pair can sensitize your imagination — or lead you into an emotional fog.

- **Conjunction:** You pick up on the slightest emotional clues and often feel overwhelmed, drained, or self-pitying. You're vulnerable and kind, with strong spiritual needs, definite psychic potential, and an active dream life. This aspect indicates imagination and creative talent. It can also produce a tendency toward escapism, alcoholism, and drug abuse.

- **Harmonious aspects:** Compassionate, intuitive, and caring, you find it difficult to say no. Although this aspect increases your creativity, harnessing it can be difficult because you're inclined to float off on a daydream. Turning fantasy into reality involves work — and that can be a problem for you.

- **Hard aspects:** You struggle with wishful thinking, irrational fears (such as hypochondria), and emotional instability, not to mention drug and alcohol abuse. But you're also sensitive, creative, and receptive.

Moon/Pluto

Pluto lends intensity to the emotional issues governed by the Moon. A major aspect between these two means that your feelings are deep and your perceptions are laser-sharp.

- **Conjunction:** You're magnetic, controlling, possessive, intense, and compulsive. You resist minor changes. But when it's time for major changes, you understand the need and do just fine.

✔ **Harmonious aspects:** You handle big changes with ease. You have deep emotions and a compelling need, from time to time, to purge yourself of old feelings. Doing so brings relief.

✔ **Hard aspects:** You're inhibited about expressing your emotions, and you tend to hold back. People struggle to gain your trust, and you may manipulate situations in an effort to gain the upper hand. Occasionally, domestic upheavals and power struggles rock your life.

Aspects to Mercury

Mercury represents the way you think, your curiosity, the way you express yourself, and your intellect.

Mercury/Venus

Lovely Venus, the muse of the zodiac, bestows grace of expression on Mercury's mental gymnastics.

✔ **Conjunction:** You express yourself with charm and humor. You may have literary ability, and you love to talk, which is lucky because you're a confirmed gossip.

✔ **Harmonious aspects:** You're alert, charming, diplomatic, and a skilled communicator.

✔ **Hard aspect (sort of):** Mercury and Venus are never farther than 76° apart, so they can't form a square or opposition. But they can be semi-square — a 45° angle that enhances your creative abilities and can stimulate you to be critical of those you love the most.

Mercury/Mars

When the ruler of the intellect teams up with the planet of aggression, you get a sharp, assertive, lawyer-like mind.

✔ **Conjunction:** You have a lively, argumentative mind, strongly held opinions, and the intellectual authority to win most of your debates — whether you know anything about the topic or not.

✔ **Harmonious aspects:** You're forthright and mentally active, with a quick mind and the ability to make clear decisions.

✔ **Hard aspects:** You respond immediately and sometimes recklessly. You also have a sharp tongue and a tendency to be combative.

Mercury/Jupiter

Mercury is the planet of mental abilities, while expansive Jupiter makes anything bigger and better. This pair can inspire grand ideas or distracted excess.

- ✔ **Conjunction:** You're smart, philosophical, open-minded, and able to see the big picture. You ask the big questions, juggle dozens of interests, and have the ability to influence others. Gathering information and mastering new skills makes you happy.

- ✔ **Harmonious aspects:** You're intelligent and good-humored, optimistic yet clear-eyed, with a variety of interests. You're a persuasive speaker.

- ✔ **Hard aspects:** You're filled with exciting ideas and good intentions. But you tend to exaggerate and leap to conclusions, and your judgment can be off-base.

Mercury/Saturn

Fleet-footed Mercury rules the thinking process. Demanding Saturn is the planet of structure and self-control. They work well together if Mercury can use Saturn's discipline to put thoughts into action.

- ✔ **Conjunction:** You're a serious person with a rational mind, a dry sense of humor, and an appreciation for useful knowledge.

- ✔ **Harmonious aspects:** You're well-organized, methodical, reserved, and intelligent, with a natural understanding of how to focus your mind and absorb information.

- ✔ **Hard aspects:** You don't take things lightly, even when you should. Though you're an effective planner, you may also be inflexible, melancholy, and uncomfortable with new ideas.

Mercury/Uranus

Mercury represents the way you think, while Uranus is a lightning rod that attracts inspiration from out of the blue. Depending on how the two interact, they can bring out the brilliant inventor, the mad scientist, or the talkative eccentric from down the street.

- ✔ **Conjunction:** This is the Eureka! aspect — you're a progressive thinker prone to sudden insights and startling ideas. You have an unconventional mind, a novel way of expressing yourself, and even a touch of genius.

- ✔ **Harmonious aspects:** Unusual ideas excite you. Your mind is inventive, unconstrained, and bright, and you express yourself in a lively and original way.

✔ **Hard aspects:** Sometimes brilliant, sometimes just nervous and impatient, you have an erratic mind. You rebel against authority, routine, and convention, and in so doing you create tension and conflict. You also have a spontaneous, ingenious intellect that can take you far.

Mercury/Neptune

Mercury thinks, while Neptune dreams. Mercury can help turn Neptune's fantasies into realities, while Neptune brings insight and flights of fancy to Mercury's ideas.

✔ **Conjunction:** You're a visionary with an inspired imagination, a dreamer sensitive to mood and language, and a multitalented artist and poet who can create a mood through words alone. But when you get obsessed with an idée fixe, you can lose touch with reality.

✔ **Harmonious aspects:** You have a discriminating mind, an artistic imagination, and an imaginative manner of expressing yourself.

✔ **Hard aspects:** Fantasy and reality vie for your attention, and it isn't always clear which one is winning. At your best, you're creative, intuitive, and visionary. But you may also be disorganized and oblivious, with a destructive tendency to see only what you want to see.

Mercury/Pluto

When Pluto, the zodiac's detective, connects with quick-thinking Mercury, the combination gives you a commanding mind and the ability to concentrate.

✔ **Conjunction:** You're analytical, focused, and skilled at digging up secrets. With your penetrating intelligence, you can be a gifted researcher, investigative reporter, or detective. This aspect brings insight and writing ability, along with obsessive thoughts.

✔ **Harmonious aspects:** You're an astute, creative thinker who can dig beneath the surface and who's willing to grapple with important issues.

✔ **Hard aspects:** You're thoughtful, observant, and curious, as well as tense and combative, with a distinct tendency to brood.

Aspects to Venus

Venus symbolizes love, relationships, art, pleasure, possessions, and money.

Venus/Mars

Venus is the planet of allure. Mars stimulates desire. Together they stir up the forces of passion and sensuality.

✔ **Conjunction:** Demonstrative and magnetic, you radiate sexuality, vitality, and charisma. You have no trouble attracting others because people want to be near you. But you like to see sparks fly and may unconsciously create tumultuous relationships.

✔ **Harmonious aspects:** You're attractive, genial, loving, and likely to find romantic fulfillment.

✔ **Hard aspects:** You aren't sure what you want, especially in romantic relationships. As a result, your love life may be troubled by arguments, unhappiness, and tension.

Venus/Jupiter

When amorous Venus meets generous Jupiter in a birth chart, the result is an outpouring of affection, a love of luxury, and an appreciation of art and beauty.

✔ **Conjunction:** This is a lucky aspect. Because you're affectionate and generous, you attract love, friendship, and even money — which is amazing, considering how reckless, undisciplined, and self-indulgent you can be. This aspect also confers artistic ability.

✔ **Harmonious aspects:** This fortunate aspect increases your ability to attract attention, to make money, and to choose the right mate.

✔ **Hard aspects:** You go overboard. You may eat or drink or spend to excess, be unreasonably demanding, or simply blow your feelings out of proportion. One way or another, extravagance is an issue.

Venus/Saturn

Restrictive Saturn inhibits affectionate Venus. This aspect grounds and strengthens your feelings — but also brings suffering and delays in love.

✔ **Conjunction:** Emotionally inhibited and afraid of being hurt, you take yourself too seriously to treat romance in a lighthearted way. You're most comfortable in a relationship with someone older or more established than yourself. Some people with this aspect make love a kind of obsessive pursuit. Whether you do that or not, love is an issue for you. This aspect also enhances creativity by helping you focus (the influence of Saturn) your artistic talents (given by Venus).

✔ **Harmonious aspects:** Both emotionally and financially, you value security over excitement. Responsible and loyal, you seek a solid, enduring relationship — and a well-stocked financial portfolio.

✔ **Hard aspects:** Romance can be a struggle. Defensive and afraid of rejection, you may hide behind a wall of your own creation. Even when you find a fulfilling relationship (and plenty of people with this aspect are happily married), you may feel isolated and may attempt to fill that void by taking on additional responsibilities. Something similar happens with money. In both cases, fear of loss is a motivating factor.

Venus/Uranus

If amorous Venus and unconventional Uranus link up in your birth chart, you're likely to be the impetuous star of your own romantic soap opera.

- ✔ **Conjunction:** This is the lightning-bolt aspect, the one that brings an excitable personality, love at first sight, and a dramatic, often unstable love life. Like Elizabeth Taylor (married eight times) or Warren Beatty (married for the first time at age 55 after decades as Hollywood's number one playboy), you want instant attraction and fireworks all the way.

- ✔ **Harmonious aspects:** In friendship as in romance, you're drawn to people who are exciting and offbeat. You're original, artistically talented, and lucky in love. Plus, you have the enviable (but entirely unpredictable) ability to attract windfalls of cash.

- ✔ **Hard aspects:** Looking for a reliable relationship with an "appropriate" person? I doubt it. You seek the thrill of the forbidden. Out-of-the-blue love is part of your story; sudden betrayal may be another. Among the people in my files with a hard aspect between Venus and Uranus, I find one who had an affair with her sister's spouse, one who ran off with her best friend's husband, one who married her first cousin, and several who defied expectation by marrying someone of another race or nationality.

Venus/Neptune

Venus lives for romance and beauty. Glamorous Neptune encourages mystery, magic, and spiritual feelings. When they're in sync, you can walk on air, but even the conjunction can bring you back down to earth in a hurry.

- ✔ **Conjunction:** Your compassion and vivid imagination can make you an inspired artist, but they can also get you into trouble, especially in romance, because you unconsciously let your desire for love (or enlightenment) cloud your vision. You're a romantic, an idealist, and a spiritual seeker. Your ideal mate shares those inclinations.

- ✔ **Harmonious aspects:** You can be sympathetic, gentle, mystical, musical, refined, and creative. You're also prone to laziness and self-indulgence.

- ✔ **Hard aspects:** Illusion enters your life in a positive way through art, music, and film. You're also prone to starry-eyed infatuation. Being realistic about romance isn't your strength. You fall for Heathcliff every time.

Venus/Pluto

The planet of love meets the planet of obsession. You can guess what happens: Jealousy, intrigue, and passion are the watchwords for this pair.

- ✔ **Conjunction:** You're jealous, possessive, profoundly sexual, and controlling. This aspect also brings artistic and financial ability.

✔ **Harmonious aspects:** Intense but not destructive, you successfully seek to transform yourself through relationships. You attract powerful people, both in love and in business.

✔ **Hard aspects:** Ever been fixated on someone you knew wasn't good for you? I thought so. This aspect brings passion and obsession. Fortunately, it can also make you magnetically attractive.

Aspects to Mars

Mars represents your will, desires, drive, energy, and aggression.

Mars/Jupiter

The "will-do" energy of Mars is a perfect complement to the "can-do" energy of Jupiter. This is an enthusiastic pairing.

✔ **Conjunction:** Why does the most famous astrological song ever written ("Age of Aquarius," by the Fifth Dimension) suggest that we will experience peace and love "when the Moon is in the seventh house and Jupiter aligns with Mars"? Frankly, I'm not sure. I will say this, though: If Jupiter aligns with Mars in your chart, you have energy to burn, an eagerness to explore, a natural sense of timing, and the ability to fulfill your desires in an extravagant way.

✔ **Harmonious aspects:** Setting big goals comes naturally to you. You're adventurous, untiring, optimistic, and stalwart — a great combination.

✔ **Hard aspects:** Restless and extravagant, you have stamina and drive, but moderation, though frequently recommended, isn't your way.

Mars/Saturn

Hot-blooded Mars is the planet of action; somber Saturn is the lord of caution. They don't much like each other, but they can work together.

✔ **Conjunction:** At its best, this aspect brings self-discipline, endurance, and courage. At its worst, it leads to shyness, inhibition, resentment, and destructive behavior.

✔ **Harmonious aspects:** You're ambitious, decisive, industrious, and sensible. You get things done.

✔ **Hard aspects:** Impatience does you in. You feel blocked and frustrated, and it isn't easy for you to regulate your moods. Plus, you feel that you have enemies, and run-ins with authority may be all too common in your life. This can be a difficult aspect (think of River Phoenix), but positive examples abound, including Anderson Cooper, Jane Austen, and Johann Sebastian Bach.

Mars/Uranus

Impatient Mars and unpredictable Uranus: the original bad-boy combination of the zodiac. These two just can't help stirring up trouble.

- ✔ **Conjunction:** You're unrestrained and determined, with unconventional sexual attitudes, unusual desires, and great drive. But your energy is erratic, and you may be accident-prone.

- ✔ **Harmonious aspects:** Nervous and outspoken, you pursue unusual goals, seek the new, and react quickly. But do you use your considerable energy in constructive ways, or do you fritter it away? Luckily, you have the choice.

- ✔ **Hard aspects:** You're a risk-taker and a free spirit whose rebellious ways can disrupt everything around you. At its worst, this aspect stimulates truly ridiculous acting-out behavior; at its creative best, it encourages independence and adventure.

Mars/Neptune

Dreamy Neptune can spend the day in foggy reverie, while heedless Mars takes action (however ill-thought out or ineffective). Fortunately, Mars also fuels Neptune's creative plans.

- ✔ **Conjunction:** Insecure, talented, and sensitive, you have trouble focusing your energy, and you may set goals that are both idealistic and unrealistic. John Lennon had this aspect.

- ✔ **Harmonious aspects:** You're romantic, artistic, and able to direct your dreams and inspirations into action.

- ✔ **Hard aspects:** You're idealistic but easily discouraged, with a tendency to indulge in escapist behavior.

Mars/Pluto

You draw from a deep well of energy and intensity. This aspect brings ambition and endurance — in spades.

- ✔ **Conjunction:** Physically endowed with enormous reserves of energy, you're aggressive, ambitious, and hardworking. You go after what you want with stunning determination. This is a powerful aspect. Example: Hillary Rodham Clinton.

- ✔ **Harmonious aspects:** You have strong likes and dislikes, a solid sense of confidence, and the rare ability to end a relationship or a job without collapsing. You also have the ability to launch a new endeavor with amazing fervor.

> ✔ **Hard aspects:** You have strong passions, but you also have difficulty controlling them and avoiding conflict. Though you tend to sabotage yourself, you have impressive stamina and the ability to eliminate your negative behaviors and achieve what you really want: power.

Aspects to Jupiter

Jupiter represents prosperity, wisdom, abundance, extravagance, and expansion. Its placement in your horoscope tells you where you can expect good luck and opportunity.

Jupiter/Saturn

Expansive Jupiter and restrictive Saturn aren't natural allies. Mix them together, and you get tension — and determination.

> ✔ **Conjunction:** When optimistic Jupiter conjuncts pessimistic Saturn, idealism gets squashed by realism, and frustration is rampant. Your path is littered with obstacles, but your capacity for hard work is breathtaking. This difficult aspect comes around about every 20 years. You may have it in your birth chart if you were born in 1901, 1921, 1940 or 1941, 1961, 1981, or 2000.

> ✔ **Harmonious aspects:** You're sensible, cool-headed, and practical enough to recognize your limitations and to compensate with your strengths. Saturn lends you the ability to turn your most extravagant Jupiter-driven dreams into Saturnian on-the-ground realities. You can make it happen. The best therapists I know have this aspect.

> ✔ **Hard aspects:** A tug of war between the forces of expansion and the forces of restriction keeps you off balance. Restlessness, discontent, bad timing, and tension may plague you. On some deep level, you fear that your judgment is unreliable, and your confidence suffers accordingly. The opposition between Jupiter and Saturn comes around approximately ten years after the conjunction: in 1911, 1930–1931, 1951–1952, 1970–1971, 1989–1990, and 2010.

Jupiter/Uranus

Surprises abound when benevolent Jupiter meets Uranus, the planet of the unexpected. Uranus adds a maverick twist to Jupiter's open-hearted enthusiasm and ability to attract opportunities.

> ✔ **Conjunction:** You're an idealistic person who benefits from taking risks. Somehow, despite your extravagant ways, you're in the right place at the right time. This is the aspect of unusual opportunities and sudden good fortune — but, as with everything that Uranus touches, it may not come in the form you would expect.

- ✔ **Harmonious aspects:** Alert and creative, you have an original mind and you respond to opportunities that are exciting and off-beat.

- ✔ **Hard aspects:** The predetermined path and the required courses are distasteful to you. You make startling choices and may suffer when your impulsive decisions turn out to be less than prudent. You're a natural rebel.

Jupiter/Neptune

Extravagant Jupiter encourages impressionable Neptune to dream big. This aspect enhances imagination, idealism, and spirituality.

- ✔ **Conjunction:** Your spirituality, idealism, and financial well-being benefit from this aspect. But be careful that your friendly, sympathetic attitude doesn't blind you to reality. While you're blessed with a certain amount of sheer good luck, you may suffer from vagueness, self-delusion, and the tendency to zone out.

- ✔ **Harmonious aspects:** You're compassionate, gentle, insightful, creative, and lucky, with an innate attraction to spiritual pursuits.

- ✔ **Hard aspects:** You tend to scatter your efforts, you can be way too gullible, and your refusal to face reality can drive your friends to drink (a substance you should be careful not to abuse). This aspect can bring money and talent, especially of the musical variety. You may also be unrealistically idealistic, and pie-in-the-sky thinking can be a problem.

Jupiter/Pluto

Jupiter brings opportunities and expands whatever it touches — the good and the bad alike. Pluto represents the journey inward and the power of transformation.

- ✔ **Conjunction:** When these two planets are cheek by jowl, you have strong convictions and can become a powerful agent of change. One example: Bill Gates, the founder of Microsoft, who has this conjunction in the third house of communication.

- ✔ **Harmonious aspects:** When times of change roll around, you have the confidence to respond, and you generally benefit. You're well-organized and a powerful leader.

- ✔ **Hard aspects:** You want to change the world. At your best, you bravely confront the most fearsome of Goliaths — and win. But you harbor a secret desire for power, and you can be ruthless, suspicious, self-destructive, and fanatical. This is a powerful aspect that appears in the charts of powerful people.

Aspects to Saturn

Saturn symbolizes limitation, contraction, restriction, and the need for structure. Its placement tells you where you have to face reality, get organized, and go to work.

Saturn/Uranus

Tradition (Saturn) meets innovation (Uranus). Boundaries (Saturn) encounter the forces of liberation (Uranus). Needless to say, things start to pop with this combo.

- ✔ **Conjunction:** You have drive, persistence, leadership potential, and the ability to focus your most original ideas by combining the brilliance of Uranus with the practical realities of Saturn.

- ✔ **Harmonious aspects:** You're determined and decisive, able to blend the seriousness of Saturn with the originality of Uranus. This is an aspect of accomplishment.

- ✔ **Hard aspects:** Compromise is difficult. You can be egotistical, callous, and hypocritical — a real pain in the neck. At your worst, you feel that you have been denied the recognition, status, or material wealth you deserve. At your best you're a reformer, able to apply original (Uranian) ideas to old (Saturnian) problems.

Saturn/Neptune

Practical Saturn follows directions. Dreamy Neptune wanders around in a daze, soaking up impressions and dissolving boundaries. Depending on whether they're working with or against each other, they either strengthen the forces of perception or cause you to become completely unfocused.

- ✔ **Conjunction:** If the two planets are well-matched, you're disciplined, sensible, and creative. If stern Saturn dominates Neptune, you distrust your intuition and squash your creative impulses. If woozy Neptune is dominant, you struggle in your efforts to be neat, organized, and in control.

- ✔ **Harmonious aspects:** Your Neptunian idealism and your Saturnian sense of reality combine forces, giving you the ability to direct your imagination in a practical, real-world way.

- ✔ **Hard aspects:** Emotionally, you hold back. You don't trust people easily, and you have reclusive tendencies. Plus, you have difficulty getting organized. The placement of Saturn in your chart indicates where you need structure. Chances are you know exactly what you should do. The trouble is that, thanks to mysterious Neptune, the planet of illusion, you have trouble doing it.

Saturn/Pluto

Pluto is a potent magician and the planet of deep, slow, internal change; Saturn is the taskmaster of the zodiac and the lord of discipline. When they link up in your chart, your ability to transform yourself is deepened.

- ✔ **Conjunction:** Pluto is all about transformation, but cautious Saturn, which isn't comfortable with change, restricts its action, creating compulsive behavior, hard-to-break habits, and a mother lode of resistance. To get around this intense, sometimes frustrating aspect, you need a systematic approach to problem-solving, a healthy dose of self-discipline, and an acceptance of the fact that although change may be glacial in its speed, glaciers nonetheless reshaped the world.

- ✔ **Harmonious aspects:** A trine or sextile linking Saturn and Pluto strengthens your willpower, sense of control, and confidence.

- ✔ **Hard aspects:** Obsessive thoughts or compulsive behavior may keep you in their nasty grip until you find a way to lessen their power. Although obstacles may block your way, you have the will to overcome them.

Aspects to Uranus, Neptune, and Pluto

Uranus represents individuality, eccentricity, upheaval, revolution, and the unpredictable. Neptune symbolizes the imagination, spiritual strivings, dreams, visions, and delusion. Pluto represents obsession, compulsion, death, rebirth, and transformation.

Uranus, Neptune, and Pluto, the three outer planets, travel through the zodiac so slowly that their greatest influence is on generations, not on individuals. The aspects that they form are in orb for a long time. A conjunction between any two of them, for example, lasts for years. So the mere fact of having such an aspect doesn't distinguish you. It merely makes you a member of your generation, with all the pluses and minuses that implies.

Under certain circumstances, an aspect involving the outer planets may rise to prominence in the chart of an individual. That happens when:

- ✔ Either of the planets occupies an angle or is conjunct your Ascendant or Midheaven.

- ✔ Either body makes several close aspects to other planets and in particular to the Sun, the Moon, or the ruler of your Ascendant.

- ✔ Either planet rules your Sun sign, Moon sign, or rising sign.

    Uranus governs Aquarius, Neptune presides over Pisces, and Pluto rules Scorpio.

Uranus/Neptune

Uranus, the planet of revolution, and mystical Neptune, the planet of dreams and visions, inspire you and bring you insight.

- ✔ **Conjunction:** In 1992 and 1993, Uranus and Neptune were exactly conjunct for the first time since 1821 — a trick they won't repeat until around 2163. Anyone born with this aspect is likely to have an inventive approach to social change and a nervous disposition.

- ✔ **Harmonious aspects:** If you have a trine or a sextile between Neptune and Uranus, you belong to a generation that's compassionate, utopian, and spiritually inclined.

- ✔ **Hard aspects:** You're emotional, eccentric, and totally original, especially if either planet touches a third in a significant way.

Uranus/Pluto

Unconventional Uranus and heavy-duty Pluto collaborate to promote major, sometimes revolutionary, changes.

- ✔ **Conjunction:** Ever wonder why the 1960s were so turbulent? Here's why: For the first time in 115 years, Uranus, the planet of revolution and eccentricity, was conjunct Pluto, the planet of transformation. Transiting planets affect everyone — not just babies born under their influence. If you were born during that decade — if you're a true child of the '60s — you're independent and willful, and you carry that Woodstockian sense of creative rebellion within you.

- ✔ **Harmonious aspects:** Trines and sextiles between freedom-loving Uranus and Pluto bring disruptive changes but allow you to use the energy that's released in creative ways.

- ✔ **Hard aspects:** When lightning strikes, you try to suppress your natural reactions, thereby creating, on top of everything else, an extra measure of anxiety. It's not just you: This is a generational influence. Like everyone else in your generation, you were born during America's Great Depression, and you've seen it all.

Neptune/Pluto

Visionary Neptune, monarch of the imagination, responds to dreams, music, poetry, mysticism, and the unseen. Powerful Pluto, lord of the underworld, plumbs the depths of the forbidden. Together, they make a mighty combo and inspire a heroic quest.

- ✔ **Conjunction:** This rare conjunction, which rolled around the last time in 1892 and will not reappear until the 24th century, combines Neptunian spirituality with the Plutonian drive for power and understanding. Examples: Paramahansa Yogananda, author of *Autobiography of a Yogi,* and J. R. R. Tolkien, author of *The Lord of the Rings.*

✔ **Harmonious aspects:** Since around 1928, Neptune and Pluto have been roughly sextile, an aspect that links the mystical yearnings of Neptune with the transformative urge of Pluto, creating an upsurge of interest in spirituality and the occult.

✔ **Hard aspects:** An unusual concern with sexuality or the supernatural can arise from the blocked energy of this charged aspect. Obsession is likely — but the direction of that obsession depends on the individual. Two examples, born a week apart, are Queen Victoria, who lent her name to an era known for its repressive ways, and Walt Whitman, whose poetry is suffused with joyous sexuality and uninhibited love.

Chapter 14

A Guide to Interpreting Your Birth Chart

Most astrologers agree that Sun sign astrology, which describes types rather than individuals, is insufficient for most purposes. But Sun sign astrology can claim one advantage: It's simple. A full astrological chart, on the other hand, with its web of planets, signs, houses, and aspects, is as complex as an actual human being — and just as difficult to understand.

Fortunately, you don't have to be psychic to be an astrologer. But you do need a system, especially when you're starting out. This chapter provides such a system.

Step One: Finding Overall Patterns

Leaf through a pile of birth charts, and you may notice that in some the planets are huddled together in one part of the circle, while in others they're scattered around the wheel like numbers on a clock. These groupings, which have nothing to do with the specific planets and signs involved, can be amazingly revealing. Astrologers have developed two main ways of assessing the configurations of an astrological chart:

> ✔ **Hemisphere analysis:** So easy that a child can do it, this method divides the chart circle in half both horizontally and vertically and counts the number of planets on each side.

> ✔ **Pattern analysis:** This method, pioneered by astrologer Marc Edmund Jones in his *Guide to Horoscope Interpretation,* analyzes the way the planets are strewn around the wheel of the horoscope.

Both methods rely only on patterns, not on specific signs and planets.

Hemisphere analysis

A quick glance at your horoscope provides an easy entry into interpretation — and all you have to do is count. First locate the *horizon line* in your chart — the line running from the Ascendant to the Descendant, as shown in Figure 14-1. (Turn to Chapter 11 for more on your Ascendant and Descendant.) If a large majority of your planets — seven or more — are above the horizon, you're an extrovert who looks to the external world for recognition and endorsement. If most of your planets populate the area below the line, you're an introvert who needs privacy, seeks personal fulfillment, and may be uncomfortable in public life.

Now divide your chart in half vertically or along the *meridian,* which runs from your Midheaven, or M.C., at the twelve o'clock spot on your chart to your I.C. at the six o'clock spot (see Figure 14-1). That line splits the horoscope into two sectors: the eastern hemisphere on the left and the western hemisphere on the right. If most of your planets lie on the eastern or left side of the horoscope, you have the enviable ability to make things happen, to create your own opportunities. You're highly independent, but you may also be intolerant of people who can't seem to call the shots the way you can.

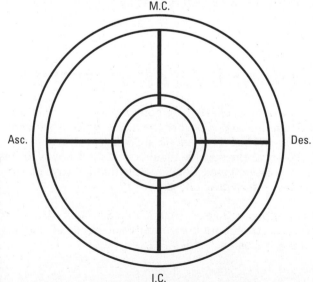

Figure 14-1: Dividing your chart by the horizon and the meridian.

If your chart leans to the right, so to speak, with seven or more planets on the western or right side of the circle, you're more dependent on circumstances. You need to grab the moment when it comes, and you may feel that you must bend to the demands of others in order to succeed. Most people, including the greatest of the great, have planets on both sides of the meridian.

The Ascendant symbolizes your surface personality. The Descendant represents your approach to marriage and partnerships. The Midheaven, or M.C., depicts your ambition and public image. The imum coeli, or I.C., indicates your attitude toward home and family.

Pattern analysis

In 1941, astrologer Marc Edmund Jones (a Libran) identified seven planetary patterns which, like hemispheric division, operate without regard to specific signs and planets. Ever since then, students of astrology have been exploring the meaning of those patterns. Here they are:

> ✔ **The bundle:** If all your planets are concentrated within four signs or 120° (a *trine*), you have a bundle chart, regardless of which signs are involved or where on the wheel that bundle of planets happens to fall. This pattern, shown in Figure 14-2, grants you a clear focus, unwavering interests, confidence, and personal strength. It also limits you: You're strong where you're strong and thoroughly unconscious (or uninterested) where you aren't. George W. Bush is an example.

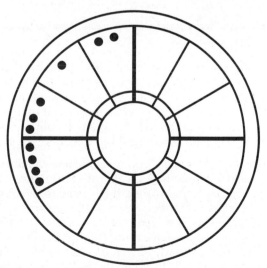

Figure 14-2:
The bundle
pattern.

Two singleton sensations

Whenever you find a birth chart with a true singleton — that is, a bucket chart with one planet sitting apart from all the others — you have found a key to the person. Consider these examples from my files:

✔ **Lulu (not her real name), the hostess with the mostest.** With three planets in charismatic Leo, she attracts people wherever she goes, throws the best dinner parties I've ever been invited to, and looks like the queen of confidence. She's also one of the most successful, compassionate women I know. But she has been married and divorced several times, has had more boyfriends than the rest of my friends combined, and is obsessed with relationships. Why? She has a bucket chart with nine planets on the eastern side balanced by the emotional, security-seeking Moon on the other. Thanks to the nine planets, she's active and autonomous, a real doer. But with the Moon smack in the middle of her seventh house of partnership, her emotional

well-being revolves around relationships. That's what the location of the singleton indicates: The focus of a life.

✔ **Dr. X (not his real name), the most entertaining psychiatrist I know.** His warm personality comes from his Leo Ascendant. His interest in psychiatry clearly comes from his singleton Moon which, like Dr. Freud's Moon, is in the eighth house of intimacy, secrets, psychoanalysis, regeneration (or healing), and occult knowledge. In his work as a therapist, Dr. X is a master at creating an easy intimacy with his patients that allows him to unearth their secrets. In his private life, the Moon spurs him on to explore areas most doctors won't admit even thinking about — areas such as psychic awareness, palmistry (his palm was read for the first time when he was 5 years old), astrology (that's how we became friends), and all manner of spiritual techniques. Once again, the singleton planet is the key.

✔ **The bowl:** If your planets cover more than 120° but no more than 180° (or half the zodiac), you have a bowl chart, as shown in Figure 14-3. This highly motivating pattern can create a frustrating feeling that something is missing, combined with a steely determination to fill that void. These people are activists. Examples include Abraham Lincoln, Vincent van Gogh, Amelia Earhart, Donald Trump, and Billie Jean King.

✔ **The bucket:** A bucket chart is like a bowl except that one planet (or sometimes two in close conjunction) is separated from the rest, as Figure 14-4 shows. That singleton planet, the handle of the bucket, becomes the focus of the chart. Because its needs are always paramount, Marc Edmund Jones compared that lone planet to a toothache. It demands attention — and sometimes it hurts. That's because its role is essentially to balance the rest of the chart. Its importance is so extreme that, both by sign and by house, it frequently describes a person in an uncanny way.

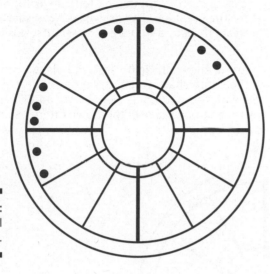

Figure 14-3:
The bowl
pattern.

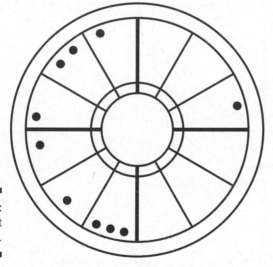

Figure 14-4:
The bucket
pattern.

✔ **The locomotive:** If the ten planets in your chart line up neatly over two-thirds of the zodiac, as shown in Figure 14-5, you've got drive, stamina, and practicality. The two most important planets are the first and the last — the locomotive, which leads the planetary parade when the chart is rotated in a clockwise direction, and the caboose, which picks up the rear.

✔ **The splash:** Just like it sounds, the planets in this pattern are sprinkled more or less evenly around the entire wheel, with blank spots here and there only because there are ten planets and 12 signs. Figure 14-6 shows

an example of the splash pattern. With this pattern, a wealth of life experience is yours for the grabbing. The drawback? You scatter your energy and your interests the way a fruit tree scatters its blossoms on a windy day.

✔ **The splay:** In this pattern, shown in Figure 14-7, the planets are distributed unevenly over the entire chart, with at least one clump of three or more planets. People with this pattern — like Al Gore and Fidel Castro — are individualistic, with a strong sense of their own interests and a refusal to bow to public opinion.

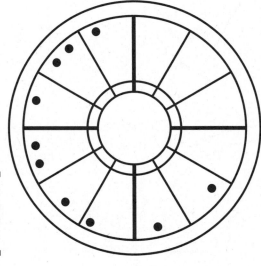

Figure 14-5:
The
locomotive
pattern.

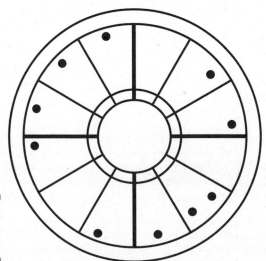

Figure 14-6:
The splash
pattern.

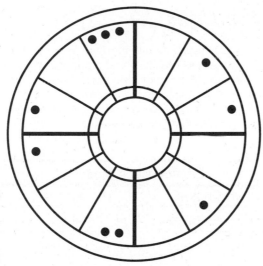

Figure 14-7:
The splay
pattern.

✔ **The seesaw:** If you have two groups of opposing planets separated by a couple of empty houses on each side, as shown in Figure 14-8, you're always riding up and down on the seesaw of circumstance and experience. An excellent mediator, judge, and administrator, you can view things objectively because you're supremely aware of the two sides of your own nature. You may also feel internally split because you have two sets of needs and two sets of talents, and you may find it difficult to satisfy both. Examples include writer Dave Eggers and performers Frank Sinatra, Mariah Carey, and Queen Latifah.

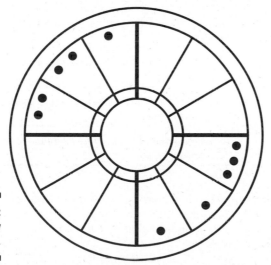

Figure 14-8:
The seesaw
pattern.

Considering the signs

After mulling over the large patterns of hemispheric division and overall design in your chart, you're ready to assess the signs and planets according to element and mode. Begin by counting the planets in each *element* (fire, earth, air, and water) and in each *mode* (cardinal, fixed, and mutable). Table 14-1 shows you which is which. If you know the time of your birth, include your Ascendant and Midheaven for a total of 12 distinct components.

Table 14-1		Elements and Modes		
	Fire	*Earth*	*Air*	*Water*
Cardinal	Aries	Capricorn	Libra	Cancer
Fixed	Leo	Taurus	Aquarius	Scorpio
Mutable	Sagittarius	Virgo	Gemini	Pisces

Most people are more or less balanced, with two to four planets in each element. If you have five or more planets in signs of one element (or quality), the traits associated with that element or quality are emphasized. Check out Table 14-2 for explanations of what such an abundance may mean for you.

Table 14-2	Emphasis by Element
With a Preponderance of Planets in . . .	**You Are . . .**
Fire signs	Active, adventurous, spirited, assertive, a natural leader
Earth signs	Practical, sensual, stable, prudent, hard-working, security-minded
Air signs	Communicative, intellectual, sociable, fueled by ideas and conversation
Water signs	Sensitive, impassioned, impressionable, compassionate, and insightful

When classifying the components of a chart, keep in mind that the Sun, Moon, and Ascendant are more influential than the other placements and therefore deserve extra weight. Some astrologers even count them twice, just to make sure they get their due.

The modes (or qualities) work the same way as the elements. Most people have a rough balance. But if you have a pileup of planets in one particular mode, those traits are emphasized. Table 14-3 tells you more.

Table 14-3	Emphasis by Mode
With a Preponderance of Planets in . . .	*You Are . . .*
Cardinal signs	Action-oriented, brave, willing to take the initiative
Fixed signs	Unyielding, determined, focused, opposed to change
Mutable signs	Flexible, adaptable, and open to change

Planets in houses: A minor point

By assuming parallels between the houses and the signs, so that the first house is equivalent to Aries, the second house to Taurus, and so on, you can classify the houses in revealing ways, as in Table 14-4. To consider your chart in this way, count how many planets you have in each trio of houses.

For an example, turn to Chapter 13 and take a look at Oprah Winfrey's chart. With three planets in the second house, one in the sixth house, and two in the tenth, a majority of her planets are in the houses of substance, which might help explain how an idealistic Aquarian got to be one of the richest women on the planet.

Table 14-4	House Classifications	
Houses	*Group Name*	*Characteristics*
1, 5, and 9	Houses of Life (fire houses)	Fiery; dynamic; motivated to enjoy life and to squeeze as much juice as possible out of experience
2, 6, and 10	Houses of Substance (earth houses)	Practical; fond of systems and methods; motivated to seek security and recognition
3, 7, and 11	Houses of Relationship (air houses)	Communicative; other-oriented; motivated to create fulfilling relationships of all sorts
4, 8, and 12	Houses of Emotion (water houses)	Emotional; responsive; discerning; motivated to explore family connections and the past

Although the house divisions from Table 14-4 don't endow you with the same abilities and characteristics that the signs possess, they direct your interests in ways that can balance an otherwise out-of-whack chart.

For example, a person who has no planets in earth signs lacks practical abilities (and will have to struggle to make up for that lack). The presence of planets in the second, sixth, and tenth houses can counteract that inability by providing motivation. Such placements can't turn an aspiring poet into an accountant with an investment portfolio and a 401(k). But they can stimulate the poet to find some form of security (from planets in the second house), to get organized (from planets in the sixth house), and to seek public recognition (from planets in the tenth house).

You can also find parallels between the houses and the qualities, or modes, as outlined in Table 14-5.

Table 14-5	House Qualities	
Houses	**Group Name**	**Characteristics**
1, 4, 7, and 10	Angular (cardinal) Houses	Enterprising, active
2, 5, 8, and 11	Succedent (fixed) Houses	Stable, determined
3, 6, 9, and 12	Cadent (mutable) Houses	Thoughtful, flexible

Astrologers traditionally view the angular houses (particularly the first and the tenth) as the strongest, while cadent houses (especially the sixth and the twelfth) are thought to be the weakest. As someone with many cadent planets, I always found that analysis discouraging until I learned about Michel Gauquelin, a French scientist who found statistical significance in certain planetary placements. Gauquelin noted the following trends:

✔ Aggressive Mars is often prominent in the horoscopes of successful athletes.

✔ The Moon, ruler of mood and instinct, plays an important role in writers' horoscopes.

✔ Somber Saturn, the lord of structure and consistency, is conspicuous in the charts of scientists.

✔ Jovial Jupiter, the planet of extravagance, is prominent in the horoscopes of actors.

These planets were often located in areas of the horoscope sometimes known as the *Gauquelin zones.* Those areas of power include large portions of the cadent houses, with the twelfth and the ninth ranking as the most important. Despite traditional astrology, which states otherwise, cadent planets aren't necessarily weak at all.

Step Two: Five Main Components of a Birth Chart

After looking at the overall patterns of your chart, you're ready to check out the specific signs and planets. To get a sense of your chart without drowning in detail, concentrate on these factors:

- **The Sun:** The Sun determines your basic identity — your motivations, needs, will, and individuality. Its sign describes the way you express these important aspects of yourself. Its house determines the area of greatest concern to you as well as the area in which you can most effectively express yourself.

- **The Moon:** The Moon describes your emotions, subconscious, instincts, habits, and memory. The sign it's in determines the way you experience the emotional side of your nature. Its placement by house points to the area of life that's most essential to your emotional well-being.

- **The rising sign or Ascendant:** The Ascendant describes the surface level of your personality — the face you show the world. (See Chapter 11 for more about rising signs.)

- **The ruling planet:** The planet that rules your Ascendant is the ruler of your chart, regardless of its location and regardless of anything else happening in your horoscope. As the ruler, it contributes both to your sense of self and to the impression you give others. Table 14-6 shows you the rising signs and their ruling planets. Turn to Chapter 9 or 10 for more insight into your ruling planet.

Table 14-6	Rising Signs and Rulerships	
If Your Rising Sign Is . . .	*You Strike People as . . .*	*And Your Ruling Planet Is . . .*
Aries	Impetuous, strong-willed	Mars
Taurus	Stable, sensuous	Venus
Gemini	Verbal, high-strung	Mercury
Cancer	Emotional, responsive	Moon
Leo	Confident, exuberant	Sun
Virgo	Methodical, discerning	Mercury
Libra	Charming, appealing	Venus
Scorpio	Controlled, reserved	Pluto and/or Mars
Sagittarius	Cosmopolitan, irrepressible	Jupiter

(continued)

Table 14-6 (continued)

If Your Rising Sign Is ...	You Strike People as ...	And Your Ruling Planet Is ...
Capricorn	Respectable, proud	Saturn
Aquarius	Friendly, individualistic	Uranus and/or Saturn
Pisces	Idealistic, receptive	Neptune and/or Jupiter

One of the most revealing qualities of the ruling planet is its position by house. For instance, Jay Leno is Aquarius rising (which may explain his bizarre hair as well as his love of machinery); his ruling planet, Uranus, is in the fifth house of entertainment. Courtney Love has Libra rising. Her ruling planet, Venus (of course), is in the eighth house of sex and death. Winona Ryder has Sagittarius rising; her ruling planet is Jupiter, which can be found hiding out in her twelfth house of self-undoing. And so it goes. Now, don't get me wrong: This quick and dirty method doesn't always work in such a blatant way. But it does provide a clue to the understanding of a chart, and its message shouldn't be ignored. No matter what your ruling planet is, its house position has an influence on you. Table 14-7 tells how this important factor affects you.

Table 14-7 **Ruling Planet by House Position**

If Your Ruling Planet Is in the ...	You Are ...
First house	A personality and a self-starter
Second house	A money-maker; someone for whom values are primary
Third house	A communicator and a gossip
Fourth house	A family member and a homemaker
Fifth house	A romantic; an entertainer; a devoted parent
Sixth house	A workaholic; a worrier; a perfectionist
Seventh house	A confidante and a companion
Eighth house	An observer and a questioner
Ninth house	An explorer and a thinker
Tenth house	An achiever and a prominent person
Eleventh house	A friend and a joiner
Twelfth house	A spiritual seeker and a hermit

✔ **Stelliums:** A cluster of three or more planets in the same sign, and preferably in the same house, is known as a *stellium* (or, in England, a *satellitium*). Such a grouping is automatically important. When it appears in the same sign as the Sun, it reinforces the message of that sign. When it shows up in another sign, it adds an extra set of qualities and influences that can rival the Sun sign in importance.

The size of the stellium also makes a difference. Normally, a stellium consists of three or four planets. Seldom do you see more. But occasional planetary pileups produce monstrous stelliums, as in the case of the TV cook Rachael Ray (who has seven planets plus the Ascendant in Virgo) or the actress Jennifer Jason Leigh, whose extraordinary birth chart features seven planets, including the Sun and the Moon, in Aquarius. The scary intensity she portrays in her acting comes directly from the power of that stellium.

Step Three: Looking for Aspect Patterns

A birth chart can easily have two dozen aspects in it. Fortunately, some are more important than others. The aspects that deserve the closest attention are those that are the tightest, those that involve the Sun or the Moon, and those that weave three or more planets into a single pattern, as in these configurations:

✔ **The Grand Trine:** Three planets, each at a 120° angle to the other two, form a giant good-luck triangle called a *Grand Trine,* shown in Figure 14-9.

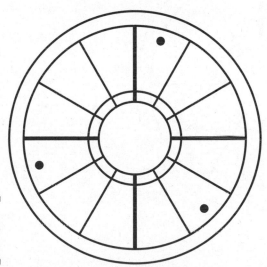

Figure 14-9:
A Grand
Trine.

A perfect Grand Trine always includes at least one planet in each sign of a given element. In those areas of life, energy flows and opportunities are abundant. For example, pop artist Andy Warhol was an attention-grabbing Leo with a Grand Trine in fire: His Moon and Uranus were in Aries, his Sun was in Leo, and his Saturn was in Sagittarius. Like most people, Andy Warhol had other areas in his chart that offered plenty of difficulties. But he used his Grand Trine to his advantage, both artistically (thanks to Saturn in the fifth house of creativity) and socially (thanks to his high-spirited Sun sign). You can take a look at his chart in Chapter 19.

Not everyone fortunate enough to have this aspect uses it so effectively. The Grand Trine, a symbol of the slacker, is notorious for bringing just enough good luck to keep you from feeling that you have to exert yourself.

✔ **The Grand Cross:** If two sets of planets in your chart oppose (or *square*) each other, as shown in Figure 14-10, you have your hands full. The *Grand Cross* is a relatively rare aspect that symbolizes tension, obstruction, and frustration.

Some people are overwhelmed by a Grand Cross. Think of Nicole Brown Simpson, O.J. Simpson's murdered wife, whose chart was positively overflowing with squares. But the Grand Cross can also be a source of incredible commitment, courage, and energy — as in the charts of Miles Davis, Stonewall Jackson, and Douglas Adams, author of *The Hitchhiker's Guide to the Galaxy*.

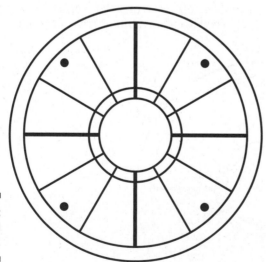

Figure 14-10:
A Grand
Cross.

✓ **The T-square:** When two planets oppose each other with a third planet square to both, as shown in Figure 14-11, they form a *T-square* — a restless, troublesome, but fairly common configuration. A T-square inevitably creates tension and dissatisfaction. It also motivates you to do something about your situation, which may be why so many successful people have T-square configurations. Oprah is one of them. Turn to her chart in Chapter 13. You'll see a classic T-square involving four planets: Pluto in Leo, Saturn in Scorpio, and the Sun and Venus in Aquarius.

✓ **The Yod, Finger of Fate, or Hand of God:** Sounds serious, doesn't it? Actually, this difficult-to-spot configuration, shown in Figure 14-12, is subtler in action than the other aspect patterns. It looks like a long, narrow triangle, with two planets at its base forming a *sextile* (a 60° angle) and a third at the *apex,* or peak, forming a 150° angle to the other two.

That 150° aspect, also called a *quincunx* or *inconjunct,* has a stop-and-go energy that creates false starts, backslides, and frustrations. It demands continual adjustment and impairs your decision-making abilities, especially in the areas affected by the planet at the apex. This aspect sets up complex dynamics within a chart. But is it lethal? No. Is it a sign of special favor from God? No. Do plenty of successful people have this aspect? Yes. (Try Meryl Streep, Winston Churchill, Quincy Jones, and Leonardo da Vinci.) Don't let the name of this aspect unhinge you.

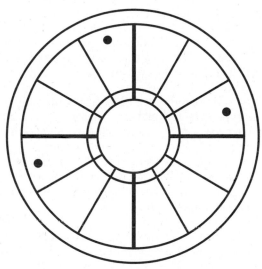

Figure 14-11:
A T-Square.

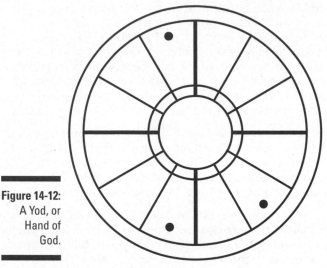

Figure 14-12:
A Yod, or
Hand of
God.

Step Four: Putting the Puzzle Together

Before you reach any wild conclusions about a chart (especially your own), make sure you've looked at everything, including the planets, the aspects, the Ascendant and Midheaven, the houses (including the ones that are empty), and anything else you can think of. For example, if asteroids interest you, by all means check them out. One of the most fascinating parts of astrology is that there's always something new to look at in a chart.

And yet you may discover that the more you delve into your chart, the more the information seems to repeat itself. You'll also unearth a few contradictions: Everyone has them in their charts, just as everyone has them in their psyches. You'll also find the occasional placement or aspect that doesn't gel with the rest of the horoscope or that simply doesn't fit the person in front of you. (Don't toss it out too quickly, especially if you're completing a chart for a friend or acquaintance. Your discomfort could be an indication that you don't know this person half as well as you think you do.)

After you weigh all these factors, you'll notice that certain characteristics seem to pop up everywhere. It's amazing how in every chart, a few themes wind their way through the entire chart. No matter where you begin — with the hemisphere balance or the element countdown, with the Sun sign or with that peculiar stellium in the fifth house — the same theme keeps coming around again and again. And the entire chart starts to click into place. That's when you know you're becoming an astrologer.

Part IV
Using Astrology Right Now

The 5th Wave
By Rich Tennant

APPLIANCE ASTROLOGY

"You can bake and grind nuts, but I'd stay away from pureeing and don't even go near your panini grill until after June 15th."

In this part . . .

*P*roviding insight into your personality isn't the only
application of astrology. It can also help you understand your relationships, give you a sense of the large patterns of your life, and show you how to time your actions
for maximum benefit. In this part, I discuss all that. I also
talk about one of the great astrological bug-a-bears of all
time: Retrograde Mercury, which has a nasty reputation
for turning ordinary activities into adventures in chaos.
I tell you how to take advantage of this much maligned
transit. That's what this part of the book is about: The
here-and-now practical application of astrology.

Chapter 15

The Sun Sign Combinations

A strology does not judge. All 12 signs are equally worthy. That's the official line. In reality, everyone has preferences. Peering out from within the confines of your own horoscope, you can't help feeling that some signs are easier to get along with than others. In this chapter, I talk about the Sun sign combinations — the ones that feel natural from day one, and the ones that make you crazy. "How do I love thee?" There are 78 ways — one for each pair of Sun signs.

In the pages that follow, I talk about each combination under the sign that comes first in the zodiac. If you're a fiery Aries and your beloved is a peace-loving Libra, turn to Aries for a description of the dynamics of your relationship. And if you're a sentimental Pisces involved with a workaholic Virgo, look up your relationship under that sign. Since Pisces is the last sign in the zodiac, every relationship you have (except for one with a fellow fish) is classified under the other sign. It may not be fair. But that's the way it is.

Aries in Love

Lusty and exuberant, you're passionate, idealistic, and devoted, especially when you're in love. You're also impatient, and you don't like to feel hemmed in. Lovers who try to control your behavior quickly lose favor with you, as do friends who call too often or demand too much intimacy. Here's how you do with other signs of the zodiac:

> ✔ **Aries + Aries:** Think of chili peppers, saxophones, and volcanoes — everything hot. This fast-moving, action-oriented, competitive combo leads to fireworks — both when you want them and when you don't. Example: Matthew Broderick and Sarah Jessica Parker.

- **Aries + Taurus:** The impetuous Ram is feisty, motivated, and hot-to-trot; the steady, stubborn, seductive Bull is unhurried and immovable. As with all next-door-neighbor combinations, the differences in style and tempo can drive you crazy. Example: Spencer Tracy (Aries) and Katharine Hepburn (Taurus).

- **Aries + Gemini:** You're both high-spirited and easily bored, with a million interests and a love for activities of all sorts. Aries is straightforward and physical, while inconstant Gemini lives in his or her head. Nonetheless, this is a terrific combo. Example: Warren Beatty (Aries) and Annette Bening (Gemini).

- **Aries + Cancer:** You're both dynamic and expressive. Cancer is sensitive and fearful, while hot-tempered Aries is dominating, spontaneous, and courageous. But Aries isn't tuned in emotionally — to the continual frustration of the moody, intuitive Crab.

- **Aries + Leo:** Two fire signs together generate a lot of warmth. Except for occasional outbursts of ego by either party, it doesn't get any better than this merry, high-spirited match. Example: Jennifer Garner (Aries) and Ben Affleck (Leo).

- **Aries + Virgo:** The rambunctious Ram prefers to leap first and look later; the inhibited Virgin wants to mull things over. Aries says it like it is, direct and to the point; analytical Virgo thinks before speaking and tries to be sensitive (but often fails). Both signs have legitimate complaints about the other. Example: Tabitha (Aries) and Stephen King (Virgo).

- **Aries + Libra:** Opposites attract in this combo. Aries brings impassioned energy, curiosity, and enthusiasm to the mix; Libra adds intelligence, courtesy, and charm. Even though the differences between you aren't to be dismissed — Aries is spontaneous and direct while Libra is thoughtful and restrained — this is nonetheless a recipe for romance.

- **Aries + Scorpio:** Sexually, this combo is off the charts. But dashing Aries is straightforward, while jealous Scorpio is anything but. As a rule, this pairing is asking for trouble.

- **Aries + Sagittarius:** Two fire signs egging each other on makes for a classic high-energy, good-time combo, assuming that you don't burn yourselves out. Even though the fights may be fierce, laughter gets you through — unless it doesn't, in which case neither of you has the patience to patch things up.

- **Aries + Capricorn:** The Goat initially gets off on the adventure of being with such a reckless, blustery creature. But Capricorns are relentlessly grown-up, and Rams are perpetual adolescents overflowing with gusto and half-baked plans. Most of the time, the thrill fades.

- **Aries + Aquarius:** Although these two signs are sextile, this isn't as happy a duo as you might expect. Visionary Aquarius is thinking about the future; Aries is brash, bold, and be-here-now. A strong Venus/Mars tie can be a big help.

✔ **Aries + Pisces:** The fluid, sympathetic Fish can tame the dominating Ram for a while. But what happens at the inevitable moment when emotional Pisces needs a little nurturing? The Ram is on the lam. Protect yourself, Pisces. Look elsewhere.

If you're in love with an Aries, don't be shy, subtle, or hesitant. Flirt boldly. Suggest something casual and spur-of-the-moment. Leave no doubt in Aries' mind that you're interested. If your efforts fall flat, pull back instantly and try being unavailable. Above all, don't beg, plead, or whine. Aries has no patience for small-time behavior or any form of neediness.

Taurus in Love

Possessive, faithful, and not always as mellow as you'd like to be, you require physical contact, emotional and financial security, and domestic comfort. Once you find someone who shares your sensuality and basic values, you're content. You can happily while away your time just being together, doing nothing. Troubles arise when your partner wants a change of pace. Inevitably, you resist. You're the immovable object. Learn to bend.

✔ **Taurus + Taurus:** Assuming one of you has the gumption to make the first move, this could be a long-term love-in. But when disagreements emerge, you lock horns. You'll encounter big passion and big fights, but this combo is a definite go.

✔ **Taurus + Gemini:** Effervescent Gemini loosens up the stolid Bull. Gemini loves change and jumps into it without hesitation, while conservative Taurus is uncomfortable with change and tries to avoid it. As always, neighboring signs can be problematic. Check for Mercury, Venus, or the Moon in each other's signs.

✔ **Taurus + Cancer:** Welcome home. Taurus is sensual, loving, and security-minded; Cancer is intuitive, nurturing, and security-minded. A perfect, harmonious match.

✔ **Taurus + Leo:** Reliable Taurus wants to have a normal life, a regular bedtime, and a growing bank account. Demanding Leo wants to live large. And neither of you gives an inch.

✔ **Taurus + Virgo:** You both value practical solutions, even if sensible Taurus takes longer to get there than efficient Virgo. In addition to sharing values, comfort-loving Taurus calms Virgo's frazzled nerves, while goal-oriented Virgo prods Taurus into action. A fine combination.

✔ **Taurus + Libra:** You're both ruled by sexy Venus, yet what a difference there is between you! Intellectual Libra values refinement, music, soft lighting; earthy Taurus wants to skip the preliminaries and get to it. When the thrill of the moment fades, you have little to say to each other.

✔ **Taurus + Scorpio:** Passion's playground. Scorpio bubbles over with erotic ideas; Taurus goes along. Scorpio's love of secrecy, melodrama, and control receives a cooler welcome from the Bull, who moves slowly and is considerably more upfront. When troubles arise, you're equally stubborn. Example: Jessica Lange (Taurus) and Sam Shepard (Scorpio).

✔ **Taurus + Sagittarius:** Sexually, you're a match, at least for a while. Otherwise, you're so different it's astonishing that you ever got together at all. Sagittarius collects frequent-flyer miles, wants more than the usual amount of personal space, and hungers for stimulation; Taurus gardens, needs loads of cuddling (and a cozy den), and loves to stay home, making this a difficult combo.

✔ **Taurus + Capricorn:** A fine match you've got here. You have similar values, an appreciation for physical comfort, a desire for financial prosperity, a shared work ethic, and a frequently reinforced belief in the healing power of sex. Example: Coretta Scott King (Taurus) and Martin Luther King, Jr. (Capricorn).

✔ **Taurus + Aquarius:** Airy, eccentric Aquarius is all about ideas; conservative, stable Taurus is rooted in the real world. Both are rigid. This isn't a good long-term prospect, despite the notable example of Alice B. Toklas (Taurus) and Gertrude Stein (Aquarius). (For more about this couple, flip to the sidebar "Incompatible? You be the judge.")

✔ **Taurus + Pisces:** Earthy Taurus is essentially physical; dreamy Pisces is metaphysical. Yet these two share similar rhythms, tastes, and romantic notions. Examples: Sid Vicious (Taurus) and Nancy Spungen (Pisces), Robert (Taurus) and Elizabeth Barrett Browning (Pisces).

Head over heels for a Taurus? Hang around. Be patient. Avoid arguments. Reveal no deep-seated neuroses. And give Taurus a chance to feel comfortable. Security is essential for Taurus. To give your Bull a safe haven, provide rich food, soft touches, lazy afternoons, good wine, leisurely walks in the woods, and every reason to feel relaxed. Taurus responds to scent and texture, so wear silk, velvet, cashmere, tweed — anything touchable. That's where Taurus lives.

Gemini in Love

Wanton Gemini, the last living proponent of casual sex, flirts outrageously, connects easily, and moves on at warp speed when things fall apart. Because you love variety and relish intellectual challenges, you seek out witty, up-to-date people who share your delight in easy banter and constant stimulation. You're lively, enchanting, and flighty — yet another victim of the grass-is-always-greener myth.

- **Gemini + Gemini:** Despite the overall level of nervous energy that you generate together, you amuse and engage one another. And you never have to deal with those bleak silences that descend on the relationships of others. This is a definite talk-fest.

- **Gemini + Cancer:** Easily distracted Twins are emotional lightweights, capable of denying their feelings for years on end; moody Crabs, Olympic gold-medal champions of the weeping event, want to connect emotionally, preferably at home. Look for strong planetary ties because this is ordinarily not a match made in heaven. Example: Wallis Simpson (Gemini) and Edward VIII (Cancer).

- **Gemini + Leo:** These two playful revelers truly enjoy each other. But they may unconsciously compete for center stage, which Leo requires and Gemini, an incessant talker, hates to relinquish. Also, Leo is loyal to a fault, while Gemini . . . well, consider this example: John F. Kennedy (Gemini) and Jacqueline Kennedy (Leo).

- **Gemini + Virgo:** Smart and tart, you click immediately and you can't stop talking. But Gemini believes in free association and the benefits of serendipity, while Virgo is the mindset behind Mapquest. Ultimately, you get on each other's nerves.

- **Gemini + Libra:** This wonderful combination promotes affectionate flirting and conversation that never stops. Even though it isn't the most passionate liaison, by and large you can't go wrong. Example: Paul McCartney (Gemini) and Linda Eastman (Libra).

- **Gemini + Scorpio:** Scorpio considers sex the central mystery of life. Gemini, a lustier sign than is often acknowledged, enjoys it without getting all emotional about it. Soon jealous Scorpio is feeling wounded, while flighty Gemini, now immersed in the crossword puzzle, can't help wondering what the problem is. Example: Nicole Kidman (Gemini) and Keith Urban (Scorpio).

- **Gemini + Sagittarius:** Despite an occasional bout of head-butting, this freedom-loving, loquacious pair is on the same wavelength. Advice: Fill your schedules with varied activities and plenty of travel; pile reading material and notebooks on the bedside tables; and don't get hung up on togetherness, because that's not where this independent couple lives. Example: Angelina Jolie (Gemini) and Brad Pitt (Sagittarius).

- **Gemini + Capricorn:** Somber Capricorns take themselves seriously; easygoing Geminis, though self-absorbed, take things lightly and are always trotting off in new directions. Not an easy combo. Examples: Jean-Paul Sartre (Gemini) and Simone de Beauvoir (Capricorn), Johnny Depp (Gemini), and Vanessa Paradis (Capricorn).

✔ **Gemini + Aquarius:** You may be soul mates. You're both sociable and fun-loving, and you both have hyperactive minds (though Aquarius wants to discuss social issues, while Gemini has ideas about less highfalutin' topics). Neither of you is in touch emotionally, so when times are tough, the glue that holds you together may weaken.

✔ **Gemini + Pisces:** Laid-back Pisces wants to sleep in; Gemini likes to get an early start. Mystical Pisces wants to analyze your dreams; Gemini prefers to explore the blogosphere. You come from different planets. Clashes are inevitable, but you're both able to bend. Examples: Laurie Anderson (Gemini) and Lou Reed (Pisces).

If a Gemini is on your mind, be upbeat, up-to-date, unpredictable, and available. Gemini is quick-witted, curious, well-informed, and game for anything. To capture Gemini's attention, exhibit those same qualities. Don't be morose. Don't bemoan the sad state of affairs in the world today. Don't complain. Don't demand that your dates be scheduled weeks in advance. Above all, remember that Gemini values lively conversation. Wonder why Geminis have a reputation for infidelity? It's because they're so easily bored.

Cancer in Love

Cancer has a talent for intimacy and caring. When you're in love, you blithely ignore the most obvious flaws while homing in on your beloved's hidden potential. Loving, generous, sentimental, and maternal, you need to be with someone who shares your drive and your willingness to explore complex emotional issues. When you find such a person, you're totally supportive — even when the reverse isn't true. You also have a tendency to cling. The smothering mother is a Cancerian archetype for good reason: Sometimes you can't let go, not even a teensy bit.

✔ **Cancer + Cancer:** You're intuitive and responsive, with plenty of energy and drive. Give it a go. But remember: Emotions run high during full Moons, and you both feel the pull. Examples: Rogers and Hammerstein, Barnum and Bailey, literary critics Diana and Lionel Trilling.

✔ **Cancer + Leo:** The domineering Lion loves passion, adventure, and five-star hotels; the moody Crab wants a quieter life in a cozy cottage covered in vines. If Leo is willing to downsize expectations and Cancer is ready to stroke the Lion's fragile ego and take a chance, you can find common ground. Examples: Kevin Bacon (Cancer) and Kyra Sedgwick (Leo).

✔ **Cancer + Virgo:** After you establish some trust, Cancer helps Virgo relax, and Virgo helps Cancer feel more secure. Problems arise with emotional issues. Supersensitive Cancer wants to discuss feelings, while critical Virgo prefers to skip the emotional stuff (unless it can be approached in a calm and systematic way) and make practical plans.

↙ **Cancer + Libra:** Domestic Cancer and artistic Libra have a fabulous time decorating a house together. But Cancer's emotional sensitivities cause logical Libra to pull back. Like other signs that square each other, this isn't a simpatico pairing, though Libra's desire to be mated — combined with Cancer's need to nest — can be a mitigating factor.

↙ **Cancer + Scorpio:** You're both in touch with your feelings and in love with love. You probably have a deeply intuitive relationship, though problems may arise when Scorpio can't cope with the quick ebb and flow of Cancerian emotions. Scorpio feelings, while deep, change slowly; Cancer feelings are in constant flux. Examples: Tom Hanks (Cancer) and Rita Wilson (Scorpio), Princess Diana (Cancer) — or Camilla Parker-Bowles (Cancer) — and Prince Charles (Scorpio).

↙ **Cancer + Sagittarius:** Cancer wants to love, nourish, and possess; Sagittarius can't be possessed. Though you may love each other intensely, you're completely different. Be warned. Examples: Frida Kahlo (Cancer) and Diego Rivera (Sagittarius), Tom Cruise (Cancer) and Katie Holmes (Sagittarius).

↙ **Cancer + Capricorn:** Like every pair of opposites, this one has pluses and minuses. Moody Cancer has an intuitive sense for how things ought to be done; sensible Capricorn prefers to go by the book. That's a small difference, given that Capricorn helps Cancer feel protected, Cancer helps Capricorn feel loved, and you share a reverence for tradition and family.

↙ **Cancer + Aquarius:** Warm, nurturing Cancer with cool, detached Aquarius? Not recommended, though some couples have defied the odds. Example: Nancy (Cancer) and Ronald Reagan (Aquarius).

↙ **Cancer + Pisces:** You're equally sensitive. Great feeling flows between you, your rhythms are similar, and you may even share a rare psychic connection. This is a perfect match, though Cancer, who loves to rescue, may find it difficult to overcome the famed Piscean ability to self-destruct. Examples: George Sand (Cancer) and Frederic Chopin (Pisces), Courtney Love (Cancer) and Kurt Cobain (Pisces).

If you fall for a Cancer, think roses, kisses, chocolate, and candlelight. A monogamist at heart, Cancer is tender and amorous — the real deal. Go to the ocean. Go dancing. Go anywhere by moonlight. Some signs do these things because they think they should. Cancerians do them because they respond to these traditional symbols — and because they crave intimacy. Three suggestions: Ask about your Crab's entire family tree; prove that you can cook; and be willing to discuss your emotions — in glorious detail.

Leo in Love

Uninhibitedly sexual, you're romantic, generous, witty, manipulative, loyal, and, despite your confident appearance, desperately in need of love. When

someone wins your heart, you want that person in your life forever. But you demand to be wooed in just the right way, insist on holding the reins of power, and can be interfering and controlling. Despite your bad behavior, you're so radiant and likable that you get away with everything.

- **Leo + Leo:** You have big, theatrical personalities, and your house is filled with laughter. But you also have big, thirsty egos in need of constant infusions of applause and praise. Sexually, you're dynamite. Still, the question remains: Who's the king of this castle? A tough call. Example: Antonio Banderas and Melanie Griffith.

- **Leo + Virgo:** Flamboyant Leo makes grand gestures; uptight Virgo focuses on details. This isn't an easy duo. Ideally, one or both of you has at least one planet in the other's sign to bridge the considerable distance between you. Example: Jennifer Lopez (Leo with Venus in Virgo) and Marc Anthony (Virgo with Mars in Leo).

- **Leo + Libra:** Libra is a flirt; Leo likes to play games — it works. Though Leo is more dramatic than even-tempered Libra, these two stimulate and delight each other. Example: Zelda (Leo) and F. Scott Fitzgerald (Libra).

- **Leo + Scorpio:** Leo blazes, Scorpio burns; both are drama queens. Fiery, intense, entertaining, and involving, this passionate, complicated alliance generates good times and major battles — fire and ice. Examples: Ted Hughes (Leo) and Sylvia Plath (Scorpio), Arnold Schwarzenegger (Leo) and Maria Shriver (Scorpio), Bill (Leo) and Hillary Rodham Clinton (Scorpio).

- **Leo + Sagittarius:** This fiery, exuberant combo offers laughter galore, an abundance of passion, and shared adventures in the world at large. Loyal Leo, who wants to do everything together, should remember that free-wheeling Sagittarius needs to be let off the leash once in a while, and upfront Sagittarius has to get used to the fact that melodramatic Leo needs to be a star.

- **Leo + Capricorn:** Flamboyant Leo loves grand gestures, overstated emotions, and dramatic scenarios. Conservative Capricorn prefers to stay cool by underplaying his or her reactions. But they both adore luxurious surroundings and the finer things in life. If you have plenty of money, this match can work.

- **Leo + Aquarius:** If expressive Leo can accept the Water Bearer's eccentric ways (and friends) and if freedom-loving Aquarius has no problem showering the needy Lion with adoration, this can be a match. Leo must also give up some control though, because Aquarius resists being marshaled into someone else's plan.

- **Leo + Pisces:** Pisces is bewitched by the fiery confidence of the audacious Lion, who in turn is swept away by the expressive, impractical Fish. Initially, quixotic Pisces feels protected by Leo (who wants to make everything okay). But in the end, the Fish (who has screwed things up in a way that Leo can scarcely believe) feels criticized and judged. Leave this relationship alone.

To capture the heart of a Leo, look great, exude confidence, and open your wallet. Leo expects flowers after the first date, and after that the stakes rise. It's not a matter of greed; Leo just wants to be sure of your feelings. So don't think that you can get away with second-class goods — Leo knows the difference. Plus, Leo is a glutton for affection, attention, and compliments. You can't be too brazen — Leo frogs think they're princes; Leo princes think they're kings; Leo kings think they're gods. You can't lay it on too thick.

Virgo in Love

You're understanding, easy to talk to, and far sexier than your virginal symbol suggests. But your idealistic standards are impossibly high, and mere mortals have trouble making the cut. When someone does prove worthy, you're warm, worshipful, devoted, and helpful. Unfortunately, you often have to learn the hard way that well-meaning suggestions and advice, no matter how gently delivered, pack a terrible punch.

- **Virgo + Virgo:** Your minds work in similar ways. Assuming your perfectionist compulsions can coexist, this is a happy, healthy union.

- **Virgo + Libra:** Analytical Virgo and thoughtful Libra connect mentally. But efficient, industrious Virgo aims for perfection, while ever-so-slightly lazy Libra needs more down time and yearns for romance even when there's laundry to be done. As always with neighboring signs, look for planets in the other person's sign. Example: Jada Pinkett Smith (Virgo with Venus in Libra) and Will Smith (Libra with Mars in Virgo).

- **Virgo + Scorpio:** This is an admirable match. Virgo is earthy enough to satisfy Scorpio's lustier moments, while Scorpio, a skilled detective who loves to dig into the meanings of things, can meet Virgo on his or her own intellectual ground. Example: Mary Matalin (Virgo) and James Carville (Scorpio).

- **Virgo + Sagittarius:** A sizzling, erotic charge runs between you, and you connect mentally. But extravagant Sagittarius likes to talk big and deal with the small stuff later (if at all), while prudent Virgo prefers to keep it real and attend to the details. After the initial fascination fades, the differences may be too great to overcome, as is often the case with two signs that square each other.

- **Virgo + Capricorn:** Two signs of the same element understand each other. You have great rapport, no effort required. You're both practical, methodical, accomplished, and ardent. This match is an excellent bet for a durable and congenial relationship.

- **Virgo + Aquarius:** Virgo's unique, well-stocked mind excites brilliant Aquarius, whose rebellious ways help virtuous Virgo loosen up. You have fun together, and you click intellectually. But neither of you is at

home in the gooey realm of emotions, meaning that when problems come up in that sphere, you both feel ill at ease.

✔ **Virgo + Pisces:** You fascinate each other because you're polar opposites. Virgo needs order, schedules, and reasons. Intuitive Pisces reacts instinctively and has a deep and abiding attraction to chaos. Naturally, Virgo wins the arguments. But easygoing Pisces has ways of not going along at all. It's a contest of equals: Anal-compulsive meets passive-aggressive.

To entice a Virgo, admire his intelligence; bring articles; engage in word play; and flatter his astute mind. Between the sheets, Virgo can be absolutely red-hot, but Virgo is also a control freak — as uptight as they come. So avoid messy emotions. In fact, avoid messes of all kinds. And remember: Virgo is always concerned about appropriate behavior and proper appearance, so no affection in public, please.

Libra in Love

You're gregarious, attractive, and a natural flirt. Born to be mated, you're restrained in public, amorous in private, and thoroughly identified with the object of your affection. As a single person, you're romantic, charming, and popular. But being part of a duo is essential to your fulfillment, and ultimately you're happy to leave the dating life behind.

✔ **Libra + Libra:** The downside to this duo is that if you feel ambivalent about the same issues, you can flounder in indecision forever. Otherwise, you're both creative, courteous, logical, and likable. This is a conversation that never stops. Example: Tim Robbins and Susan Sarandon.

✔ **Libra + Scorpio:** Although these two signs share a longing for romance, Scorpio craves emotional intensity and melodrama, while even-handed Libra yearns for serenity. Unless Libra has planets in Scorpio, the initial attraction is strong, but the long-term connection isn't.

✔ **Libra + Sagittarius:** Though the independent Archer's need for adventure may cause Libra a few jealous moments, Libra's charm reels the wandering gypsy back in. A fine pairing despite the weirdness of this example: Soon-yi Previn (Libra) and Woody Allen (Sagittarius).

✔ **Libra + Capricorn:** Old-fashioned romance appeals to you both, and you adore being part of a couple. But you both tend to repress emotions. When issues arise, as they inevitably do, the challenge is to admit that there's a problem and to deal with it.

✔ **Libra + Aquarius:** You could talk all night. Your mental connection is extraordinary. Other aspects of love leave something to be desired. Look for a strong Mars/Venus tie. John Lennon (Libra) and Yoko Ono (Aquarius) didn't have that planetary bond. But her Ascendant in his Sun sign and his Moon in her Sun sign helped knit them together.

✔ **Libra + Pisces:** You seem to be soul mates, but you aren't. Mysterious Pisces is a seething mass of soul, and Libra, though temptingly romantic on the surface, is cool, calm, and uncomfortable with emotions. After a while, the sensitive Fish feels ignored, while Libra, never the energy capital of the zodiac, feels exhausted.

In love with a Libra? Be smart, stylish, cultured, and good-looking. Take Libra to scenic places — Libra melts in the presence of natural beauty. Try not to be needy (Libra responds only when it matters, so don't cry wolf) or jealous (Libra flirts like mad and attracts admirers everywhere). And don't be loud or lewd: Libra can't stand it. They can stand healthy disagreement, though. In fact, they often thrive on it. That's because Libra is actually looking for a relationship, not a clone.

Scorpio in Love

You're intense, devoted, and fascinated by the game of love. You think of romance in mythic terms, demand grand passion (sexually and otherwise), and often fall into the quicksand of obsession. Because you radiate sex appeal and have such a compelling presence, other people often become fixated on you. (Note, however, that though Scorpio has a well-deserved reputation as the sexiest sign in the zodiac, many Scorpios also struggle with sexual problems that range from sexoholic excess to impotence, with a full complement of bizarre detours in between.) Still, the bottom line is this: You expect love (and sex) to transform you — and that's exactly what happens.

✔ **Scorpio + Scorpio:** Communication is eerily easy, and sex is erotic beyond imagining. But should there be even a hint of suspicion or jockeying for power, the psychic warfare is unbearable. This can be a match for the ages, or an exercise in tortured excess. Example: Larry and Althea Flynt.

✔ **Scorpio + Sagittarius:** Scorpio is complicated and covert; Sagittarius is direct and honest. Scorpio seeks total immersion; Sagittarius wants independence. The Sun signs are stunningly different. But when at least one partner has planets in the other's sign, the attraction is compelling. Examples: Pablo Picasso (Scorpio with the Moon in Sagittarius) and Françoise Gilot (Sagittarius).

- ✔ **Scorpio + Capricorn:** These serious, lusty signs seem different because Scorpio dives deep into the tropical sea of emotion, while Capricorn, though prone to sulking, prefers to skate lightly on the frozen surface. In fact, Scorpio gives Capricorn permission to have feelings, Capricorn protects the ever-emotive Scorpio, and you both feel like you have come home. Example: Mike Nichols (Scorpio) and Diane Sawyer (Capricorn).

- ✔ **Scorpio + Aquarius:** Fixed signs don't submit easily. Then again, you don't respect people who do. The problem is that Scorpio seeks attachment, is absorbed by emotional complexity, and leads from the heart, while Aquarius, however mentally vibrant, prefers a little emotional distance. This is a volatile mix. Example: Demi Moore (Scorpio) and Ashton Kutcher (Aquarius).

- ✔ **Scorpio + Pisces:** You're both sensual, intuitive, and emotionally aware. As a rule, possessive Scorpio is more at ease with the ways of the world than the out-of-this-world Fish. But Scorpio longs for magic, and imaginative Pisces can make it happen. Examples: Goldie Hawn (Scorpio) and Kurt Russell (Pisces).

If you're fixated on a Scorpio, be passionate and expressive. Sing Gershwin or Cole Porter. Invite Scorpio over to see Casablanca. Watch an eclipse together. When the object of your affections enters your domain, exploit your home-court advantage. Feel free to play games, to imply, and to pull back. Scorpio loves that stuff. Be secretive, suggestive, manipulative, and ever-so-slightly aggressive — and at the same time, be emotionally available. Make eye contact. Let Scorpions know how fascinating they are. Really, no one compares.

Sagittarius in Love

You cherish your freedom, long for adventure, and take "Don't fence me in" as your personal creed. It goes without saying that relationships are an issue. When a relationship challenges you or introduces you to a wider world, you're intrigued and excited. Unpredictability attracts you. But too many rules, too many formal dinners, and too much domesticity drive you to despair.

- ✔ **Sagittarius + Sagittarius:** Like two Don Quixotes, you understand each other well. Eternally young at heart, you share adventures, aspirations, and the ability to amuse each other. But you tend to dream the impossible dream and may fail to address concrete issues when they arise. Make frequent reality checks.

- ✔ **Sagittarius + Capricorn:** Capricorn is charmed by the Archer's madcap ways, while jaunty Sagittarius is amazed at how organized and grown-up the Goat is. Like two neighboring countries, you can either go to war or

establish a cultural exchange. It helps if one of you has a planet or two in the other's sign. Example: John F. Kennedy, Jr. (Sagittarius) and Carolyn Bessette Kennedy (Capricorn).

- **Sagittarius + Aquarius:** You're both lively, broad-minded, and unregimented. But neither of you has much talent for domesticity — or togetherness. Prepare for a life of takeout dinners, offbeat friends, late-night videos, and all-night chatter.

- **Sagittarius + Pisces:** You are two seekers, each with an inclination to dream. But Sagittarius deflates the fragile Piscean ego, while sensitive Pisces, though bewitching, can become strangely passive, which fiery Sagittarius can't abide. A questionable couple at best.

To snag a Sagittarius, don't come on too strong. Clichéd courting gestures make the Archer squirm. Instead, be casual, witty, lighthearted, and spontaneous. Spur-of-the-moment outings work in your favor; laying down too many rules works against you. Remember that Sagittarius wants to be a free spirit and delights in the unexpected. So keep your passport up-to-date. Be willing to be daring. And don't rush Sagittarians: No matter what they say, most of them are commitment-phobic. They need to relax into relationships.

Capricorn in Love

Conservative and classy, you want a traditional relationship with all the trappings. You aren't particularly interested in wild flings, which isn't to say that you're uninterested in sex. On the contrary, as an earth sign, you're a highly hormonal, high-stamina lover. But random sex seems meaningless to you. You're a devoted spouse, an attentive parent, a true friend, a loyal son or daughter — the whole shebang. You seek ever-after commitment and nothing less.

- **Capricorn + Capricorn:** You're both ambitious, committed, and lusty. But you run the danger of leading a life so upright, work-oriented, and tightly scheduled that you never have any fun apart from sex. (Even there, you aren't the most creative lovers on the planet.) And if either one of you gets depressed, you're in trouble.

- **Capricorn + Aquarius:** Capricorn is a traditionalist who believes in systems; progressive Aquarius is a maverick who likes to overturn them. Capricorn worries and feels despondent; Aquarius believes that the future is bright. Chances are you irritate each other. This can be a disaster — unless one of you has a planet or two in the other's sign.

✔ **Capricorn + Pisces:** Enterprising Capricorn knows how to handle the workaday world but can get bogged down in it; compassionate Pisces, who has other values, specializes in escaping from (or ignoring) the requirements of reality. But Pisces can lift Capricorn's spirits, and Capricorn can help Pisces get a toe or two on the ground. You inspire and support each other.

Fixated on a Capricorn? Cool and contained, Capricorn follows the rules. You should, too. Dress with class, be polite, be successful, be admiring. Offer up respectable, high-class activities — theatre, art exhibits, lectures. Don't jump into bed right away. Don't be aggressive. Don't be vulgar. Don't nag. Let things unfold naturally. And be patient: Capricorn represses emotions and generally takes things slowly. But Capricorn plays for keeps.

Aquarius in Love

A friendly, unconventional sort who's intrigued by everyone, you connect easily but superficially, and you value your freedom. Despite your reputation for bohemian behavior, when you find someone you respect, you willingly make the commitment — which doesn't mean that you intend to give up your independence or your eccentric ways. (Those are forever.) You can be as passionate as anyone else (and kinkier than most), but much as you enjoy it, you aren't a slave to sex. You live in your head.

✔ **Aquarius + Aquarius:** Ah, the people you meet, the causes you support, and the parties you throw. Not to mention the way you decorate your house. You're unfettered, unorthodox, opinionated, and visionary — a couple unlike any other. Mentally, you connect. Romantically, it's another story. But maybe that doesn't matter. Like other air sign combinations, you can easily be swept away on a sea of conversation.

✔ **Aquarius + Pisces:** This match is initially enticing but disappointing in the long run — gentle Pisces is way too sensitive to be with someone as detached and cerebral as the Water Bearer. But don't tell that to Paul Newman and Joanne Woodward. He has the Sun in Aquarius and the Moon in Pisces. She has the Sun in Pisces and the Moon in Aquarius. We should all be so lucky.

If you're beguiled by an Aquarius, prepare to meet more eccentrics than you thought existed outside of the Land of Oz. Aquarius collects them. Your mission is to strike the Water Bearer as irreplaceable and fascinating enough to add to the collection. There's no need to present yourself falsely or to iron out the kinks. On the contrary. Be independent (but available). Express your opinions. And be yourself — the more unorthodox, the better. A dozen roses? No, no, no. An invitation to a midnight ramble through the meat-packing district? That could work.

Pisces in Love

Gestures — the moonlit stroll, the mariachi singers — mean the world to you. You're a romantic who wants a cosmically connected, karmically generated, some-enchanted-evening union with a soul mate. Though your intuition is pinpoint accurate at other times, when you're in love you can be amazingly gullible, stunningly dependent, and more demanding than you may realize. Ruled by your emotions, you're also generous, erotic, affectionate, supportive, and kind.

> ✔ **Pisces + Pisces:** Same-sign unions are a mixed blessing because they magnify both the strengths and the weaknesses of the sign. Two dreamy Pisceans can communicate in ways that other signs can't even imagine. But practicality eludes you. Does that matter? Ultimately, it probably does. Example: George Harrison and Patti Boyd. (When their marriage crumbled, she wed his Aries friend, Eric Clapton.)

If you fall for a Pisces, be romantic. Pisces wants to be swept away, but not á la Tarzan and Jane. Being too aggressive may work short term (Pisces can be passive), but over the long run, it won't sit well. Pisces wants love to mean a coming together of twin souls, two companions against the slings and arrows of everyday life. Pisces also wants sentimental gifts, candlelit dinners, Valentine's remembrances, the whole bit. What Pisces doesn't want is advice. No matter how you phrase it, Pisces hears it as criticism, so lay off.

Finding Other Planetary Ties

What if your sign and your beloved's aren't compatible? Should your next stop be Match.com? Not necessarily. Conjunctions or other close aspects between the Moon in one chart and the Sun in another — or between the two Moons — breed emotional understanding. Close aspects (up to and including oppositions) that link Venus in one chart with Mars in another kindle sexual attraction. Ascendants of agreeable signs make for personalities that mesh.

The more conjunctions, sextiles, and trines that you see between the planets of one chart and the planets of another, the better. Squares and oppositions, problematical though they can be, are still a tie, and they can provide the right amount of friction.

The only planetary aspects that scarcely matter are conjunctions of Saturn and Saturn, Uranus and Uranus, Neptune and Neptune, Pluto and Pluto. These planets orbit the Sun so sluggishly that they define generations, not individuals. The fact that your Neptune is conjunct your beloved's doesn't mean that you're karmically destined to be together. It means that you're about the same age — which isn't much of a tie. But it isn't nothing either, as anyone who has ever attended a high school reunion can attest.

Incompatible? You be the judge

The actors and civil rights activists Ruby Dee (Scorpio) and Ossie Davis (Sagittarius) were born under neighboring — and hence incompatible — signs. Fortunately, her Ascendant and Venus are in his Sun sign, Sagittarius; her Moon conjuncts his Venus; and they both were born with the Moon in Aquarius. Even though their Sun signs aren't an ideal pairing, the marriage, which was also a working partnership, lasted 57 years — until his death.

Or consider Gertrude Stein, the avant-garde Aquarian writer, and her companion, Alice B. Toklas, a Taurus. They met in 1907 in Paris, where Gertrude entertained everyone from Picasso to Hemingway in her famous salon, and they stayed together until Gertrude's death in 1946. Although the earthy Bull and the airy Water Bearer don't usually mix, the connection between them was immediate. As Gertrude wrote when she described their meeting in *The Autobiography of Alice B. Toklas* (which she composed in Alice's voice, as if Alice herself had penned it), "I have met several great people but I have only known three first class geniuses and in each case on sight within me something rang."

I know what that something was. It was Alice's Mars, closely conjunct Gertrude's Venus and exactly opposite her Uranus. In the dominion of the heart, that bolt-from-the-blue connection — along with a series of harmonious trines linking the two charts — quickly prevailed over the warring Sun signs.

The other two geniuses that Alice met, by the way, were Pablo Picasso and the philosopher Alfred North Whitehead. Personally, I never doubted that Alice might have responded to Picasso, who clearly had a way with women. But Alfred North Whitehead? I wasn't so sure. So I tracked down his birthday, and guess what? Whitehead's Venus in Aquarius was conjunct Alice's Mars, and his Pluto in Taurus was exactly conjunct her Venus. I'm certain that when they met something within her rang.

Chapter 16

The Times of Our Lives: Transits

*O*nce upon a time, astrology was the province of the privileged. Kings and pharaohs consulted astrologers, not because they were fascinated by the intricacies of personality but because they wanted to know when to wage war, when to stockpile grain, when to build a temple, and when to marry. They wanted to know, in short, how to lead their lives. Astrology provided some answers.

Today, anyone can take advantage of the wisdom astrology has to offer. You can glean some of that wisdom from your birth chart — and some of it from the current position of the planets. *Transiting planets* are the planets as they appear in the sky now. As they wheel across the zodiac, they trigger your birth planets, presenting you with challenges and opportunities. Transiting Saturn is conjunct your Moon? Be prepared to combat depression. Uranus is crossing your Midheaven? Get ready for an upheaval in your career. Every time a planet in the sky forms an aspect to a planet or an angle in your birth chart, it stirs up a different area of your psyche.

Sad to say, this book isn't long enough to consider every transit. I'm leaving out the transits through the houses. I ignore transiting squares (they're stressful) as well as sextiles and trines (they're helpful). And I entirely omit aspects made by transiting Venus, Mercury, and the Sun because they move so fast that their influence is fleeting. (The Moon whizzes through the signs at an even faster clip. But it's so close that it exerts an influence anyway, which is why I devote Chapter 17 to lunar transits.)

In this chapter, I focus on the slower-moving planets, beginning with Mars and ending with Pluto. I consider the conjunctions and oppositions that those planets make to your natal chart. And I try, as best I can, to highlight the possibilities that they open up for you. Transits don't change your natal chart. Like it or not, your birth chart is eternal. But they can help you achieve the potential contained within your horoscope. And that, as they say, is priceless.

Investigating Transits

To identify the transits in effect now, turn to the Appendix at the back of this book and look up the current position of the planets. The planetary tables in the Appendix tell you what sign each planet is in. Jot down the positions of the planets from Mars to Pluto. Then make a copy of your birth chart and position the transiting planets around it. As models, look at Figures 16-2 and 16-3, which present Anne Morrow Lindbergh's chart. In each case, the inner wheel represents the birth chart, and the outer wheel shows the location of the transiting planets.

To know exactly where the transiting planets are and whether they're within a degree or two of your birth planets, you need to consult a professional, wander about on the Web, or — better yet — buy an astrological calendar, which can tell you the precise position of the planets at a glance. The best ones are *Llewellyn's Daily Planetary Guide* and *Jim Maynard's Celestial Guide* and *Celestial Influences* calendars.

Showing the importance of transits

Anne Morrow Lindbergh was the author of 14 books, the mother of six children, and the wife of the aviator Charles Lindbergh, who flew across the Atlantic Ocean by himself in 1927 and became an instant international hero (though his reputation was sullied later on when he accepted an award from the Nazi government). Unlike many wives of famous men, she became famous in her own right — which is exactly what you would expect from someone with a tenth house as packed as hers. Figure 16-1 shows her extraordinary birth chart.

After Lindbergh's triumphant solo flight, he became a goodwill ambassador to Latin America. In December 1927, he visited Mexico, where he met Anne, whose father was the American ambassador. A year and a half later, they married. Figure 16-2 shows Anne's chart in the center surrounded by the transits for her initial meeting with Charles. Notice that Jupiter, the bringer of opportunity, and Uranus, the lord of the unexpected, are conjunct in her seventh house of marriage. Any astrologer could have told her that she would meet someone soon and that he would be an unusual person.

The inner chart is the birth chart. The planets in the outer circle represent the transits.

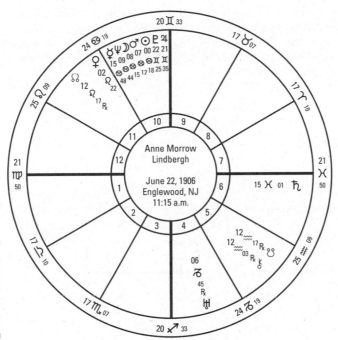

Figure 16-1:
Anne
Morrow
Lindbergh's
birth chart.

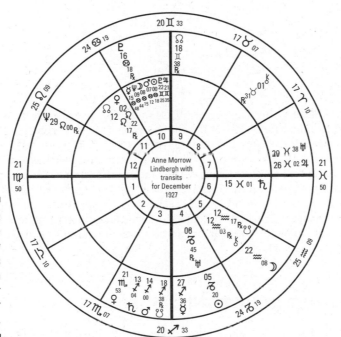

Figure 16-2:
Anne
Morrow
Lindbergh's
chart with
transits for
December
1927.

When they married, Uranus was still in her seventh house. Almost three years later, tragedy struck when the Lindberghs' 20-month-old baby was kidnapped and killed. The murderer's trial, known as "the trial of the century," was arguably bigger than O.J. Simpson's. Her transits at the time of the kidnapping are shown in Figure 16-3.

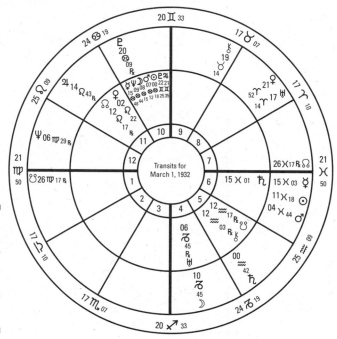

Figure 16-3:
Anne
Morrow
Lindbergh's
chart with
transits for
March, 1932.

Notice that Saturn, the planet of restriction, is now in her fifth house of children, and Uranus, the planet of the unexpected, is in her eighth house of death and transformation. Those two transits, I should point out, aren't nearly enough to trigger such an exceedingly rare and terrible loss. After all, everyone who had an Ascendant in the neighborhood of 21° Virgo also experienced those transits. A birth chart must show the potential for an event in order for it to happen. And there it is: The close opposition of her natal Uranus to her natal Sun, Moon, Mars, and Neptune clearly introduces the possibility of violence. The transits acted on the possibilities already there in her remarkable chart.

Following your transits

To follow your transits, make a copy of the empty chart on the Cheat Sheet and place your birth planet in the appropriate sections. (See Chapter 3 for more information on constructing your birth chart.) Then position the transiting

planets around the outer rim. You'll see right away that there's a lot going on. Mars is here, Saturn is there, Pluto and Jupiter are together in a third place. So how can you tell which transits to concentrate on?

Here's the rule: The transits that pack the biggest wallop are those made by the slowest planets — Saturn, Uranus, Neptune, and Pluto — to the Sun, the Moon, the Ascendant, and the faster planets. Contacts made by the faster planets are usually short-lived. Contacts made by the slower planets to the slower planets (such as Uranus opposite your Pluto or Neptune conjunct your Saturn) may be too subtle to detect (unless the natal planet happens to occupy a prominent position in your chart). But contacts made by a slow planet to one of your personal planets — Pluto conjunct your Moon, Uranus opposite your Sun, and so on — signify the chapters of your life.

Tracking Mars

Mars is associated with vitality, initiative, passion, force, anger, and aggression. Mars stirs your desires and prods you to take action. As a rule, Mars spends about two months in a sign, taking about two years to travel through the zodiac and return to the position that it occupied at your birth. But those figures are only averages because, like the other planets, Mars sometimes slows down, turns retrograde, and spends several months in one sign (see Chapter 18 for more on retrograde planets). To show you how varied its schedule can be, in 1997, Mars sped through Scorpio in about six weeks. But when it returned to that sign in 1999, it lingered there for over five months. Naturally, the more time it spends in a sign, the more it energizes the planets it contacts there.

The major transits of Mars are as follows:

✔ **Mars conjunct the Sun:** You feel determined, aggressive, and brave. But act quickly (and try to avoid angry outbursts). This energetic transit usually lasts only a few days, although occasionally, when Mars goes retrograde, it can carry a longer, hardier charge.

✔ **Mars opposite the Sun:** You're energetic but embattled. This is a don't-mess-with-me transit.

✔ **Mars conjunct the Moon:** You're feisty, expressive, and in no mood to repress your powerful emotions or peevish irritations, which somehow just pop out. Just remember that a little self-awareness goes a long way.

✔ **Mars opposite the Moon:** Take care. Your emotional outpourings — which feel externally caused — can quickly escalate into confrontation. Count to ten.

✔ **Mars conjunct Mercury:** You feel impatient, excited, and filled with ideas. You express your opinions with confidence — and aggression. A hint of competition or hostility may sneak into your communications.

- ✓ **Mars opposite Mercury:** You argue, you debate, you take no prisoners. You're quick to respond, but you may also feel frustrated, beleaguered, confrontational, and hostile. Be careful of what you say.

- ✓ **Mars conjunct Venus:** Your sex drive, ability to love, and artistic impulses are working overtime. You're at your most irresistible.

- ✓ **Mars opposite Venus:** Socially and sexually, you're in the mood for love. But your strategies for getting together with other people may be less than successful. You run the risk of being too assertive or uncooperative — or of attracting people who are behaving in a similarly out-of-balance fashion.

- ✓ **Mars conjunct natal Mars:** Mars returns. The hero's journey begins anew as a fresh wave of energy and desire washes over you. Your challenge is to harness that energy. This transit, which occurs every two years, marks the end of one energy cycle and the beginning of another. This is the moment to pursue a new interest, invent a project, and stay open to possibilities that arrive unbidden. Transiting Mars can also generate hostility, so watch your temper.

- ✓ **Mars opposite natal Mars:** Though your stamina is high, you may not find it easy to use your energy in a constructive, consistent manner. Something you've been involved in for about a year has reached a critical point. Much effort is required, and your temper could flare out of control.

- ✓ **Mars conjunct Jupiter:** The universe supports your grandest visions by prodding you to get off the couch and do something to actualize them. You're motivated to take action. Under this encouraging, expansive transit, you also benefit from travel and education.

- ✓ **Mars opposite Jupiter:** This can be a fortunate transit. You have plenty of energy, and you're buoyant and optimistic. But you run the risk of promising too much, overestimating your capabilities, and overreacting.

- ✓ **Mars conjunct Saturn:** Because you have a strong sense of limitations and bristle at the obstructions you face, this tends to be a challenging transit. It can also be a time of great accomplishment, thanks to your increased ability to get organized and to focus.

- ✓ **Mars opposite Saturn:** This transit calls for caution, diligence, and responsible behavior. Alas, you're likely to act rashly, resist the dictates of others, and express your authority awkwardly. Plus you're irritable and you feel sorry for yourself.

- ✓ **Mars conjunct Uranus:** You act impulsively, rebelling against constraints and sometimes taking off in unanticipated directions. During the few days when Mars is conjunct your birth Uranus, buckle your seat belt and avoid skateboarding. As usual with Uranus, the rule is simple: Expect the unexpected, and be safe.

- ✓ **Mars opposite Uranus:** Tension, strain, accidents, and unpredictable events can interrupt your plans. Don't take reckless chances during this agitating transit. And be sure to back up your computer files.

- **Mars conjunct Neptune:** Your dream life picks up, and you seek inspiration. Artistic, spiritual, or healing activities excite you. But be careful about drugs and alcohol, and avoid making big decisions — your judgment may be skewed.

- **Mars opposite Neptune:** Vivid dreams and artistic inspiration characterize this transit. But your efforts to get something done in the workaday world could go awry. You may feel taken advantage of, confused, or out of the loop.

- **Mars conjunct Pluto:** Your attempts to pursue your ambitions and express your personal power in interactions with others receive a boost.

- **Mars opposite Pluto:** In your desire to establish yourself, you run the risk of stumbling into power struggles.

- **Mars conjunct the Ascendant:** You express yourself effectively, as long as you avoid sounding angry, and you're motivated to take steps on your own behalf. Following the conjunction to the Ascendant, Mars travels through your first house, boosting your physical energy and lending you a boldness that you may not normally feel.

- **Mars opposite the Ascendant:** You may feel angry or upset. After forming the opposition to your Ascendant, Mars travels through your seventh house for about two months, highlighting issues concerning marriage or business partnerships and underscoring your unwillingness to be passive. But arguments and tension upset you, and you may take out your frustration on those to whom you feel the closest.

- **Mars conjunct the Midheaven:** This transit, along with the two-month-long sojourn of Mars in your tenth house, motivates you to chase after your professional desires. It also increases your impatience. Try not to be belligerent.

- **Mars opposite the Midheaven:** Your professional efforts fizzle out or are rebuffed, and your attention goes elsewhere. As Mars conjuncts your I.C. (which is directly opposite your Midheaven) and travels through your fourth house, it awakens your interest in home and family and energizes your domestic life. Hidden conflicts emerge.

Mars transits are energizing. When Mars is traveling through a house, you find the energy to take action in that area. You benefit from taking a courageous approach.

Activating Jupiter

Jupiter spins through the zodiac in slightly fewer than 12 years, spending about a year in each sign. Its transits are among the most eagerly anticipated — and the most disappointing. As the planet of expansion, opportunity, generosity, and prosperity, Jupiter can bring happiness, growth, and success. As the planet

of philosophy, religion, and education, it can stimulate an exploration of belief and the pursuit of knowledge. But despite its reputation as the lord of abundance and the bringer of good fortune, Jupiter doesn't necessarily deliver the sweepstake's prize patrol to your door, and people who sit around passively waiting for their wishes to come true under its influence are bound to be dissatisfied. The problem is that while genial Jupiter may lead you right up to the doors of opportunity, it also prompts feelings of contentment and self-indulgence. Instead of trying to push those doors open, many people lean back to enjoy the transit and thereby miss it.

In my experience, a Jupiter transit is a trumpet call to arms. When you see Jupiter poised on the brink of your Sun sign, about to contact your career-oriented Midheaven, or entering your seventh house of marriage, you know that opportunities are available in those arenas. But you have to do your part. To get the most out of Jupiter, make a legitimate effort to learn something, to tackle an old dilemma in a novel way, or to find time for the things you always say you want to do. When you take action under a Jupiter transit, rewards inevitably follow.

A transit can only activate the potential that already exists in your chart.

- **Jupiter conjunct the Sun:** Seize the opportunity to branch out during this year of growth, but be warned: If life is going well, you may be tempted to do nothing. If life isn't going your way, you may become disheartened or cynical. Don't let Jupiter lull you into complacency. This is the time to reach out, be generous, and take risks.

- **Jupiter opposite the Sun:** Opportunities are available, but you run the risk of overextending yourself, overdramatizing your situation, or simply promising too much.

- **Jupiter conjunct the Moon:** This transit brings expanded sensitivity and a greater flow of emotions — which is pleasant if your birth Moon makes mostly harmonious aspects to other planets but exhausting if your Moon is afflicted by squares and oppositions.

- **Jupiter opposite the Moon:** Why does every emotional blip — every minor snub, every disappointment, and every little boost — feel utterly seismic? The answer is that, thanks to Jupiter, you're supersensitive, with a tendency to inflate your feelings and overreact.

- **Jupiter conjunct Mercury:** Jupiter enlivens your intellect and expands your ability to express yourself. You speak up freely and travel happily.

- **Jupiter opposite Mercury:** Seek knowledge. Read vociferously. Write daily. And remember that overconfidence can be a problem. Don't talk too much, and postpone making important decisions.

- **Jupiter conjunct Venus:** Your social life blossoms. You express your affections easily, attract love, and enjoy the arts. This fortunate transit even improves your earning ability.

✔ **Jupiter opposite Venus:** You're attractive to others, and your social life is active but not necessarily satisfying. Perhaps you're trying too hard. You may also be spending too much.

✔ **Jupiter conjunct Mars:** You're courageous, passionate, busy, and filled with vitality. Being assertive produces excellent results.

✔ **Jupiter opposite Mars:** You feel energetic but frustrated, and you may find it difficult to repress your hostility. Demands are numerous, and disagreements may arise.

✔ **Jupiter conjunct natal Jupiter:** Jupiter circles back to its birth position every 12 years, renewing your optimism. This can be a lucky, adventurous time during which travel, education, and philosophical explorations bring fulfillment. Your efforts to brush past old boundaries pay off, and you have some fun along the way. But beware: Jupiter can also promote self-satisfaction, laziness, and smug indifference.

✔ **Jupiter opposite natal Jupiter:** You're in a generous, exuberant mood, but you may be merrier than the situation merits. Watch out for overindulgence.

✔ **Jupiter conjunct Saturn:** You may become supremely conscious of your fears and limitations, but they have less of a charge. You find the help you need, or you figure out a way to get organized, or you finally buckle down and do something about your problems.

✔ **Jupiter opposite Saturn:** As much as you want to break out of your old patterns, circumstances may not permit it. However tempted you may be by new acquaintances and fresh opportunities, your responsibilities are ongoing. Your best move is to accept your obligations.

✔ **Jupiter conjunct Uranus:** Unusual opportunities present themselves to you, and you have the courage to take a leap and express your individuality. This is an exciting time of positive change.

✔ **Jupiter opposite Uranus:** Surprising opportunities may bring a longed-for chance to break away from confining circumstances. Overconfidence leads nowhere, but there's something to be said for taking a calculated risk.

✔ **Jupiter conjunct Neptune:** Your mystical side, spiritual interests, supernatural ability, and imagination are enlarged. Possible problems include excessive daydreaming, substance abuse, and the refusal to accept reality.

✔ **Jupiter opposite Neptune:** Accepting reality isn't easy — and you probably aren't even trying. Your imagination may be soaring, but your judgment is poor. You're impractical and easily deceived. If you've ever struggled with substance abuse, you must be vigilant now.

✔ **Jupiter conjunct Pluto:** Your ambition and personal power are enlarged, and your labors bear fruit. In the past, you may have journeyed through the underworld of sorrow, fear, or isolation. If so, you now return to the light.

- ✔ **Jupiter opposite Pluto:** Your desire for power can get out of hand, and obstacles may block your way. At this moment of transition, you may feel as if you have little control or that you're caught in a power struggle.

- ✔ **Jupiter conjunct the Ascendant:** You're open, ebullient, and even lucky. During the year or so when Jupiter contacts your Ascendant and travels through your first house, you're outgoing and receptive, and people respond to you positively. The bad news: Weight gain is a distinct possibility.

- ✔ **Jupiter opposite the Ascendant:** You easily connect with others, and your relationships flourish. During the year or so when Jupiter opposes the Ascendant and inhabits the seventh house, you could attract a new partner, either business or personal, into your life.

- ✔ **Jupiter conjunct the Midheaven:** Jupiter's conjunction with the Midheaven, followed by a yearlong sojourn in your tenth house, can bring success, an enlarged role in the world, and career options galore. Take advantage of them.

- ✔ **Jupiter opposite the Midheaven:** Family relationships improve. This is a fine year to move, invest in real estate, focus on domestic pursuits, and heal family wounds.

Jupiter transits bring growth, opportunity, and the danger of indolence.

Coping with Saturn

People who know something about astrology tend to look forward to Jupiter's transits — and view Saturn's transits with alarm. Saturn takes almost 30 years to whirl through the zodiac. It spends about two and a half years in each sign, and it's associated with duty, discipline, effort, obstructions, limitations, boundaries, and lessons learned. Gloomy Saturn can bring despair, apathy, and a dangerous case of the blues. But just as Jupiter doesn't necessarily deliver matchless love, best-selling first novels, or winning lottery tickets, Saturn doesn't necessarily beget misery. It can bring responsibility in the form of a better job, limitation in the form of a committed relationship, and the enhanced self-esteem that accompanies self-discipline. To benefit from a Saturn transit, you need to create structure, get organized, and figure out how to manage your time.

Transits, by definition, are transitory. They don't last long, so you must act promptly to take advantage of them.

- ✔ **Saturn conjunct the Sun:** You reap what you sow: That's the message of this challenging and sometimes discouraging transit. Saturn stimulates your ambitions, increases your need for security, forces you to learn discipline, and may confront you with your weaknesses. But it can also bring security, fulfillment, and recognition for work well done.

✔ **Saturn opposite the Sun:** Pessimism and low vitality characterize this difficult transit, which takes place approximately 14 years after Saturn conjuncts the Sun. Other people may oppose your efforts. Be patient.

Note: The squares of Saturn to the Sun, which occur seven years before and after the opposition, are also trying.

✔ **Saturn conjunct the Moon:** Worries afflict you. You may feel melancholy, misunderstood, unloved, or unlucky — not to mention filled with self-doubt. You're imprisoned momentarily in the abyss, where the time is always right for confiding in a journal, talking to a therapist, and reminding yourself that this too shall pass.

✔ **Saturn opposite the Moon:** Insecurity, bitterness, and stressful relationships may cause you to withdraw during this isolating time. Though you may wish for sympathy from others, you aren't likely to get it. Avoid self-pity and take practical steps.

✔ **Saturn conjunct Mercury:** You're in a thoughtful and possibly pessimistic mood that favors study, concentration, and regular schedules. This is the ideal time to read *War and Peace, Moby Dick,* or any other massive classics you've been avoiding.

✔ **Saturn opposite Mercury:** Circumstances may cause you to question your ideas or to look for a more effective communication style.

✔ **Saturn conjunct Venus:** Weak relationships may crumble. You may feel lonely, inhibited, unloved, and underfunded. And yet a new, more serious relationship can begin, possibly with an older person. This is also a fine time to launch an artistic project.

✔ **Saturn opposite Venus:** Breaking up is hard to do, even if it's the only move to make. Healthy relationships survive this stressful transit. But even then the blinders come off as you face the truth.

✔ **Saturn conjunct Mars:** Your efforts are frustrated, provoking you to feel resentful and overburdened. If anger is an issue for you, learn to manage it now. This is also an excellent time to hire a trainer or to join a gym. You're being challenged to learn control. If you act methodically, you can accomplish a lot.

✔ **Saturn opposite Mars:** This transit can be rough, especially if you're the sort of person who collects enemies. Obstacles impede your progress as Saturn forces you to accept reality, take appropriate action, and — worst of all — be patient.

✔ **Saturn conjunct Jupiter:** Even though the opportunities that arise during this tedious time may not be flashy, they're nonetheless real. During a Saturn transit, facing reality is essential. Although you may need to streamline or limit your goals in some way, Saturn rewards your efforts.

✔ **Saturn opposite Jupiter:** Luck isn't with you, though it isn't against you, either. Instead, this is a time of restricted growth, dampened enthusiasm, industriousness, and acceptance of the status quo.

✔ **Saturn conjunct Saturn:** Saturn returns. This is a pivotal moment, a time to face reality. Saturn returns to the position it occupied in your birth chart when you're between the ages of 28 to 30, 58 to 60, and 88 to 90. The first Saturn return represents the true onset of adulthood. During this typically trying time, you're forced to face the truth about yourself, stop messing around, and grow up. The second and third returns represent further turning points, during which you must admit to your dissatisfactions and prepare for a new phase in your life. In each case, Saturn encourages you to confront your fears, acknowledge the obstacles in your path, name your ambitions, and change your habits.

✔ **Saturn opposite Saturn:** This transit, which forces you to see yourself in relationship to the larger world, can be upsetting, especially the first time around, when you're about 14 years old. Subsequent experiences occur roughly at ages 44 and 74. In each instance, you may feel lonely and insecure. What helps? Focusing on specific tasks and practical efforts can increase your sense of security. The message: persevere.

✔ **Saturn conjunct Uranus:** Though you may feel constrained, it's pointless to rebel. Instead, seek controlled ways of expressing your individuality, which will allow you to sail through this transit with aplomb.

✔ **Saturn opposite Uranus:** Born free? That's not the way it feels. Events conspire to make you feel as if your options are limited, but don't underestimate the positive power of Saturn. Saturn supports organization and self-discipline. It rewards you by allowing you to develop the most idiosyncratic and original aspects of your self.

✔ **Saturn conjunct Neptune:** You may feel steadier and more in control during this introspective phase — or you may be pessimistic and creatively stymied. If you've been troubled by alcohol or drug abuse, you'll likely be forced to come to terms with it.

✔ **Saturn opposite Neptune:** You may feel beset by confusion, uncertainty, and despondency. Dreams can come true, yet you feel disappointed. This transit presents yet another chance to accept reality (sigh) and grow up.

✔ **Saturn conjunct Pluto:** Issues of control and manipulation arise during this long-term, transformative transit. Despite restrictive and frustrating circumstances, you can find a way to acknowledge your mistakes (or obsessions) and rethink your purpose. As always with Saturn, reaching these goals requires you to acknowledge the realities of your situation.

✔ **Saturn opposite Pluto:** Your desire to control your circumstances and pursue your goals collides with external pressures, which may be more powerful than you are. An obsession that may have you in its grip needs to be broken, and yet you may feel incapable of doing so. Look to areas of your life that are going well and focus on those.

✔ **Saturn conjunct the Ascendant:** You strike people as dependable and trustworthy, and greater responsibility may come to you as a result. Though you may feel restrained and overworked during this difficult time, this transit brings some benefits. It improves your ability to concentrate, stimulates you to regulate your behavior (making this the ideal time to start a sensible diet), and encourages you to rethink your ambitions. At the same time, you're beginning a seven-year stretch known as the *obscurity cycle,* which is characterized by introspection and a search for personal growth.

✔ **Saturn opposite the Ascendant:** This transit marks a turning point in the way you relate to the world. It may bring dissatisfactions to the surface and disrupt relationships, both personal and professional. Established relationships (if they aren't solid) may break up. New alliances are likely to be with people who are older or more authoritative. Though relationships are likely to be a challenge during the next two and a half years, the good news is that you're beginning a seven-year period of opportunity and accomplishment known as the *activity cycle.* For 14 years, your focus has been primarily internal; now you're opening up to the world.

✔ **Saturn conjunct the Midheaven:** With this transit, the seven-year *influence cycle* begins. If you've been paying your dues, you can expect to reach a peak of recognition and responsibility. This is a time of success and prominence during which you establish your place in the world. But if you've been slacking off, this transit could herald a wave of failure and defeat. If that's your situation, remember that Saturn always responds positively to increased structure.

✔ **Saturn opposite the Midheaven:** Issues regarding home and family beg for attention. Though you may feel weighed down by family needs and the burden of the past, you should know that you're beginning another component of the Saturn cycle. Having just completed the seven-year obscurity cycle, which is described earlier in this section, you're now entering the *emergence cycle,* a more creative and exciting time. A move is also a possibility.

As the planet of limitation and loss, Saturn requires a clear-eyed assessment of your situation. It also brings responsibility and rewards hard work.

Unpredictable Uranus

When Uranus rides into town, life gets interesting. As the planet of revolution, invention, electricity, individuality, and eccentricity, Uranus disrupts the usual flow of events and is associated with unforeseen occurrences and

unusual people. Uranus takes 84 years — about a lifetime — to traverse the zodiac. (Turn to Chapter 10 for more information about the outer planets.)

- **Uranus conjunct the Sun:** You're in a holding pattern, but you aren't going to be there long. Your need to express your individuality propels you toward once-in-a-lifetime change. If you're on track, this transit shouldn't be traumatic. But if you're drifting, stuck, or otherwise off your path, this transit augurs disruptive change — one way or another. If you don't initiate alterations on your own, you can expect it to arrive unbidden from external sources. Act now.

- **Uranus opposite the Sun:** This disruptive transit supports innovative thinking and ushers in a creative, explosive era of change and instability. Digging in your heels against it won't work. Flexibility is required.

- **Uranus conjunct the Moon:** Intuitive flashes bring insight during this moody, unstable transit. Look for emotional storms, shifts in family dynamics, or a sudden urge for independence.

- **Uranus opposite the Moon:** Feelings of restriction and a need to break from the past make this a time of emotional fluctuations and revolutionary changes.

- **Uranus conjunct Mercury:** Though you may feel overscheduled and frantic, rigid thinking holds you back. Fresh insights and facts compel you to abolish tired ideas and patterns of communication. Uranus triggers your ability to think in an original way. Carry a notebook.

- **Uranus opposite Mercury:** You're mentally active and physically nervous, and you may have trouble sleeping. Tackling your problems in the same old way leads to the same old result. Willingly or not, you must try a new approach.

- **Uranus conjunct Venus:** If the sizzle has gone out of a relationship you value, you can no longer be passive about it. Reinvigorate it or look elsewhere. If you're alone, you could meet someone new in an unexpected way, and that person won't be like anyone else you know. Relationships that carry a hint of unpredictability appeal to you. Boring old alliances, no matter how worthy or rooted in history, don't.

- **Uranus opposite Venus:** In your desire to escape boredom, you — or your partner — may be tempted by a relationship that seems to offer greater pizzazz. But will this new union last? I wouldn't bet on it.

- **Uranus conjunct Mars:** You're restless, anxious for change, and ready to take the initiative: that's the positive part. You're also angrier than usual and likely to act rashly and make impulsive decisions. Plus, you're accident-prone.

- **Uranus opposite Mars:** Something needs to change during this volatile period, but your actions may be erratic because you aren't sure what you want. Controlling your animosity and competitive feelings can be tricky, and you may provoke the opposition of others. Yet those outer influences may provide just the kick you need.

✔ **Uranus conjunct Jupiter:** Rare opportunities and startling changes in circumstances mark this conjunction. In one chart from my files, this transit coincided with the loss of a family member and an unplanned pregnancy. In another case, it brought a disruptive but positive cross-country move. In a third instance, a woman rocketed to professional prominence when Uranus conjoined her tenth-house Jupiter — and plunged to Earth a year later when Saturn contacted her Sun and she received the dreaded pink slip.

✔ **Uranus opposite Jupiter:** A need for independence and an urge to take a risk characterize this unruly influence. Fresh possibilities may tantalize (or frustrate) you. In your desire to lead a bigger life, you make some astonishing choices. Surprise your friends by all means — but don't let your optimism (or grandiosity) run away with your common sense.

✔ **Uranus conjunct Saturn:** You feel boxed in and tense and no longer able to tolerate the constraints you put on yourself. Uranus acts as a catalyst, forcing you to shed old fears, limitations, and even jobs in search of a less confining sense of self.

✔ **Uranus opposite Saturn:** You feel uneasy and anxious. Old habits die, and outworn patterns crumble under the onslaught of forces beyond your control.

✔ **Uranus conjunct natal Uranus:** The Uranus return occurs when you're 84 years old. It symbolizes a complete cycle of individuality and can stimulate you to seek a new expression of your most essential self.

✔ **Uranus opposite natal Uranus:** This unsettling, anxiety-provoking, midlife-crisis transit, which happens around age 42, encourages you to take risks and boosts your desire to rebel against the status quo.

✔ **Uranus conjunct Neptune:** If you were born in the early 1990s, you may have undergone this perplexing, sensitizing transit as a child. (Episodes of psychic awareness may be traced to this influence.) However, if you're old enough to remember 1993 (Hint: President Bill Clinton was inaugurated), you won't experience this transit in your lifetime.

✔ **Uranus opposite Neptune:** If you're feeling the effects of this transit, you're probably in your 70s. The advantage of aging, aside from getting into the movies at a discount, is that you worry less about what other people think and more about what matters to you. Amazing dreams, modern music, and nontraditional spiritual pursuits have a surprising appeal. Avoid get-rich-quick schemes.

✔ **Uranus conjunct Pluto:** This heavy-duty transit can bring transitions that are unforeseen and momentous. However, unless you're over 100 years old, you aren't going to experience it.

✔ **Uranus opposite Pluto:** Old patterns and obsessions fall by the wayside with this transit, especially if Pluto is prominent in your horoscope.

- ✔ **Uranus conjunct the Ascendant:** Altering your appearance, acting in an abrupt or unpredictable manner, and emphasizing your greatest eccentricities are methods of expressing your insistent need for personal freedom. This transit can also coincide with unexpected recognition.

- ✔ **Uranus opposite the Ascendant:** Whether you initiate these changes or someone else does, unexpected shake-ups in relationships clear the way for greater freedom and individuality. The people who attract you now are markedly different from your usual type.

- ✔ **Uranus conjunct the Midheaven:** Career upheavals can open a dramatic chapter in your life if you have the courage to respond. When an unusual opportunity presents itself, grab it. Don't let unresolved feelings of inferiority keep you from fulfilling your destiny.

- ✔ **Uranus opposite the Midheaven:** Unexpected events and challenges can turn your domestic life upside down and alter your social status or professional relationships. A sudden move isn't impossible.

Uranus, the planet of upheaval, brings unexpected changes and can be associated with chaos and disorientation, as well as liberation.

Nebulous Neptune

Magical, mysterious Neptune is befuddling and inspiring. It dissolves boundaries, spawns illusions, encourages compassion, and stimulates the imagination. Unlike Uranus, Neptune's influence can be difficult to detect, because it comes wrapped in a haze of confusion. When something's happening but you don't know what it is, look to Neptune, which takes about 164 years to travel through the zodiac. The Appendix presents its itinerary.

- ✔ **Neptune conjunct the Sun:** Self-pity, moodiness, and a diminished sense of self-esteem are the downsides of this lengthy transit. It can also fortify your idealism, compassion, vision, and psychic sensitivity.

- ✔ **Neptune opposite the Sun:** Your ability to deceive yourself (or to allow yourself to be deceived) is at a peak during this vaguely mystifying transit. Though your confidence may waver, sometimes wandering in the wilderness is all you can do. You're looking for a more compassionate sense of self.

- ✔ **Neptune conjunct the Moon:** You're empathetic, forgiving, and highly attuned to the emotional environment around you, be it positive or negative. To defend yourself against illusion, set limits and pay close attention to your intuition.

✔ **Neptune opposite the Moon:** Emotional uncertainty, the urge to escape, and unfamiliar obsessions may afflict you. You're easily deluded, so be cautious about falling in love or devoting yourself to a spiritual advisor with an answer for everything. Don't let others erode your trust in yourself.

✔ **Neptune conjunct Mercury:** If you're a poet, artist, or musician, you're going to love this transit. But be prepared: The imaginative boost occurs at the expense of the ordinary things you count on Mercury for — like making intelligent decisions or remembering to pay your bills.

✔ **Neptune opposite Mercury:** Think you're communicating clearly? Think you've come up with a foolproof plan to eradicate war, hunger, or terrorism? Think again. Neptune stimulates your artistic impulses, but it also foments an atmosphere in which misguided thinking can thrive.

✔ **Neptune conjunct Venus:** You're acutely sensitive and primed to fall in love. But does the object of your devotion return your affection? Is the relationship as perfect as you imagine? Remember, please, that Neptune is the planet of delusion. Similarly, if you tumble into the trap of self-pity and become convinced that you'll always be alone, dismiss that feeling and put your trust in art, music, poetry, and the universe.

✔ **Neptune opposite Venus:** You feel riled up, especially (but not solely) about your love life. Romantic visions dance in your head, yet you're unwilling or unable to fulfill those dreams. This transit, like the conjunction of Neptune and Venus, stimulates wishful thinking in a big way.

✔ **Neptune conjunct Mars:** If you're angry or envious, or you're wasting your abilities, you dissipate your energy. By acting intuitively and marshalling your talents, you lay the groundwork for success. Pay attention to coincidence and luck, whether good or bad. The outer world mirrors your inner reality and tells you whether you're on the right path.

✔ **Neptune opposite Mars:** Confused about what you want? Observe yourself as your suppressed desires rise into awareness and express themselves in your actions. And watch, too, when you respond negatively to other people. Those reactions reflect your shadow, the dark side of your personality.

✔ **Neptune conjunct Jupiter:** You fantasize about a multitude of possibilities. And so, without even realizing it, you open yourself up to new experiences. Your idealism, compassion, and faith in life grow.

✔ **Neptune opposite Jupiter:** You're sympathetic, idealistic, and open to experience — but you're out of touch with reality. Don't buy that bridge.

✔ **Neptune conjunct Saturn:** The rigid rules and regulations you live by aren't working anymore, and you need to update them with a more inspired, less fearful set of bylaws. Remind yourself that everyone who was born within a few months of you is experiencing this transit. And be sensible about money.

✔ **Neptune opposite Saturn:** Old fears and blockages appear, and you have to face them squarely. This is a challenging but not necessarily negative time, for Neptune can dispel the limitations of the past.

✔ **Neptune conjunct Uranus:** In the 21st century, this generational transit affects only the elderly. It's likely to produce altered states of consciousness, a vision of freedom, and an outbreak of eccentricity.

✔ **Neptune opposite Uranus:** Vague dissatisfaction of the midlife-crisis kind afflicts you. If you've been in a rut, even if it's one you dug yourself, you may try to redefine yourself through exciting experiences.

✔ **Neptune conjunct natal Neptune:** If you're experiencing this transit, you're too young (still an infant) or too ancient (164) to worry about it.

✔ **Neptune opposite natal Neptune:** This transit happens at age 82, about two years before Uranus returns. It can coincide with increased confusion, but it can also strengthen your imagination and spiritual awareness.

✔ **Neptune conjunct Pluto:** This conjunction isn't going to happen in your lifetime.

✔ **Neptune opposite Pluto:** This transit exerts a subtle influence that increases awareness and encourages you to rethink various aspects of your life, including psychological issues you've tried to repress.

✔ **Neptune conjunct the Ascendant:** Neptune dissolves the boundaries of the external personality, leaving you unfocused or lost in a reverie. Consciously or not, you may alter your image. At worst, you're self-destructive. At best, you're intuitive and creative. Art, music, film, dream analysis, and spiritual exploration are healthy outlets. And there's nothing wrong with daydreaming.

✔ **Neptune opposite the Ascendant:** If you're in a satisfying relationship, the two of you develop a form of communication that's virtually clairvoyant. But if your relationship is shaky, secrecy and deception can bring the house down. Pay attention to nuance.

✔ **Neptune conjunct the Midheaven:** The boundaries of your career are dissolving. Mysterious goings-on in the office may worry you and cause you to consider other career options. Satisfaction may come through spiritual matters, film, photography, music, art, oceanography, and anything that involves the healing professions. But beware, for you may also be subject to delusion, as often occurs with Neptune.

✔ **Neptune opposite the Midheaven:** Confusion or dissatisfaction with your career, your parents, or your home life clouds your decision-making ability. To find purpose and resolution, listen to your inner voice. Or talk to your grandparents. As always with Neptune, help can be found through art, music, spiritual pursuits, and long walks on the beach.

Neptune dissolves boundaries, creates confusion, invites illusion, and sensitizes the imagination.

Power-Hungry Pluto

In 2006, astronomers reclassified Pluto as a dwarf planet. This may make a difference to astrophysicists (though I can't see why it should). Astrologers essentially don't care. In our interpretation of the universe, Pluto is associated with power, regeneration, and the underworld of the psyche — a place where alchemy is the operative metaphor and size is deeply, truly meaningless. Plutonian transits, which last for two or three years, coincide with periods of profound change.

✔ **Pluto conjunct the Sun:** Your awareness increases. You become obsessed with your potential and are ultimately unwilling to be anyone other than your most powerful self. Inappropriate relationships and jobs can drop away during this critical period. Also important: Unresolved issues regarding your father or other authority figures need to be addressed. In the first half of the 21st century, only Sagittarius, Capricorn, Aquarius, and Pisces will experience this transit.

✔ **Pluto opposite the Sun:** Circumstances force you to take control of your destiny. Relationships may suffer. Despite opposition or conflicts with authority, you're determined to act in the most powerful possible way. Above all, you seek recognition. Constructive action leads to success; vengeful, fear-based, or egotistical behavior backfires. Over the next couple of years, a new phase of your life begins.

✔ **Pluto conjunct the Moon:** Powerful emotional forces are swirling around you. You may even have to deal with a death in the family. Concerns that you may have ignored since childhood reemerge, including issues regarding your mother. Confronting issues of dependency and inferiority brings healing and catharsis.

✔ **Pluto opposite the Moon:** Emotional turmoil and changing family circumstances provoke shifts in your domestic environment. Facing the truth is the only option, painful though it may be.

✔ **Pluto conjunct Mercury:** Take yourself seriously. Your mental capacity is developing, and your insights are more penetrating than ever before. You're able to influence others through the spoken or written word.

✔ **Pluto opposite Mercury:** Differences in opinion, problems in communication, and obsessive (or depressive) thoughts may disturb you. Secrets may be revealed. You also have a chance to communicate in a more forceful way.

✔ **Pluto conjunct Venus:** Jealousy, resentment, or obsessive love may have you in its grip. Unconsciously you seek a profound connection, and you can probably find it during this intense — and occasionally miserable — period.

✔ **Pluto opposite Venus:** An emotional crisis can cause a relationship to either crumble or deepen. Disputes, a clash of value, or unresolved

sexual issues may need to be addressed. Also, financial problems may hound you.

✔ **Pluto conjunct Mars:** Increased determination and ambition open many doors. Your increased ability to focus enables you to act with greater effect. Although you need to find ways to manage your anger, your energy is transformed.

✔ **Pluto opposite Mars:** Upsetting events or circumstances beyond your control force you to take action and to channel your anger in constructive ways.

✔ **Pluto conjunct Jupiter:** Expand the boundaries of your life, and you can utterly transform it. Opportunities pop up through education, travel, religion, or the law.

✔ **Pluto opposite Jupiter:** Your desire for success and power motivates you to widen your horizons. Be aware that overestimating yourself is a distinct possibility. Also, if you're religious, you may experience a crisis of faith.

✔ **Pluto conjunct Saturn:** Shedding your self-imposed chains is far from easy. This conjunction ushers in a period of intense self-examination and results in permanent change.

✔ **Pluto opposite Saturn:** Outside forces thwart your efforts and force you to alter your plans during this time of unasked-for change. As always with Saturn, you benefit from self-control and hard work.

✔ **Pluto conjunct Uranus:** If you've repressed your individuality, it reemerges now. Simple rebelliousness leads nowhere. If you have overplayed the flamboyant role, you're ready to tone down your eccentricities. If you've tried to hide your most idiosyncratic self, embrace it now. You'll find unexpected fulfillment.

✔ **Pluto opposite Uranus:** Surprising circumstances propel you into the future, forcing you to come to terms with who you are and who you want to be.

✔ **Pluto conjunct Neptune:** Your dreams, beliefs, and ideals are slowly shifting.

✔ **Pluto opposite Neptune:** Unless you're well over 100 years old, this transit isn't one you have to worry about.

✔ **Pluto conjunct natal Pluto:** Not possible.

✔ **Pluto opposite natal Pluto:** Not possible (unless you're 123 years old).

✔ **Pluto conjunct the Ascendant:** You're no longer willing to deny or suppress your personal power. A stronger self-image fortifies your resolution and spurs you to initiate change.

✔ **Pluto opposite the Ascendant:** You demand to be recognized for the powerful person you are, and you want to make an impact on the world. If a relationship is holding you down in any way, it must go.

> ✔ **Pluto conjunct the Midheaven:** Your career (or your role in the community) enters an era of slow, major shift.
>
> ✔ **Pluto opposite the Midheaven:** Habits need to change. Over the next few years, your circumstances at home and your relationship with your parents will undergo a deep shift.

Pluto brings disintegration, regeneration, and metamorphosis. External conflicts with power and internal rumbles within the psyche characterize these transformative transits.

Warning: The Astrologer's Curse

If you're anything like me, you may discover that knowing the rudiments of transits can fill you with fear. Sooner or later, you'll notice a troublesome transit approaching and you'll start to panic as worst-case scenarios haunt your imagination. Weeks or months later, you may be surprised to realize that not one of the disasters has occurred. Major events, whether positive or negative, require a confluence of influences, which is why the longer you follow the transits, the more restrained you're likely to become in your predictions.

The rules of transit interpretation are simple:

> ✔ **If the configurations in your birth chart don't make a certain event possible, it won't happen, no matter what the transits.** Unpredictable Uranus dancing through your second house of finances cheek to cheek with bountiful Jupiter brings a lottery bonanza if and only if your birth chart is littered with aspects for making easy money. The predisposition has to be there.
>
> ✔ **Even with a birth predisposition, a single transit seldom correlates with a life-altering event.** Those dramatic situations arise from a collection of influences, all pointing in a similar direction.
>
> ✔ **Any transit has several possible interpretations.** Nothing is predestined. But the energy of the transit must be expressed. The way that occurs depends on circumstances and on the choices you make.

Here's a case where foreseeing catastrophe would have been so easy — and so wrong. Imagine a person whose Sun, Ascendant, and several planets are being pummeled not only by Saturn but also by Uranus, Neptune, and Pluto. Even individually, those distant worlds have been known to make astrologers twitch. When they all act up at once, it's hard not to get nervous.

So I wonder what I would have said in 1993 if Toni Morrison, whose chart is reproduced in Figure 16-4, had asked me for a consultation. Her birth chart is in the interior part of the wheel. The transiting planets are in the outer part.

Looking at that chart, I would have noticed that Saturn, the planet of lessons, was transiting back and forth over her Sun (and had twice made an exact conjunction with it earlier that year); that Uranus and Neptune, traveling in tandem in the ninth house, were conjunct her Saturn and opposed to her natal Pluto; and that transiting Pluto had been dueling with her Ascendant for about a year and was approaching an exact opposition.

Observing all of this, I might have uttered cheerful words about transformation (Pluto) and responsibility (Saturn). I certainly would have told her that Saturn transiting through the tenth house often correlates with professional success. But secretly, I would have been worried. Like a lot of people, I find it easy to imagine catastrophe.

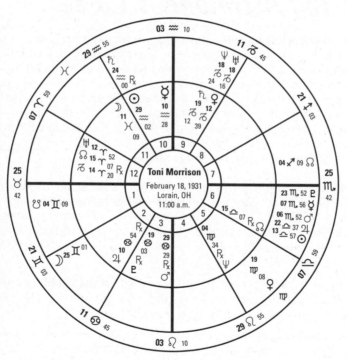

Figure 16-4: Toni Morrison's natal chart. Her birth chart is on the inner part of the wheel. The planets scattered around the outer rim represent the transits for 1993.

So what actually happened to Toni Morrison in 1993? She won the Nobel Prize for Literature. And sure enough, with Saturn in her Sun sign, she had indeed reaped what she had sown.

The most self-destructive mistake you can make as an astrologer is to allow your knowledge of transits to become a source of anxiety. Take it from me: Most of the terrifying things that astrologers agonize over never come to pass. Don't waste your time worrying about them.

Chapter 17

The Lunar Advantage: Using Astrology in Daily Life

Do you know where the Moon is right now? Without looking out the window, do you remember its phase? Can you name the sign of the zodiac that it inhabits? Do you know whether it's waxing or waning?

Don't feel bad if you don't know the answer to any of these questions. Except when the Moon is full, most people don't have a clue about where it is or what it's doing. But thousands of years ago, men and women on every continent worshipped the Moon and were attentive to all its phases. In those early cultures, storytellers created a cast of lunar deities, each of whom reflected a different phase of the moon. In Greece, for example, tomboy Artemis, patron of girls, was a goddess of the New Moon; Hera, queen of the gods, and Demeter, mother of Persephone, ruled the Full Moon; and Hecate, a goddess of a certain age, reigned over witchcraft and the waning lunar crescent. Unlike ourselves, the people of long ago who worshipped those goddesses observed the Moon carefully and were fully aware of its location. Over time, they discovered that the monthly journey of the Moon as it waxed and waned both reflected and supported the pattern of human activity.

That ancient knowledge is within your grasp. When you understand the Moon and its fundamental changes, you can choose dates that strengthen your intentions, avoid dates that could lead to frustration or failure, and live your life according to the rhythms of the cosmos. This chapter tells you how — and when — to seize the day.

Timing Your Actions by the Light of the Moon

How many phases of the Moon are there? It depends on who you ask. In India, astrologers identify 27 "lunar mansions." The great 20th century astrologer (and musician) Dane Rudhyar counted eight phases: New, Crescent, First Quarter, Disseminating, Full, Gibbous, Last Quarter, and Balsamic (no relationship to the vinegar). Ancient goddess worshippers, like their contemporary Pagan and Wiccan equivalents, generally acknowledged three phases: waxing, full, and waning. Today, most people recognize the following four phases of the Moon:

- **New:** A time of increasing energy and new beginnings. New Moons are especially powerful when they coincide with solar eclipses, something that usually happens twice a year.

- **First Quarter:** A time of growth, friction, and action.

- **Full:** A time of illumination when ongoing situations come to a head, emotions are heightened, and major events take place. Full Moons are especially dramatic and revealing when they're also lunar eclipses.

- **Last Quarter:** A time of completion, release, and fading vitality.

By taking note of these natural rhythms, you can time your activities to maximum advantage — and you don't need an astrological calendar either. Just glance at the Moon whenever you're out at night, and soon, knowing its phase will become second nature to you. Table 17-1 describes the approximate appearance and orientation of the Moon along with the actions best suited to each phase.

Table 17-1	What to Do by the Light of the Moon	
Phase of the Moon	*Appearance*	*Recommended Activities*
New Moon	Invisible at first; then it appears as a sliver with the tips of the crescent pointing east. Rises at dawn, sets at sunset.	Begin; make wishes; set goals; start projects; plant seeds; initiate endeavors.
First Quarter Moon	A semicircle with the flat side facing east (on the left) and the curved side facing west. Rises at noon. High in the sky after sunset. Sets around midnight.	Take action; develop projects; take essential steps; make decisions; deal with conflict.

Phase of the Moon	Appearance	Recommended Activities
Full Moon	A glowing orb. Rises at sunset. High in the sky at midnight. Sets around dawn.	Assess progress as emotions run high and things come to fruition; make adjustments; deal with the fallout.
Last Quarter Moon	A semicircle with the flat side facing west (on the right) and the curved side facing east. Rises at midnight. High in the sky before dawn.	Finish up; wind down; reflect; retreat.

Once a year, there's a New Moon in your sign. Regardless of whether it comes before or after your birthday, the highly charged period between those two days is ideal for setting yearly goals and taking the initial steps toward fulfilling them. If the New Moon happens to fall right on your birthday, congratulations. The coming year promises to be a time of new beginnings.

Using the Moon in the Signs

A helpful way to stay in sync with the Moon is to track its journey through the zodiac. To do this, use the Moon table in the Appendix, which tells you exactly when the Moon changes sign for every year from 1930 to 2012. Or get an astrological calendar. Personally, I wouldn't be without one.

Although the Appendix has the minimum amount of information you need to follow the Moon through the signs, astrological calendars contain a great deal more. Two of the best are *Llewellyn's Daily Planetary Guide* and *Jim Maynard's Celestial Guide* or *Celestial Influences Calendars*. These calendars, both of which are available in a variety of sizes, also tell you the phases of the Moon, the aspects it forms with other planets, the timing of eclipses, and the exact moment when the Moon enters each sign of the zodiac. If you can't find these calendars in your favorite bookstore, visit The Astrology Center of America at www.astroamerica.com to order them.

Knowing the location of the Moon is a lot of fun. Over the years, I've found that I enjoy certain lunar placements more than others. As a writer, I love Moon in Gemini. I always hope to accomplish a lot on those few days — even though experience has shown me that Moon in Gemini pulls in out-of-town visitors and unavoidable engagements more than any other sign and sets the phone to ringing in a way that seems beyond my control. Nonetheless, when I do sit at my desk on those days, the words pour out.

Getting advice from the Internet

A perceptive monthly or weekly horoscope can help you align yourself with the cosmos. Here are two of my favorites:

✔ **Susan Miller's Astrology Zone:** Her monthly forecasts, available at `www.astrology zone.com`, are warm, motivating, deeply informed, and amazingly specific. She discusses New Moons and Full Moons and is especially savvy about eclipses. You can't go wrong.

✔ **Rob Brezsny's Free Will Astrology News-letter:** He doesn't talk about the planets or use astrological jargon. He tells stories — parables — and they don't always hit the spot. When they do, they reverberate in the mind for days. Check him out at `www.freewillastrology.com`.

I love Moon in Virgo, too: It's ideal for taking care of business — and cleaning the house. I'm not the most efficient person on the planet, but you'd never know it on these days.

Watching the Moon as you go about your everyday activities casts them in an interesting light. But I want to emphasize the importance of doing this in a casual, nonobsessive way. Otherwise, you run the risk of getting so involved with the heavens that you lose sight of events right here on Earth.

That said, here's how to make the most of the Moon's journey through each sign:

✔ **Moon in Aries:** Be bold. Assert yourself, start short-term projects, do anything that requires a blast of energy and a spark of courage. Watch out for temper tantrums.

✔ **Moon in Taurus:** Be practical. Begin long-term projects, garden, pay your bills. Concentrate on jobs that call for patience. Listen to your body. Take a walk in the woods.

✔ **Moon in Gemini:** Converse, read, write in your journal, take pictures. Buy books, magazines, and stationery. Run errands, take short trips, change your mind.

✔ **Moon in Cancer:** Stay home. Cook, redecorate, call your mother. Spend time with people you love. Shop for antiques. Walk on the beach. Go outside and gaze up at the stars.

✔ **Moon in Leo:** Let the good times roll. Be romantic, cavort with children, learn the tango, attend the theatre, throw a party, dare to approach high-status people. Be confident.

- **Moon in Virgo:** Take care of the mundane. Scrub the floor, visit the dentist, go to the vet, attend to the nitpicky details you otherwise avoid. This might not sound fun, but the Moon in Virgo is incredibly useful — and it comes around every month.

- **Moon in Libra:** Indulge yourself. Go to a concert or museum, do something artistic, have a beauty treatment, smooth over disagreements. Form a business partnership. Sign a peace treaty. Get married.

- **Moon in Scorpio:** Expect intense encounters. Have sex, see your therapist, read a mystery novel, file your taxes, pay your debts, get insurance, investigate anything.

- **Moon in Sagittarius:** Explore. Travel, attend a class, talk to a lawyer, pursue spiritual or philosophical interests, take a bike ride, go the gym, alter your routine.

- **Moon in Capricorn:** Be businesslike. Print out your résumé, prepare a contract, do tasks that involve corporations or other large organizations. Talk to an older person. Investigate the past. Do your duty.

- **Moon in Aquarius:** Socialize. Volunteer for a cause. Go online, buy software, get together with friends, see an independent film, visit a planetarium. Do something unusual.

- **Moon in Pisces:** Relax. Meditate, take a nap, space out, listen to music, go swimming, analyze your dreams. Have an intimate talk or a good cry.

Tracking the Moon in the Houses

Tracking the Moon through the houses of your birth chart is another way to tap into its power. However, you can only do this if you know the time of your birth and have identified your rising sign or Ascendant. (For instructions on how to figure that out, see Chapter 11.)

Say, for example, that you have Leo rising — that is, Leo on the cusp of your first house. When the Moon is in that sign, it's traveling through your first house. Once it swings into Virgo, it enters your second house. And so on.

At any given moment, the Moon is in one sign of the zodiac and one house of your chart. If you want to get persnickety about it, you could figure out exactly when the Moon will hit the precise degree of each house cusp. But who has time for that? Not me. I suggest that you simply note the sign on the cusp of each house. When the Moon enters that sign, that's your cue to turn your attention to the matters of that house. For example:

- **Moon in the first house:** Do something for yourself. Get a haircut or a manicure. Schedule an interview, a first date, or a presentation at work. Your visibility is high, so present yourself with flair. You'll make a positive impression.

✔ **Moon in the second house:** Greater security means greater peace of mind. Practical and financial matters demand your notice. Pay bills. Meet with a financial advisor. Have a yard sale. Make important purchases. And if you're involved with construction in any way, get to work.

✔ **Moon in the third house:** Feeling restless? Run some errands. Go to the library. Gather information. Make phone calls. Talk to the neighbors. Get together with brothers and sisters. Take a short trip. This position favors reading, writing, and anything having to do with school.

✔ **Moon in the fourth house:** Focus on home, family, parents, and the past.

✔ **Moon in the fifth house:** Romance, recreation, creative pursuits, and anything having to do with children are enhanced during these few days.

✔ **Moon in the sixth house:** The emphasis is on work, health, and the routines of daily life. Clear your desk. Organize your files. Catch up on everything you let slide. Also: Start a diet. Go to the gym. Get a checkup. Take care of yourself.

✔ **Moon in the seventh house:** If you're married, set your needs aside and focus on your mate. If you have a business partner or you deal with the public at large, put your attention there. This house is all about cooperation, but it also rules your adversaries. When the Moon is in the seventh house, other people are in control — like it or not.

✔ **Moon in the eighth house:** When the Moon is in the domain of sex, death, regeneration, and other people's money, you could have an affair, rob a bank, visit a mortuary, or just — you know — see your shrink, perhaps about your compulsive behaviors or feelings of dependency. Whatever you do, the emotional charge is likely to be intense. This is the house of transformation.

✔ **Moon in the ninth house:** Anything that involves publishing, education, religion, or the law moves forward now. It's all about expanding your vision. Traveling to faraway places definitely helps.

✔ **Moon in the tenth house:** The emphasis is on career, community affairs, and your public image. Send out your résumé. Give a speech. Be in the world.

✔ **Moon in the eleventh house:** See friends. Let them remind you of your most cherished aspirations. Or join a group. Whether it's the Audubon Society or the Democratic Party, you benefit from the association.

✔ **Moon in the twelfth house:** Retreat. Rejuvenate yourself with solitude and sleep. This is the house of the unconscious and of self-undoing. So heed your dreams — and don't do anything rash.

Making the Most of Momentous Lunar Influences

The Moon cruises through the zodiac faster than any other planet, so worrying about it as it spins through one sign after another can drive you crazy. Most transits of the Moon make no difference whatsoever and can be safely ignored. Nevertheless, a few monthly lunar transits offer opportunities that are too valuable to miss. Here are the top five monthly influences:

- **The Moon in your Sun sign:** Your personal power is at its peak. You are your most charismatic self during these few days, making them a fine time to schedule important meetings, blind dates, or anything that requires you to be at your outgoing best.

- **The Moon in the sign opposite your Sun sign:** Your personal power is weak. You're at the beck and call of others, and your plans are likely to be scuttled or interrupted. Expect interference.

- **The Moon in your Moon sign:** Your emotions flow freely, whether you want them to or not. You're more sensitive and easily hurt than usual, but you're also more attuned to emotional subtleties and unconscious motivations. Listen to your intuition.

- **Dark of the Moon:** At the end of the lunar cycle, the Moon is so close to the Sun that it's invisible. During this period of decrease, attempts to launch new ventures fizzle, and hopelessness often abounds. Instead of exerting yourself in a fruitless attempt to influence events, put the finishing touches on undertakings that are nearing conclusion. Also, get plenty of sleep, secure in the knowledge that the New Moon means a fresh start.

- **New Moon:** Make wishes, set goals, and inaugurate new projects.

Finally, I want to mention one other momentous lunar influence: the eclipse. If you've ever watched an eclipse, you know how eerie it can be. A solar eclipse, which takes place during a New Moon, literally turns day to night. A lunar eclipse, which happens during the Full Moon, seems to erase the Moon from the sky. No wonder ancient people told so many myths about them.

Followers of astrology also have myths, one of which is that eclipses always bring bad news. That's flat out false. But people are afraid of change, and change is what eclipses are about. When an eclipse — or a series of eclipses — hits your chart, it brings a burst of cosmic energy that can shake things up. I've seen eclipses usher in hideous divorces, and I've seen them bring true love. Eclipses slam some doors shut — and open others. And sometimes, they do nothing much at all . . . until later. An eclipse can have a delayed effect.

A good astrological calendar will tell you when — and where — to expect an eclipse. Notice its location by sign and by house. Those are the areas where change is on its way.

Avoiding the Void

Picture this: The Moon spins into a new sign — let's say Taurus — and begins to connect with the planets. It conjuncts Jupiter in the evening (a splendid sight), trines Venus a few minutes later, squares the Sun the next morning, opposes Mars at noon, conjuncts Saturn during *All Things Considered,* and then sextiles Mercury. After that . . . nothing: No more major aspects. A few hours later, it enters Gemini, and the process begins anew.

That span, between the Moon's last major aspect in one sign and its entrance into the next, can last anywhere from a few seconds to a day or longer. During that time, the Moon is said to be *void-of-course.* If the word "void" makes you nervous, you sense the problem. When the Moon is void-of-course, things fall apart and judgment goes awry. Though ordinary activities are unaffected, business deals made during that time tend to crumble, and decisions, however carefully made, turn out to be wrong-headed.

The usual advice for a void-of-course Moon is to postpone anything important (like a job interview, wedding, or presidential campaign) and to avoid jumping into anything new. But let's get real: You'd have to be unnaturally vigilant to live that way. The Moon goes void-of-course every couple of days, and to worry about it on a regular basis is insane. I used to dismiss it entirely. And then one day a publisher called out of the blue, asked me to write a book on a subject I love, and requested a meeting. I agreed to the suggested time even though the Moon was void-of-course. The meeting couldn't have been more exciting. We hit it off perfectly, saw eye to eye on everything, and enthusiastically agreed to terms. Yet the project died. Would it have made a difference if I'd scheduled the meeting for another time? Perhaps not. Nonetheless, after that disappointment I began to pay attention to the void-of-course Moon, and I have found that it does indeed have an effect.

Still, most of the time, I ignore it. But when I'm scheduling an event I care about, launching a long-term enterprise, planning a vital interview, or making a large purchase (cars and appliances count; paperback books don't), I check my handy astrological calendar and — if at all possible — I avoid the void.

Chapter 18

Retrograde Hell? The Truth Revealed

*I*t's amazing how many people there are who can't cast a horoscope, don't know their rising signs, and yet practically have panic attacks over the retrograde movement of Mercury. These supposedly sinister periods, during which that little planet appears to travel backward, arrive regularly three or four times a year. And yes, they do usher in a volley of setbacks, misunderstandings, irritations, and minor disruptions. Worse yet, they stir up a storm of fear and anxiety in the hearts of astrology fans everywhere. But is this reaction called for? In a word, no. Retrograde motion isn't a tragedy. It isn't a disaster. It isn't even a cause for alarm. It's a respite and a gift from the cosmos — but only if you understand its purpose and use it appropriately. In this chapter, I tell you what you need to know to grapple calmly and rationally with retrograde movements.

Retrograde Revealed

When a planet is *retrograde,* it looks like it's reeling backward through the zodiac. In truth, the planets move forward constantly, but that's not the way it looks. Although the Sun and the Moon clearly revolve in the same direction all year every year, the planets seem to follow a less consistent pattern. On a regular schedule, each of the planets appears to slow down, reverse direction, and retrace its path, arcing backward across the zodiac. For weeks or months at a time (depending on the planet), it wheels against the planetary tide. Then once again, it seems to slow down, turn around, and resume normal movement (which is referred to as *going direct*).

When ancient astronomers saw the heavenly bodies whirling backward, they invented all kinds of schemes to account for the phenomenon. In the second century BCE, for example, astronomers in Greece were convinced that the planets looped around their usual orbits on little spheres carved from the purest crystal. Needless to say, they were wrong. The planets never actually switched direction.

Retrograde motion is solely a perception — an illusion caused by the fact that the planets, including Earth, are always in motion, tracing arcs across the sky as they loop around the Sun at varying speeds. You can experience the same disconcerting effect in a train. If two trains pull out of the station together but your train is moving faster, the train on the adjacent track appears to slide backward. That backward motion, like the retrograde motion of the planets, is an optical illusion.

Successfully Handling Retrograde Mercury

Here's a typical scenario from my life: The phone rings. I pick it up hesitantly (because, like most people, I have a teeny bit of telephone ESP). And indeed, it's one of the usual suspects calling in a frenzy after having experienced one frustration too many. The final straw may be a lost ATM card, an endless wait in the doctor's office, a missed appointment, a computer crash, the inability to rent an apartment at 1977 prices, a voice mail disaster, or another harrowing descent into an HMO inferno. Listening to the litany, I know what's coming. My faithful follower is about to ask this question: Is Mercury retrograde?

Often, the answer is yes. Tiny Mercury, the planet nearest the Sun, appears to change direction more frequently than any other planet. It goes into "reverse" three or four times a year for around three weeks at a stretch. During those irksome interludes — and particularly at the beginning and end — you can expect small mishaps, petty annoyances, and all sorts of miscommunication. When Mercury is retrograde, messages disappear in cyberspace, straightforward statements are misinterpreted, people forget appointments and lose papers, and answering machines, faxes, copiers, computers, and cellphones threaten to strike.

Making the best of it

Why crazy things happen when Mercury is retrograde, I can't claim to know. Astrology, to my way of thinking, is a system of metaphor, a symbolic cosmic language that reflects our lives the way the sea reflects the sky. So even though none of the planets ever actually spin backward, their apparent turn-around subtly affects our reactions, our perceptions, and our experiences.

When Mercury is retrograde, vexation abounds. Yet despite what you may have heard — and despite the inventory of possible woes I listed earlier in the chapter — retrograde Mercury isn't to be feared. It's a lesser force, not a tsunami. It forces you to slow down (because you're stuck in a traffic jam), to be flexible (because your flight just got canceled), to check on things you might normally ignore (because your package should have arrived by now). It encourages you to try another approach. Thus it offers something most people desperately need: a timeout, a chance to pick up the pieces.

When Mercury is retrograde, do *not*

- Launch an important project.
- Purchase a computer, a cellphone, a Blackberry, or any other communication device, including expensive fountain pens.
- Buy a car, a boat, or a home.
- Move into a new dwelling.
- Start a job.
- Begin a relationship.
- Sign a contract.
- Expect things to go smoothly.
- Try to fight the fates. Forcing things to happen on your schedule only creates further mayhem.

To get the most out of Mercury retrograde, breathe a sigh of relief and get off that treadmill. You've been given a reprieve. All you have to do is

- Review.
- Revise. (Mercury retrograde is invaluable for writers.)
- Reconsider. (If a former lover or an old problem reappears, Mercury retrograde can help you resolve the situation.)
- Revisit the past.
- Change your mind.
- Confirm your reservations.
- Check the facts.
- Make repairs.
- Do tasks you've been postponing.
- Correct mistakes.
- Get organized.
- Catch up on all forms of correspondence.

✔ Clear the decks.

✔ Send cards and packages early. (When Mercury is retrograde, mail may not arrive on time.)

✔ Carry a book or magazine at all times. (When Mercury is retrograde, your chances of having to wait in a line or being caught in a traffic jam increase exponentially. And don't count on your cellphone to keep you entertained: It's likely to transmit only static.)

Knowing when the hullabaloo is coming

Table 18-1 shows you when (and where) Mercury is retrograde from the first day of 2007 to the last day of 2012. The dates for each retrograde period correspond to the degrees of the zodiac listed in the "Location" column.

For example, the first line for the year 2007 shows that Mercury is retrograde from February 14 until March 7, during which time it wheels backward from 10° Pisces — its location on February 14 — to 25° Aquarius, where it ends up on March 7. At that point on March 7 it ceases to be retrograde. For a brief moment, Mercury seemingly stands still. Then it goes direct, moving forward once more in the usual way. Months pass. From its starting point at 25° Aquarius, Mercury spins happily through one-third of the zodiac. And then, on June 15, it changes direction once again, this time at 11° Cancer. And so the cycle begins anew.

Table 18-1	Retrograde Mercury	
Year	*Dates*	*Location*
2007	Feb. 14–Mar. 7	10° Pisces–25° Aquarius
2007	June 15–July 9	11° Cancer–2° Cancer
2007	Oct. 12–Nov. 1	9° Scorpio–23° Libra
2008	Jan. 28–Feb. 18	23° Aquarius–8° Aquarius
2008	May 26–June 14	21° Gemini–12° Gemini
2008	Sept. 24–Oct. 15	22° Libra–7° Libra
2009	Jan. 11–Feb. 1	7° Aquarius–21° Capricorn
2009	May 7–30	1° Gemini–22° Taurus
2009	Sept. 6–29	6° Libra–21° Virgo
2009	Dec. 26–31	21° Capricorn–19° Capricorn
2010	Jan. 1–15	18° Capricorn–5° Capricorn

Year	Dates	Location
2010	Apr. 17–May 11	12° Taurus–2° Taurus
2010	Aug. 20–Sept. 12	19° Virgo–5° Virgo
2010	Dec. 10–30	5° Capricorn–19° Sagittarius
2011	Mar. 30–Apr. 23	24° Aries–12° Aries
2011	Aug. 3–26	1° Virgo–18° Leo
2011	Nov. 24–Dec. 13	20° Sagittarius–3° Sagittarius
2012	Mar. 12–Apr. 4	6° Aries–23° Pisces
2012	July 14–Aug. 8	12° Leo–1° Leo
2012	Nov. 6–26	4° Sagittarius–18° Scorpio

Sometimes the weeks when Mercury is retrograde slip by so quietly that you barely notice. Other times, retrograde Mercury generates such a blizzard of delays and obstructions that you just can't miss its baleful influence. What makes the difference? The answer is easy: location, location, location. Look to see where Mercury is when it goes retrograde. If it's in your Sun sign, Moon sign, Mercury sign, or rising sign, you'll feel its impact. Similarly, when Mercury begins or ends its retrograde cycle within one or two degrees of a planet in your horoscope, you're likely to be affected. In both cases, get ready to revel in the rhythm of retrograde. And don't forget to bring a book.

Looking Out for Retrograde Venus

In Meso-American astrology, Venus ruled. The Aztecs and Mayans kept careful note of its rising and setting, its arrival as the morning star and as the evening star, its regular disappearances, and its intervals of retrograde motion, which occur every year and a half for about six weeks. According to Aztec astrologers, those retrograde weeks were dangerous times, especially in the political arena. Astrologers today generally see retrograde Venus as a time of uncertainty, distraction, misinterpretation, passivity, and unfulfilled desires in two areas: romance and finance.

It sounds bad, yet in reality, the effects are subtle. It seems to me that life is too short to worry excessively about this particular transit. In a strange way, I even find it comforting. For example, if your love life is less than spectacular — if it's nonexistent — then retrograde Venus gives you license to forget about it for a while and turn your mind to other matters. What a relief.

I do, however, have two iron-clad pieces of advice:

✔ Don't get married when Venus is retrograde (unless both you and your intended have retrograde Venus in your birth chart).

✔ Don't make any major financial commitments when Venus is retrograde — especially for a loan, a mortgage, a fur coat, an original piece of artwork, an emerald ring (emerald is the gem of Taurus, which Venus rules), or anything beloved by Venus (except for flowers, chocolates, and valentines).

Table 18-2 tells you when (and where) Venus is retrograde from 2007 to 2012. (2008 and 2011 aren't listed because Venus doesn't go retrograde during these years.)

Table 18-2	Retrograde Venus	
Year	*Dates*	*Location*
2007	July 27–Sept. 8	2° Virgo–16° Leo
2009	Mar. 6–Apr. 17	15° Aries–29° Pisces
2010	Oct. 8–Nov. 18	13° Scorpio–27° Libra
2012	May 15–June 27	23° Gemini–7° Gemini

Watching Out for Retrograde Mars

I love Mars, the red planet. Easily recognizable in the sky by its pale pink tint, it stimulates activity, prods us to take the initiative, and fills us with courage. Mars is enterprising, dynamic, determined, and dominating. True, it's also the planet of hostility and war. But without it, nothing would ever get done.

I like to think that in my chart, and in yours, the energy that motivates Mars can be funneled in positive directions. If nothing else, it thrives at the gym — and I'm not talking about yoga or the stationary bicycle. Mars prefers kickboxing. Let's be honest: Mars wants to fight. The harder you work out, the better.

But when Mars is retrograde, that energy is diverted. Roadblocks pop up out of nowhere, and the anger and belligerence associated with the warrior planet are driven underground. So progress slows down, even at the gym. Instigating new pursuits leads nowhere, and taking the offensive — or trying to — can create unanticipated consequences.

Aggressive Mars goes retrograde every 22 months for about 11 weeks. During those times, the cardinal rule is simple: Don't launch a crusade or go to war, metaphorically or otherwise.

Table 18-3 tells you when (and where) Mars is retrograde from 2007 to 2012. (It doesn't go retrograde at all during 2011.)

Table 18-3		Retrograde Mars
Year	*Dates*	*Location*
2007	Nov. 15–Dec. 31	12° Cancer–0° Cancer
2008	Jan. 1–Jan. 30	29° Gemini–24° Gemini
2009	Dec. 20–Dec. 31	19° Leo–18° Leo
2010	Jan. 1–Mar. 10	18° Leo–0° Leo
2012	Jan. 24–Apr. 14	23° Virgo–3° Virgo

The Other Planets

Past Mars, the planets are retrograde for months on end, and the whole matter becomes unimportant. Most of the time, there's no reason to get bent out of shape about retrograde planets beyond Mars.

I recommend paying attention to the retrograde motion of the outer planets under only two circumstances:

✔ **When five or six planets are retrograde at once.** Those are times when new endeavors inch forward at glacial speed. How do you know when planets are retrograde? I regret to say that this book can't help you. But any good astrological calendar can. The best ones are Llewellyn's Astrological Calendars (I'm partial to the *Daily Planetary Guide*) and the *Celestial Guide* and *Celestial Influences* calendars published by Jim Maynard.

✔ **When a planet turns retrograde or direct right on top of (or opposite to) your birth planet.** For instance, if Saturn (or any other planet) goes retrograde at 10° Leo and you happen to have a planet right there, you can expect to suffer the consequences. A problem from the past, something you thought was totally over, could arise. You'll have to contend with the same issues all over again. Your best and only move, taking your cue from Saturn, is to face reality.

Retrograde Mercury, Venus, and Mars in the birth chart

Years ago, I was under the impression that when a planet was retrograde, its energy was weakened. I changed my opinion when I noticed that some of the smartest, most articulate people I know have Mercury retrograde in their birth charts, as do some of my favorite writers — icons like M. F. K. Fisher, Robert Frost, Gabriel Garcia Marquez, Henry Miller, Philip Roth, Dylan Thomas, and J. R. R. Tolkien. Clearly, Mercury retrograde in a birth chart doesn't negate the ability to communicate. Rather, it bends your intellect inward, deepens it, increases your need for reflection, causes greater concern about exactly how you're communicating, and makes you a more independent and contemplative thinker. My guess is that writers with Mercury retrograde spend more time mulling things over and revising than other writers.

If you have retrograde Venus in your birth chart, you may be shy, uncertain, and hesitant to express affection, especially around potential partners. Romance isn't a lighthearted romp for you — much as you wish it were. It's complex and problematic, a matter for serious reflection, and as a result, you may hold yourself back in romantic situations. But don't despair. Venus retrograde doesn't deny romance. It merely slows it down. For instance, I know a good-hearted man with Venus retrograde who married a woman from another country — but never lived with or slept with her — simply to help her get a visa. He later found his true love — and his first "wife" was a guest at his second wedding.

Retrograde Mars makes an issue of aggression by forcing you to acknowledge your anger and focus it constructively. Some people with a retrograde Mars — Lizzie Borden comes to mind — never find a way to do this. Others succeed triumphantly. This list of world-class warriors speaks for itself: Franklin Delano Roosevelt, Billie Jean King, Jesse Jackson, and Martin Luther King, Jr. They all have Mars retrograde.

Part V
The Part of Tens

The 5th Wave   By Rich Tennant

"Let me give you a tip. Forget the racing form— try to get hold of the horse's birth chart."

In this part . . .

In this part, I tell you the traditional markers associated with ten different talents. I also show you how to use astrology as a guide to making important decisions in life, such as when to buy a computer, when to get married, and when to simply take it easy for a while. May you discover within these pages one of the great gifts of astrology: something fabulous about yourself and your potential that you didn't know.

Chapter 19

Ten Talents You Can Spot in a Chart

. . . .

In This Chapter

▶ Recognizing special talents in a birth chart

▶ Seeing astrology in action

. . . .

*W*here do extraordinary qualities come from? What goes into the chart of a world-class beauty, a groundbreaking artist, a celebrity, or a billionaire? These people obviously have something special . . . and maybe you do too. In the following sections, I reveal the astrological secrets behind great gifts.

Artistic Ability

Every sign has its complement of artists. But the all-time greats — geniuses like Leonardo da Vinci and Pablo Picasso — belong to a category all their own. Here are some indicators of artistic talent:

✔ **By sign:** Taurus, Libra, and Leo sustain artistic talent. Look for the Sun, Moon, Ascendant, Midheaven, or Venus in those signs.

✔ **By planet:** A prominent Venus and Neptune quicken the aesthetic sense and the imagination.

✔ **By house:** An active fifth house accentuates your need to be creative.

A planet is *prominent* when it's within 8° of your Ascendant or Midheaven; when it occupies an angle (that is, it's in the first, fourth, seventh, or tenth house of your chart); or when it makes close aspects to other planets.

A house is *active* either when it holds one or more planets or when its ruler is in a prominent position.

Consider the chart of Mexican artist Frida Kahlo (see Figure 19-1). During her lifetime, she wasn't as famous as her muralist husband, Diego Rivera. In recent years, her anguished, colorful canvases have attracted many admirers, and her fame has skyrocketed. Here's how her chart stacks up to the factors described earlier in this section:

✔ **By sign:** Two of the three signs on the list are central in Kahlo's chart. Taurus holds the Moon and the Midheaven, while Leo is the home of her Ascendant and her Mercury. Only Libra is vacant.

✔ **By planet:** Both Venus and Neptune are prominent in her chart. Venus rules her Midheaven, conjuncts Pluto, and sextiles her Ascendant. Neptune is closely conjunct her Sun.

✔ **By house:** Two planets — Uranus, the planet of originality, and Mars — inhabit the fifth house (along with the South Node). Also, the ruler of the fifth house, Jupiter, is conjunct her Sun in the sign of its exaltation, making it exceptionally well-placed.

Frida Kahlo struggled with heart-rending difficulties during her short life, but lack of artistic talent was not among them.

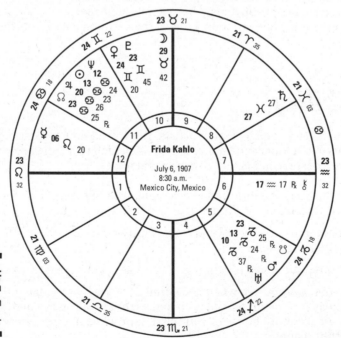

Figure 19-1:
Frida
Kahlo's birth
chart.

Athletic Prowess

Mighty Mars, the planet of aggression, figures strongly in the charts of athletes, who are statistically more likely than nonathletes to have Mars within striking distance of either the Midheaven or the Ascendant. (The specific areas near the Midheaven are the ninth house and first ten degrees of the tenth. The sensitive areas near the Ascendant are the twelfth house and the first ten degrees of the first house.) You see these positions in the charts of Muhammad Ali and Tiger Woods, both Capricorns. Ali has a tenacious Mars in Taurus conjunct the Midheaven. Tiger has a similar setup, with an impatient Mars in Gemini conjunct his Midheaven.

Mars can also be prominent for other reasons. For instance, I don't know whether Lance Armstrong has an angular Mars. Angularity depends on birth time, and I don't have that information about him. I do know this: His Mars in Aquarius aspects all but one of his other planets, making it very active indeed.

Mars can also dominate a chart in the opposite situation: When it makes no aspects whatsoever. Such a solitary planet, unhampered by other planets with competing agendas, operates without interference and can consequently be the strongest influence in a chart.

I don't want to suggest that Mars is the only planet that affects athletic ability. A well-placed Sun gives vitality. Mercury lends quickness. Jupiter, Uranus, and Pluto confer power. Athleticism, like other talents, is an amalgamation of many factors.

Finally, although gifted athletes are born under every sign of the zodiac, fire and earth signs are slightly more common among them than air and water. Athletes, like artists, benefit from a touch of Leo — not because it advances athletic ability (Leos, I have noticed, can be amazingly klutzy) but because it stimulates the love of performance. And *that* is definitely part of the game.

Beauty (Or the Power of Attraction)

If Mars promotes athletic ability, Venus amplifies beauty, particularly when it is

✔ Conjunct the Ascendant, the Sun, the Moon, the Midheaven, or the ruler of the Ascendant.

✔ In the first or tenth house.

✔ In Taurus or Libra, the signs it rules.

Brooke Shields, for instance, was a recognized beauty even as an infant, when her modeling career began. Her Venus sits at the top of her chart, conjoining her Midheaven. Angelina Jolie, whose very name advertises her prettiness, has Venus closely conjunct her Ascendant.

Not everyone with a prominent Venus boasts a gorgeous face. What they do have is even more valuable: the power of attraction. An example is former President Bill Clinton. He's a Leo (of course) with Venus in the first house in sociable Libra, the sign it rules. His Venus makes four conjunctions and two sextiles. So he easily attracts admirers. Hillary Rodham Clinton, on the other hand, has Venus in Scorpio, the sign of its detriment. With Venus conjunct her ruling planet (Mercury), she can be charming. But her Venus squares Saturn, Pluto, and Mars and makes an irritating (135°) angle to the Moon and Ascendant. Not surprisingly, as a public personality, she has to work harder to make her case.

Celebrity Appeal

Known for his silk-screened portraits and provocative paintings of Campbell's soup cans (and electric chairs), Andy Warhol is also remembered for his prescient statement, "In the future, everyone will be famous for 15 minutes." Well, that was easy for him to say. He had all the ingredients that celebrity appeal requires (see Figure 19-2):

- ✔ Planets conjunct the Midheaven and/or in the tenth house
- ✔ Planets conjunct the Ascendant and/or in the first house
- ✔ A touch of Leo

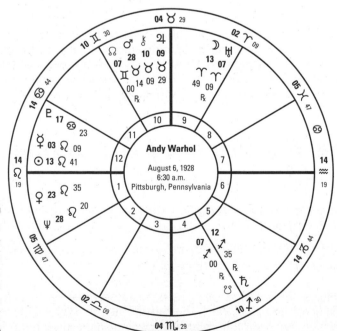

Figure 19-2: Andy Warhol's birth chart. He got his 15 minutes and more.

Specifically, he had Jupiter (and Chiron) conjunct the Midheaven, Mars in the tenth house, the Sun closely conjunct the Ascendant, and two planets — Venus and Neptune, the planets of art — in the first house. Plus, he had four planets and the Ascendant in Leo. Fame was his birthright.

Why is Paris Hilton a celebrity? I don't think it's that sex video (not that I've seen it). Nor is it her wealth (although her second house of money is loaded). It's something else: She has the astrological fingerprint for fame (see Figure 19-3). Planets conjunct the Midheaven? She's got two of them, including Jupiter, her ruling planet. Plus, Pluto is in the tenth house. Planets conjunct the Ascendant? Glamorous Neptune is right there. And, sure enough, she's got some Leo going on: the Moon and the North Node in the eighth house of sex and other people's money. Her fame is no accident.

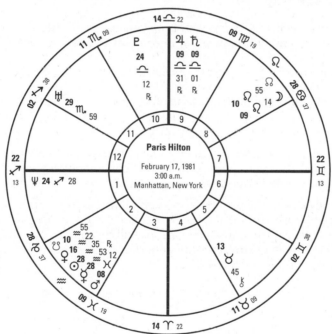

Figure 19-3:
Paris
Hilton's
birth chart.

Healing Hands

Doctors, nurses, acupuncturists, kind-hearted dentists, and others with the desire to heal share certain astrological characteristics:

> ✔ **By sign:** Cancer, Scorpio, and Pisces, the water signs, promote empathy. Virgo encourages an intellectual curiosity about health and healing techniques. Aquarius heightens humanitarian concern.

- **By planet:** Research has shown that doctors often have Saturn conjunct or opposite the Ascendant or Midheaven. Pluto, the planet of transformation, and Mars also figure heavily in the charts of healers.

- **By house:** The most crucial placements related to health are the sixth house of health and service; the eighth house of surgery, research, death, and rebirth; and the twelfth house of secrets and hospitals.

A house is powerful if it holds one or more planets, but even an empty house can be vital. If the ruler of that house is conjunct the Sun, Moon, Ascendant, or Midheaven, the matters of that house gain importance.

Business Savvy

How are Fortune 500 CEOs different from you and me (other than the fact that they fly around in private jets)? Here's how to spot executive ability:

- **By sign:** Taurus, Virgo, and Capricorn are the preeminent signs of business. Equally important is Scorpio, the sign of power politics, covert operations, and self-control. In business, as in other areas, you can also expect to see a little Leo. That's because Leos long to be on top, and they'll happily put in hours — make that years — of overtime to achieve that noble goal.

- **By planet:** Saturn, well-situated by sign, house, and aspect, grants organizational ability; Mercury provides skill in communication; and Mars fuels the competitive drive.

- **By house:** Look for planets in the tenth house of reputation, the sixth house of work, the second house of money, and the eighth house of investment. Those houses support executive ability. Also, planets in the first house can bestow considerable charisma, which is often the defining trait of a successful CEO.

Jack Welch, chairman and CEO of General Electric for 20 years, shows many of these traits (see Figure 19-4):

- **By sign:** With planets in all three earth signs, a Capricorn Ascendant, and the Sun in Scorpio, Welch shows clear organizational ability.

- **By planet:** Saturn rules his Ascendant and is therefore his ruling planet. Mercury is conjunct his Midheaven. But his most notable planet is his commanding, ambitious Mars. It's angular (in the first house), closely conjunct his Ascendant, well-aspected, and in the sign of its exaltation, all of which makes him exceptionally competitive and aggressive.

- **By house:** His Sun is in the tenth house of career and public life and is conjunct expansive Jupiter, which is another mark of leadership ability. His Moon is in the eighth house of investments, along with two other planets, and his ruler, Saturn, is in the second house of money.

Say what you will about the corporate world, that's where Jack Welch belongs.

Figure 19-4:
Jack
Welch's
birth chart.

Making Money

These are the traditional markers that point to the ability to amass money and material goods, whether through your own efforts or through sheer good luck:

- Planets in the second and eighth houses.
- Powerful, well-aspected planets ruling the second and eighth houses.
- A well-placed Jupiter. If you're lucky, it will connect with the second and eighth houses.

A glance at Jack Welch's chart (Figure 19-4) shows just what you might expect: He has four planets in the second and eighth houses, including Saturn, the ruler of his Ascendant. The ruler of his second house, Neptune, is conjunct the Moon in the eighth house. The ruler of his eighth house, Mercury, is conjunct the Midheaven. As for Jupiter, it's powerful by sign (because it's in Sagittarius, the sign it rules); by house (because it's in the tenth house of reputation); and by aspect (because it's conjunct his Sun).

Psychic Ability

Whether you call it extrasensory perception, clairvoyance, a sixth sense, or plain old intuition, psychic ability isn't as rare as you might think. Here's how to find it:

- **By sign:** Pisces, Scorpio, and Cancer bolster psychic ability. Sagittarius can also foster a tendency in that direction.

- **By planet:** Neptune and the Moon keep the channels of reception open (especially when they're conjunct). A prominent Uranus can bring flashes of insight and understanding. Pluto also boosts perception, especially if it aspects the Sun, Moon, Mercury, or the Ascendant. I'm not sure it's actually psychic, but if your powers of observation are acute, no one can tell the difference.

- **By house:** The twelfth, eighth, and fourth houses carry the most weight.

A classic illustration of psychic ability gone wild is the renowned healer Edgar Cayce, who worked as a "psychic diagnostician" (his term) by entering a trance and suggesting cures for clients he had never even met.

His chart (Figure 19-5) showed all the indications of psychic ability. He had the Sun and three planets in Pisces, three planets in the eighth house, a Moon/Neptune conjunction in the tenth house, and Uranus rising.

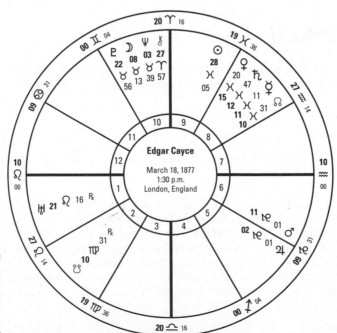

Figure 19-5: Edgar Cayce's birth chart.

Becoming an Astrologer

Becoming a skilled astrologer has nothing to do with psychic ability. Astrology is an accumulated body of knowledge — not the mystic ability to intercept messages from the spirit world. Anyone can learn it. But you're more likely to be interested if you have some of the following in your chart:

✔ A prominent Uranus.

✔ Activity in Aquarius and/or an active eleventh house. When I began studying astrology, I heard that two specific degrees often showed up in astrologers' charts: 25° Aquarius and 25° Leo. I'm not sure I believe that.

✔ Activity in Scorpio and/or the eighth house. Scorpio is subtle and incisive. It feels at home with contradictions and hidden motivations, and it loves to ferret out a mystery — and that's what astrology is all about.

Case in point: Isabel M. Hickey, whose 1970 book, *Astrology: A Cosmic Science,* 2nd edition (CRCS Publications, 1992), has inspired generations of astrologers. Look what she had going for her (see Figure 19-6): Uranus rising in her first house; Saturn in Aquarius; a Scorpio Ascendant; the Sun in Leo at 25°, one of the so-called astrologer's degrees; and a sensitive Moon/Neptune conjunction in the eighth house.

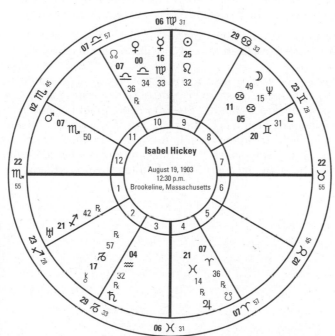

Figure 19-6: Isabel Hickey, astrologer extraordinaire.

Writing

It's astonishing how many people fantasize about writing. Here's what it takes to be a success:

- ✔ **By sign:** Great writers are born under every sign of the zodiac, but Gemini is especially haunted by the urge to write. Having the Sun, Moon, Mercury, Ascendant, or Midheaven in the sign of the Twins encourages writing ability.

- ✔ **By planet:** Becoming a successful writer requires a robust Mercury. Mercury is strong if it rules the Ascendant or Midheaven, if it's in Gemini or Virgo, if it makes close aspects to other planets, and if it's in the third, sixth, ninth, or tenth houses. Don't fret if your Mercury is retrograde. That placement is so common among the authors I admire that I've started to wonder whether it's actually an advantage.

  Saturn, the planet of self-discipline, is essential. Imaginative Neptune can be pivotal, especially in writing poetry, fiction, and song lyrics.

  The Moon is arguably the most important planet, as the researcher Michel Gauquelin discovered. He found that creative writers are more likely than nonwriters to have the Moon in one of the so-called zones of power: either overhead (that is, in the ninth house or conjunct the Midheaven in the tenth) or rising (in the first house conjunct the Ascendant or in the twelfth house of secrets and solitude).

- ✔ **By house:** Look for activity in the third house of communication, the ninth house of publication, and the fifth house of creativity.

To observe this in real life, take a look at novelist Toni Morrison's chart (see Chapter 16). She doesn't have every one of the characteristics listed above. Then again, no one does. But her Mercury is conjunct her Midheaven; Venus, the ruler of her Ascendant, is in the ninth house of publication conjunct Saturn; two planets are in the third house (with one more knocking at the gate); and Neptune, the planet of the imagination, is located in the fifth house of creativity. By becoming a writer, she fulfilled the potential of her chart.

Chapter 20

Ten (Plus One) Ways to Use Astrology in Your Life: The Art of Timing

In This Chapter

▶ Making your move when the time is right

▶ Knowing when to hold back and wait

*I*f timing is everything, then astrology is the key to success — not natal astrology, which has to do with your birth chart, but *electional astrology,* the intricate, high-pressure art of choosing a favorable date in advance. By applying its principles, you can choose auspicious times, avoid problematical ones, align yourself with the cosmos, and increase your chances of having a happy outcome. In this chapter, I show you how.

To partake of the wonders of celestial timing, you must have an astrological calendar. I like *Llewellyn's Daily Planetary Guide* and *Jim Maynard's Celestial Guide* and *Celestial Influences* calendars, but there are others. You can take a close look at them online and order them through the Astrology Center of America at www.astroamerica.com.

Getting Married

More than any other event, a request to choose a wedding date can cause an astrologer to leaf frantically through the ephemeris in quest of the perfect day and then to throw her arms up in despair. Given the marriage statistics, it won't surprise you to hear that ideal days are hard to come by — and that even astrologers get divorced.

Still, certain celestial events improve your chances of making it past your paper anniversary. One of the most encouraging is a transit of Jupiter through your seventh house of marriage. The problem is that Jupiter only returns to your seventh house every twelve years, and you may not want to wait that long.

Some astrological influences, on the other hand, occur fairly frequently and are worth waiting for. Here's what to look for when you name the day:

- Make certain that Venus, the planet of love, is direct. If it happens to be retrograde, postpone your wedding for a few weeks. (See Chapter 18 for more about retrograde Venus.)

- Choose a day when Mercury is direct, not retrograde. With retrograde Mercury, misunderstandings and problems in communication are likely to arise, either immediately or down the line. Also, it's never a good idea to sign a contract when Mercury is retrograde. Marriage, whatever else it may be, is a legal agreement — and you *will* have to sign on the dotted line.

- Choose the position of the Moon with care. A New Moon, with the Sun and the Moon conjunct, classically signals a new beginning. The best possible Moon for a wedding is a New Moon in your sign (or your partner's), in your seventh house of marriage, or in Libra.

  As an example, take a look at Nicole Kidman's chart in Chapter 3. She has Scorpio rising. So Taurus is on the cusp of her seventh house. Thus, if she were to get married a third time, she might want to do it after a New Moon in Taurus.

- If a New Moon isn't possible, for whatever reasons, at least get married when the Moon is *waxing* — that is, when it's between New and Full, becoming larger and more luminous every night. A *waning* Moon has passed its peak of luminosity and is on the downward slide, getting smaller and dimmer every moment. Who needs that symbolism?

- Look for an auspicious angle between the Sun and the Moon. A sextile (60°) or trine (120°) creates harmony. A tight 90° square or 180° opposition generates tension and conflict.

- Look for trines and sextiles involving the Moon, Venus, and Jupiter — the more the better.

- Make sure the Moon isn't void-of-course. And make sure that your schedule has room for error, just in case the flower girl is late.

The Moon is *void-of-course* when it has made its last major aspect in one sign but has not yet entered the next. The void-of-course period always comes at the end of the Moon's journey through a sign. To avoid a void-of-course Moon, schedule an event shortly after the Moon enters a new sign. (For more about the void-of-course Moon, turn to Chapter 17.)

Going on a First Date

In the real world, if someone you're interested in asks you out, the last thing you want to do is announce that the Moon is waning, so you'd rather wait two weeks for that mojito. On the other hand, if you have any control over the matter, you might decide that you don't mind waiting. Here's how to schedule a date that might lead to another:

✔ Pay attention to the Moon. Look for a *waxing* Moon, meaning a Moon that's somewhere between New and Full. Make certain that the Moon is not void-of-course because relationships begun under a void-of-course Moon are less likely to go the distance. And choose a moon sign that's either warm and sensitive — like Cancer, Pisces, or Taurus — or fun, like Gemini, Leo, or Sagittarius.

✔ Look for harmonious aspects — that is, conjunctions, sextiles, or trines — between the Moon and Venus. Any good astrological calendar will list these. (For more about aspects, turn to Chapter 13.)

✔ Watch your planetary transits. Jupiter in your fifth house is a propitious influence that can ease the misery of dating even for those who hate the process. It spends about a year in your fifth house — but it only comes around every twelve years, so it behooves you to take advantage of it.

✔ Look at the transits of the Sun, the Moon, Venus, or Mars through that sector of your horoscope.

✔ A once-a-year New Moon in your fifth house of romance is definitely a door to romance, as is the once-a-year Full Moon that takes place six months later. Don't be shy.

Opening a Business

Launching a business isn't so different from starting a marriage, and some of the same rules apply. To wit:

✔ Make sure that Mercury, the planet that rules contracts, isn't retrograde. The same goes for Venus, the planet of money.

✔ Start your enterprise on or shortly after a New Moon. A New Moon in your second house (or in Taurus) is ideal if the business is primarily financial or if it involves material objects. (A New Moon in the second house is also the right time to ask for a raise.) A New Moon in your sixth house (or in Virgo) is perfect if your business is service-oriented. And a New Moon in the tenth house (or in Capricorn) supports public awareness of your business and guarantees that you'll be recognized in your field.

- Look for beneficial aspects (sextiles and trines) between Saturn and Jupiter. Saturn rules structures and organizations; Jupiter rules luck and expansion. You want them working together. Avoid squares and oppositions involving those two planets.

An astrological calendar can tell you when an aspect is exact or at its peak. But an aspect between two planets often creates a buzz even before the crucial moment, when the aspect is approaching. It's like Christmas: You can feel it in the air well in advance of the actual day. Afterwards, the energy diminishes quickly. I suggest that you scan ahead in your calendar to see if any major aspects are approaching. Be aware that if you open your business on a Wednesday, and Thursday there's an opposition between Saturn and Jupiter, you'll feel the tension.

- To make sure that your brainchild gets noticed, launch your enterprise — by which I mean put up your shingle, cut the ribbon, sign the articles of incorporation, shake hands with your partner — around midday. That way, you can be sure that there are planets near the top of the chart. Win or lose, you won't go unnoticed.

Scheduling a Meeting

The way you schedule a meeting depends entirely on what you wish to accomplish. Follow these rules:

- If you hope the meeting will help you inaugurate a program, introduce a new set of goals, involve a staff member who hasn't previously participated in this area, or make a case for organizational change, schedule the meeting when the Moon is New or, at minimum, waxing.

- To encourage brainstorming, look for a conjunction, sextile, or trine between Mercury and Uranus, the planet of originality. The Moon in Gemini also encourages an explosion of ideas.

- If you want the meeting to reach a final decision about an issue that's been on the table many times before, schedule it for a time when the Moon is close to full. Full Moons can be times of high emotion. They're very illuminating — they reveal that which has been hidden and they bring things to a head. If that's what you have in mind, go ahead.

- Make sure the Moon isn't void-of-course and that Mercury isn't retrograde.

On the other hand, if you're scheduling a meeting to discuss a proposal you thoroughly oppose, here's what to do:

- Schedule the meeting during a waning Moon, preferably during the last few days of the lunar cycle.

- Make certain that the Moon is void-of-course. Many ideas may be floated at the meeting. Much discussion may occur. But guess what? Nothing will come of any of it.

Throwing a Party

Once again, it depends on what you have in mind. If you plan to hire a DJ and throw open the doors to anyone you've ever met, these are the rules:

- Let the Moon be in Leo (first choice), Gemini, or Sagittarius, followed by Libra, Aquarius, or Aries. The fire and air signs are boisterous and engaging. They may not generate as much intimacy as other signs, but under their happy influence, the good times roll.

- Look to Venus and Jupiter. If they make conjunctions, sextiles, or trines to the Sun and the Moon, that's good news

- To be certain that stern Saturn won't squeeze the fun right out of your fête, make sure that it doesn't make a close conjunction, square, or opposition to the Sun, the Moon, Venus, Mars, or Jupiter.

On the other hand, if you want to host a quiet family dinner or a champagne brunch for your dearest friends, Moon in Cancer, Taurus, or Pisces aren't bad choices, ensuring that everyone will feel at home, cared for, and well-fed.

Purchasing a Computer

Follow these three simple rules when buying a computer:

- Make sure that Mercury, the planet of communication, isn't retrograde. Okay, I know I keep mentioning this influence. It's always important, but there are times — I admit it — when you can bend the rules. Not in this case, though. Do not — I repeat, do *not* — purchase a computer (or a car) when Mercury is spinning backward.

- Make sure that Uranus and Mars aren't doing anything unfortunate. High-tension squares, oppositions, and conjunctions, especially to Mercury or the Moon, are just the sort of thing you don't want to see.

- Check that the Moon isn't void-of-course.

It isn't necessary, but an Aquarian influence — perhaps in the form of the Sun or Moon in that sign — makes sure that your technology is cutting edge.

Buying a House

Considering that buying a house is the largest purchase most people will ever make, it's smart to get the planets on your side — beginning with Jupiter, the lord of abundance. Once every 12 years, Jupiter travels through your fourth house. That's the single best influence for investing in real estate.

But maybe you can't wait that long. And maybe you can't wait for the right economic market to come along either. If you need to buy or sell a house now, take these suggestions:

✔ Begin the process of buying with a New Moon in your fourth house or a New Moon in Cancer. A Full Moon can also work — especially if you're selling.

✔ Make sure the Moon is waxing when you buy a house. If it's in Taurus, Cancer, or the sign that's on the cusp of your fourth house, so much the better. When you sell a house, it's okay if the Moon is waning.

✔ Look for auspicious aspects (trines and sextiles) involving the Sun, the Moon, and any planets moving through your fourth house.

✔ To make sure that the sale goes through, never sign a contract when Mercury is retrograde — and make sure that the Moon isn't void-of-course.

Having Surgery

First, let me be clear: If you need an operation immediately, you need it immediately. Listen to your doctor.

But perhaps you're undergoing elective surgery. Or maybe your doctor has given you a choice. That happened to me when I broke my arm in a foreign country (where I didn't speak the language). My doctor told me I could have my elbow operated on right away or I could fly home and have the operation here. Either way, she said that I had to have the operation within a week.

In a situation like that, how do you decide? These are the rules:

TIP

- ✔ Make sure the Moon isn't in the sign that corresponds to the part of your body being operated on. Thus, if you're going to have surgery on your arm, avoid the Moon in Gemini. If you're planning to have knee surgery, make sure the Moon isn't in Capricorn. And so on.

  For a description of the signs and the parts of the bodies associated with them, see Chapter 1.

- ✔ Some people recommend avoiding Moon in Scorpio for any kind of surgery. The astrologer Susan Miller notes that for cosmetic surgery it's smart to avoid Mars in either Aries, which rules the face, or Taurus, which rules the neck.

- ✔ Don't have surgery when the Moon is full.

- ✔ Avoid retrograde Mercury, Venus, or Mars, if possible.

- ✔ Look for trines and sextiles to the Sun, the Moon, and the planet that rules the sign on the cusp of your eighth house (of surgery).

- ✔ Look for positive influences, such as Jupiter or Venus in your sixth house of health.

Starting a Diet or an Exercise Program

Going on a diet is a cheerless activity under any circumstances. The least you can do is give yourself a celestial head start. Here's how:

- ✔ Once a year, there's a New Moon in your sixth house of health. A New Moon helps you usher in a new habit, so that's a perfect time for beginning a diet or exercise program (or both).

- ✔ A Full Moon in your sixth house can also be beneficial. It can help you release an old habit — like compulsive eating or an addiction to 300-calorie chai lattes.

- ✔ Saturn, the planet of self-discipline, can help you stick to a diet and create new, healthier habits. Look for Saturn to form conjunctions, trines, and sextiles with the Sun and the Moon.

- ✔ Saturn also supports your efforts if it's traveling through your sixth house, your first house, or your Sun sign, even though any of these transits may correspond to difficult times in your life. The silver lining is that they can also bring increased willpower, control, and accomplishment.

- ✔ Mars in the sixth house gives you a boost of energy — ideal for getting to the gym and making it a habit.

Writing a Novel or Screenplay

I often work in the writers' room of a private library, so I know how many people are struggling with novels, screenplays, and other writing projects. I see them all the time, shuffling their index cards, marking up their print-outs, staring disconsolately at the screens of their laptops, or playing solitaire. I sympathize. Writing projects are like diets: easy to begin and easy to put aside. Here's how to better your odds of completing your project:

✔ Begin a creative writing project when there's a New Moon in your third house; a New Moon in the fourth house (if you're penning a memoir); a New Moon in the fifth house (especially if you're working on a screenplay); a New Moon in the ninth house (of publication); or a New Moon in Gemini.

✔ Begin when Mercury is direct. If Mercury happens to be in Gemini, in Virgo, in your Sun sign, or in the same sign as your natal Mercury, that's a plus.

✔ Look for an active Uranus if you need to generate some original ideas; an active Neptune when you want to stretch your imagination; and an active Pluto when you're ready to dig into emotionally complex material.

✔ Take advantage of Mercury's retrograde periods by using them to revise.

Laying Low

You can only push so hard. Then, at a certain point, the universe pushes back and you need to get some rest. For example:

✔ A New Moon or Full Moon in your twelfth house is a clear message that you need to withdraw. The Sun's annual monthly passage through that sector of your chart is a wonderful time to schedule a retreat.

✔ It's also wise to withdraw when the Moon is in the sign preceding your own. Thus, if you're a Scorpio, the Moon's journey through Libra is a time to pull back, to meditate, and to catch up on your sleep, content in the knowledge that when the Moon enters Scorpio two or three days later, you'll receive a boost — and you'll be fully rested and ready to take advantage of it.

That's what astrological timing is about. It isn't about fate. It's about using the stars to maximum advantage.

Appendix

Planetary Tables

● ●

*T*his appendix gives the location, by sign, of the Sun, the Moon, the planets, the Nodes of the Moon, and the asteroid Chiron between 1930 and 2012.

The tables list the day and time for every entrance (or ingress) into a new sign for each of these celestial bodies. The tables are in the following order:

- Table A 1: The Sun
- Table A 2: The Moon
- Table A 3: The Nodes of the Moon
- Table A 4: Mercury
- Table A 5: Venus
- Table A 6: Mars
- Table A 7: Jupiter
- Table A 8: Saturn
- Table A 9: Uranus
- Table A 10: Neptune
- Table A 11: Pluto
- Table A 12: Chiron

The first column in each table tells you the sign the planet is entering. (The Cheat Sheet at the beginning of this book lists the symbol for each sign.) The second column gives the date when the planet moves into that sign. The third column shows the time when the shift takes place. Time is written in military style, so 0:18 means 18 minutes after midnight, 16:09 is 4:09 in the afternoon, and 23:57 is 11:57 at night. In some cases, the letter "R" follows the time. This R stands for retrograde. It tells you that on that particular day, the planet was retrograde. It doesn't tell you when the planet went retrograde or when it ceased to be retrograde and went direct. (See Chapter 18 for the retrograde dates of Mercury, Venus, and Mars for the years 2007 to 2012.)

The tables in this appendix use eastern standard time. If you weren't born in eastern standard time, you have to make adjustments. Let's say you were born in Chicago. Since Illinois observes central standard time, Chicago is one hour behind the East Coast — that is, it's one hour earlier there. To account for that difference, you have to subtract one hour from the times listed in the tables.

For example, Pluto swung into Sagittarius on January 17, 1995, at 4:16 in the morning, EST. In Chicago, that momentous event occurred one hour earlier, at 3:16 a.m. In Denver, it was 2:16. In Los Angeles, it was 1:16. And so on.

The following is a partial list of the adjustments you have to make, depending on where you were born:

If You Were Born In	*Do This*
Central standard time	Subtract 1 hour
Mountain standard time	Subtract 2 hours
Pacific standard time	Subtract 3 hours
Alaska standard time	Subtract 4 hours
Hawaii standard time	Subtract 5 hours
Most of Brazil and Argentina	Add 2 hours
British Isles and western Africa	Add 5 hours
Western Europe	Add 6 hours
Middle East, Norway, and South Africa	Add 7 hours
India	Add 10½ hours
China	Add 13 hours
Australia	Add 12–15 hours

And don't forget about daylight saving time. If it was in operation at the time of your birth, or if you're looking up the current position of the planets during daylight saving time, you must subtract an additional hour. For many years, daylight saving time began at 2 a.m. on the first Sunday in April and ended at 2 a.m. on the last Sunday in October. That has changed. As of 2007, DST extends from the second Sunday in March to the first Sunday in November.

Note, too, that the tables in this appendix cover the years from 1930 to 2012 — even when it doesn't look that way. The Pluto Table (A 11) begins in 1937 with the entrance of Pluto into Leo on October 7. Before that, Pluto was in the previous sign — Cancer. Similarly, the last entries for Pluto are in 2008. On January 25 it enters Capricorn. On June 14 it slips back into Sagittarius. (Notice the R next to that entry, indicating that it's retrograde on that day.) Finally, on November 26 it reenters Capricorn, where it remains until well past 2012. No further entries are required.

Table A 1 — The Sun

1930

♒ Jan 20 13:33
♓ Feb 19 4:00
♈ Mar 21 3:30
♉ Apr 20 15:06
♊ May 21 14:42
♋ Jun 21 22:53
♌ Jul 23 9:42
♍ Aug 23 16:26
♎ Sept 23 13:36
♏ Oct 23 22:26
♐ Nov 22 19:34
♑ Dec 22 8:40

1931

♒ Jan 20 19:18
♓ Feb 19 9:40
♈ Mar 21 9:06
♉ Apr 20 20:40
♊ May 21 20:15
♋ Jun 22 4:28
♌ Jul 23 15:21
♍ Aug 23 22:10
♎ Sept 23 19:23
♏ Oct 24 4:16
♐ Nov 23 1:25
♑ Dec 22 14:30

1932

♒ Jan 21 1:07
♓ Feb 19 15:28
♈ Mar 20 14:54
♉ Apr 20 2:28
♊ May 21 2:07
♋ Jun 21 10:23
♌ Jul 22 21:18
♍ Aug 23 4:06
♎ Sept 23 1:16
♏ Oct 23 10:04
♐ Nov 22 7:10
♑ Dec 21 20:14

1933

♒ Jan 20 6:53
♓ Feb 18 21:16
♈ Mar 20 20:43
♉ Apr 20 8:18
♊ May 21 7:57
♋ Jun 21 16:12
♌ Jul 23 3:05
♍ Aug 23 9:52
♎ Sept 23 7:01
♏ Oct 23 15:48
♐ Nov 22 12:53
♑ Dec 22 1:58

1934

♒ Jan 20 12:37
♓ Feb 19 3:02

♈ Mar 21 2:28
♉ Apr 20 14:00
♊ May 21 13:35
♋ Jun 21 21:48
♌ Jul 23 8:42
♍ Aug 23 15:32
♎ Sept 23 12:45
♏ Oct 23 21:36
♐ Nov 22 18:44
♑ Dec 22 7:49

1935

♒ Jan 20 18:28
♓ Feb 19 8:52
♈ Mar 21 8:18
♉ Apr 20 19:50
♊ May 21 19:25
♋ Jun 22 3:38
♌ Jul 23 14:33
♍ Aug 23 21:24
♎ Sept 23 18:38
♏ Oct 24 3:29
♐ Nov 23 0:35
♑ Dec 22 13:37

1936

♒ Jan 21 0:12
♓ Feb 19 14:33
♈ Mar 20 13:58
♉ Apr 20 1:31
♊ May 21 1:07
♋ Jun 21 9:22
♌ Jul 22 20:18
♍ Aug 23 3:11
♎ Sept 23 0:26
♏ Oct 23 9:18
♐ Nov 22 6:25
♑ Dec 21 19:27

1937

♒ Jan 20 6:01
♓ Feb 18 20:21
♈ Mar 20 19:45
♉ Apr 20 7:19
♊ May 21 6:57
♋ Jun 21 15:12
♌ Jul 23 2:07
♍ Aug 23 8:58
♎ Sept 23 6:13
♏ Oct 23 15:07
♐ Nov 22 12:17
♑ Dec 22 1:22

1938

♒ Jan 20 11:59
♓ Feb 19 2:20
♈ Mar 21 1:43
♉ Apr 20 13:15
♊ May 21 12:50

♋ Jun 21 21:04
♌ Jul 23 7:57
♍ Aug 23 14:46
♎ Sept 23 12:00
♏ Oct 23 20:54
♐ Nov 22 18:06
♑ Dec 22 7:13

1939

♒ Jan 20 17:51
♓ Feb 19 8:09
♈ Mar 21 7:28
♉ Apr 20 18:55
♊ May 21 18:27
♋ Jun 22 2:39
♌ Jul 23 13:37
♍ Aug 23 20:31
♎ Sept 23 17:49
♏ Oct 24 2:46
♐ Nov 22 23:59
♑ Dec 22 13:06

1940

♒ Jan 20 23:44
♓ Feb 19 14:04
♈ Mar 20 13:24
♉ Apr 20 0:51
♊ May 21 0:23
♋ Jun 21 8:36
♌ Jul 22 19:34
♍ Aug 23 2:29
♎ Sept 22 23:46
♏ Oct 23 8:39
♐ Nov 22 5:49
♑ Dec 21 18:55

1941

♒ Jan 20 5:34
♓ Feb 18 19:56
♈ Mar 20 19:20
♉ Apr 20 6:50
♊ May 21 6:23
♋ Jun 21 14:33
♌ Jul 23 1:26
♍ Aug 23 8:17
♎ Sept 23 5:33
♏ Oct 23 14:27
♐ Nov 22 11:38
♑ Dec 22 0:44

1942

♒ Jan 20 11:24
♓ Feb 19 1:47
♈ Mar 21 1:11
♉ Apr 20 12:39
♊ May 21 12:09
♋ Jun 21 20:16
♌ Jul 23 7:07
♍ Aug 23 13:58

♎ Sept 23 11:16
♏ Oct 23 20:15
♐ Nov 22 17:30
♑ Dec 22 6:40

1943

♒ Jan 20 17:19
♓ Feb 19 7:40
♈ Mar 21 7:03
♉ Apr 20 18:32
♊ May 21 18:03
♋ Jun 22 2:12
♌ Jul 23 13:05
♍ Aug 23 19:55
♎ Sept 23 17:12
♏ Oct 24 2:08
♐ Nov 22 23:22
♑ Dec 22 12:29

1944

♒ Jan 20 23:07
♓ Feb 19 13:27
♈ Mar 20 12:49
♉ Apr 20 0:18
♊ May 20 23:51
♋ Jun 21 8:02
♌ Jul 22 18:56
♍ Aug 23 1:46
♎ Sept 22 23:02
♏ Oct 23 7:56
♐ Nov 22 5:08
♑ Dec 21 18:15

1945

♒ Jan 20 4:54
♓ Feb 18 19:15
♈ Mar 20 18:37
♉ Apr 20 6:07
♊ May 21 5:40
♋ Jun 21 13:52
♌ Jul 23 0:45
♍ Aug 23 7:35
♎ Sept 23 4:50
♏ Oct 23 13:44
♐ Nov 22 10:55
♑ Dec 22 0:04

1946

♒ Jan 20 10:45
♓ Feb 19 1:09
♈ Mar 21 0:33
♉ Apr 20 12:02
♊ May 21 11:34
♋ Jun 21 19:44
♌ Jul 23 6:37
♍ Aug 23 13:26
♎ Sept 23 10:41
♏ Oct 23 19:35
♐ Nov 22 16:46

♑ Dec 22 5:53

1947

♒ Jan 20 16:32
♓ Feb 19 6:52
♈ Mar 21 6:13
♉ Apr 20 17:39
♊ May 21 17:09
♋ Jun 22 1:19
♌ Jul 23 12:14
♍ Aug 23 19:09
♎ Sept 23 16:29
♏ Oct 24 1:26
♐ Nov 22 22:38
♑ Dec 22 11:43

1948

♒ Jan 20 22:18
♓ Feb 19 12:37
♈ Mar 20 11:57
♉ Apr 19 23:25
♊ May 20 22:58
♋ Jun 21 7:11
♌ Jul 22 18:08
♍ Aug 23 1:03
♎ Sept 22 22:22
♏ Oct 23 7:18
♐ Nov 22 4:29
♑ Dec 21 17:33

1949

♒ Jan 20 4:09
♓ Feb 18 18:27
♈ Mar 20 17:48
♉ Apr 20 5:17
♊ May 21 4:51
♋ Jun 21 13:03
♌ Jul 22 23:57
♍ Aug 23 6:48
♎ Sept 23 4:06
♏ Oct 23 13:03
♐ Nov 22 10:16
♑ Dec 21 23:23

1950

♒ Jan 20 10:00
♓ Feb 19 0:18
♈ Mar 20 23:35
♉ Apr 20 10:59
♊ May 21 10:27
♋ Jun 21 18:36
♌ Jul 23 5:30
♍ Aug 23 12:23
♎ Sept 23 9:44
♏ Oct 23 18:45
♐ Nov 22 16:03
♑ Dec 22 5:13

(continued)

Table A 1 — The Sun (continued)

1951
♒ Jan 20 15:52
♓ Feb 19 6:10
♈ Mar 21 5:26
♉ Apr 20 16:48
♊ May 21 16:15
♋ Jun 22 0:25
♌ Jul 23 11:21
♍ Aug 23 18:16
♎ Sept 23 15:37
♏ Oct 24 0:36
♐ Nov 22 21:51
♑ Dec 22 11:00

1952
♒ Jan 20 21:38
♓ Feb 19 11:57
♈ Mar 20 11:14
♉ Apr 19 22:37
♊ May 20 22:04
♋ Jun 21 6:13
♌ Jul 22 17:07
♍ Aug 23 0:03
♎ Sept 22 21:24
♏ Oct 23 6:22
♐ Nov 22 3:36
♑ Dec 21 16:43

1953
♒ Jan 20 3:21
♓ Feb 18 17:41
♈ Mar 20 17:01
♉ Apr 20 4:25
♊ May 21 3:53
♋ Jun 21 12:00
♌ Jul 22 22:52
♍ Aug 23 5:45
♎ Sept 23 3:06
♏ Oct 23 12:06
♐ Nov 22 9:22
♑ Dec 21 22:31

1954
♒ Jan 20 9:11
♓ Feb 18 23:32
♈ Mar 20 22:53
♉ Apr 20 10:20
♊ May 21 9:47
♋ Jun 21 17:54
♌ Jul 23 4:45
♍ Aug 23 11:36
♎ Sept 23 8:55
♏ Oct 23 17:56
♐ Nov 22 15:14
♑ Dec 22 4:24

1955
♒ Jan 20 15:02
♓ Feb 19 5:19
♈ Mar 21 4:35
♉ Apr 20 15:58
♊ May 21 15:24
♋ Jun 21 23:31
♌ Jul 23 10:25
♍ Aug 23 17:19
♎ Sept 23 14:41
♏ Oct 23 23:43
♐ Nov 22 21:01
♑ Dec 22 10:11

1956
♒ Jan 20 20:48
♓ Feb 19 11:05
♈ Mar 20 10:20
♉ Apr 19 21:43
♊ May 20 21:13
♋ Jun 21 5:24
♌ Jul 22 16:20
♍ Aug 22 23:15
♎ Sept 22 20:35
♏ Oct 23 5:34
♐ Nov 22 2:50
♑ Dec 21 15:59

1957
♒ Jan 20 2:39
♓ Feb 18 16:58
♈ Mar 20 16:16
♉ Apr 20 3:41
♊ May 21 3:10
♋ Jun 21 11:21
♌ Jul 22 22:15
♍ Aug 23 5:08
♎ Sept 23 2:26
♏ Oct 23 11:24
♐ Nov 22 8:39
♑ Dec 21 21:49

1958
♒ Jan 20 8:28
♓ Feb 18 22:48
♈ Mar 20 22:06
♉ Apr 20 9:27
♊ May 21 8:51
♋ Jun 21 16:57
♌ Jul 23 3:50
♍ Aug 23 10:46
♎ Sept 23 8:09
♏ Oct 23 17:11
♐ Nov 22 14:29
♑ Dec 22 3:40

1959
♒ Jan 20 14:19
♓ Feb 19 4:38
♈ Mar 21 3:55
♉ Apr 20 15:17
♊ May 21 14:42
♋ Jun 21 22:50
♌ Jul 23 9:45
♍ Aug 23 16:44
♎ Sept 23 14:08
♏ Oct 23 23:11
♐ Nov 22 20:27
♑ Dec 22 9:34

1960
♒ Jan 20 20:10
♓ Feb 19 10:26
♈ Mar 20 9:43
♉ Apr 19 21:06
♊ May 20 20:34
♋ Jun 21 4:42
♌ Jul 22 15:37
♍ Aug 22 22:34
♎ Sept 22 19:59
♏ Oct 23 5:02
♐ Nov 22 2:18
♑ Dec 21 15:26

1961
♒ Jan 20 2:01
♓ Feb 18 16:16
♈ Mar 20 15:32
♉ Apr 20 2:55
♊ May 21 2:22
♋ Jun 21 10:30
♌ Jul 22 21:24
♍ Aug 23 4:19
♎ Sept 23 1:42
♏ Oct 23 10:47
♐ Nov 22 8:08
♑ Dec 21 21:19

1962
♒ Jan 20 7:58
♓ Feb 18 22:15
♈ Mar 20 21:30
♉ Apr 20 8:51
♊ May 21 8:17
♋ Jun 21 16:24
♌ Jul 23 3:18
♍ Aug 23 10:12
♎ Sept 23 7:35
♏ Oct 23 16:40
♐ Nov 22 14:02
♑ Dec 22 3:15

1963
♒ Jan 20 13:54
♓ Feb 19 4:09
♈ Mar 21 3:20
♉ Apr 20 14:36
♊ May 21 13:58
♋ Jun 21 22:04
♌ Jul 23 8:59
♍ Aug 23 15:58
♎ Sept 23 13:24
♏ Oct 23 22:29
♐ Nov 22 19:49
♑ Dec 22 9:02

1964
♒ Jan 20 19:41
♓ Feb 19 9:57
♈ Mar 20 9:10
♉ Apr 19 20:27
♊ May 20 19:50
♋ Jun 21 3:57
♌ Jul 22 14:53
♍ Aug 22 21:51
♎ Sept 22 19:17
♏ Oct 23 4:21
♐ Nov 22 1:39
♑ Dec 21 14:50

1965
♒ Jan 20 1:29
♓ Feb 18 15:48
♈ Mar 20 15:05
♉ Apr 20 2:26
♊ May 21 1:50
♋ Jun 21 9:56
♌ Jul 22 20:48
♍ Aug 23 3:43
♎ Sept 23 1:06
♏ Oct 23 10:10
♐ Nov 22 7:29
♑ Dec 21 20:40

1966
♒ Jan 20 7:20
♓ Feb 18 21:38
♈ Mar 20 20:53
♉ Apr 20 8:12
♊ May 21 7:32
♋ Jun 21 15:33
♌ Jul 23 2:23
♍ Aug 23 9:18
♎ Sept 23 6:43
♏ Oct 23 15:51
♐ Nov 22 13:14
♑ Dec 22 2:28

1967
♒ Jan 20 13:08
♓ Feb 19 3:24
♈ Mar 21 2:37
♉ Apr 20 13:55
♊ May 21 13:18
♋ Jun 21 21:23
♌ Jul 23 8:16
♍ Aug 23 15:12
♎ Sept 23 12:38
♏ Oct 23 21:44
♐ Nov 22 19:04
♑ Dec 22 8:16

1968
♒ Jan 20 18:54
♓ Feb 19 9:09
♈ Mar 20 8:22
♉ Apr 19 19:41
♊ May 20 19:06
♋ Jun 21 3:13
♌ Jul 22 14:07
♍ Aug 22 21:03
♎ Sept 22 18:26
♏ Oct 23 3:30
♐ Nov 22 0:49
♑ Dec 21 14:00

1969
♒ Jan 20 0:38
♓ Feb 18 14:55
♈ Mar 20 14:08
♉ Apr 20 1:27
♊ May 21 0:50
♋ Jun 21 8:55
♌ Jul 22 19:48
♍ Aug 23 2:43
♎ Sept 23 0:07
♏ Oct 23 9:11
♐ Nov 22 6:31
♑ Dec 21 19:44

1970
♒ Jan 20 6:24
♓ Feb 18 20:42
♈ Mar 20 19:56
♉ Apr 20 7:15
♊ May 21 6:37
♋ Jun 21 14:43
♌ Jul 23 1:37
♍ Aug 23 8:34
♎ Sept 23 5:59
♏ Oct 23 15:04
♐ Nov 22 12:25
♑ Dec 22 1:36

1971
♒ Jan 20 12:13
♓ Feb 19 2:27
♈ Mar 21 1:38
♉ Apr 20 12:54
♊ May 21 12:15
♋ Jun 21 20:20
♌ Jul 23 7:15
♍ Aug 23 14:15
♎ Sept 23 11:45
♏ Oct 23 20:53
♐ Nov 22 18:14
♑ Dec 22 7:24

1972
♒ Jan 20 17:59

Table A 1   The Sun *(continued)*

♓ Feb 19 8:11	♊ May 20 17:21	♍ Aug 22 18:41	♐ Nov 21 22:11	**1989**
♈ Mar 20 7:21	♋ Jun 21 1:24	♎ Sept 22 16:09	♑ Dec 21 11:23	♒ Jan 19 21:07
♉ Apr 19 18:37	♌ Jul 22 12:18	♏ Oct 23 1:18		♓ Feb 18 11:21
♊ May 20 18:00	♍ Aug 22 19:18	♐ Nov 21 22:41	**1985**	♈ Mar 20 10:28
♋ Jun 21 2:06	♎ Sept 22 16:48	♑ Dec 21 11:56	♒ Jan 19 21:58	♉ Apr 19 21:39
♌ Jul 22 13:03	♏ Oct 23 1:58		♓ Feb 18 12:07	♊ May 20 20:54
♍ Aug 22 20:03	♐ Nov 21 23:22	**1981**	♈ Mar 20 11:14	♋ Jun 21 4:53
♎ Sept 22 17:33	♑ Dec 21 12:35	♒ Jan 19 22:36	♉ Apr 19 22:26	♌ Jul 22 15:45
♏ Oct 23 2:41		♓ Feb 18 12:52	♊ May 20 21:43	♍ Aug 22 22:46
♐ Nov 22 0:03	**1977**	♈ Mar 20 12:03	♋ Jun 21 5:44	♎ Sept 22 20:20
♑ Dec 21 13:13	♒ Jan 19 23:14	♉ Apr 19 23:19	♌ Jul 22 16:36	♏ Oct 23 5:35
	♓ Feb 18 13:30	♊ May 20 22:39	♍ Aug 22 23:36	♐ Nov 22 3:05
1973	♈ Mar 20 12:42	♋ Jun 21 6:45	♎ Sept 22 21:07	♑ Dec 21 16:22
♒ Jan 19 23:48	♉ Apr 19 23:57	♌ Jul 22 17:40	♏ Oct 23 6:22	
♓ Feb 18 14:01	♊ May 20 23:14	♍ Aug 23 0:38	♐ Nov 22 3:51	**1990**
♈ Mar 20 13:12	♋ Jun 21 7:14	♎ Sept 22 22:05	♑ Dec 21 17:08	♒ Jan 20 3:02
♉ Apr 20 0:30	♌ Jul 22 18:04	♏ Oct 23 7:13		♓ Feb 18 17:14
♊ May 20 23:54	♍ Aug 23 1:00	♐ Nov 22 4:36	**1986**	♈ Mar 20 16:19
♋ Jun 21 8:01	♎ Sept 22 22:29	♑ Dec 21 17:51	♒ Jan 20 3:46	♉ Apr 20 3:27
♌ Jul 22 18:56	♏ Oct 23 7:41		♓ Feb 18 17:58	♊ May 21 2:37
♍ Aug 23 1:53	♐ Nov 22 5:07	**1982**	♈ Mar 20 17:03	♋ Jun 21 10:33
♎ Sept 22 23:21	♑ Dec 21 18:23	♒ Jan 20 4:31	♉ Apr 20 4:12	♌ Jul 22 21:22
♏ Oct 23 8:30		♓ Feb 18 18:47	♊ May 21 3:28	♍ Aug 23 4:21
♐ Nov 22 5:54	**1978**	♈ Mar 20 17:56	♋ Jun 21 11:30	♎ Sept 23 1:56
♑ Dec 21 19:08	♒ Jan 20 5:04	♉ Apr 20 5:07	♌ Jul 22 22:24	♏ Oct 23 11:14
	♓ Feb 18 19:21	♊ May 21 4:23	♍ Aug 23 5:26	♐ Nov 22 8:47
1974	♈ Mar 20 18:34	♋ Jun 21 12:23	♎ Sept 23 2:59	♑ Dec 21 22:07
♒ Jan 20 5:46	♉ Apr 20 5:50	♌ Jul 22 23:15	♏ Oct 23 12:14	
♓ Feb 18 19:59	♊ May 21 5:08	♍ Aug 23 6:15	♐ Nov 22 9:44	**1991**
♈ Mar 20 19:07	♋ Jun 21 13:10	♎ Sept 23 3:46	♑ Dec 21 23:02	♒ Jan 20 8:47
♉ Apr 20 6:19	♌ Jul 23 0:00	♏ Oct 23 12:58		♓ Feb 18 22:58
♊ May 21 5:36	♍ Aug 23 6:57	♐ Nov 22 10:23	**1987**	♈ Mar 20 22:02
♋ Jun 21 13:38	♎ Sept 23 4:25	♑ Dec 21 23:38	♒ Jan 20 9:40	♉ Apr 20 9:08
♌ Jul 23 0:30	♏ Oct 23 13:37		♓ Feb 18 23:50	♊ May 21 8:20
♍ Aug 23 7:29	♐ Nov 22 11:05	**1983**	♈ Mar 20 22:52	♋ Jun 21 16:19
♎ Sept 23 4:58	♑ Dec 22 0:21	♒ Jan 20 10:17	♉ Apr 20 9:58	♌ Jul 23 3:11
♏ Oct 23 14:11		♓ Feb 19 0:31	♊ May 21 9:10	♍ Aug 23 10:13
♐ Nov 22 11:38	**1979**	♈ Mar 20 23:39	♋ Jun 21 17:11	♎ Sept 23 7:48
♑ Dec 22 0:56	♒ Jan 20 11:00	♉ Apr 20 10:50	♌ Jul 23 4:06	♏ Oct 23 17:05
	♓ Feb 19 1:13	♊ May 21 10:06	♍ Aug 23 11:10	♐ Nov 22 14:36
1975	♈ Mar 21 0:22	♋ Jun 21 18:09	♎ Sept 23 8:45	♑ Dec 22 3:54
♒ Jan 20 11:36	♉ Apr 20 11:35	♌ Jul 23 5:04	♏ Oct 23 18:01	
♓ Feb 19 1:50	♊ May 21 10:54	♍ Aug 23 12:07	♐ Nov 22 15:29	**1992**
♈ Mar 21 0:57	♋ Jun 21 18:56	♎ Sept 23 9:42	♑ Dec 22 4:46	♒ Jan 20 14:32
♉ Apr 20 12:07	♌ Jul 23 5:49	♏ Oct 23 18:54		♓ Feb 19 4:43
♊ May 21 11:24	♍ Aug 23 12:47	♐ Nov 22 16:18	**1988**	♈ Mar 20 3:48
♋ Jun 21 19:26	♎ Sept 23 10:16	♑ Dec 22 5:30	♒ Jan 20 15:24	♉ Apr 19 14:57
♌ Jul 23 6:22	♏ Oct 23 19:28		♓ Feb 19 5:35	♊ May 20 14:12
♍ Aug 23 13:24	♐ Nov 22 16:54	**1984**	♈ Mar 20 4:39	♋ Jun 20 22:14
♎ Sept 23 10:55	♑ Dec 22 6:10	♒ Jan 20 16:05	♉ Apr 19 15:45	♌ Jul 22 9:09
♏ Oct 23 20:06		♓ Feb 19 6:16	♊ May 20 14:57	♍ Aug 22 16:10
♐ Nov 22 17:31	**1980**	♈ Mar 20 5:24	♋ Jun 20 22:57	♎ Sept 22 13:43
♑ Dec 22 6:46	♒ Jan 20 16:49	♉ Apr 19 16:38	♌ Jul 22 9:51	♏ Oct 22 22:57
	♓ Feb 19 7:02	♊ May 20 15:58	♍ Aug 22 16:54	♐ Nov 21 20:26
1976	♈ Mar 20 6:10	♋ Jun 21 0:02	♎ Sept 22 14:29	♑ Dec 21 9:43
♒ Jan 20 17:25	♉ Apr 19 17:23	♌ Jul 22 10:58	♏ Oct 22 23:44	
♓ Feb 19 7:40	♊ May 20 16:42	♍ Aug 22 18:00	♐ Nov 21 21:12	**1993**
♈ Mar 20 6:50	♋ Jun 21 0:47	♎ Sept 22 15:33	♑ Dec 21 10:28	♒ Jan 19 20:23
♉ Apr 19 18:03	♌ Jul 22 11:42	♏ Oct 23 0:46		♓ Feb 18 10:35

(continued)

Table A 1   The Sun *(continued)*

♈ Mar 20 9:41
♉ Apr 19 20:49
♊ May 20 20:02
♋ Jun 21 4:00
♌ Jul 22 14:51
♍ Aug 22 21:50
♎ Sept 22 19:22
♏ Oct 23 4:37
♐ Nov 22 2:07
♑ Dec 21 15:26

1994
♒ Jan 20 2:07
♓ Feb 18 16:22
♈ Mar 20 15:28
♉ Apr 20 2:36
♊ May 21 1:48
♋ Jun 21 9:48
♌ Jul 22 20:41
♍ Aug 23 3:44
♎ Sept 23 1:19
♏ Oct 23 10:36
♐ Nov 22 8:06
♑ Dec 21 21:23

1995
♒ Jan 20 8:00
♓ Feb 18 22:11
♈ Mar 20 21:14
♉ Apr 20 8:21
♊ May 21 7:34
♋ Jun 21 15:34
♌ Jul 23 2:30
♍ Aug 23 9:35
♎ Sept 23 7:13
♏ Oct 23 16:32
♐ Nov 22 14:01
♑ Dec 22 3:17

1996
♒ Jan 20 13:52
♓ Feb 19 4:01
♈ Mar 20 3:03
♉ Apr 19 14:10
♊ May 20 13:23
♋ Jun 20 21:24
♌ Jul 22 8:19
♍ Aug 22 15:23
♎ Sept 22 13:00
♏ Oct 22 22:19
♐ Nov 21 19:49
♑ Dec 21 9:06

1997
♒ Jan 19 19:43

♓ Feb 18 9:51
♈ Mar 20 8:55
♉ Apr 19 20:03
♊ May 20 19:18
♋ Jun 21 3:20
♌ Jul 22 14:15
♍ Aug 22 21:19
♎ Sept 22 18:56
♏ Oct 23 4:15
♐ Nov 22 1:48
♑ Dec 21 15:07

1998
♒ Jan 20 1:46
♓ Feb 18 15:55
♈ Mar 20 14:55
♉ Apr 20 1:57
♊ May 21 1:05
♋ Jun 21 9:03
♌ Jul 22 19:55
♍ Aug 23 2:59
♎ Sept 23 0:37
♏ Oct 23 9:59
♐ Nov 22 7:34
♑ Dec 21 20:56

1999
♒ Jan 20 7:37
♓ Feb 18 21:47
♈ Mar 20 20:46
♉ Apr 20 7:46
♊ May 21 6:52
♋ Jun 21 14:49
♌ Jul 23 1:44
♍ Aug 23 8:51
♎ Sept 23 6:31
♏ Oct 23 15:52
♐ Nov 22 13:25
♑ Dec 22 2:44

2000
♒ Jan 20 13:23
♓ Feb 19 3:33
♈ Mar 20 2:35
♉ Apr 19 13:40
♊ May 20 12:49
♋ Jun 20 20:48
♌ Jul 22 7:43
♍ Aug 22 14:49
♎ Sept 22 12:28
♏ Oct 22 21:47
♐ Nov 21 19:19
♑ Dec 21 8:37

2001
♒ Jan 19 19:16
♓ Feb 18 9:27
♈ Mar 20 8:31
♉ Apr 19 19:36
♊ May 20 18:44
♋ Jun 21 2:38
♌ Jul 22 13:26
♍ Aug 22 20:27
♎ Sept 22 18:04
♏ Oct 23 3:26
♐ Nov 22 1:00
♑ Dec 21 14:21

2002
♒ Jan 20 1:02
♓ Feb 18 15:13
♈ Mar 20 14:16
♉ Apr 20 1:20
♊ May 21 0:29
♋ Jun 21 8:24
♌ Jul 22 19:15
♍ Aug 23 2:17
♎ Sept 22 23:55
♏ Oct 23 9:18
♐ Nov 22 6:54
♑ Dec 21 20:14

2003
♒ Jan 20 6:53
♓ Feb 18 21:00
♈ Mar 20 20:00
♉ Apr 20 7:03
♊ May 21 6:12
♋ Jun 21 14:10
♌ Jul 23 1:04
♍ Aug 23 8:08
♎ Sept 23 5:47
♏ Oct 23 15:08
♐ Nov 22 12:43
♑ Dec 22 2:04

2004
♒ Jan 20 12:42
♓ Feb 19 2:50
♈ Mar 20 1:49
♉ Apr 19 12:50
♊ May 20 11:59
♋ Jun 20 19:57
♌ Jul 22 6:50
♍ Aug 22 13:53
♎ Sept 22 11:30
♏ Oct 22 20:49
♐ Nov 21 18:22
♑ Dec 21 7:42

2005
♒ Jan 19 18:22
♓ Feb 18 8:32
♈ Mar 20 7:33
♉ Apr 19 18:37
♊ May 20 17:47
♋ Jun 21 1:46
♌ Jul 22 12:41
♍ Aug 22 19:45
♎ Sept 22 17:23
♏ Oct 23 2:42
♐ Nov 22 0:15
♑ Dec 21 13:35

2006
♒ Jan 20 0:15
♓ Feb 18 14:25
♈ Mar 20 13:25
♉ Apr 20 0:25
♊ May 20 23:31
♋ Jun 21 7:25
♌ Jul 22 18:17
♍ Aug 23 1:22
♎ Sept 22 23:03
♏ Oct 23 8:26
♐ Nov 22 6:01
♑ Dec 21 19:21

2007
♒ Jan 20 6:00
♓ Feb 18 20:08
♈ Mar 20 19:07
♉ Apr 20 6:06
♊ May 21 5:11
♋ Jun 21 13:06
♌ Jul 23 0:00
♍ Aug 23 7:07
♎ Sept 23 4:51
♏ Oct 23 14:15
♐ Nov 22 11:49
♑ Dec 22 1:07

2008
♒ Jan 20 11:43
♓ Feb 19 1:49
♈ Mar 20 0:48
♉ Apr 19 11:50
♊ May 20 11:00
♋ Jun 20 18:59
♌ Jul 22 5:54
♍ Aug 22 13:02
♎ Sept 22 10:44
♏ Oct 22 20:08
♐ Nov 21 17:44
♑ Dec 21 7:03

2009
♒ Jan 19 17:40
♓ Feb 18 7:45
♈ Mar 20 6:43
♉ Apr 19 17:44
♊ May 20 16:50
♋ Jun 21 0:45
♌ Jul 22 11:35
♍ Aug 22 18:38
♎ Sept 22 16:18
♏ Oct 23 1:43
♐ Nov 21 23:22
♑ Dec 21 12:46

2010
♒ Jan 19 23:27
♓ Feb 18 13:35
♈ Mar 20 12:32
♉ Apr 19 23:29
♊ May 20 22:33
♋ Jun 21 6:28
♌ Jul 22 17:21
♍ Aug 23 0:26
♎ Sept 22 22:08
♏ Oct 23 7:34
♐ Nov 22 5:14
♑ Dec 21 18:38

2011
♒ Jan 20 5:18
♓ Feb 18 19:25
♈ Mar 20 18:20
♉ Apr 20 5:17
♊ May 21 4:20
♋ Jun 21 12:16
♌ Jul 22 23:11
♍ Aug 23 6:20
♎ Sept 23 4:04
♏ Oct 23 13:30
♐ Nov 22 11:07
♑ Dec 22 0:29

2012
♒ Jan 20 11:09
♓ Feb 19 1:17
♈ Mar 20 0:14
♉ Apr 19 11:11
♊ May 20 10:15
♋ Jun 20 18:08
♌ Jul 22 5:00
♍ Aug 22 12:06
♎ Sept 22 9:48
♏ Oct 22 19:13
♐ Nov 21 16:49
♑ Dec 21 6:11

Table A-2 — The Moon

1930

♒ Jan 1 13:29	♐ May 13 4:39	♏ Sept 24 10:07	♌ Feb 1 22:24	♋ Jun 16 8:38
♓ Jan 4 2:05	♑ May 15 13:39	♐ Sept 26 14:34	♍ Feb 3 21:57	♌ Jun 18 12:36
♈ Jan 6 13:27	♒ May 18 1:04	♑ Sept 28 22:48	♎ Feb 5 21:54	♍ Jun 20 15:32
♉ Jan 8 21:59	♓ May 20 13:34	♒ Oct 1 10:09	♏ Feb 8 0:04	♎ Jun 22 18:23
♊ Jan 11 2:34	♈ May 23 0:56	♓ Oct 3 22:48	♐ Feb 10 5:21	♏ Jun 24 21:34
♋ Jan 13 3:35	♉ May 25 9:15	♈ Oct 6 10:52	♑ Feb 12 13:39	♐ Jun 27 1:26
♌ Jan 15 2:37	♊ May 27 14:07	♉ Oct 8 21:14	♒ Feb 15 0:14	♑ Jun 29 6:35
♍ Jan 17 1:57	♋ May 29 16:26	♊ Oct 11 5:29	♓ Feb 17 12:23	♒ Jul 1 13:56
♎ Jan 19 3:44	♌ May 31 17:45	♋ Oct 13 11:29	♈ Feb 20 1:21	♓ Jul 4 0:10
♏ Jan 21 9:25	♍ Jun 2 19:37	♌ Oct 15 15:19	♉ Feb 22 13:54	♈ Jul 6 12:40
♐ Jan 23 18:56	♎ Jun 4 23:04	♍ Oct 17 17:26	♊ Feb 25 0:13	♉ Jul 9 1:14
♑ Jan 26 6:53	♏ Jun 7 4:30	♎ Oct 19 18:43	♋ Feb 27 6:47	♊ Jul 11 11:14
♒ Jan 28 19:35	♐ Jun 9 11:56	♏ Oct 21 20:32	♌ Mar 1 9:25	♋ Jul 13 17:30
♓ Jan 31 7:59	♑ Jun 11 21:20	♐ Oct 24 0:23	♍ Mar 3 9:21	♌ Jul 15 20:41
♈ Feb 2 19:23	♒ Jun 14 8:39	♑ Oct 26 7:27	♎ Mar 5 8:32	♍ Jul 17 22:22
♉ Feb 5 4:49	♓ Jun 16 21:12	♒ Oct 28 17:54	♏ Mar 7 9:03	♎ Jul 20 0:06
♊ Feb 7 11:08	♈ Jun 19 9:15	♓ Oct 31 6:23	♐ Mar 9 12:30	♏ Jul 22 2:56
♋ Feb 9 13:55	♉ Jun 21 18:35	♈ Nov 2 18:34	♑ Mar 11 19:39	♐ Jul 24 7:18
♌ Feb 11 14:00	♊ Jun 24 0:00	♉ Nov 5 4:37	♒ Mar 14 6:03	♑ Jul 26 13:22
♍ Feb 13 13:14	♋ Jun 26 1:57	♊ Nov 7 11:58	♓ Mar 16 18:26	♒ Jul 28 21:24
♎ Feb 15 13:50	♌ Jun 28 2:06	♋ Nov 9 17:05	♈ Mar 19 :24	♓ Jul 31 7:45
♏ Feb 17 17:45	♍ Jun 30 2:28	♌ Nov 11 20:45	♉ Mar 21 19:44	♈ Aug 2 20:10
♐ Feb 20 1:49	♎ Jul 2 4:47	♍ Nov 13 23:42	♊ Mar 24 6:19	♉ Aug 5 9:05
♑ Feb 22 13:13	♏ Jul 4 9:56	♎ Nov 16 2:27	♋ Mar 26 14:04	♊ Aug 7 20:01
♒ Feb 25 1:57	♐ Jul 6 17:49	♏ Nov 18 5:36	♌ Mar 28 18:29	♋ Aug 10 3:10
♓ Feb 27 14:13	♑ Jul 9 3:49	♐ Nov 20 10:00	♍ Mar 30 19:58	♌ Aug 12 6:31
♈ Mar 2 1:08	♒ Jul 11 15:23	♑ Nov 22 16:42	♎ Apr 1 19:49	♍ Aug 14 7:25
♉ Mar 4 10:19	♓ Jul 14 3:57	♒ Nov 25 2:23	♏ Apr 3 19:50	♎ Aug 16 7:45
♊ Mar 6 17:16	♈ Jul 16 16:26	♓ Nov 27 14:33	♐ Apr 5 21:52	♏ Aug 18 9:10
♋ Mar 8 21:34	♉ Jul 19 2:54	♈ Nov 30 3:06	♑ Apr 8 3:20	♐ Aug 20 12:47
♌ Mar 10 23:25	♊ Jul 21 9:39	♉ Dec 2 13:32	♒ Apr 10 12:40	♑ Aug 22 18:58
♍ Mar 12 23:54	♋ Jul 23 12:22	♊ Dec 4 20:32	♓ Apr 13 0:49	♒ Aug 25 3:38
♎ Mar 15 0:43	♌ Jul 25 12:19	♋ Dec 7 0:31	♈ Apr 15 13:48	♓ Aug 27 14:27
♏ Mar 17 3:46	♍ Jul 27 11:34	♌ Dec 9 2:53	♉ Apr 18 1:50	♈ Aug 30 2:56
♐ Mar 19 10:24	♎ Jul 29 12:18	♍ Dec 11 5:04	♊ Apr 20 11:56	♉ Sept 1 15:59
♑ Mar 21 20:40	♏ Jul 31 16:05	♎ Dec 13 8:05	♋ Apr 22 19:42	♊ Sept 4 3:43
♒ Mar 24 9:05	♐ Aug 2 23:24	♏ Dec 15 12:19	♌ Apr 25 1:04	♋ Sept 6 12:15
♓ Mar 26 21:24	♑ Aug 5 9:34	♐ Dec 17 17:54	♍ Apr 27 4:10	♌ Sept 8 16:47
♈ Mar 29 8:00	♒ Aug 7 21:26	♑ Dec 20 1:11	♎ Apr 29 5:35	♍ Sept 10 18:04
♉ Mar 31 16:24	♓ Aug 10 10:03	♒ Dec 22 10:44	♏ May 1 6:26	♎ Sept 12 17:43
♊ Apr 2 22:42	♈ Aug 12 22:32	♓ Dec 24 22:35	♐ May 3 8:14	♏ Sept 14 17:40
♋ Apr 5 3:11	♉ Aug 15 9:38	♈ Dec 27 11:29	♑ May 5 12:35	♐ Sept 16 19:39
♌ Apr 7 6:09	♊ Aug 17 17:46	♉ Dec 29 22:52	♒ May 7 20:37	♑ Sept 19 0:48
♍ Apr 9 8:11	♋ Aug 19 22:02		♓ May 10 8:02	♒ Sept 21 9:18
♎ Apr 11 10:17	♌ Aug 21 22:58	**1931**	♈ May 12 20:57	♓ Sept 23 20:28
♏ Apr 13 13:45	♍ Aug 23 22:13	♊ Jan 1 6:34	♉ May 15 8:54	♈ Sept 26 9:09
♐ Apr 15 19:49	♎ Aug 25 21:58	♋ Jan 3 10:21	♊ May 17 18:26	♉ Sept 28 22:07
♑ Apr 18 5:07	♏ Aug 28 0:11	♌ Jan 5 11:32	♋ May 20 1:26	♊ Oct 1 10:03
♒ Apr 20 16:58	♐ Aug 30 6:04	♍ Jan 7 12:06	♌ May 22 6:27	♋ Oct 3 19:38
♓ Apr 23 5:23	♑ Sept 1 15:35	♎ Jan 9 13:48	♍ May 24 10:07	♌ Oct 6 1:49
♈ Apr 25 16:10	♒ Sept 4 3:27	♏ Jan 11 17:40	♎ May 26 12:51	♍ Oct 8 4:34
♉ Apr 28 0:08	♓ Sept 6 16:06	♐ Jan 13 23:51	♏ May 28 15:08	♎ Oct 10 4:50
♊ Apr 30 5:26	♈ Sept 9 4:21	♑ Jan 16 8:02	♐ May 30 17:48	♏ Oct 12 4:17
♋ May 2 8:54	♉ Sept 11 15:18	♒ Jan 18 18:04	♑ Jun 1 22:07	♐ Oct 14 4:51
♌ May 4 11:32	♊ Sept 14 0:01	♓ Jan 21 5:55	♒ Jun 4 5:23	♑ Oct 16 8:18
♍ May 6 14:11	♋ Sept 16 5:42	♈ Jan 23 18:55	♓ Jun 6 16:01	♒ Oct 18 15:39
♎ May 8 17:30	♌ Sept 18 8:18	♉ Jan 26 7:10	♈ Jun 9 4:44	♓ Oct 21 2:32
♏ May 10 22:06	♍ Sept 20 8:45	♊ Jan 28 16:18	♉ Jun 11 16:54	♈ Oct 23 15:21
	♎ Sept 22 8:43	♋ Jan 30 21:09	♊ Jun 14 2:22	♉ Oct 26 4:12

(continued)

Table A-2 — The Moon (continued)

Sign	Date	Time	Sign	Date	Time	Sign	Date	Time	Sign	Date	Time	Sign	Date	Time
♊	Oct 28	15:48	♓	Mar 5	18:15	♒	Jul 18	0:44	♑	Nov 29	10:16	♎	Apr 8	23:00
♋	Oct 31	1:26	♈	Mar 8	5:35	♓	Jul 20	6:34	♒	Dec 1	11:46	♏	Apr 11	0:32
♌	Nov 2	8:39	♉	Mar 10	18:19	♈	Jul 22	15:52	♓	Dec 3	17:08	♐	Apr 13	0:52
♍	Nov 4	13:08	♊	Mar 13	7:03	♉	Jul 25	3:54	♈	Dec 6	2:35	♑	Apr 15	1:54
♎	Nov 6	15:03	♋	Mar 15	17:46	♊	Jul 27	16:26	♉	Dec 8	14:41	♒	Apr 17	5:02
♏	Nov 8	15:21	♌	Mar 18	0:56	♋	Jul 30	3:07	♊	Dec 11	3:26	♓	Apr 19	10:54
♐	Nov 10	15:39	♍	Mar 20	4:18	♌	Aug 1	10:57	♋	Dec 13	15:28	♈	Apr 21	19:14
♑	Nov 12	17:52	♎	Mar 22	4:56	♍	Aug 3	16:15	♌	Dec 16	2:13	♉	Apr 24	5:31
♒	Nov 14	23:40	♏	Mar 24	4:35	♎	Aug 5	19:56	♍	Dec 18	11:09	♊	Apr 26	17:18
♓	Nov 17	9:32	♐	Mar 26	5:07	♏	Aug 7	22:49	♎	Dec 20	17:32	♋	Apr 29	5:58
♈	Nov 19	22:08	♑	Mar 28	8:08	♐	Aug 10	1:32	♏	Dec 22	20:53	♌	May 1	18:06
♉	Nov 22	11:00	♒	Mar 30	14:30	♑	Aug 12	4:38	♐	Dec 24	21:42	♍	May 4	3:41
♊	Nov 24	22:12	♓	Apr 2	0:05	♒	Aug 14	8:54	♑	Dec 26	21:31	♎	May 6	9:17
♋	Nov 27	7:09	♈	Apr 4	11:53	♓	Aug 16	15:13	♒	Dec 28	22:23	♏	May 8	11:07
♌	Nov 29	14:06	♉	Apr 7	0:44	♈	Aug 19	0:18	♓	Dec 31	2:16	♐	May 10	10:43
♍	Dec 1	19:16	♊	Apr 9	13:27	♉	Aug 21	11:56				♑	May 12	10:15
♎	Dec 3	22:44	♋	Apr 12	0:47	♊	Aug 24	0:33	**1933**			♒	May 14	11:46
♏	Dec 6	0:43	♌	Apr 14	9:22	♋	Aug 26	11:50	♈	Jan 2	10:13	♓	May 16	16:34
♐	Dec 8	2:04	♍	Apr 16	14:21	♌	Aug 28	20:03	♉	Jan 4	21:36	♈	May 19	0:45
♑	Dec 10	4:18	♎	Apr 18	16:00	♍	Aug 31	0:58	♊	Jan 7	10:19	♉	May 21	11:26
♒	Dec 12	9:10	♏	Apr 20	15:33	♎	Sept 2	3:32	♋	Jan 9	22:16	♊	May 23	23:31
♓	Dec 14	17:50	♐	Apr 22	14:57	♏	Sept 4	5:06	♌	Jan 12	8:27	♋	May 26	12:12
♈	Dec 17	5:49	♑	Apr 24	16:15	♐	Sept 6	7:00	♍	Jan 14	16:42	♌	May 29	0:33
♉	Dec 19	18:45	♒	Apr 26	21:04	♑	Sept 8	10:11	♎	Jan 16	23:03	♍	May 31	11:06
♊	Dec 22	5:59	♓	Apr 29	5:55	♒	Sept 10	15:16	♏	Jan 19	3:24	♎	Jun 2	18:15
♋	Dec 24	14:22	♈	May 1	17:46	♓	Sept 12	22:31	♐	Jan 21	5:54	♏	Jun 4	21:25
♌	Dec 26	20:16	♉	May 4	6:46	♈	Sept 15	8:01	♑	Jan 23	7:18	♐	Jun 6	21:32
♍	Dec 29	0:41	♊	May 6	19:20	♉	Sept 17	19:34	♒	Jan 25	8:57	♑	Jun 8	20:33
♎	Dec 31	4:17	♋	May 9	6:34	♊	Sept 20	8:14	♓	Jan 27	12:31	♒	Jun 10	20:41
			♌	May 11	15:47	♋	Sept 22	20:13	♈	Jan 29	19:21	♓	Jun 12	23:50
1932			♍	May 13	22:13	♌	Sept 25	5:32	♉	Feb 1	5:40	♈	Jun 15	6:51
♏	Jan 2	7:24	♎	May 16	1:32	♍	Sept 27	11:07	♊	Feb 3	18:05	♉	Jun 17	17:12
♐	Jan 4	10:15	♏	May 18	2:15	♎	Sept 29	13:22	♋	Feb 6	6:13	♊	Jun 20	5:25
♑	Jan 6	13:37	♐	May 20	1:48	♏	Oct 1	13:44	♌	Feb 8	16:16	♋	Jun 22	18:07
♒	Jan 8	18:44	♑	May 22	2:12	♐	Oct 3	14:02	♍	Feb 10	23:43	♌	Jun 25	6:17
♓	Jan 11	2:49	♒	May 24	5:31	♑	Oct 5	16:00	♎	Feb 13	4:59	♍	Jun 27	17:01
♈	Jan 13	14:07	♓	May 26	12:57	♒	Oct 7	20:44	♏	Feb 15	8:46	♎	Jun 30	1:11
♉	Jan 16	3:02	♈	May 29	0:09	♓	Oct 10	4:26	♐	Feb 17	11:42	♏	Jul 2	5:57
♊	Jan 18	14:47	♉	May 31	13:05	♈	Oct 12	14:36	♑	Feb 19	14:22	♐	Jul 4	7:32
♋	Jan 20	23:22	♊	Jun 3	1:32	♉	Oct 15	2:24	♒	Feb 21	17:29	♑	Jul 6	7:15
♌	Jan 23	4:39	♋	Jun 5	12:21	♊	Oct 17	15:03	♓	Feb 23	21:56	♒	Jul 8	7:05
♍	Jan 25	7:47	♌	Jun 7	21:14	♋	Oct 20	3:26	♈	Feb 26	4:42	♓	Jul 10	9:01
♎	Jan 27	10:07	♍	Jun 10	4:06	♌	Oct 22	13:57	♉	Feb 28	14:20	♈	Jul 12	14:31
♏	Jan 29	12:43	♎	Jun 12	8:41	♍	Oct 24	21:03	♊	Mar 3	2:18	♉	Jul 14	23:49
♐	Jan 31	16:07	♏	Jun 14	11:00	♎	Oct 27	0:15	♋	Mar 5	14:43	♊	Jul 17	11:44
♑	Feb 2	20:39	♐	Jun 16	11:45	♏	Oct 29	0:30	♌	Mar 8	1:18	♋	Jul 20	0:25
♒	Feb 5	2:48	♑	Jun 18	12:31	♐	Oct 30	23:40	♍	Mar 10	8:42	♌	Jul 22	12:19
♓	Feb 7	11:15	♒	Jun 20	15:12	♑	Nov 1	23:54	♎	Mar 12	13:03	♍	Jul 24	22:36
♈	Feb 9	22:17	♓	Jun 22	21:25	♒	Nov 4	3:06	♏	Mar 14	15:27	♎	Jul 27	6:44
♉	Feb 12	11:05	♈	Jun 25	7:34	♓	Nov 6	10:06	♐	Mar 16	17:18	♏	Jul 29	12:21
♊	Feb 14	23:27	♉	Jun 27	20:08	♈	Nov 8	20:24	♑	Mar 18	19:47	♐	Jul 31	15:27
♋	Feb 17	9:02	♊	Jun 30	8:35	♉	Nov 11	8:33	♒	Mar 20	23:39	♑	Aug 2	16:40
♌	Feb 19	14:49	♋	Jul 2	19:07	♊	Nov 13	21:13	♓	Mar 23	5:16	♒	Aug 4	17:22
♍	Feb 21	17:25	♌	Jul 5	3:18	♋	Nov 16	9:32	♈	Mar 25	12:49	♓	Aug 6	19:10
♎	Feb 23	18:22	♍	Jul 7	9:33	♌	Nov 18	20:35	♉	Mar 27	22:32	♈	Aug 8	23:41
♏	Feb 25	19:20	♎	Jul 9	14:12	♍	Nov 21	5:08	♊	Mar 30	10:13	♉	Aug 11	7:45
♐	Feb 27	21:39	♏	Jul 11	17:27	♎	Nov 23	10:08	♋	Apr 1	22:50	♊	Aug 13	18:57
♑	Mar 1	2:06	♐	Jul 13	19:38	♏	Nov 25	11:38	♌	Apr 4	10:16	♋	Aug 16	7:32
♒	Mar 3	9:00	♑	Jul 15	21:35	♐	Nov 27	10:58	♍	Apr 6	18:33	♌	Aug 18	19:22

Table A-2 — The Moon *(continued)*

♍	Aug 21	5:07	**1934**			♊	May 13	22:38	
♎	Aug 23	12:29	♌	Jan 2	8:56	♋	May 16	9:17	
♏	Aug 25	17:45	♍	Jan 4	21:09	♌	May 18	21:55	
♐	Aug 27	21:21	♎	Jan 7	7:20	♍	May 21	10:35	
♑	Aug 29	23:52	♏	Jan 9	14:11	♎	May 23	20:43	
♒	Sept 1	2:00	♐	Jan 11	17:18	♏	May 26	2:52	
♓	Sept 3	4:44	♑	Jan 13	17:37	♐	May 28	5:28	
♈	Sept 5	9:15	♒	Jan 15	16:56	♑	May 30	6:12	
♉	Sept 7	16:35	♓	Jan 17	17:17	♒	Jun 1	6:55	
♊	Sept 10	3:01	♈	Jan 19	20:28	♓	Jun 3	9:06	
♋	Sept 12	15:25	♉	Jan 22	3:26	♈	Jun 5	13:31	
♌	Sept 15	3:30	♊	Jan 24	13:54	♉	Jun 7	20:17	
♍	Sept 17	13:13	♋	Jan 27	2:24	♊	Jun 10	5:14	
♎	Sept 19	19:51	♌	Jan 29	15:12	♋	Jun 12	16:14	
♏	Sept 21	23:59	♍	Feb 1	3:00	♌	Jun 15	4:53	
♐	Sept 24	2:49	♎	Feb 3	13:00	♍	Jun 17	17:51	
♑	Sept 26	5:23	♏	Feb 5	20:31	♎	Jun 20	4:59	
♒	Sept 28	8:27	♐	Feb 8	1:14	♏	Jun 22	12:25	
♓	Sept 30	12:27	♑	Feb 10	3:23	♐	Jun 24	15:54	
♈	Oct 2	17:51	♒	Feb 12	3:57	♑	Jun 26	16:24	
♉	Oct 5	1:18	♓	Feb 14	4:27	♒	Jun 28	16:02	
♊	Oct 7	11:18	♈	Feb 16	6:39	♓	Jun 30	16:38	
♋	Oct 9	23:29	♉	Feb 18	12:03	♈	Jul 2	19:39	
♌	Oct 12	12:02	♊	Feb 20	21:16	♉	Jul 5	1:47	
♍	Oct 14	22:24	♋	Feb 23	9:22	♊	Jul 7	10:55	
♎	Oct 17	5:07	♌	Feb 25	22:13	♋	Jul 9	22:20	
♏	Oct 19	8:27	♍	Feb 28	9:46	♌	Jul 12	11:07	
♐	Oct 21	9:54	♎	Mar 2	19:02	♍	Jul 15	0:07	
♑	Oct 23	11:13	♏	Mar 5	1:59	♎	Jul 17	11:47	
♒	Oct 25	13:48	♐	Mar 7	6:58	♏	Jul 19	20:31	
♓	Oct 27	18:17	♑	Mar 9	10:22	♐	Jul 22	1:28	
♈	Oct 30	0:40	♒	Mar 11	12:36	♑	Jul 24	3:03	
♉	Nov 1	8:53	♓	Mar 13	14:25	♒	Jul 26	2:43	
♊	Nov 3	19:02	♈	Mar 15	17:00	♓	Jul 28	2:20	
♋	Nov 6	7:05	♉	Mar 17	21:46	♈	Jul 30	3:46	
♌	Nov 8	19:58	♊	Mar 20	5:51	♉	Aug 1	8:25	
♍	Nov 11	7:24	♋	Mar 22	17:13	♊	Aug 3	16:48	
♎	Nov 13	15:13	♌	Mar 25	6:03	♋	Aug 6	4:13	
♏	Nov 15	18:52	♍	Mar 27	17:44	♌	Aug 8	17:08	
♐	Nov 17	19:34	♎	Mar 30	2:37	♍	Aug 11	5:59	
♑	Nov 19	19:24	♏	Apr 1	8:35	♎	Aug 13	17:33	
♒	Nov 21	20:21	♐	Apr 3	12:37	♏	Aug 16	2:51	
♓	Nov 23	23:50	♑	Apr 5	15:45	♐	Aug 18	9:12	
♈	Nov 26	6:13	♒	Apr 7	18:43	♑	Aug 20	12:27	
♉	Nov 28	15:03	♓	Apr 9	21:52	♒	Aug 22	13:18	
♊	Dec 1	1:45	♈	Apr 12	1:40	♓	Aug 24	13:08	
♋	Dec 3	13:53	♉	Apr 14	6:56	♈	Aug 26	13:44	
♌	Dec 6	2:49	♊	Apr 16	14:41	♉	Aug 28	16:55	
♍	Dec 8	15:00	♋	Apr 19	1:26	♊	Aug 30	23:55	
♎	Dec 11	0:19	♌	Apr 21	14:10	♋	Sept 2	10:40	
♏	Dec 13	5:27	♍	Apr 24	2:20	♌	Sept 4	23:32	
♐	Dec 15	6:49	♎	Apr 26	11:32	♍	Sept 7	12:16	
♑	Dec 17	6:08	♏	Apr 28	17:07	♎	Sept 9	23:23	
♒	Dec 19	5:37	♐	Apr 30	20:02	♏	Sept 12	8:19	
♓	Dec 21	7:15	♑	May 2	21:53	♐	Sept 14	15:03	
♈	Dec 23	12:15	♒	May 5	0:06	♑	Sept 16	19:36	
♉	Dec 25	20:43	♓	May 7	3:26	♒	Sept 18	22:06	
♊	Dec 28	7:43	♈	May 9	8:09	♓	Sept 20	23:14	
♋	Dec 30	20:07	♉	May 11	14:24	♈	Sept 23	0:13	

♉	Sept 25	2:47	♒	Feb 2	13:26
♊	Sept 27	8:33	♓	Feb 4	12:47
♋	Sept 29	18:14	♈	Feb 6	12:49
♌	Oct 2	6:44	♉	Feb 8	15:22
♍	Oct 4	19:31	♊	Feb 10	21:35
♎	Oct 7	6:20	♋	Feb 13	7:24
♏	Oct 9	14:31	♌	Feb 15	19:35
♐	Oct 11	20:32	♍	Feb 18	8:33
♑	Oct 14	1:04	♎	Feb 20	21:02
♒	Oct 16	4:32	♏	Feb 23	8:04
♓	Oct 18	7:10	♐	Feb 25	16:40
♈	Oct 20	9:28	♑	Feb 27	22:05
♉	Oct 22	12:34	♒	Mar 2	0:16
♊	Oct 24	17:58	♓	Mar 4	0:13
♋	Oct 27	2:46	♈	Mar 5	23:40
♌	Oct 29	14:42	♉	Mar 8	0:43
♍	Nov 1	3:36	♊	Mar 10	5:11
♎	Nov 3	14:41	♋	Mar 12	13:52
♏	Nov 5	22:32	♌	Mar 15	1:48
♐	Nov 8	3:33	♍	Mar 17	14:51
♑	Nov 10	6:57	♎	Mar 20	3:08
♒	Nov 12	9:52	♏	Mar 22	13:44
♓	Nov 14	12:56	♐	Mar 24	22:24
♈	Nov 16	16:26	♑	Mar 27	4:49
♉	Nov 18	20:46	♒	Mar 29	8:41
♊	Nov 21	2:47	♓	Mar 31	10:14
♋	Nov 23	11:25	♈	Apr 2	10:31
♌	Nov 25	22:54	♉	Apr 4	11:18
♍	Nov 28	11:52	♊	Apr 6	14:35
♎	Nov 30	23:39	♋	Apr 8	21:49
♏	Dec 3	8:06	♌	Apr 11	8:52
♐	Dec 5	12:53	♍	Apr 13	21:47
♑	Dec 7	15:09	♎	Apr 16	10:01
♒	Dec 9	16:34	♏	Apr 18	20:09
♓	Dec 11	18:31	♐	Apr 21	4:06
♈	Dec 13	21:51	♑	Apr 23	10:13
♉	Dec 16	2:56	♒	Apr 25	14:43
♊	Dec 18	9:58	♓	Apr 27	17:40
♋	Dec 20	19:11	♈	Apr 29	19:26
♌	Dec 23	6:37	♉	May 1	21:09
♍	Dec 25	19:32	♊	May 4	0:26
♎	Dec 28	7:59	♋	May 6	6:50
♏	Dec 30	17:41	♌	May 8	16:55
			♍	May 11	5:26
1935			♎	May 13	17:48
♐	Jan 1	23:27	♏	May 16	3:54
♑	Jan 4	1:44	♐	May 18	11:13
♒	Jan 6	2:04	♑	May 20	16:20
♓	Jan 8	2:17	♒	May 22	20:08
♈	Jan 10	4:03	♓	May 24	23:13
♉	Jan 12	8:25	♈	May 27	1:59
♊	Jan 14	15:43	♉	May 29	4:59
♋	Jan 17	1:37	♊	May 31	9:11
♌	Jan 19	13:27	♋	Jun 2	15:44
♍	Jan 22	2:19	♌	Jun 5	1:19
♎	Jan 24	14:59	♍	Jun 7	13:26
♏	Jan 27	1:46	♎	Jun 10	2:00
♐	Jan 29	9:11	♏	Jun 12	12:35
♑	Jan 31	12:47	♐	Jun 14	19:57

(continued)

Table A-2 — The Moon *(continued)*

Sign	Date	Time
♑	Jun 17	0:21
♒	Jun 19	2:56
♓	Jun 21	4:56
♈	Jun 23	7:21
♉	Jun 25	10:54
♊	Jun 27	16:06
♋	Jun 29	23:26
♌	Jul 2	9:13
♍	Jul 4	21:08
♎	Jul 7	9:52
♏	Jul 9	21:15
♐	Jul 12	5:27
♑	Jul 14	10:03
♒	Jul 16	11:53
♓	Jul 18	12:30
♈	Jul 20	13:33
♉	Jul 22	16:21
♊	Jul 24	21:42
♋	Jul 27	5:43
♌	Jul 29	16:04
♍	Aug 1	4:07
♎	Aug 3	16:55
♏	Aug 6	4:57
♐	Aug 8	14:25
♑	Aug 10	20:10
♒	Aug 12	22:22
♓	Aug 14	22:19
♈	Aug 16	21:55
♉	Aug 18	23:07
♊	Aug 21	3:25
♋	Aug 23	11:17
♌	Aug 25	22:00
♍	Aug 28	10:20
♎	Aug 30	23:08
♏	Sept 2	11:22
♐	Sept 4	21:48
♑	Sept 7	5:08
♒	Sept 9	8:44
♓	Sept 11	9:15
♈	Sept 13	8:20
♉	Sept 15	8:10
♊	Sept 17	10:48
♋	Sept 19	17:27
♌	Sept 22	3:50
♍	Sept 24	16:18
♎	Sept 27	5:05
♏	Sept 29	17:06
♐	Oct 2	3:41
♑	Oct 4	12:02
♒	Oct 6	17:20
♓	Oct 8	19:27
♈	Oct 10	19:20
♉	Oct 12	18:53
♊	Oct 14	20:17
♋	Oct 17	1:21
♌	Oct 19	10:35
♍	Oct 21	22:44
♎	Oct 24	11:31
♏	Oct 26	23:15
♐	Oct 29	9:17
♑	Oct 31	17:31
♒	Nov 2	23:38
♓	Nov 5	3:20
♈	Nov 7	4:54
♉	Nov 9	5:29
♊	Nov 11	6:52
♋	Nov 13	10:56
♌	Nov 15	18:51
♍	Nov 18	6:10
♎	Nov 20	18:52
♏	Nov 23	6:36
♐	Nov 25	16:08
♑	Nov 27	23:28
♒	Nov 30	5:00
♓	Dec 2	9:03
♈	Dec 4	11:53
♉	Dec 6	14:03
♊	Dec 8	16:36
♋	Dec 10	20:54
♌	Dec 13	4:07
♍	Dec 15	14:33
♎	Dec 18	2:58
♏	Dec 20	15:03
♐	Dec 23	0:45
♑	Dec 25	7:27
♒	Dec 27	11:46
♓	Dec 29	14:42
♈	Dec 31	17:15

1936

Sign	Date	Time
♉	Jan 2	20:11
♊	Jan 5	0:04
♋	Jan 7	5:29
♌	Jan 9	13:02
♍	Jan 11	23:05
♎	Jan 14	11:10
♏	Jan 16	23:38
♐	Jan 19	10:11
♑	Jan 21	17:19
♒	Jan 23	21:02
♓	Jan 25	22:35
♈	Jan 27	23:36
♉	Jan 30	1:37
♊	Feb 1	5:39
♋	Feb 3	11:58
♌	Feb 5	20:26
♍	Feb 8	6:48
♎	Feb 10	18:45
♏	Feb 13	7:24
♐	Feb 15	18:56
♑	Feb 18	3:21
♒	Feb 20	7:46
♓	Feb 22	8:55
♈	Feb 24	8:35
♉	Feb 26	8:51
♊	Feb 28	11:30
♋	Mar 1	17:25
♌	Mar 4	2:20
♍	Mar 6	13:18
♎	Mar 9	1:26
♏	Mar 11	14:03
♐	Mar 14	2:06
♑	Mar 16	11:51
♒	Mar 18	17:52
♓	Mar 20	19:59
♈	Mar 22	19:31
♉	Mar 24	18:37
♊	Mar 26	19:31
♋	Mar 28	23:52
♌	Mar 31	8:04
♍	Apr 2	19:07
♎	Apr 5	7:31
♏	Apr 7	20:05
♐	Apr 10	8:03
♑	Apr 12	18:23
♒	Apr 15	1:49
♓	Apr 17	5:37
♈	Apr 19	6:20
♉	Apr 21	5:37
♊	Apr 23	5:37
♋	Apr 25	8:22
♌	Apr 27	15:03
♍	Apr 30	1:22
♎	May 2	13:43
♏	May 5	2:16
♐	May 7	13:54
♑	May 9	22:27
♒	May 12	7:47
♓	May 14	12:52
♈	May 16	15:14
♉	May 18	15:47
♊	May 20	16:12
♋	May 22	18:19
♌	May 24	23:41
♍	May 27	8:48
♎	May 29	20:38
♏	Jun 1	9:11
♐	Jun 3	20:37
♑	Jun 6	6:03
♒	Jun 8	13:17
♓	Jun 10	18:27
♈	Jun 12	21:46
♉	Jun 14	23:48
♊	Jun 17	1:30
♋	Jun 19	4:09
♌	Jun 21	9:06
♍	Jun 23	17:15
♎	Jun 26	4:23
♏	Jun 28	16:53
♐	Jul 1	4:27
♑	Jul 3	13:34
♒	Jul 5	19:56
♓	Jul 8	0:10
♈	Jul 10	3:10
♉	Jul 12	5:46
♊	Jul 14	8:38
♋	Jul 16	12:28
♌	Jul 18	17:58
♍	Jul 21	1:54
♎	Jul 23	12:31
♏	Jul 26	0:54
♐	Jul 28	12:56
♑	Jul 30	22:24
♒	Aug 2	4:25
♓	Aug 4	7:36
♈	Aug 6	9:21
♉	Aug 8	11:11
♊	Aug 10	14:12
c ♋	Aug 12	18:52
♌	Aug 15	1:20
♍	Aug 17	9:44
♎	Aug 19	20:17
♏	Aug 22	8:36
♐	Aug 24	21:09
♑	Aug 27	7:35
♒	Aug 29	14:12
♓	Aug 31	17:06
♈	Sept 2	17:43
♉	Sept 4	18:04
♊	Sept 6	19:54
♋	Sept 9	0:16
♌	Sept 11	7:13
♍	Sept 13	16:20
♎	Sept 16	3:12
♏	Sept 18	15:32
♐	Sept 21	4:24
♑	Sept 23	15:53
♒	Sept 25	23:53
♓	Sept 28	3:39
♈	Sept 30	4:10
♉	Oct 2	3:25
♊	Oct 4	3:37
♋	Oct 6	6:29
♌	Oct 8	12:45
♍	Oct 10	22:01
♎	Oct 13	9:19
♏	Oct 15	21:47
♐	Oct 18	10:38
♑	Oct 20	22:37
♒	Oct 23	8:00
♓	Oct 25	13:28
♈	Oct 27	15:09
♉	Oct 29	14:34
♊	Oct 31	13:49
♋	Nov 2	15:00
♌	Nov 4	19:37
♍	Nov 7	4:00
♎	Nov 9	15:15
♏	Nov 12	3:52
♐	Nov 14	16:33
♑	Nov 17	4:20
♒	Nov 19	14:11
♓	Nov 21	21:04
♈	Nov 24	0:37
♉	Nov 26	1:29
♊	Nov 28	1:11
♋	Nov 30	1:40
♌	Dec 2	4:43
♍	Dec 4	11:31
♎	Dec 6	21:55
♏	Dec 9	10:28
♐	Dec 11	23:07
♑	Dec 14	10:25
♒	Dec 16	19:42
♓	Dec 19	2:43
♈	Dec 21	7:26
♉	Dec 23	10:05
♊	Dec 25	11:24
♋	Dec 27	12:36
♌	Dec 29	15:14
♍	Dec 31	20:45

1937

Sign	Date	Time
♎	Jan 3	5:55
♏	Jan 5	17:58
♐	Jan 8	6:43
♑	Jan 10	17:53
♒	Jan 13	2:25
♓	Jan 15	8:28
♈	Jan 17	12:48
♉	Jan 19	16:07
♊	Jan 21	18:54
♋	Jan 23	21:38
♌	Jan 26	1:08
♍	Jan 28	6:30
♎	Jan 30	14:49
♏	Feb 2	2:10
♐	Feb 4	14:59
♑	Feb 7	2:34
♒	Feb 9	11:23
♓	Feb 11	16:10
♈	Feb 13	19:12
♉	Feb 15	21:34
♊	Feb 18	0:22
♋	Feb 20	4:04
♌	Feb 22	8:51
♍	Feb 24	15:04
♎	Feb 26	23:26
♏	Mar 1	10:23
♐	Mar 3	23:08
♑	Mar 6	11:23
♒	Mar 8	20:36
♓	Mar 11	1:50
♈	Mar 13	4:00
♉	Mar 15	4:54
♊	Mar 17	6:19
♋	Mar 19	9:25
♌	Mar 21	14:35
♍	Mar 23	21:44
♎	Mar 26	6:47
♏	Mar 28	17:51
♐	Mar 31	6:32
♑	Apr 2	19:16
♒	Apr 5	5:38
♓	Apr 7	11:59

Table A-2 — The Moon (continued)

♈ Apr 9 14:28	♓ Aug 21 22:28	**1938**	♐ May 14 17:40	♏ Sept 25 19:57
♉ Apr 11 14:39	♈ Aug 24 3:23	♒ Jan 3 4:31	♑ May 17 5:51	♐ Sept 28 4:02
♊ Apr 13 14:34	♉ Aug 26 6:57	♓ Jan 5 15:07	♒ May 19 18:37	♑ Sept 30 15:20
♋ Apr 15 16:02	♊ Aug 28 10:01	♈ Jan 7 23:29	♓ May 22 6:08	♒ Oct 3 3:58
♌ Apr 17 20:11	♋ Aug 30 13:03	♉ Jan 10 5:06	♈ May 24 14:35	♓ Oct 5 15:27
♍ Apr 20 3:16	♌ Sept 1 16:21	♊ Jan 12 7:50	♉ May 26 19:17	♈ Oct 8 0:22
♎ Apr 22 12:51	♍ Sept 3 20:34	♋ Jan 14 8:21	♊ May 28 20:52	♉ Oct 10 6:43
♏ Apr 25 0:21	♎ Sept 6 2:48	♌ Jan 16 8:09	♋ May 30 20:52	♊ Oct 12 11:10
♐ Apr 27 13:05	♏ Sept 8 11:59	♍ Jan 18 9:13	♌ Jun 1 21:09	♋ Oct 14 14:31
♑ Apr 30 1:56	♐ Sept 10 23:59	♎ Jan 20 13:27	♍ Jun 3 23:21	♌ Oct 16 17:19
♒ May 2 13:08	♑ Sept 13 12:52	♏ Jan 22 21:55	♎ Jun 6 4:35	♍ Oct 18 20:09
♓ May 4 20:57	♒ Sept 15 23:51	♐ Jan 25 9:51	♏ Jun 8 13:01	♎ Oct 20 23:43
♈ May 7 0:47	♓ Sept 18 7:19	♑ Jan 27 22:58	♐ Jun 10 23:57	♏ Oct 23 5:00
♉ May 9 1:32	♈ Sept 20 11:31	♒ Jan 30 11:00	♑ Jun 13 12:21	♐ Oct 25 12:54
♊ May 11 0:56	♉ Sept 22 13:49	♓ Feb 1 20:58	♒ Jun 16 1:07	♑ Oct 27 23:39
♋ May 13 1:00	♊ Sept 24 15:46	♈ Feb 4 4:54	♓ Jun 18 13:02	♒ Oct 30 12:08
♌ May 15 3:27	♋ Sept 26 18:24	♉ Feb 6 10:58	♈ Jun 20 22:40	♓ Nov 2 0:09
♍ May 17 9:19	♌ Sept 28 22:14	♊ Feb 8 15:08	♉ Jun 23 4:50	♈ Nov 4 9:35
♎ May 19 18:34	♍ Oct 1 3:29	♋ Feb 10 17:26	♊ Jun 25 7:25	♉ Nov 6 15:41
♏ May 22 6:18	♎ Oct 3 10:31	♌ Feb 12 18:33	♋ Jun 27 7:27	♊ Nov 8 19:03
♐ May 24 19:10	♏ Oct 5 19:55	♍ Feb 14 19:57	♌ Jun 29 6:45	♋ Nov 10 20:59
♑ May 27 7:53	♐ Oct 8 7:44	♎ Feb 16 23:28	♍ Jul 1 7:24	♌ Nov 12 22:50
♒ May 29 19:13	♑ Oct 10 20:47	♏ Feb 19 6:37	♎ Jul 3 11:09	♍ Nov 15 1:38
♓ Jun 1 3:58	♒ Oct 13 8:37	♐ Feb 21 17:33	♏ Jul 5 18:49	♎ Nov 17 6:03
♈ Jun 3 9:22	♓ Oct 15 17:03	♑ Feb 24 6:28	♐ Jul 8 5:45	♏ Nov 19 12:26
♉ Jun 5 11:36	♈ Oct 17 21:32	♒ Feb 26 18:36	♑ Jul 10 18:22	♐ Nov 21 20:56
♊ Jun 7 11:46	♉ Oct 19 23:09	♓ Mar 1 4:13	♒ Jul 13 7:05	♑ Nov 24 7:38
♋ Jun 9 11:31	♊ Oct 21 23:40	♈ Mar 3 11:16	♓ Jul 15 18:55	♒ Nov 26 19:58
♌ Jun 11 12:44	♋ Oct 24 0:47	♉ Mar 5 16:29	♈ Jul 18 5:02	♓ Nov 29 8:30
♍ Jun 13 17:01	♌ Oct 26 3:42	♊ Mar 7 20:33	♉ Jul 20 12:31	♈ Dec 1 19:02
♎ Jun 16 1:08	♍ Oct 28 9:01	♋ Mar 9 23:46	♊ Jul 22 16:43	♉ Dec 4 2:01
♏ Jun 18 12:31	♎ Oct 30 16:47	♌ Mar 12 2:23	♋ Jul 24 17:54	♊ Dec 6 5:18
♐ Jun 21 1:25	♏ Nov 2 2:48	♍ Mar 14 5:05	♌ Jul 26 17:26	♋ Dec 8 6:07
♑ Jun 23 13:58	♐ Nov 4 14:46	♎ Mar 16 9:00	♍ Jul 28 17:17	♌ Dec 10 6:17
♒ Jun 26 0:54	♑ Nov 7 3:50	♏ Mar 18 15:53	♎ Jul 30 19:35	♍ Dec 12 7:37
♓ Jun 28 9:37	♒ Nov 9 16:19	♐ Mar 21 2:01	♏ Aug 2 1:49	♎ Dec 14 11:27
♈ Jun 30 5:50	♓ Nov 12 2:07	♑ Mar 23 14:32	♐ Aug 4 12:02	♏ Dec 16 18:13
♉ Jul 2 19:34	♈ Nov 14 7:59	♒ Mar 26 2:56	♑ Aug 7 0:33	♐ Dec 19 3:31
♊ Jul 4 21:15	♉ Nov 16 10:12	♓ Mar 28 12:52	♒ Aug 9 13:15	♑ Dec 21 14:39
♋ Jul 6 21:53	♊ Nov 18 10:10	♈ Mar 30 19:33	♓ Aug 12 0:45	♒ Dec 24 2:59
♌ Jul 8 22:59	♋ Nov 20 9:47	♉ Apr 1 23:43	♈ Aug 14 10:34	♓ Dec 26 15:41
♍ Jul 11 2:15	♌ Nov 22 10:55	♊ Apr 4 2:33	♉ Aug 16 18:25	♈ Dec 29 3:14
♎ Jul 13 9:04	♍ Nov 24 14:56	♋ Apr 6 5:07	♊ Aug 18 23:51	♉ Dec 31 11:47
♏ Jul 15 19:36	♎ Nov 26 22:22	♌ Apr 8 8:04	♋ Aug 21 2:39	
♐ Jul 18 8:20	♏ Nov 29 8:46	♍ Apr 10 11:51	♌ Aug 23 3:27	**1939**
♑ Jul 20 20:50	♐ Dec 1 21:05	♎ Apr 12 17:02	♍ Aug 25 3:43	♊ Jan 2 16:19
♒ Jul 23 7:20	♑ Dec 4 10:07	♏ Apr 15 0:21	♎ Aug 27 5:26	♋ Jan 4 17:20
♓ Jul 25 15:21	♒ Dec 6 22:40	♐ Apr 17 10:19	♏ Aug 29 10:26	♌ Jan 6 16:32
♈ Jul 27 21:15	♓ Dec 9 9:21	♑ Apr 19 22:31	♐ Aug 31 19:28	♍ Jan 8 16:08
♉ Jul 30 1:31	♈ Dec 11 16:55	♒ Apr 22 11:11	♑ Sept 3 7:30	♎ Jan 10 18:11
♊ Aug 1 4:29	♉ Dec 13 20:50	♓ Apr 24 21:53	♒ Sept 5 20:10	♏ Jan 12 23:54
♋ Aug 3 6:34	♊ Dec 15 21:42	♈ Apr 27 5:08	♓ Sept 8 7:28	♐ Jan 15 9:10
♌ Aug 5 8:35	♋ Dec 17 21:03	♉ Apr 29 9:01	♈ Sept 10 16:40	♑ Jan 17 20:44
♍ Aug 7 11:54	♌ Dec 19 20:48	♊ May 1 10:45	♉ Sept 12 23:54	♒ Jan 20 9:15
♎ Aug 9 17:58	♍ Dec 21 22:57	♋ May 3 11:51	♊ Sept 15 5:23	♓ Jan 22 21:51
♏ Aug 12 3:37	♎ Dec 24 4:53	♌ May 5 13:42	♋ Sept 17 9:09	♈ Jan 25 9:42
♐ Aug 14 15:59	♏ Dec 26 14:45	♍ May 7 17:17	♌ Sept 19 11:26	♉ Jan 27 19:29
♑ Aug 17 4:37	♐ Dec 29 3:12	♎ May 9 23:06	♍ Sept 21 13:01	♊ Jan 30 1:50
♒ Aug 19 15:05	♑ Dec 31 16:17	♏ May 12 7:16	♎ Sept 23 15:19	♋ Feb 1 4:22

(continued)

Table A-2 The Moon (continued)

Sign	Date	Time	Sign	Date	Time	Sign	Date	Time	Sign	Date	Time	Sign	Date	Time
♌	Feb 3	4:06	♋	Jun 17	16:06	♊	Oct 30	2:31	♓	Mar 7	8:07	♒	Jul 19	11:22
♍	Feb 5	3:02	♌	Jun 19	16:58	♋	Nov 1	8:41	♈	Mar 9	21:01	♓	Jul 21	20:58
♎	Feb 7	3:29	♍	Jun 21	17:56	♌	Nov 3	13:01	♉	Mar 12	9:44	♈	Jul 24	9:02
♏	Feb 9	7:22	♎	Jun 23	20:30	♍	Nov 5	15:57	♊	Mar 14	20:53	♉	Jul 26	21:56
♐	Feb 11	15:24	♏	Jun 26	1:25	♎	Nov 7	18:03	♋	Mar 17	4:57	♊	Jul 29	9:04
♑	Feb 14	2:41	♐	Jun 28	8:39	♏	Nov 9	20:14	♌	Mar 19	9:15	♋	Jul 31	16:32
♒	Feb 16	15:22	♑	Jun 30	17:53	♐	Nov 11	23:41	♍	Mar 21	10:20	♌	Aug 2	20:20
♓	Feb 19	3:52	♒	Jul 3	4:54	♑	Nov 14	5:42	♎	Mar 23	9:47	♍	Aug 4	21:50
♈	Feb 21	15:23	♓	Jul 5	17:17	♒	Nov 16	15:00	♏	Mar 25	9:33	♎	Aug 6	22:50
♉	Feb 24	1:19	♈	Jul 8	5:50	♓	Nov 19	3:00	♐	Mar 27	11:31	♏	Aug 9	0:46
♊	Feb 26	8:47	♉	Jul 10	16:27	♈	Nov 21	15:36	♑	Mar 29	17:00	♐	Aug 11	4:29
♋	Feb 28	13:06	♊	Jul 12	23:20	♉	Nov 24	2:23	♒	Apr 1	2:13	♑	Aug 13	10:15
♌	Mar 2	14:30	♋	Jul 15	2:16	♊	Nov 26	10:09	♓	Apr 3	14:11	♒	Aug 15	18:07
♍	Mar 4	14:17	♌	Jul 17	2:30	♋	Nov 28	15:11	♈	Apr 6	3:10	♓	Aug 18	4:10
♎	Mar 6	14:26	♍	Jul 19	2:07	♌	Nov 30	18:34	♉	Apr 8	15:39	♈	Aug 20	16:14
♏	Mar 8	17:00	♎	Jul 21	3:10	♍	Dec 2	21:23	♊	Apr 11	2:32	♉	Aug 23	5:17
♐	Mar 10	23:23	♏	Jul 23	7:04	♎	Dec 5	0:22	♋	Apr 13	11:04	♊	Aug 25	17:13
♑	Mar 13	9:35	♐	Jul 25	14:10	♏	Dec 7	3:57	♌	Apr 15	16:44	♋	Aug 28	1:53
♒	Mar 15	22:01	♑	Jul 27	23:51	♐	Dec 9	8:32	♍	Apr 17	19:34	♌	Aug 30	6:31
♓	Mar 18	10:31	♒	Jul 30	11:15	♑	Dec 11	14:51	♎	Apr 19	20:23	♍	Sept 1	7:57
♈	Mar 20	21:41	♓	Aug 1	23:41	♒	Dec 13	23:42	♏	Apr 21	20:33	♎	Sept 3	7:54
♉	Mar 23	6:58	♈	Aug 4	12:22	♓	Dec 16	11:14	♐	Apr 23	21:48	♏	Sept 5	8:16
♊	Mar 25	14:15	♉	Aug 6	23:47	♈	Dec 19	0:03	♑	Apr 26	1:50	♐	Sept 7	10:36
♋	Mar 27	19:19	♊	Aug 9	8:06	♉	Dec 21	11:32	♒	Apr 28	9:39	♑	Sept 9	15:45
♌	Mar 29	22:15	♋	Aug 11	12:21	♊	Dec 23	19:37	♓	Apr 30	20:56	♒	Sept 11	23:51
♍	Mar 31	23:39	♌	Aug 13	13:09	♋	Dec 26	0:03	♈	May 3	9:52	♓	Sept 14	10:25
♎	Apr 3	0:48	♍	Aug 15	12:19	♌	Dec 28	2:05	♉	May 5	22:12	♈	Sept 16	22:43
♏	Apr 5	3:21	♎	Aug 17	12:04	♍	Dec 30	3:29	♊	May 8	8:34	♉	Sept 19	11:45
♐	Apr 7	8:47	♏	Aug 19	14:20				♋	May 10	16:33	♊	Sept 22	0:05
♑	Apr 9	17:47	♐	Aug 21	20:14	**1940**			♌	May 12	22:22	♋	Sept 24	9:57
♒	Apr 12	5:33	♑	Aug 24	5:33	♎	Jan 1	5:44	♍	May 15	2:18	♌	Sept 26	16:09
♓	Apr 14	18:04	♒	Aug 26	17:09	♏	Jan 3	9:36	♎	May 17	4:40	♍	Sept 28	18:41
♈	Apr 17	5:13	♓	Aug 29	5:42	♐	Jan 5	15:12	♏	May 19	6:12	♎	Sept 30	18:46
♉	Apr 19	18:15	♈	Aug 31	18:15	♑	Jan 7	22:30	♐	May 21	8:00	♏	Oct 2	18:12
♊	Apr 21	20:16	♉	Sept 3	5:47	♒	Jan 10	7:42	♑	May 23	11:35	♐	Oct 4	18:54
♋	Apr 24	0:43	♊	Sept 5	15:02	♓	Jan 12	19:03	♒	May 25	18:19	♑	Oct 6	22:28
♌	Apr 26	3:55	♋	Sept 7	20:52	♈	Jan 15	7:56	♓	May 28	4:39	♒	Oct 9	5:44
♍	Apr 28	6:26	♌	Sept 9	23:11	♉	Jan 17	20:15	♈	May 30	17:18	♓	Oct 11	16:18
♎	Apr 30	9:02	♍	Sept 11	23:09	♊	Jan 20	5:32	♉	Jun 2	5:44	♈	Oct 14	4:50
♏	May 2	12:36	♎	Sept 13	22:39	♋	Jan 22	10:35	♊	Jun 4	15:49	♉	Oct 16	17:49
♐	May 4	18:11	♏	Sept 15	23:43	♌	Jan 24	12:10	♋	Jun 6	23:02	♊	Oct 19	5:59
♑	May 7	2:34	♐	Sept 18	4:02	♍	Jan 26	12:12	♌	Jun 9	4:00	♋	Oct 21	16:18
♒	May 9	13:41	♑	Sept 20	12:11	♎	Jan 28	12:43	♍	Jun 11	7:41	♌	Oct 23	23:51
♓	May 12	2:09	♒	Sept 22	23:24	♏	Jan 30	15:17	♎	Jun 13	10:43	♍	Oct 26	4:10
♈	May 14	13:41	♓	Sept 25	12:00	♐	Feb 1	20:36	♏	Jun 15	13:31	♎	Oct 28	5:37
♉	May 16	22:28	♈	Sept 28	0:22	♑	Feb 4	4:27	♐	Jun 17	16:34	♏	Oct 30	5:25
♊	May 19	4:06	♉	Sept 30	11:29	♒	Feb 6	14:21	♑	Jun 19	20:44	♐	Nov 1	5:21
♋	May 21	7:23	♊	Oct 2	20:38	♓	Feb 9	1:58	♒	Jun 22	3:15	♑	Nov 3	7:22
♌	May 23	9:33	♋	Oct 5	3:16	♈	Feb 11	14:49	♓	Jun 24	12:55	♒	Nov 5	13:03
♍	May 25	11:51	♌	Oct 7	7:10	♉	Feb 14	3:36	♈	Jun 27	1:13	♓	Nov 7	22:46
♎	May 27	15:06	♍	Oct 9	8:46	♊	Feb 16	14:10	♉	Jun 29	13:52	♈	Nov 10	11:13
♏	May 29	19:47	♎	Oct 11	9:15	♋	Feb 18	20:46	♊	Jul 2	0:15	♉	Nov 13	0:13
♐	Jun 1	2:15	♏	Oct 13	10:18	♌	Feb 20	23:19	♋	Jul 4	7:10	♊	Nov 15	12:00
♑	Jun 3	10:50	♐	Oct 15	13:36	♍	Feb 22	23:11	♌	Jul 6	11:12	♋	Nov 17	21:52
♒	Jun 5	21:40	♑	Oct 17	20:22	♎	Feb 24	22:29	♍	Jul 8	13:44	♌	Nov 20	5:38
♓	Jun 8	10:05	♒	Oct 20	6:40	♏	Feb 26	23:13	♎	Jul 10	16:07	♍	Nov 22	11:11
♈	Jun 10	22:10	♓	Oct 22	19:05	♐	Feb 29	2:54	♏	Jul 12	19:07	♎	Nov 24	14:25
♉	Jun 13	7:43	♈	Oct 25	7:28	♑	Mar 2	10:02	♐	Jul 14	23:05	♏	Nov 26	15:44
♊	Jun 15	13:32	♉	Oct 27	18:09	♒	Mar 4	20:07	♑	Jul 17	4:17	♐	Nov 28	16:18

Table A-2 — The Moon *(continued)*

Col 1	Col 2	Col 3	Col 4	Col 5
♑ Nov 30 17:50	♎ Apr 10 5:54	♍ Aug 22 14:53	**1942**	♉ May 13 1:37
♒ Dec 2 22:12	♏ Apr 12 5:31	♎ Aug 24 18:21	♋ Jan 1 11:42	♊ May 15 13:15
♓ Dec 5 6:35	♐ Apr 14 5:07	♏ Aug 26 20:49	♌ Jan 3 22:32	♋ May 18 1:49
♈ Dec 7 18:26	♑ Apr 16 6:38	♐ Aug 28 23:13	♍ Jan 6 7:42	♌ May 20 14:21
♉ Dec 10 7:27	♒ Apr 18 11:31	♑ Aug 31 2:18	♎ Jan 8 14:48	♍ May 23 1:07
♊ Dec 12 19:08	♓ Apr 20 20:07	♒ Sept 2 6:39	♏ Jan 10 19:24	♎ May 25 8:22
♋ Dec 15 4:20	♈ Apr 23 7:34	♓ Sept 4 12:52	♐ Jan 12 21:31	♏ May 27 11:32
♌ Dec 17 11:16	♉ Apr 25 20:23	♈ Sept 6 21:28	♑ Jan 14 22:07	♐ May 29 11:39
♍ Dec 19 16:35	♊ Apr 28 9:11	♉ Sept 9 8:32	♒ Jan 16 22:52	♑ May 31 10:43
♎ Dec 21 20:37	♋ Apr 30 20:56	♊ Sept 11 21:06	♓ Jan 19 1:43	♒ Jun 2 10:59
♏ Dec 23 23:30	♌ May 3 6:34	♋ Sept 14 9:09	♈ Jan 21 8:08	♓ Jun 4 14:14
♐ Dec 26 1:36	♍ May 5 13:06	♌ Sept 16 18:36	♉ Jan 23 18:18	♈ Jun 6 21:11
♑ Dec 28 3:58	♎ May 7 16:11	♍ Sept 19 0:29	♊ Jan 26 6:44	♉ Jun 9 7:16
♒ Dec 30 8:09	♏ May 9 16:34	♎ Sept 21 3:17	♋ Jan 28 19:03	♊ Jun 11 19:11
1941	♐ May 11 15:49	♏ Sept 23 4:24	♌ Jan 31 5:37	♋ Jun 14 7:50
♓ Jan 1 15:35	♑ May 13 16:03	♐ Sept 25 5:24	♍ Feb 2 13:57	♌ Jun 16 20:19
♈ Jan 4 2:34	♒ May 15 19:15	♑ Sept 27 7:44	♎ Feb 4 20:18	♍ Jun 19 7:33
♉ Jan 6 15:28	♓ May 18 2:33	♒ Sept 29 12:17	♏ Feb 7 0:56	♎ Jun 21 16:04
♊ Jan 9 3:27	♈ May 20 13:34	♓ Oct 1 19:18	♐ Feb 9 4:06	♏ Jun 23 20:50
♋ Jan 11 12:33	♉ May 23 2:26	♈ Oct 4 4:37	♑ Feb 11 6:19	♐ Jun 25 22:09
♌ Jan 13 18:39	♊ May 25 15:10	♉ Oct 6 15:52	♒ Feb 13 8:27	♑ Jun 27 21:30
♍ Jan 15 22:45	♋ May 28 2:36	♊ Oct 9 4:23	♓ Feb 15 11:50	♒ Jun 29 21:00
♎ Jan 18 2:00	♌ May 30 12:15	♋ Oct 11 16:53	♈ Feb 17 17:46	♓ Jul 1 22:46
♏ Jan 20 5:04	♍ Jun 1 19:38	♌ Oct 14 3:29	♉ Feb 20 2:57	♈ Jul 4 4:10
♐ Jan 22 8:16	♎ Jun 4 0:17	♍ Oct 16 10:36	♊ Feb 22 14:47	♉ Jul 6 13:22
♑ Jan 24 12:01	♏ Jun 6 2:13	♎ Oct 18 13:54	♋ Feb 25 3:15	♊ Jul 9 1:10
♒ Jan 26 17:06	♐ Jun 8 2:24	♏ Oct 20 14:25	♌ Feb 27 14:06	♋ Jul 11 13:51
♓ Jan 29 0:34	♑ Jun 10 2:32	♐ Oct 22 14:00	♍ Mar 1 22:06	♌ Jul 14 2:08
♈ Jan 31 11:02	♒ Jun 12 4:41	♑ Oct 24 14:40	♎ Mar 4 3:23	♍ Jul 16 13:08
♉ Feb 2 23:41	♓ Jun 14 10:33	♒ Oct 26 18:02	♏ Mar 6 6:50	♎ Jul 18 22:02
♊ Feb 5 12:09	♈ Jun 16 20:30	♓ Oct 29 0:51	♐ Mar 8 9:28	♏ Jul 21 4:02
♋ Feb 7 21:57	♉ Jun 19 9:03	♈ Oct 31 10:38	♑ Mar 10 12:08	♐ Jul 23 6:58
♌ Feb 10 4:07	♊ Jun 21 21:44	♉ Nov 2 22:19	♒ Mar 12 15:30	♑ Jul 25 7:38
♍ Feb 12 7:21	♋ Jun 24 8:51	♊ Nov 5 10:52	♓ Mar 14 20:09	♒ Jul 27 7:37
♎ Feb 14 9:07	♌ Jun 26 17:55	♋ Nov 7 23:26	♈ Mar 17 2:41	♓ Jul 29 8:49
♏ Feb 16 10:52	♍ Jun 29 1:03	♌ Nov 10 10:49	♉ Mar 19 11:39	♈ Jul 31 12:55
♐ Feb 18 13:37	♎ Jul 1 6:17	♍ Nov 12 19:29	♊ Mar 21 23:00	♉ Aug 2 20:47
♑ Feb 20 17:54	♏ Jul 3 9:34	♎ Nov 15 0:22	♋ Mar 24 11:33	♊ Aug 5 7:54
♒ Feb 23 0:02	♐ Jul 5 11:13	♏ Nov 17 1:40	♌ Mar 26 23:04	♋ Aug 7 20:30
♓ Feb 25 8:18	♑ Jul 7 12:21	♐ Nov 19 0:53	♍ Mar 29 7:36	♌ Aug 10 8:39
♈ Feb 27 18:54	♒ Jul 9 14:36	♑ Nov 21 0:11	♎ Mar 31 12:36	♍ Aug 12 19:09
♉ Mar 2 7:23	♓ Jul 11 19:42	♒ Nov 23 1:46	♏ Apr 2 14:54	♎ Aug 15 3:31
♊ Mar 4 20:12	♈ Jul 14 4:35	♓ Nov 25 7:09	♐ Apr 4 16:04	♏ Aug 17 9:38
♋ Mar 7 7:04	♉ Jul 16 16:30	♈ Nov 27 16:26	♑ Apr 6 17:41	♐ Aug 19 13:35
♌ Mar 9 14:19	♊ Jul 19 5:10	♉ Nov 30 4:18	♒ Apr 8 20:56	♑ Aug 21 15:46
♍ Mar 11 17:51	♋ Jul 21 16:15	♊ Dec 2 17:00	♓ Apr 11 2:19	♒ Aug 23 17:07
♎ Mar 13 18:51	♌ Jul 24 0:48	♋ Dec 5 5:22	♈ Apr 13 9:49	♓ Aug 25 18:55
♏ Mar 15 19:03	♍ Jul 26 7:03	♌ Dec 7 16:43	♉ Apr 15 19:18	♈ Aug 27 22:39
♐ Mar 17 20:08	♎ Jul 28 11:41	♍ Dec 10 2:12	♊ Apr 18 6:37	♉ Aug 30 5:29
♑ Mar 19 23:25	♏ Jul 30 15:09	♎ Dec 12 8:46	♋ Apr 20 19:10	♊ Sept 1 15:40
♒ Mar 22 5:34	♐ Aug 1 17:49	♏ Dec 14 11:51	♌ Apr 23 7:21	♋ Sept 4 4:00
♓ Mar 24 14:30	♑ Aug 3 20:17	♐ Dec 16 12:10	♍ Apr 25 17:02	♌ Sept 6 16:15
♈ Mar 27 1:39	♒ Aug 5 23:32	♑ Dec 18 11:26	♎ Apr 27 22:50	♍ Sept 9 2:31
♉ Mar 29 14:14	♓ Aug 8 4:51	♒ Dec 20 11:53	♏ Apr 30 0:59	♎ Sept 11 10:05
♊ Apr 1 3:06	♈ Aug 10 13:13	♓ Dec 22 15:33	♐ May 2 1:03	♏ Sept 13 15:19
♋ Apr 3 14:44	♉ Aug 13 0:32	♈ Dec 24 23:24	♑ May 4 1:04	♐ Sept 15 18:58
♌ Apr 5 23:26	♊ Aug 15 13:09	♉ Dec 27 10:43	♒ May 6 2:56	♑ Sept 17 21:48
♍ Apr 8 4:21	♋ Aug 18 0:37	♊ Dec 29 23:27	♓ May 8 7:44	♒ Sept 20 0:27
	♌ Aug 20 9:15		♈ May 10 15:31	♓ Sept 22 3:34

(continued)

Table A-2 — The Moon *(continued)*

Sign	Date	Time
♈	Sept 24	7:57
♉	Sept 26	14:34
♊	Sept 29	0:05
♋	Oct 1	12:03
♌	Oct 4	0:35
♍	Oct 6	11:13
♎	Oct 8	18:33
♏	Oct 10	22:46
♐	Oct 13	1:10
♑	Oct 15	3:13
♒	Oct 17	6:01
♓	Oct 19	10:05
♈	Oct 21	15:37
♉	Oct 23	22:52
♊	Oct 26	8:18
♋	Oct 28	20:00
♌	Oct 31	8:48
♍	Nov 2	20:19
♎	Nov 5	4:21
♏	Nov 7	8:27
♐	Nov 9	9:47
♑	Nov 11	10:18
♒	Nov 13	11:48
♓	Nov 15	15:28
♈	Nov 17	21:30
♉	Nov 20	5:38
♊	Nov 22	15:35
♋	Nov 25	3:17
♌	Nov 27	16:09
♍	Nov 30	4:29
♎	Dec 2	13:55
♏	Dec 4	19:06
♐	Dec 6	20:34
♑	Dec 8	20:07
♒	Dec 10	19:57
♓	Dec 12	21:56
♈	Dec 15	3:04
♉	Dec 17	11:16
♊	Dec 19	21:46
♋	Dec 22	9:46
♌	Dec 24	22:35
♍	Dec 27	11:10
♎	Dec 29	21:44
1943		
♏	Jan 1	4:40
♐	Jan 3	7:34
♑	Jan 5	7:35
♒	Jan 7	6:42
♓	Jan 9	7:03
♈	Jan 11	10:21
♉	Jan 13	17:22
♊	Jan 16	3:39
♋	Jan 18	15:53
♌	Jan 21	4:44
♍	Jan 23	17:03
♎	Jan 26	3:47
♏	Jan 28	11:51
♐	Jan 30	16:34
♑	Feb 1	18:15
♒	Feb 3	18:10
♓	Feb 5	18:07
♈	Feb 7	20:00
♉	Feb 10	1:17
♊	Feb 12	10:25
♋	Feb 14	22:24
♌	Feb 17	11:18
♍	Feb 19	23:20
♎	Feb 22	9:30
♏	Feb 24	17:25
♐	Feb 26	22:59
♑	Mar 1	2:19
♒	Mar 3	3:56
♓	Mar 5	4:54
♈	Mar 7	6:41
♉	Mar 9	10:53
♊	Mar 11	18:39
♋	Mar 14	5:51
♌	Mar 16	18:41
♍	Mar 19	6:43
♎	Mar 21	16:21
♏	Mar 23	23:23
♐	Mar 26	4:23
♑	Mar 28	8:05
♒	Mar 30	10:57
♓	Apr 1	13:27
♈	Apr 3	16:17
♉	Apr 5	20:37
♊	Apr 8	3:41
♋	Apr 10	14:03
♌	Apr 13	2:39
♍	Apr 15	14:59
♎	Apr 18	0:41
♏	Apr 20	7:04
♐	Apr 22	10:56
♑	Apr 24	13:40
♒	Apr 26	16:21
♓	Apr 28	19:36
♈	Apr 30	23:39
♉	May 3	4:57
♊	May 5	12:16
♋	May 7	22:17
♌	May 10	10:39
♍	May 12	23:21
♎	May 15	9:44
♏	May 17	16:19
♐	May 19	19:33
♑	May 21	21:00
♒	May 23	22:23
♓	May 26	0:58
♈	May 28	5:16
♉	May 30	11:25
♊	Jun 1	19:29
♋	Jun 4	5:45
♌	Jun 6	18:03
♍	Jun 9	7:03
♎	Jun 11	18:22
♏	Jun 14	1:59
♐	Jun 16	5:36
♑	Jun 18	6:30
♒	Jun 20	6:33
♓	Jun 22	7:36
♈	Jun 24	10:52
♉	Jun 26	16:52
♊	Jun 29	1:27
♋	Jul 1	12:13
♌	Jul 4	0:39
♍	Jul 6	13:45
♎	Jul 9	1:44
♏	Jul 11	10:40
♐	Jul 13	15:37
♑	Jul 15	17:07
♒	Jul 17	16:46
♓	Jul 19	16:30
♈	Jul 21	18:08
♉	Jul 23	22:53
♊	Jul 26	7:04
♋	Jul 28	18:04
♌	Jul 31	6:43
♍	Aug 2	19:45
♎	Aug 5	7:51
♏	Aug 7	17:40
♐	Aug 10	0:08
♑	Aug 12	3:09
♒	Aug 14	3:36
♓	Aug 16	3:06
♈	Aug 18	3:32
♉	Aug 20	6:40
♊	Aug 22	13:34
♋	Aug 25	0:07
♌	Aug 27	12:49
♍	Aug 30	1:47
♎	Sept 1	13:33
♏	Sept 3	23:20
♐	Sept 6	6:38
♑	Sept 8	11:13
♒	Sept 10	13:18
♓	Sept 12	13:46
♈	Sept 14	14:09
♉	Sept 16	16:14
♊	Sept 18	21:42
♋	Sept 21	7:10
♌	Sept 23	19:34
♍	Sept 26	8:30
♎	Sept 28	19:56
♏	Oct 1	5:04
♐	Oct 3	12:03
♑	Oct 5	17:11
♒	Oct 7	20:39
♓	Oct 9	22:44
♈	Oct 12	0:12
♉	Oct 14	2:26
♊	Oct 16	7:07
♋	Oct 18	15:28
♌	Oct 21	3:12
♍	Oct 23	16:10
♎	Oct 26	3:38
♏	Oct 28	12:14
♐	Oct 30	18:14
♑	Nov 1	22:37
♒	Nov 4	2:10
♓	Nov 6	5:16
♈	Nov 8	8:10
♉	Nov 10	11:32
♊	Nov 12	16:31
♋	Nov 15	0:22
♌	Nov 17	11:27
♍	Nov 20	0:21
♎	Nov 22	12:19
♏	Nov 24	21:09
♐	Nov 27	2:35
♑	Nov 29	5:43
♒	Dec 1	8:01
♓	Dec 3	10:36
♈	Dec 5	14:00
♉	Dec 7	18:30
♊	Dec 10	0:32
♋	Dec 12	8:46
♌	Dec 14	19:37
♍	Dec 17	8:22
♎	Dec 19	20:55
♏	Dec 22	6:46
♐	Dec 24	12:44
♑	Dec 26	15:24
♒	Dec 28	16:21
♓	Dec 30	17:17
1944		
♈	Jan 1	19:34
♉	Jan 3	23:58
♊	Jan 6	6:44
♋	Jan 8	15:48
♌	Jan 11	2:58
♍	Jan 13	15:38
♎	Jan 16	4:29
♏	Jan 18	15:27
♐	Jan 20	22:53
♑	Jan 23	2:26
♒	Jan 25	3:09
♓	Jan 27	2:48
♈	Jan 29	3:15
♉	Jan 31	6:07
♊	Feb 2	12:17
♋	Feb 4	21:40
♌	Feb 7	9:20
♍	Feb 9	22:08
♎	Feb 12	10:54
♏	Feb 14	22:24
♐	Feb 17	7:15
♑	Feb 19	12:33
♒	Feb 21	14:27
♓	Feb 23	14:09
♈	Feb 25	13:31
♉	Feb 27	14:36
♊	Feb 29	19:06
♋	Mar 3	3:38
♌	Mar 5	15:19
♍	Mar 8	4:18
♎	Mar 10	16:55
♏	Mar 13	4:12
♐	Mar 15	13:31
♑	Mar 17	20:13
♒	Mar 19	23:55
♓	Mar 22	0:59
♈	Mar 24	0:42
♉	Mar 26	1:01
♊	Mar 28	3:58
♋	Mar 30	10:59
♌	Apr 1	21:54
♍	Apr 4	10:49
♎	Apr 6	23:22
♏	Apr 9	10:12
♐	Apr 11	19:02
♑	Apr 14	1:56
♒	Apr 16	6:46
♓	Apr 18	9:28
♈	Apr 20	10:35
♉	Apr 22	11:29
♊	Apr 24	13:59
♋	Apr 26	19:49
♌	Apr 29	5:36
♍	May 1	18:04
♎	May 4	6:40
♏	May 6	17:18
♐	May 9	1:27
♑	May 11	7:33
♒	May 13	12:10
♓	May 15	15:35
♈	May 17	18:03
♉	May 19	20:15
♊	May 21	23:26
♋	May 24	5:04
♌	May 26	14:04
♍	May 29	1:58
♎	May 31	14:37
♏	Jun 3	1:32
♐	Jun 5	9:27
♑	Jun 7	14:41
♒	Jun 9	18:12
♓	Jun 11	20:58
♈	Jun 13	23:41
♉	Jun 16	2:52
♊	Jun 18	7:11
♋	Jun 20	13:28
♌	Jun 22	22:25
♍	Jun 25	9:58
♎	Jun 27	22:40
♏	Jun 30	10:10
♐	Jul 2	18:38
♑	Jul 4	23:42
♒	Jul 7	2:14
♓	Jul 9	3:39
♈	Jul 11	5:18
♉	Jul 13	8:16
♊	Jul 15	13:11

Table A-2 — The Moon (continued)

♋ Jul 17 20:21	♊ Nov 29 6:55	♓ Apr 8 20:10	♒ Aug 21 3:32	**1946**
♌ Jul 20 5:51	♋ Dec 1 10:17	♈ Apr 10 20:38	♓ Aug 23 7:05	♑ Jan 2 7:11
♍ Jul 22 17:24	♌ Dec 3 16:53	♉ Apr 12 19:40	♈ Aug 25 8:30	♒ Jan 4 16:38
♎ Jul 25 6:08	♍ Dec 6 3:04	♊ Apr 14 19:31	♉ Aug 27 9:34	♓ Jan 6 23:47
♏ Jul 27 18:16	♎ Dec 8 15:28	♋ Apr 16 22:14	♊ Aug 29 11:47	♈ Jan 9 4:56
♐ Jul 30 3:50	♏ Dec 11 3:42	♌ Apr 19 4:52	♋ Aug 31 16:00	♉ Jan 11 8:25
♑ Aug 1 9:42	♐ Dec 13 13:50	♍ Apr 21 15:03	♌ Sept 2 22:20	♊ Jan 13 10:42
♒ Aug 3 12:10	♑ Dec 15 21:22	♎ Apr 24 3:15	♍ Sept 5 6:36	♋ Jan 15 12:32
♓ Aug 5 12:35	♒ Dec 18 2:44	♏ Apr 26 15:52	♎ Sept 7 16:48	♌ Jan 17 15:04
♈ Aug 7 12:43	♓ Dec 20 6:39	♐ Apr 29 3:56	♏ Sept 10 4:48	♍ Jan 19 19:40
♉ Aug 9 14:19	♈ Dec 22 9:42	♑ May 1 14:40	♐ Sept 12 17:37	♎ Jan 22 3:31
♊ Aug 11 18:38	♉ Dec 24 12:24	♒ May 3 23:06	♑ Sept 15 5:11	♏ Jan 24 14:40
♋ Aug 14 2:03	♊ Dec 26 15:26	♓ May 6 4:21	♒ Sept 17 13:19	♐ Jan 27 3:27
♌ Aug 16 12:08	♋ Dec 28 19:44	♈ May 8 6:25	♓ Sept 19 17:19	♑ Jan 29 15:18
♍ Aug 19 0:01	♌ Dec 31 2:19	♉ May 10 6:24	♈ Sept 21 18:11	♒ Feb 1 0:23
♎ Aug 21 12:45		♊ May 12 6:12	♉ Sept 23 17:53	♓ Feb 3 6:32
♏ Aug 24 1:13	**1945**	♋ May 14 7:51	♊ Sept 25 18:32	♈ Feb 5 10:38
♐ Aug 26 11:52	♍ Jan 2 11:49	♌ May 16 12:57	♋ Sept 27 21:38	♉ Feb 7 13:47
♑ Aug 28 19:12	♎ Jan 4 23:44	♍ May 18 21:56	♌ Sept 30 3:47	♊ Feb 9 16:45
♒ Aug 30 22:44	♏ Jan 7 12:13	♎ May 21 9:43	♍ Oct 2 12:34	♋ Feb 11 19:59
♓ Sept 1 23:14	♐ Jan 9 22:55	♏ May 23 22:21	♎ Oct 4 23:17	♌ Feb 13 23:50
♈ Sept 3 22:27	♑ Jan 12 6:28	♐ May 26 10:11	♏ Oct 7 11:24	♍ Feb 16 5:03
♉ Sept 5 22:28	♒ Jan 14 10:57	♑ May 28 20:24	♐ Oct 10 0:17	♎ Feb 18 12:36
♊ Sept 8 1:14	♓ Jan 16 13:27	♒ May 31 4:35	♑ Oct 12 12:33	♏ Feb 20 23:05
♋ Sept 10 7:47	♈ Jan 18 15:21	♓ Jun 2 10:25	♒ Oct 14 22:07	♐ Feb 23 11:41
♌ Sept 12 17:50	♉ Jan 20 17:48	♈ Jun 4 13:51	♓ Oct 17 3:34	♑ Feb 26 0:01
♍ Sept 15 6:00	♊ Jan 22 21:35	♉ Jun 6 15:23	♈ Oct 19 5:09	♒ Feb 28 9:34
♎ Sept 17 18:48	♋ Jan 25 3:05	♊ Jun 8 16:15	♉ Oct 21 4:30	♓ Mar 2 15:25
♏ Sept 20 7:11	♌ Jan 27 10:33	♋ Jun 10 18:02	♊ Oct 23 3:49	♈ Mar 4 18:23
♐ Sept 22 18:16	♍ Jan 29 20:09	♌ Jun 12 22:20	♋ Oct 25 5:11	♉ Mar 6 20:08
♑ Sept 25 2:55	♎ Feb 1 7:46	♍ Jun 15 6:07	♌ Oct 27 9:55	♊ Mar 8 22:12
♒ Sept 27 8:10	♏ Feb 3 20:22	♎ Jun 17 17:06	♍ Oct 29 18:12	♋ Mar 11 1:29
♓ Sept 29 9:58	♐ Feb 6 7:57	♏ Jun 20 5:36	♎ Nov 1 5:08	♌ Mar 13 6:14
♈ Oct 1 9:30	♑ Feb 8 16:29	♐ Jun 22 17:27	♏ Nov 3 17:29	♍ Mar 15 12:32
♉ Oct 3 8:46	♒ Feb 10 21:12	♑ Jun 25 3:14	♐ Nov 6 6:18	♎ Mar 17 20:40
♊ Oct 5 9:59	♓ Feb 12 22:52	♒ Jun 27 10:36	♑ Nov 8 18:35	♏ Mar 20 7:04
♋ Oct 7 14:56	♈ Feb 14 23:12	♓ Jun 29 15:51	♒ Nov 11 4:59	♐ Mar 22 19:30
♌ Oct 10 0:03	♉ Feb 17 0:05	♈ Jul 1 19:29	♓ Nov 13 12:05	♑ Mar 25 8:18
♍ Oct 12 12:04	♊ Feb 19 3:01	♉ Jul 3 22:04	♈ Nov 15 15:24	♒ Mar 27 18:51
♎ Oct 15 0:55	♋ Feb 21 8:42	♊ Jul 6 0:20	♉ Nov 17 15:48	♓ Mar 30 1:26
♏ Oct 17 13:03	♌ Feb 23 16:58	♋ Jul 8 3:10	♊ Nov 19 15:02	♈ Apr 1 4:16
♐ Oct 19 23:50	♍ Feb 26 3:13	♌ Jul 10 7:43	♋ Nov 21 15:14	♉ Apr 3 4:56
♑ Oct 22 8:48	♎ Feb 28 14:57	♍ Jul 12 14:58	♌ Nov 23 18:12	♊ Apr 5 5:25
♒ Oct 24 15:19	♏ Mar 3 3:32	♎ Jul 15 1:13	♍ Nov 26 0:59	♋ Apr 7 7:21
♓ Oct 26 18:53	♐ Mar 5 15:45	♏ Jul 17 13:29	♎ Nov 28 11:18	♌ Apr 9 11:37
♈ Oct 28 19:54	♑ Mar 8 1:37	♐ Jul 20 1:36	♏ Nov 30 23:43	♍ Apr 11 18:20
♉ Oct 30 19:45	♒ Mar 10 7:40	♑ Jul 22 11:29	♐ Dec 3 12:30	♎ Apr 14 3:13
♊ Nov 1 20:28	♓ Mar 12 9:50	♒ Jul 24 18:16	♑ Dec 6 0:23	♏ Apr 16 14:03
♋ Nov 4 0:04	♈ Mar 14 9:32	♓ Jul 26 22:27	♒ Dec 8 10:34	♐ Apr 19 2:30
♌ Nov 6 7:44	♉ Mar 16 8:54	♈ Jul 29 1:07	♓ Dec 10 18:20	♑ Apr 21 15:28
♍ Nov 8 18:59	♊ Mar 18 10:04	♉ Jul 31 3:29	♈ Dec 12 23:15	♒ Apr 24 2:56
♎ Nov 11 7:45	♋ Mar 20 14:31	♊ Aug 2 6:23	♉ Dec 15 1:30	♓ Apr 26 10:54
♏ Nov 13 19:48	♌ Mar 22 22:32	♋ Aug 4 10:23	♊ Dec 17 2:03	♈ Apr 28 14:45
♐ Nov 16 6:02	♍ Mar 25 9:11	♌ Aug 6 15:53	♋ Dec 19 2:27	♉ Apr 30 15:31
♑ Nov 18 14:20	♎ Mar 27 21:15	♍ Aug 8 23:24	♌ Dec 21 4:30	♊ May 2 15:03
♒ Nov 20 20:47	♏ Mar 30 9:50	♎ Aug 11 9:21	♍ Dec 23 9:44	♋ May 4 15:23
♓ Nov 23 1:18	♐ Apr 1 22:08	♏ Aug 13 21:24	♎ Dec 25 18:45	♌ May 6 18:04
♈ Nov 25 3:57	♑ Apr 4 8:51	♐ Aug 16 9:56	♏ Dec 28 6:43	♍ May 8 23:57
♉ Nov 27 5:22	♒ Apr 6 16:28	♑ Aug 18 20:31	♐ Dec 30 19:32	♎ May 11 8:53

(continued)

Table A-2   The Moon *(continued)*

♏ May 13 20:08	♎ Sept 25 0:40	♋ Feb 2 8:38	♊ Jun 16 21:21	♉ Oct 29 5:16
♐ May 16 8:46	♏ Sept 27 9:12	♌ Feb 4 9:01	♋ Jun 18 21:32	♊ Oct 31 9:36
♑ May 18 21:42	♐ Sept 29 20:32	♍ Feb 6 9:42	♌ Jun 20 21:06	♋ Nov 2 12:32
♒ May 21 9:31	♑ Oct 2 9:29	♎ Feb 8 12:39	♍ Jun 22 22:01	♌ Nov 4 15:03
♓ May 23 18:39	♒ Oct 4 21:27	♏ Feb 10 19:28	♎ Jun 25 1:51	♍ Nov 6 17:55
♈ May 26 0:05	♓ Oct 7 6:09	♐ Feb 13 6:15	♏ Jun 27 9:17	♎ Nov 8 21:42
♉ May 28 2:03	♈ Oct 9 11:05	♑ Feb 15 19:12	♐ Jun 29 19:46	♏ Nov 11 3:03
♊ May 30 1:54	♉ Oct 11 13:20	♒ Feb 18 7:38	♑ Jul 2 8:03	♐ Nov 13 10:33
♋ Jun 1 1:29	♊ Oct 13 14:37	♓ Feb 20 17:57	♒ Jul 4 20:50	♑ Nov 15 20:37
♌ Jun 3 2:39	♋ Oct 15 16:23	♈ Feb 23 1:58	♓ Jul 7 9:03	♒ Nov 18 8:45
♍ Jun 5 6:57	♌ Oct 17 19:35	♉ Feb 25 8:08	♈ Jul 9 19:34	♓ Nov 20 21:16
♎ Jun 7 14:57	♍ Oct 20 0:35	♊ Feb 27 12:47	♉ Jul 12 3:12	♈ Nov 23 7:53
♏ Jun 10 2:04	♎ Oct 22 7:33	♋ Mar 1 15:59	♊ Jul 14 7:17	♉ Nov 25 15:06
♐ Jun 12 14:50	♏ Oct 24 16:41	♌ Mar 3 18:00	♋ Jul 16 8:14	♊ Nov 27 18:55
♑ Jun 15 3:39	♐ Oct 27 4:03	♍ Mar 5 19:46	♌ Jul 18 7:34	♋ Nov 29 20:31
♒ Jun 17 15:16	♑ Oct 29 16:59	♎ Mar 7 22:51	♍ Jul 20 7:19	♌ Dec 1 21:30
♓ Jun 20 0:43	♒ Nov 1 5:36	♏ Mar 10 4:51	♎ Jul 22 9:33	♍ Dec 3 23:23
♈ Jun 22 7:19	♓ Nov 3 15:32	♐ Mar 12 14:34	♏ Jul 24 15:41	♎ Dec 6 3:14
♉ Jun 24 10:56	♈ Nov 5 21:28	♑ Mar 15 3:00	♐ Jul 27 1:40	♏ Dec 8 9:24
♊ Jun 26 12:07	♉ Nov 7 23:49	♒ Mar 17 15:35	♑ Jul 29 14:01	♐ Dec 10 17:49
♋ Jun 28 12:10	♊ Nov 10 0:07	♓ Mar 20 1:57	♒ Aug 1 2:50	♑ Dec 13 4:14
♌ Jun 30 12:47	♋ Nov 12 0:15	♈ Mar 22 9:23	♓ Aug 3 14:49	♒ Dec 15 16:16
♍ Jul 2 15:45	♌ Nov 14 1:53	♉ Mar 24 14:29	♈ Aug 6 1:20	♓ Dec 18 4:59
♎ Jul 4 22:21	♍ Nov 16 6:05	♊ Mar 26 18:16	♉ Aug 8 9:43	♈ Dec 20 16:37
♏ Jul 7 8:41	♎ Nov 18 13:12	♋ Mar 28 21:26	♊ Aug 10 15:17	♉ Dec 23 1:11
♐ Jul 9 21:20	♏ Nov 20 22:58	♌ Mar 31 0:22	♋ Aug 12 17:49	♊ Dec 25 5:47
♑ Jul 12 10:05	♐ Nov 23 10:44	♍ Apr 2 3:30	♌ Aug 14 18:06	♋ Dec 27 7:03
♒ Jul 14 21:17	♑ Nov 25 23:40	♎ Apr 4 7:39	♍ Aug 16 17:49	♌ Dec 29 6:41
♓ Jul 17 6:15	♒ Nov 28 12:30	♏ Apr 6 13:56	♎ Aug 18 19:04	♍ Dec 31 6:47
♈ Jul 19 12:59	♓ Nov 30 23:30	♐ Apr 8 23:12	♏ Aug 20 23:44	
♉ Jul 21 17:35	♈ Dec 3 7:05	♑ Apr 11 11:08	♐ Aug 23 8:34	**1948**
♊ Jul 23 20:18	♉ Dec 5 10:48	♒ Apr 13 23:51	♑ Aug 25 20:31	♎ Jan 2 9:10
♋ Jul 25 21:44	♊ Dec 7 11:30	♓ Apr 16 10:47	♒ Aug 28 9:18	♏ Jan 4 14:51
♌ Jul 27 22:57	♋ Dec 9 10:50	♈ Apr 18 18:26	♓ Aug 30 21:03	♐ Jan 6 23:41
♍ Jul 30 1:32	♌ Dec 11 10:46	♉ Apr 20 22:56	♈ Sept 2 7:03	♑ Jan 9 10:41
♎ Aug 1 7:05	♍ Dec 13 13:09	♊ Apr 23 1:28	♉ Sept 4 15:10	♒ Jan 11 22:54
♏ Aug 3 16:23	♎ Dec 15 19:07	♋ Apr 25 3:22	♊ Sept 6 21:18	♓ Jan 14 11:35
♐ Aug 6 4:36	♏ Dec 18 4:43	♌ Apr 27 5:44	♋ Sept 9 1:12	♈ Jan 16 23:44
♑ Aug 8 17:23	♐ Dec 20 16:48	♍ Apr 29 9:15	♌ Sept 11 3:03	♉ Jan 19 9:42
♒ Aug 11 4:23	♑ Dec 23 5:50	♎ May 1 14:24	♍ Sept 13 3:51	♊ Jan 21 16:01
♓ Aug 13 12:41	♒ Dec 25 18:29	♏ May 3 21:35	♎ Sept 15 5:16	♋ Jan 23 18:23
♈ Aug 15 18:37	♓ Dec 28 5:43	♐ May 6 7:09	♏ Sept 17 9:11	♌ Jan 25 18:00
♉ Aug 17 22:59	♈ Dec 30 14:31	♑ May 8 18:55	♐ Sept 19 16:49	♍ Jan 27 16:56
♊ Aug 20 2:22		♒ May 11 7:41	♑ Sept 22 3:58	♎ Jan 29 17:29
♋ Aug 22 5:06	**1947**	♓ May 13 19:20	♒ Sept 24 16:38	♏ Jan 31 21:27
♌ Aug 24 7:38	♉ Jan 1 20:06	♈ May 16 3:56	♓ Sept 27 4:24	♐ Feb 3 5:26
♍ Aug 26 10:54	♊ Jan 3 22:26	♉ May 18 8:51	♈ Sept 29 13:58	♑ Feb 5 16:30
♎ Aug 28 16:15	♋ Jan 5 22:28	♊ May 20 10:51	♉ Oct 1 21:15	♒ Feb 8 4:59
♏ Aug 31 0:49	♌ Jan 7 21:53	♋ May 22 11:27	♊ Oct 4 2:44	♓ Feb 10 17:37
♐ Sept 2 12:31	♍ Jan 9 22:45	♌ May 24 12:18	♋ Oct 6 6:47	♈ Feb 13 5:37
♑ Sept 5 1:24	♎ Jan 12 2:54	♍ May 26 14:50	♌ Oct 8 9:41	♉ Feb 15 16:08
♒ Sept 7 12:41	♏ Jan 14 11:15	♎ May 28 19:54	♍ Oct 10 11:57	♊ Feb 17 23:56
♓ Sept 9 20:46	♐ Jan 16 23:03	♏ May 31 3:42	♎ Oct 12 14:31	♋ Feb 20 4:09
♈ Sept 12 1:49	♑ Jan 19 12:10	♐ Jun 2 13:54	♏ Oct 14 18:45	♌ Feb 22 5:07
♉ Sept 14 5:03	♒ Jan 22 0:37	♑ Jun 5 1:51	♐ Oct 17 1:53	♍ Feb 24 4:22
♊ Sept 16 7:45	♓ Jan 24 11:23	♒ Jun 7 14:38	♑ Oct 19 12:14	♎ Feb 26 4:05
♋ Sept 18 10:42	♈ Jan 26 20:10	♓ Jun 10 2:47	♒ Oct 22 0:39	♏ Feb 28 6:24
♌ Sept 20 14:13	♉ Jan 29 2:45	♈ Jun 12 12:34	♓ Oct 24 12:45	♐ Mar 1 12:41
♍ Sept 22 18:38	♊ Jan 31 6:52	♉ Jun 14 18:45	♈ Oct 26 22:31	♑ Mar 3 22:50

Table A-2 The Moon *(continued)*

≈ Mar 6 11:14	♑ Jul 18 14:13	♐ Nov 29 22:52	♍ Apr 9 10:32	♌ Aug 21 20:08
♓ Mar 8 23:53	≈ Jul 21 1:02	♑ Dec 2 4:16	♎ Apr 11 10:48	♍ Aug 23 21:56
♈ Mar 11 11:33	♓ Jul 23 13:13	≈ Dec 4 12:32	♏ Apr 13 10:27	♎ Aug 25 22:24
♉ Mar 13 21:40	♈ Jul 26 1:57	♓ Dec 6 23:46	♐ Apr 15 11:23	♏ Aug 27 23:20
♊ Mar 16 5:45	♉ Jul 28 13:34	♈ Dec 9 12:30	♑ Apr 17 15:16	♐ Aug 30 2:00
♋ Mar 18 11:14	♊ Jul 30 22:01	♉ Dec 12 0:09	≈ Apr 19 22:59	♑ Sept 1 7:05
♌ Mar 20 13:58	♋ Aug 2 2:20	♊ Dec 14 8:44	♓ Apr 22 10:08	≈ Sept 3 14:37
♍ Mar 22 14:42	♌ Aug 4 3:13	♋ Dec 16 14:01	♈ Apr 24 23:01	♓ Sept 6 0:26
♎ Mar 24 15:01	♍ Aug 6 2:32	♌ Dec 18 17:03	♉ Apr 27 11:41	♈ Sept 8 12:13
♏ Mar 26 16:49	♎ Aug 8 2:30	♍ Dec 20 19:19	♊ Apr 29 22:48	♉ Sept 11 1:12
♐ Mar 28 21:46	♏ Aug 10 4:57	♎ Dec 22 21:59	♋ May 2 7:43	♊ Sept 13 13:47
♑ Mar 31 6:34	♐ Aug 12 10:49	♏ Dec 25 1:39	♌ May 4 14:11	♋ Sept 15 23:52
≈ Apr 2 18:18	♑ Aug 14 19:51	♐ Dec 27 6:29	♍ May 6 18:11	♌ Sept 18 6:04
♓ Apr 5 6:56	≈ Aug 17 7:02	♑ Dec 29 12:47	♎ May 8 20:07	♍ Sept 20 8:34
♈ Apr 7 18:28	♓ Aug 19 19:23	≈ Dec 31 21:07	♏ May 10 20:54	♎ Sept 22 8:41
♉ Apr 10 3:58	♈ Aug 22 8:05		♐ May 12 21:57	♏ Sept 24 8:20
♊ Apr 12 11:20	♉ Aug 24 20:03	*1949*	♑ May 15 0:57	♐ Sept 26 9:21
♋ Apr 14 16:41	♊ Aug 27 5:40	♓ Jan 3 7:58	≈ May 17 7:19	♑ Sept 28 13:07
♌ Apr 16 20:16	♋ Aug 29 11:34	♈ Jan 5 20:40	♓ May 19 17:26	≈ Sept 30 20:13
♍ Apr 18 22:30	♌ Aug 31 13:41	♉ Jan 8 9:03	♈ May 22 6:02	♓ Oct 3 6:19
♎ Apr 21 0:16	♍ Sept 2 13:20	♊ Jan 10 18:31	♉ May 24 18:42	♈ Oct 5 18:27
♏ Apr 23 2:49	♎ Sept 4 12:35	♋ Jan 12 23:57	♊ May 27 5:27	♉ Oct 8 7:26
♐ Apr 25 7:31	♏ Sept 6 13:34	♌ Jan 15 2:08	♋ May 29 13:39	♊ Oct 10 20:02
♑ Apr 27 15:22	♐ Sept 8 17:52	♍ Jan 17 2:52	♌ May 31 19:36	♋ Oct 13 6:51
≈ Apr 30 2:16	♑ Sept 11 1:56	♎ Jan 19 4:03	♍ Jun 2 23:53	♌ Oct 15 14:35
♓ May 2 14:44	≈ Sept 13 12:58	♏ Jan 21 6:59	♎ Jun 5 2:57	♍ Oct 17 18:42
♈ May 5 2:28	♓ Sept 16 1:27	♐ Jan 23 12:09	♏ Jun 7 5:13	♎ Oct 19 19:48
♉ May 7 11:48	♈ Sept 18 14:02	♑ Jan 25 19:22	♐ Jun 9 7:24	♏ Oct 21 19:18
♊ May 9 18:20	♉ Sept 21 1:45	≈ Jan 28 4:26	♑ Jun 11 10:40	♐ Oct 23 19:08
♋ May 11 22:38	♊ Sept 23 11:40	♓ Jan 30 15:26	≈ Jun 13 16:26	♑ Oct 25 21:10
♌ May 14 1:39	♋ Sept 25 18:46	♈ Feb 2 4:04	♓ Jun 16 1:38	≈ Oct 28 2:50
♍ May 16 4:14	♌ Sept 27 22:35	♉ Feb 4 16:57	♈ Jun 18 13:45	♓ Oct 30 12:21
♎ May 18 7:07	♍ Sept 29 23:40	♊ Feb 7 3:40	♉ Jun 21 2:30	♈ Nov 2 0:34
♏ May 20 10:56	♎ Oct 1 23:30	♋ Feb 9 10:22	♊ Jun 23 13:20	♉ Nov 4 13:37
♐ May 22 16:22	♏ Oct 3 23:58	♌ Feb 11 13:00	♋ Jun 25 21:01	♊ Nov 7 1:55
♑ May 25 0:08	♐ Oct 6 2:55	♍ Feb 13 13:05	♌ Jun 28 2:01	♋ Nov 9 12:35
≈ May 27 10:31	♑ Oct 8 9:31	♎ Feb 15 12:44	♍ Jun 30 5:27	♌ Nov 11 21:00
♓ May 29 22:46	≈ Oct 10 19:42	♏ Feb 17 13:53	♎ Jul 2 8:22	♍ Nov 14 2:42
♈ Jun 1 10:55	♓ Oct 13 8:03	♐ Feb 19 17:49	♏ Jul 4 11:22	♎ Nov 16 5:35
♉ Jun 3 20:43	♈ Oct 15 20:36	♑ Feb 22 0:50	♐ Jul 6 14:45	♏ Nov 18 6:18
♊ Jun 6 3:06	♉ Oct 18 7:54	≈ Feb 24 10:26	♑ Jul 8 19:02	♐ Nov 20 6:15
♋ Jun 8 6:28	♊ Oct 20 17:15	♓ Feb 26 21:54	≈ Jul 11 1:09	♑ Nov 22 7:19
♌ Jun 10 8:11	♋ Oct 23 0:21	♈ Mar 1 10:36	♓ Jul 13 10:01	≈ Nov 24 11:24
♍ Jun 12 9:49	♌ Oct 25 5:10	♉ Mar 3 23:33	♈ Jul 15 21:43	♓ Nov 26 19:35
♎ Jun 14 12:33	♍ Oct 27 7:53	♊ Mar 6 11:05	♉ Jul 18 10:36	♈ Nov 28 7:18
♏ Jun 16 17:03	♎ Oct 29 9:16	♋ Mar 8 19:21	♊ Jul 20 21:57	♉ Dec 1 20:22
♐ Jun 18 23:28	♏ Oct 31 10:31	♌ Mar 10 23:33	♋ Jul 23 5:52	♊ Dec 4 8:28
♑ Jun 21 7:51	♐ Nov 2 13:10	♍ Mar 13 0:24	♌ Jul 25 10:19	♋ Dec 6 18:31
≈ Jun 23 18:15	♑ Nov 4 18:39	♎ Mar 14 23:40	♍ Jul 27 12:36	♌ Dec 9 2:28
♓ Jun 26 6:23	≈ Nov 7 3:41	♏ Mar 16 23:25	♎ Jul 29 14:20	♍ Dec 11 8:31
♈ Jun 28 18:56	♓ Nov 9 15:34	♐ Mar 19 1:31	♏ Jul 31 16:44	♎ Dec 13 12:45
♉ Jul 1 5:40	♈ Nov 12 4:12	♑ Mar 21 7:04	♐ Aug 2 20:25	♏ Dec 15 15:13
♊ Jul 3 12:48	♉ Nov 14 15:24	≈ Mar 23 16:10	♑ Aug 5 1:36	♐ Dec 17 16:32
♋ Jul 5 16:07	♊ Nov 17 0:02	♓ Mar 26 3:50	≈ Aug 7 8:34	♑ Dec 19 18:00
♌ Jul 7 16:53	♋ Nov 19 6:11	♈ Mar 28 16:41	♓ Aug 9 17:45	≈ Dec 21 21:24
♍ Jul 9 17:03	♌ Nov 21 10:32	♉ Mar 31 5:29	♈ Aug 12 5:20	♓ Dec 24 4:20
♎ Jul 11 18:31	♍ Nov 23 13:48	♊ Apr 2 17:03	♉ Aug 14 18:18	♈ Dec 26 15:05
♏ Jul 13 22:28	♎ Nov 25 16:33	♋ Apr 5 2:10	♊ Aug 17 6:23	♉ Dec 29 3:58
♐ Jul 16 5:11	♏ Nov 27 19:19	♌ Apr 7 7:59	♋ Aug 19 15:15	♊ Dec 31 16:13

(continued)

Table A-2   The Moon (continued)

1950

♋ Jan 3 1:56	♉ May 14 15:59	♈ Sept 25 18:32	♑ Feb 2 21:52	♐ Jun 17 12:26
♌ Jan 5 8:58	♊ May 17 4:52	♉ Sept 28 5:08	♒ Feb 4 23:04	♑ Jun 19 11:38
♍ Jan 7 14:06	♋ May 19 16:50	♊ Sept 30 17:26	♓ Feb 7 1:29	♒ Jun 21 11:04
♎ Jan 9 18:08	♌ May 22 3:06	♋ Oct 3 5:59	♈ Feb 9 6:43	♓ Jun 23 12:49
♏ Jan 11 21:28	♍ May 24 10:50	♌ Oct 5 16:40	♉ Feb 11 15:33	♈ Jun 25 18:13
♐ Jan 14 0:16	♎ May 26 15:26	♍ Oct 7 23:54	♊ Feb 14 3:18	♉ Jun 28 3:17
♑ Jan 16 3:06	♏ May 28 17:01	♎ Oct 10 3:29	♋ Feb 16 15:51	♊ Jun 30 14:51
♒ Jan 18 7:07	♐ May 30 16:43	♏ Oct 12 4:31	♌ Feb 19 3:01	♋ Jul 3 3:27
♓ Jan 20 13:41	♑ Jun 1 16:27	♐ Oct 14 4:44	♍ Feb 21 11:43	♌ Jul 5 16:00
♈ Jan 22 23:37	♒ Jun 3 18:18	♑ Oct 16 5:55	♎ Feb 23 18:01	♍ Jul 8 3:36
♉ Jan 25 12:08	♓ Jun 5 23:57	♒ Oct 18 9:27	♏ Feb 25 22:31	♎ Jul 10 13:04
♊ Jan 28 0:43	♈ Jun 8 9:44	♓ Oct 20 15:53	♐ Feb 28 1:49	♏ Jul 12 19:19
♋ Jan 30 10:50	♉ Jun 10 22:12	♈ Oct 23 0:59	♑ Mar 2 4:29	♐ Jul 14 22:03
♌ Feb 1 17:34	♊ Jun 13 11:05	♉ Oct 25 12:03	♒ Mar 4 7:11	♑ Jul 16 22:14
♍ Feb 3 21:37	♋ Jun 15 22:45	♊ Oct 28 0:22	♓ Mar 6 10:45	♒ Jul 18 21:41
♎ Feb 6 0:19	♌ Jun 18 8:37	♋ Oct 30 13:03	♈ Mar 8 16:16	♓ Jul 20 22:29
♏ Feb 8 2:50	♍ Jun 20 16:31	♌ Nov 2 0:38	♉ Mar 11 0:33	♈ Jul 23 2:21
♐ Feb 10 5:51	♎ Jun 22 22:09	♍ Nov 4 9:21	♊ Mar 13 11:36	♉ Jul 25 10:07
♑ Feb 12 9:45	♏ Jun 25 1:19	♎ Nov 6 14:10	♋ Mar 16 0:06	♊ Jul 27 21:08
♒ Feb 14 14:57	♐ Jun 27 2:26	♏ Nov 8 15:29	♌ Mar 18 11:44	♋ Jul 30 9:42
♓ Feb 16 22:11	♑ Jun 29 2:48	♐ Nov 10 14:51	♍ Mar 20 20:39	♌ Aug 1 22:08
♈ Feb 19 8:01	♒ Jul 1 4:19	♑ Nov 12 14:25	♎ Mar 23 2:21	♍ Aug 4 9:18
♉ Feb 21 20:12	♓ Jul 3 8:51	♒ Nov 14 16:14	♏ Mar 25 5:36	♎ Aug 6 18:34
♊ Feb 24 9:03	♈ Jul 5 17:24	♓ Nov 16 21:38	♐ Mar 27 7:40	♏ Aug 9 1:24
♋ Feb 26 20:03	♉ Jul 8 5:13	♈ Nov 19 6:39	♑ Mar 29 9:51	♐ Aug 11 5:31
♌ Mar 1 3:30	♊ Jul 10 18:02	♉ Nov 21 18:08	♒ Mar 31 13:02	♑ Aug 13 7:18
♍ Mar 3 7:24	♋ Jul 13 5:34	♊ Nov 24 6:38	♓ Apr 2 17:44	♒ Aug 15 7:53
♎ Mar 5 9:00	♌ Jul 15 14:52	♋ Nov 26 19:13	♈ Apr 5 0:16	♓ Aug 17 8:52
♏ Mar 7 9:55	♍ Jul 17 22:05	♌ Nov 29 7:02	♉ Apr 7 8:52	♈ Aug 19 11:58
♐ Mar 9 11:37	♎ Jul 20 3:34	♍ Dec 1 16:53	♊ Apr 9 19:41	♉ Aug 21 18:26
♑ Mar 11 15:07	♏ Jul 22 7:27	♎ Dec 3 23:29	♋ Apr 12 8:04	♊ Aug 24 4:27
♒ Mar 13 20:52	♐ Jul 24 9:55	♏ Dec 6 2:19	♌ Apr 14 20:18	♋ Aug 26 16:44
♓ Mar 16 4:59	♑ Jul 26 11:39	♐ Dec 8 2:17	♍ Apr 17 6:07	♌ Aug 29 5:10
♈ Mar 18 15:21	♒ Jul 28 13:55	♑ Dec 10 1:16	♎ Apr 19 12:13	♍ Aug 31 16:00
♉ Mar 21 3:32	♓ Jul 30 18:19	♒ Dec 12 1:34	♏ Apr 21 14:55	♎ Sept 3 0:32
♊ Mar 23 16:28	♈ Aug 2 2:03	♓ Dec 14 5:11	♐ Apr 23 15:40	♏ Sept 5 6:49
♋ Mar 26 4:17	♉ Aug 4 13:06	♈ Dec 16 12:58	♑ Apr 25 16:20	♐ Sept 7 11:11
♌ Mar 28 13:04	♊ Aug 7 1:44	♉ Dec 19 0:10	♒ Apr 27 18:32	♑ Sept 9 14:06
♍ Mar 30 18:01	♋ Aug 9 13:27	♊ Dec 21 12:49	♓ Apr 29 23:13	♒ Sept 11 16:11
♎ Apr 1 19:41	♌ Aug 11 22:36	♋ Dec 24 1:18	♈ May 2 6:26	♓ Sept 13 18:21
♏ Apr 3 19:35	♍ Aug 14 5:03	♌ Dec 26 12:45	♉ May 4 15:47	♈ Sept 15 21:47
♐ Apr 5 19:37	♎ Aug 16 9:31	♍ Dec 28 22:41	♊ May 7 2:51	♉ Sept 18 3:41
♑ Apr 7 21:29	♏ Aug 18 12:49	♎ Dec 31 6:20	♋ May 9 15:13	♊ Sept 20 12:47
♒ Apr 10 2:24	♐ Aug 20 15:36	**1951**	♌ May 12 3:49	♋ Sept 23 0:34
♓ Apr 12 10:38	♑ Aug 22 18:23	♏ Jan 2 10:58	♍ May 14 14:44	♌ Sept 25 13:08
♈ Apr 14 21:32	♒ Aug 24 21:53	♐ Jan 4 12:38	♎ May 16 22:05	♍ Sept 28 0:05
♉ Apr 17 10:00	♓ Aug 27 3:02	♑ Jan 6 12:32	♏ May 19 1:23	♎ Sept 30 8:08
♊ Apr 19 22:54	♈ Aug 29 10:45	♒ Jan 8 12:35	♐ May 21 1:44	♏ Oct 2 13:23
♋ Apr 22 11:02	♉ Aug 31 21:19	♓ Jan 10 14:56	♑ May 23 1:07	♐ Oct 4 16:48
♌ Apr 24 20:57	♊ Sept 3 9:45	♈ Jan 12 21:05	♒ May 25 1:41	♑ Oct 6 19:30
♍ Apr 27 3:30	♋ Sept 5 21:54	♉ Jan 15 7:10	♓ May 27 5:05	♒ Oct 8 22:19
♎ Apr 29 6:25	♌ Sept 8 7:34	♊ Jan 17 19:36	♈ May 29 11:53	♓ Oct 11 1:46
♏ May 1 6:37	♍ Sept 10 13:55	♋ Jan 20 8:06	♉ May 31 21:33	♈ Oct 13 6:19
♐ May 3 5:50	♎ Sept 12 17:28	♌ Jan 22 19:12	♊ Jun 3 9:03	♉ Oct 15 12:37
♑ May 5 6:08	♏ Sept 14 19:27	♍ Jan 25 4:26	♋ Jun 5 21:31	♊ Oct 17 21:22
♒ May 7 9:22	♐ Sept 16 21:12	♎ Jan 27 11:46	♌ Jun 8 10:12	♋ Oct 20 8:43
♓ May 9 16:34	♑ Sept 18 23:49	♏ Jan 29 17:04	♍ Jun 10 21:47	♌ Oct 22 21:25
♈ May 12 3:18	♒ Sept 21 3:59	♐ Jan 31 20:16	♎ Jun 13 6:31	♍ Oct 25 9:01
	♓ Sept 23 10:09		♏ Jun 15 11:17	♎ Oct 27 17:25

Table A-2 — The Moon *(continued)*

♏	Oct 29	22:09	♌	Mar 7	7:30	♋	Jul 19	8:05	
♐	Nov 1	0:20	♍	Mar 9	19:51	♌	Jul 21	20:20	
♑	Nov 3	1:40	♎	Mar 12	6:16	♍	Jul 24	9:25	
♒	Nov 5	3:43	♏	Mar 14	14:20	♎	Jul 26	21:54	
♓	Nov 7	7:23	♐	Mar 16	20:15	♏	Jul 29	8:04	
♈	Nov 9	12:52	♑	Mar 19	0:19	♐	Jul 31	14:37	
♉	Nov 11	20:07	♒	Mar 21	2:55	♑	Aug 2	17:27	
♊	Nov 14	5:15	♓	Mar 23	4:39	♒	Aug 4	17:41	
♋	Nov 16	16:27	♈	Mar 25	6:34	♓	Aug 6	17:05	
♌	Nov 19	5:12	♉	Mar 27	10:05	♈	Aug 8	17:33	
♍	Nov 21	17:35	♊	Mar 29	16:36	♉	Aug 10	20:46	
♎	Nov 24	3:09	♋	Apr 1	2:39	♊	Aug 13	3:36	
♏	Nov 26	8:32	♌	Apr 3	15:10	♋	Aug 15	13:52	
♐	Nov 28	10:20	♍	Apr 6	3:40	♌	Aug 18	2:19	
♑	Nov 30	10:22	♎	Apr 8	13:56	♍	Aug 20	15:22	
♒	Dec 2	10:45	♏	Apr 10	21:13	♎	Aug 23	3:42	
♓	Dec 4	13:08	♐	Apr 13	2:08	♏	Aug 25	14:10	
♈	Dec 6	18:18	♑	Apr 15	5:41	♐	Aug 27	21:53	
♉	Dec 9	2:04	♒	Apr 17	8:43	♑	Aug 30	2:24	
♊	Dec 11	11:54	♓	Apr 19	11:40	♒	Sept 1	4:03	
♋	Dec 13	23:22	♈	Apr 21	14:56	♓	Sept 3	4:00	
♌	Dec 16	12:05	♉	Apr 23	19:15	♈	Sept 5	3:57	
♍	Dec 19	0:52	♊	Apr 26	1:40	♉	Sept 7	5:48	
♎	Dec 21	11:41	♋	Apr 28	11:06	♊	Sept 9	11:06	
♏	Dec 23	18:38	♌	Apr 30	23:12	♋	Sept 11	20:24	
♐	Dec 25	21:27	♍	May 3	11:57	♌	Sept 14	8:38	
♑	Dec 27	21:24	♎	May 5	22:39	♍	Sept 16	21:42	
♒	Dec 29	20:36	♏	May 8	5:49	♎	Sept 19	9:41	
♓	Dec 31	21:10	♐	May 10	9:50	♏	Sept 21	19:43	
1952			♑	May 12	12:09	♐	Sept 24	3:33	
♈	Jan 3	0:42	♒	May 14	14:14	♑	Sept 26	9:06	
♉	Jan 5	7:43	♓	May 16	17:05	♒	Sept 28	12:24	
♊	Jan 7	17:42	♈	May 18	21:07	♓	Sept 30	13:52	
♋	Jan 10	5:34	♉	May 21	2:29	♈	Oct 2	14:34	
♌	Jan 12	18:19	♊	May 23	9:37	♉	Oct 4	16:05	
♍	Jan 15	7:00	♋	May 25	19:06	♊	Oct 6	20:15	
♎	Jan 17	18:19	♌	May 28	6:59	♋	Oct 9	4:16	
♏	Jan 20	2:44	♍	May 30	19:57	♌	Oct 11	15:50	
♐	Jan 22	7:22	♎	Jun 2	7:26	♍	Oct 14	4:51	
♑	Jan 24	8:39	♏	Jun 4	15:19	♎	Oct 16	16:44	
♒	Jan 26	8:06	♐	Jun 6	19:21	♏	Oct 19	2:10	
♓	Jan 28	7:45	♑	Jun 8	20:46	♐	Oct 21	9:12	
♈	Jan 30	9:33	♒	Jun 10	21:27	♑	Oct 23	14:28	
♉	Feb 1	14:51	♓	Jun 12	23:00	♒	Oct 25	18:28	
♊	Feb 3	23:55	♈	Jun 15	2:29	♓	Oct 27	21:23	
♋	Feb 6	11:44	♉	Jun 17	8:11	♈	Oct 29	23:34	
♌	Feb 9	0:36	♊	Jun 19	16:03	♉	Nov 1	1:58	
♍	Feb 11	13:02	♋	Jun 22	2:04	♊	Nov 3	6:02	
♎	Feb 14	0:00	♌	Jun 24	14:02	♋	Nov 5	13:12	
♏	Feb 16	8:45	♍	Jun 27	3:06	♌	Nov 7	23:56	
♐	Feb 18	14:42	♎	Jun 29	15:18	♍	Nov 10	12:47	
♑	Feb 20	17:49	♏	Jul 2	0:25	♎	Nov 13	0:57	
♒	Feb 22	18:48	♐	Jul 4	5:27	♏	Nov 15	10:18	
♓	Feb 24	19:01	♑	Jul 6	7:02	♐	Nov 17	16:33	
♈	Feb 26	20:11	♒	Jul 8	6:54	♑	Nov 19	20:40	
♉	Feb 29	0:02	♓	Jul 10	6:59	♒	Nov 21	23:52	
♊	Mar 2	7:36	♈	Jul 12	8:56	♓	Nov 24	2:55	
♋	Mar 4	18:40	♉	Jul 14	13:45	♈	Nov 26	6:09	
			♊	Jul 16	21:37	♉	Nov 28	9:54	

♊	Nov 30	14:53	♓	Apr 10	0:49
♋	Dec 2	22:09	♈	Apr 12	1:19
♌	Dec 5	8:23	♉	Apr 14	1:31
♍	Dec 7	20:57	♊	Apr 16	3:27
♎	Dec 10	9:35	♋	Apr 18	8:53
♏	Dec 12	19:39	♌	Apr 20	18:27
♐	Dec 15	2:00	♍	Apr 23	6:53
♑	Dec 17	5:17	♎	Apr 25	19:40
♒	Dec 19	7:02	♏	Apr 28	6:52
♓	Dec 21	8:45	♐	Apr 30	15:52
♈	Dec 23	11:30	♑	May 2	22:55
♉	Dec 25	15:46	♒	May 5	4:12
♊	Dec 27	21:48	♓	May 7	7:46
♋	Dec 30	5:53	♈	May 9	9:49
1953			♉	May 11	11:12
♌	Jan 1	16:17	♊	May 13	13:27
♍	Jan 4	4:41	♋	May 15	18:16
♎	Jan 6	17:36	♌	May 18	2:47
♏	Jan 9	4:44	♍	May 20	14:31
♐	Jan 11	12:14	♎	May 23	3:16
♑	Jan 13	15:55	♏	May 25	14:32
♒	Jan 15	16:57	♐	May 27	23:08
♓	Jan 17	17:07	♑	May 30	5:17
♈	Jan 19	18:08	♒	Jun 1	9:45
♉	Jan 21	21:20	♓	Jun 3	13:12
♊	Jan 24	3:21	♈	Jun 5	16:01
♋	Jan 26	12:07	♉	Jun 7	18:41
♌	Jan 28	23:06	♊	Jun 9	22:03
♍	Jan 31	11:35	♋	Jun 12	3:17
♎	Feb 3	0:31	♌	Jun 14	11:27
♏	Feb 5	12:21	♍	Jun 16	22:37
♐	Feb 7	21:20	♎	Jun 19	11:16
♑	Feb 10	2:32	♏	Jun 21	22:57
♒	Feb 12	4:17	♐	Jun 24	7:48
♓	Feb 14	3:58	♑	Jun 26	13:29
♈	Feb 16	3:31	♒	Jun 28	16:51
♉	Feb 18	4:51	♓	Jun 30	19:08
♊	Feb 20	9:27	♈	Jul 2	21:23
♋	Feb 22	17:48	♉	Jul 5	0:23
♌	Feb 25	5:05	♊	Jul 7	4:42
♍	Feb 27	17:51	♋	Jul 9	10:54
♎	Mar 2	6:41	♌	Jul 11	19:28
♏	Mar 4	18:31	♍	Jul 14	6:28
♐	Mar 7	4:20	♎	Jul 16	19:04
♑	Mar 9	11:10	♏	Jul 19	7:17
♒	Mar 11	14:37	♐	Jul 21	16:59
♓	Mar 13	15:17	♑	Jul 23	23:06
♈	Mar 15	14:39	♒	Jul 26	2:03
♉	Mar 17	14:44	♓	Jul 28	3:07
♊	Mar 19	17:35	♈	Jul 30	3:56
♋	Mar 22	0:29	♉	Aug 1	5:57
♌	Mar 24	11:14	♊	Aug 3	10:10
♍	Mar 27	0:04	♋	Aug 5	16:59
♎	Mar 29	12:51	♌	Aug 8	2:16
♏	Apr 1	0:19	♍	Aug 10	13:33
♐	Apr 3	9:58	♎	Aug 13	2:08
♑	Apr 5	17:29	♏	Aug 15	14:43
♒	Apr 7	22:27	♐	Aug 18	1:30
			♑	Aug 20	8:53

(continued)

Table A-2 — The Moon (continued)

Col 1	Col 2	Col 3	Col 4	Col 5
≈ Aug 22 12:29	**1954**	♎ May 12 23:03	♍ Sept 24 3:11	♊ Feb 1 9:02
)(Aug 24 13:12	♐ Jan 1 11:39	♏ May 15 11:42	♎ Sept 26 13:11	♋ Feb 3 11:36
Υ Aug 26 12:46	♑ Jan 3 19:45	♐ May 17 23:53	♏ Sept 29 0:52	♌ Feb 5 14:28
♉ Aug 28 13:10	≈ Jan 6 1:09	♑ May 20 10:49	♐ Oct 1 13:41	♍ Feb 7 18:43
♊ Aug 30 16:07	)(Jan 8 4:43	≈ May 22 19:48	♑ Oct 4 2:04	♎ Feb 10 1:33
♋ Sept 1 22:30	Υ Jan 10 7:27	)(May 25 2:08	≈ Oct 6 11:45	♏ Feb 12 11:38
♌ Sept 4 8:05	♉ Jan 12 10:10	Υ May 27 5:32	)(Oct 8 17:17	♐ Feb 15 0:07
♍ Sept 6 19:47	♊ Jan 14 13:29	♉ May 29 6:33	Υ Oct 10 18:58	♑ Feb 17 12:34
♎ Sept 9 8:27	♋ Jan 16 18:01	♊ May 31 6:41	♉ Oct 12 18:32	≈ Feb 19 22:33
♏ Sept 11 21:05	♌ Jan 19 0:24	♋ Jun 2 7:46	♊ Oct 14 18:10	)(Feb 22 5:09
♐ Sept 14 8:32	♍ Jan 21 9:14	♌ Jun 4 11:34	♋ Oct 16 19:50	Υ Feb 24 9:06
♑ Sept 16 17:21	♎ Jan 23 20:30	♍ Jun 6 19:06	♌ Oct 19 0:41	♉ Feb 26 11:46
≈ Sept 18 22:30	♏ Jan 26 9:03	♎ Jun 9 5:59	♍ Oct 21 8:44	♊ Feb 28 14:24
)(Sept 21 0:06	♐ Jan 28 20:42	♏ Jun 11 18:30	♎ Oct 23 19:12	♋ Mar 2 17:40
Υ Sept 22 23:30	♑ Jan 31 5:26	♐ Jun 14 6:37	♏ Oct 26 7:11	♌ Mar 4 21:48
♉ Sept 24 22:45	≈ Feb 2 10:38	♑ Jun 16 17:05	♐ Oct 28 19:59	♍ Mar 7 3:09
♊ Sept 27 0:01	)(Feb 4 13:03	≈ Jun 19 1:26	♑ Oct 31 8:36	♎ Mar 9 10:20
♋ Sept 29 4:56	Υ Feb 6 14:14	)(Jun 21 7:37	≈ Nov 2 19:22	♏ Mar 11 20:04
♌ Oct 1 13:53	♉ Feb 8 15:47	Υ Jun 23 11:43	)(Nov 5 2:34	♐ Mar 14 8:13
♍ Oct 4 1:40	♊ Feb 10 18:54	♉ Jun 25 14:09	Υ Nov 7 5:42	♑ Mar 16 21:01
♎ Oct 6 14:28	♋ Feb 13 0:10	♊ Jun 27 15:41	♉ Nov 9 5:48	≈ Mar 19 7:47
♏ Oct 9 2:56	♌ Feb 15 7:35	♋ Jun 29 17:35	♊ Nov 11 4:50	)(Mar 21 14:45
♐ Oct 11 14:19	♍ Feb 17 17:00	♌ Jul 1 21:16	♋ Nov 13 4:59	Υ Mar 23 18:09
♑ Oct 13 23:51	♎ Feb 20 4:14	♍ Jul 4 3:56	♌ Nov 15 8:03	♉ Mar 25 19:31
≈ Oct 16 6:34	♏ Feb 22 16:43	♎ Jul 6 13:53	♍ Nov 17 14:52	♊ Mar 27 20:42
)(Oct 18 9:55	♐ Feb 25 5:00	♏ Jul 9 2:04	♎ Nov 20 1:02	♋ Mar 29 23:05
Υ Oct 20 10:27	♑ Feb 27 14:58	♐ Jul 11 14:19	♏ Nov 22 13:13	♌ Apr 1 3:20
♉ Oct 22 9:47	≈ Mar 1 21:07	♑ Jul 14 0:40	♐ Nov 25 2:01	♍ Apr 3 9:31
♊ Oct 24 10:04	)(Mar 3 23:32	≈ Jul 16 8:19	♑ Nov 27 14:24	♎ Apr 5 17:34
♋ Oct 26 13:24	Υ Mar 5 23:40	)(Jul 18 13:33	≈ Nov 30 1:19	♏ Apr 8 3:38
♌ Oct 28 20:55	♉ Mar 7 23:32	Υ Jul 20 17:07	)(Dec 2 9:38	♐ Apr 10 15:41
♍ Oct 31 8:04	♊ Mar 10 1:06	♉ Jul 22 19:52	Υ Dec 4 14:35	♑ Apr 13 4:40
♎ Nov 2 20:51	♋ Mar 12 5:37	♊ Jul 24 22:30	♉ Dec 6 16:23	≈ Apr 15 16:20
♏ Nov 5 9:12	♌ Mar 14 13:17	♋ Jul 27 1:41	♊ Dec 8 16:16	)(Apr 18 0:28
♐ Nov 7 20:06	♍ Mar 16 23:21	♌ Jul 29 6:10	♋ Dec 10 16:06	Υ Apr 20 4:29
♑ Nov 10 5:18	♎ Mar 19 10:57	♍ Jul 31 12:50	♌ Dec 12 17:48	♉ Apr 22 5:29
≈ Nov 12 12:31	♏ Mar 21 23:26	♎ Aug 2 22:14	♍ Dec 14 22:54	♊ Apr 24 5:24
)(Nov 14 17:17	♐ Mar 24 11:56	♏ Aug 5 10:03	♎ Dec 17 7:51	♋ Apr 26 6:09
Υ Nov 16 19:35	♑ Mar 26 22:55	♐ Aug 7 22:32	♏ Dec 19 19:43	♌ Apr 28 9:09
♉ Nov 18 20:15	≈ Mar 29 6:37	♑ Aug 10 9:20	♐ Dec 22 8:35	♍ Apr 30 14:58
♊ Nov 20 20:55	)(Mar 31 10:16	≈ Aug 12 16:54	♑ Dec 24 20:40	♎ May 2 23:26
♋ Nov 22 23:32	Υ Apr 2 10:40	)(Aug 14 21:17	≈ Dec 27 7:00	♏ May 5 10:04
♌ Nov 25 5:40	♉ Apr 4 9:43	Υ Aug 16 23:37	)(Dec 29 15:09	♐ May 7 22:19
♍ Nov 27 15:41	♊ Apr 6 9:40	♉ Aug 19 1:26	Υ Dec 31 20:56	♑ May 10 11:19
♎ Nov 30 4:06	♋ Apr 8 12:29	♊ Aug 21 3:56		≈ May 12 23:29
♏ Dec 2 16:30	♌ Apr 10 19:05	♋ Aug 23 7:50	**1955**	)(May 15 8:53
♐ Dec 5 3:09	♍ Apr 13 5:03	♌ Aug 25 13:22	♉ Jan 3 0:24	Υ May 17 14:21
♑ Dec 7 11:33	♎ Apr 15 16:58	♍ Aug 27 20:44	♊ Jan 5 2:04	♉ May 19 16:12
≈ Dec 9 17:59	♏ Apr 18 5:32	♎ Aug 30 6:12	♋ Jan 7 3:00	♊ May 21 15:56
)(Dec 11 22:46	♐ Apr 20 17:55	♏ Sept 1 17:49	♌ Jan 9 4:41	♋ May 23 15:33
Υ Dec 14 2:06	♑ Apr 23 5:11	♐ Sept 4 6:32	♍ Jan 11 8:43	♌ May 25 16:52
♉ Dec 16 4:22	≈ Apr 25 14:02	♑ Sept 6 18:10	♎ Jan 13 16:15	♍ May 27 21:16
♊ Dec 18 6:27	)(Apr 27 19:21	≈ Sept 9 2:31	♏ Jan 16 3:15	♎ May 30 5:08
♋ Dec 20 9:40	Υ Apr 29 21:08	)(Sept 11 6:55	♐ Jan 18 16:01	♏ Jun 1 15:54
♌ Dec 22 15:23	♉ May 1 20:42	Υ Sept 13 8:22	♑ Jan 21 4:09	♐ Jun 4 4:24
♍ Dec 25 0:24	♊ May 3 20:06	♉ Sept 15 8:44	≈ Jan 23 13:58	♑ Jun 6 17:21
♎ Dec 27 12:11	♋ May 5 21:30	♊ Sept 17 9:55	)(Jan 25 21:11	≈ Jun 9 5:30
♏ Dec 30 0:43	♌ May 8 2:29	♋ Sept 19 13:13	Υ Jan 28 2:19	)(Jun 11 15:32
	♍ May 10 11:23	♌ Sept 21 19:04	♉ Jan 30 6:06	Υ Jun 13 22:24

Table A-2 — The Moon (continued)

♉ Jun 16 1:50	♈ Oct 28 10:46	♑ Mar 5 15:32	♐ Jul 17 15:38	♏ Nov 29 0:34
♊ Jun 18 2:36	♉ Oct 30 13:30	♒ Mar 8 4:19	♑ Jul 20 3:40	♐ Dec 1 7:59
♋ Jun 20 2:15	♊ Nov 1 14:23	♓ Mar 10 15:11	♒ Jul 22 16:28	♑ Dec 3 17:36
♌ Jun 22 2:36	♋ Nov 3 15:11	♈ Mar 12 23:26	♓ Jul 25 4:50	♒ Dec 6 5:16
♍ Jun 24 5:26	♌ Nov 5 17:20	♉ Mar 15 5:32	♈ Jul 27 15:54	♓ Dec 8 17:57
♎ Jun 26 11:55	♍ Nov 7 21:36	♊ Mar 17 10:12	♉ Jul 30 0:40	♈ Dec 11 5:37
♏ Jun 28 22:04	♎ Nov 10 4:15	♋ Mar 19 13:47	♊ Aug 1 6:16	♉ Dec 13 14:15
♐ Jul 1 10:34	♏ Nov 12 13:12	♌ Mar 21 16:31	♋ Aug 3 8:32	♊ Dec 15 19:06
♑ Jul 3 23:29	♐ Nov 15 0:17	♍ Mar 23 18:53	♌ Aug 5 8:27	♋ Dec 17 20:52
♒ Jul 6 11:18	♑ Nov 17 12:59	♎ Mar 25 22:00	♍ Aug 7 7:50	♌ Dec 19 21:11
♓ Jul 8 21:09	♒ Nov 20 1:58	♏ Mar 28 3:19	♎ Aug 9 8:50	♍ Dec 21 21:56
♈ Jul 11 4:33	♓ Nov 22 13:10	♐ Mar 30 11:56	♏ Aug 11 13:20	♎ Dec 24 0:39
♉ Jul 13 9:20	♈ Nov 24 20:47	♑ Apr 1 23:37	♐ Aug 13 22:00	♏ Dec 26 6:09
♊ Jul 15 11:43	♉ Nov 27 0:27	♒ Apr 4 12:24	♑ Aug 16 9:47	♐ Dec 28 14:20
♋ Jul 17 12:30	♊ Nov 29 1:11	♓ Apr 6 23:37	♒ Aug 18 22:38	♑ Dec 31 0:37
♌ Jul 19 13:03	♋ Dec 1 0:46	♈ Apr 9 7:46	♓ Aug 21 10:47	**1957** ♒ Jan 2 12:25
♍ Jul 21 15:06	♌ Dec 3 1:07	♉ Apr 11 13:03	♈ Aug 23 21:30	♓ Jan 5 1:04
♎ Jul 23 20:16	♍ Dec 5 3:50	♊ Apr 13 16:30	♉ Aug 26 6:23	♈ Jan 7 13:23
♏ Jul 26 5:19	♎ Dec 7 9:48	♋ Apr 15 19:15	♊ Aug 28 12:59	♉ Jan 9 23:27
♐ Jul 28 17:24	♏ Dec 9 18:59	♌ Apr 17 22:00	♋ Aug 30 16:51	♊ Jan 12 5:44
♑ Jul 31 6:18	♐ Dec 12 6:34	♍ Apr 20 1:17	♌ Sept 1 18:14	♋ Jan 14 8:05
♒ Aug 2 17:52	♑ Dec 14 19:23	♎ Apr 22 5:36	♍ Sept 3 18:20	♌ Jan 16 7:50
♓ Aug 5 3:04	♒ Dec 17 8:19	♏ Apr 24 11:44	♎ Sept 5 19:04	♍ Jan 18 7:03
♈ Aug 7 10:00	♓ Dec 19 20:02	♐ Apr 27 20:25	♏ Sept 7 22:27	♎ Jan 20 7:55
♉ Aug 9 15:03	♈ Dec 22 5:05	♑ Apr 29 7:44	♐ Sept 10 5:46	♏ Jan 22 12:02
♊ Aug 11 18:33	♉ Dec 24 10:33	♒ May 1 20:27	♑ Sept 12 16:46	♐ Jan 24 19:52
♋ Aug 13 20:50	♊ Dec 26 12:33	♓ May 4 8:15	♒ Sept 15 5:28	♑ Jan 27 6:32
♌ Aug 15 22:34	♋ Dec 28 12:17	♈ May 6 17:05	♓ Sept 17 17:34	♒ Jan 29 18:42
♍ Aug 18 0:57	♌ Dec 30 11:36	♉ May 8 22:24	♈ Sept 20 3:47	♓ Feb 1 7:20
♎ Aug 20 5:34	**1956** ♍ Jan 1 12:31	♊ May 11 1:00	♉ Sept 22 12:01	♈ Feb 3 19:42
♏ Aug 22 13:37	♎ Jan 3 16:44	♋ May 13 2:21	♊ Sept 24 18:25	♉ Feb 6 6:37
♐ Aug 25 1:03	♏ Jan 6 1:00	♌ May 15 3:52	♋ Sept 26 23:00	♊ Feb 8 14:34
♑ Aug 27 13:57	♐ Jan 8 12:32	♍ May 17 6:40	♌ Sept 29 1:49	♋ Feb 10 18:39
♒ Aug 30 1:35	♑ Jan 11 1:33	♎ May 19 11:25	♍ Oct 1 3:24	♌ Feb 12 19:19
♓ Sept 1 10:23	♒ Jan 13 14:19	♏ May 21 18:26	♎ Oct 3 5:01	♍ Feb 14 18:17
♈ Sept 3 16:24	♓ Jan 16 1:47	♐ May 24 3:46	♏ Oct 5 8:19	♎ Feb 16 17:50
♉ Sept 5 20:36	♈ Jan 18 11:17	♑ May 26 15:11	♐ Oct 7 14:46	♏ Feb 18 20:06
♊ Sept 7 23:58	♉ Jan 20 18:11	♒ May 29 3:52	♑ Oct 10 0:48	♐ Feb 21 2:23
♋ Sept 10 3:01	♊ Jan 22 22:06	♓ May 31 16:09	♒ Oct 12 13:09	♑ Feb 23 12:27
♌ Sept 12 6:02	♋ Jan 24 23:20	♈ Jun 3 2:04	♓ Oct 15 1:25	♒ Feb 26 0:42
♍ Sept 14 9:33	♌ Jan 26 23:06	♉ Jun 5 8:22	♈ Oct 17 11:35	♓ Feb 28 13:25
♎ Sept 16 14:35	♍ Jan 28 23:17	♊ Jun 7 11:09	♉ Oct 19 19:07	♈ Mar 3 1:31
♏ Sept 18 22:18	♎ Jan 31 1:56	♋ Jun 9 11:42	♊ Oct 22 0:29	♉ Mar 5 12:20
♐ Sept 21 9:11	♏ Feb 2 8:33	♌ Jun 11 11:45	♋ Oct 24 4:23	♊ Mar 7 21:03
♑ Sept 23 22:01	♐ Feb 4 19:13	♍ Jun 13 13:03	♌ Oct 26 7:27	♋ Mar 10 2:45
♒ Sept 26 10:07	♑ Feb 7 8:08	♎ Jun 15 16:58	♍ Oct 28 10:09	♌ Mar 12 5:12
♓ Sept 28 19:12	♒ Feb 9 20:52	♏ Jun 18 0:03	♎ Oct 30 13:10	♍ Mar 14 5:20
♈ Oct 1 0:46	♓ Feb 12 7:52	♐ Jun 20 9:55	♏ Nov 1 17:24	♎ Mar 16 4:59
♉ Oct 3 3:52	♈ Feb 14 16:48	♑ Jun 22 21:43	♐ Nov 3 23:56	♏ Mar 18 6:15
♊ Oct 5 5:59	♉ Feb 16 23:48	♒ Jun 25 10:26	♑ Nov 6 9:24	♐ Mar 20 10:54
♋ Oct 7 8:23	♊ Feb 19 4:50	♓ Jun 27 22:54	♒ Nov 8 21:19	♑ Mar 22 19:34
♌ Oct 9 11:41	♋ Feb 21 7:50	♈ Jun 30 9:43	♓ Nov 11 9:51	♒ Mar 25 7:17
♍ Oct 11 16:11	♌ Feb 23 9:10	♉ Jul 2 17:26	♈ Nov 13 20:36	♓ Mar 27 20:00
♎ Oct 13 22:13	♍ Feb 25 10:05	♊ Jul 4 21:26	♉ Nov 16 4:12	♈ Mar 30 7:45
♏ Oct 16 6:23	♎ Feb 27 12:20	♋ Jul 6 22:20	♊ Nov 18 8:45	♉ Apr 1 18:11
♐ Oct 18 17:07	♏ Feb 29 17:45	♌ Jul 8 21:42	♋ Nov 20 11:18	♊ Apr 4 2:30
♑ Oct 21 5:52	♐ Mar 3 3:09	♍ Jul 10 21:34	♌ Nov 22 13:10	♋ Apr 6 8:37
♒ Oct 23 18:33		♎ Jul 12 23:54	♍ Nov 24 15:32	
♓ Oct 26 4:37		♏ Jul 15 5:56	♎ Nov 26 19:11	

(continued)

Table A-2 — The Moon *(continued)*

Sign	Date	Time	Sign	Date	Time	Sign	Date	Time	Sign	Date	Time	Sign	Date	Time
♌	Apr 8	12:24	♋	Aug 21	1:48		**1958**		♈	May 13	18:58	♓	Sept 24	20:33
♍	Apr 10	14:13	♌	Aug 23	3:51	♊	Jan 2	7:21	♉	May 16	7:50	♈	Sept 27	8:07
♎	Apr 12	15:08	♍	Aug 25	3:26	♋	Jan 4	13:22	♊	May 18	19:14	♉	Sept 29	20:58
♏	Apr 14	16:45	♎	Aug 27	2:41	♌	Jan 6	16:21	♋	May 21	4:23	♊	Oct 2	9:50
♐	Apr 16	20:43	♏	Aug 29	3:45	♍	Jan 8	17:59	♌	May 23	11:14	♋	Oct 4	21:00
♑	Apr 19	4:08	♐	Aug 31	8:07	♎	Jan 10	19:52	♍	May 25	16:00	♌	Oct 7	4:50
♒	Apr 21	14:53	♑	Sept 2	16:05	♏	Jan 12	23:02	♎	May 27	18:55	♍	Oct 9	8:49
♓	Apr 24	3:23	♒	Sept 5	2:50	♐	Jan 15	3:49	♏	May 29	20:33	♎	Oct 11	9:44
♈	Apr 26	15:22	♓	Sept 7	15:04	♑	Jan 17	10:13	♐	May 31	21:54	♏	Oct 13	9:11
♉	Apr 29	1:18	♈	Sept 10	3:45	♒	Jan 19	18:22	♑	Jun 3	0:23	♐	Oct 15	9:09
♊	May 1	8:47	♉	Sept 12	15:57	♓	Jan 22	4:42	♒	Jun 5	5:34	♑	Oct 17	11:23
♋	May 3	14:08	♊	Sept 15	2:26	♈	Jan 24	17:03	♓	Jun 7	14:24	♒	Oct 19	17:04
♌	May 5	17:54	♋	Sept 17	9:49	♉	Jan 27	5:56	♈	Jun 10	2:20	♓	Oct 22	2:19
♍	May 7	20:37	♌	Sept 19	13:31	♊	Jan 29	16:47	♉	Jun 12	15:12	♈	Oct 24	14:10
♎	May 9	22:57	♍	Sept 21	14:11	♋	Jan 31	23:41	♊	Jun 15	2:31	♉	Oct 27	3:07
♏	May 12	1:48	♎	Sept 23	13:33	♌	Feb 3	2:37	♋	Jun 17	11:04	♊	Oct 29	15:49
♐	May 14	6:13	♏	Sept 25	13:40	♍	Feb 5	3:11	♌	Jun 19	17:04	♋	Nov 1	3:09
♑	May 16	13:13	♐	Sept 27	16:27	♎	Feb 7	3:23	♍	Jun 21	21:22	♌	Nov 3	12:02
♒	May 18	23:12	♑	Sept 29	22:59	♏	Feb 9	5:03	♎	Jun 24	0:42	♍	Nov 5	17:45
♓	May 21	11:20	♒	Oct 2	9:04	♐	Feb 11	9:11	♏	Jun 26	3:30	♎	Nov 7	20:16
♈	May 23	23:34	♓	Oct 4	21:17	♑	Feb 13	15:55	♐	Jun 28	6:11	♏	Nov 9	20:30
♉	May 26	9:43	♈	Oct 7	9:57	♒	Feb 16	0:51	♑	Jun 30	9:32	♐	Nov 11	20:03
♊	May 28	16:47	♉	Oct 9	21:48	♓	Feb 18	11:39	♒	Jul 2	14:44	♑	Nov 13	20:54
♋	May 30	21:05	♊	Oct 12	8:01	♈	Feb 21	0:02	♓	Jul 4	22:57	♒	Nov 16	0:53
♌	Jun 1	23:45	♋	Oct 14	15:54	♉	Feb 23	13:05	♈	Jul 7	10:18	♓	Nov 18	8:56
♍	Jun 4	1:59	♌	Oct 16	20:59	♊	Feb 26	0:52	♉	Jul 9	23:09	♈	Nov 20	20:28
♎	Jun 6	4:45	♍	Oct 18	23:23	♋	Feb 28	9:17	♊	Jul 12	10:46	♉	Nov 23	9:30
♏	Jun 8	8:41	♎	Oct 21	0:03	♌	Mar 2	13:27	♋	Jul 14	19:15	♊	Nov 25	22:00
♐	Jun 10	14:09	♏	Oct 23	0:31	♍	Mar 4	14:15	♌	Jul 17	0:31	♋	Nov 28	8:51
♑	Jun 12	21:36	♐	Oct 25	2:33	♎	Mar 6	13:35	♍	Jul 19	3:42	♌	Nov 30	17:41
♒	Jun 15	7:23	♑	Oct 27	7:41	♏	Mar 8	13:34	♎	Jul 21	6:12	♍	Dec 3	0:18
♓	Jun 17	19:15	♒	Oct 29	16:32	♐	Mar 10	15:56	♏	Jul 23	8:57	♎	Dec 5	4:31
♈	Jun 20	7:46	♓	Nov 1	4:18	♑	Mar 12	21:36	♐	Jul 25	12:25	♏	Dec 7	6:28
♉	Jun 22	18:38	♈	Nov 3	17:00	♒	Mar 15	6:28	♑	Jul 27	16:53	♐	Dec 9	7:02
♊	Jun 25	2:07	♉	Nov 6	4:38	♓	Mar 17	17:41	♒	Jul 29	22:52	♑	Dec 11	7:46
♋	Jun 27	6:00	♊	Nov 8	14:09	♈	Mar 20	6:17	♓	Aug 1	7:11	♒	Dec 13	10:38
♌	Jun 29	7:31	♋	Nov 10	21:24	♉	Mar 22	19:16	♈	Aug 3	18:14	♓	Dec 15	17:12
♍	Jul 1	8:23	♌	Nov 13	2:36	♊	Mar 25	7:20	♉	Aug 6	7:04	♈	Dec 18	3:45
♎	Jul 3	10:16	♍	Nov 15	6:07	♋	Mar 27	16:53	♊	Aug 8	19:16	♉	Dec 20	16:38
♏	Jul 5	14:10	♎	Nov 17	8:25	♌	Mar 29	22:45	♋	Aug 11	4:25	♊	Dec 23	5:09
♐	Jul 7	20:20	♏	Nov 19	10:17	♍	Apr 1	1:01	♌	Aug 13	9:43	♋	Dec 25	15:33
♑	Jul 10	4:35	♐	Nov 21	12:52	♎	Apr 3	0:54	♍	Aug 15	12:07	♌	Dec 27	23:33
♒	Jul 12	14:43	♑	Nov 23	17:29	♏	Apr 5	0:16	♎	Aug 17	13:17	♍	Dec 30	5:41
♓	Jul 15	2:32	♒	Nov 26	1:16	♐	Apr 7	1:07	♏	Aug 19	14:50		**1959**	
♈	Jul 17	15:14	♓	Nov 28	12:16	♑	Apr 9	5:01	♐	Aug 21	17:48	♎	Jan 1	10:21
♉	Jul 20	2:58	♈	Dec 1	0:56	♒	Apr 11	12:41	♑	Aug 23	22:38	♏	Jan 3	13:42
♊	Jul 22	11:34	♉	Dec 3	12:48	♓	Apr 13	23:38	♒	Aug 26	5:28	♐	Jan 5	15:56
♋	Jul 24	16:05	♊	Dec 5	22:00	♈	Apr 16	12:23	♓	Aug 28	14:25	♑	Jan 7	17:50
♌	Jul 26	17:16	♋	Dec 8	4:16	♉	Apr 19	1:16	♈	Aug 31	1:35	♒	Jan 9	20:52
♍	Jul 28	16:59	♌	Dec 10	8:23	♊	Apr 21	13:03	♉	Sept 2	14:24	♓	Jan 12	2:39
♎	Jul 30	17:20	♍	Dec 12	11:28	♋	Apr 23	22:46	♊	Sept 5	3:07	♈	Jan 14	12:09
♏	Aug 1	20:01	♎	Dec 14	14:23	♌	Apr 26	5:44	♋	Sept 7	13:22	♉	Jan 17	0:33
♐	Aug 4	1:47	♏	Dec 16	17:35	♍	Apr 28	9:40	♌	Sept 9	19:42	♊	Jan 19	13:16
♑	Aug 6	10:23	♐	Dec 18	21:30	♎	Apr 30	11:06	♍	Sept 11	22:19	♋	Jan 21	23:47
♒	Aug 8	21:01	♑	Dec 21	2:47	♏	May 2	11:14	♎	Sept 13	22:46	♌	Jan 24	7:13
♓	Aug 11	9:02	♒	Dec 23	10:19	♐	May 4	11:43	♏	Sept 15	22:49	♍	Jan 26	12:13
♈	Aug 13	21:46	♓	Dec 25	20:41	♑	May 6	14:21	♐	Sept 18	0:16	♎	Jan 28	15:54
♉	Aug 16	10:00	♈	Dec 28	9:13	♒	May 8	20:29	♑	Sept 20	4:13	♏	Jan 30	19:05
♊	Aug 18	19:51	♉	Dec 30	21:37	♓	May 11	6:27	♒	Sept 22	11:03			

Table A-2 — The Moon *(continued)*

Sign	Date	Time	Sign	Date	Time	Sign	Date	Time	Sign	Date	Time	Sign	Date	Time
♐	Feb 1	22:11	♏	Jun 16	16:38	♎	Oct 29	3:41	♋	Mar 6	12:37	♊	Jul 18	10:40
♑	Feb 4	1:29	♐	Jun 18	17:14	♏	Oct 31	5:14	♌	Mar 9	0:25	♋	Jul 20	23:09
♒	Feb 6	5:40	♑	Jun 20	17:01	♐	Nov 2	5:02	♍	Mar 11	9:47	♌	Jul 23	11:46
♓	Feb 8	11:50	♒	Jun 22	18:00	♑	Nov 4	5:05	♎	Mar 13	16:19	♍	Jul 25	23:31
♈	Feb 10	20:55	♓	Jun 24	22:09	♒	Nov 6	7:14	♏	Mar 15	20:37	♎	Jul 28	9:33
♉	Feb 13	8:47	♈	Jun 27	6:28	♓	Nov 8	12:35	♐	Mar 17	23:37	♏	Jul 30	16:55
♊	Feb 15	21:39	♉	Jun 29	18:11	♈	Nov 10	21:10	♑	Mar 20	2:14	♐	Aug 1	21:04
♋	Feb 18	8:50	♊	Jul 2	7:05	♉	Nov 13	8:04	♒	Mar 22	5:10	♑	Aug 3	22:25
♌	Feb 20	16:38	♋	Jul 4	19:03	♊	Nov 15	20:16	♓	Mar 24	9:02	♒	Aug 5	22:21
♍	Feb 22	21:06	♌	Jul 7	5:08	♋	Nov 18	8:57	♈	Mar 26	14:29	♓	Aug 7	22:42
♎	Feb 24	23:29	♍	Jul 9	13:15	♌	Nov 20	21:04	♉	Mar 28	22:13	♈	Aug 10	1:21
♏	Feb 27	1:15	♎	Jul 11	19:26	♍	Nov 23	7:08	♊	Mar 31	8:32	♉	Aug 12	7:36
♐	Mar 1	3:33	♏	Jul 13	23:33	♎	Nov 25	13:41	♋	Apr 2	20:46	♊	Aug 14	17:29
♑	Mar 3	7:06	♐	Jul 16	1:42	♏	Nov 27	16:21	♌	Apr 5	9:01	♋	Aug 17	5:43
♒	Mar 5	12:16	♑	Jul 18	2:42	♐	Nov 29	16:12	♍	Apr 7	19:02	♌	Aug 19	18:18
♓	Mar 7	19:25	♒	Jul 20	4:05	♑	Dec 1	15:11	♎	Apr 10	1:35	♍	Aug 22	5:41
♈	Mar 10	4:54	♓	Jul 22	7:41	♒	Dec 3	15:35	♏	Apr 12	5:01	♎	Aug 24	15:09
♉	Mar 12	16:37	♈	Jul 24	14:53	♓	Dec 5	19:16	♐	Apr 14	6:37	♏	Aug 26	22:24
♊	Mar 15	5:31	♉	Jul 27	1:43	♈	Dec 8	2:59	♑	Apr 16	8:01	♐	Aug 29	3:19
♋	Mar 17	17:28	♊	Jul 29	14:23	♉	Dec 10	13:56	♒	Apr 18	10:32	♑	Aug 31	6:09
♌	Mar 20	2:22	♋	Aug 1	2:24	♊	Dec 13	2:24	♓	Apr 20	14:55	♒	Sept 2	7:35
♍	Mar 22	7:28	♌	Aug 3	12:09	♋	Dec 15	15:00	♈	Apr 22	21:23	♓	Sept 4	8:51
♎	Mar 24	9:27	♍	Aug 5	19:29	♌	Dec 18	2:58	♉	Apr 25	5:50	♈	Sept 6	11:26
♏	Mar 26	9:54	♎	Aug 8	0:56	♍	Dec 20	13:29	♊	Apr 27	16:16	♉	Sept 8	16:44
♐	Mar 28	10:31	♏	Aug 10	5:00	♎	Dec 22	21:29	♋	Apr 30	4:22	♊	Sept 11	1:31
♑	Mar 30	12:49	♐	Aug 12	7:58	♏	Dec 25	2:01	♌	May 2	16:59	♋	Sept 13	13:10
♒	Apr 1	17:41	♑	Aug 14	10:18	♐	Dec 27	3:15	♍	May 5	3:59	♌	Sept 16	1:46
♓	Apr 4	1:23	♒	Aug 16	12:53	♑	Dec 29	2:38	♎	May 7	11:30	♍	Sept 18	13:07
♈	Apr 6	11:33	♓	Aug 18	16:59	♒	Dec 31	2:15	♏	May 9	15:07	♎	Sept 20	21:58
♉	Apr 8	23:32	♈	Aug 20	23:51				♐	May 11	15:55	♏	Sept 23	4:18
♊	Apr 11	12:25	♉	Aug 23	9:58	**1960**			♑	May 13	15:50	♐	Sept 25	8:42
♋	Apr 14	0:48	♊	Aug 25	22:18	♓	Jan 2	4:19	♒	May 15	16:51	♑	Sept 27	11:54
♌	Apr 16	10:55	♋	Aug 28	10:33	♈	Jan 4	10:21	♓	May 17	20:23	♒	Sept 29	14:32
♍	Apr 18	17:27	♌	Aug 30	20:33	♉	Jan 6	20:22	♈	May 20	2:55	♓	Oct 1	17:14
♎	Apr 20	20:19	♍	Sept 2	3:31	♊	Jan 9	8:45	♉	May 22	12:00	♈	Oct 3	20:46
♏	Apr 22	20:34	♎	Sept 4	7:56	♋	Jan 11	21:23	♊	May 24	22:55	♉	Oct 6	2:09
♐	Apr 24	19:59	♏	Sept 6	10:53	♌	Jan 14	8:59	♋	May 27	11:06	♊	Oct 8	10:16
♑	Apr 26	20:32	♐	Sept 8	13:20	♍	Jan 16	19:03	♌	May 29	23:50	♋	Oct 10	21:18
♒	Apr 28	23:55	♑	Sept 10	16:04	♎	Jan 19	3:14	♍	Jun 1	11:38	♌	Oct 13	9:55
♓	May 1	6:58	♒	Sept 12	19:43	♏	Jan 21	8:59	♎	Jun 3	20:31	♍	Oct 15	21:40
♈	May 3	17:19	♓	Sept 15	0:54	♐	Jan 23	12:02	♏	Jun 6	1:20	♎	Oct 18	6:32
♉	May 6	5:39	♈	Sept 17	8:16	♑	Jan 25	12:59	♐	Jun 8	2:31	♏	Oct 20	12:06
♊	May 8	18:34	♉	Sept 19	18:12	♒	Jan 27	13:19	♑	Jun 10	1:48	♐	Oct 22	15:16
♋	May 11	6:57	♊	Sept 22	6:16	♓	Jan 29	14:56	♒	Jun 12	1:23	♑	Oct 24	17:28
♌	May 13	17:40	♋	Sept 24	18:49	♈	Jan 31	19:39	♓	Jun 14	3:17	♒	Oct 26	19:57
♍	May 16	1:38	♌	Sept 27	5:36	♉	Feb 3	4:16	♈	Jun 16	8:42	♓	Oct 28	23:26
♎	May 18	6:06	♍	Sept 29	13:04	♊	Feb 5	15:58	♉	Jun 18	17:33	♈	Oct 31	4:11
♏	May 20	7:24	♎	Oct 1	17:08	♋	Feb 8	4:37	♊	Jun 21	4:46	♉	Nov 2	10:27
♐	May 22	6:51	♏	Oct 3	18:54	♌	Feb 10	16:08	♋	Jun 23	17:10	♊	Nov 4	18:44
♑	May 24	6:24	♐	Oct 5	19:54	♍	Feb 13	1:35	♌	Jun 26	5:51	♋	Nov 7	5:26
♒	May 26	8:09	♑	Oct 7	21:38	♎	Feb 15	8:55	♍	Jun 28	17:53	♌	Nov 9	17:59
♓	May 28	13:42	♒	Oct 10	1:12	♏	Feb 17	14:24	♎	Jul 1	3:46	♍	Nov 12	6:24
♈	May 30	23:18	♓	Oct 12	7:06	♐	Feb 19	18:12	♏	Jul 3	10:08	♎	Nov 14	16:07
♉	Jun 2	11:37	♈	Oct 14	15:20	♑	Feb 21	20:39	♐	Jul 5	12:42	♏	Nov 16	21:53
♊	Jun 5	0:35	♉	Oct 17	1:40	♒	Feb 23	22:32	♑	Jul 7	12:34	♐	Nov 19	0:17
♋	Jun 7	12:44	♊	Oct 19	13:40	♓	Feb 26	1:04	♒	Jul 9	11:43	♑	Nov 21	1:02
♌	Jun 9	23:19	♋	Oct 22	2:22	♈	Feb 28	5:38	♓	Jul 11	12:19	♒	Nov 23	2:04
♍	Jun 12	7:50	♌	Oct 24	14:03	♉	Mar 1	13:18	♈	Jul 13	16:07	♓	Nov 25	4:49
♎	Jun 14	13:42	♍	Oct 26	22:48	♊	Mar 4	0:08	♉	Jul 15	23:48	♈	Nov 27	9:51

(continued)

Table A-2 — The Moon *(continued)*

Sign	Date	Time	Sign	Date	Time	Sign	Date	Time	Sign	Date	Time	Sign	Date	Time
♉	Nov 29	17:00	♒	Apr 9	1:03	♑	Aug 21	17:07	**1962**			♎	May 14	16:03
♊	Dec 2	2:01	♓	Apr 11	3:31	♒	Aug 23	18:25	♐	Jan 3	1:23	♏	May 17	3:43
♋	Dec 4	12:52	♈	Apr 13	5:55	♓	Aug 25	18:02	♑	Jan 5	5:24	♐	May 19	13:02
♌	Dec 7	1:21	♉	Apr 15	9:16	♈	Aug 27	17:49	♒	Jan 7	7:00	♑	May 21	20:08
♍	Dec 9	14:13	♊	Apr 17	14:55	♉	Aug 29	19:37	♓	Jan 9	7:53	♒	May 24	1:31
♎	Dec 12	1:10	♋	Apr 19	23:50	♊	Sept 1	0:53	♈	Jan 11	9:34	♓	May 26	5:29
♏	Dec 14	8:13	♌	Apr 22	11:43	♋	Sept 3	10:00	♉	Jan 13	13:01	♈	May 28	8:15
♐	Dec 16	11:07	♍	Apr 25	0:31	♌	Sept 5	22:01	♊	Jan 15	18:42	♉	May 30	10:17
♑	Dec 18	11:16	♎	Apr 27	11:34	♍	Sept 8	11:05	♋	Jan 18	2:39	♊	Jun 1	12:40
♒	Dec 20	10:49	♏	Apr 29	19:27	♎	Sept 10	23:33	♌	Jan 20	12:50	♋	Jun 3	16:56
♓	Dec 22	11:47	♐	May 2	0:25	♏	Sept 13	10:23	♍	Jan 23	0:53	♌	Jun 6	0:23
♈	Dec 24	15:34	♑	May 4	3:40	♐	Sept 15	18:54	♎	Jan 25	13:52	♍	Jun 8	11:12
♉	Dec 26	22:30	♒	May 6	6:24	♑	Sept 18	0:42	♏	Jan 28	1:54	♎	Jun 10	23:51
♊	Dec 29	8:01	♓	May 8	9:23	♒	Sept 20	3:43	♐	Jan 30	10:59	♏	Jun 13	11:45
♋	Dec 31	19:22	♈	May 10	12:56	♓	Sept 22	4:36	♑	Feb 1	16:09	♐	Jun 15	21:03
1961			♉	May 12	17:25	♈	Sept 24	4:40	♒	Feb 3	17:57	♑	Jun 18	3:30
♌	Jan 3	7:54	♊	May 14	23:34	♉	Sept 26	5:42	♓	Feb 5	17:53	♒	Jun 20	7:49
♍	Jan 5	20:48	♋	May 17	8:17	♊	Sept 28	9:31	♈	Feb 7	17:50	♓	Jun 22	10:59
♎	Jan 8	8:31	♌	May 19	19:45	♋	Sept 30	17:19	♉	Feb 9	19:35	♈	Jun 24	13:43
♏	Jan 10	17:09	♍	May 22	8:38	♌	Oct 3	4:43	♊	Feb 12	0:18	♉	Jun 26	16:34
♐	Jan 12	21:40	♎	May 24	20:18	♍	Oct 5	17:45	♋	Feb 14	8:20	♊	Jun 28	20:09
♑	Jan 14	22:41	♏	May 27	4:34	♎	Oct 8	6:04	♌	Feb 16	19:04	♋	Jul 1	1:19
♒	Jan 16	21:55	♐	May 29	9:11	♏	Oct 10	16:19	♍	Feb 19	7:27	♌	Jul 3	8:55
♓	Jan 18	21:32	♑	May 31	11:20	♐	Oct 13	0:21	♎	Feb 21	20:22	♍	Jul 5	19:22
♈	Jan 20	23:26	♒	Jun 2	12:45	♑	Oct 15	6:24	♏	Feb 24	8:36	♎	Jul 8	7:48
♉	Jan 23	4:51	♓	Jun 4	14:50	♒	Oct 17	10:37	♐	Feb 26	18:46	♏	Jul 10	20:05
♊	Jan 25	13:50	♈	Jun 6	18:23	♓	Oct 19	13:10	♑	Mar 1	1:38	♐	Jul 13	6:00
♋	Jan 28	1:22	♉	Jun 8	23:38	♈	Oct 21	14:36	♒	Mar 3	4:52	♑	Jul 15	12:32
♌	Jan 30	14:05	♊	Jun 11	6:40	♉	Oct 23	16:07	♓	Mar 5	5:16	♒	Jul 17	16:07
♍	Feb 2	2:48	♋	Jun 13	15:50	♊	Oct 25	19:24	♈	Mar 7	4:32	♓	Jul 19	18:00
♎	Feb 4	14:27	♌	Jun 16	3:16	♋	Oct 28	2:03	♉	Mar 9	4:40	♈	Jul 21	19:34
♏	Feb 6	23:51	♍	Jun 18	16:12	♌	Oct 30	12:30	♊	Mar 11	7:35	♉	Jul 23	21:57
♐	Feb 9	6:01	♎	Jun 21	4:32	♍	Nov 2	1:17	♋	Mar 13	14:25	♊	Jul 26	1:57
♑	Feb 11	8:50	♏	Jun 23	13:51	♎	Nov 4	13:42	♌	Mar 16	0:56	♋	Jul 28	8:00
♒	Feb 13	9:14	♐	Jun 25	19:05	♏	Nov 6	23:40	♍	Mar 18	13:33	♌	Jul 30	16:21
♓	Feb 15	8:53	♑	Jun 27	21:00	♐	Nov 9	6:51	♎	Mar 21	2:28	♍	Aug 2	2:57
♈	Feb 17	9:41	♒	Jun 29	21:18	♑	Nov 11	11:59	♏	Mar 23	14:29	♎	Aug 4	15:17
♉	Feb 19	13:21	♓	Jul 1	21:52	♒	Nov 13	15:59	♐	Mar 26	0:49	♏	Aug 7	3:56
♊	Feb 21	20:51	♈	Jul 4	0:12	♓	Nov 15	19:18	♑	Mar 28	8:46	♐	Aug 9	14:48
♋	Feb 24	7:49	♉	Jul 6	5:01	♈	Nov 17	22:10	♒	Mar 30	13:43	♑	Aug 11	22:18
♌	Feb 26	20:34	♊	Jul 8	12:27	♉	Nov 20	1:03	♓	Apr 1	15:42	♒	Aug 14	2:07
♍	Mar 1	9:12	♋	Jul 10	22:13	♊	Nov 22	4:59	♈	Apr 3	15:41	♓	Aug 16	3:17
♎	Mar 3	20:21	♌	Jul 13	9:56	♋	Nov 24	11:20	♉	Apr 5	15:25	♈	Aug 18	3:25
♏	Mar 6	5:24	♍	Jul 15	22:55	♌	Nov 26	21:01	♊	Apr 7	17:00	♉	Aug 20	4:20
♐	Mar 8	12:04	♎	Jul 18	11:39	♍	Nov 29	9:25	♋	Apr 9	22:12	♊	Aug 22	7:28
♑	Mar 10	16:19	♏	Jul 20	22:04	♎	Dec 1	22:08	♌	Apr 12	7:36	♋	Aug 24	13:34
♒	Mar 12	18:29	♐	Jul 23	4:42	♏	Dec 4	8:30	♍	Apr 14	19:57	♌	Aug 26	22:30
♓	Mar 14	19:26	♑	Jul 25	7:28	♐	Dec 6	15:25	♎	Apr 17	8:54	♍	Aug 29	9:36
♈	Mar 16	20:32	♒	Jul 27	7:41	♑	Dec 8	19:50	♏	Apr 19	20:37	♎	Aug 31	22:01
♉	Mar 18	23:25	♓	Jul 29	7:13	♒	Dec 10	22:11	♐	Apr 22	6:27	♏	Sept 3	10:46
♊	Mar 21	5:32	♈	Jul 31	7:56	♓	Dec 13	0:41	♑	Apr 24	14:20	♐	Sept 5	22:26
♋	Mar 23	15:22	♉	Aug 2	11:19	♈	Dec 15	3:44	♒	Apr 26	20:08	♑	Sept 8	7:20
♌	Mar 26	3:48	♊	Aug 4	18:04	♉	Dec 17	7:39	♓	Apr 28	23:40	♒	Sept 10	12:26
♍	Mar 28	16:30	♋	Aug 7	3:56	♊	Dec 19	12:47	♈	May 1	1:12	♓	Sept 12	14:02
♎	Mar 31	3:21	♌	Aug 9	15:59	♋	Dec 21	19:50	♉	May 3	1:49	♈	Sept 14	13:33
♏	Apr 2	11:36	♍	Aug 12	5:00	♌	Dec 24	5:26	♊	May 5	3:16	♉	Sept 16	13:01
♐	Apr 4	17:34	♎	Aug 14	17:44	♍	Dec 26	17:29	♋	May 7	7:28	♊	Sept 18	14:29
♑	Apr 6	21:52	♏	Aug 17	4:44	♎	Dec 29	6:26	♌	May 9	15:35	♋	Sept 20	19:26
			♐	Aug 19	12:44	♏	Dec 31	17:42	♍	May 12	3:11	♌	Sept 23	4:07

Table A-2 The Moon *(continued)*

♍	Sept 25	15:31
♎	Sept 28	4:08
♏	Sept 30	16:49
♐	Oct 3	4:40
♑	Oct 5	14:35
♒	Oct 7	21:22
♓	Oct 10	0:29
♈	Oct 12	0:40
♉	Oct 13	23:43
♊	Oct 15	23:50
♋	Oct 18	3:05
♌	Oct 20	10:30
♍	Oct 22	21:31
♎	Oct 25	10:13
♏	Oct 27	22:49
♐	Oct 30	10:19
♑	Nov 1	20:17
♒	Nov 4	4:02
♓	Nov 6	8:52
♈	Nov 8	10:45
♉	Nov 10	10:45
♊	Nov 12	10:43
♋	Nov 14	12:49
♌	Nov 16	18:40
♍	Nov 19	4:33
♎	Nov 21	16:58
♏	Nov 24	5:33
♐	Nov 26	16:43
♑	Nov 29	2:00
♒	Dec 1	9:26
♓	Dec 3	14:53
♈	Dec 5	18:17
♉	Dec 7	19:59
♊	Dec 9	21:07
♋	Dec 11	23:21
♌	Dec 14	4:20
♍	Dec 16	12:59
♎	Dec 19	0:41
♏	Dec 21	13:18
♐	Dec 24	0:33
♑	Dec 26	9:19
♒	Dec 28	15:42
♓	Dec 30	20:20
1963		
♈	Jan 1	23:48
♉	Jan 4	2:33
♊	Jan 6	5:14
♋	Jan 8	8:41
♌	Jan 10	14:01
♍	Jan 12	22:07
♎	Jan 15	9:05
♏	Jan 17	21:35
♐	Jan 20	9:20
♑	Jan 22	18:23
♒	Jan 25	0:14
♓	Jan 27	3:35
♈	Jan 29	5:44
♉	Jan 31	7:55
♊	Feb 2	11:03
♋	Feb 4	15:40
♌	Feb 6	22:06
♍	Feb 9	6:36
♎	Feb 11	17:18
♏	Feb 14	5:38
♐	Feb 16	17:57
♑	Feb 19	4:00
♒	Feb 21	10:23
♓	Feb 23	13:17
♈	Feb 25	14:05
♉	Feb 27	14:38
♊	Mar 1	16:39
♋	Mar 3	21:08
♌	Mar 6	4:15
♍	Mar 8	13:34
♎	Mar 11	0:35
♏	Mar 13	12:51
♐	Mar 16	1:27
♑	Mar 18	12:35
♒	Mar 20	20:21
♓	Mar 23	0:04
♈	Mar 25	0:38
♉	Mar 26	23:57
♊	Mar 29	0:13
♋	Mar 31	3:14
♌	Apr 2	9:45
♍	Apr 4	19:20
♎	Apr 7	6:49
♏	Apr 9	19:14
♐	Apr 12	7:48
♑	Apr 14	19:27
♒	Apr 17	4:34
♓	Apr 19	9:53
♈	Apr 21	11:30
♉	Apr 23	10:51
♊	Apr 25	10:06
♋	Apr 27	11:27
♌	Apr 29	16:25
♍	May 2	1:13
♎	May 4	12:42
♏	May 7	1:16
♐	May 9	13:42
♑	May 12	1:13
♒	May 14	10:51
♓	May 16	17:32
♈	May 18	20:48
♉	May 20	21:21
♊	May 22	20:53
♋	May 24	21:29
♌	May 27	0:59
♍	May 29	8:22
♎	May 31	19:09
♏	Jun 3	7:38
♐	Jun 5	20:01
♑	Jun 8	7:07
♒	Jun 10	16:22
♓	Jun 12	23:21
♈	Jun 15	3:46
♉	Jun 17	5:54
♊	Jun 19	6:44
♋	Jun 21	7:46
♌	Jun 23	10:44
♍	Jun 25	16:56
♎	Jun 28	2:41
♏	Jun 30	14:48
♐	Jul 3	3:11
♑	Jul 5	14:03
♒	Jul 7	22:36
♓	Jul 10	4:53
♈	Jul 12	9:16
♉	Jul 14	12:15
♊	Jul 16	14:27
♋	Jul 18	16:45
♌	Jul 20	20:15
♍	Jul 23	2:06
♎	Jul 25	11:02
♏	Jul 27	22:38
♐	Jul 30	11:08
♑	Aug 1	22:12
♒	Aug 4	6:25
♓	Aug 6	11:46
♈	Aug 8	15:07
♉	Aug 10	17:37
♊	Aug 12	20:16
♋	Aug 14	23:39
♌	Aug 17	4:17
♍	Aug 19	10:40
♎	Aug 21	19:25
♏	Aug 24	6:39
♐	Aug 26	19:15
♑	Aug 29	6:57
♒	Aug 31	15:37
♓	Sept 2	20:37
♈	Sept 4	22:52
♉	Sept 7	0:02
♊	Sept 9	1:46
♋	Sept 11	5:08
♌	Sept 13	10:30
♍	Sept 15	17:47
♎	Sept 18	3:00
♏	Sept 20	14:10
♐	Sept 23	2:50
♑	Sept 25	15:15
♒	Sept 28	1:03
♓	Sept 30	6:46
♈	Oct 2	8:48
♉	Oct 4	8:50
♊	Oct 6	8:58
♋	Oct 8	11:01
♌	Oct 10	15:54
♍	Oct 12	23:34
♎	Oct 15	9:24
♏	Oct 17	20:53
♐	Oct 20	9:32
♑	Oct 22	22:21
♒	Oct 25	9:20
♓	Oct 27	16:36
♈	Oct 29	19:40
♉	Oct 31	19:42
♊	Nov 2	18:48
♋	Nov 4	19:08
♌	Nov 6	22:24
♍	Nov 9	5:14
♎	Nov 11	15:07
♏	Nov 14	2:57
♐	Nov 16	15:40
♑	Nov 19	4:23
♒	Nov 21	15:51
♓	Nov 24	0:32
♈	Nov 26	5:25
♉	Nov 28	6:49
♊	Nov 30	6:14
♋	Dec 2	5:45
♌	Dec 4	7:20
♍	Dec 6	12:26
♎	Dec 8	21:21
♏	Dec 11	9:04
♐	Dec 13	21:53
♑	Dec 16	10:21
♒	Dec 18	21:29
♓	Dec 21	6:28
♈	Dec 23	12:41
♉	Dec 25	15:57
♊	Dec 27	16:58
♋	Dec 29	17:07
♌	Dec 31	18:09
1964		
♍	Jan 2	21:48
♎	Jan 5	5:10
♏	Jan 7	16:04
♐	Jan 10	4:49
♑	Jan 12	17:14
♒	Jan 15	3:48
♓	Jan 17	12:04
♈	Jan 19	18:10
♉	Jan 21	22:23
♊	Jan 24	1:05
♋	Jan 26	2:51
♌	Jan 28	4:45
♍	Jan 30	8:09
♎	Feb 1	14:25
♏	Feb 4	0:12
♐	Feb 6	12:35
♑	Feb 9	1:11
♒	Feb 11	11:39
♓	Feb 13	19:09
♈	Feb 16	0:10
♉	Feb 18	3:45
♊	Feb 20	6:48
♋	Feb 22	9:49
♌	Feb 24	13:11
♍	Feb 26	17:30
♎	Feb 28	23:46
♏	Mar 2	8:54
♐	Mar 4	20:47
♑	Mar 7	9:35
♒	Mar 9	20:35
♓	Mar 12	4:05
♈	Mar 14	8:15
♉	Mar 16	10:30
♊	Mar 18	12:26
♋	Mar 20	15:11
♌	Mar 22	19:15
♍	Mar 25	0:42
♎	Mar 27	7:48
♏	Mar 29	17:03
♐	Apr 1	4:41
♑	Apr 3	17:36
♒	Apr 6	5:24
♓	Apr 8	13:47
♈	Apr 10	18:08
♉	Apr 12	19:37
♊	Apr 14	20:06
♋	Apr 16	21:23
♌	Apr 19	0:40
♍	Apr 21	6:17
♎	Apr 23	14:08
♏	Apr 26	0:01
♐	Apr 28	11:46
♑	May 1	0:42
♒	May 3	13:06
♓	May 5	22:43
♈	May 8	4:15
♉	May 10	6:09
♊	May 12	6:01
♋	May 14	5:53
♌	May 16	7:31
♍	May 18	12:02
♎	May 20	19:41
♏	May 23	5:58
♐	May 25	18:03
♑	May 28	7:00
♒	May 30	19:32
♓	Jun 2	6:01
♈	Jun 4	13:03
♉	Jun 6	16:20
♊	Jun 8	16:50
♋	Jun 10	16:16
♌	Jun 12	16:35
♍	Jun 14	19:27
♎	Jun 17	1:54
♏	Jun 19	11:49
♐	Jun 22	0:03
♑	Jun 24	13:02
♒	Jun 27	1:22
♓	Jun 29	11:56
♈	Jul 1	19:52
♉	Jul 4	0:42
♊	Jul 6	2:43
♋	Jul 8	2:57
♌	Jul 10	3:01
♍	Jul 12	4:44
♎	Jul 14	9:41
♏	Jul 16	18:32

(continued)

Table A-2 The Moon *(continued)*

♐	Jul 19	6:28
♑	Jul 21	19:27
♒	Jul 24	7:30
♓	Jul 26	17:36
♈	Jul 29	1:25
♉	Jul 31	7:00
♊	Aug 2	10:28
♋	Aug 4	12:13
♌	Aug 6	13:11
♍	Aug 8	14:50
♎	Aug 10	18:51
♏	Aug 13	2:31
♐	Aug 15	13:44
♑	Aug 18	2:38
♒	Aug 20	14:39
♓	Aug 23	0:13
♈	Aug 25	7:15
♉	Aug 27	12:24
♊	Aug 29	16:16
♋	Aug 31	19:13
♌	Sept 2	21:36
♍	Sept 5	0:12
♎	Sept 7	4:19
♏	Sept 9	11:20
♐	Sept 11	21:47
♑	Sept 14	10:30
♒	Sept 16	22:47
♓	Sept 19	8:22
♈	Sept 21	14:44
♉	Sept 23	18:46
♊	Sept 25	21:46
♋	Sept 28	0:39
♌	Sept 30	3:52
♍	Oct 2	7:42
♎	Oct 4	12:44
♏	Oct 6	19:57
♐	Oct 9	6:02
♑	Oct 11	18:32
♒	Oct 14	7:15
♓	Oct 16	17:33
♈	Oct 19	0:05
♉	Oct 21	3:24
♊	Oct 23	5:03
♋	Oct 25	6:37
♌	Oct 27	9:14
♍	Oct 29	13:25
♎	Oct 31	19:24
♏	Nov 3	3:25
♐	Nov 5	13:43
♑	Nov 8	2:06
♒	Nov 10	15:08
♓	Nov 13	2:28
♈	Nov 15	10:10
♉	Nov 17	13:57
♊	Nov 19	14:58
♋	Nov 21	15:04
♌	Nov 23	15:59
♍	Nov 25	19:02
♎	Nov 28	0:54
♏	Nov 30	9:31
♐	Dec 2	20:24
♑	Dec 5	8:53
♒	Dec 7	21:57
♓	Dec 10	10:00
♈	Dec 12	19:12
♉	Dec 15	0:33
♊	Dec 17	2:21
♋	Dec 19	2:02
♌	Dec 21	1:31
♍	Dec 23	2:42
♎	Dec 25	7:04
♏	Dec 27	15:11
♐	Dec 30	2:20
1965		
♑	Jan 1	15:06
♒	Jan 4	4:04
♓	Jan 6	16:06
♈	Jan 9	2:08
♉	Jan 11	9:10
♊	Jan 13	12:48
♋	Jan 15	13:35
♌	Jan 17	12:57
♍	Jan 19	12:55
♎	Jan 21	15:28
♏	Jan 23	22:01
♐	Jan 26	8:32
♑	Jan 28	21:21
♒	Jan 31	10:17
♓	Feb 2	21:56
♈	Feb 5	7:43
♉	Feb 7	15:24
♊	Feb 9	20:36
♋	Feb 11	23:14
♌	Feb 13	23:54
♍	Feb 16	0:05
♎	Feb 18	1:45
♏	Feb 20	6:45
♐	Feb 22	15:57
♑	Feb 25	4:17
♒	Feb 27	17:14
♓	Mar 2	4:38
♈	Mar 4	13:45
♉	Mar 6	20:49
♊	Mar 9	2:14
♋	Mar 11	6:03
♌	Mar 13	8:23
♍	Mar 15	9:55
♎	Mar 17	12:04
♏	Mar 19	16:32
♐	Mar 22	0:37
♑	Mar 24	12:07
♒	Mar 27	0:59
♓	Mar 29	12:32
♈	Mar 31	21:19
♉	Apr 3	3:29
♊	Apr 5	7:55
♋	Apr 7	11:24
♌	Apr 9	14:23
♍	Apr 11	17:14
♎	Apr 13	20:38
♏	Apr 16	1:42
♐	Apr 18	9:31
♑	Apr 20	20:24
♒	Apr 23	9:04
♓	Apr 25	21:02
♈	Apr 28	6:12
♉	Apr 30	12:03
♊	May 2	15:26
♋	May 4	17:39
♌	May 6	19:50
♍	May 8	22:47
♎	May 11	3:04
♏	May 13	9:10
♐	May 15	17:32
♑	May 18	4:20
♒	May 20	16:50
♓	May 23	5:14
♈	May 25	15:19
♉	May 27	21:48
♊	May 30	0:58
♋	Jun 1	2:05
♌	Jun 3	2:47
♍	Jun 5	4:33
♎	Jun 7	8:29
♏	Jun 9	15:04
♐	Jun 12	0:10
♑	Jun 14	11:20
♒	Jun 16	23:51
♓	Jun 19	12:29
♈	Jun 21	23:29
♉	Jun 24	7:16
♊	Jun 26	11:18
♋	Jun 28	12:20
♌	Jun 30	11:59
♍	Jul 2	12:11
♎	Jul 4	14:43
♏	Jul 6	20:38
♐	Jul 9	5:53
♑	Jul 11	17:29
♒	Jul 14	6:08
♓	Jul 16	18:45
♈	Jul 19	6:13
♉	Jul 21	15:14
♊	Jul 23	20:48
♋	Jul 25	22:53
♌	Jul 27	22:37
♍	Jul 29	21:55
♎	Jul 31	22:54
♏	Aug 3	3:20
♐	Aug 5	11:49
♑	Aug 7	23:22
♒	Aug 10	12:09
♓	Aug 13	0:37
♈	Aug 15	11:57
♉	Aug 17	21:27
♊	Aug 20	4:20
♋	Aug 22	8:04
♌	Aug 24	9:01
♍	Aug 26	8:36
♎	Aug 28	8:52
♏	Aug 30	11:54
♐	Sept 1	19:00
♑	Sept 4	5:51
♒	Sept 6	18:34
♓	Sept 9	6:56
♈	Sept 11	17:50
♉	Sept 14	2:56
♊	Sept 16	10:06
♋	Sept 18	15:01
♌	Sept 20	17:35
♍	Sept 22	18:30
♎	Sept 24	19:15
♏	Sept 26	21:47
♐	Sept 29	3:42
♑	Oct 1	13:29
♒	Oct 4	1:48
♓	Oct 6	14:14
♈	Oct 9	0:54
♉	Oct 11	9:16
♊	Oct 13	15:40
♋	Oct 15	20:27
♌	Oct 17	23:51
♍	Oct 20	2:13
♎	Oct 22	4:21
♏	Oct 24	7:31
♐	Oct 26	13:09
♑	Oct 28	22:05
♒	Oct 31	9:49
♓	Nov 2	22:23
♈	Nov 5	9:21
♉	Nov 7	17:29
♊	Nov 9	22:54
♋	Nov 12	2:29
♌	Nov 14	5:13
♍	Nov 16	7:55
♎	Nov 18	11:10
♏	Nov 20	15:37
♐	Nov 22	21:57
♑	Nov 25	6:45
♒	Nov 27	18:03
♓	Nov 30	6:40
♈	Dec 2	18:22
♉	Dec 5	3:11
♊	Dec 7	8:27
♋	Dec 9	10:57
♌	Dec 11	12:08
♍	Dec 13	13:35
♎	Dec 15	16:33
♏	Dec 17	21:40
♐	Dec 20	5:01
♑	Dec 22	14:27
♒	Dec 25	1:44
♓	Dec 27	14:17
♈	Dec 30	2:40
1966		
♉	Jan 1	12:46
♊	Jan 3	19:06
♋	Jan 5	21:40
♌	Jan 7	21:50
♍	Jan 9	21:34
♎	Jan 11	22:53
♏	Jan 14	3:08
♐	Jan 16	10:39
♑	Jan 18	20:45
♒	Jan 21	8:26
♓	Jan 23	20:58
♈	Jan 26	9:33
♉	Jan 28	20:43
♊	Jan 31	4:43
♋	Feb 2	8:41
♌	Feb 4	9:14
♍	Feb 6	8:11
♎	Feb 8	7:50
♏	Feb 10	10:15
♐	Feb 12	16:33
♑	Feb 15	2:26
♒	Feb 17	14:25
♓	Feb 20	3:05
♈	Feb 22	15:30
♉	Feb 25	2:53
♊	Feb 27	12:03
♋	Mar 1	17:48
♌	Mar 3	19:57
♍	Mar 5	19:36
♎	Mar 7	18:48
♏	Mar 9	19:47
♐	Mar 12	0:18
♑	Mar 14	8:55
♒	Mar 16	20:35
♓	Mar 19	9:19
♈	Mar 21	21:33
♉	Mar 24	8:32
♊	Mar 26	17:41
♋	Mar 29	0:23
♌	Mar 31	4:12
♍	Apr 2	5:31
♎	Apr 4	5:40
♏	Apr 6	6:30
♐	Apr 8	9:54
♑	Apr 10	17:02
♒	Apr 13	3:42
♓	Apr 15	16:13
♈	Apr 18	4:27
♉	Apr 20	15:00
♊	Apr 22	23:27
♋	Apr 25	5:48
♌	Apr 27	10:09
♍	Apr 29	12:50
♎	May 1	14:31
♏	May 3	16:23
♐	May 5	19:52
♑	May 8	2:12
♒	May 10	11:52

Table A-2 — The Moon (continued)

♓ May 12 23:55	♒ Sept 23 22:48	♏ Jan 31 20:44	♎ Jun 15 16:58	♍ Oct 28 8:19
♈ May 15 12:15	♓ Sept 26 10:48	♐ Feb 3 0:55	♏ Jun 17 19:25	♎ Oct 30 10:31
♉ May 17 22:49	♈ Sept 28 23:29	♑ Feb 5 7:10	♐ Jun 19 21:20	♏ Nov 1 10:26
♊ May 20 6:40	♉ Oct 1 11:47	♒ Feb 7 15:17	♑ Jun 21 23:46	♐ Nov 3 9:51
♋ May 22 12:00	♊ Oct 3 22:43	♓ Feb 10 1:19	♒ Jun 24 4:11	♑ Nov 5 10:44
♌ May 24 15:37	♋ Oct 6 7:12	♈ Feb 12 13:17	♓ Jun 26 11:49	♒ Nov 7 14:45
♍ May 26 18:22	♌ Oct 8 12:25	♉ Feb 15 2:19	♈ Jun 28 22:53	♓ Nov 9 22:42
♎ May 28 21:00	♍ Oct 10 14:27	♊ Feb 17 14:16	♉ Jul 1 11:43	♈ Nov 12 9:58
♏ May 31 0:11	♎ Oct 12 14:29	♋ Feb 19 22:48	♊ Jul 3 23:39	♉ Nov 14 22:52
♐ Jun 2 4:38	♏ Oct 14 14:21	♌ Feb 22 3:04	♋ Jul 6 8:47	♊ Nov 17 11:40
♑ Jun 4 11:10	♐ Oct 16 15:59	♍ Feb 24 4:04	♌ Jul 8 14:58	♋ Nov 19 23:13
♒ Jun 6 20:21	♑ Oct 18 20:55	♎ Feb 26 3:44	♍ Jul 10 19:07	♌ Nov 22 8:47
♓ Jun 9 7:57	♒ Oct 21 5:41	♏ Feb 28 4:09	♎ Jul 12 22:20	♍ Nov 24 15:46
♈ Jun 11 20:26	♓ Oct 23 17:20	♐ Mar 2 6:53	♏ Jul 15 1:17	♎ Nov 26 19:48
♉ Jun 14 7:29	♈ Oct 26 6:03	♑ Mar 4 12:35	♐ Jul 17 4:22	♏ Nov 28 21:13
♊ Jun 16 15:26	♉ Oct 28 18:05	♒ Mar 6 21:03	♑ Jul 19 7:59	♐ Nov 30 21:10
♋ Jun 18 20:05	♊ Oct 31 4:28	♓ Mar 9 7:41	♒ Jul 21 12:59	♑ Dec 2 21:25
♌ Jun 20 22:29	♋ Nov 2 12:43	♈ Mar 11 19:53	♓ Jul 23 20:28	♒ Dec 4 23:57
♍ Jun 23 0:08	♌ Nov 4 18:36	♉ Mar 14 8:54	♈ Jul 26 7:00	♓ Dec 7 6:19
♎ Jun 25 2:23	♍ Nov 6 22:10	♊ Mar 16 21:19	♉ Jul 28 19:40	♈ Dec 9 16:43
♏ Jun 27 6:04	♎ Nov 8 23:54	♋ Mar 19 7:10	♊ Jul 31 8:00	♉ Dec 12 5:32
♐ Jun 29 11:31	♏ Nov 11 0:53	♌ Mar 21 13:04	♋ Aug 2 17:32	♊ Dec 14 18:18
♑ Jul 1 18:51	♐ Nov 13 2:36	♍ Mar 23 15:08	♌ Aug 4 23:26	♋ Dec 17 5:23
♒ Jul 4 4:14	♑ Nov 15 6:37	♎ Mar 25 14:50	♍ Aug 7 2:36	♌ Dec 19 14:21
♓ Jul 6 15:39	♒ Nov 17 14:03	♏ Mar 27 14:10	♎ Aug 9 4:34	♍ Dec 21 21:21
♈ Jul 9 4:16	♓ Nov 20 0:53	♐ Mar 29 15:08	♏ Aug 11 6:44	♎ Dec 24 2:27
♉ Jul 11 16:03	♈ Nov 22 13:31	♑ Mar 31 19:11	♐ Aug 13 9:52	♏ Dec 26 5:36
♊ Jul 14 0:51	♉ Nov 25 1:37	♒ Apr 3 2:49	♑ Aug 15 14:18	♐ Dec 28 7:09
♋ Jul 16 5:44	♊ Nov 27 11:31	♓ Apr 5 13:29	♒ Aug 17 20:17	♑ Dec 30 8:11
♌ Jul 18 7:27	♋ Nov 29 18:50	♈ Apr 8 1:57	♓ Aug 20 4:18	
♍ Jul 20 7:47	♌ Dec 2 0:02	♉ Apr 10 14:56	♈ Aug 22 14:47	**1968**
♎ Jul 22 8:38	♍ Dec 4 3:48	♊ Apr 13 3:15	♉ Aug 25 3:21	♒ Jan 1 10:24
♏ Jul 24 11:32	♎ Dec 6 6:43	♋ Apr 15 13:37	♊ Aug 27 16:08	♓ Jan 3 15:35
♐ Jul 26 17:04	♏ Dec 8 9:18	♌ Apr 17 20:54	♋ Aug 30 2:34	♈ Jan 6 0:45
♑ Jul 29 1:04	♐ Dec 10 12:13	♍ Apr 20 0:42	♌ Sept 1 9:08	♉ Jan 8 13:02
♒ Jul 31 11:02	♑ Dec 12 16:30	♎ Apr 22 1:41	♍ Sept 3 12:07	♊ Jan 11 1:54
♓ Aug 2 22:36	♒ Dec 14 23:19	♏ Apr 24 1:19	♎ Sept 5 13:03	♋ Jan 13 12:54
♈ Aug 5 11:15	♓ Dec 17 9:17	♐ Apr 26 1:27	♏ Sept 7 13:44	♌ Jan 15 21:09
♉ Aug 7 23:38	♈ Dec 19 21:39	♑ Apr 28 3:54	♐ Sept 9 15:40	♍ Jan 18 3:11
♊ Aug 10 9:38	♉ Dec 22 10:07	♒ Apr 30 9:57	♑ Sept 11 19:43	♎ Jan 20 7:47
♋ Aug 12 15:41	♊ Dec 24 20:14	♓ May 2 19:47	♒ Sept 14 2:08	♏ Jan 22 11:28
♌ Aug 14 17:50	♋ Dec 27 2:58	♈ May 5 8:10	♓ Sept 16 10:53	♐ Jan 24 14:23
♍ Aug 16 17:35	♌ Dec 29 6:57	♉ May 7 21:09	♈ Sept 18 21:46	♑ Jan 26 16:57
♎ Aug 18 17:05	♍ Dec 31 9:33	♊ May 10 9:08	♉ Sept 21 10:20	♒ Jan 28 20:06
♏ Aug 20 18:24		♋ May 12 19:11	♊ Sept 23 23:21	♓ Jan 31 1:16
♐ Aug 22 22:51	**1967**	♌ May 15 2:49	♋ Sept 26 10:45	♈ Feb 2 9:39
♑ Aug 25 6:37	♎ Jan 2 12:04	♍ May 17 7:52	♌ Sept 28 18:41	♉ Feb 4 21:15
♒ Aug 27 16:56	♏ Jan 4 15:16	♎ May 19 10:31	♍ Sept 30 22:38	♊ Feb 7 10:09
♓ Aug 30 4:48	♐ Jan 6 19:28	♏ May 21 11:30	♎ Oct 2 23:34	♋ Feb 9 21:34
♈ Sept 1 17:27	♑ Jan 9 0:53	♐ May 23 12:06	♏ Oct 4 23:14	♌ Feb 12 5:50
♉ Sept 4 5:59	♒ Jan 11 8:05	♑ May 25 13:58	♐ Oct 6 23:32	♍ Feb 14 11:02
♊ Sept 6 16:52	♓ Jan 13 17:45	♒ May 27 18:44	♑ Oct 9 2:04	♎ Feb 16 14:21
♋ Sept 9 0:26	♈ Jan 16 5:48	♓ May 30 3:18	♒ Oct 11 7:45	♏ Feb 18 17:00
♌ Sept 11 4:01	♉ Jan 18 18:39	♈ Jun 1 15:07	♓ Oct 13 16:38	♐ Feb 20 19:48
♍ Sept 13 4:25	♊ Jan 21 5:38	♉ Jun 4 4:04	♈ Oct 16 3:58	♑ Feb 22 23:12
♎ Sept 15 3:33	♋ Jan 23 12:51	♊ Jun 6 15:52	♉ Oct 18 16:41	♒ Feb 25 3:37
♏ Sept 17 3:34	♌ Jan 25 16:20	♋ Jun 9 1:18	♊ Oct 21 5:38	♓ Feb 27 9:42
♐ Sept 19 6:21	♍ Jan 27 17:36	♌ Jun 11 8:19	♋ Oct 23 17:27	♈ Feb 29 18:14
♑ Sept 21 12:52	♎ Jan 29 18:33	♍ Jun 13 13:24	♌ Oct 26 2:40	♉ Mar 3 5:28

(continued)

Table A-2   The Moon (continued)

Sign	Date	Time	Sign	Date	Time	Sign	Date	Time	Sign	Date	Time	Sign	Date	Time
♊	Mar 5	18:17	♉	Jul 17	14:30	♈	Nov 28	17:26	♑	Apr 8	0:04	♐	Aug 20	19:12
♋	Mar 8	6:21	♊	Jul 20	3:13	♉	Dec 1	3:58	♒	Apr 10	2:46	♑	Aug 22	21:49
♌	Mar 10	15:27	♋	Jul 22	15:31	♊	Dec 3	16:06	♓	Apr 12	6:41	♒	Aug 24	22:36
♍	Mar 12	20:51	♌	Jul 25	1:55	♋	Dec 6	4:43	♈	Apr 14	12:13	♓	Aug 26	23:03
♎	Mar 14	23:23	♍	Jul 27	10:10	♌	Dec 8	17:02	♉	Apr 16	19:43	♈	Aug 29	0:57
♏	Mar 17	0:33	♎	Jul 29	16:32	♍	Dec 11	3:59	♊	Apr 19	5:28	♉	Aug 31	5:50
♐	Mar 19	1:54	♏	Jul 31	21:11	♎	Dec 13	12:08	♋	Apr 21	17:17	♊	Sept 2	14:23
♑	Mar 21	4:34	♐	Aug 3	0:11	♏	Dec 15	16:31	♌	Apr 24	5:51	♋	Sept 5	1:57
♒	Mar 23	9:16	♑	Aug 5	1:57	♐	Dec 17	17:27	♍	Apr 26	16:57	♌	Sept 7	14:36
♓	Mar 25	16:15	♒	Aug 7	3:37	♑	Dec 19	16:32	♎	Apr 29	0:43	♍	Sept 10	2:20
♈	Mar 28	1:32	♓	Aug 9	6:46	♒	Dec 21	15:59	♏	May 1	4:49	♎	Sept 12	12:01
♉	Mar 30	12:55	♈	Aug 11	12:53	♓	Dec 23	18:01	♐	May 3	6:19	♏	Sept 14	19:25
♊	Apr 2	1:40	♉	Aug 13	22:36	♈	Dec 26	0:02	♑	May 5	6:57	♐	Sept 17	0:42
♋	Apr 4	14:13	♊	Aug 16	10:51	♉	Dec 28	9:57	♒	May 7	8:28	♑	Sept 19	4:14
♌	Apr 7	0:28	♋	Aug 18	23:15	♊	Dec 30	22:11	♓	May 9	12:04	♒	Sept 21	6:31
♍	Apr 9	7:04	♌	Aug 21	9:40				♈	May 11	18:09	♓	Sept 23	8:22
♎	Apr 11	10:01	♍	Aug 23	17:21	**1969**			♉	May 14	2:28	♈	Sept 25	10:55
♏	Apr 13	10:32	♎	Aug 25	22:45	♋	Jan 2	10:53	♊	May 16	12:41	♉	Sept 27	15:29
♐	Apr 15	10:23	♏	Aug 28	2:38	♌	Jan 4	22:55	♋	May 19	0:30	♊	Sept 29	23:05
♑	Apr 17	11:23	♐	Aug 30	5:40	♍	Jan 7	9:42	♌	May 21	13:12	♋	Oct 2	9:52
♒	Apr 19	14:57	♑	Sept 1	8:22	♎	Jan 9	18:32	♍	May 24	1:07	♌	Oct 4	22:25
♓	Apr 21	21:46	♒	Sept 3	11:19	♏	Jan 12	0:32	♎	May 26	10:07	♍	Oct 7	10:21
♈	Apr 24	7:32	♓	Sept 5	15:27	♐	Jan 14	3:19	♏	May 28	15:05	♎	Oct 9	19:48
♉	Apr 26	19:22	♈	Sept 7	21:49	♑	Jan 16	3:39	♐	May 30	16:30	♏	Oct 12	2:19
♊	Apr 29	8:11	♉	Sept 10	7:06	♒	Jan 18	3:17	♑	Jun 1	16:07	♐	Oct 14	6:33
♋	May 1	20:50	♊	Sept 12	18:54	♓	Jan 20	4:21	♒	Jun 3	16:03	♑	Oct 16	9:35
♌	May 4	7:54	♋	Sept 15	7:28	♈	Jan 22	8:43	♓	Jun 5	18:13	♒	Oct 18	12:21
♍	May 6	15:58	♌	Sept 17	18:25	♉	Jan 24	17:13	♈	Jun 7	23:36	♓	Oct 20	15:26
♎	May 8	20:21	♍	Sept 20	2:15	♊	Jan 27	4:53	♉	Jun 10	8:06	♈	Oct 22	19:17
♏	May 10	21:30	♎	Sept 22	7:00	♋	Jan 29	17:36	♊	Jun 12	18:48	♉	Oct 25	0:32
♐	May 12	20:53	♏	Sept 24	9:39	♌	Feb 1	5:29	♋	Jun 15	6:52	♊	Oct 27	8:00
♑	May 14	20:31	♐	Sept 26	11:30	♍	Feb 3	15:40	♌	Jun 17	19:35	♋	Oct 29	18:13
♒	May 16	22:22	♑	Sept 28	13:44	♎	Feb 6	0:00	♍	Jun 20	7:53	♌	Nov 1	6:35
♓	May 19	3:53	♒	Sept 30	17:11	♏	Feb 8	6:18	♎	Jun 22	18:03	♍	Nov 3	19:00
♈	May 21	13:14	♓	Oct 2	22:21	♐	Feb 10	10:23	♏	Jun 25	0:31	♎	Nov 6	4:59
♉	May 24	1:15	♈	Oct 5	5:35	♑	Feb 12	12:28	♐	Jun 27	3:00	♏	Nov 8	11:18
♊	May 26	14:12	♉	Oct 7	15:07	♒	Feb 14	13:30	♑	Jun 29	2:44	♐	Nov 10	14:30
♋	May 29	2:43	♊	Oct 10	2:43	♓	Feb 16	15:03	♒	Jul 1	1:49	♑	Nov 12	16:08
♌	May 31	13:53	♋	Oct 12	15:23	♈	Feb 18	18:48	♓	Jul 3	2:26	♒	Nov 14	17:53
♍	Jun 2	22:52	♌	Oct 15	3:08	♉	Feb 21	2:02	♈	Jul 5	6:16	♓	Nov 16	20:52
♎	Jun 5	4:49	♍	Oct 17	11:58	♊	Feb 23	12:41	♉	Jul 7	13:53	♈	Nov 19	1:32
♏	Jun 7	7:30	♎	Oct 19	17:05	♋	Feb 26	1:11	♊	Jul 10	0:31	♉	Nov 21	7:52
♐	Jun 9	7:42	♏	Oct 21	19:05	♌	Feb 28	13:12	♋	Jul 12	12:47	♊	Nov 23	15:59
♑	Jun 11	7:05	♐	Oct 23	19:32	♍	Mar 2	23:07	♌	Jul 15	1:29	♋	Nov 26	2:10
♒	Jun 13	7:46	♑	Oct 25	20:13	♎	Mar 5	6:34	♍	Jul 17	13:42	♌	Nov 28	14:22
♓	Jun 15	11:42	♒	Oct 27	22:43	♏	Mar 7	11:56	♎	Jul 20	0:20	♍	Dec 1	3:14
♈	Jun 17	19:50	♓	Oct 30	3:54	♐	Mar 9	15:48	♏	Jul 22	8:04	♎	Dec 3	14:17
♉	Jun 20	7:25	♈	Nov 1	11:51	♑	Mar 11	18:40	♐	Jul 24	12:10	♏	Dec 5	21:30
♊	Jun 22	20:22	♉	Nov 3	22:01	♒	Mar 13	21:09	♑	Jul 26	13:09	♐	Dec 8	0:43
♋	Jun 25	8:43	♊	Nov 6	9:48	♓	Mar 16	0:04	♒	Jul 28	12:34	♑	Dec 10	1:20
♌	Jun 27	19:30	♋	Nov 8	22:26	♈	Mar 18	4:27	♓	Jul 30	12:30	♒	Dec 12	1:27
♍	Jun 30	4:26	♌	Nov 11	10:45	♉	Mar 20	11:20	♈	Aug 1	14:55	♓	Dec 14	2:56
♎	Jul 2	11:10	♍	Nov 13	20:55	♊	Mar 22	21:12	♉	Aug 3	21:02	♈	Dec 16	6:56
♏	Jul 4	15:20	♎	Nov 16	3:26	♋	Mar 25	9:18	♊	Aug 6	6:49	♉	Dec 18	13:35
♐	Jul 6	17:05	♏	Nov 18	6:06	♌	Mar 27	21:37	♋	Aug 8	18:57	♊	Dec 20	22:28
♑	Jul 8	17:24	♐	Nov 20	6:04	♍	Mar 30	7:54	♌	Aug 11	7:38	♋	Dec 23	9:09
♒	Jul 10	18:03	♑	Nov 22	5:20	♎	Apr 1	15:03	♍	Aug 13	19:32	♌	Dec 25	21:21
♓	Jul 12	21:03	♒	Nov 24	6:02	♏	Apr 3	19:22	♎	Aug 16	5:51	♍	Dec 28	10:20
♈	Jul 15	3:51	♓	Nov 26	9:52	♐	Apr 5	21:57	♏	Aug 18	13:54	♎	Dec 30	22:18

Table A-2 — The Moon (continued)

1970

♏ Jan 2 7:03	♍ May 13 21:10	♌ Sept 24 17:54	♉ Feb 1 10:49	♈ Jun 16 6:06
♐ Jan 4 11:33	♎ May 16 9:02	♍ Sept 27 6:53	♊ Feb 3 15:34	♉ Jun 18 8:39
♑ Jan 6 12:30	♏ May 18 17:49	♎ Sept 29 19:33	♋ Feb 5 23:07	♊ Jun 20 11:24
♒ Jan 8 11:47	♐ May 20 23:11	♏ Oct 2 6:35	♌ Feb 8 9:06	♋ Jun 22 15:30
♓ Jan 10 11:37	♑ May 23 2:13	♐ Oct 4 15:31	♍ Feb 10 20:58	♌ Jun 24 22:12
♈ Jan 12 13:48	♒ May 25 4:25	♑ Oct 6 22:10	♎ Feb 13 9:50	♍ Jun 27 8:06
♉ Jan 14 19:20	♓ May 27 6:59	♒ Oct 9 2:26	♏ Feb 15 22:22	♎ Jun 29 20:22
♊ Jan 17 4:07	♈ May 29 10:27	♓ Oct 11 4:30	♐ Feb 18 8:45	♏ Jul 2 8:46
♋ Jan 19 15:13	♉ May 31 15:03	♈ Oct 13 5:12	♑ Feb 20 15:37	♐ Jul 4 18:59
♌ Jan 22 3:40	♊ Jun 2 21:10	♉ Oct 15 6:00	♒ Feb 22 18:43	♑ Jul 7 2:03
♍ Jan 24 16:33	♋ Jun 5 5:25	♊ Oct 17 8:43	♓ Feb 24 19:05	♒ Jul 9 6:26
♎ Jan 27 4:42	♌ Jun 7 16:17	♋ Oct 19 14:59	♈ Feb 26 18:30	♓ Jul 11 9:14
♏ Jan 29 14:34	♍ Jun 10 5:02	♌ Oct 22 1:12	♉ Feb 28 18:54	♈ Jul 13 11:32
♐ Jan 31 20:50	♎ Jun 12 17:28	♍ Oct 24 13:57	♊ Mar 2 22:01	♉ Jul 15 14:10
♑ Feb 2 23:21	♏ Jun 15 3:01	♎ Oct 27 2:37	♋ Mar 5 4:47	♊ Jul 17 17:47
♒ Feb 4 23:19	♐ Jun 17 8:39	♏ Oct 29 13:15	♌ Mar 7 14:55	♋ Jul 19 22:56
♓ Feb 6 22:37	♑ Jun 19 11:04	♐ Oct 31 21:24	♍ Mar 10 3:10	♌ Jul 22 6:16
♈ Feb 8 23:17	♒ Jun 21 12:00	♑ Nov 3 3:32	♎ Mar 12 16:06	♍ Jul 24 16:09
♉ Feb 11 2:59	♓ Jun 23 13:11	♒ Nov 5 8:11	♏ Mar 15 4:31	♎ Jul 27 4:12
♊ Feb 13 10:29	♈ Jun 25 15:52	♓ Nov 7 11:33	♐ Mar 17 15:23	♏ Jul 29 16:50
♋ Feb 15 21:17	♉ Jun 27 20:35	♈ Nov 9 13:52	♑ Mar 19 23:37	♐ Aug 1 3:49
♌ Feb 18 9:53	♊ Jun 30 3:24	♉ Nov 11 15:50	♒ Mar 22 4:28	♑ Aug 3 11:32
♍ Feb 20 22:42	♋ Jul 2 12:21	♊ Nov 13 18:48	♓ Mar 24 6:07	♒ Aug 5 15:46
♎ Feb 23 10:30	♌ Jul 4 23:26	♋ Nov 16 0:23	♈ Mar 26 5:45	♓ Aug 7 17:34
♏ Feb 25 20:23	♍ Jul 7 12:11	♌ Nov 18 9:36	♉ Mar 28 5:16	♈ Aug 9 18:27
♐ Feb 28 3:38	♎ Jul 10 1:02	♍ Nov 20 21:50	♊ Mar 30 6:44	♉ Aug 11 19:55
♑ Mar 2 7:54	♏ Jul 12 11:41	♎ Nov 23 10:39	♋ Apr 1 11:51	♊ Aug 13 23:11
♒ Mar 4 9:34	♐ Jul 14 18:26	♏ Nov 25 21:05	♌ Apr 3 21:05	♋ Aug 16 4:50
♓ Mar 6 9:49	♑ Jul 16 21:19	♐ Nov 28 5:02	♍ Apr 6 9:16	♌ Aug 18 12:57
♈ Mar 8 10:16	♒ Jul 18 21:44	♑ Nov 30 10:05	♎ Apr 8 22:17	♍ Aug 20 23:19
♉ Mar 10 12:43	♓ Jul 20 21:36	♒ Dec 2 13:45	♏ Apr 11 10:28	♎ Aug 23 11:22
♊ Mar 12 18:37	♈ Jul 22 22:42	♓ Dec 4 16:55	♐ Apr 13 21:03	♏ Aug 26 0:09
♋ Mar 15 4:18	♉ Jul 25 2:18	♈ Dec 6 20:03	♑ Apr 16 5:38	♐ Aug 28 11:56
♌ Mar 17 16:40	♊ Jul 27 8:53	♊ Dec 11 3:33	♒ Apr 18 11:46	♑ Aug 30 20:54
♍ Mar 20 5:30	♋ Jul 29 18:14	♋ Dec 13 9:32	♓ Apr 20 15:07	♒ Sept 2 2:04
♎ Mar 22 16:56	♌ Aug 1 5:44	♌ Dec 15 18:21	♈ Apr 22 16:08	♓ Sept 4 3:51
♏ Mar 25 2:10	♍ Aug 3 18:34	♍ Dec 18 6:04	♉ Apr 24 16:06	♈ Sept 6 3:43
♐ Mar 27 9:07	♎ Aug 6 7:33	♎ Dec 20 19:01	♊ Apr 26 16:58	♉ Sept 8 3:37
♑ Mar 29 14:00	♏ Aug 8 18:57	♏ Dec 23 6:27	♋ Apr 28 20:43	♊ Sept 10 5:25
♒ Mar 31 17:08	♐ Aug 11 3:07	♐ Dec 25 14:27	♌ May 1 4:34	♋ Sept 12 10:21
♓ Apr 2 19:01	♑ Aug 13 7:25	♑ Dec 27 19:01	♍ May 3 16:03	♌ Sept 14 18:38
♈ Apr 4 20:32	♒ Aug 15 8:31	♒ Dec 29 21:24	♎ May 6 4:59	♍ Sept 17 5:29
♉ Apr 6 23:02	♓ Aug 17 8:01	♓ Dec 31 23:08	♏ May 8 17:03	♎ Sept 19 17:47
♊ Apr 9 4:02	♈ Aug 19 7:50	**1971**	♐ May 11 3:08	♏ Sept 22 6:33
♋ Apr 11 12:33	♉ Aug 21 9:46	♈ Jan 3 1:26	♑ May 13 11:09	♐ Sept 24 18:43
♌ Apr 14 0:16	♊ Aug 23 15:03	♉ Jan 5 5:00	♒ May 15 17:19	♑ Sept 27 4:52
♍ Apr 16 13:07	♋ Aug 25 23:58	♊ Jan 7 10:08	♓ May 17 21:39	♒ Sept 29 11:39
♎ Apr 19 0:35	♌ Aug 28 11:38	♋ Jan 9 17:09	♈ May 20 0:11	♓ Oct 1 14:36
♏ Apr 21 9:15	♍ Aug 31 0:36	♌ Jan 12 2:24	♉ May 22 1:31	♈ Oct 3 14:40
♐ Apr 23 15:15	♎ Sept 2 13:25	♍ Jan 14 13:57	♊ May 24 3:01	♉ Oct 5 13:42
♑ Apr 25 19:26	♏ Sept 5 0:54	♎ Jan 17 2:53	♋ May 26 6:26	♊ Oct 7 13:53
♒ Apr 27 22:43	♐ Sept 7 9:58	♏ Jan 19 15:04	♌ May 28 13:16	♋ Oct 9 17:10
♓ Apr 30 1:37	♑ Sept 9 15:51	♐ Jan 22 0:15	♍ May 30 23:48	♌ Oct 12 0:30
♈ May 2 4:32	♒ Sept 11 18:34	♑ Jan 24 5:32	♎ Jun 2 12:26	♍ Oct 14 11:16
♉ May 4 8:05	♓ Sept 13 18:57	♒ Jan 26 7:36	♏ Jun 5 0:36	♎ Oct 16 23:47
♊ May 6 13:17	♈ Sept 15 18:35	♓ Jan 28 8:02	♐ Jun 7 12:28	♏ Oct 19 12:31
♋ May 8 21:17	♉ Sept 17 19:21	♈ Jan 30 8:36	♑ Jun 9 17:45	♐ Oct 22 0:31
♌ May 11 8:22	♊ Sept 19 23:02		♒ Jun 11 23:03	♑ Oct 24 11:05
	♋ Sept 22 6:41		♓ Jun 14 3:01	♒ Oct 26 19:11

(continued)

Table A-2 The Moon *(continued)*

♓	Oct 28	23:57
♈	Oct 31	1:26
♉	Nov 2	0:55
♊	Nov 4	0:27
♋	Nov 6	2:15
♌	Nov 8	7:56
♍	Nov 10	17:44
♎	Nov 13	6:05
♏	Nov 15	18:49
♐	Nov 18	6:30
♑	Nov 20	16:36
♒	Nov 23	0:52
♓	Nov 25	6:48
♈	Nov 27	10:03
♉	Nov 29	11:08
♊	Dec 1	11:25
♋	Dec 3	12:51
♌	Dec 5	17:17
♍	Dec 8	1:40
♎	Dec 10	13:19
♏	Dec 13	2:01
♐	Dec 15	13:37
♑	Dec 17	23:07
♒	Dec 20	6:32
♓	Dec 22	12:10
♈	Dec 24	16:09
♉	Dec 26	18:45
♊	Dec 28	20:38
♋	Dec 30	23:01
1972		
♌	Jan 2	3:22
♍	Jan 4	10:50
♎	Jan 6	21:33
♏	Jan 9	10:03
♐	Jan 11	21:57
♑	Jan 14	7:26
♒	Jan 16	14:04
♓	Jan 18	18:28
♈	Jan 20	21:35
♉	Jan 23	0:17
♊	Jan 25	3:14
♋	Jan 27	7:01
♌	Jan 29	12:21
♍	Jan 31	19:56
♎	Feb 3	6:07
♏	Feb 5	18:18
♐	Feb 8	6:38
♑	Feb 10	16:50
♒	Feb 12	23:36
♓	Feb 15	3:11
♈	Feb 17	4:51
♉	Feb 19	6:11
♊	Feb 21	8:35
♋	Feb 23	12:52
♌	Feb 25	19:15
♍	Feb 28	3:39
♎	Mar 1	14:00
♏	Mar 4	2:00
♐	Mar 6	14:36
♑	Mar 9	1:49
♒	Mar 11	9:42
♓	Mar 13	13:39
♈	Mar 15	14:37
♉	Mar 17	14:27
♊	Mar 19	15:12
♋	Mar 21	18:26
♌	Mar 24	0:46
♍	Mar 26	9:48
♎	Mar 28	20:42
♏	Mar 31	8:48
♐	Apr 2	21:27
♑	Apr 5	9:20
♒	Apr 7	18:37
♓	Apr 9	23:58
♈	Apr 12	1:32
♉	Apr 14	0:54
♊	Apr 16	0:16
♋	Apr 18	1:46
♌	Apr 20	6:47
♍	Apr 22	15:24
♎	Apr 25	2:34
♏	Apr 27	14:56
♐	Apr 30	3:31
♑	May 2	15:29
♒	May 5	1:35
♓	May 7	8:28
♈	May 9	11:35
♉	May 11	11:47
♊	May 13	10:57
♋	May 15	11:16
♌	May 17	14:38
♍	May 19	21:56
♎	May 22	8:36
♏	May 24	21:01
♐	May 27	9:33
♑	May 29	21:13
♒	Jun 1	7:15
♓	Jun 3	14:52
♈	Jun 5	19:27
♉	Jun 7	21:15
♊	Jun 9	21:24
♋	Jun 11	21:45
♌	Jun 14	0:10
♍	Jun 16	6:03
♎	Jun 18	15:39
♏	Jun 21	3:43
♐	Jun 23	16:14
♑	Jun 26	3:36
♒	Jun 28	13:02
♓	Jun 30	20:18
♈	Jul 3	1:22
♉	Jul 5	4:25
♊	Jul 7	6:05
♋	Jul 9	7:29
♌	Jul 11	10:05
♍	Jul 13	15:16
♎	Jul 15	23:49
♏	Jul 18	11:15
♐	Jul 20	23:46
♑	Jul 23	11:10
♒	Jul 25	20:07
♓	Jul 28	2:29
♈	Jul 30	6:50
♉	Aug 1	9:57
♊	Aug 3	12:33
♋	Aug 5	15:18
♌	Aug 7	18:56
♍	Aug 10	0:23
♎	Aug 12	8:27
♏	Aug 14	19:19
♐	Aug 17	7:49
♑	Aug 19	19:38
♒	Aug 22	4:43
♓	Aug 24	10:28
♈	Aug 26	13:40
♉	Aug 28	15:43
♊	Aug 30	17:56
♋	Sept 1	21:11
♌	Sept 4	1:54
♍	Sept 6	8:15
♎	Sept 8	16:36
♏	Sept 11	3:15
♐	Sept 13	15:42
♑	Sept 16	4:07
♒	Sept 18	14:04
♓	Sept 20	20:09
♈	Sept 22	22:44
♉	Sept 24	23:27
♊	Sept 27	0:14
♋	Sept 29	2:39
♌	Oct 1	7:25
♍	Oct 3	14:31
♎	Oct 5	23:35
♏	Oct 8	10:27
♐	Oct 10	22:52
♑	Oct 13	11:44
♒	Oct 15	22:51
♓	Oct 18	6:12
♈	Oct 20	9:22
♉	Oct 22	9:37
♊	Oct 24	9:02
♋	Oct 26	9:44
♌	Oct 28	13:14
♍	Oct 30	19:59
♎	Nov 2	5:27
♏	Nov 4	16:46
♐	Nov 7	5:16
♑	Nov 9	18:11
♒	Nov 12	6:02
♓	Nov 14	14:56
♈	Nov 16	19:44
♉	Nov 18	20:53
♊	Nov 20	20:05
♋	Nov 22	19:31
♌	Nov 24	21:12
♍	Nov 27	2:24
♎	Nov 29	11:15
♏	Dec 1	22:42
♐	Dec 4	11:22
♑	Dec 7	0:06
♒	Dec 9	11:53
♓	Dec 11	21:33
♈	Dec 14	3:59
♉	Dec 16	6:59
♊	Dec 18	7:24
♋	Dec 20	6:57
♌	Dec 22	7:34
♍	Dec 24	11:03
♎	Dec 26	18:21
♏	Dec 29	5:10
♐	Dec 31	17:51
1973		
♑	Jan 3	6:30
♒	Jan 5	17:47
♓	Jan 8	3:03
♈	Jan 10	9:57
♉	Jan 12	14:24
♊	Jan 14	16:41
♋	Jan 16	17:39
♌	Jan 18	18:40
♍	Jan 20	21:24
♎	Jan 23	3:16
♏	Jan 25	12:52
♐	Jan 28	1:10
♑	Jan 30	13:54
♒	Feb 2	0:55
♓	Feb 4	9:22
♈	Feb 6	15:29
♉	Feb 8	19:53
♊	Feb 10	23:10
♋	Feb 13	1:44
♌	Feb 15	4:12
♍	Feb 17	7:31
♎	Feb 19	12:58
♏	Feb 21	21:35
♐	Feb 24	9:14
♑	Feb 26	22:04
♒	Mar 1	9:22
♓	Mar 3	17:31
♈	Mar 5	22:37
♉	Mar 8	1:51
♊	Mar 10	4:31
♋	Mar 12	7:29
♌	Mar 14	11:07
♍	Mar 16	15:42
♎	Mar 18	21:48
♏	Mar 21	6:15
♐	Mar 23	17:26
♑	Mar 26	6:16
♒	Mar 28	18:12
♓	Mar 31	2:55
♈	Apr 2	7:48
♉	Apr 4	9:58
♊	Apr 6	11:12
♋	Apr 8	13:04
♌	Apr 10	16:31
♍	Apr 12	21:47
♎	Apr 15	4:50
♏	Apr 17	13:51
♐	Apr 20	1:02
♑	Apr 22	13:49
♒	Apr 25	2:21
♓	Apr 27	12:09
♈	Apr 29	17:53
♉	May 1	20:01
♊	May 3	20:16
♋	May 5	20:35
♌	May 7	22:36
♍	May 10	3:13
♎	May 12	10:31
♏	May 14	20:09
♐	May 17	7:41
♑	May 19	20:30
♒	May 22	9:17
♓	May 24	20:05
♈	May 27	3:14
♉	May 29	6:28
♊	May 31	6:53
♋	Jun 2	6:21
♌	Jun 4	6:49
♍	Jun 6	9:51
♎	Jun 8	16:16
♏	Jun 11	1:52
♐	Jun 13	13:43
♑	Jun 16	2:37
♒	Jun 18	15:19
♓	Jun 21	2:29
♈	Jun 23	10:48
♉	Jun 25	15:37
♊	Jun 27	17:18
♋	Jun 29	17:08
♌	Jul 1	16:55
♍	Jul 3	18:31
♎	Jul 5	23:23
♏	Jul 8	8:05
♐	Jul 10	19:48
♑	Jul 13	8:45
♒	Jul 15	21:15
♓	Jul 18	8:07
♈	Jul 20	16:43
♉	Jul 22	22:41
♊	Jul 25	1:58
♋	Jul 27	3:10
♌	Jul 29	3:29
♍	Jul 31	4:35
♎	Aug 2	8:12
♏	Aug 4	15:35
♐	Aug 7	2:37
♑	Aug 9	15:30
♒	Aug 12	3:52
♓	Aug 14	14:14
♈	Aug 16	22:16
♉	Aug 19	4:14

Table A-2   The Moon *(continued)*

♊ Aug 21 8:26	**1974**	♓ May 14 18:03	♒ Sept 25 14:38	♏ Feb 2 0:53
♋ Aug 23 11:08	♉ Jan 2 23:38	♈ May 17 4:20	♓ Sept 28 3:14	♐ Feb 4 7:10
♌ Aug 25 12:49	♊ Jan 5 3:00	♉ May 19 11:10	♈ Sept 30 14:25	♑ Feb 6 16:42
♍ Aug 27 14:33	♋ Jan 7 3:28	♊ May 21 14:54	♉ Oct 2 23:39	♒ Feb 9 4:16
♎ Aug 29 17:52	♌ Jan 9 2:42	♋ May 23 16:46	♊ Oct 5 7:00	♓ Feb 11 16:45
♏ Sept 1 0:17	♍ Jan 11 2:41	♌ May 25 18:12	♋ Oct 7 12:30	♈ Feb 14 5:22
♐ Sept 3 10:24	♎ Jan 13 5:21	♍ May 27 20:25	♌ Oct 9 16:03	♉ Feb 16 17:09
♑ Sept 5 23:01	♏ Jan 15 11:54	♎ May 30 0:16	♍ Oct 11 17:56	♊ Feb 19 2:35
♒ Sept 8 11:30	♐ Jan 17 22:12	♏ Jun 1 6:10	♎ Oct 13 19:11	♋ Feb 21 8:18
♓ Sept 10 21:40	♑ Jan 20 10:47	♐ Jun 3 14:21	♏ Oct 15 21:23	♌ Feb 23 10:13
♈ Sept 13 4:56	♒ Jan 22 23:50	♑ Jun 6 0:48	♐ Oct 18 2:14	♍ Feb 25 9:37
♉ Sept 15 9:59	♓ Jan 25 12:00	♒ Jun 8 13:02	♑ Oct 20 10:44	♎ Feb 27 8:38
♊ Sept 17 13:48	♈ Jan 27 22:32	♓ Jun 11 1:43	♒ Oct 22 22:20	♏ Mar 1 9:33
♋ Sept 19 17:01	♉ Jan 30 6:41	♈ Jun 13 12:52	♓ Oct 25 10:57	♐ Mar 3 14:05
♌ Sept 21 19:56	♊ Feb 1 11:53	♉ Jun 15 20:46	♈ Oct 27 22:13	♑ Mar 5 22:39
♍ Sept 23 22:58	♋ Feb 3 14:05	♊ Jun 18 0:59	♉ Oct 30 7:00	♒ Mar 8 10:09
♎ Sept 26 3:00	♌ Feb 5 14:11	♋ Jun 20 2:21	♊ Nov 1 13:23	♓ Mar 10 22:49
♏ Sept 28 9:18	♍ Feb 7 13:52	♌ Jun 22 2:30	♋ Nov 3 18:01	♈ Mar 13 11:18
♐ Sept 30 18:47	♎ Feb 9 15:10	♍ Jun 24 3:11	♌ Nov 5 21:30	♉ Mar 15 22:52
♑ Oct 3 7:02	♏ Feb 11 19:58	♎ Jun 26 5:57	♍ Nov 8 0:18	♊ Mar 18 8:43
♒ Oct 5 19:49	♐ Feb 14 5:01	♏ Jun 28 11:40	♎ Nov 10 2:58	♋ Mar 20 15:48
♓ Oct 8 6:23	♑ Feb 16 17:16	♐ Jun 30 20:20	♏ Nov 12 6:23	♌ Mar 22 19:31
♈ Oct 10 13:29	♒ Feb 19 6:21	♑ Jul 3 7:19	♐ Nov 14 11:39	♍ Mar 24 20:21
♉ Oct 12 17:36	♓ Feb 21 18:15	♒ Jul 5 19:41	♑ Nov 16 19:42	♎ Mar 26 19:51
♊ Oct 14 20:09	♈ Feb 24 4:12	♓ Jul 8 8:25	♒ Nov 19 6:39	♏ Mar 28 20:08
♋ Oct 16 22:28	♉ Feb 26 12:11	♈ Jul 10 20:10	♓ Nov 21 19:11	♐ Mar 30 23:10
♌ Oct 19 1:25	♊ Feb 28 18:10	♉ Jul 13 5:21	♈ Nov 24 6:59	♑ Apr 2 6:08
♍ Oct 21 5:19	♋ Mar 2 21:59	♊ Jul 15 10:54	♉ Nov 26 16:05	♒ Apr 4 16:45
♎ Oct 23 10:28	♌ Mar 4 23:49	♋ Jul 17 12:56	♊ Nov 28 21:58	♓ Apr 7 5:17
♏ Oct 25 17:28	♍ Mar 7 0:33	♌ Jul 19 12:43	♋ Dec 1 1:22	♈ Apr 9 17:44
♐ Oct 28 2:58	♎ Mar 9 1:52	♍ Jul 21 12:10	♌ Dec 3 3:31	♉ Apr 12 4:53
♑ Oct 30 14:57	♏ Mar 11 5:40	♎ Jul 23 13:19	♍ Dec 5 5:40	♊ Apr 14 14:14
♒ Nov 2 3:58	♐ Mar 13 13:20	♏ Jul 25 17:45	♎ Dec 7 8:42	♋ Apr 16 21:27
♓ Nov 4 15:26	♑ Mar 16 0:41	♐ Jul 28 2:00	♏ Dec 9 13:13	♌ Apr 19 2:14
♈ Nov 6 23:19	♒ Mar 18 13:38	♑ Jul 30 13:11	♐ Dec 11 19:34	♍ Apr 21 4:42
♉ Nov 9 3:25	♓ Mar 21 1:33	♒ Aug 2 1:46	♑ Dec 14 4:04	♎ Apr 23 5:41
♊ Nov 11 4:59	♈ Mar 23 11:02	♓ Aug 4 14:26	♒ Dec 16 14:48	♏ Apr 25 6:39
♋ Nov 13 5:46	♉ Mar 25 18:09	♈ Aug 7 2:15	♓ Dec 19 3:12	♐ Apr 27 9:20
♌ Nov 15 7:20	♊ Mar 27 23:33	♉ Aug 9 12:13	♈ Dec 21 15:35	♑ Apr 29 15:08
♍ Nov 17 10:41	♋ Mar 30 3:40	♊ Aug 11 19:15	♉ Dec 24 1:45	♒ May 2 0:34
♎ Nov 19 16:15	♌ Apr 1 6:40	♋ Aug 13 22:49	♊ Dec 26 8:15	♓ May 4 12:34
♏ Nov 22 0:06	♍ Apr 3 8:56	♌ Aug 15 23:26	♋ Dec 28 11:15	♈ May 7 1:03
♐ Nov 24 10:11	♎ Apr 5 11:22	♍ Aug 17 22:43	♌ Dec 30 12:05	♉ May 9 12:03
♑ Nov 26 22:13	♏ Apr 7 15:25	♎ Aug 19 22:45		♊ May 11 20:44
♒ Nov 29 11:17	♐ Apr 9 22:27	♏ Aug 22 1:37	**1975**	♋ May 14 3:00
♓ Dec 1 23:32	♑ Apr 12 8:56	♐ Aug 24 8:34	♍ Jan 1 12:32	♌ May 16 7:38
♈ Dec 4 8:50	♒ Apr 14 21:34	♑ Aug 26 19:15	♎ Jan 3 14:21	♍ May 18 10:45
♉ Dec 6 14:08	♓ Apr 17 9:44	♒ Aug 29 7:52	♏ Jan 5 18:39	♎ May 20 13:05
♊ Dec 8 15:58	♈ Apr 19 19:20	♓ Aug 31 20:29	♐ Jan 8 1:39	♏ May 22 15:25
♋ Dec 10 15:52	♉ Apr 22 1:53	♈ Sept 3 7:58	♑ Jan 10 10:58	♐ May 24 18:51
♌ Dec 12 15:44	♊ Apr 24 6:11	♉ Sept 5 17:50	♒ Jan 12 22:03	♑ May 27 0:31
♍ Dec 14 17:20	♋ Apr 26 9:17	♊ Sept 8 1:36	♓ Jan 15 10:23	♒ May 29 9:09
♎ Dec 16 21:53	♌ Apr 28 12:03	♋ Sept 10 6:39	♈ Jan 17 23:03	♓ May 31 20:32
♏ Dec 19 5:44	♍ Apr 30 15:00	♌ Sept 12 8:54	♉ Jan 20 10:21	♈ Jun 3 9:01
♐ Dec 21 16:20	♎ May 2 18:39	♍ Sept 14 9:12	♊ Jan 22 18:23	♉ Jun 5 20:19
♑ Dec 24 4:41	♏ May 4 23:43	♎ Sept 16 9:17	♋ Jan 24 22:20	♊ Jun 8 4:49
♒ Dec 26 17:43	♐ May 7 7:05	♏ Sept 18 11:14	♌ Jan 26 23:00	♋ Jun 10 10:21
♓ Dec 29 6:10	♑ May 9 17:15	♐ Sept 20 16:46	♍ Jan 28 22:14	♌ Jun 12 13:45
♈ Dec 31 16:34	♒ May 12 5:34	♑ Sept 23 2:22	♎ Jan 30 22:13	♍ Jun 14 16:11

(continued)

Table A-2   The Moon (continued)

♎	Jun 16	18:41	♍	Oct 29	13:47	♊	Mar 7	10:56	♉	Jul 19	8:11	♈	Nov 30	6:01
♏	Jun 18	21:59	♎	Oct 31	14:55	♋	Mar 9	20:59	♊	Jul 21	20:40	♉	Dec 2	18:41
♐	Jun 21	2:34	♏	Nov 2	15:07	♌	Mar 12	2:55	♋	Jul 24	6:39	♊	Dec 5	7:38
♑	Jun 23	8:56	♐	Nov 4	16:10	♍	Mar 14	4:59	♌	Jul 26	13:18	♋	Dec 7	19:21
♒	Jun 25	17:33	♑	Nov 6	19:45	♎	Mar 16	4:44	♍	Jul 28	17:23	♌	Dec 10	5:12
♓	Jun 28	4:33	♒	Nov 9	2:59	♏	Mar 18	4:18	♎	Jul 30	20:13	♍	Dec 12	12:55
♈	Jun 30	17:02	♓	Nov 11	13:42	♐	Mar 20	5:34	♏	Aug 1	22:55	♎	Dec 14	18:13
♉	Jul 3	4:54	♈	Nov 14	2:17	♑	Mar 22	9:48	♐	Aug 4	2:03	♏	Dec 16	21:01
♊	Jul 5	13:58	♉	Nov 16	14:38	♒	Mar 24	17:19	♑	Aug 6	5:54	♐	Dec 18	21:54
♋	Jul 7	19:23	♊	Nov 19	1:14	♓	Mar 27	3:34	♒	Aug 8	10:57	♑	Dec 20	22:12
♌	Jul 9	21:50	♋	Nov 21	9:36	♈	Mar 29	15:37	♓	Aug 10	18:00	♒	Dec 22	23:48
♍	Jul 11	22:55	♌	Nov 23	15:48	♉	Apr 1	4:34	♈	Aug 13	3:49	♓	Dec 25	4:36
♎	Jul 14	0:21	♍	Nov 25	20:04	♊	Apr 3	17:15	♉	Aug 15	16:05	♈	Dec 27	13:32
♏	Jul 16	3:23	♎	Nov 27	22:48	♋	Apr 6	4:06	♊	Aug 18	4:54	♉	Dec 30	1:43
♐	Jul 18	8:32	♏	Nov 30	0:37	♌	Apr 8	11:36	♋	Aug 20	15:34			
♑	Jul 20	15:46	♐	Dec 2	2:33	♍	Apr 10	15:16	♌	Aug 22	22:31		**1977**	
♒	Jul 23	0:56	♑	Dec 4	5:58	♎	Apr 12	15:54	♍	Aug 25	2:03	♊	Jan 1	14:43
♓	Jul 25	11:58	♒	Dec 6	12:12	♏	Apr 14	15:14	♎	Aug 27	3:42	♋	Jan 4	2:12
♈	Jul 28	0:27	♓	Dec 8	21:52	♐	Apr 16	15:15	♏	Aug 29	5:05	♌	Jan 6	11:20
♉	Jul 30	12:53	♈	Dec 11	10:06	♑	Apr 18	17:43	♐	Aug 31	7:28	♍	Jan 8	18:23
♊	Aug 1	23:02	♉	Dec 13	22:39	♒	Apr 20	23:47	♑	Sept 2	11:29	♎	Jan 10	23:48
♋	Aug 4	5:17	♊	Dec 16	9:12	♓	Apr 23	9:28	♒	Sept 4	17:20	♏	Jan 13	3:44
♌	Aug 6	7:44	♋	Dec 18	16:49	♈	Apr 25	21:37	♓	Sept 7	1:11	♐	Jan 15	6:18
♍	Aug 8	7:53	♌	Dec 20	21:54	♉	Apr 28	10:37	♈	Sept 9	11:18	♑	Jan 17	8:02
♎	Aug 10	7:51	♍	Dec 23	1:28	♊	Apr 30	23:05	♉	Sept 11	23:30	♒	Jan 19	10:12
♏	Aug 12	9:30	♎	Dec 25	4:27	♋	May 3	9:53	♊	Sept 14	12:32	♓	Jan 21	14:30
♐	Aug 14	13:59	♏	Dec 27	7:28	♌	May 5	18:09	♋	Sept 17	0:07	♈	Jan 23	22:20
♑	Aug 16	21:25	♐	Dec 29	10:53	♍	May 7	23:21	♌	Sept 19	8:10	♉	Jan 26	9:41
♒	Aug 19	7:09	♑	Dec 31	15:16	♎	May 10	1:39	♍	Sept 21	12:16	♊	Jan 28	22:37
♓	Aug 21	18:32				♏	May 12	2:03	♎	Sept 23	13:28	♋	Jan 31	10:20
♈	Aug 24	7:02		**1976**		♐	May 14	2:04	♏	Sept 25	13:34	♌	Feb 2	19:11
♉	Aug 26	19:45	♒	Jan 2	21:33	♑	May 16	3:31	♐	Sept 27	14:21	♍	Feb 5	1:17
♊	Aug 29	6:53	♓	Jan 5	6:35	♒	May 18	8:02	♑	Sept 29	17:13	♎	Feb 7	5:36
♋	Aug 31	14:35	♈	Jan 7	18:21	♓	May 20	16:27	♒	Oct 1	22:49	♏	Feb 9	9:49
♌	Sept 2	18:08	♉	Jan 10	7:10	♈	May 23	4:07	♓	Oct 4	7:10	♐	Feb 11	12:11
♍	Sept 4	18:29	♊	Jan 12	18:19	♉	May 25	17:07	♈	Oct 6	17:50	♑	Feb 13	15:14
♎	Sept 6	17:38	♋	Jan 15	2:00	♊	May 28	5:22	♉	Oct 9	6:11	♒	Feb 15	18:45
♏	Sept 8	17:46	♌	Jan 17	6:15	♋	May 30	15:39	♊	Oct 11	19:14	♓	Feb 17	23:45
♐	Sept 10	20:41	♍	Jan 19	8:25	♌	Jun 1	23:37	♋	Oct 14	7:24	♈	Feb 20	7:22
♑	Sept 13	3:11	♎	Jan 21	10:11	♍	Jun 4	5:21	♌	Oct 16	16:49	♉	Feb 22	18:06
♒	Sept 15	12:51	♏	Jan 23	12:48	♎	Jun 6	9:00	♍	Oct 18	22:25	♊	Feb 25	6:50
♓	Sept 18	0:32	♐	Jan 25	16:51	♏	Jun 8	10:58	♎	Oct 21	0:26	♋	Feb 27	19:02
♈	Sept 20	13:07	♑	Jan 27	22:24	♐	Jun 10	12:07	♏	Oct 23	0:17	♌	Mar 2	4:25
♉	Sept 23	1:43	♒	Jan 30	5:34	♑	Jun 12	13:45	♐	Oct 24	23:49	♍	Mar 4	10:19
♊	Sept 25	13:13	♓	Feb 1	14:47	♒	Jun 14	17:31	♑	Oct 27	0:55	♎	Mar 6	13:34
♋	Sept 27	22:07	♈	Feb 4	2:17	♓	Jun 17	0:43	♒	Oct 29	5:05	♏	Mar 8	15:37
♌	Sept 30	3:20	♉	Feb 6	15:13	♈	Jun 19	11:32	♓	Oct 31	12:53	♐	Mar 10	17:42
♍	Oct 2	5:03	♊	Feb 9	3:16	♉	Jun 22	0:21	♈	Nov 2	23:46	♑	Mar 12	20:40
♎	Oct 4	4:39	♋	Feb 11	11:59	♊	Jun 24	12:37	♉	Nov 5	12:23	♒	Mar 15	1:00
♏	Oct 6	4:09	♌	Feb 13	16:32	♋	Jun 26	22:29	♊	Nov 8	1:21	♓	Mar 17	7:06
♐	Oct 8	5:36	♍	Feb 15	17:59	♍	Jul 1	10:46	♋	Nov 10	13:28	♈	Mar 19	15:23
♑	Oct 10	10:29	♎	Feb 17	18:14	♎	Jul 3	14:34	♌	Nov 12	23:36	♉	Mar 22	2:05
♒	Oct 12	19:10	♏	Feb 19	19:14	♏	Jul 5	17:33	♍	Nov 15	6:46	♊	Mar 24	14:39
♓	Oct 15	6:40	♐	Feb 21	22:18	♐	Jul 7	20:05	♎	Nov 17	10:34	♋	Mar 27	3:16
♈	Oct 17	19:20	♑	Feb 24	3:54	♑	Jul 9	22:49	♏	Nov 19	11:31	♌	Mar 29	13:40
♉	Oct 20	7:43	♒	Feb 26	11:48	♒	Jul 12	2:53	♐	Nov 21	11:03	♍	Mar 31	20:25
♊	Oct 22	18:51	♓	Feb 28	21:42	♓	Jul 14	9:36	♑	Nov 23	11:03	♎	Apr 2	23:39
♋	Oct 25	3:57	♈	Mar 2	9:22	♈	Jul 16	19:40	♒	Nov 25	13:30	♏	Apr 5	0:40
♌	Oct 27	10:20	♉	Mar 4	22:18				♓	Nov 27	19:47	♐	Apr 7	1:09

Table A-2 — The Moon *(continued)*

Sign	Date	Time
♑	Apr 9	2:40
♒	Apr 11	6:24
♓	Apr 13	12:49
♈	Apr 15	21:52
♉	Apr 18	9:02
♊	Apr 20	21:37
♋	Apr 23	10:25
♌	Apr 25	21:43
♍	Apr 28	5:52
♎	Apr 30	10:12
♏	May 2	11:23
♐	May 4	10:59
♑	May 6	10:54
♒	May 8	13:00
♓	May 10	18:29
♈	May 13	3:29
♉	May 15	15:04
♊	May 18	3:50
♋	May 20	16:35
♌	May 23	4:13
♍	May 25	13:31
♎	May 27	19:28
♏	May 29	21:57
♐	May 31	21:54
♑	Jun 2	21:07
♒	Jun 4	21:44
♓	Jun 7	1:35
♈	Jun 9	9:34
♉	Jun 11	20:56
♊	Jun 14	9:50
♋	Jun 16	22:28
♌	Jun 19	9:53
♍	Jun 21	19:29
♎	Jun 24	2:35
♏	Jun 26	6:42
♐	Jun 28	8:02
♑	Jun 30	7:48
♒	Jul 2	7:56
♓	Jul 4	10:31
♈	Jul 6	17:03
♉	Jul 9	3:33
♊	Jul 11	16:15
♋	Jul 14	4:50
♌	Jul 16	15:51
♍	Jul 19	0:58
♎	Jul 21	8:09
♏	Jul 23	13:13
♐	Jul 25	16:04
♑	Jul 27	17:15
♒	Jul 29	18:04
♓	Jul 31	20:23
♈	Aug 3	1:54
♉	Aug 5	11:18
♊	Aug 7	23:29
♋	Aug 10	12:04
♌	Aug 12	22:57
♍	Aug 15	7:26
♎	Aug 17	13:49
♏	Aug 19	18:35
♐	Aug 21	22:03
♑	Aug 24	0:30
♒	Aug 26	2:41
♓	Aug 28	5:46
♈	Aug 30	11:11
♉	Sept 1	19:52
♊	Sept 4	7:27
♋	Sept 6	20:03
♌	Sept 9	7:14
♍	Sept 11	15:34
♎	Sept 13	21:07
♏	Sept 16	0:45
♐	Sept 18	3:28
♑	Sept 20	6:04
♒	Sept 22	9:12
♓	Sept 24	13:30
♈	Sept 26	19:40
♉	Sept 29	4:21
♊	Oct 1	15:33
♋	Oct 4	4:09
♌	Oct 6	15:58
♍	Oct 9	0:59
♎	Oct 11	6:29
♏	Oct 13	9:11
♐	Oct 15	10:27
♑	Oct 17	11:51
♒	Oct 19	14:36
♓	Oct 21	19:26
♈	Oct 24	2:34
♉	Oct 26	11:53
♊	Oct 28	23:08
♋	Oct 31	11:40
♌	Nov 3	0:03
♍	Nov 5	10:17
♎	Nov 7	16:51
♏	Nov 9	19:42
♐	Nov 11	20:03
♑	Nov 13	19:50
♒	Nov 15	21:00
♓	Nov 18	0:58
♈	Nov 20	8:13
♉	Nov 22	18:09
♊	Nov 25	5:48
♋	Nov 27	18:20
♌	Nov 30	6:53
♍	Dec 2	18:05
♎	Dec 5	2:17
♏	Dec 7	6:33
♐	Dec 9	7:22
♑	Dec 11	6:26
♒	Dec 13	5:59
♓	Dec 15	8:09
♈	Dec 17	14:11
♉	Dec 19	23:54
♊	Dec 22	11:51
♋	Dec 25	0:30
♌	Dec 27	12:52
♍	Dec 30	0:13
1978		
♎	Jan 1	9:31
♏	Jan 3	15:35
♐	Jan 5	18:03
♑	Jan 7	17:55
♒	Jan 9	17:05
♓	Jan 11	17:50
♈	Jan 13	22:05
♉	Jan 16	6:30
♊	Jan 18	18:06
♋	Jan 21	6:50
♌	Jan 23	19:02
♍	Jan 26	5:56
♎	Jan 28	15:08
♏	Jan 30	22:04
♐	Feb 2	2:13
♑	Feb 4	3:50
♒	Feb 6	4:04
♓	Feb 8	4:47
♈	Feb 10	7:56
♉	Feb 12	14:50
♊	Feb 15	1:24
♋	Feb 17	13:56
♌	Feb 20	2:09
♍	Feb 22	12:39
♎	Feb 24	21:03
♏	Feb 27	3:28
♐	Mar 1	8:02
♑	Mar 3	10:58
♒	Mar 5	12:51
♓	Mar 7	14:46
♈	Mar 9	18:08
♉	Mar 12	0:18
♊	Mar 14	9:48
♋	Mar 16	21:49
♌	Mar 19	10:12
♍	Mar 21	20:49
♎	Mar 24	4:41
♏	Mar 26	10:01
♐	Mar 28	13:37
♑	Mar 30	16:23
♒	Apr 1	19:05
♓	Apr 3	22:20
♈	Apr 6	2:51
♉	Apr 8	9:21
♊	Apr 10	18:27
♋	Apr 13	5:59
♌	Apr 15	18:30
♍	Apr 18	5:44
♎	Apr 20	13:53
♏	Apr 22	18:39
♐	Apr 24	21:00
♑	Apr 26	22:28
♒	Apr 29	0:28
♓	May 1	4:00
♈	May 3	9:27
♉	May 5	16:52
♊	May 8	2:18
♋	May 10	13:41
♌	May 13	2:17
♍	May 15	14:15
♎	May 17	23:24
♏	May 20	4:39
♐	May 22	6:31
♑	May 24	6:41
♒	May 26	7:10
♓	May 28	9:37
♈	May 30	14:52
♉	Jun 1	22:50
♊	Jun 4	8:53
♋	Jun 6	20:30
♌	Jun 9	9:07
♍	Jun 11	21:35
♎	Jun 14	7:55
♏	Jun 16	14:28
♐	Jun 18	17:01
♑	Jun 20	16:52
♒	Jun 22	16:07
♓	Jun 24	16:57
♈	Jun 26	20:53
♉	Jun 29	4:21
♊	Jul 1	14:37
♋	Jul 4	2:33
♌	Jul 6	15:13
♍	Jul 9	3:44
♎	Jul 11	14:48
♏	Jul 13	22:47
♐	Jul 16	2:50
♑	Jul 18	3:33
♒	Jul 20	2:41
♓	Jul 22	2:26
♈	Jul 24	4:46
♉	Jul 26	10:50
♊	Jul 28	20:31
♋	Jul 31	8:28
♌	Aug 2	21:10
♍	Aug 5	9:29
♎	Aug 7	20:30
♏	Aug 10	5:11
♐	Aug 12	10:43
♑	Aug 14	13:03
♒	Aug 16	13:15
♓	Aug 18	13:04
♈	Aug 20	14:29
♉	Aug 22	19:06
♊	Aug 25	3:31
♋	Aug 27	14:59
♌	Aug 30	3:40
♍	Sept 1	15:46
♎	Sept 4	2:15
♏	Sept 6	10:38
♐	Sept 8	16:39
♑	Sept 10	20:20
♒	Sept 12	22:09
♓	Sept 14	23:09
♈	Sept 17	0:50
♉	Sept 19	4:43
♊	Sept 21	11:56
♋	Sept 23	22:31
♌	Sept 26	11:02
♍	Sept 28	23:11
♎	Oct 1	9:17
♏	Oct 3	16:48
♐	Oct 5	22:07
♑	Oct 8	1:52
♒	Oct 10	4:42
♓	Oct 12	7:12
♈	Oct 14	10:06
♉	Oct 16	14:22
♊	Oct 18	21:05
♋	Oct 21	6:52
♌	Oct 23	19:04
♍	Oct 26	7:32
♎	Oct 28	17:51
♏	Oct 31	0:52
♐	Nov 2	5:03
♑	Nov 4	7:40
♒	Nov 6	10:04
♓	Nov 8	13:06
♈	Nov 10	17:11
♉	Nov 12	22:35
♊	Nov 15	5:45
♋	Nov 17	15:16
♌	Nov 20	3:09
♍	Nov 22	15:57
♎	Nov 25	3:07
♏	Nov 27	11:40
♐	Nov 29	14:23
♑	Dec 1	15:44
♒	Dec 3	16:35
♓	Dec 5	18:36
♈	Dec 7	22:40
♉	Dec 10	4:50
♊	Dec 12	12:54
♋	Dec 14	22:50
♌	Dec 17	10:37
♍	Dec 19	23:34
♎	Dec 22	11:40
♏	Dec 24	20:32
♐	Dec 27	1:07
♑	Dec 29	2:15
♒	Dec 31	1:53
1979		
♓	Jan 2	2:08
♈	Jan 4	4:41
♉	Jan 6	10:17
♊	Jan 9	18:42
♋	Jan 11	5:14
♌	Jan 13	17:16
♍	Jan 16	6:10
♎	Jan 18	18:40
♏	Jan 21	4:51
♐	Jan 23	11:08
♑	Jan 25	13:27
♒	Jan 27	13:12
♓	Jan 29	12:25

(continued)

Table A-2 — The Moon (continued)

Sign	Date	Time	Sign	Date	Time	Sign	Date	Time	Sign	Date	Time	Sign	Date	Time
♈	Jan 31	13:11	♓	Jun 15	4:56	♒	Oct 28	0:16	♏	Mar 5	18:22	♎	Jul 17	16:55
♉	Feb 2	17:03	♈	Jun 17	7:52	♓	Oct 30	3:29	♐	Mar 8	5:38	♏	Jul 20	5:33
♊	Feb 5	0:33	♉	Jun 19	12:18	♈	Nov 1	5:09	♑	Mar 10	14:02	♐	Jul 22	16:42
♋	Feb 7	11:06	♊	Jun 21	18:23	♉	Nov 3	6:16	♒	Mar 12	18:45	♑	Jul 25	0:45
♌	Feb 9	23:25	♋	Jun 24	2:25	♊	Nov 5	8:26	♓	Mar 14	20:10	♒	Jul 27	5:34
♍	Feb 12	12:18	♌	Jun 26	12:47	♋	Nov 7	13:24	♈	Mar 16	19:41	♓	Jul 29	8:11
♎	Feb 15	0:37	♍	Jun 29	1:14	♌	Nov 9	22:14	♉	Mar 18	19:13	♈	Jul 31	9:53
♏	Feb 17	11:12	♎	Jul 1	14:08	♍	Nov 12	10:20	♊	Mar 20	20:47	♉	Aug 2	11:55
♐	Feb 19	18:51	♏	Jul 4	0:57	♎	Nov 14	23:16	♋	Mar 23	1:55	♊	Aug 4	15:10
♑	Feb 21	23:00	♐	Jul 6	7:55	♏	Nov 17	10:29	♌	Mar 25	10:58	♋	Aug 6	20:12
♒	Feb 24	0:12	♑	Jul 8	11:07	♐	Nov 19	18:56	♍	Mar 27	22:52	♌	Aug 9	3:23
♓	Feb 25	23:52	♒	Jul 10	11:59	♑	Nov 22	1:01	♎	Mar 30	11:49	♍	Aug 11	12:54
♈	Feb 27	23:54	♓	Jul 12	12:23	♒	Nov 24	5:37	♏	Apr 2	0:21	♎	Aug 14	0:32
♉	Mar 2	2:09	♈	Jul 14	13:57	♓	Nov 26	9:17	♐	Apr 4	11:35	♏	Aug 16	13:15
♊	Mar 4	7:58	♉	Jul 16	17:43	♈	Nov 28	12:17	♑	Apr 6	20:43	♐	Aug 19	1:08
♋	Mar 6	17:34	♊	Jul 18	23:59	♉	Nov 30	14:54	♒	Apr 9	3:00	♑	Aug 21	10:11
♌	Mar 9	5:47	♋	Jul 21	8:40	♊	Dec 2	18:02	♓	Apr 11	6:07	♒	Aug 23	15:32
♍	Mar 11	18:42	♌	Jul 23	19:30	♋	Dec 4	23:01	♈	Apr 13	6:40	♓	Aug 25	17:43
♎	Mar 14	6:42	♍	Jul 26	8:01	♌	Dec 7	7:09	♉	Apr 15	6:11	♈	Aug 27	18:11
♏	Mar 16	16:49	♎	Jul 28	21:06	♍	Dec 9	18:33	♊	Apr 17	6:41	♉	Aug 29	18:41
♐	Mar 19	0:38	♏	Jul 31	8:46	♎	Dec 12	7:29	♋	Apr 19	10:11	♊	Aug 31	20:50
♑	Mar 21	5:56	♐	Aug 2	17:05	♏	Dec 14	19:08	♌	Apr 21	17:52	♋	Sept 3	1:39
♒	Mar 23	8:52	♑	Aug 4	21:23	♐	Dec 17	3:36	♍	Apr 24	5:12	♌	Sept 5	9:22
♓	Mar 25	10:04	♒	Aug 6	22:28	♑	Dec 19	8:54	♎	Apr 26	18:09	♍	Sept 7	19:31
♈	Mar 27	10:47	♓	Aug 8	22:05	♒	Dec 21	12:13	♏	Apr 29	6:35	♎	Sept 10	7:22
♉	Mar 29	12:36	♈	Aug 10	22:10	♓	Dec 23	14:50	♐	May 1	17:22	♏	Sept 12	20:06
♊	Mar 31	17:08	♉	Aug 13	0:21	♈	Dec 25	17:40	♑	May 4	2:14	♐	Sept 15	8:28
♋	Apr 3	1:24	♊	Aug 15	5:41	♉	Dec 27	21:08	♒	May 6	9:03	♑	Sept 17	18:45
♌	Apr 5	12:58	♋	Aug 17	14:17	♊	Dec 30	1:32	♓	May 8	13:33	♒	Sept 20	1:30
♍	Apr 8	1:52	♌	Aug 20	1:28				♈	May 10	15:44	♓	Sept 22	4:27
♎	Apr 10	13:45	♍	Aug 22	14:11	**1980**			♉	May 12	16:24	♈	Sept 24	4:37
♏	Apr 12	23:16	♎	Aug 25	3:13	♋	Jan 1	7:29	♊	May 14	17:07	♉	Sept 26	3:53
♐	Apr 15	6:18	♏	Aug 27	15:12	♌	Jan 3	15:47	♋	May 16	19:52	♊	Sept 28	4:21
♑	Apr 17	11:23	♐	Aug 30	0:39	♍	Jan 6	2:48	♌	May 19	2:14	♋	Sept 30	7:46
♒	Apr 19	15:02	♑	Sept 1	6:33	♎	Jan 8	15:38	♍	May 21	12:32	♌	Oct 2	14:57
♓	Apr 21	17:41	♒	Sept 3	8:59	♏	Jan 11	3:55	♎	May 24	1:11	♍	Oct 5	1:19
♈	Apr 23	19:51	♓	Sept 5	9:03	♐	Jan 13	13:17	♏	May 26	13:37	♎	Oct 7	13:30
♉	Apr 25	22:27	♈	Sept 7	8:29	♑	Jan 15	18:51	♐	May 29	0:05	♏	Oct 10	2:15
♊	Apr 28	2:49	♉	Sept 9	9:12	♒	Jan 17	21:25	♑	May 31	8:14	♐	Oct 12	14:37
♋	Apr 30	10:11	♊	Sept 11	12:54	♓	Jan 19	22:33	♒	Jun 2	14:29	♑	Oct 15	1:37
♌	May 2	20:56	♋	Sept 13	20:27	♈	Jan 21	23:52	♓	Jun 4	19:10	♒	Oct 17	9:54
♍	May 5	9:41	♌	Sept 16	7:25	♉	Jan 24	2:31	♈	Jun 6	22:23	♓	Oct 19	14:31
♎	May 7	21:47	♍	Sept 18	20:15	♊	Jan 26	7:11	♉	Jun 9	0:29	♈	Oct 21	15:43
♏	May 10	7:10	♎	Sept 21	9:11	♋	Jan 28	14:02	♊	Jun 11	2:22	♉	Oct 23	14:55
♐	May 12	13:25	♏	Sept 23	20:54	♌	Jan 30	23:08	♋	Jun 13	5:29	♊	Oct 25	14:17
♑	May 14	17:25	♐	Sept 26	6:36	♍	Feb 2	10:21	♌	Jun 15	11:22	♋	Oct 27	16:00
♒	May 16	20:26	♑	Sept 28	13:40	♎	Feb 4	23:04	♍	Jun 17	20:47	♌	Oct 29	21:38
♓	May 18	23:18	♒	Sept 30	17:49	♏	Feb 7	11:46	♎	Jun 20	8:55	♍	Nov 1	7:18
♈	May 21	2:30	♓	Oct 2	19:23	♐	Feb 9	22:19	♏	Jun 22	21:26	♎	Nov 3	19:31
♉	May 23	6:20	♈	Oct 4	19:28	♑	Feb 12	5:12	♐	Jun 25	8:02	♏	Nov 6	8:19
♊	May 25	11:28	♉	Oct 6	19:45	♒	Feb 14	9:45	♑	Jun 27	15:46	♐	Nov 8	20:25
♋	May 27	18:51	♊	Oct 8	22:07	♓	Feb 16	8:54	♒	Jun 29	21:04	♑	Nov 11	7:15
♌	May 30	5:08	♋	Oct 11	4:09	♈	Feb 18	8:43	♓	Jul 2	0:48	♒	Nov 13	16:10
♍	Jun 1	17:41	♌	Oct 13	14:12	♉	Feb 20	9:35	♈	Jul 4	3:46	♓	Nov 15	22:21
♎	Jun 4	6:12	♍	Oct 16	2:51	♊	Feb 22	12:58	♉	Jul 6	6:30	♈	Nov 18	1:22
♏	Jun 6	16:05	♎	Oct 18	15:44	♋	Feb 24	19:34	♊	Jul 8	9:33	♉	Nov 20	1:51
♐	Jun 8	22:15	♏	Oct 21	3:02	♌	Feb 27	5:10	♋	Jul 10	13:44	♊	Nov 22	1:27
♑	Jun 11	1:23	♐	Oct 23	12:09	♍	Feb 29	16:53	♌	Jul 12	20:03	♋	Nov 24	2:19
♒	Jun 13	3:06	♑	Oct 25	19:11	♎	Mar 3	5:40	♍	Jul 15	5:11	♌	Nov 26	6:23

Table A-2 — The Moon (continued)

♍ Nov 28 14:37	♊ Apr 7 14:47	♉ Aug 20 7:43	**1982**	♒ May 13 22:44
♎ Dec 1 2:13	♋ Apr 9 16:34	♊ Aug 22 10:18	♈ Jan 2 1:33	♓ May 16 9:46
♏ Dec 3 15:00	♌ Apr 11 21:36	♋ Aug 24 13:17	♉ Jan 4 6:02	♈ May 18 17:04
♐ Dec 6 2:57	♍ Apr 14 5:56	♌ Aug 26 17:10	♊ Jan 6 7:48	♉ May 20 20:22
♑ Dec 8 13:12	♎ Apr 16 16:38	♍ Aug 28 22:32	♋ Jan 8 8:01	♊ May 22 20:54
♒ Dec 10 21:36	♏ Apr 19 4:39	♎ Aug 31 6:02	♌ Jan 10 8:21	♋ May 24 20:38
♓ Dec 13 4:03	♐ Apr 21 17:15	♏ Sept 2 16:10	♍ Jan 12 10:37	♌ May 26 21:27
♈ Dec 15 8:21	♑ Apr 24 5:31	♐ Sept 5 4:24	♎ Jan 14 16:17	♍ May 29 0:43
♉ Dec 17 10:36	♒ Apr 26 15:57	♑ Sept 7 16:48	♏ Jan 17 1:46	♎ May 31 7:02
♊ Dec 19 11:39	♓ Apr 28 22:56	♒ Sept 10 2:58	♐ Jan 19 14:00	♏ Jun 2 16:12
♋ Dec 21 13:03	♈ May 1 1:57	♓ Sept 12 9:34	♑ Jan 22 2:51	♐ Jun 5 3:31
♌ Dec 23 16:34	♉ May 3 1:59	♈ Sept 14 12:55	♒ Jan 24 14:25	♑ Jun 7 16:12
♍ Dec 25 23:32	♊ May 5 1:01	♉ Sept 16 14:30	♓ Jan 26 23:49	♒ Jun 10 5:08
♎ Dec 28 10:05	♋ May 7 1:18	♊ Sept 18 15:59	♈ Jan 29 6:58	♓ Jun 12 16:44
♏ Dec 30 22:36	♌ May 9 4:40	♋ Sept 20 18:39	♉ Jan 31 12:03	♈ Jun 15 1:20
	♍ May 11 11:55	♌ Sept 22 23:08	♊ Feb 2 15:20	♉ Jun 17 6:07
1981	♎ May 13 22:24	♍ Sept 25 5:29	♋ Feb 4 17:18	♊ Jun 19 7:34
♐ Jan 2 10:42	♏ May 16 10:37	♎ Sept 27 13:40	♌ Feb 6 18:50	♋ Jun 21 7:13
♑ Jan 4 20:41	♐ May 18 23:14	♏ Sept 29 23:53	♍ Feb 8 21:15	♌ Jun 23 6:57
♒ Jan 7 4:12	♑ May 21 11:20	♐ Oct 2 12:00	♎ Feb 11 2:02	♍ Jun 25 8:36
♓ Jan 9 9:42	♒ May 23 22:01	♑ Oct 5 0:49	♏ Feb 13 10:16	♎ Jun 27 13:30
♈ Jan 11 13:43	♓ May 26 6:05	♒ Oct 7 12:01	♐ Feb 15 21:45	♏ Jun 29 22:02
♉ Jan 13 16:45	♈ May 28 10:44	♓ Oct 9 19:32	♑ Feb 18 10:36	♐ Jul 2 9:25
♊ Jan 15 19:17	♉ May 30 12:10	♈ Oct 11 23:01	♒ Feb 20 22:15	♑ Jul 4 22:15
♋ Jan 17 22:08	♊ Jun 1 11:48	♉ Oct 13 23:43	♓ Feb 23 7:09	♒ Jul 7 11:03
♌ Jan 20 2:21	♋ Jun 3 11:38	♊ Oct 15 23:41	♈ Feb 25 13:17	♓ Jul 9 22:35
♍ Jan 22 9:02	♌ Jun 5 13:43	♋ Oct 18 0:52	♉ Feb 27 17:32	♈ Jul 12 7:49
♎ Jan 24 18:45	♍ Jun 7 19:25	♌ Oct 20 4:34	♊ Mar 1 20:50	♉ Jul 14 14:00
♏ Jan 27 6:49	♎ Jun 10 4:55	♍ Oct 22 11:05	♋ Mar 3 23:48	♊ Jul 16 17:03
♐ Jan 29 19:12	♏ Jun 12 16:54	♎ Oct 24 19:56	♌ Mar 6 2:50	♋ Jul 18 17:46
♑ Feb 1 5:37	♐ Jun 15 5:31	♏ Oct 27 6:38	♍ Mar 8 6:27	♌ Jul 20 17:35
♒ Feb 3 12:55	♑ Jun 17 17:21	♐ Oct 29 18:48	♎ Mar 10 11:34	♍ Jul 22 18:20
♓ Feb 5 17:21	♒ Jun 20 3:36	♑ Nov 1 7:46	♏ Mar 12 19:17	♎ Jul 24 21:45
♈ Feb 7 20:01	♓ Jun 22 11:44	♒ Nov 3 19:51	♐ Mar 15 6:03	♏ Jul 27 4:58
♉ Feb 9 22:11	♈ Jun 24 17:18	♓ Nov 6 4:52	♑ Mar 17 18:47	♐ Jul 29 15:48
♊ Feb 12 0:51	♉ Jun 26 20:16	♈ Nov 8 9:38	♒ Mar 20 6:53	♑ Aug 1 4:36
♋ Feb 14 4:43	♊ Jun 28 21:21	♉ Nov 10 10:44	♓ Mar 22 16:01	♒ Aug 3 17:17
♌ Feb 16 10:10	♋ Jun 30 21:57	♊ Nov 12 9:59	♈ Mar 24 21:37	♓ Aug 6 4:23
♍ Feb 18 17:34	♌ Jul 2 23:47	♋ Nov 14 9:37	♉ Mar 27 0:39	♈ Aug 8 13:21
♎ Feb 21 3:12	♍ Jul 5 4:26	♌ Nov 16 11:33	♊ Mar 29 2:44	♉ Aug 10 20:00
♏ Feb 23 14:54	♎ Jul 7 12:42	♍ Nov 18 16:53	♋ Mar 31 5:09	♊ Aug 13 0:22
♐ Feb 26 3:29	♏ Jul 10 0:02	♎ Nov 21 1:33	♌ Apr 2 8:36	♋ Aug 15 2:40
♑ Feb 28 14:46	♐ Jul 12 12:35	♏ Nov 23 12:36	♍ Apr 4 13:18	♌ Aug 17 3:40
♒ Mar 2 22:51	♑ Jul 15 0:19	♐ Nov 26 1:00	♎ Apr 6 19:26	♍ Aug 19 4:40
♓ Mar 5 3:12	♒ Jul 17 10:02	♑ Nov 28 13:53	♏ Apr 9 3:33	♎ Aug 21 7:22
♈ Mar 7 4:48	♓ Jul 19 17:26	♒ Dec 1 2:09	♐ Apr 11 14:07	♏ Aug 23 13:21
♉ Mar 9 5:22	♈ Jul 21 22:43	♓ Dec 3 12:16	♑ Apr 14 2:41	♐ Aug 25 23:11
♊ Mar 11 6:42	♉ Jul 24 2:18	♈ Dec 5 18:49	♒ Apr 16 15:18	♑ Aug 28 11:42
♋ Mar 13 10:06	♊ Jul 26 4:42	♉ Dec 7 21:31	♓ Apr 19 1:20	♒ Aug 31 0:23
♌ Mar 15 16:02	♋ Jul 28 6:41	♊ Dec 9 21:30	♈ Apr 21 7:23	♓ Sept 2 11:11
♍ Mar 18 0:20	♌ Jul 30 9:20	♋ Dec 11 20:40	♉ Apr 23 9:59	♈ Sept 4 19:24
♎ Mar 20 10:31	♍ Aug 1 13:54	♌ Dec 13 21:08	♊ Apr 25 10:48	♉ Sept 7 1:27
♏ Mar 22 22:14	♎ Aug 3 21:24	♍ Dec 16 0:38	♋ Apr 27 11:43	♊ Sept 9 5:57
♐ Mar 25 10:51	♏ Aug 6 7:58	♎ Dec 18 7:58	♌ Apr 29 14:09	♋ Sept 11 9:18
♑ Mar 27 22:52	♐ Aug 8 20:22	♏ Dec 20 18:39	♍ May 1 18:45	♌ Sept 13 11:46
♒ Mar 30 8:15	♑ Aug 11 8:20	♐ Dec 23 7:11	♎ May 4 1:32	♍ Sept 15 13:57
♓ Apr 1 13:41	♒ Aug 13 17:56	♑ Dec 25 19:59	♏ May 6 10:24	♎ Sept 17 17:03
♈ Apr 3 15:25	♓ Aug 16 0:34	♒ Dec 28 7:54	♐ May 8 21:17	♏ Sept 19 22:32
♉ Apr 5 15:04	♈ Aug 18 4:49	♓ Dec 30 18:01	♑ May 11 9:50	♐ Sept 22 7:30

(continued)

Table A-2 — The Moon (continued)

Sign	Date	Time	Sign	Date	Time	Sign	Date	Time	Sign	Date	Time	Sign	Date	Time
♑	Sept 24	19:31	♎	Feb 1	4:47	♍	Jun 15	18:38	♌	Oct 28	13:50	♉	Mar 6	13:09
♒	Sept 27	8:21	♏	Feb 3	9:32	♎	Jun 17	21:36	♍	Oct 30	16:33	♊	Mar 8	23:30
♓	Sept 29	19:18	♐	Feb 5	18:28	♏	Jun 20	2:59	♎	Nov 1	18:31	♋	Mar 11	6:48
♈	Oct 2	3:06	♑	Feb 8	6:33	♐	Jun 22	10:55	♏	Nov 3	20:53	♌	Mar 13	10:21
♉	Oct 4	8:09	♒	Feb 10	19:40	♑	Jun 24	21:08	♐	Nov 6	1:09	♍	Mar 15	10:47
♊	Oct 6	11:39	♓	Feb 13	8:02	♒	Jun 27	9:07	♑	Nov 8	8:31	♎	Mar 17	9:51
♋	Oct 8	14:39	♈	Feb 15	18:46	♓	Jun 29	21:52	♒	Nov 10	19:10	♏	Mar 19	9:49
♌	Oct 10	17:44	♉	Feb 18	3:31	♈	Jul 2	9:47	♓	Nov 13	7:41	♐	Mar 21	12:41
♍	Oct 12	21:09	♊	Feb 20	9:52	♉	Jul 4	19:05	♈	Nov 15	19:36	♑	Mar 23	19:36
♎	Oct 15	1:23	♋	Feb 22	13:31	♊	Jul 7	0:41	♉	Nov 18	5:06	♒	Mar 26	6:09
♏	Oct 17	7:21	♌	Feb 24	14:47	♋	Jul 9	2:50	♊	Nov 20	11:45	♓	Mar 28	18:37
♐	Oct 19	16:02	♍	Feb 26	14:49	♌	Jul 11	2:54	♋	Nov 22	16:10	♈	Mar 31	7:14
♑	Oct 22	3:38	♎	Feb 28	15:30	♍	Jul 13	2:43	♌	Nov 24	19:19	♉	Apr 2	18:55
♒	Oct 24	16:36	♏	Mar 2	18:51	♎	Jul 15	4:10	♍	Nov 26	22:02	♊	Apr 5	5:04
♓	Oct 27	4:12	♐	Mar 5	2:15	♏	Jul 17	8:38	♎	Nov 29	0:57	♋	Apr 7	12:59
♈	Oct 29	12:25	♑	Mar 7	13:29	♐	Jul 19	16:31	♏	Dec 1	4:41	♌	Apr 9	18:01
♉	Oct 31	17:04	♒	Mar 10	2:30	♑	Jul 22	3:11	♐	Dec 3	9:56	♍	Apr 11	20:11
♊	Nov 2	19:23	♓	Mar 12	14:47	♒	Jul 24	15:26	♑	Dec 5	17:28	♎	Apr 13	20:29
♋	Nov 4	20:59	♈	Mar 15	1:00	♓	Jul 27	4:11	♒	Dec 8	3:39	♏	Apr 15	20:41
♌	Nov 6	23:10	♉	Mar 17	9:04	♈	Jul 29	16:21	♓	Dec 10	15:53	♐	Apr 17	22:44
♍	Nov 9	2:40	♊	Mar 19	15:20	♉	Aug 1	2:37	♈	Dec 13	4:17	♑	Apr 20	4:10
♎	Nov 11	7:46	♋	Mar 21	19:52	♊	Aug 3	9:43	♉	Dec 15	14:33	♒	Apr 22	13:27
♏	Nov 13	14:42	♌	Mar 23	22:43	♋	Aug 5	13:09	♊	Dec 17	21:23	♓	Apr 25	1:26
♐	Nov 15	23:52	♍	Mar 26	0:18	♌	Aug 7	13:37	♋	Dec 20	1:02	♈	Apr 27	14:02
♑	Nov 18	11:21	♎	Mar 28	1:48	♍	Aug 9	12:49	♌	Dec 22	2:44	♉	Apr 30	1:30
♒	Nov 21	0:20	♏	Mar 30	4:57	♎	Aug 11	12:51	♍	Dec 24	4:01	♊	May 2	11:02
♓	Nov 23	12:43	♐	Apr 1	11:20	♏	Aug 13	15:44	♎	Dec 26	6:18	♋	May 4	18:26
♈	Nov 25	22:07	♑	Apr 3	21:30	♐	Aug 15	22:33	♏	Dec 28	10:27	♌	May 6	23:43
♉	Nov 28	3:31	♒	Apr 6	10:06	♑	Aug 18	8:59	♐	Dec 30	16:44	♍	May 9	3:02
♊	Nov 30	5:36	♓	Apr 8	22:30	♒	Aug 20	21:25				♎	May 11	4:54
♋	Dec 2	5:58	♈	Apr 11	8:37	♓	Aug 23	10:10	**1984**			♏	May 13	6:22
♌	Dec 4	6:26	♉	Apr 13	15:59	♈	Aug 25	22:08	♑	Jan 2	1:07	♐	May 15	8:50
♍	Dec 6	8:32	♊	Apr 15	21:15	♉	Aug 28	8:38	♒	Jan 4	11:30	♑	May 17	13:43
♎	Dec 8	13:11	♋	Apr 18	1:14	♊	Aug 30	16:49	♓	Jan 6	23:34	♒	May 19	21:55
♏	Dec 10	20:34	♌	Apr 20	4:26	♋	Sept 1	21:53	♈	Jan 9	12:15	♓	May 22	9:09
♐	Dec 13	6:27	♍	Apr 22	7:12	♌	Sept 3	23:47	♉	Jan 11	23:36	♈	May 24	21:39
♑	Dec 15	18:15	♎	Apr 24	10:04	♍	Sept 5	23:36	♊	Jan 14	7:40	♉	May 27	9:13
♒	Dec 18	7:12	♏	Apr 26	14:04	♎	Sept 7	23:13	♋	Jan 16	11:47	♊	May 29	18:23
♓	Dec 20	19:56	♐	Apr 28	20:28	♏	Sept 10	0:49	♌	Jan 18	12:49	♋	Jun 1	0:53
♈	Dec 23	6:34	♑	May 1	6:01	♐	Sept 12	6:08	♍	Jan 20	12:35	♌	Jun 3	5:19
♉	Dec 25	13:37	♒	May 3	18:09	♑	Sept 14	15:34	♎	Jan 22	13:07	♍	Jun 5	8:27
♊	Dec 27	16:49	♓	May 6	6:43	♒	Sept 17	3:45	♏	Jan 24	16:04	♎	Jun 7	11:03
♋	Dec 29	17:12	♈	May 8	17:16	♓	Sept 19	16:30	♐	Jan 26	22:12	♏	Jun 9	13:48
♌	Dec 31	16:33	♉	May 11	0:36	♈	Sept 22	4:10	♑	Jan 29	7:12	♐	Jun 11	17:26
			♊	May 13	5:03	♉	Sept 24	14:12	♒	Jan 31	18:11	♑	Jun 13	22:48
1983			♋	May 15	7:48	♊	Sept 26	22:24	♓	Feb 3	6:22	♒	Jun 16	6:41
♍	Jan 2	16:49	♌	May 17	10:01	♋	Sept 29	4:24	♈	Feb 5	19:04	♓	Jun 18	17:18
♎	Jan 4	19:44	♍	May 19	12:37	♌	Oct 1	7:54	♉	Feb 8	7:05	♈	Jun 21	5:40
♏	Jan 7	2:16	♎	May 21	16:11	♍	Oct 3	9:15	♊	Feb 10	16:39	♉	Jun 23	17:38
♐	Jan 9	12:14	♏	May 23	21:17	♎	Oct 5	9:42	♋	Feb 12	22:20	♊	Jun 26	3:04
♑	Jan 12	0:26	♐	May 26	4:27	♏	Oct 7	11:06	♌	Feb 15	0:09	♋	Jun 28	9:09
♒	Jan 14	13:26	♑	May 28	14:07	♐	Oct 9	15:21	♍	Feb 16	23:32	♌	Jun 30	12:30
♓	Jan 17	2:02	♒	May 31	2:00	♑	Oct 11	23:30	♎	Feb 18	22:39	♍	Jul 2	14:28
♈	Jan 19	13:08	♓	Jun 2	14:42	♒	Oct 14	11:00	♏	Feb 20	23:44	♎	Jul 4	16:27
♉	Jan 21	21:36	♈	Jun 5	1:59	♓	Oct 16	23:41	♐	Feb 23	4:22	♏	Jul 6	19:28
♊	Jan 24	2:40	♉	Jun 7	10:05	♈	Oct 19	11:18	♑	Feb 25	12:49	♐	Jul 9	0:03
♋	Jan 26	4:28	♊	Jun 9	14:37	♉	Oct 21	20:47	♒	Feb 28	0:02	♑	Jul 11	6:23
♌	Jan 28	4:10	♋	Jun 11	16:32	♊	Oct 24	4:10	♓	Mar 1	12:29	♒	Jul 13	14:41
♍	Jan 30	3:35	♌	Jun 13	17:21	♋	Oct 26	9:47	♈	Mar 4	1:07	♓	Jul 16	1:10

Table A-2 — The Moon *(continued)*

♈ Jul 18 13:26	♓ Nov 29 10:33	♐ Apr 8 5:18	♏ Aug 20 20:51	**1986**
♉ Jul 21 1:52	♈ Dec 1 22:42	♑ Apr 10 7:57	♐ Aug 22 23:36	♎ Jan 2 15:45
♊ Jul 23 12:10	♉ Dec 4 11:20	♒ Apr 12 14:04	♑ Aug 25 3:24	♏ Jan 4 19:44
♋ Jul 25 18:44	♊ Dec 6 22:24	♓ Apr 14 23:30	♒ Aug 27 8:31	♐ Jan 6 21:47
♌ Jul 27 21:41	♋ Dec 9 6:56	♈ Apr 17 11:18	♓ Aug 29 15:25	♑ Jan 8 22:42
♍ Jul 29 22:29	♌ Dec 11 13:08	♉ Apr 20 0:12	♈ Sept 1 0:42	♒ Jan 11 0:01
♎ Jul 31 23:03	♍ Dec 13 17:35	♊ Apr 22 13:01	♉ Sept 3 12:28	♓ Jan 13 3:39
♏ Aug 3 1:04	♎ Dec 15 20:52	♋ Apr 25 0:26	♊ Sept 6 1:27	♈ Jan 15 11:03
♐ Aug 5 5:30	♏ Dec 17 23:27	♌ Apr 27 9:10	♋ Sept 8 13:10	♉ Jan 17 22:14
♑ Aug 7 12:24	♐ Dec 20 1:58	♍ Apr 29 14:24	♌ Sept 10 21:27	♊ Jan 20 11:12
♒ Aug 9 21:25	♑ Dec 22 5:21	♎ May 1 16:22	♍ Sept 13 1:52	♋ Jan 22 23:14
♓ Aug 12 8:13	♒ Dec 24 10:47	♏ May 3 16:17	♎ Sept 15 3:34	♌ Jan 25 8:47
♈ Aug 14 20:28	♓ Dec 26 19:18	♐ May 5 15:56	♏ Sept 17 4:17	♍ Jan 27 15:51
♉ Aug 17 9:13	♈ Dec 29 6:49	♑ May 7 17:11	♐ Sept 19 5:40	♎ Jan 29 21:10
♊ Aug 19 20:31	♉ Dec 31 19:36	♒ May 9 21:38	♑ Sept 21 8:49	♏ Feb 1 1:19
♋ Aug 22 4:20		♓ May 12 5:56	♒ Sept 23 14:11	♐ Feb 3 4:31
♌ Aug 24 8:00	**1985**	♈ May 14 17:25	♓ Sept 25 21:50	♑ Feb 5 7:01
♍ Aug 26 8:32	♊ Jan 3 7:00	♉ May 17 6:23	♈ Sept 28 7:43	♒ Feb 7 9:35
♎ Aug 28 7:57	♋ Jan 5 15:18	♊ May 19 19:01	♉ Sept 30 19:35	♓ Feb 9 13:32
♏ Aug 30 8:23	♌ Jan 7 20:28	♋ May 22 6:05	♊ Oct 3 8:36	♈ Feb 11 20:21
♐ Sept 1 11:30	♍ Jan 9 23:40	♌ May 24 14:54	♋ Oct 5 20:59	♉ Feb 14 6:38
♑ Sept 3 17:55	♎ Jan 12 2:13	♍ May 26 21:06	♌ Oct 8 6:33	♊ Feb 16 19:17
♒ Sept 6 3:11	♏ Jan 14 5:07	♎ May 29 0:40	♍ Oct 10 12:09	♋ Feb 19 7:39
♓ Sept 8 14:24	♐ Jan 16 8:48	♏ May 31 2:07	♎ Oct 12 14:12	♌ Feb 21 17:25
♈ Sept 11 2:47	♑ Jan 18 13:29	♐ Jun 2 2:33	♏ Oct 14 14:13	♍ Feb 23 23:58
♉ Sept 13 15:33	♒ Jan 20 19:38	♑ Jun 4 3:34	♐ Oct 16 14:05	♎ Feb 26 4:07
♊ Sept 16 3:26	♓ Jan 23 4:02	♒ Jun 6 6:52	♑ Oct 18 15:35	♏ Feb 28 7:06
♋ Sept 18 12:36	♈ Jan 25 15:05	♓ Jun 8 13:46	♒ Oct 20 19:54	♐ Mar 2 9:51
♌ Sept 20 17:49	♉ Jan 28 3:53	♈ Jun 11 0:24	♓ Oct 23 3:27	♑ Mar 4 12:56
♍ Sept 22 19:19	♊ Jan 30 16:01	♉ Jun 13 13:11	♈ Oct 25 13:47	♒ Mar 6 16:42
♎ Sept 24 18:41	♋ Feb 2 0:59	♊ Jun 16 1:45	♉ Oct 28 1:59	♓ Mar 8 21:48
♏ Sept 26 18:04	♌ Feb 4 6:02	♋ Jun 18 12:22	♊ Oct 30 14:59	♈ Mar 11 5:03
♐ Sept 28 19:32	♍ Feb 6 8:09	♌ Jun 20 20:32	♋ Nov 2 3:31	♉ Mar 13 15:04
♑ Oct 1 0:28	♎ Feb 8 9:10	♍ Jun 23 2:32	♌ Nov 4 14:04	♊ Mar 16 3:23
♒ Oct 3 9:03	♏ Feb 10 10:49	♎ Jun 25 6:48	♍ Nov 6 21:18	♋ Mar 18 16:04
♓ Oct 5 20:19	♐ Feb 12 14:09	♏ Jun 27 9:37	♎ Nov 9 0:52	♌ Mar 21 2:38
♈ Oct 8 8:51	♑ Feb 14 19:27	♐ Jun 29 11:30	♏ Nov 11 1:31	♍ Mar 23 9:39
♉ Oct 10 21:28	♒ Feb 17 2:36	♑ Jul 1 13:22	♐ Nov 13 0:52	♎ Mar 25 13:22
♊ Oct 13 9:14	♓ Feb 19 11:38	♒ Jul 3 16:36	♑ Nov 15 0:53	♏ Mar 27 15:05
♋ Oct 15 19:00	♈ Feb 21 22:43	♓ Jul 5 22:40	♒ Nov 17 3:25	♐ Mar 29 16:20
♌ Oct 18 1:41	♉ Feb 24 11:27	♈ Jul 8 8:20	♓ Nov 19 9:42	♑ Mar 31 18:25
♍ Oct 20 4:56	♊ Feb 27 0:11	♉ Jul 10 20:44	♈ Nov 21 19:42	♒ Apr 2 22:11
♎ Oct 22 5:32	♋ Mar 1 10:23	♊ Jul 13 9:23	♉ Nov 24 8:07	♓ Apr 5 4:03
♏ Oct 24 5:08	♌ Mar 3 16:28	♋ Jul 15 19:54	♊ Nov 26 21:08	♈ Apr 7 12:12
♐ Oct 26 5:43	♍ Mar 5 18:43	♌ Jul 18 3:25	♋ Nov 29 9:23	♉ Apr 9 22:36
♑ Oct 28 9:05	♎ Mar 7 18:47	♍ Jul 20 8:29	♌ Dec 1 19:59	♊ Apr 12 10:51
♒ Oct 30 16:13	♏ Mar 9 18:47	♎ Jul 22 12:10	♍ Dec 4 4:14	♋ Apr 14 23:42
♓ Nov 2 2:50	♐ Mar 11 20:29	♏ Jul 24 15:16	♎ Dec 6 9:33	♌ Apr 17 11:10
♈ Nov 4 15:20	♑ Mar 14 0:55	♐ Jul 26 18:12	♏ Dec 8 11:56	♍ Apr 19 19:24
♉ Nov 7 3:53	♒ Mar 16 8:11	♑ Jul 28 21:21	♐ Dec 10 12:13	♎ Apr 21 23:50
♊ Nov 9 15:10	♓ Mar 18 17:50	♒ Jul 31 1:25	♑ Dec 12 11:59	♏ Apr 24 1:15
♋ Nov 12 0:31	♈ Mar 21 5:20	♓ Aug 2 7:33	♒ Dec 14 13:15	♐ Apr 26 1:16
♌ Nov 14 7:34	♉ Mar 23 18:06	♈ Aug 4 16:43	♓ Dec 16 17:50	♑ Apr 28 1:41
♍ Nov 16 12:08	♊ Mar 26 7:02	♉ Aug 7 4:41	♈ Dec 19 2:37	♒ Apr 30 4:06
♎ Nov 18 14:29	♋ Mar 28 18:13	♊ Aug 9 17:31	♉ Dec 21 14:41	♓ May 2 9:30
♏ Nov 20 15:30	♌ Mar 31 1:51	♋ Aug 12 4:28	♊ Dec 24 3:45	♈ May 4 18:01
♐ Nov 22 16:34	♍ Apr 2 5:25	♌ Aug 14 11:57	♋ Dec 26 15:44	♉ May 7 4:59
♑ Nov 24 19:17	♎ Apr 4 5:54	♍ Aug 16 16:15	♌ Dec 29 1:44	♊ May 9 17:26
♒ Nov 27 1:06	♏ Apr 6 5:10	♎ Aug 18 18:44	♍ Dec 31 9:43	♋ May 12 6:18

(continued)

Table A-2 — The Moon (continued)

♌ May 14 18:15	♋ Sept 25 16:44	♈ Feb 1 21:09	♓ Jun 16 7:54	♒ Oct 29 2:27
♍ May 17 3:45	♌ Sept 28 4:39	♉ Feb 4 3:53	♈ Jun 18 11:56	♓ Oct 31 5:19
♎ May 19 9:41	♍ Sept 30 13:57	♊ Feb 6 14:23	♉ Jun 20 19:09	♈ Nov 2 8:40
♏ May 21 12:02	♎ Oct 2 20:03	♋ Feb 9 2:55	♊ Jun 23 4:54	♉ Nov 4 13:02
♐ May 23 11:57	♏ Oct 4 23:35	♌ Feb 11 15:21	♋ Jun 25 16:22	♊ Nov 6 19:16
♑ May 25 11:15	♐ Oct 7 1:48	♍ Feb 14 2:26	♌ Jun 28 4:52	♋ Nov 9 4:10
♒ May 27 12:00	♑ Oct 9 3:52	♎ Feb 16 11:44	♍ Jun 30 17:34	♌ Nov 11 15:45
♓ May 29 15:54	♒ Oct 11 6:45	♏ Feb 18 19:04	♎ Jul 3 4:55	♍ Nov 14 4:29
♈ May 31 23:43	♓ Oct 13 11:03	♐ Feb 21 0:09	♏ Jul 5 13:03	♎ Nov 16 15:48
♉ Jun 3 10:45	♈ Oct 15 17:13	♑ Feb 23 2:57	♐ Jul 7 17:05	♏ Nov 18 23:47
♊ Jun 5 23:26	♉ Oct 18 1:35	♒ Feb 25 4:08	♑ Jul 9 17:43	♐ Nov 21 4:16
♋ Jun 8 12:16	♊ Oct 20 12:15	♓ Feb 27 5:07	♒ Jul 11 16:49	♑ Nov 23 6:32
♌ Jun 11 0:11	♋ Oct 23 0:37	♈ Mar 1 7:37	♓ Jul 13 16:36	♒ Nov 25 8:13
♍ Jun 13 10:18	♌ Oct 25 13:02	♉ Mar 3 13:11	♈ Jul 15 19:00	♓ Nov 27 10:40
♎ Jun 15 17:38	♍ Oct 27 23:20	♊ Mar 5 22:26	♉ Jul 18 1:04	♈ Nov 29 14:36
♏ Jun 17 21:36	♎ Oct 30 6:04	♋ Mar 8 10:24	♊ Jul 20 10:33	♉ Dec 1 20:06
♐ Jun 19 22:36	♏ Nov 1 9:19	♌ Mar 10 22:54	♋ Jul 22 22:13	♊ Dec 4 3:13
♑ Jun 21 22:00	♐ Nov 3 10:19	♍ Mar 13 9:55	♌ Jul 25 10:50	♋ Dec 6 12:20
♒ Jun 23 21:50	♑ Nov 5 10:49	♎ Mar 15 18:34	♍ Jul 27 23:26	♌ Dec 8 23:40
♓ Jun 26 0:13	♒ Nov 7 12:29	♏ Mar 18 0:57	♎ Jul 30 10:59	♍ Dec 11 12:30
♈ Jun 28 6:35	♓ Nov 9 16:30	♐ Mar 20 5:32	♏ Aug 1 20:09	♎ Dec 14 0:40
♉ Jun 30 16:54	♈ Nov 11 23:14	♑ Mar 22 8:48	♐ Aug 4 1:47	♏ Dec 16 9:41
♊ Jul 3 5:32	♉ Nov 14 8:24	♒ Mar 24 11:18	♑ Aug 6 3:51	♐ Dec 18 14:33
♋ Jul 5 18:19	♊ Nov 16 19:26	♓ Mar 26 13:46	♒ Aug 8 3:37	♑ Dec 20 16:07
♌ Jul 8 5:56	♋ Nov 19 7:46	♈ Mar 28 17:12	♓ Aug 10 3:01	♒ Dec 22 16:20
♍ Jul 10 15:50	♌ Nov 21 20:25	♉ Mar 30 22:46	♈ Aug 12 4:09	♓ Dec 24 17:10
♎ Jul 12 23:40	♍ Nov 24 7:46	♊ Apr 2 7:16	♉ Aug 14 8:38	♈ Dec 26 20:05
♏ Jul 15 4:58	♎ Nov 26 15:59	♋ Apr 4 18:33	♊ Aug 16 16:59	♉ Dec 29 1:37
♐ Jul 17 7:34	♏ Nov 28 20:13	♌ Apr 7 7:04	♋ Aug 19 4:19	♊ Dec 31 9:29
♑ Jul 19 8:10	♐ Nov 30 21:08	♍ Apr 9 18:28	♌ Aug 21 16:58	
♒ Jul 21 8:17	♑ Dec 2 20:28	♎ Apr 12 3:06	♍ Aug 24 5:23	**1988**
♓ Jul 23 9:59	♒ Dec 4 20:23	♏ Apr 14 8:41	♎ Aug 26 16:35	♋ Jan 2 19:17
♈ Jul 25 15:02	♓ Dec 6 22:48	♐ Apr 16 12:01	♏ Aug 29 1:49	♌ Jan 5 6:47
♉ Jul 28 0:11	♈ Dec 9 4:49	♑ Apr 18 14:21	♐ Aug 31 8:24	♍ Jan 7 19:35
♊ Jul 30 12:19	♉ Dec 11 14:10	♒ Apr 20 16:45	♑ Sept 2 12:04	♎ Jan 10 8:17
♋ Aug 2 1:04	♊ Dec 14 1:41	♓ Apr 22 20:02	♒ Sept 4 13:22	♏ Jan 12 18:39
♌ Aug 4 12:26	♋ Dec 16 14:09	♈ Apr 25 0:41	♓ Sept 6 13:37	♐ Jan 15 0:58
♍ Aug 6 21:44	♌ Dec 19 2:44	♉ Apr 27 7:06	♈ Sept 8 14:34	♑ Jan 17 3:15
♎ Aug 9 5:05	♍ Dec 21 14:30	♊ Apr 29 15:43	♉ Sept 10 17:57	♒ Jan 19 3:02
♏ Aug 11 10:36	♎ Dec 24 0:05	♋ May 2 2:39	♊ Sept 13 0:55	♓ Jan 21 2:27
♐ Aug 13 14:17	♏ Dec 26 6:06	♌ May 4 15:06	♋ Sept 15 11:22	♈ Jan 23 3:31
♑ Aug 15 16:22	♐ Dec 28 8:19	♍ May 7 3:07	♌ Sept 17 23:50	♉ Jan 25 7:36
♒ Aug 17 17:44	♑ Dec 30 7:54	♎ May 9 12:29	♍ Sept 20 12:13	♊ Jan 27 15:02
♓ Aug 19 19:52		♏ May 11 18:09	♎ Sept 22 22:58	♋ Jan 30 1:11
♈ Aug 22 0:27	**1987**	♐ May 13 20:41	♏ Sept 25 7:30	♌ Feb 1 13:06
♉ Aug 24 8:36	♒ Jan 1 6:54	♑ May 15 21:37	♐ Sept 27 13:49	♍ Feb 4 1:54
♊ Aug 26 20:00	♓ Jan 3 7:36	♒ May 17 22:42	♑ Sept 29 18:08	♎ Feb 6 14:36
♋ Aug 29 8:40	♈ Jan 5 11:51	♓ May 20 1:24	♒ Oct 1 20:51	♏ Feb 9 1:42
♌ Aug 31 20:08	♉ Jan 7 20:13	♈ May 22 6:23	♓ Oct 3 22:39	♐ Feb 11 9:36
♍ Sept 3 5:06	♊ Jan 10 7:39	♉ May 24 13:39	♈ Oct 6 0:35	♑ Feb 13 13:36
♎ Sept 5 11:33	♋ Jan 12 20:18	♊ May 26 22:55	♉ Oct 8 3:57	♒ Feb 15 14:25
♏ Sept 7 16:12	♌ Jan 15 8:45	♋ May 29 9:59	♊ Oct 10 10:03	♓ Feb 17 13:44
♐ Sept 9 19:40	♍ Jan 17 20:15	♌ May 31 22:25	♋ Oct 12 19:31	♈ Feb 19 13:35
♑ Sept 11 22:28	♎ Jan 20 6:09	♍ Jun 3 10:56	♌ Oct 15 7:34	♉ Feb 21 15:50
♒ Sept 14 1:07	♏ Jan 22 13:30	♎ Jun 5 21:24	♍ Oct 17 20:06	♊ Feb 23 21:42
♓ Sept 16 4:27	♐ Jan 24 17:35	♏ Jun 8 4:06	♎ Oct 20 6:50	♋ Feb 26 7:12
♈ Sept 18 9:33	♑ Jan 26 18:42	♐ Jun 10 6:53	♏ Oct 22 14:41	♌ Feb 28 19:12
♉ Sept 20 17:25	♒ Jan 28 18:17	♑ Jun 12 7:05	♐ Oct 24 19:57	♍ Mar 2 8:06
♊ Sept 23 4:13	♓ Jan 30 18:24	♒ Jun 14 6:45	♑ Oct 26 23:33	♎ Mar 4 20:32

Table A-2 — The Moon *(continued)*

Sign	Date	Time	Sign	Date	Time	Sign	Date	Time	Sign	Date	Time	Sign	Date	Time
♏	Mar 7	7:27	♎	Jul 19	10:22	♍	Nov 30	7:00	♊	Apr 8	20:31	♉	Aug 21	10:10
♐	Mar 9	15:59	♏	Jul 21	22:13	♎	Dec 2	19:56	♋	Apr 10	23:58	♊	Aug 23	12:39
♑	Mar 11	21:31	♐	Jul 24	6:42	♏	Dec 5	7:51	♌	Apr 13	7:31	♋	Aug 25	17:13
♒	Mar 14	0:08	♑	Jul 26	11:07	♐	Dec 7	16:55	♍	Apr 15	18:39	♌	Aug 28	0:12
♓	Mar 16	0:42	♒	Jul 28	12:25	♑	Dec 9	23:07	♎	Apr 18	7:31	♍	Aug 30	9:29
♈	Mar 18	0:45	♓	Jul 30	12:23	♒	Dec 12	3:25	♏	Apr 20	20:13	♎	Sept 1	20:47
♉	Mar 20	2:05	♈	Aug 1	12:53	♓	Dec 14	6:53	♐	Apr 23	7:38	♏	Sept 4	9:23
♊	Mar 22	6:21	♉	Aug 3	15:24	♈	Dec 16	10:03	♑	Apr 25	17:15	♐	Sept 6	21:51
♋	Mar 24	14:27	♊	Aug 5	20:43	♉	Dec 18	13:11	♒	Apr 28	0:33	♑	Sept 9	8:13
♌	Mar 27	1:54	♋	Aug 8	4:52	♊	Dec 20	16:43	♓	Apr 30	5:03	♒	Sept 11	15:02
♍	Mar 29	14:49	♌	Aug 10	15:26	♋	Dec 22	21:35	♈	May 2	6:50	♓	Sept 13	18:08
♎	Apr 1	3:05	♍	Aug 13	3:46	♌	Dec 25	4:57	♉	May 4	6:55	♈	Sept 15	18:38
♏	Apr 3	13:26	♎	Aug 15	16:52	♍	Dec 27	15:27	♊	May 6	7:03	♉	Sept 17	18:22
♐	Apr 5	21:29	♏	Aug 18	5:12	♎	Dec 30	4:09	♋	May 8	9:19	♊	Sept 19	19:16
♑	Apr 8	3:19	♐	Aug 20	14:55				♌	May 10	15:23	♋	Sept 21	22:50
♒	Apr 10	7:10	♑	Aug 22	20:49	**1989**			♍	May 13	1:30	♌	Sept 24	5:44
♓	Apr 12	9:24	♒	Aug 24	23:05	♏	Jan 1	16:34	♎	May 15	14:07	♍	Sept 26	15:32
♈	Apr 14	10:47	♓	Aug 26	23:01	♐	Jan 4	2:12	♏	May 18	2:48	♎	Sept 29	3:15
♉	Apr 16	12:31	♈	Aug 28	22:29	♑	Jan 6	8:14	♐	May 20	13:52	♏	Oct 1	15:53
♊	Apr 18	16:10	♉	Aug 30	23:22	♒	Jan 8	11:31	♑	May 22	22:54	♐	Oct 4	4:29
♋	Apr 20	23:04	♊	Sept 2	3:11	♓	Jan 10	13:31	♒	May 25	6:01	♑	Oct 6	15:45
♌	Apr 23	9:34	♋	Sept 4	10:37	♈	Jan 12	15:36	♓	May 27	11:13	♒	Oct 9	0:06
♍	Apr 25	22:16	♌	Sept 6	21:14	♉	Jan 14	18:36	♈	May 29	14:25	♓	Oct 11	4:37
♎	Apr 28	10:37	♍	Sept 9	9:48	♊	Jan 16	22:57	♉	May 31	15:59	♈	Oct 13	5:41
♏	Apr 30	20:39	♎	Sept 11	22:51	♋	Jan 19	4:57	♊	Jun 2	17:02	♉	Oct 15	4:52
♐	May 3	3:52	♏	Sept 14	11:07	♌	Jan 21	13:02	♋	Jun 4	19:17	♊	Oct 17	4:19
♑	May 5	8:54	♐	Sept 16	21:25	♍	Jan 23	23:32	♌	Jun 7	0:28	♋	Oct 19	6:09
♒	May 7	12:37	♑	Sept 19	4:45	♎	Jan 26	12:01	♍	Jun 9	9:29	♌	Oct 21	11:47
♓	May 9	15:39	♒	Sept 21	8:43	♏	Jan 29	0:49	♎	Jun 11	21:31	♍	Oct 23	21:15
♈	May 11	18:23	♓	Sept 23	9:51	♐	Jan 31	11:30	♏	Jun 14	10:11	♎	Oct 26	9:11
♉	May 13	21:22	♈	Sept 25	9:29	♑	Feb 2	18:30	♐	Jun 16	21:12	♏	Oct 28	21:56
♊	May 16	1:31	♉	Sept 27	9:29	♒	Feb 4	21:51	♑	Jun 19	5:41	♐	Oct 31	10:23
♋	May 18	8:05	♊	Sept 29	11:43	♓	Feb 6	22:52	♒	Jun 21	11:57	♑	Nov 2	21:46
♌	May 20	17:51	♋	Oct 1	17:39	♈	Feb 8	23:18	♓	Jun 23	16:36	♒	Nov 5	7:09
♍	May 23	6:12	♌	Oct 4	3:31	♉	Feb 11	0:45	♈	Jun 25	20:06	♓	Nov 7	13:25
♎	May 25	18:49	♍	Oct 6	16:01	♊	Feb 13	4:22	♉	Jun 27	22:45	♈	Nov 9	16:08
♏	May 28	5:06	♎	Oct 9	5:03	♋	Feb 15	10:40	♊	Jun 30	1:08	♉	Nov 11	16:09
♐	May 30	11:57	♏	Oct 11	16:58	♌	Feb 17	19:33	♋	Jul 2	4:19	♊	Nov 13	15:19
♑	Jun 1	15:58	♐	Oct 14	2:58	♍	Feb 20	6:34	♌	Jul 4	9:37	♋	Nov 15	15:51
♒	Jun 3	18:34	♑	Oct 16	10:44	♎	Feb 22	19:05	♍	Jul 6	18:04	♌	Nov 17	19:45
♓	Jun 5	21:00	♒	Oct 18	16:05	♏	Feb 25	7:57	♎	Jul 9	5:30	♍	Nov 20	3:54
♈	Jun 8	0:04	♓	Oct 20	18:58	♐	Feb 27	19:29	♏	Jul 11	18:09	♎	Nov 22	15:25
♉	Jun 10	4:02	♈	Oct 22	19:59	♑	Mar 2	3:58	♐	Jul 14	5:31	♏	Nov 25	4:13
♊	Jun 12	9:14	♉	Oct 24	20:22	♒	Mar 4	8:36	♑	Jul 16	14:01	♐	Nov 27	16:30
♋	Jun 14	16:19	♊	Oct 26	21:55	♓	Mar 6	9:59	♒	Jul 18	19:35	♑	Nov 30	3:26
♌	Jun 17	1:57	♋	Oct 29	2:28	♈	Mar 8	9:36	♓	Jul 20	23:07	♒	Dec 2	12:42
♍	Jun 19	14:03	♌	Oct 31	11:03	♉	Mar 10	9:25	♈	Jul 23	1:41	♓	Dec 4	19:48
♎	Jun 22	2:57	♍	Nov 2	23:02	♊	Mar 12	11:16	♉	Jul 25	4:10	♈	Dec 7	0:11
♏	Jun 24	13:58	♎	Nov 5	12:04	♋	Mar 14	16:27	♊	Jul 27	7:15	♉	Dec 9	1:59
♐	Jun 26	21:18	♏	Nov 7	23:46	♌	Mar 17	1:13	♋	Jul 29	11:32	♊	Dec 11	2:15
♑	Jun 29	1:00	♐	Nov 10	9:06	♍	Mar 19	12:39	♌	Jul 31	17:41	♋	Dec 13	2:49
♒	Jul 1	2:30	♑	Nov 12	16:12	♎	Mar 22	1:24	♍	Aug 3	2:19	♌	Dec 15	5:41
♓	Jul 3	3:33	♒	Nov 14	21:36	♏	Mar 24	14:10	♎	Aug 5	13:28	♍	Dec 17	12:19
♈	Jul 5	5:37	♓	Nov 17	1:34	♐	Mar 27	1:54	♏	Aug 8	2:05	♎	Dec 19	22:45
♉	Jul 7	9:27	♈	Nov 19	4:12	♑	Mar 29	11:25	♐	Aug 10	14:02	♏	Dec 22	11:18
♊	Jul 9	15:16	♉	Nov 21	6:02	♒	Mar 31	17:45	♑	Aug 12	23:16	♐	Dec 24	23:37
♋	Jul 11	23:08	♊	Nov 23	8:12	♓	Apr 2	20:37	♒	Aug 15	4:59	♑	Dec 27	10:10
♌	Jul 14	9:11	♋	Nov 25	12:20	♈	Apr 4	20:51	♓	Aug 17	7:45	♒	Dec 29	18:38
♍	Jul 16	21:17	♌	Nov 27	19:52	♉	Apr 6	20:07	♈	Aug 19	8:59			

(continued)

Table A-2 — The Moon (continued)

1990

Sign	Date	Time		Sign	Date	Time		Sign	Date	Time		Sign	Date	Time		Sign	Date	Time
♓	Jan 1	1:10		♑	May 13	1:21		♐	Sept 24	0:52		♍	Jan 31	10:44		♌	Jun 14	21:10
♈	Jan 3	5:56		♒	May 15	12:30		♑	Sept 26	13:36		♎	Feb 2	15:02		♍	Jun 16	23:03
♉	Jan 5	9:04		♓	May 17	20:54		♒	Sept 29	0:54		♏	Feb 4	23:01		♎	Jun 19	4:01
♊	Jan 7	11:02		♈	May 20	1:31		♓	Oct 1	8:42		♐	Feb 7	10:23		♏	Jun 21	12:18
♋	Jan 9	12:52		♉	May 22	2:42		♈	Oct 3	12:42		♑	Feb 9	23:16		♐	Jun 23	23:16
♌	Jan 11	16:02		♊	May 24	2:00		♉	Oct 5	14:06		♒	Feb 12	11:16		♑	Jun 26	11:49
♍	Jan 13	21:57		♋	May 26	1:34		♊	Oct 7	14:47		♓	Feb 14	20:59		♒	Jun 29	0:47
♎	Jan 16	7:18		♌	May 28	3:29		♋	Oct 9	16:29		♈	Feb 17	4:11		♓	Jul 1	12:51
♏	Jan 18	19:16		♍	May 30	9:08		♌	Oct 11	20:16		♉	Feb 19	9:24		♈	Jul 3	22:33
♐	Jan 21	7:44		♎	Jun 1	18:31		♍	Oct 14	2:21		♊	Feb 21	13:10		♉	Jul 6	4:52
♑	Jan 23	18:27		♏	Jun 4	6:21		♎	Oct 16	10:26		♋	Feb 23	15:56		♊	Jul 8	7:42
♒	Jan 26	2:25		♐	Jun 6	18:59		♏	Oct 18	20:24		♌	Feb 25	18:13		♋	Jul 10	8:03
♓	Jan 28	7:51		♑	Jun 9	7:12		♐	Oct 21	8:09		♍	Feb 27	20:50		♌	Jul 12	7:35
♈	Jan 30	11:34		♒	Jun 11	18:09		♑	Oct 23	21:03		♎	Mar 2	1:03		♍	Jul 14	8:12
♉	Feb 1	14:27		♓	Jun 14	3:00		♒	Oct 26	9:14		♏	Mar 4	8:08		♎	Jul 16	11:34
♊	Feb 3	17:12		♈	Jun 16	8:55		♓	Oct 28	18:22		♐	Mar 6	18:35		♏	Jul 18	18:41
♋	Feb 5	20:27		♉	Jun 18	11:43		♈	Oct 30	23:14		♑	Mar 9	7:14		♐	Jul 21	5:16
♌	Feb 8	0:51		♊	Jun 20	12:14		♉	Nov 2	0:31		♒	Mar 11	19:31		♑	Jul 23	17:55
♍	Feb 10	7:13		♋	Jun 22	12:10		♊	Nov 4	0:06		♓	Mar 14	5:11		♒	Jul 26	6:49
♎	Feb 12	16:09		♌	Jun 24	13:25		♋	Nov 6	0:07		♈	Mar 16	11:37		♓	Jul 28	18:35
♏	Feb 15	3:34		♍	Jun 26	17:42		♌	Nov 8	2:24		♉	Mar 18	15:40		♈	Jul 31	4:20
♐	Feb 17	16:07		♎	Jun 29	1:47		♍	Nov 10	7:48		♊	Mar 20	18:37		♉	Aug 2	11:32
♑	Feb 20	3:30		♏	Jul 1	13:01		♎	Nov 12	16:08		♋	Mar 22	21:27		♊	Aug 4	15:54
♒	Feb 22	11:52		♐	Jul 4	1:35		♏	Nov 15	2:39		♌	Mar 25	0:43		♋	Aug 6	17:47
♓	Feb 24	16:49		♑	Jul 6	13:39		♐	Nov 17	14:39		♍	Mar 27	4:41		♌	Aug 8	18:09
♈	Feb 26	19:16		♒	Jul 9	0:07		♑	Nov 20	3:32		♎	Mar 29	9:49		♍	Aug 10	18:35
♉	Feb 28	20:43		♓	Jul 11	8:29		♒	Nov 22	16:07		♏	Mar 31	17:01		♎	Aug 12	20:52
♊	Mar 2	22:37		♈	Jul 13	14:36		♓	Nov 25	2:32		♐	Apr 3	2:59		♏	Aug 15	2:34
♋	Mar 5	2:02		♉	Jul 15	18:29		♈	Nov 27	9:06		♑	Apr 5	15:20		♐	Aug 17	12:11
♌	Mar 7	7:24		♊	Jul 17	20:32		♉	Nov 29	11:37		♒	Apr 8	4:00		♑	Aug 20	0:34
♍	Mar 9	14:47		♋	Jul 19	21:44		♊	Dec 1	11:22		♓	Apr 10	14:18		♒	Aug 22	13:27
♎	Mar 12	0:09		♌	Jul 21	23:29		♋	Dec 3	10:27		♈	Apr 12	20:49		♓	Aug 25	0:51
♏	Mar 14	11:25		♍	Jul 24	3:17		♌	Dec 5	11:00		♉	Apr 15	0:06		♈	Aug 27	10:01
♐	Mar 16	23:56		♎	Jul 26	10:19		♍	Dec 7	14:39		♊	Apr 17	1:41		♉	Aug 29	17:00
♑	Mar 19	12:01		♏	Jul 28	20:39		♎	Dec 9	22:00		♋	Apr 19	3:17		♊	Aug 31	22:02
♒	Mar 21	21:31		♐	Jul 31	9:00		♏	Dec 12	8:28		♌	Apr 21	6:04		♋	Sept 3	1:19
♓	Mar 24	3:08		♑	Aug 2	21:08		♐	Dec 14	20:44		♍	Apr 23	10:29		♌	Sept 5	3:13
♈	Mar 26	5:15		♒	Aug 5	7:19		♑	Dec 17	9:35		♎	Apr 25	16:36		♍	Sept 7	4:35
♉	Mar 28	5:26		♓	Aug 7	14:54		♒	Dec 19	21:59		♏	Apr 28	0:34		♎	Sept 9	6:52
♊	Mar 30	5:42		♈	Aug 9	20:13		♓	Dec 22	8:48		♐	Apr 30	10:42		♏	Sept 11	11:42
♋	Apr 1	7:50		♉	Aug 11	23:55		♈	Dec 24	16:45		♑	May 2	22:55		♐	Sept 13	20:14
♌	Apr 3	12:50		♊	Aug 14	2:41		♉	Dec 26	21:09		♒	May 5	11:51		♑	Sept 16	8:04
♍	Apr 5	20:42		♋	Aug 16	5:12		♊	Dec 28	22:26		♓	May 7	23:04		♒	Sept 18	20:58
♎	Apr 8	6:44		♌	Aug 18	8:11		♋	Dec 30	22:02		♈	May 10	6:34		♓	Sept 21	8:20
♏	Apr 10	18:18		♍	Aug 20	12:33						♉	May 12	10:07		♈	Sept 23	16:56
♐	Apr 13	6:48		♎	Aug 22	19:17		**1991**				♊	May 14	11:02		♉	Sept 25	22:59
♑	Apr 15	19:15		♏	Aug 25	4:56		♌	Jan 1	21:54		♋	May 16	11:14		♊	Sept 28	3:25
♒	Apr 18	5:53		♐	Aug 27	16:57		♍	Jan 3	23:57		♌	May 18	12:30		♋	Sept 30	6:58
♓	Apr 20	12:57		♑	Aug 30	5:23		♎	Jan 6	5:33		♍	May 20	16:00		♌	Oct 2	9:58
♈	Apr 22	15:58		♒	Sept 1	15:51		♏	Jan 8	14:59		♎	May 22	22:08		♍	Oct 4	12:45
♉	Apr 24	16:03		♓	Sept 3	23:06		♐	Jan 11	3:06		♏	May 25	6:41		♎	Oct 6	16:00
♊	Apr 26	15:12		♈	Sept 6	3:23		♑	Jan 13	16:00		♐	May 27	17:21		♏	Oct 8	21:00
♋	Apr 28	15:39		♉	Sept 8	5:55		♒	Jan 16	4:04		♑	May 30	5:40		♐	Oct 11	4:58
♌	Apr 30	19:08		♊	Sept 10	8:05		♓	Jan 18	14:23		♒	Jun 1	18:42		♑	Oct 13	16:10
♍	May 3	2:18		♋	Sept 12	10:53		♈	Jan 20	22:28		♓	Jun 4	6:36		♒	Oct 16	5:04
♎	May 5	12:28		♌	Sept 14	14:52		♉	Jan 23	4:01		♈	Jun 6	15:25		♓	Oct 18	16:53
♏	May 8	0:22		♍	Sept 16	20:19		♊	Jan 25	7:06		♉	Jun 8	20:13		♈	Oct 21	1:33
♐	May 10	12:56		♎	Sept 19	3:34		♋	Jan 27	8:23		♊	Jun 10	21:36		♉	Oct 23	6:55
				♏	Sept 21	13:06		♌	Jan 29	9:03		♋	Jun 12	21:16		♊	Oct 25	10:09

Table A-2 — The Moon (continued)

♋ Oct 27 12:37	♈ Mar 5 15:07	♓ Jul 17 17:44	♒ Nov 28 16:19	♏ Apr 7 10:32
♌ Oct 29 15:20	♉ Mar 8 0:05	♈ Jul 20 6:07	♓ Dec 1 4:23	♐ Apr 9 12:10
♍ Oct 31 18:47	♊ Mar 10 7:03	♉ Jul 22 16:36	♈ Dec 3 16:49	♑ Apr 11 17:24
♎ Nov 2 23:13	♋ Mar 12 11:50	♊ Jul 24 23:44	♉ Dec 6 3:16	♒ Apr 14 2:36
♏ Nov 5 5:09	♌ Mar 14 14:20	♋ Jul 27 3:08	♊ Dec 8 10:37	♓ Apr 16 14:32
♐ Nov 7 13:21	♍ Mar 16 15:13	♌ Jul 29 3:39	♋ Dec 10 15:05	♈ Apr 19 3:14
♑ Nov 10 0:16	♎ Mar 18 15:55	♍ Jul 31 3:01	♌ Dec 12 17:47	♉ Apr 21 15:08
♒ Nov 12 13:06	♏ Mar 20 18:20	♎ Aug 2 3:17	♍ Dec 14 19:56	♊ Apr 24 1:27
♓ Nov 15 1:33	♐ Mar 23 0:13	♏ Aug 4 6:16	♎ Dec 16 22:33	♋ Apr 26 9:45
♈ Nov 17 11:08	♑ Mar 25 10:08	♐ Aug 6 12:57	♏ Dec 19 2:20	♌ Apr 28 15.39
♉ Nov 19 16:49	♒ Mar 27 22:44	♑ Aug 8 23:00	♐ Dec 21 7:42	♍ Apr 30 19:00
♊ Nov 21 19:22	♓ Mar 30 11:23	♒ Aug 11 11:06	♑ Dec 23 15:04	♎ May 2 20:20
♋ Nov 23 20:25	♈ Apr 1 22:04	♓ Aug 13 23:51	♒ Dec 26 0:43	♏ May 4 20:57
♌ Nov 25 21:37	♉ Apr 4 6:18	♈ Aug 16 12:11	♓ Dec 28 12:28	♐ May 6 22:34
♍ Nov 28 0:12	♊ Apr 6 12:33	♉ Aug 18 23:10	♈ Dec 31 1:07	♑ May 9 2:51
♎ Nov 30 4:47	♋ Apr 8 17:18	♊ Aug 21 7:36		♒ May 11 10:44
♏ Dec 2 11:33	♌ Apr 10 20:46	♋ Aug 23 12:36	**1993**	♓ May 13 21:50
♐ Dec 4 20:32	♍ Apr 12 23:09	♌ Aug 25 14:15	♉ Jan 2 12:30	♈ May 16 10:24
♑ Dec 7 7:41	♎ Apr 15 1:10	♍ Aug 27 13:46	♊ Jan 4 20:42	♉ May 18 22:16
♒ Dec 9 20:27	♏ Apr 17 4:10	♎ Aug 29 13:11	♋ Jan 7 1:10	♊ May 21 8:07
♓ Dec 12 9:19	♐ Apr 19 9:40	♏ Aug 31 14:38	♌ Jan 9 2:49	♋ May 23 15:38
♈ Dec 14 20:06	♑ Apr 21 18:40	♐ Sept 2 19:50	♍ Jan 11 3:20	♌ May 25 21:03
♉ Dec 17 3:10	♒ Apr 24 6:38	♑ Sept 5 5:06	♎ Jan 13 4:30	♍ May 28 0:46
♊ Dec 19 6:21	♓ Apr 26 19:20	♒ Sept 7 17:08	♏ Jan 15 7:42	♎ May 30 3:18
♋ Dec 21 6:54	♈ Apr 29 6:13	♓ Sept 10 5:56	♐ Jan 17 13:30	♏ Jun 1 5:22
♌ Dec 23 6:38	♉ May 1 14:09	♈ Sept 12 18:02	♑ Jan 19 21:46	♐ Jun 3 8:01
♍ Dec 25 7:24	♊ May 3 19:28	♉ Sept 15 4:47	♒ Jan 22 8:00	♑ Jun 5 12:26
♎ Dec 27 10:37	♋ May 5 23:09	♊ Sept 17 13:40	♓ Jan 24 19:47	♒ Jun 7 19:30
♏ Dec 29 17:03	♌ May 8 2:07	♋ Sept 19 19:59	♈ Jan 27 8:28	♓ Jun 10 5:57
	♍ May 10 4:56	♌ Sept 21 23:19	♉ Jan 29 20:37	♈ Jun 12 18:14
1992	♎ May 12 8:05	♍ Sept 24 0:08	♊ Feb 1 6:14	♉ Jun 15 6:19
♐ Jan 1 2:30	♏ May 14 12:15	♎ Sept 25 23:55	♋ Feb 3 11:56	♊ Jun 17 16:12
♑ Jan 3 14:09	♐ May 16 18:22	♏ Sept 28 0:44	♌ Feb 5 13:51	♋ Jun 19 23:05
♒ Jan 6 2:59	♑ May 19 3:13	♐ Sept 30 4:33	♍ Feb 7 13:29	♌ Jun 22 3:26
♓ Jan 8 15:52	♒ May 21 14:43	♑ Oct 2 12:29	♎ Feb 9 12:58	♍ Jun 24 6:18
♈ Jan 11 3:22	♓ May 24 3:25	♒ Oct 4 23:53	♏ Feb 11 14:23	♎ Jun 26 8:45
♉ Jan 13 12:00	♈ May 26 14:52	♓ Oct 7 12:38	♐ Feb 13 19:08	♏ Jun 28 11:37
♊ Jan 15 16:55	♉ May 28 23:16	♈ Oct 10 0:36	♑ Feb 16 3:20	♐ Jun 30 15:28
♋ Jan 17 18:26	♊ May 31 4:19	♉ Oct 12 10:48	♒ Feb 18 14:05	♑ Jul 2 20:49
♌ Jan 19 17:57	♋ Jun 2 6:58	♊ Oct 14 19:08	♓ Feb 21 2:12	♒ Jul 5 4:14
♍ Jan 21 17:22	♌ Jun 4 8:35	♋ Oct 17 1:36	♈ Feb 23 14:50	♓ Jul 7 14:10
♎ Jan 23 18:42	♍ Jun 6 10:28	♌ Oct 19 6:01	♉ Feb 26 3:11	♈ Jul 10 2:11
♏ Jan 25 23:32	♎ Jun 8 13:33	♍ Oct 21 8:27	♊ Feb 28 13:52	♉ Jul 12 14:37
♐ Jan 28 8:20	♏ Jun 10 18:27	♎ Oct 23 9:39	♋ Mar 2 21:16	♊ Jul 15 1:07
♑ Jan 30 20:07	♐ Jun 13 1:29	♏ Oct 25 11:04	♌ Mar 5 0:40	♋ Jul 17 8:08
♒ Feb 2 9:09	♑ Jun 15 10:50	♐ Oct 27 14:29	♍ Mar 7 0:52	♌ Jul 19 11:47
♓ Feb 4 21:51	♒ Jun 17 22:19	♑ Oct 29 21:18	♎ Mar 8 23:46	♍ Jul 21 13:24
♈ Feb 7 9:15	♓ Jun 20 11:00	♒ Nov 1 7:43	♏ Mar 10 23:40	♎ Jul 23 14:39
♉ Feb 9 18:36	♈ Jun 22 23:03	♓ Nov 3 20:13	♐ Mar 13 2:33	♏ Jul 25 17:00
♊ Feb 12 1:08	♉ Jun 25 8:28	♈ Nov 6 8:19	♑ Mar 15 9:28	♐ Jul 27 21:13
♋ Feb 14 4:31	♊ Jun 27 14:14	♉ Nov 8 18:19	♒ Mar 17 19:52	♑ Jul 30 3:27
♌ Feb 16 5:15	♋ Jun 29 16:42	♊ Nov 11 1:49	♓ Mar 20 8:11	♒ Aug 1 11:36
♍ Feb 18 4:47	♌ Jul 1 17:15	♋ Nov 13 7:19	♈ Mar 22 20:51	♓ Aug 3 21:44
♎ Feb 20 5:05	♍ Jul 3 17:37	♌ Nov 15 11:23	♉ Mar 25 8:59	♈ Aug 6 9:39
♏ Feb 22 8:11	♎ Jul 5 19:27	♍ Nov 17 14:28	♊ Mar 27 19:48	♉ Aug 8 22:22
♐ Feb 24 15:26	♏ Jul 7 23:53	♎ Nov 19 17:03	♋ Mar 30 4:14	♊ Aug 11 9:47
♑ Feb 27 2:33	♐ Jul 10 7:17	♏ Nov 21 19:52	♌ Apr 1 9:21	♋ Aug 13 17:46
♒ Feb 29 15:34	♑ Jul 12 17:16	♐ Nov 24 0:01	♍ Apr 3 11:10	♌ Aug 15 21:43
♓ Mar 3 4:11	♒ Jul 15 5:03	♑ Nov 26 6:38	♎ Apr 5 10:54	♍ Aug 17 22:41

(continued)

Table A-2 — The Moon (continued)

Column 1	Column 2	Column 3	Column 4	Column 5
♎ Aug 19 22:35	**1994**	♋ May 13 20:27	♊ Sept 24 21:41	♓ Feb 1 3:05
♏ Aug 21 23:27	♍ Jan 1 15:15	♌ May 16 5:58	♋ Sept 27 10:12	♈ Feb 3 9:12
♐ Aug 24 2:45	♎ Jan 3 18:31	♍ May 18 12:31	♌ Sept 29 19:55	♉ Feb 5 19:08
♑ Aug 26 8:58	♏ Jan 5 21:29	♎ May 20 15:54	♍ Oct 2 1:39	♊ Feb 8 7:44
♒ Aug 28 17:42	♐ Jan 8 0:34	♏ May 22 16:51	♎ Oct 4 3:56	♋ Feb 10 20:17
♓ Aug 31 4:18	♑ Jan 10 4:16	♐ May 24 16:43	♏ Oct 6 4:22	♌ Feb 13 6:31
♈ Sept 2 16:21	♒ Jan 12 9:25	♑ May 26 17:17	♐ Oct 8 4:47	♍ Feb 15 13:52
♉ Sept 5 5:09	♓ Jan 14 17:04	♒ May 28 20:19	♑ Oct 10 6:44	♎ Feb 17 19:00
♊ Sept 7 17:16	♈ Jan 17 3:42	♓ May 31 3:03	♒ Oct 12 11:09	♏ Feb 19 22:55
♋ Sept 10 2:37	♉ Jan 19 16:22	♈ Jun 2 13:31	♓ Oct 14 18:18	♐ Feb 22 2:13
♌ Sept 12 7:51	♊ Jan 22 4:34	♉ Jun 5 2:14	♈ Oct 17 3:56	♑ Feb 24 5:11
♍ Sept 14 9:20	♋ Jan 24 13:55	♊ Jun 7 15:03	♉ Oct 19 15:34	♒ Feb 26 8:14
♎ Sept 16 8:44	♌ Jan 26 19:38	♋ Jun 10 2:22	♊ Oct 22 4:28	♓ Feb 28 12:16
♏ Sept 18 8:15	♍ Jan 28 22:39	♌ Jun 12 11:29	♋ Oct 24 17:15	♈ Mar 2 18:30
♐ Sept 20 9:53	♎ Jan 31 0:34	♍ Jun 14 18:16	♌ Oct 27 4:05	♉ Mar 5 3:50
♑ Sept 22 14:54	♏ Feb 2 2:49	♎ Jun 16 22:48	♍ Oct 29 11:21	♊ Mar 7 15:55
♒ Sept 24 23:19	♐ Feb 4 6:14	♏ Jun 19 1:20	♎ Oct 31 14:46	♋ Mar 10 4:40
♓ Sept 27 10:13	♑ Feb 6 11:02	♐ Jun 21 2:32	♏ Nov 2 15:19	♌ Mar 12 15:28
♈ Sept 29 22:29	♒ Feb 8 17:16	♑ Jun 23 3:37	♐ Nov 4 14:46	♍ Mar 14 22:54
♉ Oct 2 11:13	♓ Feb 11 1:23	♒ Jun 25 6:10	♑ Nov 6 15:02	♎ Mar 17 3:18
♊ Oct 4 23:27	♈ Feb 13 11:49	♓ Jun 27 11:44	♒ Nov 8 17:48	♏ Mar 19 5:52
♋ Oct 7 9:42	♉ Feb 16 0:20	♈ Jun 29 21:07	♓ Nov 11 0:04	♐ Mar 21 7:57
♌ Oct 9 16:34	♊ Feb 18 13:05	♉ Jul 2 9:23	♈ Nov 13 9:44	♑ Mar 23 10:31
♍ Oct 11 19:36	♋ Feb 20 23:27	♊ Jul 4 22:12	♉ Nov 15 21:44	♒ Mar 25 14:10
♎ Oct 13 19:47	♌ Feb 23 5:47	♋ Jul 7 9:17	♊ Nov 18 10:41	♓ Mar 27 19:18
♏ Oct 15 19:01	♍ Feb 25 8:27	♌ Jul 9 17:43	♋ Nov 20 23:21	♈ Mar 30 2:26
♐ Oct 17 19:23	♎ Feb 27 9:06	♍ Jul 11 23:48	♌ Nov 23 10:33	♉ Apr 1 11:59
♑ Oct 19 22:42	♏ Mar 1 9:43	♎ Jul 14 4:15	♍ Nov 25 19:09	♊ Apr 3 23:49
♒ Oct 22 5:49	♐ Mar 3 11:54	♏ Jul 16 7:35	♎ Nov 28 0:22	♋ Apr 6 12:40
♓ Oct 24 16:17	♑ Mar 5 16:24	♐ Jul 18 10:09	♏ Nov 30 2:21	♌ Apr 9 0:15
♈ Oct 27 4:39	♒ Mar 7 23:15	♑ Jul 20 12:30	♐ Dec 2 2:13	♍ Apr 11 8:39
♉ Oct 29 17:20	♓ Mar 10 8:09	♒ Jul 22 15:38	♑ Dec 4 1:42	♎ Apr 13 13:20
♊ Nov 1 5:13	♈ Mar 12 18:59	♓ Jul 24 20:56	♒ Dec 6 2:52	♏ Apr 15 15:51
♋ Nov 3 15:25	♉ Mar 15 7:27	♈ Jul 27 5:31	♓ Dec 8 7:24	♐ Apr 17 15:51
♌ Nov 5 23:06	♊ Mar 17 20:29	♉ Jul 29 17:13	♈ Dec 10 16:03	♑ Apr 19 16:54
♍ Nov 8 3:47	♋ Mar 20 7:54	♊ Aug 1 6:05	♉ Dec 13 3:56	♒ Apr 21 19:38
♎ Nov 10 5:42	♌ Mar 22 15:39	♋ Aug 3 17:22	♊ Dec 15 17:00	♓ Apr 24 0:50
♏ Nov 12 6:00	♍ Mar 24 19:14	♌ Aug 6 1:31	♋ Dec 18 5:25	♈ Apr 26 8:41
♐ Nov 14 6:20	♎ Mar 26 19:46	♍ Aug 8 6:42	♌ Dec 20 16:13	♉ Apr 28 18:53
♑ Nov 16 8:34	♏ Mar 28 19:15	♎ Aug 10 10:07	♍ Dec 23 1:01	♊ May 1 6:53
♒ Nov 18 14:08	♐ Mar 30 19:41	♏ Aug 12 12:56	♎ Dec 25 7:27	♋ May 3 19:45
♓ Nov 20 23:27	♑ Apr 1 22:38	♐ Aug 14 15:53	♏ Dec 27 11:17	♌ May 6 7:55
♈ Nov 23 11:30	♒ Apr 4 4:45	♑ Aug 16 19:18	♐ Dec 29 12:45	♍ May 8 17:33
♉ Nov 26 0:14	♓ Apr 6 13:51	♒ Aug 18 23:34	♑ Dec 31 12:57	♎ May 10 22:30
♊ Nov 28 11:48	♈ Apr 9 1:09	♓ Aug 21 5:27		♏ May 13 1:53
♋ Nov 30 21:17	♉ Apr 11 13:48	♈ Aug 23 13:55	**1995**	♐ May 15 1:58
♌ Dec 3 4:33	♊ Apr 14 2:48	♉ Aug 26 1:13	♒ Jan 2 13:39	♑ May 17 1:36
♍ Dec 5 9:43	♋ Apr 16 14:41	♊ Aug 28 14:07	♓ Jan 4 16:49	♒ May 19 2:39
♎ Dec 7 13:03	♌ Apr 18 23:45	♋ Aug 31 2:00	♈ Jan 6 23:56	♓ May 21 6:40
♏ Dec 9 15:04	♍ Apr 21 4:58	♌ Sept 2 10:37	♉ Jan 9 10:58	♈ May 23 14:13
♐ Dec 11 16:39	♎ Apr 23 6:40	♍ Sept 4 15:33	♊ Jan 11 23:57	♉ May 26 0:46
♑ Dec 13 19:06	♏ Apr 25 6:18	♎ Sept 6 17:57	♋ Jan 14 12:20	♊ May 28 13:07
♒ Dec 15 23:51	♐ Apr 27 5:48	♏ Sept 8 19:26	♌ Jan 16 22:36	♋ May 31 1:59
♓ Dec 18 7:59	♑ Apr 29 7:05	♐ Sept 10 21:25	♍ Jan 19 6:39	♌ Jun 2 14:17
♈ Dec 20 19:19	♒ May 1 11:34	♑ Sept 13 0:44	♎ Jan 21 12:54	♍ Jun 5 1:36
♉ Dec 23 8:05	♓ May 3 19:47	♒ Sept 15 5:42	♏ Jan 23 17:32	♎ Jun 7 8:13
♊ Dec 25 19:46	♈ May 6 7:01	♓ Sept 17 12:31	♐ Jan 25 20:37	♏ Jun 9 12:03
♋ Dec 28 4:46	♉ May 8 19:50	♈ Sept 19 21:30	♑ Jan 27 22:26	♐ Jun 11 12:50
♌ Dec 30 10:59	♊ May 11 8:43	♉ Sept 22 8:47	♒ Jan 30 0:03	♑ Jun 13 12:05

Table A-2 — The Moon *(continued)*

Sign	Date	Time	Sign	Date	Time	Sign	Date	Time	Sign	Date	Time	Sign	Date	Time
♒	Jun 15	11:52	♑	Oct 28	2:15	♎	Mar 6	8:40	♍	Jul 18	13:16	♌	Nov 29	12:30
♓	Jun 17	14:13	♒	Oct 30	4:23	♏	Mar 8	16:05	♎	Jul 21	1:14	♍	Dec 2	1:11
♈	Jun 19	20:29	♓	Nov 1	8:17	♐	Mar 10	21:32	♏	Jul 23	10:43	♎	Dec 4	13:23
♉	Jun 22	6:35	♈	Nov 3	14:21	♑	Mar 13	1:08	♐	Jul 25	16:24	♏	Dec 6	22:38
♊	Jun 24	19:02	♉	Nov 5	22:35	♒	Mar 15	3:15	♑	Jul 27	18:17	♐	Dec 9	3:58
♋	Jun 27	7:56	♊	Nov 8	8:55	♓	Mar 17	4:50	♒	Jul 29	17:47	♑	Dec 11	6:14
♌	Jun 29	20:02	♋	Nov 10	20:57	♈	Mar 19	7:15	♓	Jul 31	17:00	♒	Dec 13	7:14
♍	Jul 2	6:35	♌	Nov 13	9:37	♉	Mar 21	11:59	♈	Aug 2	18:05	♓	Dec 15	8:44
♎	Jul 4	14:55	♍	Nov 15	21:02	♊	Mar 23	19:59	♉	Aug 4	22:33	♈	Dec 17	11:55
♏	Jul 6	20:19	♎	Nov 18	5:18	♋	Mar 26	7:06	♊	Aug 7	6:49	♉	Dec 19	17.09
♐	Jul 8	22:37	♏	Nov 20	9:40	♌	Mar 28	19:37	♋	Aug 9	17:57	♊	Dec 22	0:17
♑	Jul 10	22:43	♐	Nov 22	10:56	♍	Mar 31	7:14	♌	Aug 12	6:29	♋	Dec 24	9:14
♒	Jul 12	22:21	♑	Nov 24	10:48	♎	Apr 2	16:26	♍	Aug 14	19:07	♌	Dec 26	20:09
♓	Jul 14	23:37	♒	Nov 26	11:15	♏	Apr 4	22:57	♎	Aug 17	6:55	♍	Dec 29	8:45
♈	Jul 17	4:23	♓	Nov 28	13:59	♐	Apr 7	3:21	♏	Aug 19	16:50	♎	Dec 31	21:32
♉	Jul 19	13:20	♈	Nov 30	19:51	♑	Apr 9	6:30	♐	Aug 21	23:48		**1997**	
♊	Jul 22	1:23	♉	Dec 3	4:40	♒	Apr 11	9:09	♑	Aug 24	3:22	♏	Jan 3	8:02
♋	Jul 24	14:16	♊	Dec 5	15:35	♓	Apr 13	12:00	♒	Aug 26	4:10	♐	Jan 5	14:27
♌	Jul 27	2:07	♋	Dec 8	3:44	♈	Apr 15	15:42	♓	Aug 28	3:49	♑	Jan 7	16:55
♍	Jul 29	12:12	♌	Dec 10	16:24	♉	Apr 17	21:05	♈	Aug 30	4:15	♒	Jan 9	17:00
♎	Jul 31	20:23	♍	Dec 13	4:26	♊	Apr 20	4:54	♉	Sept 1	7:19	♓	Jan 11	16:51
♏	Aug 3	2:29	♎	Dec 15	14:09	♋	Apr 22	15:25	♊	Sept 3	14:08	♈	Jan 13	18:22
♐	Aug 5	6:14	♏	Dec 17	20:07	♌	Apr 25	3:44	♋	Sept 6	0:29	♉	Jan 15	22:40
♑	Aug 7	7:52	♐	Dec 19	22:13	♍	Apr 27	15:49	♌	Sept 8	12:54	♊	Jan 18	5:53
♒	Aug 9	8:28	♑	Dec 21	21:46	♎	Apr 30	1:27	♍	Sept 11	1:28	♋	Jan 20	15:29
♓	Aug 11	9:46	♒	Dec 23	20:52	♏	May 2	7:42	♎	Sept 13	12:51	♌	Jan 23	2:50
♈	Aug 13	13:41	♓	Dec 25	21:45	♐	May 4	11:05	♏	Sept 15	22:20	♍	Jan 25	15:26
♉	Aug 15	21:25	♈	Dec 28	2:06	♑	May 6	12:54	♐	Sept 18	5:31	♎	Jan 28	4:21
♊	Aug 18	8:40	♉	Dec 30	10:21	♒	May 8	14:39	♑	Sept 20	10:12	♏	Jan 30	15:48
♋	Aug 20	21:24		**1996**		♓	May 10	17:29	♒	Sept 22	12:39	♐	Feb 1	23:51
♌	Aug 23	9:13	♊	Jan 1	21:29	♈	May 12	22:00	♓	Sept 24	13:43	♑	Feb 4	3:44
♍	Aug 25	18:50	♋	Jan 4	9:56	♉	May 15	4:25	♈	Sept 26	14:46	♒	Feb 6	4:21
♎	Aug 28	2:15	♌	Jan 6	22:30	♊	May 17	12:48	♉	Sept 28	17:24	♓	Feb 8	3:34
♏	Aug 30	7:51	♍	Jan 9	10:29	♋	May 19	23:16	♊	Sept 30	23:01	♈	Feb 10	3:29
♐	Sept 1	11:57	♎	Jan 11	20:55	♌	May 22	11:28	♋	Oct 3	8:14	♉	Feb 12	5:56
♑	Sept 3	14:45	♏	Jan 14	4:30	♍	May 24	23:58	♌	Oct 5	20:12	♊	Feb 14	11:53
♒	Sept 5	16:47	♐	Jan 16	8:25	♎	May 27	10:33	♍	Oct 8	8:49	♋	Feb 16	21:13
♓	Sept 7	19:08	♑	Jan 18	9:07	♏	May 29	17:30	♎	Oct 10	20:00	♌	Feb 19	8:52
♈	Sept 9	23:14	♒	Jan 20	8:15	♐	May 31	20:43	♏	Oct 13	4:46	♍	Feb 21	21:38
♉	Sept 12	6:21	♓	Jan 22	8:02	♑	Jun 2	21:29	♐	Oct 15	11:07	♎	Feb 24	10:23
♊	Sept 14	16:48	♈	Jan 24	10:37	♒	Jun 4	21:45	♑	Oct 17	15:37	♏	Feb 26	21:57
♋	Sept 17	5:16	♉	Jan 26	17:16	♓	Jun 6	23:19	♒	Oct 19	18:51	♐	Mar 1	7:01
♌	Sept 19	17:19	♊	Jan 29	3:42	♈	Jun 9	3:23	♓	Oct 21	21:22	♑	Mar 3	12:38
♍	Sept 22	3:01	♋	Jan 31	16:11	♉	Jun 11	10:11	♈	Oct 23	23:50	♒	Mar 5	14:54
♎	Sept 24	9:50	♌	Feb 3	4:46	♊	Jun 13	19:16	♉	Oct 26	3:11	♓	Mar 7	14:57
♏	Sept 26	14:20	♍	Feb 5	16:22	♋	Jun 16	6:08	♊	Oct 28	8:35	♈	Mar 9	14:33
♐	Sept 28	17:30	♎	Feb 8	2:30	♌	Jun 18	18:22	♋	Oct 30	16:56	♉	Mar 11	15:37
♑	Sept 30	20:10	♏	Feb 10	10:35	♍	Jun 21	7:07	♌	Nov 2	4:16	♊	Mar 13	19:48
♒	Oct 2	22:59	♐	Feb 12	15:58	♎	Jun 23	18:37	♍	Nov 4	16:57	♋	Mar 16	3:51
♓	Oct 5	2:35	♑	Feb 14	18:29	♏	Jun 26	2:53	♎	Nov 7	4:29	♌	Mar 18	15:08
♈	Oct 7	7:41	♒	Feb 16	19:00	♐	Jun 28	7:01	♏	Nov 9	13:02	♍	Mar 21	3:59
♉	Oct 9	15:05	♓	Feb 18	19:09	♑	Jun 30	7:47	♐	Nov 11	18:26	♎	Mar 23	16:35
♊	Oct 12	1:10	♈	Feb 20	20:58	♒	Jul 2	7:05	♑	Nov 13	21:44	♏	Mar 26	3:42
♋	Oct 14	13:20	♉	Feb 23	2:08	♓	Jul 4	7:07	♒	Nov 16	0:14	♐	Mar 28	12:40
♌	Oct 17	1:46	♊	Feb 25	11:14	♈	Jul 6	9:42	♓	Nov 18	3:00	♑	Mar 30	19:07
♍	Oct 19	12:11	♋	Feb 27	23:10	♉	Jul 8	15:43	♈	Nov 20	6:34	♒	Apr 1	22:59
♎	Oct 21	19:15	♌	Mar 1	11:47	♊	Jul 11	0:52	♉	Nov 22	11:12	♓	Apr 4	0:42
♏	Oct 23	23:06	♍	Mar 3	23:13	♋	Jul 13	12:08	♊	Nov 24	17:20	♈	Apr 6	1:19
♐	Oct 26	0:56				♌	Jul 16	0:31	♋	Nov 27	1:37			

(continued)

Table A-2 — The Moon (continued)

Sign	Date	Time	Sign	Date	Time	Sign	Date	Time	Sign	Date	Time	Sign	Date	Time
♉	Apr 8	2:20	♈	Aug 20	12:45	**1998**			♑	May 14	13:39	♐	Sept 25	18:05
♊	Apr 10	5:28	♉	Aug 22	13:57	♓	Jan 2	4:56	♒	May 16	21:30	♑	Sept 28	5:30
♋	Apr 12	12:03	♊	Aug 24	17:56	♈	Jan 4	7:43	♓	May 19	3:03	♒	Sept 30	13:53
♌	Apr 14	22:22	♋	Aug 27	1:10	♉	Jan 6	10:52	♈	May 21	6:06	♓	Oct 2	18:23
♍	Apr 17	11:00	♌	Aug 29	11:19	♊	Jan 8	14:42	♉	May 23	7:06	♈	Oct 4	19:32
♎	Apr 19	23:36	♍	Aug 31	23:27	♋	Jan 10	19:43	♊	May 25	7:25	♉	Oct 6	18:57
♏	Apr 22	10:19	♎	Sept 3	12:30	♌	Jan 13	2:45	♋	May 27	8:58	♊	Oct 8	18:43
♐	Apr 24	18:32	♏	Sept 6	1:10	♍	Jan 15	12:31	♌	May 29	13:38	♋	Oct 10	20:48
♑	Apr 27	0:32	♐	Sept 8	11:54	♎	Jan 18	0:44	♍	May 31	22:21	♌	Oct 13	2:25
♒	Apr 29	4:50	♑	Sept 10	19:23	♏	Jan 20	13:34	♎	Jun 3	10:17	♍	Oct 15	11:32
♓	May 1	7:50	♒	Sept 12	23:10	♐	Jan 23	0:25	♏	Jun 5	23:06	♎	Oct 17	23:02
♈	May 3	9:59	♓	Sept 14	23:59	♑	Jan 25	7:39	♐	Jun 8	10:34	♏	Oct 20	11:36
♉	May 5	12:04	♈	Sept 16	23:25	♒	Jan 27	11:27	♑	Jun 10	19:50	♐	Oct 23	0:16
♊	May 7	15:21	♉	Sept 18	23:21	♓	Jan 29	13:08	♒	Jun 13	3:03	♑	Oct 25	12:05
♋	May 9	21:13	♊	Sept 21	1:39	♈	Jan 31	14:21	♓	Jun 15	8:31	♒	Oct 27	21:44
♌	May 12	6:33	♋	Sept 23	7:33	♉	Feb 2	16:25	♈	Jun 17	12:23	♓	Oct 30	3:58
♍	May 14	18:43	♌	Sept 25	17:12	♊	Feb 4	20:09	♉	Jun 19	14:47	♈	Nov 1	6:27
♎	May 17	7:27	♍	Sept 28	5:27	♋	Feb 7	1:57	♊	Jun 21	16:26	♉	Nov 3	6:12
♏	May 19	18:11	♎	Sept 30	18:32	♌	Feb 9	9:57	♋	Jun 23	18:39	♊	Nov 5	5:11
♐	May 22	1:51	♏	Oct 3	6:57	♍	Feb 11	20:09	♌	Jun 25	23:04	♋	Nov 7	5:39
♑	May 24	6:51	♐	Oct 5	17:43	♎	Feb 14	8:17	♍	Jun 28	6:54	♌	Nov 9	9:33
♒	May 26	10:20	♑	Oct 8	2:04	♏	Feb 16	21:13	♎	Jun 30	18:05	♍	Nov 11	17:37
♓	May 28	13:18	♒	Oct 10	7:29	♐	Feb 19	8:56	♏	Jul 3	6:45	♎	Nov 14	4:57
♈	May 30	16:18	♓	Oct 12	9:59	♑	Feb 21	17:29	♐	Jul 5	18:24	♏	Nov 16	17:41
♉	Jun 1	19:39	♈	Oct 14	10:25	♒	Feb 23	22:10	♑	Jul 8	3:27	♐	Nov 19	6:13
♊	Jun 3	23:55	♉	Oct 16	10:16	♓	Feb 25	23:42	♒	Jul 10	9:52	♑	Nov 21	17:45
♋	Jun 6	6:02	♊	Oct 18	11:26	♈	Feb 27	23:42	♓	Jul 12	14:22	♒	Nov 24	3:43
♌	Jun 8	14:58	♋	Oct 20	15:45	♉	Mar 2	0:00	♈	Jul 14	17:45	♓	Nov 26	11:14
♍	Jun 11	2:43	♌	Oct 23	0:10	♊	Mar 4	2:15	♉	Jul 16	20:33	♈	Nov 28	15:34
♎	Jun 13	15:35	♍	Oct 25	11:59	♋	Mar 6	7:27	♊	Jul 18	23:18	♉	Nov 30	16:52
♏	Jun 16	2:51	♎	Oct 28	1:05	♌	Mar 8	15:46	♋	Jul 21	2:43	♊	Dec 2	16:29
♐	Jun 18	10:39	♏	Oct 30	13:15	♍	Mar 11	2:35	♌	Jul 23	7:48	♋	Dec 4	16:28
♑	Jun 20	15:02	♐	Nov 1	23:27	♎	Mar 13	14:58	♍	Jul 25	15:34	♌	Dec 6	18:55
♒	Jun 22	17:20	♑	Nov 4	7:31	♏	Mar 16	3:51	♎	Jul 28	2:14	♍	Dec 9	1:21
♓	Jun 24	19:09	♒	Nov 6	13:33	♐	Mar 18	15:56	♏	Jul 30	14:44	♎	Dec 11	11:43
♈	Jun 26	21:38	♓	Nov 8	17:34	♑	Mar 21	1:43	♐	Aug 2	2:48	♏	Dec 14	0:16
♉	Jun 29	1:23	♈	Nov 10	19:44	♒	Mar 23	8:01	♑	Aug 4	12:18	♐	Dec 16	12:47
♊	Jul 1	6:35	♉	Nov 12	20:45	♓	Mar 25	10:43	♒	Aug 6	18:31	♑	Dec 18	23:55
♋	Jul 3	13:33	♊	Nov 14	22:05	♈	Mar 27	10:49	♓	Aug 8	22:04	♒	Dec 21	9:17
♌	Jul 5	22:45	♋	Nov 17	1:32	♉	Mar 29	10:06	♈	Aug 11	0:10	♓	Dec 23	16:45
♍	Jul 8	10:22	♌	Nov 19	8:38	♊	Mar 31	10:37	♉	Aug 13	2:04	♈	Dec 25	22:03
♎	Jul 10	23:21	♍	Nov 21	19:33	♋	Apr 2	14:10	♊	Aug 15	4:46	♉	Dec 28	1:05
♏	Jul 13	11:20	♎	Nov 24	8:29	♌	Apr 4	21:36	♋	Aug 17	8:55	♊	Dec 30	2:22
♐	Jul 15	20:02	♏	Nov 26	20:43	♍	Apr 7	8:25	♌	Aug 19	15:00	**1999**		
♑	Jul 18	0:45	♐	Nov 29	6:28	♎	Apr 9	21:04	♍	Aug 21	23:21	♋	Jan 1	3:15
♒	Jul 20	2:29	♑	Dec 1	13:38	♏	Apr 12	9:55	♎	Aug 24	10:02	♌	Jan 3	5:31
♓	Jul 22	3:00	♒	Dec 3	18:58	♐	Apr 14	21:52	♏	Aug 26	22:25	♍	Jan 5	10:49
♈	Jul 24	4:03	♓	Dec 5	23:07	♑	Apr 17	8:05	♐	Aug 29	10:55	♎	Jan 7	19:53
♉	Jul 26	6:53	♈	Dec 8	2:24	♒	Apr 19	15:41	♑	Aug 31	21:23	♏	Jan 10	7:49
♊	Jul 28	12:04	♉	Dec 10	5:00	♓	Apr 21	20:06	♒	Sept 3	4:21	♐	Jan 12	20:23
♋	Jul 30	19:38	♊	Dec 12	7:35	♈	Apr 23	21:30	♓	Sept 5	7:48	♑	Jan 15	7:28
♌	Aug 2	5:27	♋	Dec 14	11:25	♉	Apr 25	21:09	♈	Sept 7	8:52	♒	Jan 17	16:11
♍	Aug 4	17:15	♌	Dec 16	17:58	♊	Apr 27	20:55	♉	Sept 9	9:16	♓	Jan 19	22:40
♎	Aug 7	6:17	♍	Dec 19	4:00	♋	Apr 29	22:57	♊	Sept 11	10:40	♈	Jan 22	3:25
♏	Aug 9	18:50	♎	Dec 21	16:35	♌	May 2	4:49	♋	Sept 13	14:20	♉	Jan 24	6:52
♐	Aug 12	4:45	♏	Dec 24	5:07	♍	May 4	14:47	♌	Sept 15	20:48	♊	Jan 26	9:29
♑	Aug 14	10:42	♐	Dec 26	15:07	♎	May 7	3:19	♍	Sept 18	5:52	♋	Jan 28	11:57
♒	Aug 16	12:58	♑	Dec 28	21:48	♏	May 9	16:10	♎	Sept 20	16:57	♌	Jan 30	15:16
♓	Aug 18	13:01	♒	Dec 31	1:58	♐	May 12	3:48	♏	Sept 23	5:22			

Table A-2 — The Moon (continued)

Col 1	Col 2	Col 3	Col 4	Col 5
♍ Feb 1 20:37	♌ Jun 16 3:07	♋ Oct 28 15:09	♈ Mar 7 1:54	♓ Jul 19 8:44
♎ Feb 4 4:56	♍ Jun 18 7:12	♌ Oct 30 17:47	♉ Mar 9 7:01	♈ Jul 21 19:09
♏ Feb 6 16:06	♎ Jun 20 15:10	♍ Nov 1 23:07	♊ Mar 11 10:46	♉ Jul 24 2:44
♐ Feb 9 4:38	♏ Jun 23 2:18	♎ Nov 4 6:57	♋ Mar 13 13:51	♊ Jul 26 7:01
♑ Feb 11 16:10	♐ Jun 25 14:51	♏ Nov 6 16:46	♌ Mar 15 16:43	♋ Jul 28 8:30
♒ Feb 14 0:57	♑ Jun 28 3:12	♐ Nov 9 4:15	♍ Mar 17 19:48	♌ Jul 30 8:23
♓ Feb 16 6:40	♒ Jun 30 14:19	♑ Nov 11 17:00	♎ Mar 19 23:57	♍ Aug 1 8:27
♈ Feb 18 10:06	♓ Jul 2 23:34	♒ Nov 14 5:46	♏ Mar 22 6:17	♎ Aug 3 10:31
♉ Feb 20 12:29	♈ Jul 5 6:21	♓ Nov 16 16:21	♐ Mar 24 15:43	♏ Aug 5 16:04
♊ Feb 22 14:54	♉ Jul 7 10:22	♈ Nov 18 22:57	♑ Mar 27 3:51	♐ Aug 8 1:30
♋ Feb 24 18:09	♊ Jul 9 12:00	♉ Nov 21 1:26	♒ Mar 29 16:34	♑ Aug 10 13:44
♌ Feb 26 22:44	♋ Jul 11 13:26	♊ Nov 23 1:13	♓ Apr 1 3:12	♒ Aug 13 2:43
♍ Mar 1 5:04	♌ Jul 13 13:26	♋ Nov 25 0:29	♈ Apr 3 10:22	♓ Aug 15 14:41
♎ Mar 3 13:34	♍ Jul 15 16:39	♌ Nov 27 1:19	♉ Apr 5 14:29	♈ Aug 18 0:44
♏ Mar 6 0:22	♎ Jul 17 23:19	♍ Nov 29 5:11	♊ Apr 7 16:58	♉ Aug 20 8:31
♐ Mar 8 12:46	♏ Jul 20 9:30	♎ Dec 1 12:29	♋ Apr 9 19:16	♊ Aug 22 13:55
♑ Mar 11 0:54	♐ Jul 22 21:48	♏ Dec 3 22:35	♌ Apr 11 22:16	♋ Aug 24 17:00
♒ Mar 13 10:32	♑ Jul 25 10:08	♐ Dec 6 10:27	♍ Apr 14 2:19	♌ Aug 26 18:17
♓ Mar 15 16:30	♒ Jul 27 20:54	♑ Dec 8 23:14	♎ Apr 16 7:36	♍ Aug 28 18:55
♈ Mar 17 19:13	♓ Jul 30 5:27	♒ Dec 11 11:59	♏ Apr 18 14:35	♎ Aug 30 20:33
♉ Mar 19 20:09	♈ Aug 1 11:47	♓ Dec 13 23:18	♐ Apr 20 23:58	♏ Sept 2 0:55
♊ Mar 21 21:05	♉ Aug 3 16:09	♈ Dec 16 7:30	♑ Apr 23 11:47	♐ Sept 4 9:08
♋ Mar 23 23:33	♊ Aug 5 18:57	♉ Dec 18 11:45	♒ Apr 26 0:42	♑ Sept 6 20:47
♌ Mar 26 4:22	♋ Aug 7 20:52	♊ Dec 20 12:39	♓ Apr 28 12:06	♒ Sept 9 9:44
♍ Mar 28 11:34	♌ Aug 9 22:55	♋ Dec 22 11:52	♈ Apr 30 19:55	♓ Sept 11 21:34
♎ Mar 30 20:49	♍ Aug 12 2:22	♌ Dec 24 11:32	♉ May 2 23:54	♈ Sept 14 7:00
♏ Apr 2 7:49	♎ Aug 14 8:24	♍ Dec 26 13:34	♊ May 5 1:23	♉ Sept 16 14:05
♐ Apr 4 20:07	♏ Aug 16 17:40	♎ Dec 28 19:14	♋ May 7 2:14	♊ Sept 18 19:22
♑ Apr 7 8:39	♐ Aug 19 5:31	♏ Dec 31 4:36	♌ May 9 4:01	♋ Sept 20 23:16
♒ Apr 9 19:24	♑ Aug 21 17:59	**2000**	♍ May 11 7:41	♌ Sept 23 2:00
♓ Apr 12 2:35	♒ Aug 24 4:49	♐ Jan 2 16:32	♎ May 13 13:27	♍ Sept 25 4:02
♈ Apr 14 5:46	♓ Aug 26 12:50	♑ Jan 5 5:24	♏ May 15 21:16	♎ Sept 27 6:22
♉ Apr 16 6:07	♈ Aug 28 18:09	♒ Jan 7 17:53	♐ May 18 7:09	♏ Sept 29 10:30
♊ Apr 18 5:39	♉ Aug 30 21:41	♓ Jan 10 4:59	♑ May 20 19:01	♐ Oct 1 17:50
♋ Apr 20 6:27	♊ Sept 2 0:25	♈ Jan 12 13:48	♒ May 23 8:00	♑ Oct 4 4:42
♌ Apr 22 10:06	♋ Sept 4 3:09	♉ Jan 14 19:38	♓ May 25 20:07	♒ Oct 6 17:33
♍ Apr 24 17:04	♌ Sept 6 6:29	♊ Jan 16 22:25	♈ May 28 5:08	♓ Oct 9 5:36
♎ Apr 27 2:46	♍ Sept 8 10:57	♋ Jan 18 23:01	♉ May 30 10:02	♈ Oct 11 14:51
♏ Apr 29 14:12	♎ Sept 10 17:16	♌ Jan 20 22:58	♊ Jun 1 11:34	♉ Oct 13 21:06
♐ May 2 2:36	♏ Sept 13 2:08	♍ Jan 23 0:07	♋ Jun 3 11:30	♊ Oct 16 1:19
♑ May 4 15:12	♐ Sept 15 13:35	♎ Jan 25 4:09	♌ Jun 5 11:45	♋ Oct 18 4:37
♒ May 7 2:40	♑ Sept 18 2:13	♏ Jan 27 12:01	♍ Jun 7 13:57	♌ Oct 20 7:42
♓ May 9 11:16	♒ Sept 20 13:38	♐ Jan 29 23:17	♎ Jun 9 18:59	♍ Oct 22 10:52
♈ May 11 15:53	♓ Sept 22 21:51	♑ Feb 1 12:10	♏ Jun 12 2:55	♎ Oct 24 14:30
♉ May 13 16:56	♈ Sept 25 2:34	♒ Feb 4 0:31	♐ Jun 14 13:18	♏ Oct 26 19:23
♊ May 15 16:07	♉ Sept 27 4:51	♓ Feb 6 11:02	♑ Jun 17 1:26	♐ Oct 29 2:40
♋ May 17 15:39	♊ Sept 29 6:21	♈ Feb 8 19:17	♒ Jun 19 14:26	♑ Oct 31 13:02
♌ May 19 17:37	♋ Oct 1 8:31	♉ Feb 11 1:21	♓ Jun 22 2:52	♒ Nov 3 1:41
♍ May 21 23:15	♌ Oct 3 12:13	♊ Feb 13 5:23	♈ Jun 24 12:55	♓ Nov 5 14:13
♎ May 24 8:29	♍ Oct 5 17:40	♋ Feb 15 7:45	♉ Jun 26 19:19	♈ Nov 8 2:07
♏ May 26 20:05	♎ Oct 8 0:52	♌ Feb 17 9:11	♊ Jun 28 21:59	♉ Nov 10 6:12
♐ May 29 8:37	♏ Oct 10 10:01	♍ Feb 19 10:53	♋ Jun 30 22:09	♊ Nov 12 9:27
♑ May 31 21:05	♐ Oct 12 21:18	♎ Feb 21 14:21	♌ Jul 2 21:38	♋ Nov 14 11:21
♒ Jun 3 8:37	♑ Oct 15 10:04	♏ Feb 23 20:58	♍ Jul 4 22:19	♌ Nov 16 13:19
♓ Jun 5 18:00	♒ Oct 17 22:17	♐ Feb 26 7:10	♎ Jul 7 1:47	♍ Nov 18 16:15
♈ Jun 8 0:08	♓ Oct 20 7:33	♑ Feb 28 19:45	♏ Jul 9 8:48	♎ Nov 20 20:35
♉ Jun 10 2:43	♈ Oct 22 12:41	♒ Mar 2 8:14	♐ Jul 11 19:06	♏ Nov 23 2:33
♊ Jun 12 2:48	♉ Oct 24 14:25	♓ Mar 4 18:30	♑ Jul 14 7:28	♐ Nov 25 10:33
♋ Jun 14 2:14	♊ Oct 26 14:33		♒ Jul 16 20:27	♑ Nov 27 20:57

(continued)

Table A-2 — The Moon *(continued)*

Sign	Date	Time	Sign	Date	Time	Sign	Date	Time	Year/Sign	Date	Time	Sign	Date	Time
♒	Nov 30	9:26	♏	Apr 8	18:01	♎	Aug 21	3:19	**2002**			♋	May 15	6:33
♓	Dec 2	22:23	♐	Apr 10	22:47	♏	Aug 23	4:50	♍	Jan 2	18:34	♌	May 17	12:52
♈	Dec 5	9:17	♑	Apr 13	7:21	♐	Aug 25	9:59	♎	Jan 4	20:23	♍	May 19	17:01
♉	Dec 7	16:27	♒	Apr 15	19:11	♑	Aug 27	19:02	♏	Jan 6	23:41	♎	May 21	19:19
♊	Dec 9	19:50	♓	Apr 18	8:00	♒	Aug 30	6:48	♐	Jan 9	4:57	♏	May 23	20:38
♋	Dec 11	20:48	♈	Apr 20	19:18	♓	Sept 1	19:32	♑	Jan 11	12:18	♐	May 25	22:20
♌	Dec 13	21:09	♉	Apr 23	3:56	♈	Sept 4	7:58	♒	Jan 13	21:41	♑	May 28	1:54
♍	Dec 15	22:30	♊	Apr 25	10:11	♉	Sept 6	19:18	♓	Jan 16	9:00	♒	May 30	8:35
♎	Dec 18	2:01	♋	Apr 27	14:49	♊	Sept 9	4:41	♈	Jan 18	21:35	♓	Jun 1	18:37
♏	Dec 20	8:12	♌	Apr 29	18:25	♋	Sept 11	11:09	♉	Jan 21	9:47	♈	Jun 4	6:51
♐	Dec 22	16:57	♍	May 1	21:16	♌	Sept 13	14:16	♊	Jan 23	19:28	♉	Jun 6	19:07
♑	Dec 25	3:54	♎	May 3	23:50	♍	Sept 15	14:39	♋	Jan 26	1:17	♊	Jun 9	5:29
♒	Dec 27	16:25	♏	May 6	3:01	♎	Sept 17	14:00	♌	Jan 28	3:31	♋	Jun 11	13:38
♓	Dec 30	5:27	♐	May 8	8:05	♏	Sept 19	14:27	♍	Jan 30	3:40	♌	Jun 13	18:39
2001			♑	May 10	16:10	♐	Sept 21	18:02	♎	Feb 1	3:44	♍	Jun 15	22:23
♈	Jan 1	17:14	♒	May 13	3:20	♑	Sept 24	1:48	♏	Feb 3	5:35	♎	Jun 18	1:11
♉	Jan 4	1:57	♓	May 15	16:01	♒	Sept 26	13:05	♐	Feb 5	10:21	♏	Jun 20	3:42
♊	Jan 6	6:44	♈	May 18	3:41	♓	Sept 29	1:50	♑	Feb 7	18:08	♐	Jun 22	6:42
♋	Jan 8	8:09	♉	May 20	12:29	♈	Oct 1	14:08	♒	Feb 10	4:15	♑	Jun 24	11:01
♌	Jan 10	7:44	♊	May 22	18:12	♉	Oct 4	1:01	♓	Feb 12	15:53	♒	Jun 26	17:36
♍	Jan 12	7:26	♋	May 24	21:42	♊	Oct 6	10:12	♈	Feb 15	4:26	♓	Jun 29	3:00
♎	Jan 14	9:05	♌	May 27	0:12	♋	Oct 8	17:19	♉	Feb 17	16:58	♈	Jul 1	14:49
♏	Jan 16	14:02	♍	May 29	2:38	♌	Oct 10	21:54	♊	Feb 20	3:50	♉	Jul 4	3:16
♐	Jan 18	22:36	♎	May 31	5:41	♍	Oct 12	23:58	♋	Feb 22	11:16	♊	Jul 6	14:01
♑	Jan 21	9:57	♏	Jun 2	9:56	♎	Oct 15	0:26	♌	Feb 24	14:36	♋	Jul 8	21:36
♒	Jan 23	22:43	♐	Jun 4	15:58	♏	Oct 17	1:03	♍	Feb 26	14:47	♌	Jul 11	2:08
♓	Jan 26	11:39	♑	Jun 7	0:23	♐	Oct 19	3:47	♎	Feb 28	13:47	♍	Jul 13	4:41
♈	Jan 28	23:35	♒	Jun 9	11:20	♑	Oct 21	10:11	♏	Mar 2	13:51	♎	Jul 15	6:39
♉	Jan 31	9:21	♓	Jun 11	23:53	♒	Oct 23	20:26	♐	Mar 4	16:55	♏	Jul 17	9:13
♊	Feb 2	15:56	♈	Jun 14	12:03	♓	Oct 26	8:56	♑	Mar 6	23:48	♐	Jul 19	13:02
♋	Feb 4	19:00	♉	Jun 16	21:39	♈	Oct 28	21:15	♒	Mar 9	9:56	♑	Jul 21	18:26
♌	Feb 6	19:21	♊	Jun 19	3:42	♉	Oct 31	7:48	♓	Mar 11	21:56	♒	Jul 24	1:40
♍	Feb 8	18:35	♋	Jun 21	6:41	♊	Nov 2	16:12	♈	Mar 14	10:34	♓	Jul 26	11:04
♎	Feb 10	18:46	♌	Jun 23	7:55	♋	Nov 4	22:44	♉	Mar 16	23:01	♈	Jul 28	22:39
♏	Feb 12	21:51	♍	Jun 25	8:58	♌	Nov 7	3:34	♊	Mar 19	10:20	♉	Jul 31	11:17
♐	Feb 15	5:02	♎	Jun 27	11:11	♍	Nov 9	6:49	♋	Mar 21	19:06	♊	Aug 2	22:46
♑	Feb 17	15:59	♏	Jun 29	15:28	♎	Nov 11	8:53	♌	Mar 24	0:12	♋	Aug 5	7:02
♒	Feb 20	4:53	♐	Jul 1	22:13	♏	Nov 13	10:44	♍	Mar 26	1:44	♌	Aug 7	11:27
♓	Feb 22	17:45	♑	Jul 4	7:21	♐	Nov 15	13:51	♎	Mar 28	1:04	♍	Aug 9	13:03
♈	Feb 25	5:20	♒	Jul 6	18:33	♑	Nov 17	19:40	♏	Mar 30	0:21	♎	Aug 11	13:38
♉	Feb 27	15:06	♓	Jul 9	7:05	♒	Nov 20	4:55	♐	Apr 1	1:48	♏	Aug 13	15:01
♊	Mar 1	22:36	♈	Jul 11	19:36	♓	Nov 22	16:52	♑	Apr 3	6:58	♐	Aug 15	18:25
♋	Mar 4	3:24	♉	Jul 14	6:13	♈	Nov 25	5:21	♒	Apr 5	16:07	♑	Aug 18	0:15
♌	Mar 6	5:30	♊	Jul 16	13:26	♉	Nov 27	16:06	♓	Apr 8	3:57	♒	Aug 20	8:16
♍	Mar 8	5:44	♋	Jul 18	16:56	♊	Nov 30	0:04	♈	Apr 10	16:40	♓	Aug 22	18:11
♎	Mar 10	5:47	♌	Jul 20	17:43	♋	Dec 2	5:30	♉	Apr 13	4:55	♈	Aug 25	5:48
♏	Mar 12	7:43	♍	Jul 22	17:29	♌	Dec 4	9:15	♊	Apr 15	15:56	♉	Aug 27	18:32
♐	Mar 14	13:17	♎	Jul 24	18:08	♍	Dec 6	12:11	♋	Apr 18	1:01	♊	Aug 30	6:45
♑	Mar 16	23:02	♏	Jul 26	21:17	♎	Dec 8	14:57	♌	Apr 20	7:20	♋	Sept 1	16:14
♒	Mar 19	11:36	♐	Jul 29	3:44	♏	Dec 10	18:09	♍	Apr 22	10:35	♌	Sept 3	21:36
♓	Mar 22	0:28	♑	Jul 31	13:16	♐	Dec 12	22:30	♎	Apr 24	11:22	♍	Sept 5	23:16
♈	Mar 24	11:44	♒	Aug 3	0:53	♑	Dec 15	4:48	♏	Apr 26	11:15	♎	Sept 7	22:57
♉	Mar 26	20:51	♓	Aug 5	13:30	♒	Dec 17	13:43	♐	Apr 28	12:13	♏	Sept 9	22:48
♊	Mar 29	4:01	♈	Aug 8	2:05	♓	Dec 20	1:09	♑	Apr 30	16:03	♐	Sept 12	0:44
♋	Mar 31	9:23	♉	Aug 10	13:23	♈	Dec 22	13:45	♒	May 2	23:43	♑	Sept 14	5:47
♌	Apr 2	12:54	♊	Aug 12	21:59	♉	Dec 25	1:12	♓	May 5	10:46	♒	Sept 16	13:54
♍	Apr 4	14:46	♋	Aug 15	2:55	♊	Dec 27	9:39	♈	May 7	23:22	♓	Sept 19	0:18
♎	Apr 6	15:57	♌	Aug 17	4:25	♋	Dec 29	14:40	♉	May 10	11:32	♈	Sept 21	12:11
			♍	Aug 19	3:53	♌	Dec 31	17:09	♊	May 12	22:04	♉	Sept 24	0:55

Table A-2 — The Moon (continued)

Column 1	Column 2	Column 3	Column 4	Column 5
♊ Sept 26 13:26	♓ Feb 2 14:55	♒ Jun 16 19:41	♑ Oct 29 5:37	♎ Mar 7 17:31
♋ Sept 29 0:01	♈ Feb 5 0:44	♓ Jun 19 0:57	♒ Oct 31 8:41	♏ Mar 9 21:03
♌ Oct 1 6:58	♉ Feb 7 12:59	♈ Jun 21 10:06	♓ Nov 2 14:52	♐ Mar 11 23:57
♍ Oct 3 9:52	♊ Feb 10 1:45	♉ Jun 23 22:15	♈ Nov 5 0:02	♑ Mar 14 2:51
♎ Oct 5 9:51	♋ Feb 12 12:19	♊ Jun 26 11:13	♉ Nov 7 11:29	♒ Mar 16 6:10
♏ Oct 7 8:57	♌ Feb 14 19:04	♋ Jun 28 22:52	♊ Nov 10 0:14	♓ Mar 18 10:26
♐ Oct 9 9:21	♍ Feb 16 22:22	♌ Jul 1 8:13	♋ Nov 12 13:10	♈ Mar 20 16:29
♑ Oct 11 12:45	♎ Feb 18 23:48	♍ Jul 3 15:16	♌ Nov 15 0:48	♉ Mar 23 1:10
♒ Oct 13 19:51	♏ Feb 21 1:09	♎ Jul 5 20:20	♍ Nov 17 9:36	♊ Mar 25 12:35
♓ Oct 16 6:07	♐ Feb 23 3:46	♏ Jul 7 23:43	♎ Nov 19 14:42	♋ Mar 28 1:23
♈ Oct 18 18:13	♑ Feb 25 8:11	♐ Jul 10 1:48	♏ Nov 21 16:24	♌ Mar 30 13:07
♉ Oct 21 6:57	♒ Feb 27 14:24	♑ Jul 12 3:21	♐ Nov 23 16:02	♍ Apr 1 21:45
♊ Oct 23 19:17	♓ Mar 1 22:26	♒ Jul 14 5:38	♑ Nov 25 15:31	♎ Apr 4 2:52
♋ Oct 26 6:10	♈ Mar 4 8:30	♓ Jul 16 10:14	♒ Nov 27 16:48	♏ Apr 6 5:24
♌ Oct 28 14:20	♉ Mar 6 20:36	♈ Jul 18 18:20	♓ Nov 29 21:25	♐ Apr 8 6:50
♍ Oct 30 18:59	♊ Mar 9 9:38	♉ Jul 21 5:48	♈ Dec 2 5:56	♑ Apr 10 8:33
♎ Nov 1 20:28	♋ Mar 11 21:12	♊ Jul 23 18:42	♉ Dec 4 17:30	♒ Apr 12 11:33
♏ Nov 3 20:10	♌ Mar 14 5:06	♋ Jul 26 6:23	♊ Dec 7 6:26	♓ Apr 14 16:24
♐ Nov 5 20:01	♍ Mar 16 8:52	♌ Jul 28 15:17	♋ Dec 9 19:11	♈ Apr 16 23:24
♑ Nov 7 21:59	♎ Mar 18 9:43	♍ Jul 30 21:27	♌ Dec 12 6:40	♉ Apr 19 8:43
♒ Nov 10 3:27	♏ Mar 20 9:38	♎ Aug 2 1:48	♍ Dec 14 16:07	♊ Apr 21 20:10
♓ Nov 12 12:42	♐ Mar 22 10:33	♏ Aug 4 5:12	♎ Dec 16 22:46	♋ Apr 24 8:56
♈ Nov 15 0:38	♑ Mar 24 13:48	♐ Aug 6 8:11	♏ Dec 19 2:20	♌ Apr 26 21:14
♉ Nov 17 13:23	♒ Mar 26 19:51	♑ Aug 8 11:02	♐ Dec 21 3:16	♍ Apr 29 7:00
♊ Nov 20 1:25	♓ Mar 29 4:26	♒ Aug 10 14:23	♑ Dec 23 2:55	♎ May 1 13:03
♋ Nov 22 11:48	♈ Mar 31 15:04	♓ Aug 12 19:19	♒ Dec 25 3:13	♏ May 3 15:38
♌ Nov 24 20:00	♉ Apr 3 3:20	♈ Aug 15 3:00	♓ Dec 27 6:10	♐ May 5 16:08
♍ Nov 27 1:42	♊ Apr 5 16:24	♉ Aug 17 13:52	♈ Dec 29 13:08	♑ May 7 16:17
♎ Nov 29 4:54	♋ Apr 8 4:36	♊ Aug 20 2:41	**2004** ♉ Jan 1 0:02	♒ May 9 17:46
♏ Dec 1 6:15	♌ Apr 10 13:54	♋ Aug 22 14:44	♊ Jan 3 12:58	♓ May 11 21:52
♐ Dec 3 6:58	♍ Apr 12 19:07	♌ Aug 24 23:48	♋ Jan 6 1:38	♈ May 14 5:02
♑ Dec 5 8:39	♎ Apr 14 20:42	♍ Aug 27 5:27	♌ Jan 8 12:38	♉ May 16 14:57
♒ Dec 7 12:54	♏ Apr 16 20:16	♎ Aug 29 8:41	♍ Jan 10 21:37	♊ May 19 2:41
♓ Dec 9 20:46	♐ Apr 18 19:51	♏ Aug 31 11:00	♎ Jan 13 4:38	♋ May 21 15:35
♈ Dec 12 7:58	♑ Apr 20 21:20	♐ Sept 2 13:32	♏ Jan 15 9:33	♌ May 24 4:07
♉ Dec 14 20:43	♒ Apr 23 1:58	♑ Sept 4 16:51	♐ Jan 17 12:18	♍ May 26 14:52
♊ Dec 17 8:43	♓ Apr 25 10:02	♒ Sept 6 21:15	♑ Jan 19 13:24	♎ May 28 22:22
♋ Dec 19 18:30	♈ Apr 27 20:54	♓ Sept 9 3:07	♒ Jan 21 14:11	♏ May 31 2:08
♌ Dec 22 1:48	♉ Apr 30 9:26	♈ Sept 11 11:09	♓ Jan 23 16:29	♐ Jun 2 2:52
♍ Dec 24 7:05	♊ May 2 22:27	♉ Sept 13 21:50	♈ Jan 25 22:06	♑ Jun 4 2:12
♎ Dec 26 10:53	♋ May 5 10:42	♊ Sept 16 10:32	♉ Jan 28 7:46	♒ Jun 6 2:10
♏ Dec 28 13:41	♌ May 7 20:46	♋ Sept 18 23:07	♊ Jan 30 20:18	♓ Jun 8 4:38
♐ Dec 30 16:01	♍ May 10 3:31	♌ Sept 21 9:02	♋ Feb 2 9:03	♈ Jun 10 10:49
2003 ♑ Jan 1 18:42	♎ May 12 6:42	♍ Sept 23 15:04	♌ Feb 4 19:50	♉ Jun 12 20:37
♒ Jan 3 22:56	♏ May 14 7:14	♎ Sept 25 17:49	♍ Feb 7 4:03	♊ Jun 15 8:44
♓ Jan 6 5:57	♐ May 16 6:43	♏ Sept 27 18:52	♎ Feb 9 10:12	♋ Jun 17 21:37
♈ Jan 8 16:15	♑ May 18 7:03	♐ Sept 29 19:57	♏ Feb 11 14:58	♌ Jun 20 10:05
♉ Jan 11 4:48	♒ May 20 10:01	♑ Oct 1 22:21	♐ Feb 13 18:35	♍ Jun 22 21:10
♊ Jan 13 17:08	♓ May 22 16:41	♒ Oct 4 2:45	♑ Feb 15 21:14	♎ Jun 25 5:50
♋ Jan 16 2:56	♈ May 25 2:59	♓ Oct 6 9:20	♒ Feb 17 23:27	♏ Jun 27 11:13
♌ Jan 18 9:29	♉ May 27 15:32	♈ Oct 8 18:07	♓ Feb 20 2:27	♐ Jun 29 13:15
♍ Jan 20 13:32	♊ May 30 4:32	♉ Oct 11 5:05	♈ Feb 22 7:45	♑ Jul 1 13:01
♎ Jan 22 16:23	♋ Jun 1 16:27	♊ Oct 13 17:45	♉ Feb 24 16:30	♒ Jul 3 12:22
♏ Jan 24 19:09	♌ Jun 4 2:25	♋ Oct 16 6:41	♊ Feb 27 4:22	♓ Jul 5 13:26
♐ Jan 26 22:26	♍ Jun 6 9:51	♌ Oct 18 17:41	♋ Feb 29 17:12	♈ Jul 7 18:03
♑ Jan 29 2:30	♎ Jun 8 14:30	♍ Oct 21 1:01	♌ Mar 3 4:18	♉ Jul 10 2:51
♒ Jan 31 7:44	♏ Jun 10 16:39	♎ Oct 23 4:27	♍ Mar 5 12:18	♊ Jul 12 14:45
	♐ Jun 12 17:12	♏ Oct 25 5:08		♋ Jul 15 3:40
	♑ Jun 14 17:38	♐ Oct 27 4:55		♌ Jul 17 15:56

(continued)

Table A-2 — The Moon *(continued)*

Sign	Date	Time	Sign	Date	Time	Sign	Date	Time	Sign	Date	Time	Sign	Date	Time
♍	Jul 20	2:44	♌	Dec 1	5:50	♉	Apr 9	10:50	♈	Aug 21	18:01	**2006**		
♎	Jul 22	11:39	♍	Dec 3	18:00	♊	Apr 11	17:55	♉	Aug 23	20:58	♒	Jan 1	7:15
♏	Jul 24	18:08	♎	Dec 6	3:46	♋	Apr 14	4:03	♊	Aug 26	3:43	♓	Jan 3	7:43
♐	Jul 26	21:48	♏	Dec 8	9:43	♌	Apr 16	16:17	♋	Aug 28	13:57	♈	Jan 5	9:44
♑	Jul 28	22:57	♐	Dec 10	11:54	♍	Apr 19	4:27	♌	Aug 31	2:14	♉	Jan 7	14:08
♒	Jul 30	22:54	♑	Dec 12	11:42	♎	Apr 21	14:27	♍	Sept 2	14:56	♊	Jan 9	20:59
♓	Aug 1	23:34	♒	Dec 14	11:10	♏	Apr 23	21:25	♎	Sept 5	2:52	♋	Jan 12	5:50
♈	Aug 4	2:59	♓	Dec 16	12:24	♐	Apr 26	1:46	♏	Sept 7	13:10	♌	Jan 14	16:31
♉	Aug 6	10:26	♈	Dec 18	16:52	♑	Apr 28	4:33	♐	Sept 9	21:03	♍	Jan 17	4:49
♊	Aug 8	21:33	♉	Dec 21	0:52	♒	Apr 30	6:54	♑	Sept 12	1:56	♎	Jan 19	17:49
♋	Aug 11	10:20	♊	Dec 23	11:32	♓	May 2	9:43	♒	Sept 14	4:02	♏	Jan 22	5:29
♌	Aug 13	22:30	♋	Dec 25	23:38	♈	May 4	13:36	♓	Sept 16	4:24	♐	Jan 24	13:37
♍	Aug 16	8:49	♌	Dec 28	12:14	♉	May 6	19:01	♈	Sept 18	4:43	♑	Jan 26	17:31
♎	Aug 18	17:09	♍	Dec 31	0:33	♊	May 9	2:29	♉	Sept 20	6:47	♒	Jan 28	18:09
♏	Aug 20	23:37				♋	May 11	12:20	♊	Sept 22	12:07	♓	Jan 30	17:31
♐	Aug 23	4:08	**2005**			♌	May 14	0:17	♋	Sept 24	21:10	♈	Feb 1	17:46
♑	Aug 25	6:46	♎	Jan 2	11:19	♍	May 16	12:46	♌	Sept 27	9:03	♉	Feb 3	20:31
♒	Aug 27	8:08	♏	Jan 4	19:00	♎	May 18	23:30	♍	Sept 29	21:44	♊	Feb 6	2:33
♓	Aug 29	9:33	♐	Jan 6	22:44	♏	May 21	6:49	♎	Oct 2	9:24	♋	Feb 8	11:34
♈	Aug 31	12:46	♑	Jan 8	23:11	♐	May 23	10:38	♏	Oct 4	19:03	♌	Feb 10	22:44
♉	Sept 2	19:16	♒	Jan 10	22:07	♑	May 25	12:11	♐	Oct 7	2:28	♍	Feb 13	11:!4
♊	Sept 5	5:24	♓	Jan 12	21:50	♒	May 27	13:10	♑	Oct 9	7:43	♎	Feb 16	0:09
♋	Sept 7	17:50	♈	Jan 15	0:27	♓	May 29	15:09	♒	Oct 11	11:05	♏	Feb 18	12:12
♌	Sept 10	6:06	♉	Jan 17	7:06	♈	May 31	19:07	♓	Oct 13	13:05	♐	Feb 20	21:38
♍	Sept 12	16:16	♊	Jan 19	17:24	♉	Jun 3	1:20	♈	Oct 15	14:39	♑	Feb 23	3:16
♎	Sept 14	23:54	♋	Jan 22	5:42	♊	Jun 5	9:36	♉	Oct 17	17:04	♒	Feb 25	5:15
♏	Sept 17	5:25	♌	Jan 24	18:21	♋	Jun 7	19:46	♊	Oct 19	21:44	♓	Feb 27	4:56
♐	Sept 19	9:30	♍	Jan 27	6:24	♌	Jun 10	7:39	♋	Oct 22	5:41	♈	Mar 1	4:19
♑	Sept 21	12:35	♎	Jan 29	17:13	♍	Jun 12	20:22	♌	Oct 24	16:48	♉	Mar 3	5:22
♒	Sept 23	15:10	♏	Feb 1	1:51	♎	Jun 15	7:59	♍	Oct 27	5:28	♊	Mar 5	9:38
♓	Sept 25	17:55	♐	Feb 3	7:21	♏	Jun 17	16:23	♎	Oct 29	17:15	♋	Mar 7	17:38
♈	Sept 27	21:57	♑	Feb 5	9:32	♐	Jun 19	20:45	♏	Nov 1	2:29	♌	Mar 10	4:43
♉	Sept 30	4:24	♒	Feb 7	9:26	♑	Jun 21	21:52	♐	Nov 3	8:55	♍	Mar 12	17:24
♊	Oct 2	13:55	♓	Feb 9	8:59	♒	Jun 23	21:36	♑	Nov 5	13:17	♎	Mar 15	6:13
♋	Oct 5	1:54	♈	Feb 11	10:21	♓	Jun 25	22:03	♒	Nov 7	16:31	♏	Mar 17	17:59
♌	Oct 7	14:23	♉	Feb 13	15:18	♈	Jun 28	0:51	♓	Nov 9	19:22	♐	Mar 20	3:43
♍	Oct 10	1:00	♊	Feb 16	0:18	♉	Jun 30	6:45	♈	Nov 11	22:22	♑	Mar 22	10:35
♎	Oct 12	8:32	♋	Feb 18	12:13	♊	Jul 2	15:26	♉	Nov 14	2:02	♒	Mar 24	14:21
♏	Oct 14	13:10	♌	Feb 21	0:54	♋	Jul 5	2:07	♊	Nov 16	7:10	♓	Mar 26	15:32
♐	Oct 16	15:58	♍	Feb 23	12:44	♌	Jul 7	14:11	♋	Nov 18	14:42	♈	Mar 28	15:31
♑	Oct 18	18:07	♎	Feb 25	22:59	♍	Jul 10	2:57	♌	Nov 21	1:10	♉	Mar 30	16:00
♒	Oct 20	20:38	♏	Feb 28	7:21	♎	Jul 12	15:09	♍	Nov 23	13:41	♊	Apr 1	18:50
♓	Oct 23	0:13	♐	Mar 2	13:29	♏	Jul 15	0:51	♎	Nov 26	1:58	♋	Apr 4	1:14
♈	Oct 25	5:24	♑	Mar 4	17:12	♐	Jul 17	6:35	♏	Nov 28	11:33	♌	Apr 6	11:25
♉	Oct 27	12:37	♒	Mar 6	18:49	♑	Jul 19	8:26	♐	Nov 30	17:32	♍	Apr 8	23:59
♊	Oct 29	22:11	♓	Mar 8	19:32	♒	Jul 21	7:55	♑	Dec 2	20:42	♎	Apr 11	12:47
♋	Nov 1	9:53	♈	Mar 10	21:03	♓	Jul 23	7:12	♒	Dec 4	22:36	♏	Apr 14	0:09
♌	Nov 3	22:32	♉	Mar 13	1:05	♈	Jul 25	8:23	♓	Dec 7	0:44	♐	Apr 16	9:20
♍	Nov 6	10:00	♊	Mar 15	8:44	♉	Jul 27	12:54	♈	Dec 9	4:02	♑	Apr 18	16:13
♎	Nov 8	18:23	♋	Mar 17	19:44	♊	Jul 29	21:02	♉	Dec 11	8:46	♒	Apr 20	20:56
♏	Nov 10	23:05	♌	Mar 20	8:17	♋	Aug 1	7:52	♊	Dec 13	14:59	♓	Apr 22	23:44
♐	Nov 13	0:56	♍	Mar 22	20:10	♌	Aug 3	20:10	♋	Dec 15	23:01	♈	Apr 25	1:12
♑	Nov 15	1:33	♎	Mar 25	6:00	♍	Aug 6	8:54	♌	Dec 18	9:18	♉	Apr 27	2:26
♒	Nov 17	2:39	♏	Mar 27	13:29	♎	Aug 8	21:08	♍	Dec 20	21:39	♊	Apr 29	4:58
♓	Nov 19	5:38	♐	Mar 29	18:56	♏	Aug 11	7:35	♎	Dec 23	10:26	♋	May 1	10:18
♈	Nov 21	11:11	♑	Mar 31	22:48	♐	Aug 13	14:47	♏	Dec 25	21:04	♌	May 3	19:18
♉	Nov 23	19:16	♒	Apr 3	1:31	♑	Aug 15	18:13	♐	Dec 28	3:43	♍	May 6	7:20
♊	Nov 26	5:25	♓	Apr 5	3:45	♒	Aug 17	18:39	♑	Dec 30	6:35	♎	May 8	20:09
♋	Nov 28	17:10	♈	Apr 7	6:28	♓	Aug 19	17:52				♏	May 11	7:25

Table A-2 — The Moon *(continued)*

♐ May 13 15:57	♏ Sep 24 20:55	♌ Feb 1 0:15	♋ Jun 15 8:44	♊ Oct 27 19:11
♑ May 15 21:59	♐ Sep 27 8:16	♍ Feb 3 9:34	♌ Jun 17 12:25	♋ Oct 29 19:49
♒ May 18 2:20	♑ Sep 29 17:01	♎ Feb 5 21:15	♍ Jun 19 19:45	♌ Oct 31 23:48
♓ May 20 5:39	♒ Oct 1 22:24	♏ Feb 8 10:10	♎ Jun 22 6:44	♍ Nov 3 7:45
♈ May 22 8:24	♓ Oct 4 0:33	♐ Feb 10 22:01	♏ Jun 24 19:27	♎ Nov 5 18:47
♉ May 24 11:00	♈ Oct 6 0:32	♑ Feb 13 6:43	♐ Jun 27 7:24	♏ Nov 8 7:18
♊ May 26 14:19	♉ Oct 8 0:05	♒ Feb 15 11:35	♑ Jun 29 17:04	♐ Nov 10 19:59
♋ May 28 19:34	♊ Oct 10 1:07	♓ Feb 17 13:29	♒ Jul 2 0:23	♑ Nov 13 8:01
♌ May 31 3:52	♋ Oct 12 5:21	♈ Feb 19 14:06	♓ Jul 4 5:52	♒ Nov 15 18:30
♍ Jun 2 15:18	♌ Oct 14 13:38	♉ Feb 21 15:04	♈ Jul 6 9:57	♓ Nov 18 2:15
♎ Jun 5 4:09	♍ Oct 17 1:16	♊ Feb 23 17:42	♉ Jul 8 12:54	♈ Nov 20 6:24
♏ Jun 7 15:41	♎ Oct 19 14:20	♋ Feb 25 22:48	♊ Jul 10 15:10	♉ Nov 22 7:19
♐ Jun 10 0:05	♏ Oct 22 2:55	♌ Feb 28 6:30	♋ Jul 12 17:39	♊ Nov 24 6:29
♑ Jun 12 5:18	♐ Oct 24 13:54	♍ Mar 2 16:32	♌ Jul 14 21:44	♋ Nov 26 6:07
♒ Jun 14 8:33	♑ Oct 26 22:47	♎ Mar 5 4:25	♍ Jul 17 4:40	♌ Nov 28 8:24
♓ Jun 16 11:06	♒ Oct 29 5:17	♏ Mar 7 17:17	♎ Jul 19 14:54	♍ Nov 30 14:25
♈ Jun 18 13:53	♓ Oct 31 9:10	♐ Mar 10 5:37	♏ Jul 22 3:18	♎ Dec 3 1:01
♉ Jun 20 17:23	♈ Nov 2 10:46	♑ Mar 12 15:34	♐ Jul 24 15:30	♏ Dec 5 13:30
♊ Jun 22 21:49	♉ Nov 4 11:04	♒ Mar 14 21:52	♑ Jul 27 1:22	♐ Dec 8 2:11
♋ Jun 25 3:48	♊ Nov 6 11:47	♓ Mar 17 0:30	♒ Jul 29 8:14	♑ Dec 10 13:51
♌ Jun 27 12:09	♋ Nov 8 14:25	♈ Mar 19 0:41	♓ Jul 31 12:14	♒ Dec 13 0:02
♍ Jun 29 11:15	♌ Nov 10 21:34	♉ Mar 21 0:15	♈ Aug 2 15:43	♓ Dec 15 8:15
♎ Jul 2 12:06	♍ Nov 13 8:19	♊ Mar 23 1:07	♉ Aug 4 18:15	♈ Dec 17 13:53
♏ Jul 5 0:13	♎ Nov 15 21:15	♋ Mar 25 4:49	♊ Aug 6 21:02	♉ Dec 19 16:48
♐ Jul 7 9:14	♏ Nov 18 9:47	♌ Mar 27 12:05	♋ Aug 9 0:35	♊ Dec 21 17:14
♑ Jul 9 14:25	♐ Nov 20 20:16	♍ Mar 29 22:27	♌ Aug 11 5:42	♋ Dec 23 17:17
♒ Jul 11 16:46	♑ Nov 23 4:25	♎ Apr 1 10:44	♍ Aug 13 13:03	♌ Dec 25 18:51
♓ Jul 13 18:00	♒ Nov 25 10:41	♏ Apr 3 23:36	♎ Aug 15 23:04	♍ Dec 27 23:44
♈ Jul 15 19:39	♓ Nov 27 15:21	♐ Apr 6 11:57	♏ Aug 18 11:14	♎ Dec 30 8:37
♉ Jul 17 22:43	♈ Nov 29 18:30	♑ Apr 8 22:35	♐ Aug 20 23:45	**2008**
♊ Jul 20 3:37	♉ Dec 1 20:26	♒ Apr 11 6:23	♑ Aug 23 10:20	♏ Jan 1 20:31
♋ Jul 22 10:27	♊ Dec 3 22:05	♓ Apr 13 10:38	♒ Aug 25 17:35	♐ Jan 4 9:14
♌ Jul 24 19:25	♋ Dec 6 1:01	♈ Apr 15 11:47	♓ Aug 27 21:34	♑ Jan 6 20:42
♍ Jul 27 6:37	♌ Dec 8 6:51	♉ Apr 17 11:11	♈ Aug 29 23:24	♒ Jan 9 6:12
♎ Jul 29 19:28	♍ Dec 10 16:31	♊ Apr 19 10:51	♉ Sep 1 0:36	♓ Jan 11 13:44
♏ Aug 1 8:08	♎ Dec 13 5:01	♋ Apr 21 12:50	♊ Sep 3 2:30	♈ Jan 13 19:24
♐ Aug 3 18:14	♏ Dec 15 17:43	♌ Apr 23 18:38	♋ Sep 5 6:08	♉ Jan 15 23:13
♑ Aug 6 0:19	♐ Dec 18 4:10	♍ Apr 26 4:24	♌ Sep 7 12:00	♊ Jan 18 1:30
♒ Aug 8 2:47	♑ Dec 20 11:38	♎ Apr 28 16:45	♍ Sep 9 20:10	♋ Jan 20 3:05
♓ Aug 10 3:11	♒ Dec 22 16:49	♏ May 1 5:41	♎ Sep 12 6:32	♌ Jan 22 5:20
♈ Aug 12 3:22	♓ Dec 24 20:49	♐ May 3 17:48	♏ Sep 14 18:37	♍ Jan 24 9:48
♉ Aug 14 5:00	♈ Dec 27 0:04	♑ May 6 4:21	♐ Sep 17 7:21	♎ Jan 26 17:35
♊ Aug 16 9:07	♉ Dec 29 3:08	♒ May 8 12:47	♑ Sep 19 18:52	♏ Jan 29 4:35
♋ Aug 18 16:03	♊ Dec 31 6:16	♓ May 10 18:32	♒ Sep 22 3:19	♐ Jan 31 17:08
♌ Aug 21 1:34	**2007**	♈ May 12 21:19	♓ Sep 24 7:55	♑ Feb 3 4:52
♍ Aug 23 13:08	♋ Jan 2 10:14	♉ May 14 21:48	♈ Sep 26 9:22	♒ Feb 5 14:10
♎ Aug 26 2:02	♌ Jan 4 16:14	♊ May 16 21:33	♉ Sep 28 9:17	♓ Feb 7 20:46
♏ Aug 28 14:57	♍ Jan 7 1:19	♋ May 18 22:37	♊ Sep 30 9:34	♈ Feb 10 1:17
♐ Aug 31 2:00	♎ Jan 9 13:15	♌ May 21 2:57	♋ Oct 2 11:57	♉ Feb 12 4:34
♑ Sep 2 9:34	♏ Jan 12 2:08	♍ May 23 11:27	♌ Oct 4 17:27	♊ Feb 14 7:19
♒ Sep 4 13:15	♐ Jan 14 13:12	♎ May 25 23:17	♍ Oct 7 2:02	♋ Feb 16 10:12
♓ Sep 6 13:56	♑ Jan 16 20:49	♏ May 28 12:12	♎ Oct 9 12:58	♌ Feb 18 13:51
♈ Sep 8 13:22	♒ Jan 19 1:15	♐ May 31 0:07	♏ Oct 12 1:14	♍ Feb 20 19:07
♉ Sep 10 13:29	♓ Jan 21 3:48	♑ Jun 2 10:09	♐ Oct 14 13:59	♎ Feb 23 2:45
♊ Sep 12 15:59	♈ Jan 23 5:51	♒ Jun 4 18:16	♑ Oct 17 2:02	♏ Feb 25 13:05
♋ Sep 14 21:53	♉ Jan 25 8:29	♓ Jun 7 0:23	♒ Oct 19 11:51	♐ Feb 28 1:23
♌ Sep 17 7:14	♊ Jan 27 12:09	♈ Jun 9 4:27	♓ Oct 21 18:03	♑ Mar 1 13:33
♍ Sep 19 19:06	♋ Jan 29 17:17	♉ Jun 11 6:29	♈ Oct 23 20:24	♒ Mar 3 23:25
♎ Sep 22 8:07		♊ Jun 13 7:24	♉ Oct 25 20:06	

Table A-2 — The Moon (continued)

Sign	Date	Time	Sign	Date	Time	Sign	Date	Time	Sign	Date	Time	Sign	Date	Time
♓	Mar 6	5:52	♒	Jul 18	10:40	♑	Nov 29	12:48	♎	Apr 7	22:22	♍	Aug 20	9:01
♈	Mar 8	9:32	♓	Jul 20	20:08	♒	Dec 2	1:45	♏	Apr 10	4:23	♎	Aug 22	10:11
♉	Mar 10	11:14	♈	Jul 23	3:23	♓	Dec 4	13:23	♐	Apr 12	13:01	♏	Aug 24	14:16
♊	Mar 12	12:55	♉	Jul 25	8:14	♈	Dec 6	21:44	♑	Apr 15	0:28	♐	Aug 26	22:17
♋	Mar 14	15:38	♊	Jul 27	10:55	♉	Dec 9	1:52	♒	Apr 17	13:19	♑	Aug 29	9:45
♌	Mar 16	20:04	♋	Jul 29	12:12	♊	Dec 11	2:34	♓	Apr 20	0:55	♒	Aug 31	22:43
♍	Mar 19	2:25	♌	Jul 31	13:31	♋	Dec 13	1:40	♈	Apr 22	9:09	♓	Sep 3	10:58
♎	Mar 21	10:44	♍	Aug 2	15:59	♌	Dec 15	1:23	♉	Apr 24	13:46	♈	Sep 5	21:14
♏	Mar 23	21:07	♎	Aug 4	21:28	♍	Dec 17	3:36	♊	Apr 26	16:02	♉	Sep 8	5:18
♐	Mar 26	9:11	♏	Aug 7	6:27	♎	Dec 19	9:23	♋	Apr 28	17:38	♊	Sep 10	11:16
♑	Mar 28	21:43	♐	Aug 9	18:11	♏	Dec 21	18:37	♌	Apr 30	19:56	♋	Sep 12	15:20
♒	Mar 31	8:34	♑	Aug 12	6:42	♐	Dec 24	6:13	♍	May 2	23:37	♌	Sep 14	17:39
♓	Apr 2	15:55	♒	Aug 14	17:56	♑	Dec 26	18:56	♎	May 5	4:52	♍	Sep 16	18:56
♈	Apr 4	19:27	♓	Aug 17	2:47	♒	Dec 29	7:43	♏	May 7	11:48	♎	Sep 18	20:27
♉	Apr 6	20:20	♈	Aug 19	9:09	♓	Dec 31	19:27	♐	May 9	20:50	♏	Sep 20	23:51
♊	Apr 8	20:27	♉	Aug 21	13:37				♑	May 12	8:09	♐	Sep 23	6:42
♋	Apr 10	21:43	♊	Aug 23	16:49	**2009**			♒	May 14	21:02	♑	Sep 25	17:19
♌	Apr 13	1:28	♋	Aug 25	19:19	♈	Jan 3	4:50	♓	May 17	9:17	♒	Sep 28	6:07
♍	Apr 15	8:06	♌	Aug 27	21:51	♉	Jan 5	10:45	♈	May 19	18:30	♓	Sep 30	18:26
♎	Apr 17	17:10	♍	Aug 30	1:19	♊	Jan 7	13:11	♉	May 21	23:40	♈	Oct 3	4:20
♏	Apr 20	4:01	♎	Sep 1	6:45	♋	Jan 9	13:14	♊	May 24	1:34	♉	Oct 5	11:33
♐	Apr 22	16:08	♏	Sep 3	15:02	♌	Jan 11	12:41	♋	May 26	1:57	♊	Oct 7	16:47
♑	Apr 25	4:47	♐	Sep 6	2:10	♍	Jan 13	13:32	♌	May 28	2:45	♋	Oct 9	20:47
♒	Apr 27	16:27	♑	Sep 8	14:25	♎	Jan 15	17:30	♍	May 30	5:18	♌	Oct 12	0:03
♓	Apr 30	1:11	♒	Sep 11	2:19	♏	Jan 18	1:20	♎	Jun 1	10:16	♍	Oct 14	2:45
♈	May 2	5:50	♓	Sep 13	11:05	♐	Jan 20	12:30	♏	Jun 3	17:44	♎	Oct 16	5:30
♉	May 4	6:58	♈	Sep 15	16:38	♑	Jan 23	1:18	♐	Jun 6	3:24	♏	Oct 18	9:22
♊	May 6	6:18	♉	Sep 17	19:57	♒	Jan 25	13:57	♑	Jun 8	15:00	♐	Oct 20	15:49
♋	May 8	6:01	♊	Sep 19	22:17	♓	Jan 28	1:12	♒	Jun 11	3:53	♑	Oct 23	1:38
♌	May 10	8:09	♋	Sep 22	0:48	♈	Jan 30	10:25	♓	Jun 13	16:32	♒	Oct 25	14:08
♍	May 12	13:48	♌	Sep 24	4:14	♉	Feb 1	17:09	♈	Jun 16	2:51	♓	Oct 28	2:46
♎	May 14	22:47	♍	Sep 26	8:52	♊	Feb 3	21:15	♉	Jun 18	9:21	♈	Oct 30	12:57
♏	May 17	9:59	♎	Sep 28	3:06	♋	Feb 5	23:06	♊	Jun 20	11:59	♉	Nov 1	19:45
♐	May 19	22:19	♏	Sep 30	23:26	♌	Feb 7	23:43	♋	Jun 22	12:11	♊	Nov 3	23:53
♑	May 22	10:56	♐	Oct 3	10:15	♍	Feb 10	0:39	♌	Jun 24	11:50	♋	Nov 6	2:43
♒	May 24	22:52	♑	Oct 5	22:49	♎	Feb 12	3:32	♍	Jun 26	12:46	♌	Nov 8	5:22
♓	May 27	8:39	♒	Oct 8	11:03	♏	Feb 14	9:51	♎	Jun 28	16:25	♍	Nov 10	8:31
♈	May 29	14:52	♓	Oct 10	20:31	♐	Feb 16	19:54	♏	Jun 30	23:19	♎	Nov 12	12:33
♉	May 31	17:18	♈	Oct 13	2:06	♑	Feb 19	8:26	♐	Jul 3	9:11	♏	Nov 14	17:24
♊	Jun 2	17:05	♉	Oct 15	4:30	♒	Feb 21	21:07	♑	Jul 5	21:08	♐	Nov 17	0:22
♋	Jun 4	16:15	♊	Oct 17	5:26	♓	Feb 24	8:00	♒	Jul 8	10:04	♑	Nov 19	10:01
♌	Jun 6	17:00	♋	Oct 19	6:41	♈	Feb 26	16:24	♓	Jul 10	22:44	♒	Nov 21	22:11
♍	Jun 8	21:01	♌	Oct 21	9:34	♉	Feb 28	22:33	♈	Jul 13	9:39	♓	Nov 24	11:07
♎	Jun 11	4:55	♍	Oct 23	14:40	♊	Mar 3	2:58	♉	Jul 15	17:30	♈	Nov 26	22:11
♏	Jun 13	15:53	♎	Oct 25	21:48	♋	Mar 5	6:07	♊	Jul 17	21:41	♉	Nov 29	5:34
♐	Jun 16	4:20	♏	Oct 28	6:47	♌	Mar 7	8:25	♋	Jul 19	22:51	♊	Dec 1	9:24
♑	Jun 18	16:52	♐	Oct 30	17:41	♍	Mar 9	10:34	♌	Jul 21	22:28	♋	Dec 3	11:00
♒	Jun 21	4:34	♑	Nov 2	6:14	♎	Mar 11	13:45	♍	Jul 23	22:22	♌	Dec 5	12:06
♓	Jun 23	14:32	♒	Nov 4	19:02	♏	Mar 13	19:23	♎	Jul 26	0:25	♍	Dec 7	14:05
♈	Jun 25	21:48	♓	Nov 7	5:44	♐	Mar 16	4:22	♏	Jul 28	5:56	♎	Dec 9	17:47
♉	Jun 28	1:51	♈	Nov 9	12:26	♑	Mar 18	16:19	♐	Jul 30	15:10	♏	Dec 11	23:31
♊	Jun 30	3:03	♉	Nov 11	15:06	♒	Mar 21	5:07	♑	Aug 2	3:09	♐	Dec 14	7:25
♋	Jul 2	2:53	♊	Nov 13	15:11	♓	Mar 23	16:08	♒	Aug 4	16:08	♑	Dec 16	17:32
♌	Jul 4	3:15	♋	Nov 15	14:52	♈	Mar 26	0:03	♓	Aug 7	4:34	♒	Dec 19	5:39
♍	Jul 6	6:04	♌	Nov 17	16:08	♉	Mar 28	5:08	♈	Aug 9	15:24	♓	Dec 21	18:42
♎	Jul 8	12:32	♍	Nov 19	20:13	♊	Mar 30	8:36	♉	Aug 11	23:49	♈	Dec 24	6:40
♏	Jul 10	22:35	♎	Nov 22	3:20	♋	Apr 1	11:30	♊	Aug 14	5:26	♉	Dec 26	15:26
♐	Jul 13	10:50	♏	Nov 24	12:54	♌	Apr 3	14:33	♋	Aug 16	8:13	♊	Dec 28	20:13
♑	Jul 15	23:20	♐	Nov 27	0:14	♍	Apr 5	18:01	♌	Aug 18	8:56	♋	Dec 30	21:46

Table A-2 — The Moon *(continued)*

2010

♌ Jan 1 21:40	♊ May 14 8:18	♉ Sep 25 15:17	♒ Feb 1 18:22	♑ Jun 16 0:59
♍ Jan 3 21:52	♋ May 16 12:46	♊ Sep 28 1:11	♓ Feb 4 5:24	♒ Jun 18 6:48
♎ Jan 5 23:58	♌ May 18 16:06	♋ Sep 30 8:45	♈ Feb 6 17:46	♓ Jun 20 15:45
♏ Jan 8 5:00	♍ May 20 18:59	♌ Oct 2 13:20	♉ Feb 9 6:23	♈ Jun 23 3:24
♐ Jan 10 13:09	♎ May 22 21:50	♍ Oct 4 15:00	♊ Feb 11 17:21	♉ Jun 25 15:53
♑ Jan 12 23:54	♏ May 25 1:16	♎ Oct 6 14:51	♋ Feb 14 0:48	♊ Jun 28 2:56
♒ Jan 15 12:17	♐ May 27 6:16	♏ Oct 8 14:51	♌ Feb 16 4:14	♋ Jun 30 11:13
♓ Jan 18 1:17	♑ May 29 13:44	♐ Oct 10 17:09	♍ Feb 18 4:38	♌ Jul 2 16:42
♈ Jan 20 13:37	♒ Jun 1 0:07	♑ Oct 12 23:16	♎ Feb 20 4:00	♍ Jul 4 20:16
♉ Jan 22 23:40	♓ Jun 3 12:34	♒ Oct 15 9:24	♏ Feb 22 4:28	♎ Jul 6 22:53
♊ Jan 25 6:11	♈ Jun 6 0:50	♓ Oct 17 21:51	♐ Feb 24 7:46	♏ Jul 9 1:31
♋ Jan 27 9:02	♉ Jun 8 10:41	♈ Oct 20 10:23	♑ Feb 26 14:32	♐ Jul 11 4:47
♌ Jan 29 9:10	♊ Jun 10 17:10	♉ Oct 22 21:30	♒ Mar 1 0:15	♑ Jul 13 9:14
♍ Jan 31 8:23	♋ Jun 12 20:51	♊ Oct 25 6:48	♓ Mar 3 11:47	♒ Jul 15 15:30
♎ Feb 2 8:41	♌ Jun 14 22:54	♋ Oct 27 14:15	♈ Mar 6 0:14	♓ Jul 18 0:13
♏ Feb 4 11:56	♍ Jun 17 0:41	♌ Oct 29 19:39	♉ Mar 8 12:52	♈ Jul 20 11:26
♐ Feb 6 19:04	♎ Jun 19 3:12	♍ Oct 31 22:50	♊ Mar 11 0:30	♉ Jul 22 23:58
♑ Feb 9 5:44	♏ Jun 21 7:14	♎ Nov 3 0:18	♋ Mar 13 9:30	♊ Jul 25 11:34
♒ Feb 11 18:24	♐ Jun 23 13:10	♏ Nov 5 1:16	♌ Mar 15 14:32	♋ Jul 27 20:12
♓ Feb 14 7:23	♑ Jun 25 21:22	♐ Nov 7 3:28	♍ Mar 17 15:53	♌ Jul 30 1:16
♈ Feb 16 19:31	♒ Jun 28 7:52	♑ Nov 9 8:36	♎ Mar 19 15:03	♍ Aug 1 3:41
♉ Feb 19 5:54	♓ Jun 30 20:10	♒ Nov 11 17:32	♏ Mar 21 14:17	♎ Aug 3 5:05
♊ Feb 21 13:47	♈ Jul 3 8:44	♓ Nov 14 5:24	♐ Mar 23 15:44	♏ Aug 5 6:57
♋ Feb 23 18:29	♉ Jul 5 19:29	♈ Nov 16 17:59	♑ Mar 25 20:58	♐ Aug 7 10:21
♌ Feb 25 20:09	♊ Jul 8 2:51	♉ Nov 19 5:05	♒ Mar 28 6:00	♑ Aug 9 15:38
♍ Feb 27 19:53	♋ Jul 10 6:37	♊ Nov 21 13:46	♓ Mar 30 17:38	♒ Aug 11 22:48
♎ Mar 1 19:31	♌ Jul 12 7:54	♋ Nov 23 20:13	♈ Apr 2 6:16	♓ Aug 14 7:54
♏ Mar 3 21:11	♍ Jul 14 8:14	♌ Nov 26 1:00	♉ Apr 4 18:46	♈ Aug 16 19:02
♐ Mar 6 2:36	♎ Jul 16 9:24	♍ Nov 28 4:34	♊ Apr 7 6:22	♉ Aug 19 7:37
♑ Mar 8 12:13	♏ Jul 18 12:41	♎ Nov 30 7:15	♋ Apr 9 16:02	♊ Aug 21 19:53
♒ Mar 11 0:43	♐ Jul 20 18:49	♏ Dec 2 9:43	♌ Apr 11 22:37	♋ Aug 24 5:31
♓ Mar 13 13:44	♑ Jul 23 3:39	♐ Dec 4 12:59	♍ Apr 14 1:41	♌ Aug 26 11:08
♈ Mar 16 1:32	♒ Jul 25 14:38	♑ Dec 6 18:15	♎ Apr 16 1:58	♍ Aug 28 13:13
♉ Mar 18 11:30	♓ Jul 28 3:00	♒ Dec 9 2:31	♏ Apr 18 1:18	♎ Aug 30 13:25
♊ Mar 20 19:29	♈ Jul 30 15:42	♓ Dec 11 13:41	♐ Apr 20 1:50	♏ Sep 1 13:48
♋ Mar 23 1:16	♉ Aug 2 3:13	♈ Dec 14 2:15	♑ Apr 22 5:24	♐ Sep 3 16:04
♌ Mar 25 4:38	♊ Aug 4 11:54	♉ Dec 16 13:49	♒ Apr 24 12:59	♑ Sep 5 21:03
♍ Mar 27 5:57	♋ Aug 6 16:49	♊ Dec 18 22:37	♓ Apr 26 23:58	♒ Sep 8 4:42
♎ Mar 29 6:20	♌ Aug 8 18:22	♋ Dec 21 4:22	♈ Apr 29 12:34	♓ Sep 10 14:27
♏ Mar 31 7:41	♍ Aug 10 18:00	♌ Dec 23 7:50	♉ May 2 0:59	♈ Sep 13 1:50
♐ Apr 2 11:53	♎ Aug 12 17:42	♍ Dec 25 10:13	♊ May 4 12:08	♉ Sep 15 14:25
♑ Apr 4 20:07	♏ Aug 14 19:26	♎ Dec 27 12:38	♋ May 6 21:31	♊ Sep 18 3:06
♒ Apr 7 7:51	♐ Aug 17 0:34	♏ Dec 29 15:50	♌ May 9 4:35	♋ Sep 20 13:53
♓ Apr 9 20:48	♑ Aug 19 9:16	♐ Dec 31 20:21	♍ May 11 10:03	♌ Sep 22 20:55
♈ Apr 12 8:31	♒ Aug 21 20:38		♎ May 13 10:57	♍ Sep 24 23:50
♉ Apr 14 17:55	♓ Aug 24 9:11	**2011**	♏ May 15 11:31	♎ Sep 26 23:51
♊ Apr 17 1:08	♈ Aug 26 21:49	♑ Jan 3 2:39	♐ May 17 12:23	♏ Sep 28 23:05
♋ Apr 19 6:39	♉ Aug 29 9:36	♒ Jan 5 11:08	♑ May 19 15:15	♐ Sep 30 23:41
♌ Apr 21 10:42	♊ Aug 31 19:19	♓ Jan 7 21:57	♒ May 21 21:31	♑ Oct 3 3:16
♍ Apr 23 13:25	♋ Sep 3 1:50	♈ Jan 10 10:24	♓ May 24 7:24	♒ Oct 4 10:18
♎ Apr 25 15:17	♌ Sep 5 4:45	♉ Jan 12 22:36	♈ May 26 19:37	♓ Oct 7 20:13
♏ Apr 27 17:29	♍ Sep 7 4:53	♊ Jan 15 8:22	♉ May 29 8:02	♈ Oct 10 7:57
♐ Apr 29 21:36	♎ Sep 9 4:01	♋ Jan 17 14:29	♊ May 31 18:56	♉ Oct 12 20:34
♑ May 2 5:00	♏ Sep 11 4:21	♌ Jan 19 17:15	♋ Jun 3 3:37	♊ Oct 15 9:15
♒ May 4 15:52	♐ Sep 13 7:52	♍ Jan 21 18:10	♌ Jun 5 10:03	♋ Oct 17 20:37
♓ May 7 4:34	♑ Sep 15 15:30	♎ Jan 23 18:58	♍ Jun 7 14:33	♌ Oct 20 5:06
♈ May 9 16:29	♒ Sep 18 2:35	♏ Jan 25 21:15	♎ Jun 9 17:31	♍ Oct 22 9:41
♉ May 12 1:48	♓ Sep 20 15:15	♐ Jan 28 1:55	♏ Jun 11 19:34	♎ Oct 24 10:48
	♈ Sep 23 3:47	♑ Jan 30 9:04	♐ Jun 13 21:39	♏ Oct 26 10:08

(continued)

Table A-2 — The Moon *(continued)*

♐	Oct 28 9:44	♒	Jan 22 21:53	♉	Apr 20 23:05	♌	Jul 19 5:13	♏	Oct 15 19:07
♑	Oct 30 11:38	♓	Jan 25 4:11	♊	Apr 23 12:04	♍	Jul 21 12:24	♐	Oct 17 19:25
♒	Nov 1 17:08	♈	Jan 27 13:28	♋	Apr 26 0:42	♎	Jul 23 17:39	♑	Oct 19 20:41
♓	Nov 4 2:18	♉	Jan 30 1:29	♌	Apr 28 11:11	♏	Jul 25 21:29	♒	Oct 22 0:03
♈	Nov 6 14:02	♊	Feb 1 14:15	♍	Apr 30 18:03	♐	Jul 28 0:18	♓	Oct 24 6:00
♉	Nov 9 2:46	♋	Feb 4 1:04	♎	May 2 21:03	♑	Jul 30 2:30	♈	Oct 26 14:31
♊	Nov 11 15:10	♌	Feb 6 8:24	♏	May 4 21:19	♒	Aug 1 4:55	♉	Oct 29 1:16
♋	Nov 14 2:19	♍	Feb 8 12:32	♐	May 6 20:38	♓	Aug 3 8:58	♊	Oct 31 13:41
♌	Nov 16 11:17	♎	Feb 10 14:53	♑	May 8 21:00	♈	Aug 5 15:59	♋	Nov 3 2:43
♍	Nov 18 17:19	♏	Feb 12 17:02	♒	May 11 0:02	♉	Aug 8 2:28	♌	Nov 5 14:39
♎	Nov 20 20:15	♐	Feb 14 19:57	♓	May 13 6:42	♊	Aug 10 15:11	♍	Nov 7 23:35
♏	Nov 22 20:58	♑	Feb 17 0:04	♈	May 15 16:46	♋	Aug 13 3:28	♎	Nov 10 4:35
♐	Nov 24 20:58	♒	Feb 19 5:29	♉	May 18 5:04	♌	Aug 15 13:05	♏	Nov 12 6:10
♑	Nov 26 22:05	♓	Feb 21 12:30	♊	May 20 18:06	♍	Aug 17 19:33	♐	Nov 14 5:52
♒	Nov 29 2:02	♈	Feb 23 21:48	♋	May 23 6:32	♎	Aug 19 23:46	♑	Nov 16 5:36
♓	Dec 1 9:46	♉	Feb 26 9:30	♌	May 25 17:12	♏	Aug 22 2:54	♒	Nov 18 7:10
♈	Dec 3 20:51	♊	Feb 28 22:27	♍	May 28 1:06	♐	Aug 24 5:49	♓	Nov 20 11:55
♉	Dec 6 9:35	♋	Mar 2 10:08	♎	May 30 5:46	♑	Aug 26 8:59	♈	Nov 22 20:11
♊	Dec 8 21:53	♌	Mar 4 18:18	♏	Jun 1 7:31	♒	Aug 28 12:39	♉	Nov 25 7:19
♋	Dec 11 8:26	♍	Mar 6 22:26	♐	Jun 3 7:33	♓	Aug 30 17:31	♊	Nov 27 19:59
♌	Dec 13 16:48	♎	Mar 8 23:50	♑	Jun 5 7:30	♈	Sep 2 0:37	♋	Nov 30 8:55
♍	Dec 15 22:59	♏	Mar 11 0:24	♒	Jun 7 9:17	♉	Sep 4 10:41	♌	Dec 2 20:57
♎	Dec 18 3:06	♐	Mar 13 1:53	♓	Jun 9 14:21	♊	Sep 6 23:10	♍	Dec 5 6:52
♏	Dec 20 5:33	♑	Mar 15 5:24	♈	Jun 11 23:21	♋	Sep 9 11:49	♎	Dec 7 13:36
♐	Dec 22 7:02	♒	Mar 17 11:12	♉	Jun 14 11:22	♌	Sep 11 22:01	♏	Dec 9 16:51
♑	Dec 24 8:46	♓	Mar 19 19:05	♊	Jun 17 0:24	♍	Sep 14 4:31	♐	Dec 11 17:21
♒	Dec 26 12:15	♈	Mar 22 4:58	♋	Jun 19 12:34	♎	Sep 16 7:55	♑	Dec 13 16:42
♓	Dec 28 18:46	♉	Mar 24 16:44	♌	Jun 21 22:47	♏	Sep 18 9:46	♒	Dec 15 16:53
♈	Dec 31 4:49	♊	Mar 27 5:43	♍	Jun 24 18:42	♐	Sep 20 11:34	♓	Dec 17 19:49
		♋	Mar 29 18:07	♎	Jun 26 12:15	♑	Sep 22 14:20	♈	Dec 20 2:44
2012		♌	Apr 1 3:36	♏	Jun 28 15:32	♒	Sep 24 18:32	♉	Dec 22 13:25
♉	Jan 2 17:16	♍	Apr 3 8:53	♐	Jun 30 17:04	♓	Sep 27 0:24	♊	Dec 25 2:14
♊	Jan 5 5:44	♎	Apr 5 10:32	♑	Jul 2 17:50	♈	Sep 29 8:14	♋	Dec 27 15:06
♋	Jan 7 16:05	♏	Apr 7 10:18	♒	Jul 4 19:25	♉	Oct 1 18:26	♌	Dec 30 2:46
♌	Jan 9 23:35	♐	Apr 9 10:13	♓	Jul 6 23:29	♊	Oct 4 6:47		
♍	Jan 12 4:44	♑	Apr 11 12:02	♈	Jul 9 7:14	♋	Oct 6 19:46		
♎	Jan 14 8:28	♒	Apr 13 16:48	♉	Jul 11 18:30	♌	Oct 9 6:55		
♏	Jan 16 11:33	♓	Apr 16 0:38	♊	Jul 14 7:27	♍	Oct 11 14:24		
♐	Jan 18 14:29	♈	Apr 18 10:59	♋	Jul 16 19:31	♎	Oct 13 18:01		
♑	Jan 20 17:41								

Table A-3 — The Nodes of the Moon

1930		**1936**		**1942**		**1949**		**1955**	
♈	Jul 7 10:58 R	♐	Sept 14 1:29 R	♌	Nov 21 0:56 R	♈	Jan 25 18:37 R	♐	Apr 2 18:06 R
1931		**1938**		**1944**		**1950**		**1956**	
♓	Dec 28 0:23 R	♏	Mar 3 18:15 R	♋	May 11 9:29 R	♓	Jul 26 15:56 R	♏	Oct 4 4:36 R
1933		**1939**		**1945**		**1952**		**1958**	
♒	Jun 24 11:33 R	♎	Sept 11 17:46 R	♊	Dec 2 13:35 R	♒	Mar 28 5:44 R	♎	Jun 16 6:43 R
1935		**1941**		**1947**		**1953**		**1959**	
♑	Mar 8 12:38 R	♍	May 24 2:48 R	♉	Aug 2 5:23 R	♑	Oct 8 23:28 R	♍	Dec 15 12:36 R

Table A-3 — The Nodes of the Moon

1961
♌ Jun 10 15:07 R
1962
♋ Dec 22 22:33 R
1964
♊ Aug 25 5:23 R
1966
♉ Feb 19 11:41 R
1967
♈ Aug 19 12:23 R
1969
♓ Apr 19 1:54 R
1970
♒ Nov 2 3:13 R
1972
♑ Apr 27 3:03 R

1973
♐ Oct 26 21:00 R
1975
♏ Jul 9 20:20 R
1977
♎ Jan 7 13:05 R
1978
♍ Jul 5 5:41 R
1980
♌ Jan 5 9:55 R
♍ Jan 6 21:32
♌ Jan 12 13:22 R
1981
♋ Sept 20 2:20 R
♌ Sept 21 5:22
♋ Sept 24 1:32 R

1983
♊ Mar 15 21:06 R
1984
♉ Sept 11 12:02 R
1986
♈ Apr 6 0:32 R
♉ May 5 17:53
♈ May 8 12:18 R
1987
♓ Dec 2 0:14 R
1989
♒ May 22 6:55 R
1990
♑ Nov 18 14:20 R
1992
♐ Aug 1 17:07 R

1994
♏ Feb 1 4:11 R
1995
♎ Jul 31 7:32 R
1997
♍ Jan 24 19:50 R
1998
♌ Oct 20 0:52 R
2000
♋ Apr 8 19:11 R
2001
♊ Oct 12 20:48 R
2003
♉ Apr 13 18:44 R

2004
♈ Dec 26 2:31 R
2006
♓ Jun 22 4:05 R
2007
♒ Dec 18 3:06 R
2009
♑ Aug 21 14:27 R
2011
♐ Mar 3 7:39 R
2012
♏ Aug 29 22:41 R

Table A-4 — Mercury

1930
♒ Jan 2 5:25
♑ Jan 22 19:30 R
♒ Feb 15 10:08
♓ Mar 9 17:39
♈ Mar 26 18:36
♉ Apr 10 12:05
♊ May 1 0:31
♉ May 17 6:06 R
♊ Jun 14 15:09
♋ Jul 4 17:10
♌ Jul 18 21:44
♍ Aug 3 21:38
♎ Aug 26 13:04
♍ Sept 19 21:16 R
♎ Oct 10 23:45
♏ Oct 29 9:35
♐ Nov 17 0:31
♑ Dec 6 15:57
1931
♒ Feb 11 7:27
♓ Mar 2 12:28
♈ Mar 18 14:31
♉ Apr 3 8:38
♊ Jun 11 2:27
♋ Jun 26 8:49
♌ Jul 10 14:56
♍ Jul 28 18:24

♎ Oct 4 13:27
♏ Oct 21 21:08
♐ Nov 9 23:27
♑ Dec 1 19:00
♐ Dec 20 2:59 R
1932
♑ Jan 14 7:47
♒ Feb 4 21:36
♓ Feb 22 19:50
♈ Mar 9 15:21
♉ May 15 17:49
♊ Jun 2 18:05
♋ Jun 16 17:30
♌ Jul 2 3:16
♍ Jul 27 15:38
♌ Aug 10 2:31 R
♍ Sept 9 2:20
♎ Sept 25 20:15
♏ Oct 13 10:41
♐ Nov 2 15:28
1933
♑ Jan 8 5:25
♒ Jan 27 17:39
♓ Feb 14 0:06
♈ Mar 3 5:49
♓ Mar 25 16:49 R
♈ Apr 17 10:27

♉ May 10 2:42
♊ May 25 9:27
♋ Jun 8 9:12
♌ Jun 26 20:12
♍ Sept 2 0:44
♎ Sept 17 22:48
♏ Oct 6 10:04
♐ Oct 29 23:27
♏ Nov 15 21:07 R
♐ Dec 11 22:43
1934
♑ Jan 1 13:40
♒ Jan 20 6:44
♓ Feb 6 12:24
♈ Apr 14 23:14
♉ May 2 13:45
♊ May 16 18:43
♋ Jun 1 3:22
♌ Aug 9 8:49
♍ Aug 24 21:18
♎ Sept 10 6:29
♏ Sept 30 9:46
♐ Dec 6 1:42
♑ Dec 25 9:59
1935
♒ Jan 12 20:20
♓ Feb 1 6:16

♒ Feb 14 22:02 R
♓ Mar 18 16:53
♈ Apr 8 5:40
♉ Apr 24 7:29
♊ May 8 12:20
♋ May 29 14:26
♊ Jun 20 12:58 R
♋ Jul 13 17:22
♌ Aug 1 20:48
♍ Aug 16 15:39
♎ Sept 3 4:33
♏ Sept 28 10:52
♎ Oct 12 13:03 R
♏ Nov 9 20:24
♐ Nov 29 2:05
♑ Dec 18 3:28
1936
♒ Jan 5 22:32
♓ Mar 13 1:40
♈ Mar 31 0:08
♉ Apr 14 20:45
♊ Apr 30 20:30
♋ Jul 8 15:47
♌ Jul 23 10:39
♍ Aug 7 17:59
♎ Aug 27 12:43
♏ Nov 2 6:00
♐ Nov 20 19:39

♑ Dec 10 1:40
1937
♒ Jan 1 11:41
♑ Jan 9 16:28 R
♒ Feb 13 19:26
♓ Mar 6 9:06
♈ Mar 22 22:41
♉ Apr 6 20:09
♊ Jun 13 17:28
♋ Jun 30 21:21
♌ Jul 14 23:11
♍ Jul 31 16:07
♎ Oct 8 5:12
♏ Oct 25 20:14
♐ Nov 13 14:25
♑ Dec 3 18:51
1938
♐ Jan 6 16:37 R
♑ Jan 12 17:30
♒ Feb 8 8:17
♓ Feb 26 22:01
♈ Mar 14 19:02
♉ Apr 1 8:24
♈ Apr 23 8:56 R
♉ May 16 12:46
♊ Jun 7 19:32
♋ Jun 22 8:09

(continued)

Table A-4 — Mercury (continued)

♌	Jul 6	22:21
♍	Jul 26	17:55
♌	Sept 2	21:58 R
♍	Sept 10	10:38
♎	Sept 30	23:19
♏	Oct 18	7:43
♐	Nov 6	18:33

1939

♑	Jan 12	2:57
♒	Feb 1	12:57
♓	Feb 19	3:09
♈	Mar 7	4:14
♉	May 14	8:43
♊	May 30	21:45
♋	Jun 13	18:01
♌	Jun 30	1:41
♍	Sept 6	23:58
♎	Sept 23	2:48
♏	Oct 11	0:20
♐	Nov 1	2:03
♏	Dec 3	2:22 R
♐	Dec 13	14:16

1940

♑	Jan 6	2:56
♒	Jan 25	5:14
♓	Feb 11	9:01
♈	Mar 4	5:09
♓	Mar 7	20:25 R
♈	Apr 16	23:56
♉	May 6	16:14
♊	May 21	8:59
♋	Jun 4	17:29
♌	Jun 26	9:32
♋	Jul 20	20:39 R
♌	Aug 11	12:06
♍	Aug 29	6:11
♎	Sept 14	6:34
♏	Oct 3	7:14
♐	Dec 9	7:45
♑	Dec 29	4:35

1941

♒	Jan 16	17:36
♓	Feb 3	8:08
♒	Mar 6	21:22 R
♓	Mar 16	7:26
♈	Apr 12	2:19
♉	Apr 28	18:09
♊	May 12	19:50
♋	May 29	12:32
♌	Aug 6	0:57
♍	Aug 21	0:18
♎	Sept 6	18:58
♏	Sept 28	4:21
♎	Oct 29	15:34 R
♏	Nov 11	15:11
♐	Dec 2	19:11

♑	Dec 21	22:54

1942

♒	Jan 9	10:24
♓	Mar 16	19:10
♈	Apr 5	2:06
♉	Apr 20	8:42
♊	May 4	23:37
♋	Jul 12	15:24
♌	Jul 28	23:24
♍	Aug 12	20:48
♎	Aug 31	3:27
♏	Nov 6	20:44
♐	Nov 25	15:26
♑	Dec 14	17:21

1943

♒	Jan 3	3:27
♑	Jan 27	18:42 R
♒	Feb 15	14:00
♓	Mar 10	23:59
♈	Mar 28	6:19
♉	Apr 11	23:56
♊	Apr 30	10:56
♉	May 26	5:04 R
♊	Jun 13	19:46
♋	Jul 6	4:05
♌	Jul 20	11:08
♍	Aug 5	5:33
♎	Aug 26	19:36
♍	Sept 25	4:56 R
♎	Oct 11	18:27
♏	Oct 30	18:37
♐	Nov 18	8:39
♑	Dec 7	20:47

1944

♒	Feb 12	9:17
♓	Mar 2	21:45
♈	Mar 19	2:43
♉	Apr 3	12:29
♊	Jun 11	6:46
♋	Jun 26	22:40
♌	Jul 11	2:41
♍	Jul 28	18:44
♎	Oct 4	22:17
♏	Oct 22	6:33
♐	Nov 10	6:09
♑	Dec 1	10:31
♐	Dec 23	18:21 R

1945

♑	Jan 13	22:04
♒	Feb 5	4:20
♓	Feb 23	6:25
♈	Mar 11	1:45
♉	May 16	10:21
♊	Jun 4	5:30
♋	Jun 18	7:27

♌	Jul 3	10:39
♍	Jul 26	9:48
♌	Aug 17	3:50 R
♍	Sept 10	2:21
♎	Sept 27	7:08
♏	Oct 14	19:13
♐	Nov 3	18:06

1946

♑	Jan 9	9:09
♒	Jan 29	2:22
♓	Feb 15	10:43
♈	Mar 4	4:26
♓	Apr 1	13:16 R
♈	Apr 16	9:54
♉	May 11	9:29
♊	May 26	23:13
♋	Jun 9	21:00
♌	Jun 27	14:07
♍	Sept 3	11:29
♎	Sept 19	9:34
♏	Oct 7	16:21
♐	Oct 30	6:23
♏	Nov 20	15:16 R
♐	Dec 12	19:03

1947

♑	Jan 2	20:46
♒	Jan 21	16:06
♓	Feb 7	20:31
♈	Apr 15	23:31
♉	May 4	1:03
♊	May 18	8:33
♋	Jun 2	8:40
♌	Aug 10	12:40
♍	Aug 26	9:50
♎	Sept 11	15:54
♏	Oct 1	10:26
♐	Dec 7	7:32
♑	Dec 26	18:17

1948

♒	Jan 14	5:06
♓	Feb 1	19:46
♒	Feb 20	6:08 R
♓	Mar 18	3:14
♈	Apr 8	21:26
♉	Apr 24	20:38
♊	May 8	23:38
♋	May 28	5:50
♊	Jun 28	12:57 R
♋	Jul 11	15:56
♌	Aug 2	8:54
♍	Aug 17	3:44
♎	Sept 3	10:47
♏	Sept 27	2:19
♎	Oct 16	22:33 R
♏	Nov 9	21:19
♐	Nov 29	10:09

♑	Dec 18	11:46

1949

♒	Jan 6	3:53
♓	Mar 14	4:52
♈	Apr 1	11:02
♉	Apr 16	9:55
♊	May 1	21:19
♋	Jul 9	22:19
♌	Jul 25	0:20
♍	Aug 9	4:04
♎	Aug 28	10:48
♏	Nov 3	13:58
♐	Nov 22	4:06
♑	Dec 11	8:37

1950

♒	Jan 1	7:39
♑	Jan 15	2:35 R
♒	Feb 14	14:12
♓	Mar 7	17:04
♈	Mar 24	10:52
♉	Apr 8	6:13
♊	Jun 14	9:33
♋	Jul 2	9:57
♌	Jul 16	12:08
♍	Aug 1	21:44
♎	Aug 27	9:17
♍	Sept 10	14:16 R
♎	Oct 9	9:40
♏	Oct 27	5:36
♐	Nov 14	22:10
♑	Dec 4	20:57

1951

♒	Feb 9	12:50
♓	Feb 28	8:04
♈	Mar 16	6:53
♉	Apr 1	22:27
♈	May 1	16:25 R
♉	May 14	20:40
♊	Jun 9	3:43
♋	Jun 23	22:13
♌	Jul 8	8:39
♍	Jul 27	10:24
♎	Oct 2	9:25
♏	Oct 19	16:52
♐	Nov 7	23:59
♑	Dec 1	15:41
♐	Dec 12	7:39 R

1952

♑	Jan 13	1:44
♒	Feb 2	20:38
♓	Feb 20	13:55
♈	Mar 7	12:10
♉	May 14	9:43
♊	May 31	10:26
♋	Jun 14	7:22

♌	Jun 30	5:27
♍	Sept 7	7:02
♎	Sept 23	13:45
♏	Oct 11	8:05
♐	Nov 1	0:34

1953

♑	Jan 6	8:24
♒	Jan 25	14:10
♓	Feb 11	18:57
♈	Mar 2	14:21
♓	Mar 15	16:16 R
♈	Apr 17	11:48
♉	May 8	1:24
♊	May 22	22:58
♋	Jun 6	3:23
♌	Jun 26	6:01
♋	Jul 28	8:40 R
♌	Aug 11	9:04
♍	Aug 30	17:59
♎	Sept 15	16:45
♏	Oct 4	11:40
♐	Oct 31	10:49
♏	Nov 6	17:18 R
♐	Dec 10	9:48
♑	Dec 30	12:14

1954

♒	Jan 18	2:43
♓	Feb 4	13:03
♈	Apr 13	6:34
♉	Apr 30	6:26
♊	May 30	11:13
♌	Aug 7	9:44
♍	Aug 22	12:42
♎	Sept 8	3:05
♏	Sept 28	23:06
♎	Nov 4	7:37 R
♏	Nov 11	5:25
♐	Dec 4	2:02
♑	Dec 23	7:10

1955

♒	Jan 10	18:05
♓	Mar 17	15:49
♈	Apr 6	11:15
♉	Apr 21	21:57
♊	May 6	8:05
♋	Jul 13	9:44
♌	Jul 30	12:22
♍	Aug 14	8:08
♎	Sept 1	7:06
♏	Nov 8	1:57
♐	Nov 26	23:34
♑	Dec 16	1:06

1956

♒	Jan 4	4:16

Table A-4 — Mercury (continued)

♑ Feb 2 7:18 R	♎ Sept 20 20:20	♓ Mar 9 0:26	♎ Sept 17 3:19	♓ Mar 5 15:10
♒ Feb 15 1:34	♏ Oct 8 23:02	♈ Mar 25 22:52	♏ Oct 5 17:03	♈ Mar 22 2:59
♓ Mar 11 5:27	♐ Oct 30 20:16	♉ Apr 9 17:03	♐ Oct 30 2:38	♉ Apr 6 2:40
♈ Mar 28 17:41	♏ Nov 25 6:53 R	♊ May 2 23:17	♏ Nov 12 22:26 R	♊ Jun 13 7:46
♉ Apr 12 12:10	♐ Dec 13 10:42	♉ May 10 15:39 R	♐ Dec 11 10:27	♋ Jun 30 1:22
♊ Apr 29 17:41		♊ Jun 14 18:21	♑ Dec 31 19:52	♌ Jul 14 3:06
♋ Jul 6 14:02	**1960**	♋ Jul 3 22:00		♍ Jul 31 0:21
♌ Jul 21 0:35	♑ Jan 4 3:24	♌ Jul 18 1:19	**1967**	♎ Oct 7 13:04
♍ Aug 5 14:06	♒ Jan 23 1:16	♍ Aug 3 4:20	♒ Jan 19 12:05	♏ Oct 25 1:16
♎ Aug 26 8:30	♓ Feb 9 5:13	♎ Aug 26 15:33	♓ Feb 5 19:38	♐ Nov 12 20:16
♍ Sept 29 16:25 R	♈ Apr 15 21:22	♍ Sept 16 15:29 R	♈ Apr 14 9:38	♑ Dec 3 5:14
♎ Oct 11 2:30	♉ May 4 11:45	♎ Oct 10 11:44	♉ May 1 18:26	
♏ Oct 31 3:19	♊ May 18 22:27	♏ Oct 28 14:54	♊ May 15 22:27	**1971**
♐ Nov 18 16:42	♋ Jun 2 15:31	♐ Nov 16 6:07	♋ May 31 13:02	♐ Jan 2 18:36 R
♑ Dec 8 2:11	♌ Jun 30 20:14	♑ Dec 6 0:17	♌ Aug 8 17:09	♑ Jan 13 21:16
	♋ Jul 5 20:22 R		♍ Aug 24 1:17	♒ Feb 7 15:51
1957	♌ Aug 10 12:49	**1964**	♎ Sept 9 11:53	♓ Feb 26 2:57
♒ Feb 12 9:30	♍ Aug 26 22:11	♒ Feb 10 16:30	♏ Sept 29 20:46	♈ Mar 13 23:46
♓ Mar 4 6:34	♎ Sept 12 1:29	♓ Feb 29 17:50	♐ Dec 5 8:41	♉ Apr 1 9:11
♈ Mar 20 14:48	♏ Oct 1 12:17	♈ Mar 16 18:54	♑ Dec 24 15:33	♈ Apr 18 16:52 R
♉ Apr 4 18:37	♐ Dec 7 12:30	♉ Apr 1 19:57		♉ May 16 22:32
♊ Jun 12 8:40	♑ Dec 27 2:21	♊ Jun 9 10:45	**1968**	♊ Jun 7 1:45
♋ Jun 28 12:08		♋ Jun 24 12:17	♒ Jan 12 2:19	♋ Jun 21 11:25
♌ Jul 12 14:41	**1961**	♌ Jul 8 19:38	♓ Feb 1 7:57	♌ Jul 6 3:53
♍ Jul 29 20:44	♒ Jan 14 13:58	♍ Jul 27 6:35	♒ Feb 11 13:54 R	♍ Jul 26 12:03
♎ Oct 6 6:09	♓ Feb 1 16:39	♎ Oct 2 19:12	♓ Mar 17 9:45	♌ Aug 29 15:42 R
♏ Oct 23 15:50	♒ Feb 24 15:22 R	♏ Oct 20 2:11	♈ Apr 6 20:01	♍ Sept 11 1:45
♐ Nov 11 13:00	♓ Mar 18 5:16	♐ Nov 8 6:02	♉ Apr 22 11:18	♎ Sept 30 4:19
♑ Dec 2 6:19	♈ Apr 10 4:22	♑ Nov 30 14:30	♊ May 6 17:56	♏ Oct 17 12:49
♐ Dec 28 12:30 R	♉ Apr 26 9:34	♐ Dec 16 9:31 R	♋ May 29 17:44	♐ Nov 6 1:59
	♊ May 10 11:34		♊ Jun 13 17:32 R	
1958	♋ May 28 12:23	**1965**	♋ Jul 12 20:30	**1972**
♑ Jan 14 5:03	♌ Aug 3 20:15	♑ Jan 12 22:12	♌ Jul 31 1:11	♑ Jan 11 13:18
♒ Feb 6 10:21	♍ Aug 18 15:52	♒ Feb 3 4:02	♍ Aug 14 19:53	♒ Jan 31 18:46
♓ Feb 24 16:44	♎ Sept 4 17:32	♓ Feb 21 0:40	♎ Sept 1 11:59	♓ Feb 18 7:53
♈ Mar 12 12:31	♏ Sept 27 7:16	♈ Mar 8 21:19	♏ Sept 28 9:40	♈ Mar 5 11:59
♉ Apr 2 14:17	♎ Oct 21 21:29 R	♉ May 15 8:19	♎ Oct 7 17:46 R	♉ May 12 18:45
♈ Apr 10 8:51 R	♏ Nov 10 18:53	♊ Jun 1 22:47	♏ Nov 8 6:00	♊ May 29 1:46
♉ May 16 20:53	♐ Nov 30 17:54	♋ Jun 15 21:04	♐ Nov 27 7:47	♋ Jun 11 21:56
♊ Jun 5 15:59	♑ Dec 19 20:04	♌ Jul 1 10:55	♑ Dec 16 9:11	♌ Jun 28 11:52
♋ Jun 19 21:20		♍ Jul 31 6:24		♍ Sept 5 6:36
♌ Jul 4 18:46	**1962**	♌ Aug 3 3:09 R	**1969**	♎ Sept 21 7:11
♍ Jul 26 5:08	♒ Jan 7 10:08	♍ Sept 8 12:14	♒ Jan 4 7:18	♏ Oct 9 6:11
♌ Aug 23 9:31 R	♓ Mar 15 6:43	♎ Sept 25 0:49	♓ Mar 12 10:19	♐ Oct 30 14:27
♍ Sept 10 20:10	♈ Apr 2 21:32	♏ Oct 12 16:15	♈ Mar 30 4:59	♏ Nov 29 2:08 R
♎ Sept 28 17:45	♉ Apr 17 23:10	♐ Nov 2 1:04	♉ Apr 14 0:55	♐ Dec 12 18:20
♏ Oct 16 3:52	♊ May 3 1:05		♊ Apr 30 10:18	
♐ Nov 4 21:36	♋ Jul 11 2:36	**1966**	♋ Jul 7 22:58	**1973**
	♌ Jul 26 13:50	♑ Jan 7 13:26	♌ Jul 22 14:11	♑ Jan 4 9:41
1959	♍ Aug 10 14:29	♒ Jan 26 23:10	♍ Aug 6 23:21	♒ Jan 23 10:23
♑ Jan 10 11:48	♎ Aug 29 10:48	♓ Feb 13 5:17	♎ Aug 27 1:50	♓ Feb 9 14:30
♒ Jan 30 10:41	♏ Nov 4 21:20	♈ Mar 2 21:57	♍ Oct 6 21:57 R	♈ Apr 16 16:17
♓ Feb 16 21:15	♐ Nov 23 12:31	♓ Mar 21 21:34 R	♎ Oct 9 11:56	♉ May 5 21:55
♈ Mar 5 6:52	♑ Dec 12 15:51	♈ Apr 17 16:31	♏ Nov 1 11:53	♊ May 20 12:24
♉ May 12 14:48		♉ May 9 9:48	♐ Nov 20 1:00	♋ Jun 3 23:42
♊ May 28 12:35	**1963**	♊ May 24 12:59	♑ Dec 9 8:21	♌ Jun 27 1:42
♋ Jun 11 9:11	♒ Jan 1 20:10	♋ Jun 7 14:11		♋ Jul 16 3:03 R
♌ Jun 28 11:31	♑ Jan 19 23:59 R	♌ Jun 26 14:05	**1970**	♌ Aug 11 7:21
♍ Sept 4 21:28	♒ Feb 15 5:08	♍ Sept 1 5:35	♒ Feb 13 8:08	♍ Aug 28 10:22

(continued)

Table A-4 Mercury (continued)

♎	Sept 13	11:16	
♏	Oct 2	15:12	
♐	Dec 8	16:29	
♑	Dec 28	10:14	
1974			
♒	Jan 15	22:56	
♓	Feb 2	17:42	
♒	Mar 2	12:49	R
♓	Mar 17	15:11	
♈	Apr 11	10:20	
♉	Apr 27	22:10	
♊	May 11	23:55	
♋	May 29	3:03	
♌	Aug 5	6:42	
♍	Aug 20	4:04	
♎	Sept 6	0:48	
♏	Sept 27	19:20	
♎	Oct 26	18:21	R
♏	Nov 11	11:05	
♐	Dec 2	1:17	
♑	Dec 21	4:16	
1975			
♒	Jan 8	16:58	
♓	Mar 16	6:50	
♈	Apr 4	7:28	
♉	Apr 19	12:20	
♊	May 4	6:55	
♋	Jul 12	3:56	
♌	Jul 28	3:05	
♍	Aug 12	1:12	
♎	Aug 30	12:20	
♏	Nov 6	3:58	
♐	Nov 24	20:44	
♑	Dec 13	23:10	
1976			
♒	Jan 2	15:22	
♑	Jan 24	20:30	R
♒	Feb 15	14:03	
♓	Mar 9	7:02	
♈	Mar 26	10:36	
♉	Apr 10	4:29	
♊	Apr 29	18:11	
♉	May 19	14:21	R
♊	Jun 13	14:20	
♋	Jul 4	9:18	
♌	Jul 18	14:35	
♍	Aug 3	11:41	
♎	Aug 25	15:52	
♍	Sept 21	2:15	R
♎	Oct 10	9:47	
♏	Oct 28	23:55	
♐	Nov 16	14:02	
♑	Dec 6	4:25	
1977			
♒	Feb 10	18:55	
♓	Mar 2	3:09	
♈	Mar 18	6:56	
♉	Apr 2	21:46	
♊	Jun 10	16:07	
♋	Jun 26	2:07	
♌	Jul 10	7:00	
♍	Jul 28	5:15	
♎	Oct 4	4:16	
♏	Oct 21	11:23	
♐	Nov 9	12:20	
♑	Dec 1	1:43	
♐	Dec 21	2:18	R
1978			
♑	Jan 13	15:07	
♒	Feb 4	10:54	
♓	Feb 22	11:11	
♈	Mar 10	7:10	
♉	May 16	3:20	
♊	Jun 3	10:26	
♋	Jun 17	10:49	
♌	Jul 2	17:28	
♍	Jul 27	1:10	
♌	Aug 13	2:05	R
♍	Sept 9	14:23	
♎	Sept 26	11:40	
♏	Oct 14	0:30	
♐	Nov 3	2:48	
1979			
♑	Jan 8	17:33	
♒	Jan 28	7:49	
♓	Feb 14	15:38	
♈	Mar 3	16:32	
♓	Mar 28	5:39	R
♈	Apr 17	7:48	
♉	May 10	17:03	
♊	May 26	2:44	
♋	Jun 9	1:32	
♌	Jun 27	4:51	
♍	Sept 2	16:39	
♎	Sept 18	13:59	
♏	Oct 6	22:55	
♐	Oct 30	2:06	
♏	Nov 17	22:08	R
♐	Dec 12	8:34	
1980			
♑	Jan 2	3:02	
♒	Jan 20	21:18	
♓	Feb 7	3:07	
♈	Apr 14	10:58	
♉	May 2	5:56	
♊	May 16	12:06	
♋	May 31	17:05	
♌	Aug 8	22:31	
♍	Aug 24	13:47	
♎	Sept 9	21:00	
♏	Sept 29	20:16	
♐	Dec 5	14:45	
♑	Dec 24	23:46	
1981			
♒	Jan 12	10:48	
♓	Jan 31	12:35	
♒	Feb 16	3:02	R
♓	Mar 17	23:33	
♈	Apr 8	4:11	
♉	Apr 24	0:31	
♊	May 8	4:42	
♋	May 28	12:04	
♊	Jun 22	17:51	R
♋	Jul 12	16:08	
♌	Aug 1	13:30	
♍	Aug 16	7:47	
♎	Sept 2	17:40	
♏	Sept 27	6:02	
♎	Oct 13	21:09	R
♏	Nov 9	8:14	
♐	Nov 28	15:52	
♑	Dec 17	17:21	
1982			
♒	Jan 5	11:49	
♓	Mar 13	14:11	
♈	Mar 31	15:59	
♉	Apr 15	13:54	
♊	May 1	8:29	
♋	Jul 9	6:26	
♌	Jul 24	3:48	
♎	Aug 27	22:22	
♏	Nov 2	20:10	
♐	Nov 21	9:28	
♑	Dec 10	15:04	
1983			
♒	Jan 1	8:32	
♑	Jan 12	1:55	R
♒	Feb 14	4:36	
♓	Mar 6	23:23	
♈	Mar 23	15:09	
♉	Apr 7	12:04	
♊	Jun 14	3:06	
♋	Jul 1	14:18	
♌	Jul 15	15:57	
♍	Aug 1	5:22	
♎	Aug 29	1:07	
♍	Sept 5	21:30	R
♎	Oct 8	18:44	
♏	Oct 26	10:47	
♐	Nov 14	3:56	
♑	Dec 4	6:22	
1984			
♒	Feb 8	20:50	
♓	Feb 27	13:07	
♈	Mar 14	11:27	
♉	Mar 31	15:25	
♈	Apr 25	6:49	R
♉	May 15	7:33	
♊	Jun 7	10:45	
♋	Jun 22	1:39	
♌	Jul 6	13:56	
♍	Jul 26	1:49	
♎	Sept 30	14:44	
♏	Oct 17	22:01	
♐	Nov 6	7:09	
♑	Dec 1	11:29	
♐	Dec 7	16:46	R
1985			
♑	Jan 11	13:25	
♒	Feb 1	2:43	
♓	Feb 18	18:41	
♈	Mar 6	19:07	
♉	May 13	21:10	
♊	May 30	14:44	
♋	Jun 13	11:11	
♌	Jun 29	14:34	
♍	Sept 6	14:39	
♎	Sept 22	18:13	
♏	Oct 10	13:50	
♐	Oct 31	11:44	
♏	Dec 4	14:23	R
♐	Dec 12	6:05	
1986			
♑	Jan 5	15:42	
♒	Jan 24	19:33	
♓	Feb 11	0:21	
♈	Mar 3	2:22	
♓	Mar 11	12:36	R
♈	Apr 17	7:33	
♉	May 7	7:33	
♊	May 22	2:26	
♋	Jun 5	9:06	
♌	Jun 26	9:15	
♋	Jul 23	16:51	R
♌	Aug 11	16:09	
♍	Aug 29	22:28	
♎	Sept 14	21:28	
♏	Oct 3	19:19	
♐	Dec 9	19:34	
♑	Dec 29	18:09	
1987			
♒	Jan 17	8:08	
♓	Feb 3	21:31	
♒	Mar 11	16:55	R
♓	Mar 13	16:09	
♈	Apr 12	15:23	
♉	Apr 29	10:39	
♊	May 13	12:50	
♋	May 29	23:21	
♌	Aug 6	16:20	
♍	Aug 21	16:36	
♎	Sept 7	8:52	
♏	Sept 28	12:21	
♎	Oct 31	20:57	R
♏	Nov 11	16:57	
♐	Dec 3	8:33	
♑	Dec 22	12:40	
1988			
♒	Jan 10	0:28	
♓	Mar 16	5:09	
♈	Apr 4	17:04	
♉	Apr 20	1:42	
♊	May 4	14:40	
♋	Jul 12	1:42	
♌	Jul 28	16:19	
♍	Aug 12	12:29	
♎	Aug 30	15:25	
♏	Nov 6	9:57	
♐	Nov 25	5:04	
♑	Dec 14	6:53	
1989			
♒	Jan 2	14:41	
♑	Jan 28	23:06	R
♒	Feb 14	13:11	
♓	Mar 10	13:07	
♈	Mar 27	22:16	
♉	Apr 11	16:36	
♊	Apr 29	14:53	
♉	May 28	17:53	R
♊	Jun 12	3:56	
♋	Jul 5	19:55	
♌	Jul 20	4:04	
♍	Aug 4	19:54	
♎	Aug 26	1:14	
♍	Sept 26	10:28	R
♎	Oct 11	1:11	
♏	Oct 30	8:53	
♐	Nov 17	22:10	
♑	Dec 7	9:30	
1990			
♒	Feb 11	20:11	
♓	Mar 3	12:14	
♈	Mar 19	19:04	
♉	Apr 4	2:35	
♊	Jun 11	19:29	
♋	Jun 27	15:46	
♌	Jul 11	18:48	
♍	Jul 29	6:10	
♎	Oct 5	12:44	
♏	Oct 22	20:46	
♐	Nov 10	19:06	
♑	Dec 1	19:13	
♐	Dec 25	17:57	R
1991			
♑	Jan 14	3:02	
♒	Feb 5	17:20	
♓	Feb 23	21:35	

Table A-4 Mercury *(continued)*

Sign	Date	Time	
♈	Mar 11	17:40	
♉	May 16	17:45	
♊	Jun 4	21:24	
♋	Jun 19	0:40	
♌	Jul 4	1:05	
♍	Jul 26	8:00	
♌	Aug 19	16:40	R
♍	Sept 10	12:14	
♎	Sept 27	22:26	
♏	Oct 15	9:01	
♐	Nov 4	5:41	
1992			
♑	Jan 9	20:46	
♒	Jan 29	16:15	
♓	Feb 16	2:04	
♈	Mar 3	16:45	
♓	Apr 3	18:52	R
♈	Apr 14	12:35	
♉	May 10	23:10	
♊	May 26	16:16	
♋	Jun 9	13:27	
♌	Jun 27	0:11	
♍	Sept 3	3:03	
♎	Sept 19	0:41	
♏	Oct 7	5:13	
♐	Oct 29	12:02	
♏	Nov 21	14:44	R
♐	Dec 12	3:05	
1993			
♑	Jan 2	9:47	
♒	Jan 21	6:25	
♓	Feb 7	11:19	
♈	Apr 15	10:18	
♉	May 3	16:54	
♊	May 18	1:53	
♋	Jun 1	22:54	
♌	Aug 10	0:51	
♍	Aug 26	2:06	
♎	Sept 11	6:18	
♏	Sept 30	21:09	
♐	Dec 6	20:04	
♑	Dec 26	7:47	
1994			
♒	Jan 13	19:25	
♓	Feb 1	5:28	
♒	Feb 21	10:15	R
♓	Mar 18	7:04	
♈	Apr 9	11:30	
♉	Apr 25	13:27	
♊	May 9	16:08	
♋	May 28	9:52	
♊	Jul 2	18:18	R
♋	Jul 10	7:41	
♌	Aug 3	1:09	
♍	Aug 17	19:44	
♎	Sept 3	23:55	
♏	Sept 27	3:51	
♎	Oct 19	1:19	R
♏	Nov 10	7:46	
♐	Nov 29	23:38	
♑	Dec 19	1:26	
1995			
♒	Jan 6	17:17	
♓	Mar 14	16:35	
♈	Apr 2	2:29	
♉	Apr 17	2:54	
♊	May 2	10:18	
♋	Jul 10	11:58	
♌	Jul 25	17:19	
♍	Aug 9	19:13	
♎	Aug 28	21:07	
♏	Nov 4	3:50	
♐	Nov 22	17:46	
♑	Dec 11	21:57	
1996			
♒	Jan 1	13:06	
♑	Jan 17	4:37	R
♒	Feb 14	21:44	
♓	Mar 7	6:53	
♈	Mar 24	3:03	
♉	Apr 7	22:16	
♊	Jun 13	16:45	
♋	Jul 2	2:37	
♌	Jul 16	4:56	
♍	Aug 1	11:17	
♎	Aug 26	0:17	
♍	Sept 12	4:32	R
♎	Oct 8	22:13	
♏	Oct 26	20:01	
♐	Nov 14	11:36	
♑	Dec 4	8:48	
1997			
♒	Feb 9	0:53	
♓	Feb 27	22:54	
♈	Mar 15	23:13	
♉	Apr 1	8:45	
♈	May 4	20:48	R
♉	May 12	5:25	
♊	Jun 8	18:25	
♋	Jun 23	15:41	
♌	Jul 8	0:28	
♍	Jul 26	19:42	
♎	Oct 2	0:38	
♏	Oct 19	7:08	
♐	Nov 7	12:42	
♑	Nov 30	14:11	
♐	Dec 13	13:06	R
1998			
♑	Jan 12	11:20	
♒	Feb 2	10:15	
♓	Feb 20	5:22	
♈	Mar 8	3:28	
♉	May 14	21:10	
♊	Jun 1	3:07	
♋	Jun 15	0:33	
♌	Jun 30	18:52	
♍	Sept 7	20:58	
♎	Sept 24	5:13	
♏	Oct 11	21:44	
♐	Nov 1	11:02	
1999			
♑	Jan 6	21:04	
♒	Jan 26	4:32	
♓	Feb 12	10:28	
♈	Mar 2	17:50	
♓	Mar 18	4:23	R
♈	Apr 17	17:09	
♉	May 8	16:22	
♊	May 23	16:22	
♋	Jun 6	19:18	
♌	Jun 26	10:39	
♋	Jul 31	13:44	R
♌	Aug 10	23:25	
♍	Aug 31	10:15	
♎	Sept 16	7:53	
♏	Oct 5	0:12	
♐	Oct 30	15:08	
♏	Nov 9	15:13	R
♐	Dec 10	21:09	
♑	Dec 31	1:48	
2000			
♒	Jan 18	17:20	
♓	Feb 5	3:09	
♈	Apr 12	19:17	
♉	Apr 29	22:53	
♊	May 14	2:10	
♋	May 29	23:27	
♌	Aug 7	0:42	
♍	Aug 22	5:11	
♎	Sept 7	17:22	
♏	Sept 28	8:28	
♎	Nov 7	2:28	R
♏	Nov 8	16:42	
♐	Dec 3	15:26	
♑	Dec 22	21:03	
2001			
♒	Jan 10	8:26	
♓	Feb 1	2:13	
♒	Feb 6	14:57	R
♓	Mar 17	1:05	
♈	Apr 6	2:14	
♉	Apr 21	15:00	
♊	May 5	23:53	
♋	Jul 12	17:47	
♌	Jul 30	5:18	
♍	Aug 14	0:04	
♎	Aug 31	19:37	
♏	Nov 7	14:53	
♐	Nov 26	13:23	
♑	Dec 15	14:55	
2002			
♒	Jan 3	16:38	
♑	Feb 3	23:19	R
♒	Feb 13	12:20	
♓	Mar 11	18:34	
♈	Mar 29	9:44	
♉	Apr 13	5:10	
♊	Apr 30	2:15	
♋	Jul 7	5:35	
♌	Jul 21	17:41	
♍	Aug 6	4:51	
♎	Aug 26	16:10	
♍	Oct 2	4:26	R
♎	Oct 11	0:56	
♏	Oct 31	17:43	
♐	Nov 19	6:29	
♑	Dec 8	15:21	
2003			
♒	Feb 12	20:00	
♓	Mar 4	21:04	
♈	Mar 21	7:16	
♉	Apr 5	9:37	
♊	Jun 12	20:34	
♋	Jun 29	5:17	
♌	Jul 13	7:10	
♍	Jul 30	9:05	
♎	Oct 6	20:28	
♏	Oct 24	6:20	
♐	Nov 12	2:19	
♑	Dec 2	16:34	
♐	Dec 30	14:52	R
2004			
♑	Jan 14	6:02	
♒	Feb 6	23:20	
♓	Feb 25	7:58	
♈	Mar 12	4:44	
♉	Mar 31	21:27	
♈	Apr 12	20:23	R
♉	May 16	1:54	
♊	Jun 5	7:47	
♋	Jun 19	14:49	
♌	Jul 4	9:52	
♍	Jul 25	8:58	
♌	Aug 24	20:33	R
♍	Sept 10	2:38	
♎	Sept 28	9:13	
♏	Oct 15	17:57	
♐	Nov 4	9.40	
2005			
♑	Jan 9	23:09	
♒	Jan 30	0:37	
♓	Feb 16	12:46	
♈	Mar 4	20:34	
♉	May 12	4:13	
♊	May 28	5:44	
♋	Jun 11	2:03	
♌	Jun 27	23:01	
♍	Sept 4	12:52	
♎	Sept 20	11:40	
♏	Oct 8	12:15	
♐	Oct 30	4:02	
♏	Nov 26	6:53	R
♐	Dec 12	16:19	
2006			
♑	Jan 3	16:26	
♒	Jan 22	15:41	
♓	Feb 8	20:21	
♈	Apr 16	7:19	
♉	May 5	3:27	
♊	May 19	15:51	
♋	Jun 3	6:20	
♌	Jun 28	14:57	
♋	Jul 10	15:18	R
♌	Aug 10	23:09	
♍	Aug 27	14:30	
♎	Sept 12	16:07	
♏	Oct 1	23:37	
♐	Dec 8	0:51	
♑	Dec 27	15:54	
2007			
♒	Jan 15	4:24	
♓	Feb 2	4:19	
♒	Feb 26	22:00	R
♓	Mar 18	4:34	
♈	Apr 10	18:06	
♉	Apr 27	2:15	
♊	May 11	4:16	
♋	May 28	19:55	
♌	Aug 4	12:14	
♍	Aug 19	8:00	
♎	Sept 5	7:02	
♏	Sept 27	12:17	
♎	Oct 23	22:36	R
♏	Nov 11	3:40	
♐	Dec 1	7:20	
♑	Dec 20	9:42	
2008			
♒	Jan 7	23:45	
♓	Mar 14	17:45	
♈	Apr 2	12:44	
♉	Apr 17	16:06	
♊	May 2	14:59	
♋	Jul 10	15:16	
♌	Jul 26	6:48	
♍	Aug 10	5:50	
♎	Aug 28	21:49	
♏	Nov 4	10:59	
♐	Nov 23	2:08	

(continued)

Table A-4 — Mercury (continued)

♑ Dec 12	5:12		♎ Aug 25	15:17			♍ Jul 27	16:42			♌ Jul 2	0:37			♉ May 9	0:14	
2009			♍ Sep 17	22:25	R		♎ Oct 3	10:03			♍ Jul 28	12:58			♊ May 24	6:11	
♒ Jan 1	4:51		♎ Oct 9	22:45			♏ Oct 20	16:18			♌ Aug 8	4:45	R		♋ Jun 7	6:15	
♑ Jan 21	0:36	R	♏ Oct 29	12:08			♐ Nov 8	18:42			♍ Sep 9	0:58			♌ Jun 25	21:23	
♒ Feb 14	10:38		♐ Nov 15	19:27			♑ Nov 30	19:10			♎ Sep 25	16:08			♍ Aug 31	21:31	
♓ Mar 8	13:55		♑ Dec 5	12:24			♐ Dec 18	9:53	R		♏ Oct 13	5:51			♎ Sep 16	18:21	
♈ Mar 25	14:55		**2010**				**2011**				♐ Nov 2	11:54			♏ Oct 5	5:35	
♉ Apr 9	9:21		♒ Feb 10	4:05			♑ Jan 13	6:24			**2012**				♐ Oct 29	1:18	
♊ Apr 30	17:29		♓ Mar 1	8:27			♒ Feb 3	17:18			♑ Jan 8	1:33			♏ Nov 14	2:42	R
♉ May 13	18:52	R	♈ Mar 17	11:11			♓ Feb 21	15:53			♒ Jan 27	13:11			♐ Dec 10	20:39	
♊ Jun 13	21:47		♉ Apr 2	8:05			♈ Mar 9	12:46			♓ Feb 13	20:37			♑ Dec 31	9:02	
♋ Jul 3	14:19		♊ Jun 10	0:40			♉ May 15	18:18			♈ Mar 2	6:40					
♌ Jul 17	18:07		♋ Jun 25	5:31			♊ Jun 2	15:02			♓ Mar 23	8:22	R				
♍ Aug 2	18:06		♌ Jul 9	11:28			♋ Jun 16	14:08			♈ Apr 16	17:41					

Table A-5 — Venus

1930			♊ Jul 13	5:33	R	**1935**			♌ Aug 30	19:08		**1940**		
♒ Jan 2	19:22		♋ Jul 28	7:36		♒ Jan 8	17:44		♍ Sept 24	23:03		♓ Jan 18	9:00	
♓ Feb 16	17:11		♌ Sept 8	14:45		♓ Feb 1	16:36		♎ Oct 19	11:33		♒ Feb 12	0:51	
♒ Mar 12	17:34		♍ Oct 7	0:46		♒ Feb 25	19:30		♏ Nov 12	14:43		♉ Mar 8	11:25	
♉ Apr 5	21:57		♎ Nov 1	23:01		♉ Mar 22	5:29		♐ Dec 6	13:06		♊ Apr 4	13:10	
♊ Apr 30	7:37		♏ Nov 26	19:06		♊ Apr 16	2:37		♑ Dec 30	9:42		♋ May 6	13:47	
♋ May 24	23:36		♐ Dec 21	2:43		♋ May 11	17:01		**1938**			♊ Jul 5	11:17	R
♌ Jun 18	23:39		**1933**			♌ Jun 7	14:11		♒ Jan 23	6:16		♋ Jul 31	21:20	
♍ Jul 14	11:34		♑ Jan 14	4:56		♍ Jul 7	15:33		♓ Feb 16	4:00		♌ Sept 8	11:59	
♎ Aug 9	19:54		♒ Feb 7	5:30		♎ Nov 9	11:34		♒ Mar 12	4:20		♍ Oct 6	16:10	
♏ Sept 6	23:05		♓ Mar 3	6:24		♏ Dec 8	9:36		♉ Apr 5	8:46		♎ Nov 1	12:24	
♐ Oct 11	21:45		♒ Mar 27	8:58		**1936**			♊ Apr 29	18:35		♏ Nov 26	7:32	
♏ Nov 22	2:44	R	♉ Apr 20	14:00		♐ Jan 3	9:16		♋ May 24	10:56		♐ Dec 20	14:36	
1931			♊ May 14	21:47		♑ Jan 28	9:00		♌ Jun 18	11:37		**1941**		
♐ Jan 3	15:03		♋ Jun 8	8:01		♒ Feb 21	23:14		♍ Jul 14	0:44		♑ Jan 13	16:29	
♑ Feb 6	7:25		♌ Jul 2	20:29		♓ Mar 17	9:53		♎ Aug 9	11:26		♒ Feb 6	16:49	
♒ Mar 5	16:46		♍ Jul 27	11:45		♒ Apr 10	19:41		♏ Sept 6	20:36		♓ Mar 2	17:33	
♓ Mar 31	14:04		♎ Aug 21	7:23		♉ May 5	5:53		♐ Oct 13	13:49		♒ Mar 26	19:58	
♒ Apr 25	21:10		♏ Sept 15	9:54		♊ May 29	16:39		♏ Nov 15	11:07	R	♉ Apr 20	0:53	
♉ May 20	21:38		♐ Oct 10	23:32		♋ Jun 23	3:16		**1939**			♊ May 14	8:36	
♊ Jun 14	18:04		♑ Nov 6	11:02		♌ Jul 17	12:51		♐ Jan 4	16:48		♋ Jun 7	18:53	
♋ Jul 9	10:35		♒ Dec 5	13:00		♍ Aug 10	21:11		♑ Feb 6	4:20		♌ Jul 2	7:33	
♌ Aug 2	22:29		**1934**			♎ Sept 4	5:02		♒ Mar 5	8:29		♍ Jul 26	23:12	
♍ Aug 27	5:42		♓ Apr 6	4:23		♏ Sept 28	13:36		♓ Mar 31	3:34		♎ Aug 20	19:29	
♎ Sept 20	9:15		♒ May 6	3:54		♐ Oct 23	0:00		♒ Apr 25	9:28		♏ Sept 14	23:01	
♏ Oct 14	10:45		♉ Jun 2	5:11		♑ Nov 16	13:36		♉ May 20	9:13		♐ Oct 10	14:21	
♐ Nov 7	11:32		♊ Jun 28	4:38		♒ Dec 11	9:51		♊ Jun 14	5:11		♑ Nov 6	5:17	
♑ Dec 1	12:29		♋ Jul 23	13:22		**1937**			♋ Jul 8	21:25		♒ Dec 5	18:04	
♒ Dec 25	14:44		♌ Aug 17	10:45		♓ Jan 5	22:18		♌ Aug 2	9:34		**1942**		
1932			♍ Sept 10	22:32		♒ Feb 2	5:39		♍ Aug 26	16:24		♓ Apr 6	8:14	
♓ Jan 18	20:52		♎ Oct 5	2:56		♉ Mar 9	8:19		♎ Sept 19	20:02		♒ May 5	21:26	
♒ Feb 12	11:58		♏ Oct 29	2:37		♒ Apr 13	23:19	R	♏ Oct 13	21:41		♉ Jun 1	19:26	
♉ Mar 8	21:07		♐ Nov 21	23:59		♉ Jun 4	1:41		♐ Nov 6	22:41		♊ Jun 27	17:18	
♊ Apr 4	19:19		♑ Dec 15	20:39		♊ Jul 7	16:13		♑ Nov 30	23:52		♋ Jul 23	1:10	
♋ May 6	4:04					♋ Aug 4	15:14		♒ Dec 25	2:25		♌ Aug 16	22:04	

Table A-5 Venus *(continued)*

♍	Sept 10	9:38	
♎	Oct 4	13:58	
♏	Oct 28	13:40	
♐	Nov 21	11:07	
♑	Dec 15	7:53	
1943			
♒	Jan 8	5:03	
♓	Feb 1	4:02	
♒	Feb 25	7:04	
♉	Mar 21	17:24	
♊	Apr 15	15:12	
♋	May 11	6:56	
♌	Jun 7	7:09	
♍	Jul 7	18:56	
♎	Nov 9	13:25	
♏	Dec 8	2:45	
1944			
♐	Jan 2	23:43	
♑	Jan 27	22:11	
♒	Feb 21	11:40	
♓	Mar 16	21:46	
♒	Apr 10	7:09	
♉	May 4	17:04	
♊	May 29	3:39	
♋	Jun 22	14:12	
♌	Jul 16	23:47	
♍	Aug 10	8:13	
♎	Sept 3	16:16	
♏	Sept 28	1:12	
♐	Oct 22	12:07	
♑	Nov 16	2:26	
♒	Dec 10	23:47	
1945			
♓	Jan 5	14:18	
♒	Feb 2	3:07	
♉	Mar 11	6:17	
♒	Apr 7	14:15	R
♉	Jun 4	17:58	
♊	Jul 7	11:20	
♋	Aug 4	5:59	
♌	Aug 30	8:05	
♍	Sept 24	11:06	
♎	Oct 18	23:09	
♏	Nov 12	2:05	
♐	Dec 6	0:22	
♑	Dec 29	20:56	
1946			
♒	Jan 22	17:28	
♓	Feb 15	15:11	
♒	Mar 11	15:32	
♉	Apr 4	20:01	
♊	Apr 29	5:59	
♋	May 23	22:39	
♌	Jun 18	0:00	
♍	Jul 13	14:22	
♎	Aug 9	3:34	
♏	Sept 6	19:16	
♐	Oct 16	5:45	
♏	Nov 8	3:56	R
1947			
♐	Jan 5	11:45	
♑	Feb 6	0:41	
♒	Mar 5	0:09	
♓	Mar 30	17:14	
♒	Apr 24	22:03	
♉	May 19	21:06	
♊	Jun 13	16:35	
♋	Jul 8	8:30	
♌	Aug 1	20:06	
♍	Aug 26	3:17	
♎	Sept 19	7:01	
♏	Oct 13	8:49	
♐	Nov 6	9:59	
♑	Nov 30	11:23	
♒	Dec 24	14:13	
1948			
♓	Jan 17	21:14	
♒	Feb 11	13:51	
♉	Mar 8	1:59	
♊	Apr 4	7:40	
♋	May 7	3:27	
♊	Jun 29	2:58	R
♋	Aug 2	21:15	
♌	Sept 8	8:40	
♍	Oct 6	7:25	
♎	Nov 1	1:42	
♏	Nov 25	19:55	
♐	Dec 20	2:28	
1949			
♑	Jan 13	4:01	
♒	Feb 6	4:05	
♓	Mar 2	4:38	
♒	Mar 26	6:54	
♉	Apr 19	11:44	
♊	May 13	19:25	
♋	Jun 7	5:47	
♌	Jul 1	18:40	
♍	Jul 26	10:43	
♎	Aug 20	7:39	
♏	Sept 14	12:12	
♐	Oct 10	5:18	
♑	Nov 5	23:53	
♒	Dec 6	1:06	
1950			
♓	Apr 6	10:13	
♒	May 5	14:19	
♉	Jun 1	9:19	
♊	Jun 27	5:45	
♋	Jul 22	12:50	
♌	Aug 6	9:18	
♍	Sept 9	20:37	
♎	Oct 4	0:51	
♏	Oct 28	0:33	
♐	Nov 20	22:03	
♑	Dec 14	18:54	
1951			
♒	Jan 7	16:10	
♓	Jan 31	15:14	
♒	Feb 24	18:26	
♉	Mar 21	5:05	
♊	Apr 15	3:33	
♋	May 10	20:41	
♌	Jun 7	0:10	
♍	Jul 7	23:54	
♎	Nov 9	13:48	
♏	Dec 7	19:19	
1952			
♐	Jan 2	13:44	
♑	Jan 27	10:58	
♒	Feb 20	23:42	
♓	Mar 16	9:18	
♒	Apr 9	18:17	
♉	May 4	3:55	
♊	May 28	14:19	
♋	Jun 22	0:46	
♌	Jul 16	10:23	
♍	Aug 9	18:58	
♎	Sept 3	3:17	
♏	Sept 27	12:36	
♐	Oct 22	0:02	
♑	Nov 15	15:03	
♒	Dec 10	13:30	
1953			
♓	Jan 5	6:10	
♒	Feb 2	0:54	
♉	Mar 14	13:58	
♒	Mar 31	0:17	R
♉	Jun 5	5:34	
♊	Jul 7	5:30	
♋	Aug 3	20:08	
♌	Aug 29	20:35	
♍	Sept 23	22:48	
♎	Oct 18	10:27	
♏	Nov 11	13:12	
♐	Dec 5	11:24	
♑	Dec 29	7:53	
1954			
♒	Jan 22	4:20	
♓	Feb 15	2:01	
♒	Mar 11	2:22	
♉	Apr 4	6:55	
♊	Apr 28	17:03	
♋	May 23	10:04	
♌	Jun 17	12:04	
♍	Jul 13	3:43	
♎	Aug 8	19:34	
♏	Sept 6	18:29	
♐	Oct 23	17:07	
♏	Oct 27	5:42	R
1955			
♐	Jan 6	1:48	
♑	Feb 5	20:15	
♒	Mar 4	15:22	
♓	Mar 30	6:30	
♒	Apr 24	10:13	
♉	May 19	8:35	
♊	Jun 13	3:38	
♋	Jul 7	19:15	
♌	Aug 1	6:43	
♍	Aug 25	13:52	
♎	Sept 18	17:41	
♏	Oct 12	19:39	
♐	Nov 5	21:02	
♑	Nov 29	22:42	
♒	Dec 24	1:52	
1956			
♓	Jan 17	9:22	
♒	Feb 11	2:46	
♉	Mar 7	16:31	
♊	Apr 4	2:23	
♋	May 7	21:17	
♊	Jun 23	7:10	R
♋	Aug 4	4:49	
♌	Sept 8	4:23	
♍	Oct 5	22:12	
♎	Oct 31	14:40	
♏	Nov 25	8:01	
♐	Dec 19	14:07	
1957			
♑	Jan 12	15:23	
♒	Feb 5	15:16	
♓	Mar 1	15:39	
♒	Mar 25	17:46	
♉	Apr 18	22:28	
♊	May 13	6:08	
♋	Jun 6	16:35	
♌	Jul 1	5:42	
♍	Jul 25	22:10	
♎	Aug 19	19:44	
♏	Sept 14	1:20	
♐	Oct 9	20:16	
♑	Nov 5	18:46	
♒	Dec 6	10:26	
1958			
♓	Apr 6	11:00	
♒	May 5	6:59	
♉	May 31	23:07	
♊	Jun 26	18:08	
♋	Jul 22	0:26	
♌	Aug 15	20:28	
♍	Sept 9	7:35	
♎	Oct 3	11:44	
♏	Oct 27	11:26	
♐	Nov 20	8:59	
♑	Dec 14	5:55	
1959			
♒	Jan 7	3:16	
♓	Jan 31	2:28	
♒	Feb 24	5:53	
♉	Mar 20	16:55	
♊	Apr 14	16:08	
♋	May 10	10:45	
♌	Jun 6	17:43	
♍	Jul 8	7:08	
♌	Sept 19	22:01	R
♍	Sept 25	3:15	
♎	Nov 9	13:11	
♏	Dec 7	11:41	
1960			
♐	Jan 2	3:43	
♑	Jan 26	23:46	
♒	Feb 20	11:47	
♓	Mar 15	20:53	
♒	Apr 9	5:32	
♉	May 3	14:56	
♊	May 28	1:11	
♋	Jun 21	11:34	
♌	Jul 15	21:11	
♍	Aug 9	5:54	
♎	Sept 2	14:29	
♏	Sept 27	0:13	
♐	Oct 21	12:12	
♑	Nov 15	3:57	
♒	Dec 10	3:34	
1961			
♓	Jan 4	22:31	
♒	Feb 1	23:46	
♉	Jun 5	14:25	
♊	Jul 6	23:32	
♋	Aug 3	10:28	
♌	Aug 29	9:18	
♍	Sept 23	10:43	
♎	Oct 17	21:58	
♏	Nov 11	0:33	
♐	Dec 4	22:40	
♑	Dec 28	19:07	
1962			
♒	Jan 21	15:31	
♓	Feb 14	13:09	
♒	Mar 10	13:28	
♉	Apr 3	18:05	
♊	Apr 28	4:23	
♋	May 22	21:46	
♌	Jun 17	0:31	

(continued)

Table A-5 Venus *(continued)*

Sign	Date	Time	
♍	Jul 12	17:32	
♎	Aug 8	12:13	
♏	Sept 6	19:11	
1963			
♐	Jan 6	12:35	
♑	Feb 5	15:36	
♒	Mar 4	6:41	
♓	Mar 29	20:00	
♒	Apr 23	22:39	
♉	May 18	20:21	
♊	Jun 12	14:57	
♋	Jul 7	6:18	
♌	Jul 31	17:38	
♍	Aug 25	0:49	
♎	Sept 18	4:43	
♏	Oct 12	6:50	
♐	Nov 5	8:25	
♑	Nov 29	10:21	
♒	Dec 23	13:53	
1964			
♓	Jan 16	21:54	
♒	Feb 10	16:09	
♉	Mar 7	7:38	
♊	Apr 3	22:03	
♋	May 8	22:16	
♊	Jun 17	13:17	R
♋	Aug 5	3:53	
♌	Sept 7	23:53	
♍	Oct 5	13:10	
♎	Oct 31	3:54	
♏	Nov 24	20:25	
♐	Dec 19	2:02	
1965			
♑	Jan 12	3:00	
♒	Feb 5	2:41	
♓	Mar 1	2:55	
♒	Mar 25	4:54	
♉	Apr 18	9:31	
♊	May 12	17:08	
♋	Jun 6	3:39	
♌	Jun 30	16:59	
♍	Jul 25	9:51	
♎	Aug 19	8:06	
♏	Sept 13	14:50	
♐	Oct 9	11:46	
♑	Nov 5	14:36	
♒	Dec 6	23:37	
1966			
♑	Feb 6	7:46	R
♒	Feb 25	5:55	
♓	Apr 6	10:53	
♒	May 4	23:33	
♉	May 31	13:00	
♊	Jun 26	6:40	
♋	Jul 21	12:11	
♌	Aug 15	7:47	
♍	Sept 8	18:40	
♎	Oct 2	22:44	
♏	Oct 26	22:28	
♐	Nov 19	20:06	
♑	Dec 13	17:09	
1967			
♒	Jan 6	14:36	
♓	Jan 30	13:53	
♒	Feb 23	17:30	
♉	Mar 20	4:56	
♊	Apr 14	4:54	
♋	May 10	1:05	
♌	Jun 6	11:48	
♍	Jul 8	17:11	
♌	Sept 9	6:58	R
♍	Oct 1	13:07	
♎	Nov 9	11:32	
♏	Dec 7	3:48	
1968			
♐	Jan 1	17:37	
♑	Jan 26	12:35	
♒	Feb 19	23:55	
♓	Mar 15	8:32	
♒	Apr 8	16:49	
♉	May 3	1:56	
♊	May 27	12:02	
♋	Jun 20	22:20	
♌	Jul 15	7:59	
♍	Aug 8	16:49	
♎	Sept 2	1:39	
♏	Sept 26	11:45	
♐	Oct 21	0:16	
♑	Nov 14	16:48	
♒	Dec 9	17:40	
1969			
♓	Jan 4	15:07	
♒	Feb 1	23:45	
♉	Jun 5	20:48	
♊	Jul 6	17:04	
♋	Aug 3	0:30	
♌	Aug 28	21:48	
♍	Sept 22	22:26	
♎	Oct 17	9:17	
♏	Nov 10	11:40	
♐	Dec 4	9:41	
♑	Dec 28	6:04	
1970			
♒	Jan 21	2:26	
♓	Feb 14	0:04	
♒	Mar 10	0:25	
♉	Apr 3	5:05	
♊	Apr 27	15:33	
♋	May 22	9:19	
♌	Jun 16	12:49	
♍	Jul 12	7:16	
♎	Aug 8	4:59	
♏	Sept 6	20:54	
1971			
♐	Jan 6	20:00	
♑	Feb 5	9:57	
♒	Mar 3	21:24	
♓	Mar 29	9:02	
♒	Apr 23	10:44	
♉	May 18	7:48	
♊	Jun 12	1:58	
♋	Jul 6	17:02	
♌	Jul 31	4:15	
♍	Aug 24	11:25	
♎	Sept 17	15:25	
♏	Oct 11	17:43	
♐	Nov 4	19:30	
♑	Nov 28	21:41	
♒	Dec 23	1:32	
1972			
♓	Jan 16	10:01	
♒	Feb 10	5:08	
♉	Mar 6	22:25	
♊	Apr 3	17:48	
♋	May 10	8:51	
♊	Jun 11	15:08	R
♋	Aug 5	20:26	
♌	Sept 7	18:27	
♍	Oct 5	3:33	
♎	Oct 30	16:40	
♏	Nov 24	8:23	
♐	Dec 18	13:34	
1973			
♑	Jan 11	14:15	
♒	Feb 4	13:43	
♓	Feb 28	13:45	
♒	Mar 24	15:34	
♉	Apr 17	20:05	
♊	May 12	3:42	
♋	Jun 5	14:20	
♌	Jun 30	3:55	
♍	Jul 24	21:13	
♎	Aug 18	20:10	
♏	Sept 13	4:05	
♐	Oct 9	3:08	
♑	Nov 5	10:39	
♒	Dec 7	16:37	
1974			
♑	Jan 29	14:51	R
♒	Feb 28	9:25	
♓	Apr 6	9:17	
♒	May 4	15:21	
♉	May 31	2:19	
♊	Jun 25	18:44	
♋	Jul 20	23:34	
♌	Aug 14	18:47	
♍	Sept 8	5:28	
♎	Oct 2	9:27	
♏	Oct 26	9:12	
♐	Nov 19	6:56	
♑	Dec 13	4:06	
1975			
♒	Jan 6	1:39	
♓	Jan 30	1:05	
♒	Feb 23	4:53	
♉	Mar 19	16:42	
♊	Apr 13	17:26	
♋	May 9	15:11	
♌	Jun 6	5:54	
♍	Jul 9	6:06	
♌	Sept 2	10:34	R
♍	Oct 4	0:19	
♎	Nov 9	8:52	
♏	Dec 6	19:29	
1976			
♐	Jan 1	7:14	
♑	Jan 26	1:09	
♒	Feb 19	11:50	
♓	Mar 14	19:59	
♒	Apr 8	3:56	
♉	May 2	12:49	
♊	May 26	22:43	
♋	Jun 20	8:56	
♌	Jul 14	18:36	
♍	Aug 8	3:36	
♎	Sept 1	12:44	
♏	Sept 25	23:17	
♐	Oct 20	12:22	
♑	Nov 14	5:42	
♒	Dec 9	7:53	
1977			
♓	Jan 4	8:01	
♒	Feb 2	0:54	
♉	Jun 6	1:10	
♊	Jul 6	10:09	
♋	Aug 2	14:19	
♌	Aug 28	10:09	
♍	Sept 22	10:05	
♎	Oct 16	20:37	
♏	Nov 9	22:52	
♐	Dec 3	20:49	
♑	Dec 27	17:09	
1978			
♒	Jan 20	13:29	
♓	Feb 13	11:07	
♒	Mar 9	11:29	
♉	Apr 2	16:14	
♊	Apr 27	2:53	
♋	May 21	21:03	
♌	Jun 16	1:19	
♍	Jul 11	21:14	
♎	Aug 7	22:08	
♏	Sept 7	0:07	
1979			
♐	Jan 7	1:38	
♑	Feb 5	4:16	
♒	Mar 3	12:18	
♓	Mar 28	22:18	
♒	Apr 22	23:02	
♉	May 17	19:29	
♊	Jun 11	13:13	
♋	Jul 6	4:02	
♌	Jul 30	15:07	
♍	Aug 23	22:16	
♎	Sept 17	2:21	
♏	Oct 11	4:48	
♐	Nov 4	6:50	
♑	Nov 28	9:20	
♒	Dec 22	13:35	
1980			
♓	Jan 15	22:37	
♒	Feb 9	18:39	
♉	Mar 6	13:54	
♊	Apr 3	14:46	
♋	May 12	15:53	
♊	Jun 5	0:44	R
♋	Aug 6	9:25	
♌	Sept 7	12:57	
♍	Oct 4	18:07	
♎	Oct 30	5:38	
♏	Nov 23	20:35	
♐	Dec 18	1:21	
1981			
♑	Jan 11	1:48	
♒	Feb 4	1:07	
♓	Feb 28	1:01	
♒	Mar 24	2:43	
♉	Apr 17	7:08	
♊	May 11	14:45	
♋	Jun 5	1:29	
♌	Jun 29	15:20	
♍	Jul 24	9:04	
♎	Aug 18	8:44	
♏	Sept 12	17:51	
♐	Oct 8	19:04	
♑	Nov 5	7:39	
♒	Dec 8	15:52	
1982			
♑	Jan 22	21:56	R
♒	Mar 2	6:25	
♓	Apr 6	7:20	
♒	May 4	7:27	
♉	May 30	16:02	

Table A-5 — Venus (continued)

♊	Jun 25	7:13
♋	Jul 20	11:21
♌	Aug 14	6:09
♍	Sept 7	16:38
♎	Oct 1	20:32
♏	Oct 25	20:19
♐	Nov 18	18:07
♑	Dec 12	15:20

1983

♒	Jan 5	12:58
♓	Jan 29	12:31
♒	Feb 22	16:35
♉	Mar 19	4:51
♊	Apr 13	6:26
♋	May 9	5:56
♌	Jun 6	1:04
♍	Jul 10	0:25
♌	Aug 27	6:43 R
♍	Oct 5	14:35
♎	Nov 9	5:52
♏	Dec 6	11:15
♐	Dec 31	21:00

1984

♑	Jan 25	13:51
♒	Feb 18	23:53
♓	Mar 14	7:35
♒	Apr 7	15:13
♉	May 1	23:53
♊	May 26	9:40
♋	Jun 19	19:48
♌	Jul 14	5:30
♍	Aug 7	14:40
♎	Sept 1	0:07
♏	Sept 25	11:05
♐	Oct 20	0:45
♑	Nov 13	18:54
♒	Dec 8	22:26

1985

♓	Jan 4	1:23
♒	Feb 2	3:29
♉	Jun 6	3:53
♊	Jul 6	3:01
♋	Aug 2	4:10
♌	Aug 27	22:39
♍	Sept 21	21:53
♎	Oct 16	8:04
♏	Nov 9	10:08
♐	Dec 3	8:00
♑	Dec 27	4:17

1986

♒	Jan 20	0:36
♓	Feb 12	22:11
♒	Mar 8	22:32
♉	Apr 2	3:19
♊	Apr 26	14:10

♋	May 21	8:46
♌	Jun 15	13:52
♍	Jul 11	11:23
♎	Aug 7	15:46
♏	Sept 7	5:15

1987

♐	Jan 7	5:20
♑	Feb 4	22:03
♒	Mar 3	2:55
♓	Mar 28	11:20
♒	Apr 22	11:07
♉	May 17	6:56
♊	Jun 11	0:15
♋	Jul 5	14:50
♌	Jul 30	1:49
♍	Aug 23	9:00
♎	Sept 16	13:12
♏	Oct 10	15:49
♐	Nov 3	18:04
♑	Nov 27	20:51
♒	Dec 22	1:29

1988

♓	Jan 15	11:04
♒	Feb 9	8:04
♉	Mar 6	5:21
♊	Apr 3	12:07
♋	May 17	11:26
♊	May 27	2:36 R
♋	Aug 6	18:24
♌	Sept 7	6:37
♍	Oct 4	8:15
♎	Oct 29	18:20
♏	Nov 23	8:34
♐	Dec 17	12:56

1989

♑	Jan 10	13:08
♒	Feb 3	12:15
♓	Feb 27	11:59
♒	Mar 23	13:32
♉	Apr 16	17:52
♊	May 11	1:28
♋	Jun 4	12:17
♌	Jun 29	2:21
♍	Jul 23	20:31
♎	Aug 17	20:58
♏	Sept 12	7:22
♐	Oct 8	11:00
♑	Nov 5	5:13
♒	Dec 9	23:54

1990

♑	Jan 16	10:23 R
♒	Mar 3	12:52
♓	Apr 6	4:13
♒	May 3	22:52
♉	May 30	5:13

♊	Jun 24	19:14
♋	Jul 19	22:41
♌	Aug 13	17:05
♍	Sept 7	3:21
♎	Oct 1	7:13
♏	Oct 25	7:03
♐	Nov 18	4:58
♑	Dec 12	2:18

1991

♒	Jan 5	0:03
♓	Jan 28	23:44
♒	Feb 22	4:02
♉	Mar 18	16:45
♊	Apr 12	19:10
♋	May 8	20:28
♌	Jun 5	20:16
♍	Jul 11	0:06
♌	Aug 21	10:06 R
♍	Oct 6	16:15
♎	Nov 9	1:37
♏	Dec 6	2:21
♐	Dec 31	10:19

1992

♑	Jan 25	2:14
♒	Feb 18	11:40
♓	Mar 13	18:57
♒	Apr 7	2:16
♉	May 1	10:41
♊	May 25	20:18
♋	Jun 19	6:22
♌	Jul 13	16:07
♍	Aug 7	1:26
♎	Aug 31	11:09
♏	Sept 24	22:31
♐	Oct 19	12:47
♑	Nov 17	7:48
♒	Dec 8	12:49

1993

♓	Jan 3	18:54
♒	Feb 2	7:37
♉	Jun 6	5:03
♊	Jul 5	19:21
♋	Aug 1	17:38
♌	Aug 27	10:48
♍	Sept 21	9:22
♎	Oct 15	19:13
♏	Nov 8	21:07
♐	Dec 2	18:54
♑	Dec 26	15:09

1994

♒	Jan 19	11:28
♓	Feb 12	9:04
♒	Mar 8	9:28
♉	Apr 1	14:20
♊	Apr 26	1:24

♋	May 20	20:26
♌	Jun 15	2:23
♍	Jul 11	1:33
♎	Aug 7	9:36
♏	Sept 7	12:12

1995

♐	Jan 7	7:07
♑	Feb 4	15:12
♒	Mar 2	17:10
♓	Mar 28	0:10
♒	Apr 21	23:07
♉	May 16	18:22
♊	Jun 10	11:18
♋	Jul5	1:39
♌	Jul 29	12:32
♍	Aug 22	19:43
♎	Sept 16	0:01
♏	Oct 10	2:48
♐	Nov 3	5:18
♑	Nov 27	8:23
♒	Dec 21	13:23

1996

♓	Jan 14	23:30
♒	Feb 8	21:30
♉	Mar 5	21:01
♊	Apr 3	10:26
♋	Aug 7	1:15
♌	Sept 7	0:07
♍	Oct 3	22:22
♎	Oct 29	7:02
♏	Nov 22	20:34
♐	Dec 17	0:34

1997

♑	Jan 10	0:32
♒	Feb 2	23:28
♓	Feb 26	23:01
♒	Mar 23	0:26
♉	Apr 16	4:43
♊	May 10	12:20
♋	Jun 3	23:18
♌	Jun 28	13:38
♍	Jul 23	8:16
♎	Aug 17	9:31
♏	Sept 11	21:17
♐	Oct 8	3:25
♑	Nov 5	3:50
♒	Dec 11	23:39

1998

♑	Jan 9	16:03 R
♒	Mar 4	11:14
♓	Apr 6	0:38
♒	May 3	14:16
♉	May 29	18:32
♊	Jun 24	7:27
♋	Jul 19	10:17

♌	Aug 13	4:19
♍	Sept 6	14:24
♎	Sept 30	18:13
♏	Oct 24	18:06
♐	Nov 17	16:06
♑	Dec 11	13:33

1999

♒	Jan 4	11:25
♓	Jan 28	11:17
♒	Feb 21	15:49
♉	Mar 18	4:59
♊	Apr 12	8:17
♋	May 8	11:29
♌	Jun 5	16:25
♍	Jul 12	10:18
♌	Aug 15	9:12 R
♍	Oct 7	11:51
♎	Nov 8	21:19
♏	Dec 5	17:41
♐	Dec 30	23:54

2000

♑	Jan 24	14:52
♒	Feb 17	23:43
♓	Mar 13	6:36
♒	Apr 6	13:37
♉	Apr 30	21:49
♊	May 25	7:15
♋	Jun 18	17:15
♌	Jul 13	3:02
♍	Aug 6	12:32
♎	Aug 30	22:35
♏	Sept 24	10:26
♐	Oct 19	1:18
♑	Nov 12	21:14
♒	Dec 8	3:48

2001

♓	Jan 3	13:14
♒	Feb 2	14:14
♉	Jun 6	5:25
♊	Jul 5	11:44
♋	Aug 1	7:18
♌	Aug 26	23:12
♍	Sept 20	21:09
♎	Oct 15	6:42
♏	Nov 8	8:29
♐	Dec 2	6:11
♑	Dec 26	2:25

2002

♒	Jan 18	22:42
♓	Feb 11	20:18
♒	Mar 7	20:42
♉	Apr 1	1:39
♊	Apr 25	12:57
♋	May 20	8:27
♌	Jun 14	15:16

(continued)

Table A-5 — Venus (continued)

(continued from 2004)

♍ Jul 10 16:09
♎ Aug 7 4:09
♏ Sept 7 22:05

2003
♐ Jan 7 8:07
♑ Feb 4 8:27
♒ Mar 2 7:40
♓ Mar 27 13:14
♈ Apr 21 11:18
♉ May 16 5:58
♊ Jun 9 22:32
♋ Jul 4 12:39
♌ Jul 28 23:25
♍ Aug 22 6:35
♎ Sept 15 10:58
♏ Oct 9 13:56
♐ Nov 2 16:42
♑ Nov 26 20:07
♒ Dec 21 1:32

2004
♓ Jan 14 12:16
♈ Feb 8 11:20
♉ Mar 5 13:12
♊ Apr 3 9:57
♋ Aug 7 6:02
♌ Sept 6 17:16
♍ Oct 3 12:20
♎ Oct 28 19:39
♏ Nov 22 8:31

♐ Dec 16 12:10

2005
♑ Jan 9 11:56
♒ Feb 2 10:42
♓ Feb 26 10:07
♈ Mar 22 11:25
♉ Apr 15 15:37
♊ May 9 23:14
♋ Jun 3 10:18
♌ Jun 28 0:53
♍ Jul 22 20:01
♎ Aug 16 22:05
♏ Sept 11 11:14
♐ Oct 7 20:00
♑ Nov 5 3:10
♒ Dec 15 10:57 R

2006
♑ Jan 1 15:18
♒ Mar 5 3:38
♓ Apr 5 20:20
♈ May 3 5:24
♉ May 29 7:41
♊ Jun 23 19:30
♋ Jul 18 21:41
♌ Aug 12 15:20
♍ Sep 6 1:14
♎ Sep 30 5:01
♏ Oct 24 4:57
♐ Dec 17 3:02

♑ Dec 11 0:33

2007
♒ Jan 3 22:31
♓ Jan 27 22:32
♈ Feb 21 3:21
♉ Mar 17 17:00
♊ Apr 11 21:14
♋ May 8 2:27
♌ Jun 5 12:59
♍ Jul 14 13:23
♌ Aug 8 20:10 R
♍ Oct 8 1:52
♎ Nov 8 16:04
♏ Dec 5 8:28
♐ Dec 30 13:01

2008
♑ Jan 24 3:05
♒ Feb 17 11:22
♓ Mar 12 17:50
♈ Apr 6 0:35
♉ Apr 30 8:34
♊ May 24 17:51
♋ Jun 18 3:48
♌ Jul 12 13:38
♍ Aug 5 23:19
♎ Aug 30 9:41
♏ Sep 23 21:58
♐ Oct 18 13:30
♑ Nov 12 10:24

♒ Dec 7 18:36

2009
♓ Jan 3 7:35
♒ Feb 2 22:40
♓ Apr 11 7:46 R
♒ Apr 24 2:18
♉ Jun 6 4:06
♊ Jul 5 3:22
♋ Jul 31 20:27
♌ Aug 26 11:11
♍ Sep 20 8:31
♎ Oct 14 17:46
♏ Nov 7 19:23
♐ Dec 1 5:03
♑ Dec 25 13:16

2010
♒ Jan 18 9:34
♓ Feb 11 7:09
♈ Mar 7 7:33
♉ Mar 31 12:34
♊ Apr 25 0:05
♋ May 19 20:04
♌ Jun 14 3:49
♍ Jul 10 6:31
♎ Aug 6 22:47
♏ Sep 8 10:44
♎ Nov 7 22:05 R
♏ Nov 29 19:33

2011
♐ Jan 7 7:30
♑ Feb 4 0:57
♒ Mar 1 21:38
♓ Mar 27 1:52
♈ Apr 20 23:06
♉ May 15 17:11
♊ Jun 9 9:23
♋ Jul 3 23:16
♌ Jul 28 9:58
♍ Aug 21 17:10
♎ Sep 14 21:39
♏ Oct 9 0:49
♐ Nov 2 3:51
♑ Nov 26 7:35
♒ Dec 20 13:25

2012
♓ Jan 14 0:47
♈ Feb 8 1:00
♉ Mar 5 5:24
♊ Apr 3 10:17
♋ Aug 7 8:42
♌ Sep 6 9:47
♍ Oct 3 1:58
♎ Oct 28 8:03
♏ Nov 21 20:19

Table A-6 — Mars

1930		
♒ Feb 6	13:21	
♓ Mar 17	0:55	
♈ Apr 24	12:27	
♉ Jun 2	22:15	
♊ Jul 14	7:54	
♋ Aug 28	6:27	
♌ Oct 20	9:43	

1931		
♋ Feb 16	9:27	R
♌ Mar 29	22:48	
♍ Jun 10	9:58	
♎ Aug 1	11:38	
♏ Sept 17	3:43	
♐ Oct 30	7:46	
♑ Dec 9	22:11	

1932		
♒ Jan 17	19:35	
♓ Feb 24	21:36	
♈ Apr 3	2:02	
♉ May 12	5:53	
♊ Jun 22	4:19	
♋ Aug 4	14:52	
♌ Sept 20	14:43	
♍ Nov 13	16:25	

1933		
♎ Jul 6	17:03	
♏ Aug 26	1:34	
♐ Oct 9	6:35	
♑ Nov 19	2:18	
♒ Dec 27	22:43	

1934		
♓ Feb 3	23:13	
♈ Mar 14	4:09	
♉ Apr 22	10:40	
♊ Jun 2	11:21	
♋ Jul 15	16:33	
♌ Aug 30	8:43	
♍ Oct 17	23:59	
♎ Dec 11	4:32	

1935		
♏ Jul 29	12:32	
♐ Sept 16	7:59	
♑ Oct 28	13:22	
♒ Dec 6	23:34	

1936		
♓ Jan 14	8:59	
♈ Feb 21	23:09	
♉ Apr 1	16:30	
♊ May 13	4:17	
♋ Jun 25	16:53	
♌ Aug 10	4:43	
♍ Sept 26	9:51	
♎ Nov 14	9:52	

1937		
♏ Jan 5	15:39	
♐ Mar 12	22:16	
♏ May 14	17:52	R
♐ Aug 8	17:14	
♑ Sept 30	4:08	
♒ Nov 11	13:31	
♓ Dec 21	12:46	

1938		
♈ Jan 30	7:44	
♉ Mar 12	2:48	
♊ Apr 23	13:39	
♋ Jun 6	20:28	
♌ Jul 22	17:26	
♍ Sept 7	15:22	
♎ Oct 25	1:20	
♏ Dec 11	18:25	

1939		
♐ Jan 29	4:49	
♑ Mar 21	2:25	
♒ May 24	19:19	
♑ Jul 21	14:31	R
♒ Sept 23	20:13	
♓ Nov 19	10:56	

1940		
♈ Jan 3	19:05	
♉ Feb 16	20:54	
♊ Apr 1	13:41	
♋ May 17	9:45	
♌ Jul 3	5:32	
♍ Aug 19	10:58	
♎ Oct 5	9:21	
♏ Nov 20	12:16	

1941		
♐ Jan 4	14:42	
♑ Feb 17	18:32	
♒ Apr 2	6:46	
♓ May 16	0:05	
♈ Jul 2	0:17	

1942		
♉ Jan 11	17:21	
♊ Mar 7	3:04	
♋ Apr 26	1:18	
♌ Jun 13	22:56	
♍ Aug 1	3:27	
♎ Sept 17	5:11	
♏ Nov 1	17:36	
♐ Dec 15	11:51	

1943		
♑ Jan 26	14:10	
♒ Mar 8	7:42	
♓ Apr 17	5:25	
♈ May 27	4:25	
♉ Jul 7	18:05	
♊ Aug 23	18:58	

1944		
♋ Mar 28	4:54	
♌ May 22	9:16	
♍ Jul 11	21:54	
♎ Aug 28	19:23	
♏ Oct 13	7:09	
♐ Nov 25	11:11	

1945		
♑ Jan 5	14:31	
♒ Feb 14	4:58	
♓ Mar 24	22:43	
♈ May 2	15:29	
♉ Jun 11	6:52	
♊ Jul 23	3:59	
♋ Sept 7	15:56	
♌ Nov 11	16:05	
♋ Dec 26	10:04	R

1946		
♌ Apr 22	14:31	
♍ Jun 20	3:31	
♎ Aug 9	8:17	
♏ Sept 24	11:35	
♐ Nov 6	13:22	
♑ Dec 17	5:56	

1947		
♒ Jan 25	6:44	
♓ Mar 4	11:46	
♈ Apr 11	18:03	
♉ May 20	22:40	
♊ Jun 30	22:34	
♋ Aug 13	16:26	
♌ Sept 30	21:31	
♍ Dec 1	6:44	

1948		
♌ Feb 12	5:28	R
♍ May 18	15:54	
♎ Jul 17	0:25	
♏ Sept 3	8:58	
♐ Oct 17	0:43	
♑ Nov 26	16:59	

1949		
♒ Jan 4	12:50	
♓ Feb 11	13:05	
♈ Mar 21	17:02	
♉ Apr 29	21:33	
♊ Jun 9	19:57	
♋ Jul 23	0:54	
♌ Sept 6	23:51	
♍ Oct 26	19:58	
♎ Dec 26	0:23	

1950		
♍ Mar 28	6:05	R
♎ Jun 11	15:27	
♏ Aug 10	11:48	
♐ Sept 25	14:48	
♑ Nov 6	1:40	
♒ Dec 15	3:59	

1951		
♓ Jan 22	8:05	
♈ Mar 1	17:03	
♉ Apr 10	4:37	
♊ May 21	10:32	
♋ Jul 3	18:42	
♌ Aug 18	5:55	
♍ Oct 4	19:20	
♎ Nov 24	1:11	

1952		
♏ Jan 19	20:33	
♐ Aug 27	13:53	
♑ Oct 11	23:45	
♒ Nov 21	14:40	
♓ Dec 30	16:35	

1953		
♈ Feb 7	20:07	
♉ Mar 20	1:54	
♊ May 1	1:08	
♋ Jun 13	22:49	
♌ Jul 29	14:25	
♍ Sept 14	12:59	
♎ Nov 1	9:19	
♏ Dec 20	6:22	

1954		
♐ Feb 9	14:18	
♑ Apr 12	11:28	
♐ Jul 3	2:23	R
♑ Aug 24	8:22	
♒ Oct 21	7:03	
♓ Dec 4	2:41	

1955		
♈ Jan 14	23:33	
♉ Feb 26	5:22	
♊ Apr 10	18:09	
♋ May 25	19:50	
♌ Jul 11	4:22	
♍ Aug 27	5:13	
♎ Oct 13	6:20	
♏ Nov 28	20:33	

1956		
♐ Jan 13	21:28	
♑ Feb 28	15:05	
♒ Apr 14	18:40	
♓ Jun 3	2:51	
♈ Dec 6	6:24	

1957		
♉ Jan 28	9:19	
♊ Mar 17	16:34	
♋ May 4	10:22	
♌ Jun 21	7:18	
♍ Aug 8	0:27	
♎ Sept 23	23:31	
♏ Nov 8	16:04	
♐ Dec 22	20:29	

1958		
♑ Feb 3	13:57	
♒ Mar 17	2:11	
♓ Apr 26	21:31	
♈ Jun 7	1:21	
♉ Jul 21	2:03	

(continued)

Table A-6 — Mars (continued)

♊ Sept 21 0:26
♉ Oct 28 19:00 R

1959
♊ Feb 10 8:57
♋ Apr 10 4:46
♌ May 31 21:26
♍ Jul 20 6:03
♎ Sept 5 17:46
♏ Oct 21 4:40
♐ Dec 3 13:09

1960
♑ Jan 13 23:59
♒ Feb 22 23:11
♓ Apr 2 1:24
♈ May 11 2:19
♉ Jun 20 4:05
♊ Aug 1 23:32
♋ Sept 20 23:06

1961
♊ Feb 4 19:23 R
♋ Feb 7 0:25
♌ May 5 20:13
♍ Jun 28 18:47
♎ Aug 16 19:41
♏ Oct 1 15:02
♐ Nov 13 16:50
♑ Dec 24 12:50

1962
♒ Feb 1 18:06
♓ Mar 12 2:58
♈ Apr 19 11:58
♉ May 28 18:47
♊ Jul 8 22:50
♋ Aug 22 6:37
♌ Oct 11 18:54

1963
♍ Jun 3 1:30
♎ Jul 26 23:14
♏ Sept 12 4:11
♐ Oct 25 12:31
♑ Dec 5 4:03

1964
♒ Jan 13 1:13
♓ Feb 20 2:33
♈ Mar 29 6:24
♉ May 7 9:41

♊ Jun 17 6:43
♋ Jul 30 13:23
♌ Sept 15 0:22
♍ Nov 5 22:20

1965
♎ Jun 28 20:12
♏ Aug 20 7:16
♐ Oct 4 1:46
♑ Nov 14 2:19
♒ Dec 23 0:36

1966
♓ Jan 30 2:01
♈ Mar 9 7:55
♉ Apr 17 15:35
♊ May 28 17:07
♋ Jul 10 22:15
♌ Aug 25 10:52
♍ Oct 12 13:37
♎ Dec 3 19:55

1967
♏ Feb 12 7:20
♎ Mar 31 1:10 R
♏ Jul 19 17:56
♐ Sept 9 20:44
♑ Oct 22 21:14
♒ Dec 1 15:12

1968
♓ Jan 9 4:49
♈ Feb 16 22:18
♉ Mar 27 18:43
♊ May 8 9:14
♋ Jun 21 0:03
♌ Aug 5 12:07
♍ Sept 21 13:39
♎ Nov 9 1:10
♏ Dec 29 17:07

1969
♐ Feb 25 1:21
♑ Sept 21 1:35
♒ Nov 4 13:51
♓ Dec 15 9:22

1970
♈ Jan 24 16:29
♉ Mar 6 20:28
♊ Apr 18 13:59
♋ Jun 2 1:50

♌ Jul 18 1:43
♍ Sept 2 23:57
♎ Oct 20 5:57
♏ Dec 6 11:34

1971
♐ Jan 22 20:34
♑ Mar 12 5:11
♒ May 3 15:57
♓ Nov 6 7:31
♈ Dec 26 13:04

1972
♉ Feb 10 9:04
♊ Mar 26 23:30
♋ May 12 8:14
♌ Jun 28 11:09
♍ Aug 14 19:59
♎ Sept 30 18:23
♏ Nov 15 17:17
♐ Dec 30 11:12

1973
♑ Feb 12 0:51
♒ Mar 26 15:59
♓ May 7 23:09
♈ Jun 20 15:54
♉ Aug 12 9:56
♈ Oct 29 17:56 R
♉ Dec 24 3:09

1974
♊ Feb 27 5:11
♋ Apr 20 3:18
♌ Jun 8 19:54
♍ Jul 27 9:04
♎ Sept 12 14:08
♏ Oct 28 2:05
♐ Dec 10 17:05

1975
♑ Jan 21 13:49
♒ Mar 3 0:32
♓ Apr 11 14:15
♈ May 21 3:14
♉ Jun 30 22:53
♊ Aug 14 15:47
♋ Oct 17 3:44
♊ Nov 25 13:30 R

1976
♋ Mar 18 8:15

♌ May 16 6:10
♍ Jul 6 18:27
♎ Aug 24 0:55
♏ Oct 8 15:23
♐ Nov 20 18:53
♑ Dec 31 19:42

1977
♒ Feb 9 6:57
♓ Mar 19 21:19
♈ Apr 27 10:46
♉ Jun 5 22:00
♊ Jul 17 10:13
♋ Aug 31 19:20
♌ Oct 26 13:56

1978
♋ Jan 25 20:59 R
♌ Apr 10 13:50
♍ Jun 13 21:38
♎ Aug 4 4:07
♏ Sept 19 15:57
♐ Nov 1 20:20
♑ Dec 12 12:39

1979
♒ Jan 20 12:07
♓ Feb 27 15:25
♈ Apr 6 20:08
♉ May 15 23:25
♊ Jun 25 20:55
♋ Aug 8 8:28
♌ Sept 24 16:21
♍ Nov 19 16:36

1980
♌ Mar 11 15:46 R
♍ May 3 21:26
♎ Jul 10 12:59
♏ Aug 29 0:50
♐ Oct 12 1:27
♑ Nov 21 20:42
♒ Dec 30 17:30

1981
♓ Feb 6 17:48
♈ Mar 16 21:40
♉ Apr 25 2:17
♊ Jun 5 0:26
♋ Jul 18 3:54
♌ Sept 1 20:52
♍ Oct 20 20:56

♎ Dec 15 19:14

1982
♏ Aug 3 6:45
♐ Sept 19 20:20
♑ Oct 31 18:05
♒ Dec 10 1:17

1983
♓ Jan 17 8:10
♈ Feb 24 19:19
♉ Apr 5 9:03
♊ May 16 16:43
♋ Jun 29 1:54
♌ Aug 13 11:54
♍ Sept 29 19:12
♎ Nov 18 5:26

1984
♏ Jan 10 22:20
♐ Aug 17 14:50
♑ Oct 5 1:02
♒ Nov 15 13:09
♓ Dec 25 1:38

1985
♈ Feb 2 12:19
♉ Mar 15 0:06
♊ Apr 26 4:13
♋ Jun 9 5:40
♌ Jul 24 23:04
♍ Sept 9 20:31
♎ Oct 27 10:16
♏ Dec 14 13:59

1986
♐ Feb 2 1:27
♑ Mar 27 22:47
♒ Oct 8 20:01
♓ Nov 25 21:35

1987
♈ Jan 8 7:20
♉ Feb 20 9:44
♊ Apr 5 11:37
♋ May 20 22:01
♌ Jul 6 11:46
♍ Aug 22 14:51
♎ Oct 8 14:27
♏ Nov 23 22:19

Table A-6   Mars *(continued)*

1988
♐	Jan 8	10:24
♑	Feb 22	5:15
♒	Apr 6	16:44
♓	May 22	2:42
♈	Jul 13	15:00
♓	Oct 23	17:02 R
♈	Nov 1	7:57

1989
♉	Jan 19	3:11
♊	Mar 11	3:51
♋	Apr 28	23:37
♌	Jun 16	9:10
♍	Aug 3	8:35
♎	Sept 19	9:38
♏	Nov 4	0:29
♐	Dec 17	23:57

1990
♑	Jan 29	9:10
♒	Mar 11	10:54
♓	Apr 20	17:09
♈	May 31	2:11
♉	Jul 12	9:44
♊	Aug 31	6:40
♉	Dec 14	2:46 R

1991
♊	Jan 20	20:15
♋	Apr 2	19:49
♌	May 26	7:19
♍	Jul 15	7:36
♎	Sept 1	1:38
♏	Oct 16	14:05
♐	Nov 28	21:19

1992
♑	Jan 9	4:47
♒	Feb 17	23:38
♓	Mar 27	21:04
♈	May 5	16:36
♉	Jun 14	10:56
♊	Jul 26	13:59
♋	Sept 12	1:05

1993
♌	Apr 27	18:40
♍	Jun 23	2:42
♎	Aug 11	20:10
♏	Sept 26	21:15
♐	Nov 9	0:29
♑	Dec 19	19:34

1994
♒	Jan 27	23:05
♓	Mar 7	6:01
♈	Apr 14	13:02
♉	May 23	17:37
♊	Jul 3	17:30
♋	Aug 16	14:15
♌	Oct 4	10:48
♍	Dec 12	6:32

1995
♌	Jan 22	18:48 R
♍	May 25	11:09
♎	Jul 21	4:21
♏	Sept 7	2:00
♐	Oct 20	16:02
♑	Nov 30	8:57

1996
♒	Jan 8	6:02
♓	Feb 15	6:50
♈	Mar 24	10:12
♉	May 2	13:16
♊	Jun 12	9:42
♋	Jul 25	13:32
♌	Sept 9	15:02
♍	Oct 30	2:13

1997
♎	Jan 3	3:10
♍	Mar 8	14:49 R
♎	Jun 19	3:30
♏	Aug 14	3:42
♐	Sept 28	17:22
♑	Nov 9	0:33
♒	Dec 18	1:37

1998
♓	Jan 25	4:26
♈	Mar 4	11:18
♉	Apr 12	20:05
♊	May 23	22:42
♋	Jul 6	4:00
♌	Aug 20	14:16
♍	Oct 7	7:28
♎	Nov 27	5:10

1999
♏	Jan 26	6:59
♎	May 5	16:32 R
♏	Jul 4	22:59
♐	Sept 2	14:29
♑	Oct 16	20:35
♒	Nov 26	1:56

2000
♓	Jan 3	22:01
♈	Feb 11	20:04
♉	Mar 22	20:25
♊	May 3	14:18
♋	Jun 16	7:30
♌	Jul 31	20:21
♍	Sept 16	19:19
♎	Nov 3	21:00
♏	Dec 23	9:37

2001
♐	Feb 14	15:06
♑	Sept 8	12:51
♒	Oct 27	12:19
♓	Dec 8	16:52

2002
♈	Jan 18	17:53
♉	Mar 1	10:05
♊	Apr 13	12:36
♋	May 28	6:43
♌	Jul 13	10:23
♍	Aug 29	9:38
♎	Oct 15	12:38
♏	Dec 1	9:26

2003
♐	Jan 16	23:22
♑	Mar 4	16:17
♒	Apr 21	18:48
♓	Jun 16	21:25
♈	Dec 16	8:24

2004
♉	Feb 3	5:04
♊	Mar 21	2:39
♋	May 7	3:45
♌	Jun 23	15:50
♍	Aug 10	5:14
♎	Sept 26	4:15
♏	Nov 11	0:11
♐	Dec 25	11:04

2005
♑	Feb 6	13:32
♒	Mar 20	13:02
♓	Apr 30	21:58
♈	Jun 11	21:30
♉	Jul 28	0:12 R

2006
♊	Feb 17	17:43
♋	Apr 13	19:58
♌	Jun 3	13:42
♍	Jul 22	13:52
♎	Sep 7	23:18
♏	Oct 23	11:37
♐	Dec 11	0:33

2007
♑	Jan 16	15:53
♒	Feb 25	8:32
♓	Apr 6	3:49
♈	May 15	9:06
♉	Jun 24	16:26
♊	Aug 7	1:01
♋	Sep 28	18:54
♊	Dec 31	11:00 R

2008
♋	Mar 4	5:01

♌	May 9	15:19
♍	Jul 1	11:21
♎	Aug 19	5:03
♏	Oct 3	23:33
♐	Nov 16	3:26
♑	Dec 27	2:30

2009
♒	Feb 4	10:55
♓	Mar 14	22:19
♈	Apr 22	8:44
♉	May 31	16:18
♊	Jul 11	21:55
♋	Aug 25	12:15
♌	Oct 16	10:32

2010
♍	Jun 7	1:11
♎	Jul 29	18:46
♏	Sep 14	17:37
♐	Oct 28	1:47
♑	Dec 7	18:48

2011
♒	Jan 15	17:41
♓	Feb 22	20:05
♈	Apr 1	23:50
♉	May 11	2:03
♊	Jun 20	21:49
♋	Aug 3	4:21
♌	Sep 18	20:50
♍	Nov 10	23:14

2012
♎	Jul 3	7:31
♏	Aug 23	10:24
♐	Oct 6	22:20
♑	Nov 16	21:35
♒	Dec 25	19:48
♐	Dec 15	23:37

Table A-7 — Jupiter

1930 ♋ Jun 26 17:42	**1948** ♑ Nov 15 5:38	**1962** ♓ Mar 25 17:07	♊ Aug 23 5:24 / ♉ Oct 16 15:24 R	**1994** ♐ Dec 9 5:54
1931 ♌ Jul 17 2:52	**1949** ♒ Apr 12 14:18 / ♑ Jun 27 13:29 R / ♒ Nov 30 15:08	**1963** ♈ Apr 3 22:19	**1977** ♊ Apr 3 10:42 / ♋ Aug 20 7:43 / ♊ Dec 30 18:50 R	**1996** ♑ Jan 3 2:22
1932 ♍ Aug 11 2:16	**1950** ♓ Apr 15 3:58 / ♒ Sept 14 21:23 R / ♓ Dec 1 14:57	**1964** ♉ Apr 12 1:52	**1978** ♋ Apr 11 19:12 / ♌ Sept 5 3:31	**1997** ♒ Jan 21 10:13
1933 ♎ Sept 10 0:11	**1951** ♈ Apr 21 9:57	**1965** ♊ Apr 22 9:32 / ♋ Sept 20 23:40 / ♊ Nov 16 22:08 R	**1979** ♋ Feb 28 18:35 R / ♌ Apr 20 3:30 / ♍ Sept 29 5:23	**1998** ♓ Feb 4 5:52
1934 ♏ Oct 10 23:55	**1952** ♉ Apr 28 15:50	**1966** ♋ May 5 9:52 / ♌ Sept 27 8:19	**1980** ♎ Oct 27 5:10	**1999** ♈ Feb 12 20:23 / ♉ Jun 28 4:29 / ♈ Oct 23 0:48 R
1935 ♐ Nov 8 21:56	**1953** ♊ May 9 10:33	**1967** ♋ Jan 15 22:50 R / ♌ May 23 3:21 / ♍ Oct 19 5:51	**1981** ♏ Nov 26 21:19	**2000** ♉ Feb 14 16:40 / ♊ Jun 30 2:35
1936 ♑ Dec 2 3:39	**1954** ♋ May 23 23:43	**1968** ♌ Feb 26 22:33 R / ♍ Jun 15 9:44 / ♎ Nov 15 17:44	**1982** ♐ Dec 25 20:57	**2001** ♋ Jul 12 19:03
1937 ♒ Dec 19 23:06	**1955** ♌ Jun 12 19:07 / ♍ Nov 16 22:59	**1969** ♍ Mar 30 16:36 R / ♎ Jul 15 8:30 / ♏ Dec 16 10:55	**1984** ♑ Jan 19 10:04	**2002** ♌ Aug 1 12:20
1938 ♓ May 14 2:46 / ♒ Jul 29 22:01 R / ♓ Dec 29 13:34	**1956** ♌ Jan 17 21:04 R / ♍ Jul 7 14:01 / ♎ Dec 12 21:17	**1970** ♎ Apr 30 1:43 R / ♏ Aug 15 12:58	**1985** ♒ Feb 6 10:35	**2003** ♍ Aug 27 4:26
1939 ♈ May 11 9:08 / ♓ Oct 29 19:44 R / ♈ Dec 20 12:03	**1957** ♍ Feb 19 10:37 R / ♎ Aug 6 21:11	**1971** ♐ Jan 14 3:49 / ♏ Jun 4 21:12 R / ♐ Sept 11 10:33	**1986** ♓ Feb 20 11:05	**2004** ♎ Sept 24 22:23
1940 ♉ May 16 2:54	**1958** ♏ Jan 13 7:52 / ♎ Mar 20 14:13 R / ♏ Sept 7 3:52	**1972** ♑ Feb 6 14:37 / ♐ Jul 24 11:42 R / ♑ Sept 25 13:20	**1987** ♈ Mar 2 13:41	**2005** ♏ Oct 25 21:52
1941 ♊ May 26 7:48	**1959** ♐ Feb 10 8:46 / ♏ Apr 24 9:10 R / ♐ Oct 5 9:40	**1973** ♒ Feb 23 4:28	**1988** ♉ Mar 8 10:44 / ♊ Jul 21 19:00 / ♉ Nov 30 15:53 R	**2006** ♐ Nov 23 21:52
1942 ♋ Jun 10 5:36	**1960** ♑ Mar 1 8:10 / ♐ Jun 9 20:52 R / ♑ Oct 25 22:01	**1974** ♓ Mar 8 6:11	**1989** ♊ Mar 10 22:26 / ♋ Jul 30 18:50	**2007** ♑ Dec 18 15:11
1943 ♌ Jun 30 16:46	**1961** ♒ Mar 15 3:01 / ♑ Aug 12 3:54 R / ♒ Nov 3 21:49	**1975** ♈ Mar 18 11:47	**1990** ♌ Aug 18 2:30	**2009** ♒ Jan 5 10:40
1944 ♍ Jul 25 20:04		**1976** ♉ Mar 26 5:25	**1991** ♍ Sept 12 1:00	**2010** ♓ Jan 17 21:10 / ♈ Jun 6 1:27 / ♓ Sep 8 23:49 R
1945 ♎ Aug 25 1:06			**1992** ♎ Oct 10 8:26	**2011** ♈ Jan 22 12:11 / ♉ Jun 4 8:55
1946 ♏ Sept 25 5:19			**1993** ♏ Nov 10 3:15	**2012** ♊ Jun 11 12:21
1947 ♐ Oct 23 22:00				

Table A-8 — Saturn

1932
♒ Feb 23 21:47
♉ Aug 13 6:14 R
♒ Nov 19 21:10

1935
♓ Feb 14 9:08

1937
♈ Apr 25 1:29
♓ Oct 17 22:41 R

1938
♈ Jan 14 5:31

1939
♉ Jul 6 0:45
♈ Sept 22 0:18 R

1940
♉ Mar 20 4:40

1942
♊ May 8 14:39

1944
♋ Jun 20 2:48

1946
♌ Aug 2 9:42

1948
♍ Sept 18 23:36

1949
♌ Apr 2 22:38 R
♍ May 29 7:59

1950
♎ Nov 20 10:50

1951
♍ Mar 7 7:12 R
♎ Aug 13 11:44

1953
♏ Oct 22 10:36

1956
♐ Jan 12 13:46
♏ May 13 22:45 R
♐ Oct 10 10:11

1959
♑ Jan 5 8:33

1962
♒ Jan 3 14:01

1964
♓ Mar 23 23:18
♒ Sept 16 16:04 R
♓ Dec 16 0:39

1967
♈ Mar 3 16:32

1969
♉ Apr 29 17:24

1971
♊ Jun 18 11:09

1972
♉ Jan 9 22:43 R
♊ Feb 21 9:53

1973
♋ Aug 1 17:20

1974
♊ Jan 7 15:26 R
♋ Apr 18 17:34

1975
♌ Sept 16 23:57

1976
♋ Jan 14 8:16 R
♌ Jun 5 0:09

1977
♍ Nov 16 21:43

1978
♌ Jan 4 19:44
♍ Jul 26 7:02

1980
♎ Sept 21 5:48

1982
♏ Nov 29 5:29

1983
♎ May 6 14:29 R
♏ Aug 24 6:54

1985
♐ Nov 16 21:10

1988
♑ Feb 13 18:51
♐ Jun 10 0:22 R
♑ Nov 12 4:26

1991
♒ Feb 6 13:51

1993
♓ May 20 23:58
♒ Jun 30 3:28 R

1994
♓ Jan 28 18:43

1996
♈ Apr 7 3:49

1998
♉ Jun 9 1:07

♈ Oct 25 13:41 R

1999
♉ Feb 28 20:26

2000
♊ Aug 9 21:26
♉ Oct 15 19:44 R

2001
♊ Apr 20 16:59

2003
♋ Jun 3 20:28

2005
♌ Jul 16 7:30

2007
♍ Sep 2 8:48

2009
♎ Oct 29 12:08

2010
♍ Apr 7 13:50 R
♎ Jul 21 10:10

2012
♏ Oct 5 15:33

Table A-9   Uranus

1934	♊ Nov 12 8:27 R	**1962**	♏ Sept 8 0:16	**1996**
♉ Jun 6 10:41	**1949**	♌ Jan 10 0:53 R	**1981**	♒ Jan 12 2:13
♈ Oct 9 19:37 R	♋ Jun 9 23:08	♍ Aug 9 20:19	♐ Feb 17 4:02	**2003**
1935	**1955**	**1968**	♏ Mar 20 18:15 R	♓ Mar 10 15:53
♉ Mar 27 21:57	♌ Aug 24 13:04	♎ Sept 28 11:10	♐ Nov 16 7:05	♒ Sept 14 22:47 R
1941	**1956**	**1969**	**1988**	♓ Dec 30 4:14
♊ Aug 7 10:32	♋ Jan 27 20:57 R	♍ May 20 15:51 R	♑ Feb 14 19:11	**2010**
♉ Oct 4 21:08 R	♌ Jun 9 20:48	♎ Jun 24 5:36	♐ May 26 20:17 R	♈ May 27 20:43
1942	**1961**	**1974**	♑ Dec 2 10:35	♓ Aug 13 22:36 R
♊ May 14 23:04	♍ Nov 1 11:01	♏ Nov 21 4:32	**1995**	**2011**
1948		**1975**	♒ Apr 1 7:11	♈ Mar 11 19:49
♋ Aug 30 10:40		♎ May 1 12:46 R	♑ Jun 8 20:42 R	

Table A-10   Neptune

1942	*1956*	*1970*	*1998*	*2012*
♎ Oct 3 12:01	♎ Mar 11 20:53 R	♐ Jan 4 14:55	♒ Jan 28 21:52	♓ Feb 3 14:02
1943	♏ Oct 19 4:27	♏ May 2 20:30 R	♑ Aug 22 19:13 R	
♍ Apr 17 5:56 R	*1957*	♐ Nov 6 11:32	♒ Nov 27 20:19	
♎ Aug 2 14:10	♎ Jun 15 15:07 R	*1984*	*2011*	
1955	♏ Aug 6 3:25	♑ Jan 18 21:55	♓ Apr 4 8:50	
♏ Dec 24 10:22		♐ Jun 22 20:10 R	♒ Aug 4 21:53 R	
		♑ Nov 21 8:21		

Table A-11 — Pluto

1937				1956				1971				1984				2008			
♌	Oct 7	7:08		♍	Oct 20	1:12		♎	Oct 5	1:15		♎	May 18	9:35	R	♑	Jan 25	21:36	
♋	Nov 25	4:13	R	**1957**				**1972**				♏	Aug 27	23:44		♐	Jun 14	0:13	R
1938				♌	Jan 14	21:45	R	♍	Apr 17	2:49	R	**1995**				♑	Nov 26	20:02	
♌	Aug 3	12:56		♍	Aug 18	23:23		♎	Jul 30	6:39		♐	Jan 17	4:16					
1939				**1958**				**1983**				♏	Apr 20	21:56	R				
♋	Feb 7	8:00	R	♌	Apr 11	9:58	R	♏	Nov 5	16:07		♐	Nov 10	14:11					
♌	Jun 13	23:46		♍	Jun 10	13:50													

Table A-12   Chiron

1933
♊ Jun 6 21:16
♉ Dec 22 2:52 R

1934
♊ Mar 23 8:54

1937
♋ Aug 27 12:03
♊ Nov 22 21:23 R

1938
♋ May 28 7:29

1940
♌ Sept 29 22:25
♋ Dec 27 0:22 R

1941
♌ Jun 16 13:22

1943
♍ Jul 26 17:30

1944
♎ Nov 17 22:08

1945
♍ Mar 23 22:14 R
♎ Jul 22 11:15

1946
♏ Nov 10 2:04

1948
♐ Nov 28 7:51

1951
♑ Feb 8 20:20
♐ Jun 18 8:21 R
♑ Nov 8 11:17

1955
♒ Jan 27 11:27

1960
♓ Mar 26 8:40
♒ Aug 19 1:30 R

1961
♓ Jan 20 20:51

1968
♈ Apr 1 2:09
♓ Oct 18 17:33 R

1969
♈ Jan 30 3:14

1976
♉ May 28 6:12
♈ Oct 13 17:43 R

1977
♉ Mar 28 14:07

1983
♊ Jun 21 8:56
♉ Nov 29 8:17 R

1984
♊ Apr 10 23:20

1988
♋ Jun 21 4:41

1991
♌ Jul 21 10:55

1993
♍ Sept 3 12:34

1995
♎ Sept 9 9:31

1996
♏ Dec 29 6:23

1997
♎ Apr 4 11:40 R
♏ Sept 2 22:30

1999
♐ Jan 7 5:34
♏ Jun 1 4:41 R
♐ Sept 21 21:38

2001
♑ Dec 11 18:09

2005
♒ Feb 21 12:39
♑ Jul 31 22:38 R
♒ Dec 5 20:10

2010
♓ Apr 20 2:27
♒ Jul 20 4:48 R

2011
♓ Feb 28 14:55

Index

Notes

Notes

Notes

Notes

BUSINESS, CAREERS & PERSONAL FINANCE

0-7645-9847-3

0-7645-2431-3

Also available:
- Business Plans Kit For Dummies
  0-7645-9794-9
- Economics For Dummies
  0-7645-5726-2
- Grant Writing For Dummies
  0-7645-8416-2
- Home Buying For Dummies
  0-7645-5331-3
- Managing For Dummies
  0-7645-1771-6
- Marketing For Dummies
  0-7645-5600-2

- Personal Finance For Dummies
  0-7645-2590-5*
- Resumes For Dummies
  0-7645-5471-9
- Selling For Dummies
  0-7645-5363-1
- Six Sigma For Dummies
  0-7645-6798-5
- Small Business Kit For Dummies
  0-7645-5984-2
- Starting an eBay Business For Dummies
  0-7645-6924-4
- Your Dream Career For Dummies
  0-7645-9795-7

HOME & BUSINESS COMPUTER BASICS

0-470-05432-8

0-471-75421-8

Also available:
- Cleaning Windows Vista For Dummies
  0-471-78293-9
- Excel 2007 For Dummies
  0-470-03737-7
- Mac OS X Tiger For Dummies
  0-7645-7675-5
- MacBook For Dummies
  0-470-04859-X
- Macs For Dummies
  0-470-04849-2
- Office 2007 For Dummies
  0-470-00923-3

- Outlook 2007 For Dummies
  0-470-03830-6
- PCs For Dummies
  0-7645-8958-X
- Salesforce.com For Dummies
  0-470-04893-X
- Upgrading & Fixing Laptops For Dummies
  0-7645-8959-8
- Word 2007 For Dummies
  0-470-03658-3
- Quicken 2007 For Dummies
  0-470-04600-7

FOOD, HOME, GARDEN, HOBBIES, MUSIC & PETS

0-7645-8404-9

0-7645-9904-6

Also available:
- Candy Making For Dummies
  0-7645-9734-5
- Card Games For Dummies
  0-7645-9910-0
- Crocheting For Dummies
  0-7645-4151-X
- Dog Training For Dummies
  0-7645-8418-9
- Healthy Carb Cookbook For Dummies
  0-7645-8476-6
- Home Maintenance For Dummies
  0-7645-5215-5

- Horses For Dummies
  0-7645-9797-3
- Jewelry Making & Beading For Dummies
  0-7645-2571-9
- Orchids For Dummies
  0-7645-6759-4
- Puppies For Dummies
  0-7645-5255-4
- Rock Guitar For Dummies
  0-7645-5356-9
- Sewing For Dummies
  0-7645-6847-7
- Singing For Dummies
  0-7645-2475-5

INTERNET & DIGITAL MEDIA

0-470-04529-9

0-470-04894-8

Also available:
- Blogging For Dummies
  0-471-77084-1
- Digital Photography For Dummies
  0-7645-9802-3
- Digital Photography All-in-One Desk Reference For Dummies
  0-470-03743-1
- Digital SLR Cameras and Photography For Dummies
  0-7645-9803-1
- eBay Business All-in-One Desk Reference For Dummies
  0-7645-8438-3
- HDTV For Dummies
  0-470-09673-X

- Home Entertainment PCs For Dummies
  0-470-05523-5
- MySpace For Dummies
  0-470-09529-6
- Search Engine Optimization For Dummies
  0-471-97998-8
- Skype For Dummies
  0-470-04891-3
- The Internet For Dummies
  0-7645-8996-2
- Wiring Your Digital Home For Dummies
  0-471-91830-X

* Separate Canadian edition also available
† Separate U.K. edition also available

Available wherever books are sold. For more information or to order direct: U.S. customers visit www.dummies.com or call 1-877-762-2974. U.K. customers visit www.wileyeurope.com or call 0800 243407. Canadian customers visit www.wiley.ca or call 1-800-567-4797.

SPORTS, FITNESS, PARENTING, RELIGION & SPIRITUALITY

0-471-76871-5

0-7645-7841-3

Also available:

- Catholicism For Dummies
  0-7645-5391-7
- Exercise Balls For Dummies
  0-7645-5623-1
- Fitness For Dummies
  0-7645-7851-0
- Football For Dummies
  0-7645-3936-1
- Judaism For Dummies
  0-7645-5299-6
- Potty Training For Dummies
  0-7645-5417-4
- Buddhism For Dummies
  0-7645-5359-3

- Pregnancy For Dummies
  0-7645-4483-7 †
- Ten Minute Tone-Ups For Dummies
  0-7645-7207-5
- NASCAR For Dummies
  0-7645-7681-X
- Religion For Dummies
  0-7645-5264-3
- Soccer For Dummies
  0-7645-5229-5
- Women in the Bible For Dummies
  0-7645-8475-8

TRAVEL

0-7645-7749-2

0-7645-6945-7

Also available:

- Alaska For Dummies
  0-7645-7746-8
- Cruise Vacations For Dummies
  0-7645-6941-4
- England For Dummies
  0-7645-4276-1
- Europe For Dummies
  0-7645-7529-5
- Germany For Dummies
  0-7645-7823-5
- Hawaii For Dummies
  0-7645-7402-7

- Italy For Dummies
  0-7645-7386-1
- Las Vegas For Dummies
  0-7645-7382-9
- London For Dummies
  0-7645-4277-X
- Paris For Dummies
  0-7645-7630-5
- RV Vacations For Dummies
  0-7645-4442-X
- Walt Disney World & Orlando
  For Dummies
  0-7645-9660-8

GRAPHICS, DESIGN & WEB DEVELOPMENT

0-7645-8815-X

0-7645-9571-7

Also available:

- 3D Game Animation For Dummies
  0-7645-8789-7
- AutoCAD 2006 For Dummies
  0-7645-8925-3
- Building a Web Site For Dummies
  0-7645-7144-3
- Creating Web Pages For Dummies
  0-470-08030-2
- Creating Web Pages All-in-One Desk
  Reference For Dummies
  0-7645-4345-8
- Dreamweaver 8 For Dummies
  0-7645-9649-7

- InDesign CS2 For Dummies
  0-7645-9572-5
- Macromedia Flash 8 For Dummies
  0-7645-9691-8
- Photoshop CS2 and Digital
  Photography For Dummies
  0-7645-9580-6
- Photoshop Elements 4 For Dummies
  0-471-77483-9
- Syndicating Web Sites with RSS Feeds
  For Dummies
  0-7645-8848-6
- Yahoo! SiteBuilder For Dummies
  0-7645-9800-7

NETWORKING, SECURITY, PROGRAMMING & DATABASES

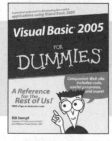

0-7645-7728-X

0-471-74940-0

Also available:

- Access 2007 For Dummies
  0-470-04612-0
- ASP.NET 2 For Dummies
  0-7645-7907-X
- C# 2005 For Dummies
  0-7645-9704-3
- Hacking For Dummies
  0-470-05235-X
- Hacking Wireless Networks
  For Dummies
  0-7645-9730-2
- Java For Dummies
  0-470-08716-1

- Microsoft SQL Server 2005 For Dummies
  0-7645-7755-7
- Networking All-in-One Desk Reference
  For Dummies
  0-7645-9939-9
- Preventing Identity Theft For Dummies
  0-7645-7336-5
- Telecom For Dummies
  0-471-77085-X
- Visual Studio 2005 All-in-One Desk
  Reference For Dummies
  0-7645-9775-2
- XML For Dummies
  0-7645-8845-1

HEALTH & SELF-HELP

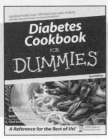

0-7645-8450-2

0-7645-4149-8

Also available:
- Bipolar Disorder For Dummies
  0-7645-8451-0
- Chemotherapy and Radiation
  For Dummies
  0-7645-7832-4
- Controlling Cholesterol For Dummies
  0-7645-5440-9
- Diabetes For Dummies
  0-7645-6820-5* †
- Divorce For Dummies
  0-7645-8417-0 †

- Fibromyalgia For Dummies
  0-7645-5441-7
- Low-Calorie Dieting For Dummies
  0-7645-9905-4
- Meditation For Dummies
  0-471-77774-9
- Osteoporosis For Dummies
  0-7645-7621-6
- Overcoming Anxiety For Dummies
  0-7645-5447-6
- Reiki For Dummies
  0-7645-9907-0
- Stress Management For Dummies
  0-7645-5144-2

EDUCATION, HISTORY, REFERENCE & TEST PREPARATION

0-7645-8381-6

0-7645-9554-7

Also available:
- The ACT For Dummies
  0-7645-9652-7
- Algebra For Dummies
  0-7645-5325-9
- Algebra Workbook For Dummies
  0-7645-8467-7
- Astronomy For Dummies
  0-7645-8465-0
- Calculus For Dummies
  0-7645-2498-4
- Chemistry For Dummies
  0-7645-5430-1
- Forensics For Dummies
  0-7645-5580-4

- Freemasons For Dummies
  0-7645-9796-5
- French For Dummies
  0-7645-5193-0
- Geometry For Dummies
  0-7645-5324-0
- Organic Chemistry I For Dummies
  0-7645-6902-3
- The SAT I For Dummies
  0-7645-7193-1
- Spanish For Dummies
  0-7645-5194-9
- Statistics For Dummies
  0-7645-5423-9

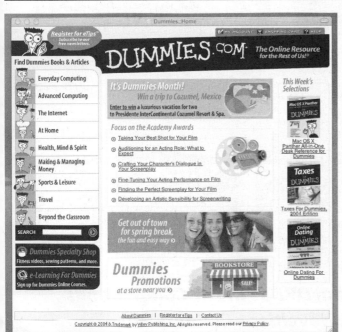

Get smart @ dummies.com®
- **Find a full list of Dummies titles**
- **Look into loads of FREE on-site articles**
- **Sign up for FREE eTips e-mailed to you weekly**
- **See what other products carry the Dummies name**
- **Shop directly from the Dummies bookstore**
- **Enter to win new prizes every month!**

* Separate Canadian edition also available

† Separate U.K. edition also available

Available wherever books are sold. For more information or to order direct: U.S. customers visit www.dummies.com or call 1-877-762-2974.
U.K. customers visit www.wileyeurope.com or call 0800 243407. Canadian customers visit www.wiley.ca or call 1-800-567-4797.